Abandoning Vietnam

Abandoning Vietnam

How America Left and South Vietnam Lost Its War

James H. Willbanks

University Press of Kansas

© 2004 by the University Press of Kansas
All rights reserved

Published by the University Press of Kansas (Lawrence, Kansas 66049), which was
organized by the Kansas Board of Regents and is operated and funded by Emporia State
University, Fort Hays State University, Kansas State University, Pittsburg State
University, the University of Kansas, and Wichita State University

Library of Congress Cataloging-in-Publication Data

Willbanks, James H., 1947–
    Abandoning Vietnam : how America left and South Vietnam lost its war / James H.
Willbanks
        p. cm. — (Modern war studies)
    Includes bibliographical references and index.
    ISBN 0-7006-1331-5 (alk. paper)
    1. Vietnamese Conflict, 1961–1975. 2. Vietnamese Conflict, 1961–1975—United States.
I. Title. II. Series.
    DS557.7.W55 2004
    959.704′3373—dc22

                                                                        2004003407

British Library Cataloguing-in-Publication Data is available.
Printed in the United States of America
10 9 8 7 6 5 4 3 2

The paper used in this publication meets the minimum requirements of the American
National Standard for Permanence of Paper for Printed Library Materials Z39.48–1984.

This book is dedicated to Lt. Col. William B. Nolde, U.S. Army, killed in An Loc eleven hours before the cease-fire went into effect in January 1973; Warrant Officer Anthony Dal Pozzo Jr., U.S. Army helicopter pilot from the 1st Aviation Brigade, killed one hour and fifteen minutes after the cease-fire; and Cpls. Darwin Judge and Charles McMahon Jr., U.S. Marines, both killed during the U.S. evacuation of Saigon in April 1975. It is also dedicated to my father, James E. Willbanks, U.S. Army (Ret.), a great soldier who fought on the frozen battlefields of Korea as a member of the 15th Infantry Regiment, 3rd Infantry Division.

Contents

(Photo insert follows p. 162)

Illustrations

MAPS

CHARTS

TABLES

Acknowledgments

I would like to thank the many archivists, librarians, and historians who assisted in the research of this study. In particular, I would like to thank the staffs of the Center of Military History, Washington, D.C.; the U.S. Army Military History Institute, Carlisle Barracks, Pennsylvania; the National Archives, College Park, Maryland; the Texas Tech University Center for the Study of the Vietnam Conflict, Lubbock, Texas; the Lyndon Baines Johnson Presidential Library in Austin, Texas; the Richard Nixon Library and Birthplace, Yorba Linda, California; and the Combined Arms Research Library, Fort Leavenworth, Kansas. Without their generous assistance, this project would never have been completed.

I would like to extend a special thanks to the Gerald R. Ford Presidential Library in Ann Arbor, Michigan, for the research grant that made it possible to examine the extensive papers and files covering the events of 1974–75 and the subsequent fall of South Vietnam.

I would also like to thank Ms. Robin Kern for her superb work on the maps in this book; her professionalism and skill added much to the finished product.

I will always be indebted to Professor Ted Wilson of the University of Kansas for his guidance, encouragement, and friendship throughout the duration of this project. His wise counsel was invaluable.

And lastly, I would like to thank my wife, Diana, for her steadfast support in this and all my endeavors; she has been my partner and best friend for thirty-five years.

Introduction

For many Americans, the enduring symbol of the end of U.S. involvement in Southeast Asia is that of the helicopter landing on the roof of the embassy in Saigon in April 1975 to extract the last group of Americans departing Vietnam as the Communist forces closed in on the city. Louis Fanning described the scene as the "spectacle of a dying nation . . . the death of the Republic of Vietnam portrayed in living color."[1] Although the image clearly symbolizes the fall of South Vietnam and the failure of U.S. policy in Southeast Asia, one must look at a much earlier period to find the seeds of defeat in this tragic conflict. This study examines U.S. actions in Vietnam during the years 1968–75 with foreknowledge of their ignominious ending. It focuses on President Richard Nixon's Vietnamization program, the Paris peace negotiations, the subsequent withdrawal of American forces, and the contribution of these actions to the eventual fall of South Vietnam. The study begins by examining the events that led to a change in U.S. strategy in 1969 and the subsequent initiation of Vietnamization. After discussing the implementation of that policy, it assesses the combat performance of the Republic of Vietnam Armed Forces (RVNAF) during the period 1969–74 and addresses the reasons for the sudden and total collapse of those forces in 1975. Finally, the study asks whether the final collapse was inevitable or if the United States, by taking different measures and/or a different strategy, could have prevailed and ensured the survival of South Vietnam as a free and independent nation.

The genesis of the change in U.S. strategy in Vietnam that led to American withdrawal can be traced to 1968, when Richard M. Nixon was elected president of the United States. He had promised to "end the war and win the peace" in Vietnam, and shortly after taking office he announced the policy of "Vietnamization," whereby the war would be turned over to the South Vietnamese forces so that American troops could be withdrawn. Although his policy encompassed a wide range of American activities in South Vietnam, Under Secretary of State U. Alexis

Johnson defined it for the House Subcommittee on Foreign Operations and Related Activities in 1970 as follows: "Vietnamization is on the nonmilitary side what is usually embraced in the term 'pacification;' that is, the extension of Government control, Government services and the presence of the Government within the countryside. On the military side, Vietnamization means improving the training, improving the equipment, and improving, in general, the capabilities of the Vietnamese forces to deal with the enemy they face."[2]

This study will emphasize the military aspects of Vietnamization. However, doing so is difficult without also focusing on the activities and events in Washington, Hanoi, and Paris, as well as those in Saigon and on the South Vietnamese battlefield. We must consider the political situation in the United States and the peace negotiations in Paris in order to properly contextualize Vietnamization within U.S. strategy in South Vietnam. Additionally, because the policy was not pursued in a vacuum, we must consider the actions and reactions of the North Vietnamese in Hanoi.

The ultimate objective of the Vietnamization program was to strengthen the armed forces of South Vietnam and bolster the Thieu government to make the South Vietnamese capable of standing alone against their Communist opponents. When the Nixon administration initiated the program in 1969, a buildup of the South Vietnamese forces began that ultimately increased the RVNAF from 825,000 troops to over 1 million by 1972. The buildup included massive military aid that modernized the South Vietnamese armed forces and provided them with new weapons, vehicles, and aircraft. In addition, an extensive training program was instituted to increase the combat capabilities of the South Vietnamese forces and their leaders. During the buildup and training, President Nixon began withdrawing American troops from South Vietnam. By the end of 1971, only 139,000 U.S. military personnel remained in country. Nixon hoped to proceed with the Vietnamization program to the point that eventually all American forces could be withdrawn. Concurrent with the Vietnamization program and the phased withdrawal of American combat troops, President Nixon and Henry Kissinger intensified secret negotiations with North Vietnamese representatives in Paris. These negotiations, coupled with the Vietnamization program, became the twin pillars of Nixon's strategy to achieve "peace with honor" and an end to the war in South Vietnam.

In 1971 the Vietnamization program received its first real test during Operation Lam Son 719, in which South Vietnamese forces invaded North Vietnamese base areas along the Ho Chi Minh Trail in Laos. The poorly executed operation resulted in a significant setback for the revamped RVNAF and demonstrated serious shortcomings that plagued the South Vietnamese armed forces in a number of key areas. Following the debacle in Laos, American advisers attempted to make necessary corrections. While these efforts were ongoing, the Vietnamization program received its severest test. On 30 March 1972 the North Vietnamese Army (NVA) launched a massive invasion of South Vietnam.[3] The three-pronged assault was designed to strike a knockout blow against the South Vietnamese government and its armed forces. Using conventional tactics and advanced Soviet and Chinese weaponry not previously deployed in the South during the Vietnam War, the North Vietnamese struck hard at Quang Tri, Kontum, and An Loc with a total of fourteen infantry divisions and twenty-six separate regiments (120,000 troops and approximately twelve hundred tanks and other armored vehicles).

Under this onslaught, the South Vietnamese forces reeled and almost broke. However, with the massive support of U.S. air power, they eventually stabilized their defenses and ultimately went on the counteroffensive. President Nixon bombed North Vietnam and mined the harbors, thus cutting off outside support to Hanoi and drastically reducing supplies to the North Vietnamese forces in the South. By September 1972 the South Vietnamese forces had retaken most of the territory lost during the initial assault.

The victory, nearly a disaster, was touted by Nixon and his administration as proof positive that Vietnamization had worked and that the South Vietnamese were ready to assume the entire burden of their own defense. It served as a justification by which Nixon could withdraw all forces from South Vietnam with at least the appearance of not having abandoned America's allies in Southeast Asia.

Meanwhile, peace negotiations in Paris had broken down: the North Vietnamese walked out of the talks. To bring them back to the table, Nixon commenced what became known as the Christmas bombing. Shortly thereafter, the North Vietnamese returned and the peace talks resumed in January 1973; Nixon subsequently canceled the bombing campaign. A tentative peace agreement was reached 23 January, and the formal document was signed 27 January, with the cease-fire scheduled to begin the next day.

The last U.S. troops departed Vietnam on 29 March 1973, in accordance with the peace agreement. The American prisoners of war were returned and Nixon declared that "peace with honor" had been achieved and that South Vietnam's integrity as a nation had been secured. Effectively, the United States was washing its hands of the situation, leaving the South Vietnamese on their own.

Although open large-scale combat seldom occurred in South Vietnam during the next two years, a constant level of small-scale armed confrontation persisted between the South Vietnamese forces and the North Vietnamese Army, which used this time to consolidate its hold over the southern territories left under Communist control by the signing of the cease-fire agreement. Additionally, the NVA mounted a massive effort to resupply and reinforce its units remaining in South Vietnam with fresh forces and equipment from the North.

At the same time, American military aid to South Vietnam dropped drastically. After the return of the American prisoners of war, U.S. support activities shifted to Thailand, leaving only a handful of American technicians and a small Defense Attache Office in Saigon. The South Vietnamese subsequently sustained several body blows, beginning with the resignation of Nixon in August 1974. The following October, the U.S. Congress appropriated only $700 million for the defense of South Vietnam and Cambodia, indicating that the amount would be drastically cut in the

future. With the departure of Saigon's patron from the White House and the reduction in military aid, the United States appeared to be turning away from its former allies in Southeast Asia.

This perception was not lost on the North Vietnamese. In December 1974 they
launched a probing attack against Phuoc Long Province in the Central Highlands
to test South Vietnamese strength and the U.S. response. The operation's results
far exceeded NVA expectations: by May the entire province had fallen. Although
the U.S. government had repeatedly pledged support to the Thieu government if
the North Vietnamese attempted to take over the country, such support was not
forthcoming. Congress had further reduced military aid to Saigon and made it very
clear that the United States would not reintroduce American troops into the war.
Emboldened, the North Vietnamese expanded the scope of their offensive operations. When President Nguyen Van Thieu, alarmed at the NVA advances, committed what proved to be a fatal strategic error and pulled his forces back to the
coastal plains, the Central Highlands fell under Communist control virtually by
default.

The North Vietnamese pressed the attack farther to the north in Military Region I. Thieu's subsequent withdrawal order demoralized the South Vietnamese
forces, and the retreat soon turned into a rout. Pleiku, Hue, and Da Nang fell; by
the first of April, Communist troops were rolling down Route 1 toward Saigon. Although the South Vietnamese put up a desperate defense at Xuan Loc (in Military
Region III, less than seventy kilometers from Saigon), the battle proved to be the
last stand of a dying army. Shortly thereafter the resistance of the South Vietnamese
forces totally collapsed. On 30 April, North Vietnamese tanks rolled into Saigon
and the war was over.

Although South Vietnam fell in just fifty-five days, the final North Vietnamese
victory was merely the culmination of a long, slow process that had begun with
Nixon's presidential election and the initiation of the Vietnamization program. The
president's new strategy received an early setback with the Lam Son 719 debacle.
However, when the South Vietnamese, although nearly overwhelmed in the beginning, eventually withstood an all-out NVA invasion in 1972, the victory contributed to a sequence of events that led to the signing of the Paris Peace Accords
and the subsequent withdrawal of all U.S. troops. Nixon's policies ended the war,
but only for the United States, and those policies, as carried out, coupled with the
subsequent limitations imposed on the White House by a hostile U.S. Congress,
laid the foundation for the destruction of the South Vietnamese nation. In the end,
Vietnamization achieved neither peace nor honor.

1

Vietnamization

1968 AND THE TET OFFENSIVE

The Year of the Monkey, 1968, proved to be the pivotal point of the Vietnam War. During the Tet holiday truce of that year, North Vietnamese Army and Viet Cong (VC) forces launched a large-scale attack across the length and breadth of South Vietnam. Beginning in the last days of January, they attacked or shelled thirty-six out of forty-four provincial capitals, five out of six autonomous cities, and 64 out of 242 district towns in the Republic of Vietnam. The extent and violence of these attacks shocked the American public; earlier, they had been led by U.S. military and political leaders to believe that the corner had been turned in the struggle against the Communists in Vietnam.

Despite the surprise achieved by the Communists, U.S. and South Vietnamese forces reacted quickly to the new threat, driving back the enemy and regaining control of the situation in most areas. Only in Saigon and the imperial capital of Hue did the actual fighting last more than a week. In the end, the offensive resulted in a military defeat for the Communist forces, who paid a terrible price for their initial successes. Estimates put the VC and North Vietnamese casualties at between 32,000 and 58,000 killed. While the actual casualty figures may be debatable, most authorities agree that the Viet Cong suffered greatly during the Tet fighting and ceased to be a significant military threat for the remainder of the war.[1] Nevertheless, at the strategic level, the offensive proved to be a psychological victory for the Communist forces. President Lyndon B. Johnson was shaken by the intensity and magnitude of the enemy offensive. When Gen. William C. Westmoreland, U.S. commander in Vietnam, asked for 206,000 more troops, many influential Americans, both in and out of the U.S. government, including many of those who had previously supported the war effort, began to question continued American involvement in a Southeast Asian war that now appeared unwinnable. The antiwar

5

movement gained new strength. On 31 March a stricken president announced he would not run for reelection. Johnson ordered a halt to U.S. bombing of North Vietnam above the twentieth parallel and at the same time proposed peace negotiations with the Communists. Saying that he was launching a "peace offensive," Johnson sent former ambassador Averell Harriman to Paris to begin talks with the North Vietnamese.[2] This portended a profound change in both American attitude toward the war and official U.S. strategy. It was clear that there was no "light at the end of the tunnel," and many Americans came to the conclusion that it was time to end the war in South Vietnam one way or the other.

NIXON ON THE CAMPAIGN TRAIL

While Johnson was trying to deal with the ramifications of the Tet offensive, Richard M. Nixon was campaigning hard for the office that the president would soon vacate. Nixon made the war in Vietnam a major element of his platform in the 1968 presidential election. On 5 March, in a speech at the American Legion Hall in Hampton, New Hampshire, Nixon said, "I pledge to you new leadership that will end the war and win the peace in the Pacific."[3] Despite his later protestations to the contrary, candidate Nixon gave many voters the impression that he had a "secret plan" for ending the war.[4] In a radio statement on 8 March he said, "It is essential that we end this war, and end it quickly . . . but it is essential that we end it such a way that we can win the peace."[5] Campaigning in Wisconsin later that month, he clarified his position, proclaiming, "The nation's objective should be to help the South Vietnamese fight the war and not fight it for them. . . . If they do not assume the majority of the burden in their own defense, they cannot be saved."[6]

In trying to devise a means to end the war, Nixon faced the same problems that confronted Lyndon Johnson. Escalation and commitment of increased numbers of American troops had not worked; the 1968 Tet offensive demonstrated that fact only too clearly. Stalemate was unacceptable because an increasingly restive American public would no longer tolerate a long-term commitment to an unwinnable war. The answer was to get out of Vietnam, but the question—a political one—was how to do it gracefully without abandoning South Vietnam to the Communists. Nixon wrestled privately with this problem, maintaining a relatively low profile in public about the Vietnam issue in the wake of Johnson's 31 March announcement that he would not run for reelection. Nixon told the *New York Times* that he would withhold any criticism of Johnson in order to see what the president's "peace offensive" might garner from the North Vietnamese.[7]

On 26 July, Nixon flew to Washington at President Johnson's request for briefings on Vietnam from Secretary of State Dean Rusk and National Security Adviser Walt W. Rostow. After the briefings, Johnson explained to Nixon what he was trying to accomplish in the negotiations with the North Vietnamese; the president was bitter that the Communists had not responded more favorably to his peace overture. Rusk warned Nixon that in his opinion "panic" would set in throughout Asia if the United States were to withdraw from Vietnam without an "honorable" peace settlement. Nixon said that he would continue to support American goals in South Vietnam and "pledged not to undercut Johnson's negotiating position just in case the Communists came around. . . ."[8]

On 3 August 1968, Nixon revealed more of his own thinking about how to solve the Vietnam puzzle when he sent his ideas about ending the war to the GOP platform committee meeting at the Republican National Convention in Miami. He wrote that "the war must be ended . . . ," but warned "it must be ended honorably, consistent with America's limited aims and with the long-term requirements of peace in Asia."[9] Then, for the first time, he became more specific about how to achieve this peace with honor. He advocated continuing to wage the war until the enemy agreed to an honorable peace, while at the same time improving the armament and training of Army of the Republic of Vietnam (ARVN) troops. Nixon later described his thoughts at the time: "As they [the South Vietnamese forces] are phased in, American troops can—and should be—phased out. This phasing out will save American lives and cut American costs."[10]

On 7 August at the Republican National Convention, Nixon officially received the nomination of his party for president. His Democratic opponent was Vice President Hubert H. Humphrey of Minnesota. During the ensuing election campaign, Humphrey, according to Nixon biographer Stephen E. Ambrose, was "trapped" because he could not break with Johnson on Vietnam, and thus he could not take a more "dovish" approach to the war that would have given the voters a clear choice between him and Nixon.[11] Nixon instructed his key staff thinkers and writers "to put the Vietnam monkey on Humphrey's back, not Johnson's."[12] At the same time, he avoided making any more substantive comments on how to bring the war to an end, making it difficult for Humphrey to attack him on specifics. It was a masterful political move, and Humphrey quickly became the target of everyone who hated the Johnson administration and its continuation of the war and/or its inability to achieve victory. The war was a hot campaign issue, as demonstrated by the disastrous Democratic convention in Chicago that resulted in rioting in the streets.

Nixon learned that President Johnson was preparing to announce a new bombing pause. Realizing that the pause would be a boon to Humphrey, he made a peremptory announcement that he would support the bombing halt and promised to "not play politics with this war."[13] His promise was hollow, since both parties had been "playing politics" with the war since the beginning of the conflict. Nixon managed to diffuse some of the impact of Johnson's announcement, but the bombing halt still resulted in a surge of support for Humphrey and the Democrats. The boost was short-lived, however, because on 2 November, President Nguyen Van Thieu of South Vietnam announced that his government would not participate in the Paris peace talks. His announcement effectively undercut Johnson's peace initiative and any potential political windfall for Hubert Humphrey and the Democrats.[14]

NIXON VICTORIOUS

On 5 November, despite a last-minute flurry of activity by the Democrats, Nixon won 43.4 percent of the popular vote to Humphrey's 42.7 percent, securing 301 electoral votes to his challenger's 191. Johnson's problems were now Nixon's, and having won a victory promising to end the war, the president-elect had to make good on that pledge and create a workable plan that would achieve the promised "peace with honor." Historian George C. Herring suggests that Nixon clearly perceived that his political future and place in history would be determined by his ability to extricate the nation from Vietnam.[15] Nixon remarked to one of his advisers, "I'm not going to end up like LBJ, holed up in the White House afraid to show my face on the street. I'm going to stop that war. Fast."[16] In the end, he would not find it such an easy task.

On 11 November, Nixon went to the White House for another foreign policy briefing from Johnson and his advisers. The main topic was the Vietnam War. Nixon was briefed by Secretary of State Rusk, Secretary of Defense Clark M. Clifford, National Security Adviser Rostow, Director of Central Intelligence Richard M. Helms, and Chairman of the Joint Chiefs of Staff Earle G. Wheeler. According to Nixon, "[T]hey all emphasized that the United States must see the war through to a successful conclusion—with negotiations if possible, but with continued fighting if necessary." The briefers also warned that "an American bug-out, or a negotiated settlement that could be interpreted as a defeat, would have a devastatingly detrimental effect" on U.S. allies and friends in Asia and around the world.[17]

Clifford offered the president-elect three alternatives to consider as he prepared to assume his new office: Nixon could continue the fighting without pursuing negotiations; he could hold private unilateral negotiations with Hanoi; or he could pressure Thieu to go to Paris to participate in the negotiations. Clifford recommended the last option, saying that President Johnson could help set the stage for this approach by notifying Thieu that the talks would go on, with or without him. Clifford thought that the South Vietnamese president would thus be forced to participate. At the same time, Clifford said, Johnson should take measures to reduce the level of combat and begin a troop withdrawal as he prepared to leave office. Clifford felt that such a course would be "a major step to end the war" and Nixon could "clean up the details" after his inauguration.[18] Despite Clifford's recommendations, Nixon later wrote in his memoirs that Johnson and his advisers "had no new approaches to recommend to me."[19] Nevertheless, after the meeting, he told the press that he would fully support the policies of the outgoing president and that the Johnson administration would speak for his new administration during the following two months until his inauguration; he said he hoped that the one-voice policy would lead to "some very significant action and progress toward peace."[20]

On 25 November, Nixon met with Harvard professor Henry Kissinger at his White House transition office in the Hotel Pierre in New York. The president-elect discussed ideas on foreign policy with the man he was considering for the post of national security adviser, talking about NATO, the Soviet Union, China, and the Middle East. When they came to the topic of Vietnam, both agreed that they needed to rethink the whole diplomatic and military policy on Vietnam in order "to avoid the trap Johnson had fallen into" of devoting virtually all the president's foreign policy time and energy to just one country.[21] To both men, the war in Vietnam was part of the much larger issue of American security and influence around the world. Nixon recalled that he felt a "strong intuition about Henry Kissinger, and I decided on the spot that he should be my National Security Adviser."[22] Two days later, Nixon offered Kissinger the position and Kissinger accepted. The alliance between Nixon and his new national security adviser would have a tremendous impact on the conduct of the war in Vietnam and, ultimately, on the continued existence of South Vietnam as a sovereign nation.

On 12 December, Nixon met once again with President Johnson in the White House to discuss the situation in Vietnam, and once again Johnson urged Nixon to stay the course. The president-elect promised that he would do so and promised further that he would ensure that Johnson received the credit he deserved when the war was brought to a successful end.[23]

Later that month, Nixon and his new national security adviser made their first overture to the North Vietnamese negotiators in Paris. Using French businessman Jean Sainteny as an intermediary, Nixon and Kissinger sent the North Vietnamese a message that the new president was interested in a negotiated end to the war. The North Vietnamese responded that the chief obstacle to meaningful negotiations was continued U.S. support of the Thieu government and their "absurd demands."[24] Nixon, "neither surprised, nor discouraged" by the less-than-auspicious beginning for the new administration, later described his mind-set about Vietnam as he prepared to move into the White House: "I began my presidency with three fundamental premises regarding Vietnam. First, I would have to prepare public opinion for the fact that total military victory was no longer possible. Second, I would have to act on what my conscience, my experience, and my analysis told me was true about the need to keep our commitment. To abandon South Vietnam to the Communists now would cost us inestimably in our search for a stable, structured, and lasting peace. Third, I would have to end the war as quickly as was honorably possible."[25]

He also claimed that he had ruled out a quick military victory and "was prepared to take most of my first year in office to arrive at a negotiated agreement" that would preserve the independence of South Vietnam.[26] Little did the new chief executive realize that reaching an agreement with the North Vietnamese would take three more years and 20,552 American lives.

NIXON ASSUMES OFFICE

On 20 January 1969, Richard Milhous Nixon was sworn in as the thirty-seventh president of the United States. In his inaugural address, he reiterated his desire to reach a peaceful settlement in Vietnam, but made clear his determination to see the war through to an honorable conclusion. "To all those who would be tempted by weakness," Nixon warned, "let us leave no doubt that we will be as strong as we need to be for as long as we need to be."[27]

On his first full day in office, Nixon got down to business. He issued National Security Study Memorandum 1 (NSSM 1), titled "Situation in Vietnam." The six-page, single-spaced document, which was sent to selected members of the new administration, requested responses to twenty-nine major questions and fifty subsidiary queries about the situation in Southeast Asia. Among those receiving the memorandum were the Department of Defense, the Department of State, the Central Intelligence Agency, the Joint Chiefs of Staff, the U.S. Embassy in Saigon, and Headquarters U.S. Military Assistance Command, Vietnam (MACV), also in Saigon. The questions covered six broad categories: negotiations (questions 1–4), the enemy situation (5–10), the state of the armed forces of South Vietnam (11–13), the status of the pacification effort (14–20), the political situation in South Vietnam (21–23), and American objectives (24–29).[28]

NSSM 1 was Nixon's attempt to arrive at some workable strategy by seeking divergent views that would yield a comprehensive estimate of the situation in South Vietnam. According to Henry Kissinger, the memorandum was designed "to sharpen any disagreements so that we could pinpoint the controversial questions and the different points of view."[29] The thrust of the questions indicated some of the new president's chief concerns: the viability of the Thieu government and the capability of the South Vietnamese to continue the fight after any U.S. withdrawal. The genesis of these concerns was an intelligence assessment that Nixon had seen in December before taking office; in this report, the CIA had been very critical of the Thieu government and the capabilities of the South Vietnamese armed forces.[30]

Historian William M. Hammond maintains that Nixon's worries about South Vietnamese capabilities were given even more impetus when, shortly after NSSM 1 was issued, the new president had occasion to review "Vietnam Has the Resources But Lacks the Motivation to Win," an unsigned memorandum thought to be authored by a knowledgeable South Vietnamese.[31] The author of the document asserted that South Vietnam's problems were so severe that it could never survive if the United States withdrew too quickly from the war and that the Americans would have to avoid troop withdrawal timetables and continue to ensure the integrity of South Vietnam until that nation could stand on its own.[32] Faced with the pessimistic assessments in both the CIA report and the unsigned memo, Nixon wanted to get a clearer picture of the situation in Southeast Asia. NSSM 1 was designed to do just that.

If Nixon wanted divergent views and opinions on the war, he certainly got them in the wide range of responses to what became known in the administration as the "29 questions." Kissinger and his staff summarized the responses to NSSM 1 in a forty-four page paper that was circulated to the National Security Council Review Group on 14 March 1969.[33] This report revealed general agreement among most respondents that the Republic of Vietnam (RVN) could not in the foreseeable future defend against both the Viet Cong and the North Vietnamese Army. In the same vein, most respondents concurred that the Government of Vietnam (GVN) probably could not stand up to serious political competition from the National Liberation Front (NLF). They also agreed that the enemy, although seriously weakened by losses during the Tet offensive, was still a viable force and capable of being refurbished and reinforced from North Vietnam.

Despite similar assessments about the short-term future in Vietnam, respondents to NSSM 1 strongly disagreed in other areas. Conflicting responses reflected two schools of thought, differing primarily on assessment of progress achieved to that point and the long-range prognosis for the situation in Southeast Asia. The more optimistic school of thought, best represented by the MACV response, and shared by Ambassador Ellsworth Bunker in Saigon, the Joint Chiefs of Staff at the Pentagon, and Adm. John S. McCain Jr. (commander in chief of the U.S. Pacific Forces), held that the North Vietnamese had agreed to peace talks in Paris because of their military weakness, that pacification gains were real and "should hold up," and that the "tides are favorable."[34]

Gen. Creighton W. Abrams Jr., who had succeeded Gen. William C. Westmoreland in July 1968 as commander of MACV (COMUSMACV), had routed NSSM 1 down to each of his four corps senior advisers for reply (South Vietnam was divided into four corps tactical zones [CTZ], each having a U.S. general officer as operational commander of U.S. forces who also served as senior adviser to the ARVN corps commander). The replies from the corps senior advisers varied, but generally they took the same stance as that of Lt. Gen. Richard G. Stilwell, I Corps Tactical Zone in the north, who wrote "that significant strides have been made in the improvement of ARVN forces [during 1968]."[35] The lone dissenter among the corps senior advisers was Lt. Gen. Walter T. Kerwin Jr., from III Corps Tactical Zone (the eleven provinces that surrounded Saigon), who reported that he saw "no marked improvement" of the South Vietnamese forces in III Corps during 1968 and rated only one-third of the maneuver battalions in the region as "effective."[36] Despite Kerwin's concerns, he and the other corps senior advisers were unanimous in one respect: they all agreed that the South Vietnamese, after a sufficient buildup, would be able to "contain" the Viet Cong threat. Kerwin, although agreeing in principle with his colleagues, qualified his concurrence by saying that he believed that continued American air and artillery support would be needed for ARVN to prevail, even against the Viet Cong. Although the senior advisers agreed that the Vietnamese forces would eventually be able to handle the ongoing insurgency, they were also unanimous in doubting that ARVN could withstand a combined onslaught by the VC and the North Vietnamese without continued American aid and assistance.

General Abrams's staff at MACV incorporated the comments of the corps senior advisers into its response to the president on NSSM 1.[37] Many of the pessimistic comments, including Kerwin's critical appraisal, were omitted or at least downplayed in the final MACV assessment. Much of the final report was based on a restatement of previously submitted statistical indicators of success in upgrading Saigon's forces. Still, the MACV report, which stressed the need to continue American air and ground support to the South Vietnamese, was not entirely optimistic. Although the report emphasized that significant progress was being made in modernizing ARVN, Abrams echoed the comments of his corps senior advisers, warning that "the RVNAF [Republic of Vietnam Armed Forces] simply are not capable of attaining the level of self-sufficiency and overwhelming force superiority that would be required to counter combined Viet Cong insurgency and North Vietnamese Army main force offensives."[38] Accordingly, Abrams stressed that any proposed American troop withdrawal had to be accompanied by a similar North Vietnamese withdrawal. Although Abrams would repeatedly emphasize this point on many subsequent occasions, in the end his warnings fell on deaf ears when compared to the political necessity of getting U.S. troops out of South Vietnam, with or without a North Vietnamese withdrawal.

Differing strongly with the more optimistic aspects of the MACV response to NSSM 1 were the reports of the Central Intelligence Agency, civilians in the Defense Department, and, to a lesser degree, the State Department. Their reports were highly critical of Saigon's military capabilities and asserted that the small improvements in the RVNAF had "produced essentially a stalemate."[39] The civilians in the Defense Department went so far as to say that the South Vietnamese could not be expected to contain even the Viet Cong, let alone a combined enemy threat, without continued and full American support. Members of this group generally agreed that pacification gains were "inflated and fragile"; that the Communists had gone to Paris for political and strategic reasons—to cut costs and to pursue their aims through negotiation—rather than because they faced defeat on the battlefield; and that a compromise settlement was the only solution in Vietnam.

Thus, there existed two drastically divergent projections for the long-term future of South Vietnam and its military forces. What had been meant as a means to clarify the perspective on the Vietnam situation had only obfuscated the view for the new president. Henry Kissinger wrote, "The answers [to NSSM 1] made clear that there was no consensus as to facts, much less as to policy."[40]

Nixon faced a serious dilemma. He was not prepared to unilaterally withdraw and award South Vietnam to the Communists, but he had also promised to end the war and bring the troops home. As Henry Kissinger subsequently observed in his memoirs: "The Nixon Administration entered office determined to end our involvement in Vietnam. But it soon came up against the reality that had also bedeviled its predecessor. For nearly a generation the security and progress of free peoples had depended on confidence in America. We could not simply walk away from an enterprise involving two administrations, five allied countries, and thirty-one thousand dead as if we were switching a television channel."[41]

The new president had to devise a strategy to get the United States out of Vietnam, without "simply walk[ing] away." South Vietnam's survival remained an objective, but the primary goal was getting the United States out of Vietnam. Nixon and his advisers began to focus on a way the United States could disengage itself from the conflict and at the same time give the South Vietnamese at least a chance of survival after the American departure. The task was acknowledged as being difficult, and perhaps even impossible in the long run. Henry Kissinger later revealed the thought process emerging in the White House:

> We recognized from the beginning the uncertainty that the South Vietnamese could be sufficiently strengthened to stand on their own with the time span that domestic opposition to American involvement would allow. Therefore a negotiated settlement has always been preferable. Rather than run the risk of South Vietnam crumbling around our remaining forces, a peace settlement would end the war with an act of policy and leave the future of South Vietnam to the historical process. We could heal the wounds in this country as our men left peace behind on the battlefield and a healthy interval for South Vietnam's fate to unfold.[42]

Despite the uncertainty involved in trying to strengthen the South Vietnamese armed forces, the president and his closest advisers, particularly Secretary of Defense Melvin R. Laird and Secretary of State William P. Rogers, realized that this was the only feasible course of action if the United States were ever to escape from Vietnam. Accordingly, Nixon ordered American representatives to take a "highly forceful approach" to cause President Thieu and the South Vietnamese government to assume greater responsibility for the war.[43]

Unspoken, but still clear to all involved, was the implication that the RVNAF would assume greater combat responsibility prior to a resultant withdrawal of American forces, which by this time totaled 543,000 troops in country. In a 25 January National Security Council meeting, the subject of troop withdrawals was discussed. General Wheeler, chairman of the Joint Chiefs of Staff, remarked during the meeting that a small reduction of U.S. forces would help the president diplomatically and "convey the image of a self-confident South Vietnam."[44] Subsequently, Wheeler wrote Abrams at MACV that on the basis of this meeting and later conversations with Secretary of Defense Laird, troop reductions were imminent, but "public discussion of withdrawal or troop reduction in Vietnam should be limited to mutual withdrawal within the context of the Paris negotiations"; he further urged Abrams to "quietly put the damper on any public discussion [of troop withdrawals] by senior U.S. officers."[45] By this time, Abrams and Ambassador Bunker had already met with President Thieu on 17 January to discuss formally the possibility of American troop redeployments under the new Nixon administration. The wheels had been set in motion to remove the United States from Vietnam once and for all. What remained was to devise a means by which the United States did not appear to be abandoning South Vietnam to the Communists.

LAIRD GOES TO SAIGON

To get a better feel for the situation on the ground in Southeast Asia, Nixon directed Laird to go to South Vietnam to make a firsthand assessment. Laird, accompanied by General Wheeler, arrived on 5 March 1969 in Saigon, where they were briefed by senior MACV officers. The MACV staff emphasized the view that significant improvements were being made in the South Vietnamese armed forces. Laird declared his satisfaction but instructed General Abrams to speed up the program for turning over the bulk of the war effort to the Saigon forces. Abrams reiterated his original warning that the South Vietnamese could not stand alone against a combined threat. Nevertheless, Laird, citing political pressures at home, directed Abrams to prepare plans to put the new policy into action "before the time given the new administration runs out. . . ."[46]

Laird returned to Washington convinced, despite Abrams's warning and the contrary recommendations of his own staff who had responded so negatively to NSSM 1, that the South Vietnamese could eventually take over prosecution of the entire war, thus permitting a complete U.S. withdrawal. Secretary of Defense Laird, a well-respected Republican who had served seventeen years in the House, was anxious to end the war because he realized the traditional post-election grace period afforded a new president by the public, the press, and Congress would be short-lived. Antiwar sentiment on Capitol Hill was growing, and Laird knew that Nixon would feel the brunt if he did not end the war quickly. Moreover, if the war in Vietnam continued much longer, Laird reasoned that it would bleed American strength and credibility around the world in places far more important to U.S. security than Southeast Asia. He believed that any effort to prolong the conflict would lead to strife and controversy capable of seriously damaging Nixon's ability to achieve an honorable settlement. Recognizing that the war could last into the foreseeable future, he wanted to end U.S. involvement as soon as possible. Therefore, according to Deputy Assistant Secretary of Defense Jerry Friedheim, Laird was "more interested in ending the war in Vietnam rather than winning it."[47]

On 13 March, Laird reported the findings from his trip in a memorandum to the new president. He was convinced that Nixon had no choice but to turn the war over to the South Vietnamese in order to extricate U.S. forces and placate both the resurgent antiwar movement and Americans who just wanted the war to go away. He proposed a plan designed to make the South Vietnamese armed forces capable of dealing not only with the ongoing insurgency, but also with a continuing North Vietnamese presence in the South. He disagreed with Abrams that U.S. withdrawals had to be tied to commensurate Communist withdrawals and argued that the large U.S. effort stifled South Vietnamese initiative and prevented them from taking over more of the war effort. He felt that the "orientation" of American senior commanders in Vietnam seemed "to be more on operations than on assisting the South Vietnamese to acquire the means to defend themselves."[48] Laird wanted the senior U.S. military leaders in South Vietnam to begin shifting their focus from fighting the war to preparing the South Vietnamese to stand on their own. The secretary of defense concluded that Saigon's forces were improving steadily and that the time had come to transfer even more responsibility to them. Accordingly, he recommended withdrawing 50,000–70,000 American troops in 1969.

In a National Security Council meeting on 28 March, the president and his advisers discussed Laird's recommendations. Gen. Andrew Goodpaster, then serving as General Abrams's deputy in Saigon, reported to the president that substantial improvement in the South Vietnamese forces had already been made and that MACV was in fact close to "de-Americanizing" the war. According to Henry Kissinger, Laird took exception to Goodpaster's term "de-Americanizing" and suggested that what was needed was a more "positive" term like "Vietnamization" to put the emphasis on the right issues; thus, "Vietnamization" became the embodiment of Nixon's efforts to turn over the war to the South Vietnamese.[49]

Laird later described the objective of the new program before the House Armed Services Committee as "the effective assumption by the RVNAF of a larger share of combat operations from American forces" so that "U.S. forces can be in fact withdrawn in substantial numbers."[50] Such statements were clearly aimed at selling the new policy to Congress and the American public. Alexander M. Haig, then a member of Nixon's National Security Council, later described Laird's plan as a "stroke of public relations genius," but pointed out that it was "a program designed to mollify American critics of the war, not a policy for the effective defense of South Vietnam."[51]

Laird, who became the chief proponent for Vietnamization, was later characterized by Kissinger as being as "skeptical about the utility of negotiations as about the possibility of military victory; and he was politically astute. His major concern was to get the United States out of Vietnam before we lost too much domestic support. But he wanted to do so without a collapse of the South Vietnamese. Hence his all-out advocacy of Vietnamization. He generally supported a hard line in negotiations and the most rapid possible pace of troop withdrawals. He had convinced himself that Vietnamization would work; it became his top priority."[52]

Laird's dogged promotion of Vietnamization and the accompanying U.S. troop withdrawals would later bring him into conflict with the president's national security adviser (for reasons which will be explained later), but in April 1969, Laird's recommendations completely convinced Nixon, who later wrote, "It was on the basis of Laird's enthusiastic advocacy that we undertook the policy of Vietnamization."[53] Convincing the president to endorse the approach may not have taken very much. Alexander Haig maintains that Nixon had begun talking about troop withdrawals within five days of his inauguration and found the answer he was looking for in Laird's plan.[54] Vietnamization would enable the president to initiate a gradual reduction of combat operations by U.S. troops, with the ultimate goal of complete withdrawal. However, he realized that American forces could not be pulled out precipitously. Although the situation was improving in South Vietnam, a significant level of fighting persisted. Thus, American forces would have to maintain combat operations to gain the necessary time to make the RVNAF sufficiently strong enough to continue the fighting alone.

In early April 1969, Nixon set forth planning guidance for the new policy in National Security Study Memorandum 36 (NSSM 36), which directed "the preparation of a specific timetable for Vietnamizing the war."[55] The timetable was to address "all aspects of U.S. military, para-military, and civilian involvement in Vietnam, including combat and combat support forces, advisory personnel, and all forms of equipment." The stated objective of the requested plan was "the progressive transfer . . . of the fighting effort" from American to South Vietnamese forces.

Nixon's directive was based on a number of assumptions. First, it assumed that, lacking progress in the Paris peace talks, any U.S. withdrawal would be unilateral and unaccompanied by comparable NVA reductions. This assumption was a significant change from previous ones, because it meant that the South Vietnamese would have to take on both the NVA and the VC. Second, it was assumed that the withdrawal schedule would depend on the operational situation in South Vietnam; the U.S. withdrawals would be justified on a "cut and try" basis, and General Abrams would have to make periodic assessments of their effects before launching the next phase of troop reductions. Third, the directive assumed that the South Vietnamese forces would willingly shoulder more military responsibility for the war. Based on these three assumptions, the American troop presence in South Vietnam was to be reduced by phased troop withdrawals to the eventual point that only a support and advisory mission remained. The troop withdrawals would begin 1 July 1969.

Thus, the Nixon administration, despite assessments from a wide range of government agencies that the RVNAF could never combat a combined VC-NVA threat, devised a strategy to prepare the South Vietnamese to do just that, instructing the American command in Vietnam to develop plans for turning over the entire ground war effort to Saigon. All that remained to institute the new strategy was a public announcement.

MIDWAY, GUAM, AND THE NIXON DOCTRINE

On 8 June 1969, President Nixon met with South Vietnamese president Nguyen Van Thieu at Midway and publicly proclaimed for the first time the new American policy of "Vietnamization." Nixon stated that there would be a steady buildup and improvement of South Vietnamese forces and institutions, accompanied by increased military pressure on the enemy, while American troops were gradually withdrawn. The ultimate objective was to strengthen ARVN capabilities and bolster the Thieu government so that the South Vietnamese could stand on their own against the Communists. Nixon announced that he was pulling out 25,000 troops and that he would pull out more at "regular intervals" thereafter. According to the president, withdrawal of U.S. forces was contingent on three factors: (1) the progress in training and equipping the South Vietnamese forces, (2) the progress in the Paris negotiations, and (3) the level of enemy activity.[56] Nixon later stated in his memoirs that the Midway announcement initiated "an irreversible process, the conclusion of which would be the departure of all Americans from Vietnam."[57]

Privately, President Thieu was not pleased with the American president's announcement. According to Nixon, Thieu realized what U.S. withdrawals would mean and was "deeply troubled" about the implications of an American departure from the war, but Nixon later claimed he privately assured Thieu through Ambassador Ellsworth Bunker that "our support for him was steadfast."[58]

Despite the concerns of the South Vietnamese about the new policy, Henry Kissinger recorded that "Nixon was jubilant. He considered the announcement [of Vietnamization] a political triumph. He thought that it would buy him the time necessary for developing our strategy."[59] A later memorandum revealed that Nixon hoped that his new policy of Vietnamizing the war would demonstrate to the American people that he "had ruled out a purely U.S. solution to the problem in South Vietnam and indeed had a plan to end the war."[60]

In order to solidify the new strategy, Nixon met with Laird and General Wheeler upon his return from Midway to discuss a formal mission change for General Abrams and MACV. The current mission statement, which had been issued by President Johnson, was to "defeat" the enemy and "force" his withdrawal from South Vietnam. As a result of the discussions following the Midway announcement, a new order that would take effect on August 15 charged Abrams with (1) providing "maximum assistance" to strengthen the armed forces of South Vietnam, (2) increasing the support to the pacification effort, and (3) reducing the flow of supplies to the enemy down the Ho Chi Minh Trail.[61] With this order, the entire thrust of U.S. efforts in South Vietnam changed, as will be discussed in detail later.

On 25 July 1969, President Nixon visited Guam as part of a tour of Asia. During a press conference there, he announced a new foreign policy for the United States. He stated that "as far as the problems of military defense, except for the threat of a major power involving nuclear weapons, that the U.S. is going to encourage and has a right to expect that this problem will be increasingly handled by, and the responsibility for it taken by, the Asian nations themselves."[62] His new policy, which was really just a wider application of the Vietnamization concept, quickly became known as the "Guam Doctrine." However, according to Henry Kissinger, the president worked hard to get the press to describe it as the "Nixon Doctrine."[63] Nixon's new doctrine was based on three fundamentals: willingness to negotiate, strength, and partnership. He asserted that East and West should find ways to live together and that relationships between the West and Communist countries should be opened and maintained in order to achieve a lasting peace. Accordingly, Nixon stated that the United States would continue to honor its commitments, but that its partners would be expected to carry their share of the load. As Secretary of Defense Laird put it, "[W]hile a major American role remains indispensable, other nations can and should assume greater responsibilities."[64]

The Vietnamization program fell into line with the Nixon Doctrine. According to historian Joan Hoff, the new doctrine was aimed at "southern tier" third world countries in East Asia and provided "essentially a rationale for retrenchment, but it came to represent the formal institutionalization of Vietnamization."[65] The United States was prepared to provide South Vietnam with aid and assistance so that the South Vietnamese forces could eventually take over the war and American troops could be withdrawn. The administration believed that helping South Vietnam to stand on its own feet would provide additional proof that the United States always honored its commitments to friends and allies, and could well work toward developing a sense of regional self-confidence, self-reliance, and cooperation even after U.S. forces were withdrawn. Vietnamization thus conceived provided the first step in implementing the Nixon Doctrine. Nixon clearly felt that the way the war in Vietnam was finally ended would have an enduring impact on American foreign policy initiatives in the future.

On 30 July, on the way home from his Asian tour, Nixon made a surprise stop in Saigon. No formal announcements were made before the stop, and Nixon was whisked by helicopter directly to Doc Lap (Independence) Palace to visit with Thieu. There he told the South Vietnamese president that the United States would not desert his country and that withdrawals were necessary to maintain American public support, promising that they would be carried out according to a "systematic timetable."[66]

Having sought to reassure the South Vietnamese, Nixon then prepared to explain his plan to the American public. In a nationally televised speech to the nation on 3 November 1969, Nixon described his new policy to the American people. He said, "We have adopted a plan which we have worked out in cooperation with the South Vietnamese for the complete withdrawal of all U.S. combat ground forces, and their replacement by South Vietnamese forces on an orderly scheduled timetable. This withdrawal will be made from strength and not from weakness." He further explained, "The precipitant withdrawal of all American forces from Vietnam would be a disaster, not only for South Vietnam but for the United States and the cause of peace. Ultimately, this would cost lives, which would not bring peace but more war."[67]

Vietnamization thus became a way for Nixon to reduce the pressure on his new administration for complete withdrawal, providing more time with which to pursue a negotiated peace while continuing to build-up the South Vietnamese forces. It was, as Henry Kissinger described it, "a plan to end the war" designed to offer the United States "a prospect of honorable disengagement that was not hostage to the other side's cooperation."[68] In time, Vietnamization became part of a wider strategy that Nixon later described as "part of his overall plan to end the war."[69] Nixon's plan included the following goals:

- Reverse the "Americanization" of the war that had occurred from 1965 to 1968 and concentrate instead on Vietnamization.

- Give more priority to pacification so that the South Vietnamese could be better able to extend their control over the countryside.
- Reduce the invasion threat by destroying enemy sanctuaries and supply lines in Cambodia and Laos.
- Withdraw the half million American troops from Vietnam in a way that would not bring collapse in the South.
- Negotiate a cease-fire and a peace treaty.
- Demonstrate our willingness and determination to stand by our ally if the peace agreement was violated by Hanoi, and assure South Vietnam that it would continue to receive our military aid as Hanoi did from its allies, the Soviet Union and, to a lesser extent, China.

Nixon and his advisers optimistically perceived that Vietnamization could bring the additional benefit of a quicker end to the war. Aside from strengthening Thieu's forces so that they could assume more responsibility for the fighting, the policy also might encourage the North Vietnamese to be more receptive to a negotiated peace. According to Nixon, "If the enemy feels that we are going to stay there long enough for the South Vietnamese to be strong enough to handle their own defense, then I think they have a real incentive to negotiate, because if they have to negotiate with a strong, vigorous South Vietnamese government, the deal they make with them isn't going to be as good as the deal they might get now."[70]

The public support for Vietnamization was initially extremely positive. Many Americans responded very favorably to the new policy, hoping that the initial withdrawal of 25,000 troops was a prelude to an eventual complete withdrawal of all U.S. forces from South Vietnam.[71] Many in the American press also were encouraged by Nixon's change in strategy, and while some columnists like Rowland Evans and Robert Novak were concerned about the ability of the South Vietnamese to take over the war effort, the media reports and commentaries preceding and immediately following the announcement of Nixon's new strategy were generally favorable.[72] Such support would prove short-lived.

PRECURSORS TO VIETNAMIZATION

Despite Nixon's rhetoric to the contrary, what he called "Vietnamization" was not an entirely new idea.[73] It was first discussed in 1967 after nearly three years of full-scale U.S. combat involvement in South Vietnam. General Westmoreland, then MACV commander, spoke in November 1967 during a National Press Club speech of gradually turning over the fighting to the South Vietnamese. He said that in 1968 the United States would undertake "Phase III" of its war strategy, which would include an upgrading of the South Vietnamese Regional and Popular Forces, providing ARVN with new equipment to prepare it to "take on an ever-increasing share of the war," and transferring "a major share" of the frontline defense of the

DMZ to the South Vietnamese forces. He further stated that during "Phase IV" U.S. forces could "begin to phase down" as ARVN developed its capabilities and began to "take charge of the final mopping up of the Vietcong" and "show[ed] that it can handle the Vietcong."[74] The objective of this plan was to upgrade the South Vietnamese forces so that they could handle a continued Viet Cong insurgency after the departure of U.S. forces. The plan, however, did not envision that the South Vietnamese armed forces would be able to deal with North Vietnam's army.

Measures under this plan had already been initiated when Nixon took office. So by the time that Nixon, Laird, and Kissinger had formulated their new strategy for ending the war, the strategic ingredients were already in place and the process was ongoing. Former ARVN general Nguyen Duy Hinh has suggested that the considerable development of the RVNAF in the year before Nixon assumed office may have been an important factor that influenced the new president's thinking when he considered ways to end the war for the Americans.[75]

However, a key difference distinguished the plans that Westmoreland initiated and those ordered by Nixon: under the Nixon and Laird plan, the South Vietnamese would be expected to fight both the Viet Cong and the North Vietnamese Army after the eventual withdrawal of U.S. troops. The distinction would prove critical during the period between the policy's initiation and the ultimate defeat of the South Vietnamese in 1975.

2

Implementing the New Strategy

THE NEW STRATEGY

As the man charged with executing Nixon's new strategy, Gen. Creighton Abrams, commander of U.S. Military Assistance Command, Vietnam, was given what Henry Kissinger called "one of the most thankless tasks ever assigned an American general," the dismantling of a force more than half a million men strong, while maintaining security and training another army to take over.[1] Kissinger described the situation that Abrams faced: "It was painful to see General Abrams, epitome of the combat commander, obviously unhappy, yet nevertheless agreeing to a withdrawal of 25,000 combat troops. He knew then that he was doomed to a rearguard action, that the purpose of his command would increasingly become logistic redeployment and not success in battle. He could not possibly achieve the victory that had eluded us at full strength while our forces were constantly dwindling. It remained to sell this proposition to President Thieu."[2] Despite the difficulties and potential dangers involved, Abrams accepted his marching orders and began the disengagement of American forces and the Vietnamization of the war.

The Vietnamization program would be implemented in three phases. In the first phase, responsibility for the bulk of the ground combat against Viet Cong and North Vietnamese forces would be turned over gradually to the RVNAF. During this phase, the United States would continue to provide air, naval, and logistical support. The second phase, the development of RVNAF's capability to achieve self-reliance, involved increasing their artillery, air, and naval assets, as well as providing other support activities. Designed to proceed simultaneously with the first phase, the second phase would require much more time. Even after the bulk of U.S. combat forces were withdrawn, U.S. forces would continue to provide support, security, and training personnel. The third phase involved the reduction of the American presence to a strictly military advisory role, with a small security element remaining for protection. The advisory effort would gradually dwindle as South Vietnam grew in strength until such American military presence was no longer required.

The timetable for completion of each phase was open-ended, and no date was set for the withdrawal of all U.S. forces. The president felt that setting such a date would remove the incentive for the Communists to negotiate; by specifying the date, Washington would lose a bargaining tool—the threat of a continued U.S. military presence—to extract concessions from the Communists at the Paris talks.

The new strategy, as conceived by Nixon and Laird, always contemplated leaving a residual force. Addressing the House Subcommittee on Department of Defense Appropriations in February 1970, Laird stated: "Under the Vietnamization program in the third phase, we anticipate that a military assistance mission will remain in Vietnam. This will not be as large a force as the one we have in Korea at the present time, nor will it be a large force like the one we have in Europe. It would be a military assistance mission, and we have this requirement for some time to come."[3] The South Vietnamese took statements such as this and many more like it as evidence of a promise that the United States would not desert them. As the cries for complete U.S. withdrawal increased in volume in America, the idea of a residual U.S. force would eventually be abandoned, a change that would have a devastating impact on the fortunes of South Vietnam.

THE SOUTH VIETNAMESE FORCES

While U.S. units continued to conduct combat operations against the Communist forces, the new Vietnamization policy focused initially on modernizing and developing the South Vietnamese armed forces. The effort included an increase in RVNAF force structure with an emphasis on improving firepower and mobility.

Prior to the initiation of that policy South Vietnam's forces were relatively small. As 1968 drew to a close, RVNAF consisted of four branches of service: the Army of Vietnam (ARVN), the Vietnamese Air Force (VNAF), the Vietnamese Navy (VNN), and the Vietnamese Marine Corps (VNMC). In addition to the services were specialized units and commands, such as the Airborne Division, the Capital Military District, the Special Forces, and the Training Command (see chart 1).

The South Vietnamese armed forces were directed by the Joint General Staff in Saigon. The chief of the Joint General Staff, overall commander of the RVNAF, headed the deputy chiefs of staff for personnel, logistics, political warfare, and operations. The next level of command under the Joint General Staff in the Army of South Vietnam included the four regional corps commanders, each overseeing one of the four corps tactical zones (I, II, III, and IV CTZ) (see map 1). The corps commanders directed military operations within their respective CTZs (CTZ designations were changed to military regions, or MRs, in 1971; e.g., I Corps Tactical Zone became Military Region I). Each corps commander was assigned from two to three

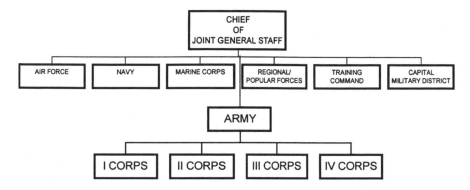

Chart 1. RVNAF Military Organization, 1966–67. Note: Airborne Division and Special Forces also came under direct command of the Joint General Staff. Adapted from Ngo Quang Truong, *Indochina Monographs: RVNAF and U.S. Operational Cooperation and Coordination* (Washington, D.C.: U.S. Army Center of Military History, 1980), 21.

of the ten regular ARVN infantry divisions. The 1st and 2nd infantry divisions were deployed to the I CTZ south of the Demilitarized Zone (DMZ); the 22nd and 23rd to the II CTZ in the Central Highlands; the 5th, 10th (later renamed the 18th), and 25th to the III CTZ; and the 7th, 9th, and 21st to the IV CTZ in the Delta.

In addition to the divisional forces, a total of twenty ranger battalions were parceled out to the respective corps headquarters, where they usually served as the corps reserve. The general (strategic) reserve, which operated under the direction of the Joint General Staff, included the Airborne and Marine divisions. Although the Vietnamese Marines were titularly under the command of the Vietnamese Navy, they actually fought as part of the South Vietnamese ground forces, normally operating under the direction of the I Corps commander. In all, 141 RVNAF maneuver battalions operated throughout South Vietnam in 1968.[4]

Along with the regular ARVN and marine ground forces were the Regional and Popular Forces (RF/PF), territorial units of local militia responsible for the protection of hamlets, villages, and important government installations. The RF were organized into companies of about 100 men each and the PF into platoons of about 40 men each. All RF companies and PF platoons were placed under operational control of the sector commander in the province in which they were located. By June 1968 total RF strength consisted of 197,900 men organized into 1,053 companies and twelve battalion headquarters; PF strength at that time totaled 164,300 men assigned to 4,861 platoons.[5] Because of the expansion of the pacification effort following the Tet offensive, the RF/PF had more members in 1968 than in previous years.

The Vietnamese Air Force was small compared to ARVN. By 1968 it numbered only 17,000 personnel. The primary VNAF combat aircraft at that time was the A-1 Skyraider, a Korean War era propeller-driven fighter-bomber. The primary

Table 1. Republic of Vietnam Armed Forces, 1968

Organization	Members
Army of the Republic of Vietnam (ARVN)	321,056
Vietnamese Marine Corps (VNMC)	8,271
Vietnamese Air Force (VNAF)	17,198
Vietnamese Navy (VNN)	17,178
Regional Forces (RF)	185,871
Popular Forces (PF)	167,640
Total members	717,214

Source: Nguyen Duy Hinh, *Indochina Monographs: Vietnamization and the Cease-Fire* (Washington, D.C.: U.S. Army Center of Military History, 1980), 32.

cargo aircraft was the C-47, which was World War II vintage. VNAF was also equipped with H-34 helicopters.

The Vietnamese Navy, like the VNAF, was also relatively small in comparison to ARVN. The navy was responsible for limited coastal defense and riverine operations in the Delta. The VNN, numbering 12,000 in 1965, had risen to only 17,000 by 1968. By that time, it was equipped with river patrol boats, miscellaneous landing craft, high-speed coastal patrol craft, and a few sea patrol ships such as destroyers.

By the end of 1968, even before the institution of the Vietnamization effort, the Republic of Vietnam Armed Forces constituted a formidable force that included over 700,000 men under arms. The totals by service are shown in table 1.

EARLY EFFORTS TO MODERNIZE THE RVNAF

Although improving and modernizing the RVNAF was not a new effort in 1969, the task had been of only secondary importance during earlier years, when U.S. military leaders focused on the conduct of operations by American units in the field. With the election of Richard Nixon and his subsequent emphasis on Vietnamization, the effort to strengthen and modernize the South Vietnamese forces became a top priority for MACV.

Even before Nixon assumed office, plans had been developed to increase the size of the RVNAF. In early April 1968 the U.S. Department of Defense ordered MACV to develop a modernization plan for the South Vietnamese armed forces. The resulting plan, which became known as the May-68 Plan, addressed three goals. The first goal was to develop the RVNAF into a balanced force with command, administration, and self-support capabilities to continue the fighting successfully after the withdrawal of U.S. and NVA troops. Achieving a balanced, capable force required an expanded air force and navy, as well as additional logistical elements. Some support would continue to be provided by U.S. forces. The second goal was to modernize the RVNAF by replacing obsolete weapons with M-16 rifles and M-60 machine guns. Obsolete or defective vehicles and signal equipment were to be replaced by more modern vehicles and radios. The third goal was

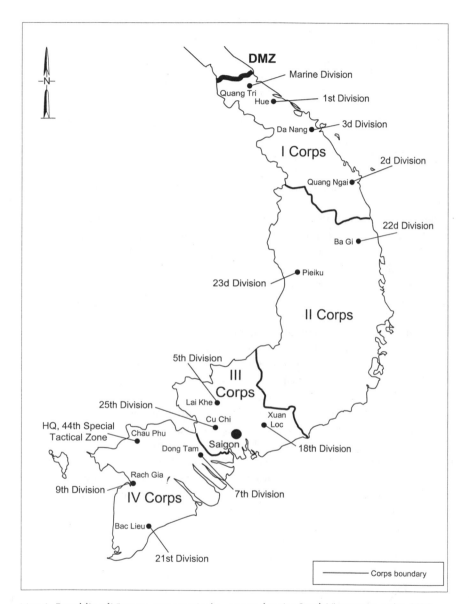

Map 1. Republic of Vietnam corps tactical zones and major South Vietnamese units, 1972.

to plan for turning over U.S. equipment to the RVNAF as U.S. forces withdrew from Vietnam.[6]

As noted earlier, most of the previous force structure increases had involved increasing the size of ARVN, while the South Vietnamese air force, navy, and marine corps had grown very little. The disparate growth resulted when U.S. planners consciously decided that American forces would cover the latter services' short-comings in capabilities. However, as the United States began peace talks with the North Vietnamese and the decision was made to transfer more of the responsibility for the war to the South Vietnamese, it became apparent that the other South Vietnamese services would have to be modernized and increased in size to replace the combat capability that would be lost when the U.S. Air Force, Navy, and Marine Corps withdrew. Thus, the May-68 Plan addressed not only the modernization of ARVN, but also focused on increasing the capabilities of the VNAF, VNN, and VNMC.

The May-68 Plan, and those that followed, envisioned that a "residual" U.S. force would remain and continue to provide supplemental combat and logistical support during the restructuring and modernization of the RVNAF forces.[7] Importantly, the plan was based upon the assumption of a mutual U.S.-North Vietnamese troop withdrawal from South Vietnam, an assumption that would eventually disappear.

When the plan was submitted by MACV to the Defense Department, Secretary Clark Clifford directed that it be modified to emphasize "maximizing fox-hole strength," rather than focusing on making the RVNAF self-sufficient by increasing the number of logistical support units. For domestic political reasons, Clifford wanted to increase Saigon's visibility in the fighting in the field. Accordingly, on 25 June 1968, Deputy Secretary of Defense Paul Nitze sent the chairman of the Joint Chiefs a memorandum directing that the May Plan be modified in light of the secretary's wishes. He suggested that the plan be revised to reflect two phases. During "Phase I," MACV should provide all assistance, particularly in the logistical area, necessary to ensure that the RVNAF assumed a greater share of the combat role in the field. In "Phase II," which would run concurrently, MACV would take measures to support the development of a self-sufficient South Vietnamese force structure "capable of meeting insurgency requirements that could remain if North Vietnam and U.S. forces withdrew."[8] As U.S. Army historian Jeffrey J. Clarke points out, at no time during the discussions of the May-68 Plan or in the subsequent guidance provided by Clifford and Nitze did any of the parties, including MACV, ever consider the "prospect of a unilateral American withdrawal that would leave South Vietnam facing a combined Viet Cong and North Vietnamese threat."[9]

With the inauguration of Richard Nixon, the plans to modernize the RVNAF and turn over more combat responsibility took on a new urgency. Despite the previously mentioned warnings about trying to build a South Vietnamese force to combat both the VC insurgency and the North Vietnamese Army, Nixon and Laird were adamant in demanding proposals for doing just that. With the initial guidance provided in National Security Study Memorandum 36 and the official announcement of Vietnamization at Midway in June 1969, President Nixon made it very clear that he wanted the war turned over to the South as quickly as possible. To do so, military planners focused on three areas to improve the RVNAF combat capability. The first two, increasing the size of the force and providing modern weapons and equipment proved easier than the third, which involved upgrading the quality and capabilities of the South Vietnamese fighting force in the field.

IMPROVEMENTS IN FORCE STRUCTURE AND EQUIPMENT

When Nixon met with President Thieu at Midway in June 1969 and announced the initiation of the Vietnamization policy, Thieu expressed significant concerns about the capabilities of his forces in light of the inevitable U.S. troop withdrawals. He was seriously troubled by the assumption behind the new policy that an improved RVNAF could combat both the VC insurgency and NVA mainforce units in South Vietnam. Accordingly, Thieu and his generals drew up some proposals of their own.

The South Vietnamese wanted to increase their manpower from 875,000 to over 1 million. Concerned about the potential for North Vietnamese tank attacks across the DMZ, they also wanted to increase their armor capability by forming two new armored brigades and three more armored cavalry squadrons. As part of this effort, they hoped to exchange their gasoline-powered M-113 armored personnel carriers for more modern diesel models and their outdated M-41 light tanks for the newer and more capable M-48 main battle tanks.

Additionally, Saigon proposed to establish a new territorial artillery branch with sixty-five 105-mm howitzer batteries (390 field pieces) and eighteen 155-mm howitzer batteries (108 field pieces). The increased capability would greatly enhance fire support for territorial security forces and permit the existing division and corps artillery units to be more mobile and thus more responsive to the regular maneuver units.

Not only did Thieu want to improve ARVN, he also wanted to increase the capabilities of his other forces. He asked for more financial support in order to increase the territorial forces. He requested that VNAF's entire fleet of old C-47 transport aircraft be replaced with newer, larger C-130s, and that additional funding be provided for three new air units, totaling ninety-five new specialized aircraft for search and rescue, commando operations, and coastal and river surveillance. He also asked for eight new radar stations, two Hawk antiaircraft missile batteries, and eleven air defense artillery battalions. He wanted the United States to fund more and larger vessels for the South Vietnamese navy and pay for the activation of three more South Vietnamese marine battalions and the subsequent formation of a VNMC division. In addition to requesting support for increasing the size and capabilities of his forces, Thieu also asked for more funding to pay for increased living standards for his troops, which would include pay raises and free messing for all servicemen. Obviously, Thieu's requests represented a significant increase in U.S. funding for the RVNAF.[10]

Laird asked Abrams to review Thieu's requests and recommend what should be done about them. After studying the issues with his staff, Abrams replied to Laird that he supported an increase in the size of the RVNAF force structure, as well as some of the material improvements, but disapproved of the requests for new air, armor, artillery, and air defense units. His rationale was that these improvements were unnecessary in light of the support provided by U.S. forces. He regarded Thieu's request for additional financial support for his servicemen as an "internal South Vietnamese problem."[11]

Adm. John S. McCain, commander of the Pacific Forces and Abrams's immediate superior, and the Joint Chiefs of Staff agreed with Abrams's recommendations on Thieu's requests. The Joint Chiefs' endorsement to the secretary of defense said that existing South Vietnamese equipment "appeared adequate in terms of current requirements and the limited Vietnamese technical capability," but noted that "as these capabilities improve and if operational needs change, more sophisticated weapon systems should be considered for introduction into the RVNAF."[12]

On 18 August 1969, Laird approved Abrams's recommendations on force structure increases for the RVNAF. These became known collectively as the "Midway increase." With his approval Laird provided additional guidance to Abrams and the Joint Chiefs of Staff, charging them to review all ongoing and projected programs for improving the RVNAF in order to make it capable of dealing with a combined Viet Cong-North Vietnamese threat. He asked them not only to consider force structure and equipment improvements, but also to examine new ways of improving leadership and training and to develop new strategies and tactics best suited to South Vietnamese capabilities.[13] Laird's directive represented a drastic change in the planning guidance under which the Pentagon and MACV headquarters in Saigon had been working. Despite repeated dire warnings to the contrary that the South Vietnamese could not handle a combined threat, it became obvious that for domestic political reasons the Saigon forces would eventually have to contend with both threats on their own.

On 2 September, Abrams responded to Laird's guidance. He pointed out in very direct terms that proposed modernization and improvement programs, even with the Midway increase, would not permit the South Vietnamese to handle the current combined threat. Citing poor leadership, high desertion rates, and corruption in the upper ranks of the RVNAF, Abrams reported that he thought that the South Vietnamese forces could not be improved either quantitatively or qualitatively to the extent necessary to deal with a combined threat; he clearly stated his opinion that what the secretary of defense wanted simply could not be done.[14]

Laird could not accept Abrams's assessment, because if he did, it meant that he would have to admit that the United States could never gracefully exit Vietnam, particularly in light of the increasingly obvious fact that the North Vietnamese were not going to agree to a bilateral withdrawal of U.S. and NVA troops from South Vietnam. The best that the United States could hope for was to build-up the South Vietnamese so that they could hold on for at least a decent interval after the American troops had been withdrawn. Accordingly, Laird wanted to accelerate efforts to increase the combat capabilities of the RVNAF. On 10 November, he directed the Joint Chiefs of Staff to come up with a new plan, a "Phase III" plan, that would, one way or the other, create a South Vietnamese military force that could "maintain at least current levels of security."[15] He told the military planners to assume unilateral U.S. withdrawals that would reduce American military strength first to a "support force" of between 190,000 and 260,000 troops by July 1971 and then to a much smaller advisory force by July 1973. He was effectively telling the planners for a third time to come up with a viable Vietnamization program, but with the new caveat that they were not to assume a large residual U.S. support force.

Laird's orders finally came through loud and clear; the resultant military response from Saigon was more to his liking. Abrams and his staff, realizing that the die was cast with regard to eventual U.S. withdrawal and despite their great misgivings, apparently attempted to devise the best plan possible given Laird's adamant directives. In order to comply with the secretary's orders, the military planners assumed a reduced Viet Cong threat and a declining NVA presence in South Vietnam, while virtually ignoring Hanoi's forces based just outside the borders of South Vietnam.[16]

Having made these somewhat questionable assumptions, MACV submitted its new recommendations at the end of December. In January 1970 the Joint Chiefs included them in the revised Phase III RVNAF Improvement and Modernization Plan, which called for an increase in RVNAF strength to 1,061,505 over a three-year period (mid-1970 to mid-1973). The plan also called for ten new artillery battalions, twenty-four truck companies, and six more helicopter squadrons for the RVNAF.

Laird and his staff thought that this plan was finally a step in the right direction, but they were concerned that MACV planners still had not accepted the fact that there would be no large residual American support force and suspected that the military was trying to stall the withdrawal process.[17] Accordingly, in mid-February 1970, Laird flew to Saigon to meet with Abrams and Thieu to impress upon them the urgency of the situation. He voiced disappointment about the lack of any new or fresh approaches from MACV regarding the implementation of the Vietnamization program. While in Saigon, he met separately with senior South Vietnamese generals who expressed concern with the Phase III plan. Specifically, they reiterated earlier requests for additional artillery, to include long-range 175-mm artillery pieces and air defense artillery, and again asked for financial assistance to improve the lot of their soldiers.[18]

When Laird returned to Washington, he ordered the Joint Chiefs of Staff to reevaluate the proposed Phase III plan in light of the South Vietnamese requests and to come up with a more comprehensive plan. Two months later, the Joint Chiefs submitted the revised plan, which became known as the Consolidated RVNAF Improvement and Modernization Plan, or CRIMP (table 2 shows the evolution of RVNAF force structure plans). The plan, which covered the 1970–72 fiscal years, raised the total supported South Vietnamese military force structure to an even 1.1 million. Laird approved the first two years of the plan, but deferred approval of the remainder until he had a better assessment of the long-range military situation in South Vietnam and the financial situation in the United States.[19]

CRIMP had a significant impact on the entire RVNAF, but, as in the past, ARVN got the largest share of the improvements. Under CRIMP, ARVN eventually received 155-mm and 175-mm long range artillery pieces, M-42 and M-55 antiaircraft weapons, M-48 tanks, and a host of other sophisticated equipment and weapons systems. By the end of 1969, the United States had supplied 1,200 tanks and armored vehicles, 30,000 machine guns, 4,000 mortars, 20,000 radios, and

Table 2. Evolution of RVNAF Force Structure Plans

RVNAF	FY-68 Final	May-68 Plan	Phase I	Phase I (Modified)	Phase II	Phase II Accelerated		Accelerated Midway Package			Phase III
						DOD APPR FY 69–73	1ST REV FY 69–72	FY 70	FY 71	FY 72	FY 73
ARVN	321,056	358,766	359,897	366,897	363,831	374,132	374,132	387,835	390,799	395,799	448,953
VNN	17,178	19,157	19,344	21,044	26,100	19,344	28,700	31,645	31,645	33,122	39,742
VNMC	8,271	8,920	8,920	8,920	9,304	9,304	9,304	13,070	13,070	13,070	14,402
VNAF	17,198	21,705	20,987	22,487	32,587	32,587	32,587	35,786	35,786	35,786	64,507
RF	185,871	213,927	213,927	252,927	245,632	252,927	252,927	270,497	275,670	275,670	324,561
PF	167,640	178,140	178,140	178,140	178,140	178,140	178,140	214,840	239,390	239,390	206,028
Total	717,214	801,215	800,615	850,415	855,594	866,434	875,790	953,673	986,360	992,837	1,100,000[a]

Source: Nguyen Duy Hinh, Indochina Monographs: Vietnamization and the Cease-Fire (Washington, D.C.: U.S. Army Center of Military History, 1980), 32.
[a] Includes 1,807 unassigned troops.

25,000 jeeps and trucks.[20] The new equipment and weapons received in the two years following the approval of CRIMP enabled ARVN to activate an additional infantry division (3rd Infantry Division), as well as a number of smaller units, including twenty-five border ranger battalions, numerous artillery battalions, four armored cavalry squadrons, three tank battalions, two armored brigade headquarters, and three antiaircraft battalions. By the beginning of 1972, the South Vietnamese army strength would increase to 450,000, comprised of 171 infantry battalions, 58 artillery battalions, 22 armored cavalry and tank squadrons, and 60 artillery battalions.[21]

The regular forces benefitted greatly from CRIMP, but so too did the territorial Regional and Popular Forces. As Vietnamization gained momentum, MACV and Washington planned to fill the gaps left by departing U.S. divisions with an expansion of the RF/PF, who they hoped could take over the major share of territorial security and support of the pacification program. Expansion of the territorial forces involved a significant increase in numbers and improved equipment. Under CRIMP, the RF and PF received newer, more modern weapons, including M-16 rifles, M-60 machine guns, and M-79 grenade launchers, all of which were vast improvements over the hodgepodge of older cast-off weapons with which they previously had been armed. The influx of 105-mm howitzers eventually enabled the Joint General Staff to activate a total of 174 territorial artillery sections in support of the RF, PF, and border ranger forces.[22] The great enhancement of fire support available to the territorial forces was significant in that it reduced the burden on the regular artillery forces, who could then focus on supporting the regular maneuver battalions in their combat operations. In addition to the new equipment, the manpower strength of the Regional and Popular Forces was increased in an attempt to get more government troops into the countryside to support the pacification effort. The command structure of the Regional Forces was reorganized and several RF Group Commands were formed.

The Vietnamese Air Force also benefitted greatly under CRIMP, growing from 17,000 in late 1968 to 37,000 by the end of 1969, and ultimately to 64,000 by 1973. A significant upgrade in aircraft and command and control capability accompanied this increase in the number of personnel. In 1968 A-37 and F-5A jet fighter-bombers began to replace the VNAF's older propeller-driven attack aircraft, thus vastly increasing VNAF ground support capability. Its cargo hauling capability was also improved with the upgrading of the C-47 fleet initially to C-119 aircraft, and eventually to C-123 and C-7 aircraft. The helicopter fleet was greatly enlarged and improved as U.S. Army aviation units began to redeploy, turning over their aircraft and equipment to newly activated Vietnamese helicopter squadrons (unlike the U.S. arrangement of the army owning most of the troop-carrying and attack helicopters, VNAF owned all the helicopters in the South Vietnamese inventory). Late in 1972, as the United States prepared for total withdrawal, VNAF, under the provisions of a special program called Enhance Plus, would receive thirty-two C-130A cargo planes, each having four engines, and additional C-7 cargo planes, F-5A fighter-bombers, and helicopters.

During the Vietnamization period, the Vietnamese Air Force grew to six times its 1964 strength and, by 1973, operated a total of 1,700 aircraft, including over 500 helicopters. By then VNAF had six air divisions, which included a total of ten A-37 fighter-bomber squadrons, three A-1H attack helicopter squadrons, three F-5E fighter-bomber squadrons, seventeen UH-1 helicopter squadrons, four CH-47 helicopter squadrons, ten liaison and observation squadrons, three C-7 squadrons, four AC-47, AC-119, and EC-47 squadrons, and other additional training units.[23] In terms of equipment, VNAF would be one of the most powerful air forces in Southeast Asia by the time of the U.S. withdrawal in 1973.

The Vietnamese Navy also underwent significant expansion during the Vietnamization period. The navy, which numbered only 17,000 sailors in 1968, would reach 40,000 by 1972. To increase the capability of the VNN and to meet the goals of the Vietnamization program, MACV instituted two new programs in 1969. The first was called the Accelerated Turnover of Assets (ACTOV), which was designed to rapidly increase naval strength and training and, at the same time, accelerate turnover of ships and combat responsibility from the U.S. Navy to the South Vietnamese navy. The second program, the Accelerated Turnover of Logistics (ACTOVLOG), was aimed at increasing naval logistical support capabilities.

Under ACTOV, the Vietnamese Navy initiated an extensive recruiting and training program. Vietnamese specialists and sailors served aboard U.S. Navy ships for on-the-job training. Once a U.S. ship was designated for eventual turnover to the VNN, the crew became a combined U.S.-South Vietnamese crew. The objective was to provide the VNN with a new ship, but only after the South Vietnamese crew was ready and able to handle its operation. Under this program, the VNN received two small cruisers in May 1969. Shortly thereafter, the U.S. Navy Riverine Force began to turn over its vessels and river patrol responsibilities to the VNN. By mid-1970, over five hundred U.S. brown-water navy boats had been transferred to the South Vietnamese. In September of that year, the VNN took over the ships and mission of the Market Time coastal interdiction program, which was designed to halt seaborne infiltration of supplies to Communist troops in the South.

The second enhancement effort, ACTOVLOG, was designed to improve the naval logistics infrastructure and support capabilities. Under ACTOV and ACTOVLOG, the Vietnamese Navy grew rapidly, and by 1972 operated a fleet of over 1,700 ships and boats of all types, including sea patrol craft, large cargo ships, coastal and river patrol craft, and amphibious ships.

In terms of materiel and modern equipment, Vietnamization worked. By 1970, the armed forces of South Vietnam had made a quantum leap in terms of modernization to become one of the largest and best-equipped military forces in the world.

THE U.S. ADVISORY EFFORT

Unfortunately, however, South Vietnam required more than equipment and sheer numbers as it prepared to assume ultimate responsibility for the war. To improve

the quality of the ARVN force, MACV increasingly placed more emphasis on training and the advisory effort. U.S. advisers operated in essentially three areas: they
advised South Vietnamese combat units, served in the training base, and worked
in the provincial pacification programs.

MACV headquarters provided the advisory function to the Joint General Staff
(JGS), the senior headquarters of the Republic of Vietnam Armed Forces. However, only a part of MACV headquarters staff personnel actually served in a true
advisory capacity. In 1970, only 397 out of 1,668 authorized spaces in MACV's
fifteen staff agencies were designated officially as "advisers" to the GVN and the
JGS.[24] Nevertheless, as the war continued and more U.S. forces were withdrawn,
the MACV staff agencies became increasingly involved in advisory functions.

As previously stated, just below the JGS level were four South Vietnamese
corps commanders who were responsible for the four corps tactical zones (later,
military regions) of South Vietnam. Initially, their U.S. counterparts were the senior U.S. commanders in each of the corps tactical zones.[25] In this capacity, the senior U.S. commander was assisted by two deputies. His deputy for Civil Operations and Rural Development Support (CORDS) was the principal adviser to the
ARVN corps commander in the area of pacification and development. Additionally, the senior U.S. commander had another deputy, who served as the senior adviser to the corps commander and was actually the chief of the U.S. Army Advisory Group attached to the ARVN corps headquarters. As such, he and his staff
provided assistance, advice, and support to the corps commander and his staff in
command, administration, combat operations, training, intelligence, logistics, political warfare, and civil affairs.

Later, as additional U.S. units and the senior American field force headquarters were withdrawn, the advisory structure changed. During 1971–72, four regional assistance commands were established. The regional assistance commander,
usually a U.S. Army major general, became the senior adviser to the South Vietnamese corps commander in the respective military region. The exception to this
was in II Corps, where civilian John Paul Vann was named the senior adviser. Because a civilian technically could not command U.S. military forces, his headquarters was redesignated Second Regional Assistance Group (rather than "Command"). Vann had a military deputy, an army brigadier general, who exercised
command on his behalf. Otherwise, Vann functioned the same as the other regional
assistance commanders.

The mission of the regional assistance commanders was to assist ARVN corps
commanders in developing and maintaining an effective military capability by advising and supporting RVNAF military and paramilitary commanders and staffs at
all levels in the corps in military operations, training, intelligence, personnel management, and combat support and combat service support activities. To accomplish
this, the regional assistance commander had a staff who worked directly with the
ARVN corps staff. He also exercised operational control over the subordinate advisory groups and the pacification advisory organizations in the military region. As

such, he and his personnel provided advice, assistance, and support at each echelon of South Vietnamese command in planning and executing combat operations
and coordinated pacification and development programs within the military region.

Below the senior U.S. adviser in each military region were two types of advisory teams: province advisory teams and division advisory teams. Each of the forty-
four provinces in South Vietnam was headed by a province chief, usually a South
Vietnamese army or marine colonel, who supervised the provincial government apparatus and also commanded the provincial Regional and Popular Forces. Under
the CORDS program initiated in 1967 an advisory system was established to assist the province chiefs in administering the pacification program.[26] The province
chief's American counterpart was the province senior adviser, who was either military or civilian, depending on the security situation of the respective province. The
province senior adviser and his staff were responsible for advising the province chief
in civil and military aspects of the South Vietnamese pacification and development
programs. The province senior adviser's staff, which was made up of both U.S. military and civilian personnel, was divided into two parts: the first dealt with area and
community development, to include public health and administration, civil affairs,
education, agriculture, psychological operations, and logistics; the second dealt with
plans and operations, focusing on preparing plans and directing military operations
of the territorial forces and associated support within the province.

The province chief exercised his authority through district chiefs. In order to
provide advice and support to the district chiefs, the province senior adviser supervised the district senior advisers, who each had a staff of about eight members
(although the actual size in each case depended on the particular situation in that
district). The district-level advisory teams assisted the district chief in the military and civil aspects of the pacification and rural development program. Additionally, the district team (and/or assigned mobile assistance training teams) advised and trained the Regional and Popular Forces in the district. By the end of
1967, a total of 4,000 U.S. military and civilian personnel were participating in the
CORDS advisory effort. When Vietnamization was officially declared in 1969,
total U.S. Army advisory strength stood at about 13,500, with half assigned to
CORDS organizations.[27] The increased number of advisers resulted from the expansion of the pacification program following the 1968 Tet offensive. Chart 2
shows the organization of the CORDS team at province level.

Other U.S. advisers assisted the RVNAF regular forces. In January 1969,
MACV, in an attempt to upgrade the capability of the regular ARVN divisions, initiated the Division Combat Assistance Team (DCAT) concept. The plan placed an
emphasis on reducing the number of tactical advisers in the field and changing their
mission from "advising to combat support coordination" at the ARVN division
level.[28] The DCAT's mission was to advise and assist the ARVN division commander and his staff in command, administration, training, tactical operations, intelligence, security, logistics, and certain elements of political warfare.[29] The division senior adviser, usually a U.S. Army colonel, exercised control over the

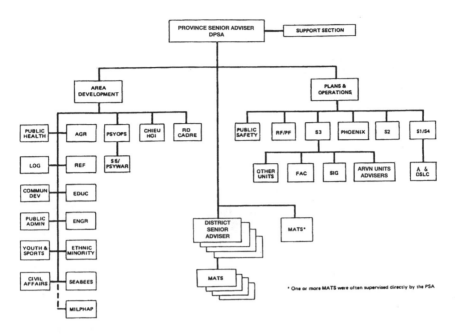

Chart 2. Province Advisory Team, 1968. Adapted from Ngo Quang Truong, *Indochina Monographs: RVNAF and U.S. Operational Cooperation and Coordination* (Washington, D.C.: U.S. Army Center of Military History, 1980), 154.

division staff advisers and the regimental and battalion advisory teams, which were selectively reduced in strength beginning in 1969 (depending on the ARVN division and the level of enemy activity in its respective operating area).[30]

Each ARVN division usually had three infantry regiments, one artillery regiment, and several separate battalions, such as the cavalry squadron and the engineer battalion. Normally, each of the regimental advisory teams was composed of eight to twelve U.S. Army personnel (their numbers eventually lessened when the drawdown of U.S. forces in country resulted in fewer assigned advisers). The regimental teams were usually headed by a U.S. Army lieutenant colonel and included various mixes of officers and noncommissioned officers (NCOs). The separate battalion advisory teams usually consisted of one or two specialists who advised the South Vietnamese in their respective functional areas (e.g., cavalry, intelligence, engineering, etc.).

Elite ARVN troops, such as the airborne and ranger units, were organized generally along the same lines as regular ARVN units (although the highest echelon of command in the ranger units was the group, roughly equivalent to a regiment). Each of these elite groups was accompanied by an American advisory team, which was headed by a colonel and was similar to but somewhat larger than those found with the regular ARVN regiments. The advisory structure for the Vietnamese Marine Corps was similar to ARVN, but the advisers were U.S. Marine Corps personnel. (Chart 3 depicts the U.S. advisory chain of command in 1969–70.)

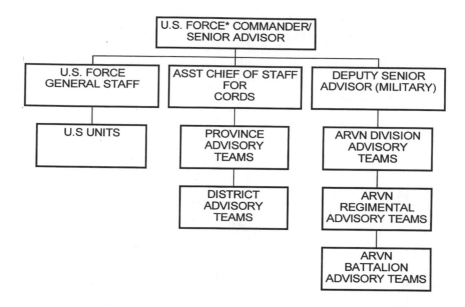

*Senior U.S. Commander (usually Field Force or Corps) in Corps Tactical Zone.

Chart 3. U.S. Advisory Chain of Command, 1969–70. From Cao Van Vien, et al., *Indochina Monographs: The U.S. Adviser* (Washington, D.C.: U.S. Army Center of Military History, 1980), 132.

U.S. Army advisers neither commanded nor exercised any operational control over any part of the ARVN forces. Their mission was to provide professional military advice and assistance to their counterpart South Vietnamese commanders and staffs in the areas of training, combat operations, intelligence, security, logistics, and psychological/civil affairs operations. Ideally, the advisory teams would work themselves out of a job over time as ARVN and the VNMC began to assume more and more responsibility for planning and executing their own operations. However, as later chapters demonstrate, the intended result was not achieved.

TRAINING

In addition to those assigned to the CORDS effort and to the combat units in the field, a significant number of advisers was assigned to work with the RVNAF training base in an effort to improve the quality of training for the South Vietnamese forces. By the end of 1972, the RVNAF would become the largest and most modern military force in Southeast Asia, but even a vast amount of the best equipment in the world would be meaningless if the soldiers, sailors, marines, and airmen lacked the knowledge, leadership, or motivation to use it in the field against the enemy. Theoretically, training the Vietnamese had received high priority through-out the war, but in practice too little attention had been given this critical function prior to the initiation of Vietnamization.[31] Even with the new policy in place, im-proving South Vietnamese training proved to be an uphill battle.

At the beginning of 1968, the ARVN training system consisted of fifty-six training centers of various types and sizes, including nine national training centers, thirty-seven provincial training centers, and ten divisional training centers (the Air-borne and Marine divisions had their own training centers). This extensive sys-tem of schools and training facilities was under the control of the RVNAF Cen-tral Training Command (CTC), which had first been established in 1966. CTC was advised and supported by the MACV Training Directorate in the development of an effective military training system for the RVNAF. As such the directorate pro-vided U.S. advisers at the RVNAF schools and training centers, where they assisted RVNAF commandants in the preparation and conduct of training programs.

At first glance, the RVNAF training system of schools and training centers in 1968 was an impressive arrangement, but deeper investigation revealed that it was less than effective in producing the leaders and soldiers necessary to successfully prosecute the war. Prior to 1969, MACV had made numerous proposals to the Viet-namese Joint General Staff and Central Training Command for improving the per-sonnel capacity and effectiveness of the South Vietnamese training facilities, but the RVNAF high command paid little attention to these recommendations. As the 1969 MACV "Command Overview" stated, "Despite CTC and MACV efforts, little progress was made in 1969 in these areas due to the complex personnel changes required, JGS reluctance to give the program a high priority, and refusal by RVN field commanders to release experienced officers and NCOs from opera-tional responsibilities."[32]

By early 1970, the U.S. authorities were so disturbed by the situation that the army chief of staff dispatched a fact-finding team led by Brig. Gen. Donnelly Bolton to tour RVNAF training facilities in Vietnam, provide an objective assess-ment of the training capabilities of the South Vietnamese, and examine the state of U.S. training assistance.[33] Bolton's team found the efforts of both the South Viet-namese and the U.S. military training advisers in Vietnam to be insufficient. The MACV Training Directorate, the U.S. military staff directorate responsible for pro-viding advisers to RVNAF training facilities, was at only 70 percent of assigned strength, and all the U.S. training advisory detachments in the field were likewise short-staffed. Another issue was the quality of advisory personnel assigned to train the South Vietnamese at the RVNAF schools: it appeared to the team that often those deemed unfit to serve in more prestigious operational and staff positions were placed in the RVNAF training billets. Col. (later Maj. Gen.) Stan L. McClellan, a member of the Bolton team wrote, "It was clear that top professionals were not being assigned to training advisory duties."[34]

General Abrams agreed with the findings of the Bolton team and urged Bolton to recommend to the Joint Chiefs of Staff that they send more and better training advisers to Vietnam. He was very concerned with filling the ranks of his advisory teams with personnel at their authorized grade level (i.e., lieutenant colonels in positions specifying lieutenant colonels, and so forth), thereby reducing the number of low-ranking advisers with little or no combat experience.[35] Abrams told the team, "It's time that they [the Joint Chiefs of Staff] recognize in Washington that the day of the U.S. fighting force involvement in South Vietnam is at an end. All we have time for now is to complete the preparation of South Vietnam to carry on the task."[36]

At the same time that Abrams was trying to convince the Joint Chiefs of Staff of the critical importance of the training mission in South Vietnam, he was pressuring the RVNAF high command to make improvements to their training system. In a March 1970 letter to Gen. Cao Van Vien, chief of the Joint General Staff, Abrams urged senior South Vietnamese commanders to get behind the training effort. He wrote, "Arrangements for support of CTC activities must be widened and accelerated. As a first order of effort it is essential to enlist the personal interest and assistance of corps, divisional tactical area, and sector commanders each of whom . . . is a user of the product of the training system, and should contribute to improving the quality of the product."[37]

Due in large part to Abrams's urging and the realization that U.S. forces were in fact going to be withdrawn, the RVNAF high command began to put more emphasis on improving their training system. The fact that the United States contributed $28 million to expanding and improving the South Vietnamese training facilities also helped. Eventually there would be a total of thirty-three major military and service schools, thirteen national and regional training centers, and fourteen division training centers (see map 2). By 1970, the South Vietnamese leaders began to transfer experienced officers and noncommissioned officers to the training centers. Although field commanders only reluctantly gave up their veteran small-unit leaders, by the end of 1971 nearly half of the South Vietnamese training instructors were men with combat experience. Also, by this time the number of U.S. training advisory personnel had increased, and by the end of 1971, more than 3,500 U.S. advisers were directly involved in training at most of the training centers and major RVNAF schools.[38]

IMPROVING THE ADVISORY EFFORT'S EFFECTIVENESS

Even as the South Vietnamese began to realize the necessity of upgrading their training programs, the quality of U.S. advisers remained an issue, not just in the training centers, but at all levels, including the field units and the CORDS teams. In December 1969, as the Vietnamization policy began to gather momentum and the various changes in force structure, equipment, and training were instituted, Secretary Laird, realizing the criticality of advisers to the Vietnamization process, asked the service secretaries to study options for upgrading the advisory effort.[39] Prior to this time, many in the U.S. Army regarded service as an adviser as much

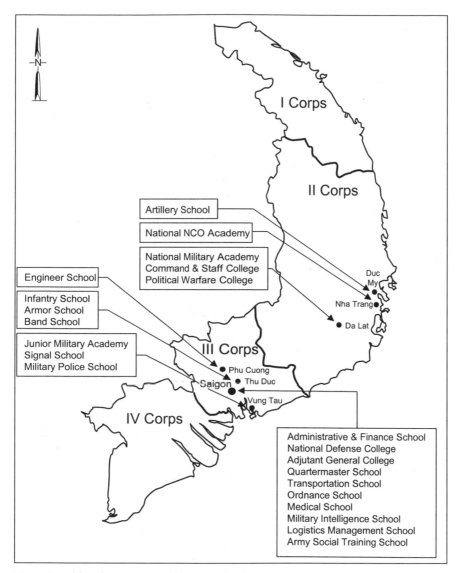

Map 2. Republic of Vietnam Armed Forces schools, 1969.

less desirable than field command with a U.S. unit, and many officers and noncommissioned officers avoided advisory duty.[40]

More often than not, advisers were chosen largely because they happened to be available for overseas duty when rotation or casualties created vacant advisory billets.[41] For those selected, the training program was limited to a six-week course at Fort Bragg, North Carolina, and in some instances, a follow-on eleven-week

Vietnamese language course. Thus, many who tried to do their best as advisers nevertheless lacked the experience, training, or, in a large number of cases, the inclination to be an adviser.

Laird set out to change the situation; he wanted to install the best people as advisers. He did not get much help initially from the army; Secretary of the Army Stanley Resor said he would continue to study the problem, but did not offer any useful solutions.[42] The army was trying to deal with severe personnel problems. The demands of the war resulted in army officers and noncommissioned officers returning to Vietnam for multiple tours, some separated by less than a year, and the call for advisers only exacerbated the strain on the personnel system. Nevertheless, Abrams, who clearly agreed with Laird on the critical nature of the advisory role, continued to urge that more emphasis be placed on assigning qualified officers with combat experience to adviser duty. He demanded "guys who can lead/influence . . . the business of pacification," officers who "feel empathy toward the Vietnamese . . . appreciate their good points and understand their weaknesses"; he wanted advisers "who can pull ideas and actions out of the Vietnamese" in pursuit of two major goals: "pacification and upgrading the RVNAF."[43]

Laird, supporting his commander in the field and recognizing that Vietnamization would fail miserably if the right people were not involved in upgrading the training of the South Vietnamese forces, demanded that the advisory posts be filled. Accordingly, he ordered the service secretaries to send "only the most highly qualified" personnel to be advisers.[44] Eventually the services complied, sending "an infusion of top-flight military professionals into South Vietnam's training advisory effort" by the end of 1970.[45] The situation would improve as more American units departed, reducing the number of available nonadvisory assignments and freeing up for advisory duty large numbers of those officers who would have gone to U.S. units. During 1969, the overall strength of the field advisory teams increased from about 7,000 to 11,900, and then to 14,332 in 1970.[46] Table 3 shows the approximate U.S. field advisory strength in 1969–70.

SOUTH VIETNAMESE RESISTANCE TO VIETNAMIZATION

The South Vietnamese distaste for the implications of the word "Vietnamization" warrants further discussion. Thieu and many of his generals took exception to the whole concept and connotation that the ARVN forces were "finally" stepping up to assume responsibility for the war. To the South Vietnamese who had been fighting the Communists since the 1950s, the idea that the war would now be "Vietnamized" was insulting. As far as they were concerned, they had been bearing the brunt of the fight with the Communists before the Americans arrived, and it became increasingly clear that they would bear it long after the Americans departed. The perception held a great deal of truth. Even though American combat troops had taken on the Communist main forces and incurred serious casualties in the

Table 3. Approximate Field Advisory Strength, 1969–70

Type	I CTZ	II CTZ	III CTZ	IV CTZ	Total
Combat advisers					
Corps	203	272	372	312	1,159
Division	194	136	261	227	818
Regiment	24	24	27	27	102
Armored cavalry regiment		44	35	24	103
Infantry battalion	82	86	144	126	438
Marine battalion	36				36
Ranger battalion		12	39	25	76
Other commands	21	46	85	92	244
Total	560	620	963	833	2,976
Support advisers					
Logistics					390
School/training					1,524
Total					1,914
CORDS advisers					
CORDS	736	1,516	1,455	1,976	5,683
Mobile training teams	275	622	619	789	2,305
Total	1,011	2,138	2,074	2,765	7,988
Component advisers					
Air Force advisory group					494
Naval advisory group					960
Total					1,454
Total of all advisers					14,332

Source: USMACV, "Command History, 1970," 2:VII-63–79.

process, South Vietnamese casualties had always exceeded those of U.S. troops (see table 4). As former ARVN major general Nguyen Duy Hinh wrote, "It was the Vietnamese who had sacrificed and suffered the most. . . . In my opinion, Vietnamization was not a proper term to be used in Vietnam, especially when propaganda was an important weapon."[47] The propaganda issue was particularly important because the Communists had long claimed that the South Vietnamese armed forces were merely "puppet troops of the American imperialists."

Consequently, President Thieu and his generals, and even the South Vietnamese press, did not speak openly of Vietnamization. Because it frowned on the implications of Vietnamization, the South Vietnamese government designed no additional programs of its own to facilitate the process. General Hinh wrote, "South Vietnam continued to fight as it had always fought. Old plans and programs [for RVNAF improvement] were kept unchanged, except perhaps for a new sense of urgency and emphasis instilled by the U.S. decision to phase down and eventually withdraw its forces."[48]

Despite the South Vietnam leaders' distaste for "Vietnamization" as both a term and a concept, they nevertheless eventually accepted the new American policies with "a mixture of confidence and concern."[49] It became clear that President Nixon and Secretary of Defense Laird planned to withdraw all U.S. troops, but Thieu and his generals felt some small confidence, particularly in light of the

Table 4. Military Casualty Comparison

	Killed in Action, U.S.	Killed in Action, RVNAF	Wounded in Action, U.S.	Wounded in Action, RVNAF
1960	—	2,223	—	2,788
1961	11	4,004	2	5,449
1962	31	4,457	41	7,195
1963	78	5,665	218	11,488
1964	147	7,457	522	17,017
1965	1,369	11,242	3,308	23,118
1966	5,008	11,953	16,526	20,975
1967	9,377	12,716	32,370	29,448
1968	14,589	27,915	46,797	70,696
1969	9,414	21,833	32,940	65,276
1970	4,221	23,346	15,211	71,582
1971	1,381	22,738	4,767	60,939
1972	300	39,587	587	109,960
1973	237	27,901	24	131,936
1974	207	31,219	—	155,735
Total	46,370	254,256	153,313	783,602

Source: Jeffrey J. Clarke, Advice and Support: The Final Years (Washington, D.C.: Center of Military History, 1988), 275.

RVNAF's qualified success during the 1968 Tet offensive. Although the Communists had surprised the Saigon command, the RVNAF had eventually recovered and, in concert with the U.S. forces in country, inflicted severe casualties on the Communist forces. The Communists' inability to cause a general uprising of the people against the Saigon government also encouraged Thieu. He and his field commanders came to believe that they could carry on the war in the absence of the Americans, but this tenuous confidence was based on the assumption that "the U.S. would continue to help financially, materially, technologically, and even spiritually, if not with manpower."[50] One former South Vietnamese general wrote after the war that his countrymen had believed all along that "U.S. forces would continue to stand behind the RVNAF with their support to fill in the gaps that the RVNAF were still unable or did not have enough time to do by themselves."[51] Later, when it became apparent that the United States would no longer help the South Vietnamese, the reality deeply shook the confidence of President Thieu and his forces, contributing toward the panic that led to the final defeat.

3

The RVNAF in Action

THE COMBAT SITUATION—1969

When the United States began prosecuting Vietnamization in earnest, South Vietnamese troop strength expanded rapidly, new and more modern equipment was delivered, and the advisory effort improved. However, these upgrades were not conducted in a vacuum—the war continued unabated. Thus, the transition to South Vietnamese responsibility for the war, including aforementioned changes in force structure and extensive modernization and training efforts, took place while both the U.S. forces and the RVNAF continued to do battle with the North Vietnamese and Viet Cong in the field.

Even as the Nixon administration took office and began to develop what would become the Vietnamization strategy, the Communists demonstrated that they were not going to give the new American president and his advisers any breathing room. The North Vietnamese launched a country-wide offensive in February 1969. The primary targets for the new attacks were U.S. forces and installations; lines of communications and the pacification program served as secondary targets.[1] Although Communist forces attacked over 125 major targets and conducted smaller sapper raids and mortar attacks on 400 others, they failed to achieve the same stunning results that operational surprise had yielded in the initial stages of the 1968 Tet offensive. This time, better allied intelligence and the reduced strength of the Communist forces due to losses sustained in the previous year's offensive enabled the allies to deal very effectively with the new attacks. Nevertheless, a surge of allied casualties prompted Nixon to respond in March by ordering the secret bombing of Communist sanctuaries in Cambodia.

The possibility of bombing the North Vietnamese buildup in Cambodia had been under discussion for some time.[2] However, Secretary of Defense Laird had opposed the option as a potential political nightmare for the administration and strongly urged the president to pursue Vietnamization and accelerate American troop withdrawals. Always highly attuned to the domestic political situation, Laird opposed widening the war in any way and believed that the bombing of Cambodia would be counterproductive to the effort to disengage the United States from the war.[3] Kissinger agreed, advising Nixon to give negotiations a chance.[4] However, when Communist forces struck Saigon with a rocket attack in March, Nixon gave the green light for Operation Menu, the secret bombing of Cambodia. Over the next fifteen months, 3,630 secret B-52 raids were conducted against suspected Communist positions in Cambodia.[5] Events would eventually prove the wisdom of Laird's counsel against any secret attempts to widen the war.

Despite potentially disastrous political consequences, the secret bombing had a positive impact in the long run in a purely military sense, for it reduced the availability of outside support to the Communist forces in South Vietnam.[6] Realizing that time was at a premium as he put the finishing touches on the Vietnamization policy, Nixon hoped that the secret bombing would weaken the Communist forces in the South and provide more time for the new policy to work.

In the same vein, General Abrams, attempting to provide a protective screen for the Vietnamization effort, ordered U.S. forces to keep the North Vietnamese and Viet Cong off balance to prevent them from mounting any prolonged action that might interfere with the process of upgrading the RVNAF to assume greater responsibility for the war. Abrams broke his forces into small platoon- and company-sized task forces and ordered them to concentrate on extensive patrolling and night operations, a tactic he described as "getting into his [the enemy's] system."[7]

The emphasis on small unit operations, however, did not mean an end to large-scale battles involving U.S. troops. As President Nixon and his advisers made final preparations for announcing the initiation of Vietnamization at Midway, the 101st Airborne Division launched an assault into the A Shau Valley in an effort to clean out North Vietnamese Base Area 611, a major Communist logistical support area. The operation was a follow-on to Operation Dewey Canyon, conducted in the same area earlier in the year by elements of the 1st Marine Division. The paratroopers of the 101st ran into a large enemy force and a major battle ensued for Ap Bia Hill (Hill 939), which later became known as "Hamburger Hill." The action resulted in 56 Americans killed and 630 enemy dead.[8] The battle, although a tactical success in keeping the NVA off balance, provoked a public outcry in the United States over heavy American casualties and the seemingly meaningless nature of a struggle that saw such a bloody expenditure of lives only to have U.S. forces abandon the battlefield shortly after the fighting ended. The American press gave wide coverage to Senator Edward Kennedy's comment that the battle was "senseless and irresponsible" and his charge that "President Nixon has told us, without question, that we seek no military victory, that we seek only peace. How can we justify sending our boys against a hill a dozen times, finally taking it, and then withdrawing a week later?"[9] The *New York Times* said after the battle, "The public is certainly entitled to raise questions about the current aggressive posture of the United States military in South Vietnam."[10] Many Americans perceived the battle of Hamburger Hill as a symbol of the Nixon administration's failure to make any substantive changes to the American approach in South Vietnam, and the president came under severe criticism for a seeming lack of strategy.[11]

In response to those growing increasingly weary of continued loss of U.S. lives for apparently meaningless real estate, Nixon and Laird prepared to announce plans to Vietnamize the war as a prelude to an orderly U.S. withdrawal. However, the administration needed time to institute the new policy, and Nixon, desirous of achieving "peace with honor," had to make sure that there were no more Hamburger Hills. Accordingly, he sent word to Abrams to take measures to hold down U.S. casualties.[12]

U.S. TROOP WITHDRAWALS

Shortly after American units battled with the enemy at Hamburger Hill and while fighting continued at many other hot spots around South Vietnam, President Nixon announced his Vietnamization policy and associated plans to reduce the number of American combat troops in Vietnam. Now Abrams had to wrestle with the prickly issue of how to prepare the South Vietnamese forces to take over even as he continued to prosecute the war in the field. Both of these demanding tasks had to be handled while President Nixon and Secretary Laird continued to push for greater and faster troop reductions.

As previously noted, discussions about U.S. troop withdrawals had begun shortly after President Nixon's inauguration.[13] En route to Midway in June 1969 to announce the initiation of Vietnamization, members of the administration held a meeting in Honolulu to devise a withdrawal strategy. Attendees included Nixon, Kissinger, Laird, Secretary of State Rogers, Ambassadors Ellsworth Bunker and Henry Cabot Lodge, Gen. Earle Wheeler, and General Abrams. Kissinger recorded that the "military approached the subject [of troop withdrawal] with a heavy heart. . . . it would make victory impossible and even an honorable outcome problematical."[14] Prior to this meeting, General Abrams had questioned the size and pace of any contemplated withdrawals. According to Abrams biographer Lewis Sorley, the U.S. commander believed his troops were beginning to enjoy more success in combating the Communist forces and naturally wanted to retain them to press the advantage. However, Sorley maintains, Abrams "also had the sensitivity to understand the political realities in the United States and what they portended in terms of continued support for prosecution of the war."[15] Therefore, once the decision was made to begin the troop withdrawals, Abrams gave it his wholehearted support, realizing that the U.S. commitment had to be downsized in order to turn the war over to the South Vietnamese.[16] Nevertheless, the U.S. commander still had concerns about the timing and wisdom of withdrawing troops when the enemy's strength appeared to be waning. In response, General Wheeler had assured Abrams on two separate occasions that any American redeployments would take into consideration the situation on the battlefield.[17]

Despite the concerns of the operational commander, the president decided to announce the first withdrawal increment at Midway and proceed with the disengagement of U.S. forces. Further reductions were to be based on three criteria: the level of enemy activity, progress in the Paris peace talks, and the strengthening of the RVNAF.[18] Kissinger wrote: "Henceforth, we [the United States] would be in a race between the decline in our combat capabilities and the improvement of South Vietnamese forces—a race whose outcome was at best uncertain."[19]

Nevertheless, after Nixon announced the first U.S. troop withdrawal at Midway, he was "jubilant" and considered the announcement a "political triumph."[20] He thought it would accomplish several significant aims. First, he hoped the initial withdrawal would quiet the antiwar critics and buy the administration time to further develop its strategy; second, he thought it would send a signal to the North Vietnamese that the United States was serious about seeking peace in Southeast Asia. Nixon and his advisers would be proved wrong on all counts.

Former secretary of defense Clark Clifford gave Nixon and Laird new motivation to expand their U.S. troop withdrawal plans. In July 1969, he published an article in *Foreign Affairs* that urged the unilateral withdrawal of 100,000 troops by the end of the year, and of all other personnel by the end of 1970, leaving only logistics and air force personnel.[21] Nixon, never one to shrink from a challenge, stated at a press conference that he could improve upon Clifford's schedule.[22] The president's statement received a great deal of attention in the press and effectively committed the United States to a unilateral withdrawal from South Vietnam, thus removing the promise of troop reductions as a bargaining chip for Kissinger in his dealings with the North Vietnamese in Paris. The consequences for the peace negotiations and the eventual cease-fire agreement would be serious.

The first redeployment of 25,000 U.S. troops promised by President Nixon was accomplished by 27 August 1969, when the last troops from the 1st and 2nd brigades of the 9th Infantry Division departed the Mekong Delta. In the months following the Midway announcement, discussions continued about the size and pace of the U.S. withdrawal. Laird had formulated several options for the rest of 1969 that ranged from withdrawing a low of 50,000 troops to a high of 100,000; in between were various combinations of numbers and forces. In a memorandum to the president, Laird cautioned him to be careful about withdrawing too many troops too quickly, as this would have serious consequences for the pacification program.[23] Laird's warning proved timely. On 6 August, as soldiers from the 9th Infantry Division prepared to depart South Vietnam, the Communists attacked Cam Ranh Bay, followed five days later by additional attacks on more than one hundred cities, towns, and bases across South Vietnam. An official North Vietnamese history of the war revealed that the Politburo in Hanoi had concluded after the Midway announcement that the United States had "lost its will to fight in Vietnam"; thus, the Communists, believing they were in a position to dictate the degree and intensity of combat, launched the new round of attacks.[24]

When Nixon had made his announcement in June about the initial U.S. troop withdrawal, he emphasized that the level of enemy activity would be one of the criteria for further reductions. These new Communist attacks clearly went against Nixon's conditions; his subsequent announcement that he was delaying a decision about additional troop withdrawals caused an uproar in both Congress and the media. On 12 September, the National Security Council met to discuss the situation. Kissinger reported that "a very natural response from us would have been to stop bringing soldiers home, but by now withdrawal had gained its own momentum."[25] Kissinger had sent the president a memorandum two days before the meeting, expressing concern about the administration's "present course" in South Vietnam. He warned that "Withdrawals of U.S. troops will become like salted peanuts to the American public; the more U.S. troops come home, the more will be demanded. This could eventually result, in effect, in demands for a unilateral withdrawal. . . . The more troops are withdrawn, the more Hanoi will be encouraged."[26] Time would prove Kissinger to be right, but during the NSC meeting he was the only dissenter to the decision to proceed with the scheduled troop reductions. On 16 September, Nixon ordered a second increment of 35,000 American troops to be redeployed by December. According to Kissinger, the withdrawals became "inexorable . . . [and] the President never again permitted the end of a withdrawal period to pass without announcing a new increment for the next."[27]

On 15 December, Nixon ordered a third increment of 50,000 to be redeployed prior to April 1970. On 20 April 1970, he announced that even though 110,000 U.S. troops had been scheduled to be redeployed during the first three increments, a total of 115,000 had actually departed Vietnam. The second phase of the withdrawal, from April 1970 to April 1971, would reduce the total U.S. strength by a further 150,000. By the end of 1970, only about 344,000 U.S. troops remained in South Vietnam. The 9th Infantry Division, the 3rd Brigade of the 82nd Airborne Division, the 1st Infantry Division, the 3rd Marine Division, two brigades of the 25th Infantry Division, and the entire 4th Infantry Division had been redeployed (table 5 depicts the schedule of U.S. troop unit withdrawals from South Vietnam). As these U.S. forces prepared to depart, they suspended combat operations and passed responsibility for their respective operational areas to the RVNAF.

From the initial announcement of U.S. troop withdrawals in June 1969 to the end of November 1972, the United States brought home fourteen increments, reducing total U.S. strength in Vietnam from a peak of 543,400 to a residual force of 27,000 (see table 6).[28]

ABRAMS PREPARES TO TURN OVER THE WAR

As Henry Kissinger pointed out, the U.S. troop withdrawals gathered a momentum of their own; any attempt by the president to modify the schedule, even when he may have been so inclined because of the battlefield situation in South Vietnam, provoked vigorous reaction by Congress, the media, and the antiwar element. Thus,

Table 5. Redeployment of Major U.S. Army Units from Vietnam

Unit	Redeployed	Main Area of Operations In Country
9th Infantry Division (2 brigades)	Aug. 1969	IV CTZ (Corps Tactical Zone)
3rd Brigade	Sep. 1970	
3rd Brigade, Eighty-second Airborne Division	Dec. 1969	I CTZ
1st Infantry Division (3 brigades)	April 1970	III CTZ
199th Infantry Brigade	Oct. 1970	III CTZ
25th Infantry Division (3 brigades)	Nov. 1970	III CTZ
4th Infantry Division (2 brigades)	Dec. 1970	II CTZ
3rd Brigade	April 1970	
1st Cavalry Division (3 brigades)	April 1971	I, II, and III CTZ
11th Armored Cavalry Regiment	April 1971	III CTZ
1st Brigade, Fifth Infantry Division	Sep. 1971	III CTZ
173rd Airborne Brigade	Sep. 1971	III and II CTZ
23rd Infantry Division (3 brigades)	Nov. 1971	I CTZ
101st Airborne Division	March 1972	I CTZ
1st Airborne Brigade	Jan. 1972	
2nd Airborne Brigade	Feb. 1972	
3rd Airborne Brigade	Dec. 1971	

Source: Nguyen Duy Hinh, *Indochina Monographs: Vietnamization and the Cease-Fire* (Washington, D.C.: U.S. Army Center of Military History, 1980), p. 23.

once the initial departure of U.S. forces began, the RVNAF was forced to assume more responsibility for the war, regardless of the progress of Vietnamization and pacification. Such was the situation that confronted General Abrams. While still fighting a war, he had to increase the efforts to prepare the RVNAF to fill the void on the battlefield left by the redeploying U.S. forces. He was essentially fighting for time. Accordingly, he hoped to retain "a balanced combat capability and as much capability for as long as possible."[29]

When Abrams assumed command of MACV from General Westmoreland in July 1968, he had fully realized that something had to be done to improve the combat capabilities of the South Vietnamese armed forces. Even before President Nixon had announced Vietnamization as the new U.S. policy in South Vietnam, General Abrams had taken measures to increase the effectiveness of the RVNAF training base, which had not historically been the focus of MACV's efforts. Abrams had inherited the long-standing U.S. mission of closing with and defeating the Communists to force them to withdraw from South Vietnam, but with Nixon's announcement of his Vietnamization policy, the mission, as previously described, and focus of MACV changed drastically.

On 7 July 1969, the president met with Kissinger, Laird, Rogers, Wheeler, John Mitchell, and Gen. Robert E. Cushman Jr. (a marine officer who was deputy director of the CIA) aboard the presidential yacht *Sequoia*.[30] The purpose of the meeting was to discuss an apparent lull in the fighting in South Vietnam. The number of enemy attacks in South Vietnam had diminished after the Hamburger Hill

Table 6. U.S. Troop Redeployments from Vietnam

	Dates	Forces Redeployed	Forces Remaining
1	July–Aug. 1969	25,000	519,000
2	Sep.–Dec. 1969	35,000	484,000
3	Jan.–Apr. 1970	50,000	434,000
4	July–Oct. 1970	50,000	384,000
5	Nov.–Dec. 1970	40,000	344,000
6	Jan.–Apr. 1971	60,000	284,000
7	May–June 1971	29,300	254,000
8	July–Aug. 1971	28,700	226,000
9	Sep.–Nov. 1971	42,000	184,000
10	Dec.–Jan. 1972	45,000	139,000
11	Feb.–Apr. 1972	70,000	69,000
12	May–June 1972	20,000	49,000
13	July–Sep. 1972	10,000	39,000
14	Oct.–Nov. 1972	12,000	27,000

Sources: Nguyen Duy Hinh, *Indochina Monographs: Vietnamization and the Cease-Fire* (Washington, D.C.: U.S. Army Center of Military History, 1980), 27; Larry A. Niksch, *Vietnamization: The Program and Its Problems* (Washington, D.C.: Library of Congress, Congressional Research Service, January 1972), A-1.

battle, and U.S. casualties had reached their lowest level of the year. According to Kissinger, the discussion centered around determining why the level of fighting had dropped off—whether it was due to Hanoi's exhaustion, a new negotiating strategy, or an attempt by Hanoi to achieve de-escalation by tacit understanding?[31] Kissinger later wrote, "It was symptomatic of the intellectual confusion of the period that in the relief felt when a military lull eased both casualties and domestic pressures, no one asked the question whether the lull might not reflect the fact that our strategy was succeeding and should therefore be continued."[32] Instead, there was "unanimity" that the situation provided an excellent opportunity to reciprocate by de-escalating U.S. operations in South Vietnam; at the same time, MACV efforts could be brought into better accord with the Vietnamization effort. Nixon agreed and authorized Secretary of Defense Laird to issue new guidelines to General Abrams.

The result was a new mission statement for MACV that emphasized the desire of the United States "to assist the Republic of Vietnam Armed forces to take over an increasing share of combat operations."[33] The mission statement (which was to go into effect on 15 August 1969) charged Abrams and his command to focus on (1) providing "maximum assistance" to the South Vietnamese to strengthen their forces, (2) supporting the pacification effort, and (3) reducing the flow of supplies to the enemy.[34] Abrams was also told once again to hold down U.S. casualties. Henry Kissinger later reported that Nixon changed his mind about these orders and attempted to rescind them. However, Secretary Laird said the orders had already been sent, and they were allowed to stand.[35] If Kissinger's account is accurate and the president did try to rescind the orders, Nixon did not reveal why he had second thoughts about the official mission change for MACV. Perhaps he was worried about interfering in military matters, or perhaps he did not want to signal the North Vietnamese that the United States was beginning to reduce the level of its commitment to the war. Nevertheless, the president let the orders stand and reiterated the new guidance in person when he made a surprise visit to Vietnam later in August. There, he stressed the shift in focus for U.S. forces, saying that "the primary mission of American troops is to enable the South Vietnamese forces to assume the full responsibility for the security of South Vietnam."[36] Notably, the president did not make this new guidance public until a nationally televised speech in November.

General Abrams, who had previously expressed misgivings about the accelerated U.S. troop withdrawals, understood his marching orders and stepped up measures to improve the combat capabilities of the South Vietnamese units.[37] The problem was not a new one for Abrams, who, since his assumption of command in 1968, had been concerned with what were essentially two different wars being fought by the U.S. and South Vietnamese forces. Abrams had sought to end the division of roles and missions between American and South Vietnamese combat forces through the adoption of a single combined allied strategy, thus eliminating "the tacit existence of two separate strategies, attrition and pacification."[38] He described this approach as "a strategy focused upon protecting the population so that the civil government can establish its authority as opposed to an earlier conception of the purpose of the war—destruction of the enemy's forces."[39] The "one war" concept was formalized in the MACV Objectives Plan approved in March 1969.

Abrams and Ambassador Bunker convinced President Thieu that Abrams's approach was the right way to proceed and secured his agreement that the MACV Objectives Plan should serve as the basis of the allied forces' efforts in South Vietnam. The decision was made official when Abrams and Gen. Cao Van Vien, chief of the South Vietnamese Joint General Staff, signed the Combined Campaign Plan, which specified that the "RVNAF must participate fully within its capabilities in all types of operations . . . to prepare for the time when it must assume the entire responsibility."[40] The plan further established population security and support of pacification as the primary objectives of the American and South Vietnamese forces.

As soon as the new plan was signed, Abrams set out to make sure that MACV forces fully accepted his "one war" concept, forever eliminating the division of labor that too often had fragmented allied efforts. Abrams had already begun shifting the focus of MACV when he received the official change of mission from President Nixon. Armed with the new "one war" combined strategy and urged by his commander in chief to Vietnamize the war, Abrams hoped to bring the combat situation under control while at the same time shifting the preponderance of the responsibility for the war to the South Vietnamese as American troop withdrawals increased in size and frequency.

By the time that Abrams received his new orders, he had already initiated programs to expand RVNAF force structure and provide more modern weapons to the South Vietnamese, as discussed above. While these improvements were being made, Abrams turned his focus on increasing the combat capabilities of the

RVNAF in the field, in part by having South Vietnamese troops fight side by side with the American troops in combined field operations.

American and South Vietnamese units had conducted combined operations prior to the adoption of the "one war" policy in 1969, but during earlier operations, the South Vietnamese troops usually filled a secondary, supporting role on the periphery of the main action. Many American combat commanders were reluctant to operate with South Vietnamese units and typically regarded ARVN as no more than "an additional burden" that had to be taken in tow, more "apt to cause problems . . . than be helpful."[41] Although the situation changed somewhat for the better after the 1968 Tet offensive, Abrams, faced with the urgent task of Vietnamizing the war, ordered closer cooperation between American and South Vietnamese forces. The hope was that American units would serve as models for Saigon's soldiers by more closely integrating the operations of the two national forces. Such integration had worked very well in South Korea and had eventually improved the fighting abilities of the Republic of Korea armed forces. Abrams and his advisers manifestly hoped that the Korean model would also work with the South Vietnamese.[42] As the South Vietnamese forces became more capable on the battlefield, they could assume a greater share of the burden as U.S. combat forces were steadily drawn down. One former ARVN general described the approach, noting that

> by participating in combat operations hand-in-hand with American units, Vietnamese forces — regular and territorial — would acquire valuable and practical experience which could hardly be acquired in a training center. Thus, combined and joint operations offered ARVN units not only the chance to observe American methods of operations, American use of firepower and mobility assets, and American leadership in action, but also offered the fringe benefits of additional combat support which could not otherwise be made available from Vietnamese resources. This was in fact a very special type of on-the-job or in-action training in which U.S. units performed the role of instructor by giving real life, positive examples of combat actions and counteractions in various tactical situations and types of terrain; and the ARVN units under their tutelage benefitted from observing and emulating the U.S. units.[43]

Unfortunately, the initiative to integrate the South Vietnamese troops into the main battle effort would prove to be uneven, varying from corps tactical zone to corps tactical zone. Several possible reasons exist. Some senior U.S. commanders were wary of the South Vietnamese troops and Abrams's "one war" concept. However, General Davidson, who was Abrams's J-2 intelligence officer at MACV, took exception to those blaming this wariness for the shortcomings of the Vietnamization effort. He wrote: "It has become conventional wisdom to claim that the new concept suffered severely because Abrams' senior commanders refused to support it. This is nonsense. In many cases the general officers in Vietnam agreed with Abrams's strategy and carried it out with dedication. Even those who disagreed with the concept dutifully, if unenthusiastically, gave it their full support. Abrams himself would accept no less, and he had the power of enforcement."[44] Davidson may have understated the resistance to the plan; it is not clear that all of Abrams's senior commanders thought that his new concept was a good idea, but there is also no doubt that Abrams had their careers in his hand and they had to get on board with his ideas or suffer the consequences. Still, some U.S. commanders were more aggressive than others in trying to make the new program work.

The South Vietnamese themselves proved to be another factor contributing to the disparate results of the new program. Leadership ability, fighting spirit, and tactical acumen varied throughout the South Vietnamese armed forces. Not all RVNAF units and commanders were prepared to keep their end of the bargain. Thus, the "one war" approach achieved more success in some areas than others.

"ONE WAR"

In I Corps, Lt. Gen. Richard G. Stilwell, the U.S. XXIV Corps commander, worked very closely with the 1st ARVN division commander, Maj. Gen. (later Lt. Gen.) Ngo Quang Truong, integrating the South Vietnamese units into operational plans as full partners.[45] Under what was essentially a U.S.-ARVN combined command, the South Vietnamese forces operated closely with the U.S. 3rd Marine Division, the 101st Airborne Division (Airmobile), and the 1st Brigade of the 5th Infantry Division (Mechanized) in Quang Tri and Thua Thien provinces. After Stilwell was replaced by Maj. Gen. Melvin Zais later in 1969, the new commander continued Stilwell's emphasis on combined operations, and other U.S. forces in I Corps stepped up their cooperative efforts with ARVN. In the southern half of the zone, the U.S. 23rd Infantry Division routinely conducted combined operations with 2nd Infantry Division (ARVN) in Quang Tin and Quang Ngai provinces. The U.S. 1st Marine Division, defending the Da Nang area, conducted combined operations with the South Vietnamese Quang Da Special Zone forces and the 51st ARVN Infantry Regiment. Abrams was extremely pleased with the performance of the ARVN forces in I Corps; later in 1969, he ordered the U.S. 1st Cavalry Division south, reoriented remaining American combat forces in the region toward area security, and eventually sent home one of the two American marine divisions located there.

In II Corps Tactical Zone, U.S. commanders also pursued combined operations, but with less success. Prior to late 1968 and early 1969, cooperation between the U.S. and ARVN forces in II Corps had been largely ineffective. The U.S. forces concerned themselves with enemy mainforce units in outlying areas of the Central Highlands, while the ARVN forces limited their activities to pacification support in the lowland coastal areas and population centers. With the institution of the "one war" concept by General Abrams, Lt. Gen. William R. Peers, commander of I Field Force, and his counterpart, Lt. Gen. Lu Lan, commander of ARVN II Corps, agreed that it was time to devise a means of exploiting the advantages of each national force while minimizing their respective disadvantages.[46] They jointly established the "Pair Off" program, which called for each ARVN unit to be closely and continually affiliated with a U.S. counterpart unit. Operations were to be conducted jointly, regardless of the size of unit each force could commit, and coordination and cooperation were effected from corps to battalion and districts. The "Pair Off" program was seen as a means of upgrading ARVN combat effectiveness and preparing ARVN units in II Corps for a larger share of the combat burden.[47] As such, this concept was later expanded to include Vietnamese artillery and other combat support units. Under this program, the U.S. 4th Infantry Division and the U.S. 173rd Airborne Brigade joined forces with the ARVN 22nd and 23rd infantry divisions.

Peers and Lan ordered the U.S. 4th Infantry Division and two ARVN regiments to hold the Communist forces at bay along the border while they concentrated the efforts of the remaining U.S. and ARVN units on restoring and expanding Saigon's control of the coastal population, including traditionally contested Binh Dinh and Phu Yen provinces. After the initiation of the "Pair Off" program, three significant combined operations were conducted in II Corps, and each achieved a modest level of success. However, this approach did not work as well as the combined operations in I Corps for a number of reasons. First, the two corps-level headquarters, unlike those in I Corps, were not co-located, making coordination more difficult. Additionally, the ARVN field commanders in II Corps were not as enthusiastic about working with U.S. forces as were Major General Truong and his fellow ARVN commanders in I Corps. Despite early gains in improving the confidence and capabilities of ARVN units in II Corps, the "Pair Off" program was abandoned in late 1969.

In the IV Corps Tactical Zone (Mekong Delta), the main U.S. presence was the 9th Infantry Division, which had arrived in country in 1967. Prior to 1969, the U.S. division seldom worked with the three ARVN divisions in the region or the territorial units. Moreover, Maj. Gen. Julian J. Ewell, the 9th Infantry Division commander, believed that the South Vietnamese forces in the Delta were ineffective and warned that the South Vietnamese were not ready to take control of the U.S. division's area of operations.[48] Therefore, many were surprised by the selection of the 9th as the first American division to be redeployed to the United States after the Midway announcement. As Jeffrey Clarke points out, the decision was, at the very least, partly a political move designed to gain support for the Nixon administration's Vietnamization policy by fulfilling the promise to bring home combat troops rather than just support personnel.[49] Despite Ewell's warnings about South Vietnamese military capabilities in the Delta, the withdrawal of the 9th also made sense strategically. By 1969, the enemy situation in the Delta was fairly stable, since the area's Viet Cong forces had been severely weakened during the 1968 Tet offensive. Additionally, the Delta was at the far end of the North Vietnamese supply route and could not be reinforced easily. Should trouble arise, General Abrams

responsibility for the war. Programs such as "Pair Off" and "Dong Tien" were designed to help bolster RVNAF leadership and combat skills, but they could not fully repair long-term ills in the South Vietnamese system.

Despite continuing difficulties and concerns, Vietnamization had made progress in several areas by the end of 1969. Because of the modernization effort, all ARVN units had been equipped with M-16 rifles, which replaced the older, heavier M-1s, and had received M-79 grenade launchers and M-60 machine guns. The redeployment of U.S. troops had forced the RVNAF to assume more responsibility for the war, as the number of battalion-sized operations conducted by the South Vietnamese almost doubled between 1968 and 1969. Still, combat performance of the South Vietnamese was uneven at best. Some units, like the 51st ARVN Infantry Battalion, did very well against their Communist opponents, while others, like the 22nd ARVN Infantry Division, were largely ineffective in the field (the 22nd had conducted 1,800 ambushes during the summer months of 1969 and netted only six enemy killed).[58]

The MACV Office of Information publicized the increased participation of the RVNAF, emphasizing that in time the South Vietnamese forces would be able to stand on their own.[59] Despite these claims, many advisers felt that the South Vietnamese were still too dependent on U.S. forces for support and worried about their ability to carry on the war by themselves after the Americans withdrew.[60] The MACV public relations statements were correct in one sense—it was clear that time would be necessary before the South Vietnamese could stand on their own against the North Vietnamese. The key question to many was whether there was enough time left before all U.S. units were withdrawn.

PACIFICATION

While the South Vietnamese regular forces struggled to assume more responsibility for the fight against the Communists in the field, the pacification effort, a companion piece of Nixon's Vietnamization policy, continued in the battle for the "hearts and minds" of the South Vietnamese people. The emphasis on pacification had actually preceded the initiation of the Vietnamization program. Early groundwork for this effort had been laid in 1967 with the development of the Civil Operations and Rural Development Support (CORDS) program headed by Robert W. Komer.[61] The program had traditionally taken a back seat to the "bigger" war in the field between the U.S. combat units and the forces of the NVA and VC. The shock of the 1968 Communist Tet offensive highlighted the need to increase the emphasis on, and assets applied to, pacification of the countryside. Komer's successor, William E. Colby, later wrote that the United States "had finally discovered that the main element of the war was the war at the village, rather than the war between battalions."[62]

During the 1968 Communist offensive, all the forces that had been committed to the pacification program had to be redeployed for the defense of provincial capitals and district towns. Once the enemy offensive ran its course, the Saigon government turned its attention once again to securing the rural areas. Consequently, a special three-month "Accelerated Pacification Campaign" was launched in November 1968 to "make coordinated and concerted use of all military, governmental, and police resources to bring about maximum security for the rural areas."[63] Because the brief campaign was successful by most measurements, the Saigon government and U.S. officials instituted the 1969 Pacification and Development Plan to take advantage of the advances made during the previous effort.

According to General Abrams, the key to pacification was "to provide meaningful, continuing security for the Vietnamese people."[64] The new pacification plan, or the Special Campaign as it was referred to by the South Vietnamese, called first for the expansion of secure areas; the second stage called for the government of South Vietnam to take measures to develop the rural areas, maintain law and order, and build the local economies.[65] Thus, security became the initial focus of the pacification effort; without a secure environment, all other programs were doomed to failure.

Two instrumental factors set the stage for further success by Saigon in the pacification effort, particularly in regard to improving the rural security situation. First, the Communist forces, still suffering from the effects of the 1968 battles, lacked sufficient strength to contest the new efforts by the Saigon government in the rural areas, at least during the latter half of 1969.[66] The temporary weakness greatly enhanced Saigon's opportunity to make gains. Second, the People's Self-Defense Force (PSDF) had increased in strength and popularity. Organized prior to 1968 to provide a structure for local self-defense, the force had languished from lack of participation at the hamlet and village level. Somewhat ironically, the PSDF received a significant boost from the Tet offensive. Many South Vietnamese villagers, who heretofore had been at best ambivalent about joining Saigon's fight against the Communists, were shocked by what they saw as the excesses of the Communists during the 1968 attacks and joined the PSDF, taking up arms to protect their towns, villages, and hamlets. By the end of 1969, over three million members had volunteered for the PSDF. Thus, as former ARVN general Nguyen Duy Hinh asserts, the PSDF movement succeeded in rallying the popular masses to support Saigon's pacification effort and contributed greatly to the maintenance of local security.[67]

As security increased, the villagers who had fled their homes to escape the fighting began to return. As they did, the populated and secure areas controlled by Saigon began to expand rapidly. By 1971, approximately 2 million refugees either returned to their home villages or were resettled elsewhere with government assistance; this number included 200,000 Vietnamese who had fled Cambodia.[68]

Ambassador Ellsworth Bunker wrote President Nixon that the pacification program had flourished in 1969 because President Thieu, for the first time, took a

While the bombing campaign planning was underway, the North Vietnamese agreed to secret talks in Paris between their representatives, Xuan Thuy and Mai Van Bo, and Kissinger. Nixon told Kissinger to be firm with the North Vietnamese. He was to remind the Communists that U.S. troop withdrawals had begun and that the United States was prepared to accept the result of free elections. If Hanoi was not prepared to reciprocate, Kissinger was to reiterate the previously issued ultimatum and tell them "that if by November 1 no major progress has been made toward a solution, we will be compelled—with great reluctance—to take measures of the greatest consequences."[83] The secret negotiations began on 4 August 1969. Kissinger made no headway with Xuan Thuy, who demanded the complete withdrawal of all American forces from South Vietnam, the removal of President Thieu, and the establishment of a coalition government composed of the Communist Provisional Revolutionary Government and the remnants of the Saigon administration. As Kissinger wrote later, he and Xuan Thuy "had achieved little except to restate established positions."[84]

The North Vietnamese provided a harsher response to Nixon's peace overtures on 6 August, when, as previously described, the Communist forces attacked more than one hundred villages, towns, and cities in South Vietnam. Kissinger later wrote, "The most generous interpretation [of the new attacks] could not avoid the conclusion that Hanoi did not believe in gestures, negotiation, goodwill, or reciprocity."[85] On 23 August, Nixon announced that he was delaying the decision on additional troop withdrawals.

On 25 August, Ho's reply to the president's July letter arrived. It was, in Nixon's words, a "cold rebuff."[86] Ho wrote that "the United States must cease the war of aggression and withdraw their troops from South Vietnam, respect the right of the population of the South and of the Vietnamese nation to dispose of themselves, without foreign influence."[87] Hanoi's answer was unequivocal; as Kissinger wrote, the "North Vietnamese were less interested in stopping the fighting than in winning it."[88] It appeared that any attempt to achieve a negotiated settlement would be immediately rejected.

However, the situation became more uncertain on 4 September when Ho Chi Minh died. What this meant for the war was unclear. Many in Congress and the media urged Nixon to declare a cease-fire, but he was not prepared to go that far. Instead, he suspended military operations for the day of Ho's funeral, an act that prompted more speculation about an armistice.

While trying to ascertain what Ho's death meant for his peace initiatives, Nixon also had to deal with an increasingly volatile domestic situation. The antiwar protesters had been quieted somewhat by the Midway announcement and subsequent withdrawal of the 9th Infantry Division from the Mekong Delta. However, Laird warned Nixon in early September, "I believe this may be an illusory phenomenon. The actual and potential antipathy for the war is, in my judgement, significant and increasing."[89] Laird was proven to be correct. The death of Ho Chi Minh and the possibility of an armistice gave those who wanted the United States to get out of Vietnam renewed vigor. Antiwar sentiment grew in the press, in Congress, and on the streets of America. Congressmen rushed to introduce resolutions designed to disengage the United States from Vietnam, and the Senate Foreign Relations Committee called a new round of hearings on the war. Antiwar activists called for a "Moratorium to End the War in Vietnam" to express a broad protest against the war on 15 October, 15 November, and so on until America was out of Vietnam.

In an attempt to undercut the effects of the Moratorium and to send a signal to the new leadership in Hanoi, Nixon announced on 16 September that he was withdrawing another sixty thousand troops from Vietnam by 15 December. He pointed out that this additional withdrawal was a significant step and that "the time for meaningful negotiations has therefore arrived."[90] Three days later, he said that because of the withdrawal, draft calls for November and December would be canceled, and on 1 December the first draft lottery would be held.[91] By these actions, Nixon was trying to send a message to both the North Vietnamese and the antiwar movement.

Nixon found himself in a very difficult position. He knew he could not simply withdraw all U.S. troops without abrogating the American commitment to South Vietnam and risking its loss to the Communists. Thus, he had to continue to fight the war in the field, while at the same time trying to win a favorable settlement at the peace talks. Concurrently, he had to bolster public support for the war at home until he could achieve the negotiated settlement. However, as Nixon biographer Stephen Ambrose points out, "The war had always been a hard sell; once Nixon began to withdraw, it was nearly an impossible one."[92] Maintaining support for the war effort proved a difficult challenge, particularly given Nixon's antipathy for dissidents. Nixon knew he had to get U.S. troops out of Vietnam, but he was not prepared to show any weakness or even give the appearance that he was kowtowing to the antiwar protesters.

On 26 September, Nixon reignited the fury of the dissenters at a press conference. When asked his view of the Moratorium, he replied, "As far as that kind of activity is concerned, we expect it. However, under no circumstances will I be affected whatever by it."[93] Despite his denials that the protesters had any influence on his decision making, it appears that they had an effect the dissidents did not anticipate: the more vocal and violent the protests, the more bellicose Nixon's attitude.

On 30 September, in a meeting with Republican congressional leaders, the president made a veiled reference to Duck Hook and his ultimatum to the North Vietnamese. He said the next sixty days would be crucial and further stated, "I can't tell you everything that will be going on, because if there is to be any chance of success, it will have to be done in secret. All I can tell you is this: I am doing my damnedest to end the war . . . I won't make it hard for the North Vietnamese if they genuinely want a settlement, but I will not be the first President of the United States to lose a war."[94] In a meeting with nine Republican senators, he let out the Duck Hook secret, admitting that a blockade of Haiphong and invasion of North Vietnam were under consideration. The next day, the story appeared in a Rowland Evans and Robert Novak newspaper column; Nixon had leaked the story himself to get the attention of the new North Vietnamese leadership in Hanoi.[95]

Secretary of Defense Laird and Secretary of State Rogers were shocked by the column and urged the president not to implement the plan. They pointed out the very low casualty rates over the previous few months and noted the improved performance of the South Vietnamese as a result of the stepped-up Vietnamization program.[96] They pleaded with Nixon not to escalate the war. Undeterred, Nixon responded by sending a memo to Kissinger, saying, "It would be very helpful if a propaganda offensive could be launched, constantly repeating what we have done in offering peace in Vietnam in preparation for what we may have to do later."[97] Nixon was preparing to increase the stakes if the call for a negotiated settlement did not work.

Nixon's actions had predictable effects on the antiwar dissidents both in and out of the government. Senator William Fulbright announced new hearings on the war and said that Nixon had been in office for nine months, but had not made any "progress in delivering on his campaign promises to give birth to his plans to end the war."[98] Other congressmen, such as Senators John Sherman Cooper, Gaylord Nelson, Mike Mansfield, Edward Kennedy, and Eugene McCarthy also severely criticized Nixon and his policies, as did the public. The presidents of seventy-nine colleges signed a letter to Nixon urging him to step up the troop withdrawals. Angry protests were held at Berkeley, Penn, Cornell, Duke, and on many other campuses around the country, and picketers carried signs in front of the White House denouncing Nixon and the war.

Nixon provided an answer to the protesters in his public response to a letter he had received from Randy Dicks, a Georgetown University student who questioned the president's refusal to be swayed by the Moratorium's appeal to conscience and urged him to "take note of the will of the people." Nixon replied that there was little to be learned from the student demonstrations and further wrote: "Whatever the issue, to allow government policy to be made in the streets would destroy the democratic process. . . . [by giving] the decision, not to the majority, . . . but to those with the loudest voices. Others can say of Vietnam, 'Get out now;' when asked how, they can give the simple, flip answer: 'By sea.' They can ignore the consequences. . . . [but] history would rightly condemn a President who took such a course."[99]

On 15 October, the Moratorium occurred as scheduled. Thousands of protesters marched in cities across the country, including Chicago, Denver, San Francisco, and Los Angeles. Over 100,000 people in Boston, 200,000 in New York City, and more than 250,000 in Washington participated. Some of Nixon's advisers were disturbed that the Moratorium brought out the middle class and the middle-aged in great numbers, but the president put out the word that he was unmoved by the demonstrations and had spent the afternoon watching a football game on television. Privately, Nixon claimed that the protests "destroyed whatever small possibility may have still existed of ending the war in 1969."[100]

That evening, Nixon began working on a major speech to be delivered on 3 November. Nixon perceived that he had two options regarding South Vietnam: he could accede to the protesters' demands and accelerate the U.S. troop withdrawals unilaterally; or he could escalate the war in an attempt to force the North Vietnamese to meaningful negotiated peace. While drafting his speech, the president received a great deal of advice. On 17 October, Kissinger, who had been strongly affected by the strength of the Moratorium, urged the president not to escalate until the North Vietnamese had a chance to respond to the 1 November deadline.[101] That same day, Nixon met with the British guerrilla-warfare expert Sir Robert Thompson.[102] The president asked Thompson what he thought about a potential U.S. escalation. Thompson was "clearly not in favor of escalation" because of the furor it would cause around the world; he further replied that he thought Vietnamization was the proper course of action. He realized that this approach meant a continuation of U.S. involvement in South Vietnam beyond Nixon's proclaimed target date of the end of 1970, but believed that it was critical for the United States "to see it through."[103]

Nixon later indicated that in crafting his decision about escalation and the 1 November deadline he considered three factors: the rapidly declining American casualty figures (and the subsequent hue and cry that would be raised if he decided to escalate the war, causing the casualties to increase); the death of Ho Chi Minh and any new possibilities that might arise from the new leadership in Hanoi; and the advice that he received from Sir Robert Thompson.[104] He wrote, "In view of these three factors, and recognizing that the Moratorium had undercut the credibility of the ultimatum, I began to think more in terms of stepping up Vietnamization while continuing the fighting at its present level rather than trying to increase it. In many respects Vietnamization would be far more damaging to the Communists than an escalation that, as Thompson had pointed out, would not solve the basic problem of South Vietnamese preparedness, and that would stir up serious domestic problems in America."[105]

Nixon continued to receive more advice as the 3 November speech grew closer. Secretary of State Rogers urged the president to concentrate on peace, emphasizing the Paris talks. Kissinger advised him to take a hard line, stressing the prospects of Vietnamization. Senate Majority Leader Mike Mansfield sent him a memorandum that urged the president to consider the impact of the war on the home front, writing, "The continuance of the war in Vietnam, in my judgment, endangers the future of this nation. . . . Most serious are the deep divisions within our society to which this conflict of dubious origins and purpose is contributing."[106]

Armed with all this advice, Nixon flew to Camp David on 24 October for a long weekend. There he worked twelve to fourteen hours a day writing and rewriting sections of the speech. Upon his return to Washington, he continued to work on the address, going through twelve drafts in the process. While the president honed his speech, speculation about what he would say became widespread. Many believed that he would announce new troop withdrawals, and some even hoped he would announce a unilateral cease-fire.

On Monday night, 3 November 1969, President Richard Nixon appeared on national television and radio to explain the administration's position. Nixon's message was that the United States was "going to keep our commitment in Vietnam." The United States would continue fighting until either the Communists agreed to negotiate a fair and honorable peace or the South Vietnamese were able to defend themselves on their own—whichever came first. The pace of American troop withdrawals would be based on the principles of the Nixon Doctrine and be linked to the progress of Vietnamization, the level of enemy activity, and developments on the negotiating front.

Saying that the obstacle to peace was not the president of the United States or South Vietnam, he pointed out that efforts had been made to negotiate with the North Vietnamese. However, the "other side" had refused to show "the least willingness to join us in seeking a just peace." He predicted that Hanoi would not cooperate "while it is convinced that all it has to do is wait for our next concession, and our next concession after that one, until it gets everything it wants."

Thus, unable to foresee any gains in the negotiating arena, the president emphasized the progress that was being made in Vietnamizing the war. He explained that he had changed General Abrams's orders, had reduced bombing operations by 20 percent, and had withdrawn sixty thousand men, while greatly improving ARVN's equipment and training. Consequently, infiltration was down, as were American casualties. Despite this success, he warned that the pace of future U.S. withdrawals would be tied to the level of enemy infiltration; and that if enemy activity and U.S. casualties increased, "I shall not hesitate to take strong and effective measures. . . . This is not a threat. This is a statement of policy."

Having laid out his plan, the president then asked for the support of the American people, saying:

And so tonight—to you, the great silent majority of my fellow Americans— I ask for your support. I pledged in my campaign for the presidency to end the war in a way that we could win the peace. I have initiated a plan of action which will enable me to keep that pledge. The more support I can have from the American people, the sooner that pledge can be redeemed; for the more divided we are at home, the less likely the enemy is to negotiate at Paris. Let us be united for peace. Let us also be united against defeat. Because let us understand: North Vietnam cannot defeat or humiliate the United States. Only Americans can do that.[107]

Nixon was extremely pleased with the speech and wrote in his *Memoirs* that "very few speeches actually influence the course of history."[108] This was hyperbole at its best, for the president had announced no startling revelations and had merely said that he was going to keep on doing what he had been doing for the previous nine months. Public response to the speech was mixed. The media, for the most part, was not kind to the president. Representative of the print media response was James Reston of the *New York Times,* who wrote, "It was a speech that seemed to be designed not to persuade the opposition, but to overwhelm it, and the chances are that this will merely divide and polarize the debaters in the United States, without bringing the enemy into serious negotiations."[109] The electronic media was no less critical. Bill Lawrence, ABC Television's national affairs editor, observed that the president's speech was "nothing new" politically and appealed, he said, to those who were moved by words rather than deeds; he concluded that the speech would make little difference to voters six months in the future.[110]

The American public responded more favorably. If Nixon intended to solidify his support, he did so with the "silent majority" remark, which apparently struck a chord. A Gallup telephone poll taken immediately after the speech showed 77 percent approval, and more than fifty thousand overwhelmingly supportive telegrams and thirty thousand letters of a similar nature poured into the White House.[111] This flood of public backing for the president's policies also had an impact on Congress. By November 12, 300 members of the House of Representatives—119 Democrats and 181 Republicans—had cosponsored a resolution of support for Nixon's Vietnam policies, and 58 senators—21 Democrats and 37 Republicans—had signed letters expressing similar sentiments.[112] Nixon concluded that he had the public support he needed to continue his policy of waging war in Vietnam while negotiating for peace in Paris until the war could be brought to "an honorable and successful conclusion."[113] However, Nixon was under no illusion that this momentary outpouring of support would last and realized that "under the constant pounding from the media and our critics in Congress, people would soon be demanding that new actions be taken to produce progress and end the war."[114]

Nixon's 3 November speech had made no concessions to the protesters, and the New Mobilization Committee to End the War in Vietnam responded with a call for a two-day protest. These demonstrations far surpassed even the expectations of those who had planned them. The events began on 13 November with a dramatic "March against Death," in which a single file of 40,000 people walked in silence from Arlington National Cemetery to the White House and Capitol. The protest reached its climax on 15 March when between 250,000 and 300,000 participants marched from the Capitol down Pennsylvania Avenue to the Washington Monument; many marchers carried placards reading "Silent Majority for Peace." The demonstrations of the November Moratorium were extremely peaceful in nature and, with the October Moratorium, demonstrated the growing strength of the antiwar movement and the increasing involvement of mainstream Americans.

The Nixon administration ended 1969 confronted by stalemate on virtually every front with respect to the war in Vietnam—on the battlefield, at the negotiating table, and on the American home front. Short of a complete unilateral withdrawal, the only way to break these impasses was to make Vietnamization work. Vietnamization and its companion program, pacification, were beginning to show glimmers of success; however, the pace of change was extremely slow. Nixon had been running the war for a year, and over 475,000 U.S. troops still remained in

Southeast Asia and another 9,145 had been killed. Still, a Gallup poll reported that by November, only one out of five Americans supported an immediate withdrawal from South Vietnam.[115] The key question was how rapidly that percentage would shift—would the American people give Nixon and his administration the time needed to complete the process of Vietnamization? Another critical question was whether the policy itself was a practical solution, given South Vietnam's political leadership and the many problems that plagued both the military and South Vietnamese society at large.

4

Raising the Stakes

"TALKING AND FIGHTING"

In 1969, the North Vietnamese modified their strategy in the South. Documents captured later in the war revealed that the Communists had concluded after the 1968 Tet offensive that launching a general offensive had been too costly. In April 1969, the North Vietnamese leadership in the South announced to their troops in Directive 53: "Never again and under no circumstances are we to risk our entire military force for just an offensive. On the contrary, we should endeavor to preserve our military potential for future campaigns."[1] In July, the Communist high command issued Resolutions 9 and 14, which closely examined the mistakes and shortcomings of the Tet offensive and called for a more economical means of continuing the fight. Resolution 9 was a critical self-analysis, noting both the failure of the 1968 "General Offensive-General Uprising" in achieving its overall objectives and the ineffectiveness of Communist proselytizing activities during the campaign.[2] Resolution 14 called for a de-emphasis of mainforce warfare and a return to small-scale actions by local force guerrillas, stating: "We secure victory not through a one-blow offensive, and not through a phase of attack, not even through a series of attacks culminating in a final kill. . . . Victory will come to us, not suddenly, but in a complicated and torturous way."[3] The result of these directives was a change in strategy called *dua danh va dua dam*, whereby the Communists would "talk and fight."[4] While their negotiators pursued Communist objectives in Paris, North Vietnamese and Viet Cong troops would keep the pressure on the U.S. and South Vietnamese forces on the battlefield. However, this pressure, with some exceptions, was to be applied primarily through the use of mortar and sapper attacks, rather than large-scale conventional attacks like those conducted in 1968. The North Vietnamese hoped to "hang in there" and wait out Nixon and the United States.[5]

Due to this change in tactics and emphasis, the level of fighting in South Vietnam subsided substantially during the last months of 1969 and the first part of

1970. However, State Department officials in Saigon warned in a January 1970 estimate of enemy strategy that the Communists remained confident in their ability to prolong the war until they won.[6] Henry Kissinger made a similar assessment in a 7 January memorandum to the president in which he asserted that, in his opinion, "Hanoi would play for time until enough American forces had left to allow it to challenge Saigon's armed forces on a more equal basis."[7] Although the level of combat in South Vietnam tapered off during the first three months of 1970, Secretary of Defense Laird told the president in an April memo that he believed the reduction in combat intensity on the battlefield more likely resulted from North Vietnamese design than from American and South Vietnamese efforts. He emphasized his perspective that the Communists still retained the strength and ability to raise the level of combat, but were probably waiting until American forces had departed before launching another major attack.[8]

Meanwhile, Vietnamization continued at an uneven pace. In his April memo to the president, Secretary Laird said that the South Vietnamese continued to lack effective military and civilian leadership and suffered from chronic instability.[9] A *Newsweek* article around the same time made a similar assessment of the Vietnamization program. Acknowledging that the modernization effort was progressing reasonably well—over 500 gunboats had been turned over to the South Vietnamese navy, 1,200 VNAF pilots were in training with the U.S. Air Force, and a number of new and modern weapons had been issued to ARVN, including M-16 rifles, M-60 machine guns, and M-79 grenade launchers—the article noted that until the South Vietnamese armed forces faced the enemy on their own, the "report card must remain a blank."[10]

The continued strength of the Communists and their intractability at the Paris negotiations, coupled with the slow progress of Vietnamization, effectively resulted in a stalemate in South Vietnam. This stalemate, part of North Vietnam's plan, was becoming a contentious issue in the United States, even among those Americans who supported President Nixon's policies. Among the antiwar dissidents, the failure of the administration to end the conflict and bring all the troops home resulted in an upward spiral of renewed demonstrations against Nixon and the war.

By April 1970, Nixon had become frustrated with the lack of progress in South Vietnam. In an attempt to "drop a bombshell on the gathering storm of anti-war protests," he announced on 20 April a phased withdrawal of another 150,000 U.S. troops to be completed over the next year.[11] In his speech, Nixon was upbeat, saying that gains in training and equipping the South Vietnamese had "substantially exceeded our original expectations"; thus he could announce this new major withdrawal because Vietnamization was working so well. He stressed that by April 1971 he would have cut in half the number of American troops in Vietnam. However, he warned Hanoi that "If I conclude increased enemy action jeopardized our remaining forces in Vietnam, I shall not hesitate to take strong and effective measures to deal with the situation."[12]

By announcing new troop reductions, Nixon hoped to satisfy the growing demand in the United States for an end to American involvement in Southeast Asia. However, he also hoped that the timetable for the phased reductions would allay any fears in Saigon about accelerated withdrawals. Nevertheless, the announcement did not please General Abrams, who thought that it made U.S. forces in South Vietnam vulnerable to new attacks by the Communists and might adversely affect the progress of Vietnamization.[13] From a purely military standpoint, Abrams was correct; but politically, Nixon had to do something to quiet the protesters and the growing questions from the American public.

Nixon still wanted to achieve a negotiated settlement in Vietnam. He had hoped that his 3 November speech would convince the North Vietnamese that he was serious about continuing the war in South Vietnam if they refused to negotiate. The Communists, however, observed the U.S. withdrawals and concluded that the pressure on Nixon to get out of South Vietnam would only continue to increase. Therefore, the Communists could achieve their objectives by a continuation of "fighting and talking," by waiting out the American president until he had eventually withdrawn all U.S. troops. Then they could take over South Vietnam without worrying about American interference.

Angry that the NVA had not taken his warnings to heart and come to the negotiating table in good faith, Nixon decided that he needed a display of force "to show the enemy that we were still serious about our commitment in Vietnam."[14] Events in Cambodia gave him the opportunity for which he yearned.

CAMBODIA AND THE HO CHI MINH TRAIL

While Communist activity in South Vietnam had declined in early 1970, it had, if anything, increased in Cambodia and Laos. Prince Norodom Sihanouk of Cambodia had previously maintained his country's neutrality, despite permitting the North Vietnamese and Viet Cong to use Cambodian territory along its entire border with Vietnam for resupply routes and staging areas to support operations into South Vietnam. Moreover, Sihanouk had permitted supplies to land at the port of Sihanoukville and cross overland to the Communist border bases; by this time in the war, an estimated 85 percent of total supplies to the Communist forces in South Vietnam traveled via the sea and land route.[15] On 18 March 1970, while Sihanouk was vacationing in Paris, his premier, Gen. Lon Nol, engineered a bloodless coup and promptly demanded that the North Vietnamese and Viet Cong leave Cambodia. The Communists refused to relinquish their sanctuaries and, in conjunction with their Cambodian allies, the Khmer Rouge, launched a wave of attacks to secure a strip of Cambodian territory ten to fifteen kilometers wide practically all along the South Vietnamese frontier. The inexperienced Cambodian army was no match for the Communist forces, and it soon appeared that the North Vietnamese and Khmer Rouge troops were going to take all of Cambodia east of the Mekong River. Lon Nol requested assistance from the United States.

The sanctuaries and Communist supply routes along the Vietnamese-Cambodian border had long been a thorn in the side of the allied war effort. A delegation of U.S. congressmen had traveled to Vietnam in 1968 and reported that the North Vietnamese and Viet Cong were using the eastern provinces of Cambodia as troop-concentration areas, training centers, and logistics bases.[16] The area also included the southern portion of the Ho Chi Minh Trail, a network of trails, bicycle paths, roads (some capable of handling heavy truck, tank, and armored personnel traffic), base camps, and storage facilities that extended along the Cambodian and Laotian borders from North Vietnam to just west of Saigon (see map 3). An intelligence report in early 1970 estimated that an average of 4,000 tons of war equipment and supplies moved down the Ho Chi Minh Trail each month to the Communist forces operating out of numerous military bases in Cambodia.

These bases were essentially safe havens for the Communist forces, who could launch operations into South Vietnam and then withdraw into the relative safety of Cambodia, where they could not be pursued by American ground troops. Gen. Dave Richard Palmer best described the problem: "Two-thirds of South Vietnam's population lived in the southern two military regions, both of which bordered Cambodia. Fourteen major North Vietnamese bases stood inside Cambodia, three neighboring the Fourth Corps area and seven by the Third Corps. Some were within 35 miles of Saigon. As long as they remained 'off-limits' to Allied forces, it was as if a loaded and cocked pistol was being held to the head of South Vietnam."[17]

President Nixon had authorized secret bombings in 1969 to attack the Cambodian sanctuaries, but the trail and base area complex proved resistant to attack from the air. The B-52 raids slowed down infiltration through the area, but did not stop North Vietnamese use of the trail complex or the staging areas. By the time of the Cambodian coup in 1970, an estimated 40,000–60,000 NVA troops were in Cambodia, and they were expanding toward the central provinces of Kompong Cham, Prey Veng, and Svay Rieng, which would put them within striking distance of Phnom Penh.[18]

The United States could not allow the North Vietnamese to take Cambodia, because that would essentially outflank South Vietnam. The whole of Cambodia would become a sanctuary for the North Vietnamese forces, and the overland route from Sihanoukville would be opened to full-scale resupply efforts. The situation was critical, not only for the U.S. forces remaining in South Vietnam, but also for the RVNAF as more American troops withdrew, leaving the South Vietnamese to their own devices. As General Palmer wrote after the war, "So long as Hanoi persisted in aggression, so long as the NVA enjoyed sanctuaries within easy striking distance of Saigon . . . then so long would war or the threat of imminent invasion cast a dark shadow across South Vietnam."[19]

Secretary of Defense Laird had visited Saigon in February 1970. While briefing him, General Abrams made a strong case for invading not only sanctuaries in Cambodia, but others in Laos as well. However, Laird was unconvinced. That month, news of secret U.S. bombing in Laos had become public, prompting an im-

Map 3. The Ho Chi Minh Trail.

mediate outcry from Congress. Laird felt that neither Nixon's critics nor a growing sector of the American people who just wanted the war to be over would accept any further widening of the war.

　　Shortly after Laird's return to the United States, the situation in Cambodia took
a turn for the worse. In a February message to the JCS, Adm. John S. McCain,

commander in chief of U.S. Pacific Forces, warned that "the Cambodian sanctuary had become a primary strategic base essential to the enemy if he is to accomplish his overall objectives against Vietnamization"; moreover, McCain warned that intelligence indicators pointed toward a major Communist offensive in Cambodia in April or May.[20] North Vietnamese troops proved his warning to be timely and accurate on 29 March when they began moving westward in the direction of Phnom Penh from their sanctuary bases in the "Fishhook," a salient that pushed into South Vietnam west of An Loc, and the "Parrot's Beak," Cambodia's Svay Rieng Province, where the border comes within thirty-three miles of Saigon. The NVA launched major ground attacks against Cambodian strongpoints all along the Cambodian-South Vietnamese border and then turned into the Cambodian interior. Within a few days, the much stronger Communist forces had pushed Lon Nol's troops completely out of the Parrot's Beak area, which was abandoned to North Vietnamese control on 10 April. By the middle of the month, the Communists seemed to be preparing to encircle Phnom Penh and the Lon Nol government appeared to be in imminent danger of falling.

Nixon and his advisers had been watching the worsening situation in Cambodia very closely. On 25 March, alarmed at the North Vietnamese assault on Lon Nol's forces, the president had charged the JCS with drafting a plan for an attack into Cambodia by either U.S. or South Vietnamese forces to relieve pressure on Phnom Penh should the Communist forces directly threaten the city.[21] The JCS passed the president's directive to General Abrams in Saigon, who prepared and submitted a plan on 30 March to Kissinger and the NSC for the president's consideration. The plan included three potential courses of action: the first was to urge the South Vietnamese to increase their cross-border raids into the enemy sanctuaries (which was already happening on a limited basis); the second option was to direct the South Vietnamese to launch larger and more effective forays into Cambodia while providing additional American artillery and air support; the final option was to initiate a full-scale attack by South Vietnamese forces accompanied by U.S. advisers into the base areas and supply depots to disrupt the enemy's command and control elements, demolish his logistical installations, and eliminate COSVN headquarters.[22] Nixon delayed a decision, and Abrams was told to put the plans on hold while the administration tried to determine what was going on inside Cambodia.

On 19 April, the president flew to Hawaii to greet the crew of *Apollo 13,* who had just returned from a near disastrous mission to the moon. While in Honolulu, Nixon received a briefing on the Cambodian situation from Admiral John S. McCain Jr., who stressed that the situation was becoming desperate. He told the president, "If you are going to withdraw another 150,000 troops from South Vietnam this year, you must protect Saigon's western flank by an invasion of the Cambodian sanctuaries."[23]

McCain's briefing was on Nixon's mind upon his return to Washington, where a heated debate ensued over what to do about the situation. On one hand, Kissinger and the Joint Chiefs of Staff, believing that Cambodia was in imminent danger of collapse, urged the president to do something to preclude that potential disaster from becoming reality. On the other hand, Secretary of State Rogers warned Nixon that U.S. intervention in Cambodia, on top of the breaking news of secret U.S. bombing in Laos, might prove to be a political nightmare for the president.

Despite the potential debacle looming in Cambodia, Nixon went ahead with his troop withdrawal announcement on 20 April. Such a move in the face of the rapidly deteriorating situation on Vietnam's flank was fraught with danger, but the administration was confronted by a conundrum, which Kissinger later described in his memoirs: "The dilemma was plain to see. Troop cuts poulticed public sores at home, but they were evaporating Hanoi's need to bargain about our disengagement. And if Vietnamization was not making good the defensive gaps created by our withdrawals, we hazarded not only the negotiating lever but South Vietnam's independence and the entire basis of our sacrifices."[24]

Nixon found himself caught between the proverbial rock and hard place. He had to continue the troop withdrawals or suffer a political disaster at home; at the same time, he also had to do something about Cambodia in order to protect the Vietnamization effort and provide time to continue the buildup of the South Vietnamese forces. The question was how to do this without igniting a firestorm of controversy at home.

On Tuesday, 21 April, the president met with Kissinger and Richard Helms, director of the Central Intelligence Agency. Helms briefed the president on the Communist attacks and emphatically warned the president that the Cambodian army faced almost certain destruction. Nixon authorized an immediate transfer of funds and military equipment for Lon Nol's army. He met later in the day with Kissinger and Laird to discuss strategic options. All three recognized that Cambodia would soon fall to the North Vietnamese and Khmer Rouge forces if nothing were done. The loss of Cambodia would bring dire consequences for the Vietnamization program, destroy Nixon's timetable for achieving "peace with honor," and undoubtedly result in a widening of the war.

Later that day, Nixon sent Kissinger a memorandum that began: "I think we need a bold move in Cambodia . . . to show that we stand with Lon Nol. . . . They [the Communists] are romping in there, and the only government in Cambodia in the last twenty-five years that had the guts to take a pro-Western and pro-American stand is ready to fall."[25] The president called an NSC meeting for the following day. Meanwhile, the White House received a long message from Ambassador Bunker and General Abrams. They emphasized the dire consequences for Vietnamization if Cambodia fell and recommended U.S.-South Vietnamese operations against the key Communist sanctuaries.[26]

During the NSC meeting the next day, Kissinger delivered a detailed report on the military situation in Cambodia. He emphasized that the Communists' defeat of Cambodia or even the expansion of their sanctuary areas would give them the capability to inflict increased casualties on U.S. forces in South Vietnam, and the resulting situation would almost certainly endanger the Vietnamization program, thereby potentially forcing a slowdown in the withdrawal of U.S. forces. Kissinger enumerated three options. The first was to do nothing, which he described in his memoirs as the "preferred course of the State and Defense departments."[27] Kissinger's preferred option, the second, was to attack the sanctuaries only with South Vietnamese forces. The last option was to use whatever forces were necessary, including American troops, to neutralize all of the base areas; this option was strongly supported by Bunker, Abrams, and the Joint Chiefs of Staff.

The consensus from the ensuing discussion was that the first option was not viable. The United States could not afford to let the Communists take Cambodia, despite the potential political fallout from any direct U.S. involvement. The use of U.S. troops was considered, but those at the meeting generally felt that the South Vietnamese should handle the ground fighting and that the United States should limit its role to air and fire support. Laird and Rogers even opposed this limited U.S. participation, but Vice President Agnew spoke up, saying that if the administration really wanted to protect Vietnamization, it should attack both sanctuaries and use whatever American troops were necessary.[28] Nixon agreed that something had to be done, but believed that the South Vietnamese should carry out the strike. He authorized American air support for the Parrot's Beak operation, but only "on the basis of demonstrated necessity."[29] He did not commit himself to an attack of the Fishhook area. Nixon later described his thought process in his memoirs: "Giving the South Vietnamese an operation of their own would be a major boost to their morale as well as provide a practical demonstration of the success of Vietnamization."[30] When the meeting adjourned, Gen. Earle Wheeler sent Abrams a message advising him to begin planning for the Cambodian operation. He said, "Our objective is to make maximum use of ARVN assets, so as to minimize U.S. involvement, and to maintain lowest possible U.S. profile. . . . U.S. advisers in Cambodia will be restricted to those required to control U.S. aircraft if and when introduced."[31]

The order to go into Cambodia was well received in Saigon by Abrams and Ambassador Bunker. The Americans had long wanted the freedom to pursue the Communists into the Cambodian sanctuaries.[32] As for the South Vietnamese, President Thieu had some reservations about sending his troops into the Communist strongholds in Cambodia, but, in fact, ARVN forces had already made limited forays into the border areas. On 27 and 28 March, an ARVN Ranger battalion, supported by artillery and tactical air support, had gone three kilometers into Kandal Province to destroy a Communist base camp. Four days later, ARVN troops penetrated sixteen kilometers into Cambodia in pursuit of the Communists. On 20 April, two thousand ARVN soldiers went into the Parrot's Beak area and killed 144 of the enemy. Now it appeared that Nixon was willing to give the green light for a much larger push into Cambodia.

After the meeting on 22 April, Kissinger received a telephone call from the president. According to Kissinger, Nixon hated to be shown up in a group as being less tough than his advisers, and in this case the president appeared to be somewhat chagrined that Agnew had been more forceful than he in the NSC meeting.[33]

Additionally, the president had been pondering what the intelligence briefers had told him about the Fishhook. They had briefed him that this area was even larger than the Parrot's Beak and reportedly contained the elusive COSVN, the supposed "nerve center" of the entire Communist effort in Southeast Asia.[34] Nixon told Kissinger that he was thinking about widening his guidance to include attacks on all the sanctuaries along the Cambodian border, not just the Parrot's Beak, as previously discussed at the NSC meeting, but also the Fishhook. Kissinger took this to mean that the president was contemplating the use of U.S. ground troops in a much broadened Cambodian operation.[35]

Later that night, Nixon called again and told Kissinger that he wanted him to convene a meeting with Adm. Thomas H. Moorer (as acting chairman of the Joint Chiefs, he was scheduled to replace Gen. Earle Wheeler in July), Helms, and Lt. Gen. Robert Cushman, deputy director of the CIA, the next morning to "discuss the feasibility of a combined U.S.-South Vietnamese operation against Fishhook, in parallel with the Parrot's Beak operation."[36]

The men met with the president on 24 April as scheduled. Moorer and Helms "were strongly in favor of an attack on the Fishhook sanctuary [and] . . . felt it would force the North Vietnamese to abandon their effort to encircle and terrorize Phnom Penh"; they reasoned that the destruction of COSVN and the Communist supply dumps would buy valuable time for Vietnamization.[37] Alexander Haig, Kissinger's military aide and a former infantry battalion commander in Vietnam, agreed with Moorer and Helms, arguing that failure to move on the Fishhook at the same time as the attack against the Parrot's Beak would permit enemy reinforcements to "flow into the Parrot's Beak from the Fishhook."[38] Therefore, he recommended that both sanctuaries be attacked, with the main attack being focused on the Fishhook. Haig had led a group of NSC analysts on a trip to Vietnam in January 1970 to study the situation, and although he had seen "hopeful signs," he concluded that the South Vietnamese forces still had some major weaknesses.[39] Accordingly, he told Nixon that while he thought that an attack into the Fishhook area was imperative, he believed that such an attack was clearly beyond the capabilities of the South Vietnamese forces by themselves. An earlier message from Abrams, which said he could not guarantee the success of the proposed raid into Cambodia without U.S. troops, backed up Haig's assessment.[40] Haig, therefore, suggested that a combined U.S.-RVNAF force make the main attack into the Fishhook, with a supporting South Vietnamese attack into the Parrot's Beak. The president agreed with the urgency of the situation and his advisers' assessments, but still demurred. The meeting broke up without a decision.

Afterward, Kissinger, at the direction of the president, notified Secretaries Laird and Rogers about what was being contemplated. Kissinger, who had less than a high opinion of the South Vietnamese capabilities, agreed with Haig and the president on the necessity for U.S. troops, but Laird and Rogers had grave reservations. They both stressed that the use of American troops would inflame the war protesters and Nixon's opponents in Congress. Nixon had already come to the conclusion that he had to act, but he still wavered. He knew Rogers and Laird were right about the probability of strong public and congressional response to what would essentially be an invasion of Cambodia. He later wrote, "I never had any illusions about the shattering effect a decision to go into Cambodia would have on public opinion. I recognized that it would mean personal and political catastrophe for me and my administration."[41] Still, he thought a successful attack into Cambodia would serve several purposes. Aside from the most obvious one of destroying Communist base camps and logistical supplies, it would demonstrate Nixon's resolve to see the war through to its completion and therefore might break the stalemate at the Paris peace talks. Additionally, and just as important, a successful operation would provide a psychological boost to the South Vietnamese and demonstrate that Vietnamization was working. At the very least, Nixon had told Kissinger, "I want to make sure that Cambodia does not go down the drain without doing something."[42]

Accordingly, the president authorized planning for the combined attack using U.S. forces as well as the South Vietnamese, but delayed final approval on launching the operation. Abrams was cabled to begin planning for a combined attack into both the Fishhook and the Parrot's Beak to "get the job done using whatever is necessary."[43]

On the evening of 26 April, Nixon met again with his principal NSC advisers to go over final deliberations about the advisability of going through with the operation. According to Kissinger, Nixon had already made up his mind, but wanted to discuss his decision with Laird and Rogers.[44] Kissinger reiterated the essence of the discussion in his memoirs:

> Could we in good conscience continue a withdrawal from Vietnam with Sihanoukville reopened and all of Cambodia turned into one big contiguous base area? Those within the Administration who balked were mostly concerned with domestic reaction. No one came up with an answer to the dilemma of how we could proceed with Vietnamization if the entire Cambodian frontier opened up to massive infiltration. Nor would inaction avoid our domestic dilemma. If we resisted, we would be charged with escalation; but if we acquiesced in the Communist takeover of Cambodia, our casualties started rising, and Vietnam began to disintegrate, we would be accused of pursuing a hopeless strategy.[45]

Laird and Rogers were vehement in their opposition to the planned invasion, but neither provided a substantive argument that swayed the president. Nevertheless, Nixon postponed the operation for twenty-four hours. According to Kissinger, Nixon delayed the attack to quiet further opposition from within the administration by giving all sides time to calm down.[46] On 28 April, the president made his final decision and Abrams was told to execute the operation. Nixon later wrote of his decision, "We would go for broke, for the big play . . . for all the marbles. . . . A joint ARVN-U.S. Force would go into the Fishhook."[47]

THE PLAN

Once Nixon arrived at the final decision to go into Cambodia, the planning was left to the military commanders in the theater of operations. On 24 April, General Abrams had flown to the corps-level headquarters of Lt. Gen. Michael Davison, commander of II Field Force, to tell him to begin planning for an attack into Cambodia. American commanders, having long wished for authority to follow the Communists into their Cambodian sanctuaries, had been working on contingency plans for just such an attack since January.[48] These contingency plans were dusted off and revised to include a combined U.S.-RVNAF operation, with American and ARVN forces attacking into the Fishhook, and the South Vietnamese attacking alone into the Parrot's Beak.

Elements of II Field Force Vietnam from III CTZ would make the main attack into the Fishhook; secondary supporting attacks would be launched from II and IV CTZs. The allied attack force numbered over fifteen thousand men (ten thousand Americans and over five thousand South Vietnamese), making it the largest combined allied action since Operation Junction City in 1967. The U.S. units involved included elements of the 1st Cavalry Division, the 25th Infantry Division, and the 11th Armored Cavalry Regiment. The South Vietnamese forces included elements of the ARVN 1st Armored Cavalry Regiment (ACR), one armored cavalry squadron each from the 5th and 25th ARVN divisions, an infantry regiment from the 25th ARVN Division, the 4th Ranger Group (four ranger battalions), the 3rd Airborne Brigade, and additional units from both II and III Corps (ARVN).

The plan in the Fishhook called for a pincer movement designed to trap elements of the 7th NVA Division operating there (an estimated seven thousand enemy soldiers). To accomplish this, the 11th Armored Cavalry Regiment would drive from the east and southeast and elements of the 1st Cavalry Division would attack from the west. Meanwhile, the 3rd ARVN Airborne Brigade would be inserted into three blocking positions to the north of the Fishhook and, on order, move south to link up with the 11th ACR and the 1st Cavalry units. At the appropriate time, heliborne forces of the 1st Cavalry would envelop the enemy's rear. In addition to trapping the 7th NVA Division, the allied forces were to comb the area for bases, fortifications, and supply caches. During this phase, U.S. forces were to find and destroy COSVN, which was thought to be located in the Fishhook. Another important objective was the town of Snuol, strategically located at the junction of Routes 7 and 13 and thought to be a main distribution point into South Vietnam for Communist supplies shipped through Sihanoukville. U.S. forces (including those advising the South Vietnamese forces) would be limited to operating at a depth of no more than thirty kilometers inside Cambodian territory.

The attack into the Parrot's Beak was to begin a day before the Fishhook operation and would involve three ARVN task forces, each composed of three infantry battalions and an armored cavalry squadron. During the initial phase of the operation, these forces, totaling 8,700 soldiers, were to surround Base Areas 706 and 367, in the tip of the Parrot's Beak. Upon completing that action, the ARVN force would turn west and north to secure the key town of Svay Rieng and to attack Base Area 354.

ANNOUNCING THE PLAN

On Thursday, 30 April, the day after South Vietnamese forces crossed the border into Cambodia, Nixon explained his reasons for approving the operation in a nationally televised speech. In what some newsmen described as a belligerent manner, he insisted that the move into Cambodia was "not an invasion" but a necessary response to North Vietnamese "aggression." He stated: "To protect our men who are in Viet-Nam and to guarantee the continued success of our withdrawal and the Vietnamization programs, I have concluded that the time has come for action. . . . In cooperation with the armed forces of South Viet-Nam, attacks are being launched this week to clean out major enemy sanctuaries on the Cambodia-Viet-Nam border. . . ." The president acknowledged that his decision to enter Cambodia would cause an uproar at home, but said that he had made his decision without regard to the political consequences. He asserted his belief that the majority of Americans favored the withdrawal of American forces and that this action would further that end, saying "Whether my party gains in November is nothing compared to the lives of 400,000 brave Americans fighting for our country and for the cause of peace and freedom in Vietnam." He concluded, "If when the chips are down, the world's most powerful nation acts like a pitiful helpless giant, the forces of totalitarianism and anarchy will threaten free nations and free institutions throughout the world."[49]

The response in America to the Cambodian operation was immediate and rapidly reached tragic proportions. An earlier leak to the media of the administration's decision to support a South Vietnamese operation into Cambodia had already produced a strong reaction in the Senate, where leading members from both parties threatened to cut off funds for action in Cambodia.[50] However, their reaction was mild compared to the one greeting Nixon's public announcement that Americans would accompany the South Vietnamese into Cambodia. An explosive outcry erupted against the administration and its policy in Southeast Asia. Nixon had promised, or at least hinted, that he was winding down the war as far as American forces were concerned; he had just announced the withdrawal of another 150,000 U.S. troops. Yet now, less than a week later, he was announcing to the nation what in effect was an invasion of Cambodia by American and South Vietnamese forces. Rather than being seen as a preventive measure dictated by the worsening military situation in Cambodia, the "incursion," despite Nixon's protestations to the contrary, looked very much like a widening of the war to many Americans. A new wave of violent protests resulted.[51]

THE CAMBODIAN INCURSION

While the protests set off by the president's announcement raged, the attack continued on schedule. On 29 April, the ARVN forces had launched their part of the operation, called *Toan Thang* (Final Victory), by attacking in division strength into the Parrot's Beak. The U.S. forces moved into the Fishhook two days later. The interval between the two attacks negated the surprise that could have been achieved by a more coordinated operation, but still both attacks went reasonably well.

Before dawn on 1 May, following lengthy preparatory strikes by allied artillery and tactical air support, lead tanks and armored personnel carriers of the 11th Armored Cavalry Regiment crossed the border into Cambodia (see map 4). The U.S. forces expected an entrenched enemy to put up a hard fight. Col. (eventually Gen.) Donn Starry, commander of the 11th, later said, "We had reports of extensive bunker systems, antitank weapons, antiaircraft guns . . . we knew that there were two NVA regiments astride the border in that area we had to go through."[52] However, enemy resistance was light. Presumably, the preponderance of the Communist forces had escaped farther into the Cambodian interior. Most contacts were the result of delaying attacks by small enemy units, rather than the large, pitched battles that the U.S. leadership expected. By 3 May, MACV reported only 8 Americans killed and 32 wounded, which were very low casualties for an operation of this size and scope. Enemy losses were reported as 476 killed, of which 160 were victims of tactical air strikes and helicopter gunship attacks.

There were exceptions to the light contact. On 2 May, Colonel Starry's 11th ACR was ordered to proceed to Snuol, where intelligence reports said an NVA battalion or more was digging in and preparing for battle. Starry entered the town with over one hundred armored vehicles, and a pitched battle ensued that lasted for two days. On the second night the surviving Communist forces slipped away. In the process of the battle, Snuol was virtually destroyed. The results of this action were inconclusive, because the retreating NVA soldiers had taken their dead and wounded with them when they escaped.

Maj. Gen. Elvy Roberts, commander of the 1st Cavalry Division, remarked at the beginning of the operation, "We think we have them [the enemy] in a bag."[53] However, the attack into the Fishhook failed to fill that "bag" with a large number of enemy soldiers. Nevertheless, the operations resulted in the capture and/or destruction of sizable quantities of enemy supplies and materiel. The attackers repeatedly came upon large weapon caches and supply dumps, one so extensive that American troops dubbed it "the City." Discovered by a battalion of the 1st Cavalry Division, this area was a two-square-mile complex that included 182 separate stocks of weapons and ammunition, eighteen mess halls, a firing range, a chicken and pig farm, and over four hundred log-covered bunkers and other shelters containing medical supplies, foodstuffs, and uniforms.[54] Later, another battalion of the 1st Cavalry Division found an even larger area that proved to be the most extensive

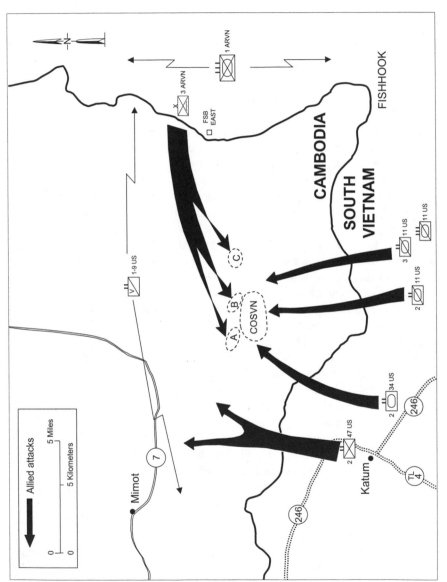

Map 4. The attack into the Fishhook, May 1970.

weapons cache ever captured in the war; the troops called it "Rock Island East."[55] A search of this area revealed more than 6.5 million rounds of antiaircraft ammunition, a half million rifle rounds, thousands of rockets, several General Motors trucks, and even telephone switchboards.

President Nixon, exhilarated by early reports of the allied successes, ordered the Joint Chiefs of Staff "to take out all the sanctuaries. . . . Knock them all out so they can't be used against us again. Ever."[56] Subsequently, units of the 25th Infantry Division invaded an area forty-eight kilometers southwest of the Fishhook, known as the Dog's Head. Additionally, two brigades of the 4th Infantry Division attacked into the Se San area, sixty kilometers west of Pleiku. By the end of May, more than thirty thousand U.S. soldiers were in Cambodia.

U.S. forces spent the rest of May and the entire month of June finding and destroying enemy cache sites. The amount of Communist supplies and equipment destroyed was staggering, but the Fishhook operation failed to achieve one of its primary objectives: the discovery and destruction of COSVN, which still eluded the allies. It was later learned that the shadowy Communist field headquarters had fled the Fishhook area on 19 March and moved west and north across the Mekong River.[57]

THE ARVN ATTACK

While most of the publicity and media attention focused on U.S. and ARVN forces assaulting the Fishhook, Nixon and his advisers' eyes were on the battles for the Parrot's Beak, which, with the exception of about one hundred American advisers, was totally a South Vietnamese show. The Parrot's Beak operation provided one of the earliest test cases for evaluating the efficacy of the South Vietnamese armed forces and the Vietnamization program. Accordingly, it was crucial that the South Vietnamese do well.

As previously stated, the South Vietnamese forces launched their assault into the Parrot's Beak on 29 April (see map 5). They crossed into the region from III Corps and IV Corps with three major objectives: engage the estimated ten to twenty thousand enemy troops operating in the area, find and destroy base facilities and supply caches, and clear Highway 1 and the Mekong River, the main land and water routes between Phnom Penh and South Vietnam.

To lead this operation, which he hoped would be a showcase for his newly revitalized armed forces, President Thieu chose Lt. Gen. Do Cao Tri, commanding general of III Corps. Tri was a dynamic and capable combat leader much respected by his officers and men. His aggressive spirit was infectious, and one ARVN general remarked that when General Tri told his subordinate commanders of the impending Parrot's Beak operation, he "could see the delight in their eyes."[58]

One of the reasons that the South Vietnamese morale was so high at the beginning of the operation was that their American advisers had received authorization to accompany the ARVN units into Cambodia; thus, the South Vietnamese

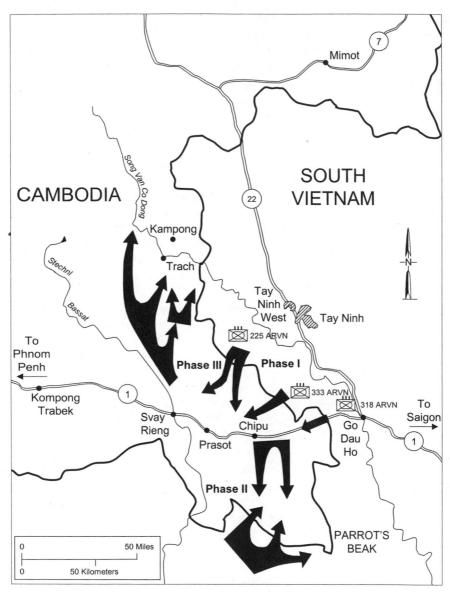

Map 5. The attack into the Parrot's Beak, May 1970.

would get the benefit of U.S. tactical air support and B-52 sorties, which the American advisers could access. Additionally, because the ARVN forces were to receive long-range artillery support from U.S. 8-inch and 175-mm guns, each ARVN task force was assigned American artillery forward observers from the U.S. 23rd Artillery Group. The involvement of the American advisers and artillery observers clearly indicated to the South Vietnamese that they would receive the full backing of the U.S. high command.[59]

Unlike the situation in the Fishhook where the attackers fought only Communist rear guards, the South Vietnamese in the Parrot's Beak made significant contact with North Vietnamese mainforce units almost immediately. Over the next few days, several intense battles raged. Tri later said that in one action his men "fought the Communists in hand-to-hand combat, using rifles, knives, and bayonets. When it was over, we had killed more than fifty of the enemy, while we suffered only five wounded."[60] At the end of the first two days' fighting, ARVN had suffered 30 killed and 70 wounded, while 375 NVA dead were claimed.

After the initial battles, the situation stabilized into one more similar to the experience in the Fishhook as the main NVA body escaped into the Cambodian interior. Against only small delaying forces, the South Vietnamese reached their initial objectives, advancing west toward the provincial capital of Svay Rieng and opening Highway 1. Shortly thereafter, the ARVN forces occupied the southern half of the Parrot's Beak. South Vietnamese reinforcements from the ARVN 9th Infantry Division, five armored cavalry squadrons, and one ranger group arrived to assist in clearing the area, bringing the total number of South Vietnamese troops in Cambodia to over 48,000.

The South Vietnamese troops in the Parrot's Beak found generally the same kind of enemy fortifications and logistical facilities that had been found in the Fishhook. At Ba Thu, fifty kilometers west of Saigon, ARVN troops seized what was apparently a center for outfitting and retraining NVA and VC units. This complex covered ten square kilometers and included hundreds of houses and bunkers connected by an extensive road network.

During May and June, the South Vietnamese conducted mobile operations in Cambodia that kept the Communists off balance and forced them out of their sanctuaries. At the same time, ARVN elements destroyed more NVA logistical supply caches and facilities. The Communists attempted limited counterattacks in early June, but they were largely ineffective. Later that month the monsoon rains began, bringing offensive action by either side to a halt and, for all practical purposes, ending the "incursion." The operation had resulted in 344 Americans killed in Cambodia, and 1,592 wounded; ARVN casualties included 818 dead and 3,553 wounded.[61]

ASSESSING THE CAMBODIAN INCURSION

Despite the furor that accompanied the Cambodian invasion in the United States, the operation was a military success. The Communist base areas and logistics stockpiles were dealt a serious blow. The allies captured an impressive array of supplies and materiel, including 16 million rounds of various caliber ammunition; 45,283 rockets; 14 million pounds of rice; 2,892 individual weapons; 5,487 land mines; 62,000 grenades; and 435 vehicles (see table 7).[62] It was estimated that the captured weapons were enough to equip at least an entire Communist division and the ammunition sufficient to supply 126 enemy battalions for up to four months in the field. Additionally, 11,700 bunkers were destroyed, and the allies claimed 11,349 enemy killed (although the CIA and many in the media found these numbers highly suspect).[63]

Noted British counterinsurgency expert Sir Robert Thompson, who visited South Vietnam shortly after the Cambodian operation, believed that the invasion achieved three important strategic results in addition to the destruction of Communist supplies. First, it prevented the North Vietnamese from immediately overrunning Cambodia and saved Phnom Penh, thereby preserving the government of Lon Nol and the existence of Cambodia as a nation (at least temporarily). It also closed Sihanoukville as an NVA supply port and forced the Communists to bring all supplies down the Ho Chi Minh Trail, thus lengthening their lifeline. Finally, according to Thompson, the invasion showed that Nixon was prepared to use American forces offensively to safeguard remaining American troops and support and protect the Vietnamization effort.[64]

For Nixon and his administration, the operation demonstrated the validity of America's Vietnamization policy. ARVN had displayed an aggressive spirit and the ability to conduct mobile operations against a well-trained, well-equipped enemy. Peter Kann of the *Wall Street Journal* reported from Cambodia in July 1970 that "Even long-time critics concede that ARVN has been operating efficiently and effectively—at least by its own standards of operation with South Vietnam. Regiments that rarely ventured out on anything more taxing than a two-day operation in South Vietnam have been constantly on the move and in contact with enemy forces for six to eight weeks in Cambodia. South Vietnamese operations in Cambodia are all the more impressive in that many have been conducted beyond the range of American logistical and firepower support."[65]

Advisers with the ARVN troops reported a marked increase in the morale of South Vietnamese soldiers, who appeared elated that the war had finally been taken out of their country and into the enemy "home" areas.[66] Although the operation had many positive aspects, all had not been perfect, including some low points such as looting by the ARVN troops at the Chup plantation and Kompong Speu.[67] However, the overall combat performance of the South Vietnamese was encouraging.

The operation gained much-needed time for the allies. The Communists were unable to launch any significant operations from the Fishhook and Parrot's Beak for the next two years. Despite having provoked controversy, the president's decision to go into Cambodia had lessened the pressure in South Vietnam. The Communist sanctuaries had been dealt a serious blow, and the NVA would need months to rebuild their Cambodian bases. Having gained more breathing room for both ARVN and further Vietnamization efforts, Nixon could carry on with his troop withdrawal schedule for the rest of 1970 and into 1971. The ARVN forces' participation in the operation had greatly raised their confidence, and they subsequently

Table 7. Materiel Captured during Cambodian Incursion, 1970

Individual weapons	2,892
Crew-served weapons	2,509
Small-arms ammunition (rounds)	16,762,167
Antiaircraft ammunition (rounds)	199,552
Mortar ammunition (rounds)	68,593
Rockets, B-40 and B-41	43,160
Recoilless rifle ammunition (rounds)	29,185
Hand grenades	62,022
Explosives (pounds)	83,000
Rockets, 107-mm and 122-mm	2,123
Land mines, all types	5,487
Vehicles, all types	435
Pharmaceutical products (pounds)	110,800
Rice (pounds)	14,046,000

Source: Data from Fact Sheet, "Impact on the Enemy of the Cambodian Operations," released in Saigon, 14 May 1970. In Southeast Asia Branch Files, U.S. Army Center of Military History, Washington, D.C.

assumed more responsibility for the war, particularly in the border areas, while the American forces prepared for redeployment to the United States.

However, not everyone thought that operation was such a success. Gen. Bruce Palmer, who served as Westmoreland's deputy at MACV, wrote after the war that the Cambodian raids "fatally wounded South Vietnam's chances to survive and remain free" and that any gains "boomeranged." "Politically," he concluded, "Cambodia not only spelled a downward spiral of public and congressional support for U.S. operations in Southeast Asia, which finally became proscribed, but also eventually resulted in a drastic diminution in U.S. military advisory effort and military aid for South Vietnam. This was probably the most damaging blow of all for Saigon."[68]

Palmer was at least partly correct. Despite the operation's military success, the Cambodian incursion had caused a firestorm of controversy at home. College students rose up almost en masse to protest what was to them a clear escalation of the war. Marches and demonstrations were held at colleges across the country, including New York, Ohio, Texas, California, Georgia, Wisconsin, and many other states. Before May was over, 57 percent of the country's 1,350 campuses experienced strikes against classes and protests involving 4.5 million students. On 4 May, National Guardsmen opened fire on a group of students demonstrating against the war at Kent State, killing four (two of whom were not involved in the protests). On 14 May 1970, ten days after the Kent State University killings, a similar incident took place at Jackson State College, a predominantly African American institution in Mississippi. After two nights of campus demonstrations, a violent confrontation ended when police and state highway patrolmen fired into a dormitory, killing two students and wounding twelve. On 8 May, over 100,000 Americans marched on Washington protesting the war; the government called out regular troops to handle the disturbance.

Congress's response to Nixon's decision to send U.S. troops into Cambodia was no less vigorous. In June, it rescinded the 1964 Tonkin Gulf Resolution, which successive administrations had used as authorization for the war. On the day that the Cambodian operation officially ended, 30 June, the Senate passed the Cooper-Church Amendment, which prohibited the expenditure of public funds for any future introduction of U.S. ground forces into Cambodia. The House rejected the amendment on 9 July, but the corresponding debate demonstrated that a growing number of those in Congress were clearly unhappy with Nixon's widening of the war.[69] By the end of August, the Senate was debating the McGovern-Hatfield Amendment, which set a deadline for American withdrawal from Southeast Asia on 31 December 1971, allowing the president to extend the deadline by sixty days in an emergency. The amendment received wide editorial support. The *Washington Post* called for its passage, saying that it would "end the shell game" in Southeast Asia.[70] Although the amendment was defeated by a vote of 55 to 39 on 1 September, similar legislation would be brought up in Congress several more times, increasing the pressure on Nixon to end the war.

The Cambodian invasion and its aftermath also had a negative impact overseas. In contrast to Nixon's assertion that U.S. influence and prestige depended on decisive action against the Communist sanctuaries, the response of American allies, in the words of British prime minister Harold Wilson, was generally one of "apprehension and anxiety."[71] In June, a secret poll conducted in four European and four Asian countries by the U.S. Information Service "showed a considerable decline in U.S. prestige—apparently as a result of the May–June operations in Cambodia—in almost all of the countries sampled."[72]

While the antiwar demonstrators, critics in Congress, and overseas observers condemned Nixon, many Americans still supported the president. A *Newsweek* poll the second week of May showed 50 percent approval of President Nixon's decision to send troops into Cambodia.[73] The White House received nearly a half million letters and cards, most of which supported the president. On 20 May, 100,000 construction workers, stevedores, tradesmen, and office clerks marched through Manhattan to display approval of Nixon and his policies in Southeast Asia.

Despite this support, Nixon knew that he was running out of time in Vietnam. He had to increase the Vietnamization effort and continue the U.S. troop withdrawals before his country tore itself apart. On 30 June, the president went on television and announced the completion of the Fishhook and Parrot's Beak operations. He said: "With American ground operations in Cambodia ended, we shall move forward with our plan to end the war in Vietnam and to secure the just peace on which all Americans are united . . . [the Cambodian incursion] will save Americans and allied forces in the future; will assure that the withdrawal of American troops from South Vietnam can proceed on schedule; will enable our progress of Vietnamization to continue on its current timetable; and should enhance the prospects for a just peace."[74]

ASSESSING THE PROGRESS OF VIETNAMIZATION

As 1970 drew to a close, military and civilian leaders on the U.S. side tried to assess the progress of Vietnamization. The RVNAF performance during the Cambodia operations, particularly in the Parrot's Beak, was greatly encouraging. The South Vietnamese had taken the offensive against entrenched North Vietnamese forces and the ARVN forces had performed reasonably well. The U.S. Army Advisory Group with III Corps (ARVN) reported that the operation "gave the South Vietnamese soldiers a psychological boost that resulted in a soaring esprit de corps." The report further stated that "of great importance was the conduct of the operation itself. Despite minor errors in planning, tactics and techniques, the operation, controlled from start to finish by South Vietnamese commanders and staffs, was an unqualified success."[75] Another after-action report from the 1st Cavalry Division rated the performance of the South Vietnamese troops in Cambodia as "excellent."[76]

The leadership of Lieutenant General Tri, called by *Time* magazine the "Patton of Parrot's Beak," was particularly encouraging; he had very effectively coordinated a complex operation.[77] Tri, for his part, was very pleased with his soldiers' performance; they had done very well against seasoned NVA troops, displaying a fighting spirit heretofore not seen among most South Vietnamese troops.

Even more than demonstrating the increased combat effectiveness of ARVN, the operation greatly improved the morale of the RVNAF and the confidence of the people of South Vietnam. Even though the ARVN forces had encountered some difficulties in Cambodia, they had met the Communists on their own turf and been successful in holding their own (albeit with U.S. combat support). This was particularly true of those units that had operated beyond the thirty kilometer limitation and therefore fought without U.S. advisers. Former ARVN Brig. Gen. Tran Dinh Tho, writing after the war, said that "to operate without U.S. advisers was a source of pride for ARVN tactical commanders. . . . [T]hey felt more self-assured of their command abilities and, in fact, they all proved that they could manage by themselves."[78] Gen. Dave Palmer agreed and later called the Cambodian incursion "a benchmark in the maturing of ARVN."[79]

President Nixon, clearly believing that the Cambodian operation validated his Vietnamization policy, wanted to spread the word that the South Vietnamese had acquitted themselves well on the battlefield. He told his advisers to devise "a positive, coordinated administration program for getting across the fact that this mission has been enormously successful. . . ."[80]

Despite this explicit guidance from the White House and the positive reports from other quarters, not all U.S. commanders in South Vietnam were so positive about the outcome of the operation and the state of Vietnamization. Lt. Gen. Arthur S. Collins Jr., the commander of I Field Force Vietnam who oversaw the northern flank of the incursion, was particularly disappointed with the performance of II

Corps commanders and troops; he concluded that ARVN was "no match" for the NVA and that developing a reliable ARVN fighting force, at least in II CTZ, would take a long time.[81]

A closer examination of the South Vietnamese performance bears out many of Collins's comments. The fighting in the Parrot's Beak had not been intense over a protracted period; after the initial clashes, the Communist forces evacuated the area without putting up much fight. The South Vietnamese troops used during the operation were mostly from more elite units, like the armored cavalry, airborne, and rangers, rather than from the mainstream of South Vietnamese troops. Even when General Tri used normal ARVN units, he organized task forces under colonels and lieutenant colonels, bypassing the much politicized division commanders and their staffs, who played almost no role in the operation.[82]

The Cambodian incursion also highlighted continuing tactical and support problems. South Vietnamese artillery still had trouble providing close and continuous fire support to the ground forces; the problem would only increase as U.S. artillery units were withdrawn and ARVN had to depend on its own artillery for support. As a result of these artillery deficiencies, ARVN commanders relied heavily on U.S. tactical air support; consequently, many advisers questioned whether the South Vietnamese forces would be able to succeed without it.[83] Another recurring problem was the inability of the South Vietnamese to handle the complex weapons systems that they had received from the U.S. Army. The armored units that participated in the Parrot's Beak were plagued by poor maintenance, gasoline shortages, inadequate spare parts, and faulty communications.[84]

These assessments also applied to other ARVN units that had not participated in the Cambodian operation. In I Corps Tactical Zone, where no cross-border operations had occurred, Lt. Gen. James W. Sutherland, U.S. XXIV Corps commander, reported that although the South Vietnamese leaders from corps to battalion were "good to excellent," they were hampered by the "lack of competent small unit leaders" and "still not ready to stand on their own."[85]

The U.S. media, while in many cases acknowledging the successes of ARVN in Cambodia, also questioned how effective the South Vietnamese forces would be in the long run. *Newsweek* noted that ARVN had developed a new confidence, but the article further stated: "Not even the intense euphoria of the Cambodian excursion can overcome low pay, corruption, and lackluster leadership."[86]

The lack of leadership continued to be a persistent problem afflicting not only small units. In fact, the more serious problem may have been at the most senior levels of the RVNAF. With the exception of a few aggressive leaders like General Tri, most of the senior ARVN officers, including division commanders and those above them, remained too politicized and were more concerned with Saigon palace intrigue and personal creature comforts than with fighting the Communists.[87] A perfect example of poor leadership at a higher level was that of the ARVN 7th Division, which had assumed responsibility for the security of the Mekong Delta from the U.S. 9th Division upon its departure from South Vietnam. By February 1970, the division, whose commanding general was by all accounts extremely weak, had "suffered severe setbacks."[88] The 7th was not an isolated case. Gen. William Westmoreland, U.S. Army chief of staff and former MACV commander, visited South Vietnam in July 1970 and saw "a need to clean house in the senior ranks of the Vietnamese Army"; he pointed out to President Thieu that there were "many young colonels capable of assuming general officer responsibilities and eager to do so" and recommended "forced retirements" for those senior officers found wanting.[89] Unfortunately, Thieu did not take this advice to heart. Senior leadership would continue to pose a serious problem for the RVNAF for the rest of the war.

Despite the overall credible performance of the RVNAF in Cambodia, serious fundamental defects clearly had to be addressed if the South Vietnamese were to stand alone once the United States had withdrawn all its forces. Poor leadership, organizational problems, politicalization of the senior officer corps, inability to provide adequate combat support, and logistical sustainment difficulties still plagued the South Vietnamese forces. Yet signs existed that Vietnamization was working. In any case, more time was necessary to cure these fundamental ills.

Following the allied operation in Cambodia in May–June 1970, South Vietnamese forces took over defense of the South Vietnam-Cambodia border in the eleven provinces closest to Saigon in Military Region III. By August 1970 ARVN had taken over the mission of securing South Vietnam's entire border with Cambodia and a large portion of the one with Laos. The only exception was a small area in the Central Highlands (Military Region II), still guarded by a brigade of the U.S. 1st Cavalry Division. By the latter part of 1970, ARVN had assumed the primary combat burden for operations around Khe Sanh and in the A Shau Valley, a traditional Communist stronghold; some ARVN units did so well that U.S. advisory teams were withdrawn.[90]

Many in the Nixon administration were encouraged by these events. Ambassador Bunker was particularly optimistic about the future success of Vietnamization. In a cable to the president in January 1971, he provided the following assessment:

1970, the first full year of Vietnamization and implementation of the Nixon Doctrine in Southeast Asia, saw an increase in confidence on the part of the GVN, RVNAF, and the people of South Viet-Nam as the favorable effects of the Cambodian operations were felt, the tempo of the war declined, U.S. troop redeployments continued, and pacification gains were consolidated and further extended. . . . The Vietnamese have seen that the relatively rapid withdrawal of our troops has brought no military defeats, but rather improved performance by their own forces. The early apprehension has now given place to a sense of satisfaction that they are approaching the point where they can go it alone. . . .[91]

Others were not so sanguine about the viability of Vietnamization, particularly as a strategy for disengagement. The controversial plan continued to be a hotly debated topic in Congress. Democratic senator Harold Hughes of Iowa said that "Vietnamization is a semantic hoax—what it denotes is simply an extension of the Johnson foreign policy. It will not get us out of Vietnam; rather it will perpetuate our involvement."[92] Senator George S. McGovern, Democrat from South Dakota, was more emphatic, saying, "As I understand the proposal, Vietnamization directs the withdrawal of American troops only as the Saigon armed forces demonstrate their ability to take over the war. Yet a preponderance of evidence indicates that the Vietnamese people do not feel the Saigon regime is worth fighting for. Without local support 'Vietnamization' becomes a plan for the permanent deployment of American combat troops, and a strategy for disengagement. . . . The policy of Vietnamization is a cruel hoax designed to screen from the American people the bankruptcy of a needless military involvement in the affairs of the Vietnamese people."[93]

Even some in the military were pessimistic about the long-range prospects for Vietnamization. An analysis prepared by members of the Army Staff for the Joint Chiefs stated the opinion that time was running out for Vietnamization. The report asserted that when the United States finally relinquished the conduct of the war to South Vietnam, the South Vietnamese armed forces would find themselves so preoccupied with providing security for the people that they would find it impossible to carry on the fight against the enemy's conventional forces, a task thus far borne by American troops. Although the report acknowledged that the destruction of enemy base areas in Cambodia might forestall a collapse of the South Vietnamese, it foresaw an eventual Communist victory.[94]

By year's end, Nixon had been bombarded by a wide range of conflicting assessments. Nevertheless, he maintained the administration line that things were getting better every day in South Vietnam. Nixon later wrote in his memoirs: "As long as the Communist troops in South Vietnam could not depend on the Cambodian sanctuaries for supplies, ammunition, and reinforcements, I felt that the ARVN forces, which had been greatly improved and strengthened by more than a year of Vietnamization, would soon be able to defend themselves and their country."[95] He took every opportunity to share this sentiment publicly. On 4 January 1971, in a televised interview with four representatives from the television networks, Nixon responded to a question from Howard K. Smith of ABC, who asked what would happen in 1972, when "our role is virtually eliminated, we are passive, we have few troops there, then the North Vietnamese attack and begin to come into control of the country. What is our policy then? Do we stand aside?" Nixon replied that by 1972, the North Vietnamese might well launch an attack, "but I am convinced that at that time . . . the South Vietnamese, based on the watershed that occurred when they jelled and became a fighting, confident unit after the Cambodian intervention, I am convinced that they will be able to hold their own and defend themselves in 1972."[96]

Although Nixon put up a positive public front, he was a realist. He was somewhat encouraged by the news from the battle front, but the upheaval at home, caused by the decision to go into Cambodia and subsequent demonstrations around the country, had increased the pressure on him to speed up the disengagement of U.S. forces from the war. He realized that the American public was becoming more war weary as the fighting continued with no end in sight.

As the president contemplated his strategy for the coming new year, the U.S. troop withdrawals continued unabated. The 3rd Brigade of the 9th Infantry Division went home in October, and in December, the 4th and 25th infantry divisions departed. By the end of 1970, only 335,000 U.S. troops remained in South Vietnam. Additionally, the III Marine Amphibious Force, the 1st Marine Division, and the 11th Armored Cavalry Regiment were all scheduled to leave in the first part of 1971. As more U.S. troops were withdrawn and further withdrawals were announced, morale among those left plummeted, and disciplinary problems, including "fragging of officers," mutinous behavior, and drug abuse, became the norm; the U.S. Army in Vietnam appeared to be in danger of disintegrating.

Thus, even though Nixon's Vietnamization policy apparently was beginning to show modest signs of progress, the president once again confronted a dilemma. He needed time to correct continuing defects in the RVNAF before South Vietnamese forces could assume complete responsibility for the war. At the same time, he had to keep up the pace of U.S. withdrawals. The war had become "Nixon's War," and he was under fire from every quarter to end U.S. involvement in Southeast Asia. However, if he withdrew American troops too quickly, the South Vietnamese were doomed. Complicating the matter, Nixon's twin policy of troop withdrawals and Vietnamization was proving incompatible with U.S. peace efforts in Paris. Kissinger wrote in his memoirs that, in addition to the "serious blow to the psychological basis for a coherent strategy" that had been inflicted by congressional discussion of the McGovern-Hatfield Amendment, "North Vietnam had another disincentive to negotiate. We were pulling out American troops so fast as to place a burden of credulity on Vietnamization; in the process we lost the bargaining leverage inherent in offering a speedup in our withdrawals in return for a genuinely free political choice by the people."[97]

At Kissinger's urging, Nixon tried another peace overture to the Communists. In a nationally televised speech on 7 October 1970, he proposed a standstill cease-fire, a halt to U.S. bombing throughout Southeast Asia, and a peace conference to bring an end to the fighting throughout Indochina. He said that he was ready to discuss a timetable for the withdrawal of all U.S. forces. He invited Hanoi to participate in a political settlement based on the will of the South Vietnamese people, but rejected the "patently unreasonable" demand that the United States dismantle the organized non-Communist forces.[98] Finally, he called for both sides to release all prisoners of war.

Nixon's proposal was significant for a number of reasons, not the least of which was that for the first time the president had said publicly he would accept a cease-fire in place, effectively decoupling the issue of a cease-fire from the question of mutual troop withdrawal. In his memoirs, Kissinger confirmed the proposal's importance, saying, "The decision to propose a standstill ceasefire in 1970 thus implied the solution of 1972. That North Vietnamese forces would remain in the South was implicit in the standstill proposal; no negotiations would be able to remove them if we had not been able to expel them with force of arms."[99] This decision would eventually have disastrous effects for South Vietnam.

The president's speech won immediate praise from all quarters in the United States, including from some of his harshest critics on Capitol Hill.[100] However, the hopes fostered by the speech were short-lived. The next day, Xuan Thuy, one of Hanoi's representatives in Paris, issued a statement rejecting Nixon's proposals out of hand and refusing even to discuss them, calling them a "great fraud" designed to "legalize and perpetuate the intervention of the United States in Indochina."[101]

On 12 October, Nixon made another announcement. He said that Vietnamization was going so well that he was speeding up the withdrawal of forty thousand troops and would have them home by Christmas. The announcement was a political move designed more for show than effect; the troops had been scheduled to come out in January 1971 anyway. Nixon claimed later that his 7 October speech and the accelerated troops withdrawal "went so far toward removing the obstacles to a settlement that they effectively silenced the domestic antiwar movement by placing the burden squarely on the North Vietnamese to begin serious negotiations."[102] Removing obstacles to peace and quelling dissent may have been his intent, but the tactic did not work. The North Vietnamese remained intractable. Lacking their agreement to discuss potential peace initiatives, the president was forced to continue both his emphasis on Vietnamization and the withdrawal of U.S. forces.

Nixon and Kissinger spent November working on strategy for the coming year. Kissinger recommended that Nixon make an announcement that he was reducing U.S. troops by another 100,000 beginning immediately and to be completed by December 1971. Thus, sufficient U.S. forces would remain to provide security for the South Vietnamese elections scheduled to be held in October. Once the elections were over, U.S. forces would be below 180,000 and the president could speed up the withdrawal by announcing smaller, more frequent reductions. Sometime in 1971, depending on the situation, the president should announce that he was ending U.S. participation in ground combat. By the summer of 1972, fewer than 50,000 American soldiers would be left in South Vietnam; that residual force would remain to assist the South Vietnamese until there was a settlement. Kissinger proposed that the North Vietnamese be offered a more rapid U.S. withdrawal in return for a cease-fire. If the North Vietnamese refused, the allies could expect a Communist offensive, probably in 1972. As Kissinger later wrote, "The outcome of the war would depend on whether the South Vietnamese, aided only by American air power, would be able to blunt the assault. Peace would thus come either at the end of 1971 or at the end of 1972—either by negotiations or by a South Vietnamese collapse."[103]

Clearly, the new year would bring new challenges for the South Vietnamese and Vietnamization. Kissinger wrote, "If we were serious about Vietnamization, we had to manage, in spite of our domestic dissent, three concurrent efforts until Saigon could stand on its own feet: American troop withdrawals; the rapid strengthening of South Vietnam forces; and the progressive weakening of the enemy."[104] These efforts would combine to give the South Vietnamese forces their next big test in 1971 during Operation Lam Son 719, when they would go into Laos with limited U.S. support and no American ground forces.

5

Lam Son 719

NVA EFFORTS ON THE HO CHI MINH TRAIL

The Cambodian incursion may have bought time for the allies, but it had an unforeseen consequence. Deprived of its sanctuaries and bases in Cambodia, Hanoi had to turn entirely to cross-country routes through Laos from North Vietnam for the resupply of its forces in the South. In order to offset the loss of the Sihanoukville overland route and the large quantities of supplies seized by U.S. and South Vietnamese forces during the Cambodian incursion, the Communists initiated a vast program to increase the capabilities of the Ho Chi Minh Trail. By 1971, the complex network of trails stretched from North Vietnam through the Mu Gia, Ban Karai, and Ban Raving Passes in the Annamite (or Truong Son) Mountains to Tchepone and Muong Nong in Laos, just across the border from Khe Sanh in Quang Tri Province. From Tchepone and Muong Nong, the men and supplies moved to two key NVA base areas, 604 and 611 (see map 6). From these base areas, the Ho Chi Minh Trail ran south toward other bases along South Vietnam's 1,300-kilometer border with Laos and Cambodia.

The North Vietnamese boasted after the war that they had constructed over 13,000 kilometers of trails and roads as part of the system, which had been built, maintained, and defended by Transportation Group 559 using an estimated 100,000 NVA and Laotian volunteers and forced laborers.[1] U.S. intelligence estimated that between 1966 and 1971, 630,000 NVA troops, 100,000 tons of foodstuffs, 400,000 weapons, and 50,000 tons of ammunition moved from North Vietnam down the Ho Chi Minh Trail.[2]

After the allied invasion of Cambodia, the NVA took additional steps not only to improve the trail, but also to fortify it to allow use without interference from U.S. or South Vietnamese forces. In the fall of 1970, twenty antiaircraft battalions were moved into Laos to provide air cover for the trail against allied aircraft.

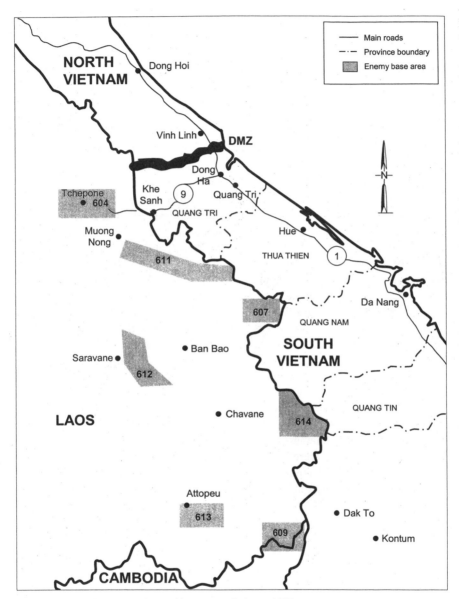

Map 6. Communist sanctuaries and base areas in Laos, 1971.

These new units came equipped with a wide range of sophisticated weaponry, including 12.7-mm and 14.5-mm machine guns, 23-mm cannons, and over two hundred antiaircraft guns (37-mm, 57-mm, 85-mm, and 100-mm). These weapons provided a significant improvement of the air defense umbrella over the Ho Chi Minh Trail. In addition to the air defense units, other NVA combat units were moved to

Laos to protect the vital supply line, bringing the total Communist troop strength there to an estimated 22,000 (7,000 NVA combat troops, 10,000 soldiers in logistics and support units, and 5,000 Communist Pathet Lao), all under a new corps command, the 70B Corps, which assumed operational control of the 304th, 308th, and 320th NVA divisions. Intelligence reports estimated that by the end of 1970 the NVA used the protection of these forces to infiltrate 6,000 combat troops every month down the trail through Laos into South Vietnam.[3] In addition to reports of increased infiltration, U.S. intelligence also had picked up indications that an unusually heavy stockpiling of weapons, ammunition, and equipment had taken place in Base Area 604 near Tchepone. Further intelligence revealed that the North Vietnamese were intent on rebuilding their sanctuaries in Cambodia.

President Nixon and his military advisers were alarmed at the buildup in Laos and the renewed enemy activity in Cambodia. Unless something was done, the North Vietnamese would soon be in position to directly threaten Quang Tri, the northernmost province in South Vietnam, and easily attack the ancient capital of Hue, only a short march from Base Area 611 through the A Shau Valley. Intelligence analysts believed that the influx of troops and new weapons in Laos and Cambodia might be in preparation for a Communist offensive against the two northern provinces in South Vietnam, either early in 1971 or, more likely, in the U.S. election year of 1972, when less than fifty thousand U.S. troops would remain in South Vietnam and Nixon would be busy running for reelection.[4] The president faced the same problem that had confronted him when the Communists had threatened Phnom Penh. He had to do something about the North Vietnamese in Laos before the enemy buildup there had a devastating effect on Vietnamization and plans for U.S. withdrawal from Southeast Asia. Nixon could not afford to wait, because U.S. strength and combat power in country were dwindling daily, and he did not think the South Vietnamese could end the buildup using only their own forces. The Laotian base areas were heavily defended and the terrain was difficult. The ground fighting would have to be done by the South Vietnamese; whether they could stand alone against the North Vietnamese Army was questionable. If Nixon waited, however, the NVA would continue its buildup until it launched an offensive at a time of its choosing.

Perusing a series of studies commissioned in November 1970, Nixon came to the conclusion that his only option was to conduct a preemptive strike against the Communists. The question was where to focus the attack. An amphibious thrust into North Vietnam, aimed at Vinh, was initially considered, but Kissinger countered with a recommendation to repeat the Cambodian incursion to take advantage of the gains made by the earlier operation. Among the locations proposed for an allied attack was the one suggested by Admiral McCain, CINCPAC, who had cabled General Abrams in October to consider an operation against the Communist logistics corridor in Laos.[5]

In early December, the JCS authorized General Abrams "to contact General Vien and effect such planning and coordination as you deem appropriate in preparation for the Laos plan."[6] A follow-on message directed Abrams to prepare contingency plans for a South Vietnamese cross-border operation into Laos via Route 9, just south of the DMZ, supported by American air forces, and for a concurrent South Vietnamese attack into Cambodia aimed at destroying a major enemy base area being developed in the Chup rubber plantation.[7]

On 10 December, Adm. Moorer, chairman of the Joint Chiefs, cabled Abrams, forwarding a message from the president. In that message, the president charged Abrams to "undertake, in coordination with the armed forces of South Vietnam and Cambodia, an intensive planning effort . . . to carry the battle to the enemy to the greatest extent possible."[8] Additionally, he informed Abrams that he was sending General Haig to Saigon to discuss the planning.

Haig arrived in Saigon on 13 December. He met with Abrams and Ambassador Bunker. They all agreed with Kissinger's assessment of the need for a new allied offensive, but General Abrams proposed a plan that he had developed in response to Admiral McCain's earlier guidance. Abrams's plan included a main attack into Laos by South Vietnamese forces to cut the Ho Chi Minh Trail. U.S. forces would set up blocking positions along the DMZ in South Vietnam and establish a forward support base adjacent to the Laotian border to support the ARVN effort to seize Tchepone.[9] The initial assault would be followed by search and clear operations to destroy Communist base areas and interdict traffic along the Ho Chi Minh Trail inside Laos. A smaller South Vietnamese supporting attack into Cambodia would seek to destroy a new enemy base area being constructed in the vicinity of the Chup rubber plantation adjacent to Military Region III.

Abrams argued that if the Communists' supply routes could be interdicted in Laos and Cambodia for just one dry season, their ability to launch a large-scale offensive in South Vietnam would be "significantly curtailed, if not eliminated, for an indefinite future."[10]

Haig returned to Washington and related Abrams's plan to Kissinger and the president. According to Kissinger, Nixon liked the plan immediately, but "was determined not to stand naked in front of his critics as he had the year before on Cambodia."[11] Therefore, he set about to build a working consensus for the offensive among his advisers. To do so, he set up a series of briefings for his cabinet members and other key advisers in which he could take them on one at a time. He targeted Laird first. On 23 December, Haig briefed Nixon again, but this time with Laird present. After the briefing, Nixon told Laird that he was in favor of the proposed operation and wanted Laird to look into the plan when he visited Saigon early in January. According to Kissinger, Laird backed the concept of a cross-border operation to cut the Ho Chi Minh Trail, arguing that it would buy at least a year and that a successful major offensive operation by the South Vietnamese without U.S. ground support would be clear evidence of the success of Vietnamization.[12] On 21 December 1970, Nixon approved the Laos operation in principle, subject to final review before execution.

Because of the modified version of the Cooper-Church Amendment, which had been passed after the Cambodian incursion, American ground troops were forbidden to cross the border. Additionally, no advisers could accompany ARVN units into Laos. U.S. support was limited to tactical air, helicopter, and long-range artillery support (operating from South Vietnamese firebases on the border). Nevertheless, the president believed that ARVN was capable of conducting these attacks in consort with the American combat forces that remained in country at the beginning of 1971. Admiral Moorer assured him that the South Vietnamese could do the job if protected by American airpower.[13]

While MACV worked on the contingency plans, Nixon and his advisers continued to discuss the proposed operations. Following Laird's return from Saigon, the president held a meeting in the Oval Office on 18 January 1971, attended by Kissinger, Laird, Rogers, Helms, Moorer, and Haig. Laird reported on his trip and conversations with Abrams, Bunker, and Thieu. In an almost three-hour briefing, Laird reviewed the military and political situation in South Vietnam and then discussed the proposed operations into Laos and Cambodia. The consensus of the ensuing discussion was that, if successful, the campaign would interrupt the North Vietnamese buildup, delay any planned Communist general offensive, gain at least six more months for the Vietnamization program to proceed, permit U.S. troop withdrawals to continue on schedule, and dissuade the Communists from further "adventures."[14] Nixon felt that a successful operation might convince the North Vietnamese to negotiate in good faith and further stressed that the operations might "prove decisive in the overall conduct of the war."[15] The discussion also focused on another important issue, one that Admiral Moorer had observed in an earlier memorandum to Laird: the operation represented the last opportunity for the South Vietnamese to mount a major operation against the enemy's sanctuaries while American forces were strong enough to provide backing.[16] Haig wrote later that those who briefed the president on the plan were optimistic about its success, but all agreed that the "key factor was all-out U.S. military support of ARVN."[17] This is a rather revealing commentary on the prevalent thinking on the state of the Vietnamization process, but as General Haig points out in his memoirs, the success of Vietnamization "had little to do with its military effectiveness. Vietnamization was a success not in Vietnam but in the United States, where as the Secretary of Defense [Laird] and his faction had hoped and intended, it has lessened opposition to the war in Congress and the news media by offering a program that promised a definitive end to American casualties. . . . [B]ut reduced American casualties had little to do with the military effectiveness of the armed forces of South Vietnam."[18] Nevertheless, Nixon gave tentative approval to proceed with the detailed planning for the cross-border operation into Laos, to be code-named Lam Son 719.

As the military planning continued, Kissinger began to have doubts about the operation. On 25 January, he met with Admiral Moorer. Kissinger reasoned that if the Tchepone area was so clearly critical to the North Vietnamese resupply effort, the Communists would no doubt fight hard to retain it. Concerned about the potential for high South Vietnamese casualties, he questioned the ability of the

ARVN forces to operate by themselves, without U.S. advisers and air controllers on the ground with them.[19] Moorer assured him that the South Vietnamese were capable of handling the attack and that U.S. airpower could isolate the battlefield to keep the force ratios at a manageable level. Kissinger reported his conversations with Moorer in a memorandum to the president and arranged for Moorer to talk to Nixon the next day. When they met, Moorer was "emphatic in his reassurances" to the president that the operation was sound, saying that "decisive" results were probable.[20]

Although the president was convinced by such projections, Secretary of State Rogers was not. In a meeting on 29 January, he urged the president to reconsider his decision, asserting that the operation was too risky. He pointed out that when General Westmoreland had looked at a similar operation while serving as MACV commander, he had estimated that four U.S. divisions would be needed to accomplish the mission. The current plan under consideration involved the use of far fewer South Vietnamese troops. Therefore, to Rogers, an ARVN defeat was almost assured, and he felt that the damage to the Vietnamization effort might be irreparable. Additionally, he believed that Nixon's opponents in Congress would charge that the operation was contrary to the spirit, if not the letter, of the Cooper-Church Amendment.[21] According to Kissinger, Nixon had already considered most of Rogers's objections and thought that the secretary of state "simply did not know what he was talking about."[22] The president ordered that the operation be launched, and the chairman of the Joint Chiefs of Staff gave the official go-ahead on 4 February 1971.[23]

THE PLAN

Lam Son 719 was to be a combined RVNAF-US operation conducted under several constraints. No joint command was established for the control of the operation.[24] The overall ground commander of the operation in Laos was Lt. Gen. Hoang Xuan Lam, commanding general of the ARVN's I Corps. His U.S. counterpart, Lt. Gen. James W. Sutherland, commanding general of XXIV Corps, would command all involved U.S. Army forces and coordinate American support for the operation. Gen. Lucius D. Clay Jr., commander of the 7th Air Force, would command and coordinate all U.S. Air Force resources supporting the operation.

The campaign was to be a spoiling attack, designed not so much to take and hold terrain objectives but rather to disrupt the enemy's plans and forestall a new offensive. The primary objective of Operation Lam Son 719 was to seize Base Area 604 in the Tchepone area, located at a strategic junction of supply routes along the Ho Chi Minh Trail about fifty kilometers from the border with South Vietnam. After securing Tchepone, the South Vietnamese would, for the remainder of the dry season, interdict the trail and destroy logistical facilities in the area. The actual invasion of Laos would commence on 8 February and last ninety days until monsoon rains forced the curtailment of operations. The attack was to be made by some of the ARVN's best troops, including the ARVN 1st Division, 1st Armored Brigade, three ranger battalions from I Corps, and most of the elite Airborne and Marine divisions from the Joint General Staff's strategic reserve. Initially, sixteen thousand South Vietnamese troops would be employed when the operation was launched; later, reinforcements would increase this number to twenty thousand. Approximately ten thousand U.S. combat, engineering, and other troops would support the operation from Quang Tri Province inside South Vietnam.

The complex plan involved four phases. In Phase I, the 1st Brigade of the U.S. 5th Infantry Division was to clear and secure Route 9 from Dong Ha to the Laotian border. Additionally, the brigade would secure Fire Support Base Vandegrift, an abandoned U.S. Marine firebase, and Khe Sanh, where a headquarters would be established to coordinate all helicopter assaults, close air support, long-range artillery fire, and logistical support. The U.S. 45th Engineer Group would repair the airfield at Khe Sanh and prepare it for C-130 traffic. The engineers would also repair Route 9 to the Laotian border. Simultaneous with the 1st Brigade, 5th Infantry Division operation, the U.S. 101st Airborne Division would take over responsibility for the ARVN 1st Infantry Division area of operation in Quang Tri and Thua Thien provinces when ARVN moved into Laos. Other U.S. forces would secure the area south of the DMZ and adjacent to the Vietnamese-Laotian border. An ARVN task force from the 1st Armored Brigade was to follow the 1st Brigade of the 5th Infantry Division and, after Khe Sanh was secured, move to the northwest to screen the northern flank.[25] The U.S. portion of Phase I was code-named Dewey Canyon II.[26]

Another aspect of Phase I was the pre-positioning of 6,500 troops from the ARVN Airborne Division and 3,000 troops from the Vietnamese Marine Corps. U.S. Air Force cargo aircraft were to move these forces to airfields at Quang Tri and Dong Ha. Phase I was expected to last from five to eight days.

Once Route 9 was secured, Phase II would begin with a three-pronged ARVN attack west along the highway to Tchepone, supported by 7th U.S. Air Force tactical air support and U.S. XXIV Corps helicopters and long-range artillery. The ARVN Airborne Division, reinforced by the 1st Armored Brigade, would make the main thrust along the highway; the ground movement and successive heliborne assaults were ultimately aimed at seizing A Luoi, the intersection of Routes 9 and 92. Once the initial objective was secured, the Airborne Division would air assault into Tchepone while the armored forces continued the attack by road to link up in Tchepone with the airborne forces. The flanks of the main attack were to be protected in the south by a parallel attack conducted by the South Vietnamese 1st Infantry Division, which would establish firebases on the high ground south of Route 9 between A Luoi and Tchepone. In the north, the South Vietnamese flanks would be protected by the 1st Ranger Group, which would conduct helicopter assaults to establish blocking positions to prevent the enemy from moving south to impede the main attack along the highway. The attack helicopters of the U.S. 2nd Squadron, 17th Cavalry (Air), were to locate and destroy antiaircraft weapons, find enemy concentrations, and carry out reconnaissance and security missions, which included the rescue of air crews downed in Laos.[27] A Vietnamese Marine brigade would be held in reserve at Khe Sanh. Two days prior to the start of Phase II, U.S. tactical air support would begin a concentrated bombing campaign (lasting from three to seven days) to suppress enemy air defenses.

Phase III, which would commence after the capture of Tchepone, called for the South Vietnamese to conduct search-and-destroy missions in Base Area 604 and throughout the area south of Tchepone. The Airborne Division was to establish blocking positions northwest of Tchepone along Route 91 and southeast of Tchepone along Route 9 in order to isolate the area. At the same time, the 1st Infantry Division was to conduct search-and-destroy operations in its assigned area just to the south of the Xe Pon River, while the 1st Ranger Group would continue its blocking and screening positions on the northern flank. The ARVN forces would be limited to a corridor no wider than fifteen miles on either side of Route 9 and to a penetration no deeper than Tchepone.

Phase IV, the final phase, addressed the withdrawal of the South Vietnamese forces from Laos. Withdrawal was to be accomplished in one of two ways, depending on the situation at the time. Under the first option, the Airborne Division would withdraw directly to the east along Route 9 to cover an attack to the southeast into Base Area 611 by the 1st Infantry Division as it headed back into South Vietnam. The second option was an attack by both divisions into Base Area 611. Both options included provisions for the insertion of RVNAF elements to stay behind and harass the enemy in Base Areas 604 and 611 after the main body of South Vietnamese troops had withdrawn.

The plan also included a deception phase. In an attempt to mislead the North Vietnamese as to the main attack, a naval task force, carrying U.S. Marines from the 31st Marine Amphibious Unit and including two aircraft carriers, would steam into the Tonkin Gulf seventy kilometers off the port city of Vinh in North Vietnam. The mission of this task force was to feign an amphibious assault on Vinh to draw North Vietnamese attention as the South Vietnamese forces entered Laos. This part of the plan apparently worked: the amphibious task force in the Tonkin Gulf did indeed get the attention of the North Vietnamese high command, giving the South Vietnamese attackers a few days' respite from a major NVA reinforcement effort in Laos.

Because Communist espionage cells were believed to be active within the RVNAF high command, Abrams had directed that the number of personnel involved in joint operational planning be held to a bare minimum.[28] Units that were to play a part in the operation were not notified until 17 January, and the Airborne Division, which was scheduled to lead the assault, was not given detailed plans until 2 February, less than a week before the scheduled D-Day of 8 February. In an attempt to preclude premature press coverage of the operation, MACV briefed American reporters off the record about the impending campaign and then imposed a brief embargo on reporting troop movements until the operation was actually launched. This proved to be a bad move, because the imposition of the embargo was itself an indication of an upcoming operation. Although the embargo was lifted on 4 February, word had leaked and speculative stories of an impending allied attack into Laos had already appeared in U.S. and international newspapers.[29]

Despite the difficulties in maintaining secrecy about the operation, U.S. and ARVN commanders were very optimistic about the potential outcome of the ambitious plan. Col. Arthur W. Pence, the senior adviser to the ARVN Airborne Division, reported after the operation: "It was apparent at this time that . . . Intelligence felt the operation would be lightly opposed and that a two-day preparation of the area prior to D-Day by tactical air would effectively neutralize the enemy antiaircraft capability, although the enemy was credited with having 170 to 200 antiaircraft weapons of mixed caliber in the operational area. The tank threat was considered minimal and the reinforcement capability was listed as fourteen days for two divisions from north of the DMZ."[30]

U.S. and ARVN commanders and planners apparently were emboldened by the modest success of the Cambodian incursion. However, three significant differences between the attack into Laos and the Cambodian incursion exerted major influence on the ultimate outcome of Lam Son 719. Although it was to be a combined operation and XXIV U.S. Corps would provide logistical support, long-range artillery, and helicopters, U.S. personnel would be prohibited from operating on the ground in Laos. Not only would no U.S. combat troops accompany ARVN forces, as they had in Cambodia, but no U.S. advisers would go with the South Vietnamese when they went into Laos. For the first time, most of ARVN would go into battle without their American counterparts, whom they had become accustomed to relying upon to coordinate U.S. air, assault helicopter, long-range artillery, and logistical support. In Lam Son, once they crossed into Laos, the South Vietnamese forces would be on their own against the NVA.

The second difference between the Laotian operation and the Cambodian incursion was that the terrain and, to a great extent, the weather would play major roles in the outcome of the battle. Whereas the terrain in Cambodia had been relatively easy to traverse, the target area for Lam Son 719 was rugged, covered by dense undergrowth and, along the Xe Pon River, which paralleled Route 9 to the south, by double-canopy jungle. Route 9 itself was an unimproved road, little better than a cart path in many places. High ground that provided excellent defensive terrain for the NVA defenders dominated the highway on both sides. The weather was also a significant factor. By the time of the operation, the northeast monsoon would be just ending and flying weather would be marginal, often limiting flight operations by helicopters and fixed-wing aircraft. Additionally, the area would be subject to intermittent rainfall, which at times could be heavy and inhibit passage of armored vehicles. Thus, terrain and weather would not favor the attacker in this operation.

The third key difference between Lam Son 719 and the Cambodian operation was that this time, despite intelligence estimates to the contrary, the enemy would stay and fight. After the battle, it became known that the NVA had long suspected an ARVN offensive into Laos adjacent to Military Region I and had begun preparations to counter such a move as early as October 1970, when its forces began to build defensive fortifications, prepare ambush sites, preregister artillery strikes on potential allied landing zones, and reposition supplies and ammunition.[31] By the time ARVN launched its operation, over 22,000 NVA troops were in the area surrounding Tchepone, and Hanoi, having ordered that Base Area 604 be held, was sending additional reinforcements that would bring the total enemy troop strength to over 36,000.[32] By the end of the campaign, the North Vietnamese were to throw elements of five divisions with supporting armor and artillery into the battle.[33]

According to Gen. Bruce Palmer, Abrams was well aware of the potential dangers posed by the differences between the Cambodian incursion and Lam Son 719. The operation may have looked very much "like sending a boy to do a man's job" in an extremely hostile environment, but the U.S. commander was counting heavily on U.S. B-52 strikes, suppressive fire by U.S. tactical air support, and the tactical mobility provided by U.S. assault helicopters accompanied by their own armed escort helicopters to "even the odds" for the South Vietnamese.[34] Palmer later described the situation as "a big gamble. Failure would bring Vietnamization into serious question and might result either in keeping U.S. forces in Vietnam longer, or in generating such pressure at home as to cause the United States to abandon its hapless ally."[35] If the plan worked, it would be a boost for the South Vietnamese and validate the Vietnamization process, but if anything went wrong, it would be a disaster for both South Vietnam and the United States.

LAM SON 719

Phase I of the operation was launched by U.S. forces at 0400, 29 January. During this operation, the 1st Brigade, 5th U.S. Mechanized Infantry Division, began clearing South Vietnam from Route 9 north to the DMZ. Additional U.S. forces reoccupied the firebase at Khe Sanh, and the 45th Engineers began refurbishing its damaged airstrip.[36] At the same time, still more American troops secured Route 9 to the border and began repairing the road. By 5 February, the U.S. forces had finished most of their tasks and had taken over security for the ARVN assembly areas near the border.

The lead ARVN forces, consisting of the 1st Armored Brigade, with two South Vietnamese airborne battalions (the 1st and 8th) and the 11th and 17th cavalry regiments, crossed the line of departure on schedule at 0700 hours, 8 February 1971 (see map 7). Unfortunately, the weather had turned bad on 6 February, forcing the cancellation of air strikes that were supposed to neutralize NVA antiaircraft guns along Route 9. Nevertheless, the 4,000-man armored column attacked west along the road as planned. Led by M-41 tanks and M-113 armored personnel carriers, the column pushed nine kilometers into Laos on the first day, but was slowed by dense jungle and huge bomb craters adjacent to the route that limited its advance. The road itself was in disrepair, and the ARVN 101st Combat Engineer Battalion had to con-

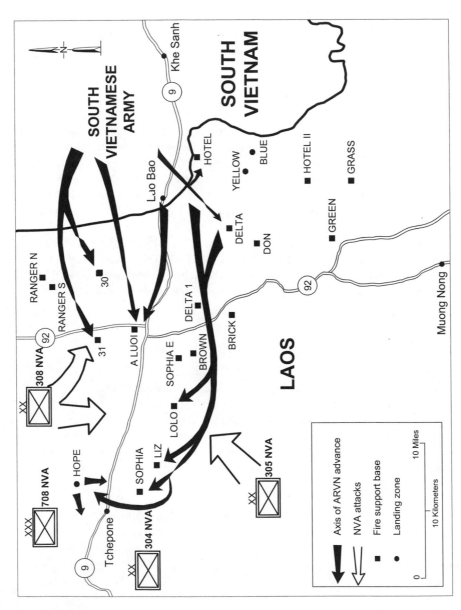

Map 7. Operation Lam Son 719, February–March 1971.

SOUTH VIETNAMESE ARMY

SOUTH VIETNAM

Khe Sanh

9

Lao Bao

HOTEL

YELLOW

BLUE

HOTEL II

GRASS

DELTA

DON

GREEN

RANGER N

RANGER S

30

31

A LUOI

DELTA 1

BRICK

92

Muong Nong

308 NVA

SOPHIA E

BROWN

XX

LOLO

LIZ

LAOS

HOPE

SOPHIA

305 NVA

XX

708 NVA

XXX

Tchepone

304 NVA

XX

9

Axis of ARVN advance

NVA attacks

Fire support base

Landing zone

10 Miles

0   10 Kilometers

struct detours where the road was totally destroyed, further slowing the progress of the armored column.[37] Meanwhile, the airborne forces inserted on the northern flank took their first objectives against sporadic enemy resistance.

The ARVN 1st Infantry Division, on the southern flank, also secured their initial objectives with little enemy contact. It was later determined that General Giap and the commander of 70B Corps were restraining their forces until they decided whether the ARVN attack along Route 9 was real or merely a deception to cover the main attack elsewhere. By 9 February, they had decided that the ARVN attack along the highway was in fact the main attack, and the commander of 70B Corps ordered the 308th ("Iron") Division, located in an assembly area near the DMZ, to begin moving toward Route 9 to reinforce the NVA units already there. Additionally, the North Vietnamese high command ordered the 2nd NVA Division to move from positions farther south to the Tchepone area to blunt the ARVN armored column on Route 9.

Heavy rains turned Route 9 into a quagmire, further impeding the advance of the South Vietnamese armored column. Nevertheless, by 10 February, the attackers had reached their first objective, A Luoi, and had linked up with an airborne battalion that had been brought in earlier that day by U.S. helicopters. The South Vietnamese main attack along the road had reached a point halfway to Tchepone, opposed only by light enemy sniper fire. At the same time, ARVN forces on both the northern and southern flanks closed on positions adjacent to A Luoi. In the north, the 3rd Airborne Brigade established two firebases (30 and 31) while the 21st and 39th Ranger battalions established two outposts, Ranger Base South and Ranger Base North, to provide early warning of any NVA reinforcement coming south along the Ho Chi Minh Trail; thus, ARVN essentially had a network of four mutually supporting bases in the north. Simultaneously, the ARVN 1st Infantry Division established five firebases (Hotel, Blue, Delta, Delta 1, and Don) south of Route 9 to secure that flank from enemy attack.

So far, the South Vietnamese had made good progress against relatively light NVA resistance. However, on 11 February, the attack ground to a halt. For reasons that were inexplicable at the time, the ARVN force just stopped attacking, which gave the North Vietnamese an opportunity to send in additional reinforcements. With elements of three infantry regiments, a tank battalion, and an artillery regiment already in the area, the NVA high command ordered four more infantry regiments and part of a tank regiment to join the battle. As these forces began to close on the area, the South Vietnamese remained stationary. It became clear that the ARVN attack needed to regain its momentum before the enemy forces gained the initiative, but General Lam and his major subordinate commanders were silent. In the absence of orders, the South Vietnamese forces in Laos sat where they were.

Furious, General Abrams went to see Gen. Cao Van Vien, chairman of the Joint General Staff, in Saigon to convince him to energize the attackers. On 16 February, Abrams and Sutherland met with Vien and Lam at Lam's forward command post in Dong Ha. At this meeting the decision was made to move the 1st ARVN Division farther west along the southern escarpment to establish firebases to support a resumed airborne-armored thrust westward along Route 9 to Tchepone; the 1st Division elements would require an estimated three to five days to get into position. The order was given, but unfortunately for the attackers, by this time, the NVA had positioned reinforcements to block the resumption of the South Vietnamese attack. ARVN had lost the initiative and never regained it for the duration of the battle.

After the operation, President Thieu was discovered to have had a hand in the halting of the ARVN attack. On 12 February, he ordered Lam to be careful as he moved west and, if he incurred 3,000 casualties, to cancel the operation.[38] Thieu was apparently worried about how potentially high casualty figures in Laos would affect the upcoming national elections in the fall. Also, he was concerned about losing the ARVN general reserve (which consisted of the Airborne Division, the 1st Armored Brigade, and the South Vietnamese marines). Perhaps more significant, these forces were effectively Thieu's palace guard and provided protection against any potential coup; thus, he was reluctant to expose them to destruction.

Having lost momentum, the South Vietnamese forces now faced new NVA reinforcements. On 18 February, the 308th NVA Division was identified in action for the first time on the northern flank. The 2nd NVA Division appeared in front of the lead ARVN units, and the 24B Regiment of the 305th NVA Division was identified by South Vietnamese troops south of Route 9. More ominous, ARVN forces began to sight enemy tanks, and an NVA prisoner stated that an NVA tank regiment was in the area. By early March, the North Vietnamese outnumbered the South Vietnamese forces by a two-to-one margin. Heavy mortar and large-caliber artillery fire increased on all South Vietnamese positions. The would-be attackers soon found themselves being attacked by a much stronger enemy than they had anticipated.

To make matters worse for the South Vietnamese, intermittent rain and dense fog repeatedly grounded all aircraft. The few helicopters that were able to fly had to do so at low altitude, making them very vulnerable to enemy ground fire. Resupplying the ARVN attack became particularly difficult and dangerous under these conditions.

On 19 February, Lam and his division commanders met with President Thieu. Lam briefed the president on the situation, stressing the sightings of new NVA units in the area. Thieu told Lam "to take his time and . . . expand search activities toward the southwest."[39] The meaningless order essentially told Lam to keep doing what he was doing, which was effectively nothing.

By 20 February, the South Vietnamese had completely lost the initiative. Supported by heavy artillery and Soviet-made T-54 and PT-76 tanks, the NVA struck hard with repeated frontal assaults against the ARVN positions, particularly the northern flank of the airborne and ranger units. Soon, virtually every South Vietnamese unit was in heavy contact with the enemy. The NVA tactics were to surround the ARVN positions and cut their aerial resupply lines with heavy antiaircraft fire, while pounding them continually with mortar, rocket, and artillery fire. Next, they would storm the positions, using combined infantry-armor assaults when possible. The ARVN forces fought back, but they were usually severely outnumbered and compounded matters by repeatedly demonstrating the inability to coordinate maneuvers with artillery fire support. Additionally, South Vietnamese artillery was of much shorter range than the NVA's 122- and 130-mm guns and could not provide effective counterbattery fire. Consequently, the South Vietnamese depended on U.S. close air support and attack helicopters for survival. Unfortunately, however, the allied air support was less effective than planners had anticipated for a number of reasons. First, as has been discussed, the bad weather often grounded both helicopters and fixed-wing support aircraft or degraded their effectiveness when they could fly. Additionally, the absence of U.S. advisers meant that the air strikes that were flown were not closely coordinated. To make matters worse, the enemy air defense system was much denser and more effective than intelligence analysts had predicted. The NVA had also learned that it could minimize the impact of U.S. tactical air support by "hugging the belts" of ARVN so that the American fighter-bombers and attack helicopters could not get at the NVA without putting their South Vietnamese allies at risk. B-52 "arc light" bombing missions were very effective, but only when the NVA massed for an attack.[40]

The NVA, with elements of four divisions, increased the intensity of its attacks on the South Vietnamese positions. The NVA had isolated the 39th Ranger Battalion at Ranger Base North on 19 February, surrounding the base with over 2,000 troops. Over a three-day period, the NVA pounded the position and then pursued the rangers as they attempted to break out. Of a total of 430 rangers when the battle started, 178 were killed or missing and 148 were wounded. The 39th was finished as a unit, but it had taken a toll on the enemy; reconnaissance photo analysts counted 639 NVA bodies on the ground around Ranger Base North.[41] The North Vietnamese then turned their attention on Ranger Base South, occupied by the 21st Battalion and the remnants of the 39th Battalion. After two days of heavy fighting, General Lam decided that the rangers' position was untenable and ordered the South Vietnamese defenders to withdraw to Fire Support Base 30. These actions rendered another ranger battalion combat ineffective and severely shook the confidence of the survivors.

One aspect of the battle at Ranger Base North set the tone for the lasting public perception of Lam Son 719. Although most of the rangers there fought valiantly, a few unscathed soldiers lost their nerve and tried to climb aboard helicopters evacuating seriously wounded soldiers. The aircrews attempted to prevent these troops from escaping the battle, but some soldiers deserted by clinging to the helicopters' skids and riding back to South Vietnam. Photographs of these individuals hanging on to the helicopters for dear life provided the enduring image of Operation Lam Son 719.[42] Many Americans protested this perception. Lt. Col. Robert F. Molinelli, commander of the 2nd Squadron, 17th Air Cavalry, which flew in support of the battle at Ranger Base North, said, "The ARVN Rangers were outnumbered six or eight to one. For three days we were unable to get supplies to them. When they were low on ammunition, they went out and took NVA rifles and fought on. When they decided to move off their hill, they beat their way right through that North Vietnamese regiment, killing them with their own guns and ammunition. . . .

Seventeen of their men [rangers] did panic and they did leave hanging on helicopter skids. There were a lot more who did not."[43] Despite such observations, the initial impression of panic-stricken ARVN soldiers fleeing the Communists proved almost impossible to overcome.

As these events unfolded, President Thieu became more and more upset with General Lam's indecision and poor conduct of the battle. On 23 February, he summoned the more dynamic Lt. Gen. Do Cao Tri, hero of the Cambodian incursion, from his III Corps headquarters to Saigon and turned over to him command of Lam Son 719. Leaving Saigon to take over his new position, Tri's helicopter crashed and he was killed. General Lam retained command of the operation in Laos.

NVA pressure did not let up. The North Vietnamese overran the 3rd Airborne Brigade at Fire Support Base (FSB) 31 on 25 February, capturing Col. Nguyen Van Tho, the brigade commander, and his entire staff. A South Vietnamese counterattack failed, but killed 250 NVA and destroyed eleven PT-76 and T-54 tanks in the process. The defense of FSB 31 and the subsequent counterattack cost the ARVN airborne forces 155 killed and over 100 captured.

Shortly thereafter, the NVA attacked Fire Support Base 30. What had become a pattern for the NVA attacks repeated itself, yielding similar results. Lt. Gen. Sutherland described the developing situation in a message to General Abrams:

I am very concerned about the discipline and morale of the airborne division. General Dong [the division commander] has developed a defeatist attitude and this same attitude is reflected in some of his subordinate commanders. For example, an operation was planned and executed today to resupply FSB 30, evacuate dead and wounded and transport some 21st Rangers to the Ranger FSB. The wounded and four bodies were evacuated. Ninety-four healthy troops, but not including all the rangers, rushed to the choppers and boarded. The airborne infantry commander was among those who managed to get aboard the choppers. I have been told, but it has not been confirmed, that the brigade commander went to FSB 30 at approximately 1800 hours to take charge of the situation. I suspect that before this night is finished, the airborne troops may walk off and abandon FSB 30.[44]

The South Vietnamese did not immediately abandon the fire support base, but it survived only a few days longer. Eventually, the base's guns were all damaged, and the 2nd Airborne Battalion was given orders to evacuate FSB 30.

On 28 February, President Thieu inserted himself in the action once again. He had decided that the mission of Lam Son 719 should shift from destroying the NVA base area to "taking" Tchepone, which by itself had no real military value. Focusing on Tchepone was purely a public relations ploy that, if accomplished, would permit Thieu to declare victory and withdraw his forces from harm's way, thereby gaining political capital for the upcoming fall elections. Accordingly, he ordered the Airborne Division to be replaced by the remainder of the Marine Division, which had been moved to Khe Sanh. Thieu's order was ludicrous. The Airborne Division, although embattled, was still in relatively good shape; no sound reason was offered for replacing them. Moreover, the Marine Division, which had never fought as a division, was an unknown quantity. To make matters worse, relieving one division with another in the face of intense enemy opposition is one of the most difficult tasks in modern warfare.

These factors were not lost on General Lam, who flew to Saigon to propose an alternate plan to Thieu. He recommended a helicopter assault into Tchepone by the 1st ARVN Infantry Division (reinforced with its 2nd Regiment, which had been moved from its previous position near the DMZ). The Marine Division would follow the 1st Division, and the Airborne Division would assume the mission of protecting the northern flank. Thieu agreed and on the next day, 1 March, informed Abrams and Ambassador Bunker of the change in the original plan.

Abrams was not happy with this development. The objective of occupying and destroying the enemy base areas in Laos had been abandoned in favor of what he saw as a meaningless effort to get South Vietnamese forces into Tchepone for political purposes, rather than sound military reasons. Nevertheless, Abrams could do nothing except acquiesce.

The NVA had gained control of the high ground overlooking Route 9 from the north, but it had paid a high price. Repeated B-52 strikes took a terrible toll on the North Vietnamese, inflicting casualties that MACV estimated as being equivalent to one combat effective NVA regiment a week.[45] The considerable losses probably prevented the North Vietnamese from massing enough forces to completely annihilate ARVN units along the highway.

From 3 to 6 March, elements of the 1st ARVN Division executed a series of heliborne assaults to the west along the southern escarpment, establishing three bases named Lolo, Liz, and Sophia. The NVA offered heavy resistance: eleven helicopters were shot down and forty-four others damaged as they brought ARVN troops into Fire Support Base Lolo. On 6 March, after a heavy pounding of the NVA positions by fighter-bombers and B-52s, two infantry battalions from the 2nd Regiment of the 1st ARVN Division were lifted by 120 U.S. UH-1 Huey helicopters from Khe Sanh to Landing Zone Hope, four kilometers northeast of Tchepone. On 7 March, South Vietnamese troops entered Tchepone. ARVN had reached its objective, but by this time, the NVA forces had increased to twelve infantry regiments, two tank battalions, an artillery regiment, and at least nineteen antiaircraft battalions.[46] The South Vietnamese forces in Laos were in a precarious situation.

On 9 March, Lam flew once again to meet with Thieu. This time he went to make a case for the withdrawal of his forces from Laos. Having stressed the exposed position of the ARVN forces, he proposed to disengage and extract them by helicopter, with the 1st Division, the westernmost unit, leaving first, followed by the Airborne, and lastly the marines.[47] General Vien agreed with Lam. Abrams and Ambassador Bunker, also in attendance, strongly disagreed with the withdrawal and urged President Thieu to reinforce his beleaguered forces in Laos with the ARVN 2nd Infantry Division, then in Quang Ngai Province, and fight it out to the finish with the Communists.[48] Abrams and Bunker argued that political and public relations had to be considered. In a message to the chairman of the Joint Chiefs, Abrams enumerated his arguments against the withdrawal: "Whether it might not appear the RVNAF forces had been forced to withdraw despite the heavy casualties inflicted on the enemy; how such a move would be interpreted by the South Vietnam, American, and international press; the effect this would have on the political situation in South Vietnam [where national elections would be held in the following fall]. . . ."[49]

Thieu, however, was unwilling to risk more casualties, as well as the potential destruction of his best division (the Airborne Division) and the bulk of his strategic reserve. Accordingly, he gave the order to terminate the operation and to begin the withdrawal. According to Gen. Bruce Palmer, Abrams privately believed that Thieu had lost his nerve and never forgave him.[50]

On 12 March, General Lam began to withdraw his forces, a difficult maneuver for a force in contact with, and outnumbered by, the enemy. By this time, the NVA had moved a total of five divisions into the area to inflict as much damage as possible on ARVN. They placed heavy antiaircraft fire on the evacuation helicopters, ambushed ARVN elements moving by road, and kept the pressure on the South Vietnamese firebases. The retreat took twelve days and was a near disaster. The NVA attempted to surround and destroy the South Vietnamese units; only U.S. tactical air support and attack helicopters prevented a complete rout.

The airborne and armored forces withdrew along Route 9 while U.S. helicopters extracted the units on the flanks. The North Vietnamese used all available options to prevent the South Vietnamese from escaping, pursuing with tanks and other armored vehicles. The ensuing panic in some South Vietnamese units was reminiscent of that shown earlier by the deserters at Ranger Base North. Lt. Col. William N. Preachey, commander of the 158th Aviation Battalion, which flew support missions for the South Vietnamese throughout most of Lam Son 719, described the nature of the South Vietnamese withdrawal:

> They [the ARVN troops] would do absolutely anything to get out of Laos. . . .
> The healthy would run over the dead and wounded. We would hover at six or seven feet and the crew chief and gunner would lay on their bellies and pull people up. If you got on the ground they would turn the helicopter over. A later tactic was to run and jump on the shoulders of people and grab on to the skids. The helicopters would go up to 3,000 or 4,000 feet, and after five or ten minutes, they'd get tired and turn loose. I can still see the bodies coming through the sky.[51]

The last ARVN troops crossed back into South Vietnam on 24 March, and the operation was officially terminated on 6 April 1971, forty-five days after the South Vietnamese forces had first entered Laos.[52]

ASSESSING LAM SON 719 AND
THE SOUTH VIETNAMESE PERFORMANCE

Assessing Lam Son 719 is difficult. On the day that his forces reached Tchepone, President Thieu proclaimed the Laotian campaign "the biggest victory ever . . . a moral, political, and psychological Dien Bien Phu."[53] Likewise, the Nixon administration began a campaign to convince the American public that, despite clear evidence to the contrary, the operation had been a success. President Nixon had reported in February that "the operation has gone according to plan" and that ARVN was "fighting in a superior way."[54] Administration spokesmen described the South Vietnamese withdrawal from Laos as merely "mobile maneuvering." This was obviously spin, but even after the war, Nixon continued to maintain that the operation had achieved its objective; he wrote in his memoirs, "[T]he net result [of Lam Son 719] was a military success but a psychological defeat," brought on by negative television coverage of the withdrawal.[55]

Although Nixon's assessment of the operation is clearly subject to debate, there is no doubt that the many commentators in the U.S. news media took almost violent exception to administration pronouncements about South Vietnamese performance and the results of the operation.[56] James McCartney wrote in the *Philadelphia Inquirer*: "The South Vietnamese have invented a new kind of warfare in Laos. They avoid fighting whenever they can, they flee an area when the Communists start showing up on the battlefield, and they consistently claim 'victory' or 'success' when the operation involved is over. . . . Many U.S. military men used to criticize the South Vietnamese for a tendency to 'cut and run' when a battle loomed in Vietnam. Now, when the South Vietnamese flee, Pentagon spokesmen are inclined to praise their 'mobility.'"[57]

The *Cleveland Plain Dealer* also challenged the administration, writing, "Rather than the military success President Nixon has acclaimed, it appears the Laos incursion was a defeat that has bolstered Hanoi's confidence."[58] A relatively balanced account of the operation in the *Philadelphia Bulletin* observed, "Without our air cover and without 51 battalions of U.S. troops holding the fort . . . [one] can only guess at how much worse the situation might have been."[59] Essentially agreeing with the most negative assessments by the U.S. news media, the North Vietnamese ridiculed the operation and called it "the heaviest defeat ever" for "Nixon and Company. . . . A fine picture of Vietnamization indeed!"[60]

An objective assessment of the Laotian campaign lies somewhere between Nixon's public pronouncements about the success of the operation and the U.S. media's portrayal of complete debacle. From a purely military standpoint, the results of the campaign were mixed. Saigon reported that the operation had cost 1,160 government troops killed, 4,271 wounded, and 240 missing. Many in the media, including the Associated Press and *Newsweek* magazine, challenged these figures and put the actual casualty count at 3,800 killed, 5,200 wounded, and 775 missing.[61] According to XXIV Corps official figures, which closely matched those reported by the media, Saigon casualties included 9,000 killed, wounded, and captured, a casualty rate of nearly 50 percent. U.S. casualties included 253 killed or missing in action and 1,149 wounded. In terms of equipment, the United States lost 108 helicopters destroyed and 618 damaged (20 percent of which were expected to never fly again).[62] The U.S. Air Force lost seven fighter-bombers, and four pilots were killed in action.[63] ARVN lost 211 trucks, 87 combat vehicles, 54 tanks, 96 artillery pieces, and all of the combat engineer equipment (bulldozers, graders, etc.) that had accompanied the attackers.[64]

The allies reported 19,043 enemy killed. They also reported 1,963 crew-served and 5,170 individual weapons captured and 106 tanks, 13 artillery pieces, 2,001 vehicles, 170,346 tons of munitions, and 1,250 tons of rice destroyed.[65] Although these results were impressive, most of them occurred in the earlier part of the campaign before the South Vietnamese lost the initiative.

Despite the casualties inflicted on the North Vietnamese and the capture or destruction of enemy supplies, the South Vietnamese combat performance had been, at best, uneven, and at worst, very poor. President Nixon, trying to put the best face on what he knew had been a near disastrous operation, credited the South Vietnamese with having done a laudable job against the best that the North Vietnamese could offer. He proclaimed: "General Abrams . . . says that some [ARVN] units did not do so well, but 18 out of 22 battalions conducted themselves with high morale, with great confidence, and they are able to defend themselves man for man against the North Vietnamese."[66] Nixon's assessment was, at best, questionable. Some units fought very well, but others, including some of the elite forces, broke and ran under heavy NVA pressure.

South Vietnamese weaknesses were only too obvious. General Abrams best summarized the situation when he gloomily concluded that "Saigon cannot sustain large scale cross-border operations . . . without external support."[67] As before, the politicized senior leadership represented a serious problem. Although Lieutenant General Lam was the overall ground commander, he was virtually ignored by the two commanders of the Airborne and Marine divisions, lieutenant generals themselves who were more accustomed, as commanders of national strategic reserve forces, to answering directly to Saigon rather than responding to a corps commander.[68] They contested Lam's orders and directives at every opportunity. Although Lam appealed to President Thieu for support, Thieu refused to reprimand Lam's subordinate commanders, even when their actions bordered on insubordination during the heat of the battle. Thieu did not wish to offend the two other generals, one of whom commanded his primary anti-coup force (the Airborne) and the other of whom commanded a large portion of his strategic reserve. Once again, political considerations proved more important than military necessity.

Lam himself was no bright shining star. As Gen. Bruce Palmer wrote after the war, Lam's "reputation as a combat commander was only mediocre, but . . . [he] was considered to be a loyal, capable administrator."[69] Prior to Lam Son 719, Lam had survived as a corps commander thanks to his political skills and his support of President Thieu. He had very little experience in directing multidivision conventional operations. The intensity of combat in Laos and the demands of the operation were too much for Lam. Lt. Col. Darron of the XXIV Corps headquarters subsequently discussed Lam's actions during the operations, concluding: "I remember seeing him one morning toward the end of the operation when things were worms in Laos. . . . He was laying back, kind of in a crucified position, leaning back against his bunker . . . looking up at the sky with his eyes closed, and he was obviously under a terrible, terrible strain. Frankly, I think he was just in over his head."[70] Lam's ineptitude was evident throughout the operation. Brig. Gen. Sidney B. Berry, assistant commander of the 101st Airborne Division, reported after the operation that "planning and coordination for Lam Son 719 were, at the Corps Commanders' level, of unacceptably low quality."[71]

Lam was woefully unprepared to conduct an operation the size and complexity of Lam Son 719, but he was not alone; unfortunately for the South Vietnamese, planning and coordination inadequacies were not limited solely to the corps commander level. ARVN commanders at all echelons displayed serious difficulties in command and control, particularly with regard to coordinating combined arms operations, including the ability to employ infantry, armor, and artillery in concert and the proper use of reserve forces. General Vien, chairman of the RVNAF Joint General Staff, described the results of these difficulties:

> Deployed in an unfavorable terrain, our 300-vehicle armored force was impotent against enemy tanks and unable to assist the Airborne Division in breaking the enemy encirclement or regaining the initiative. By contrast, the enemy armor had proved aggressive and dangerous; it had taken advantage of a familiar though unfavorable terrain to lay ambushes or close in on our strongpoints and finally combine with infantry to assault and overrun them. Our infantry units shunned maneuvers when engaged and failed to use their organic fire to destroy the enemy, relying entirely on supporting firepower. The I Corps and the division commanders involved all had reserves, but they failed to use them to overcome difficulties and regain the initiative. Even our available firepower was not properly used especially during the first month of the operation because of poor coordination.[72]

The absence of U.S. advisers was readily apparent in the increased coordination difficulties repeatedly demonstrated by the South Vietnamese forces. Many of the tasks that U.S. advisers had routinely accomplished for ARVN commanders were either not done or done poorly. Army Chief of Staff William Westmoreland wrote, "Long accustomed to working with American advisers, subordinate ARVN commanders had difficulty without them in arranging fire support and resupply. The senior American adviser and the over-all ARVN commander were operating from different bases. Several senior ARVN commanders folded, prompting President Thieu to intervene and start issuing orders himself as far down as regiment, in many cases without General Abrams' knowledge."[73]

Perhaps the gravest concern to MACV was the South Vietnamese inability to coordinate their own fire support, which led to a subsequent overreliance on external U.S. assets. Many in both MACV and the RVNAF Joint General Staff realized that only U.S. air support had stood between the South Vietnamese and a total rout in Laos. Flying against intense antiaircraft artillery and ground fire, U.S. Army helicopters flew over 160,000 sorties and U.S. tactical aircraft and B-52s flew more than 10,000 strikes in support of the South Vietnamese forces.[74] The South Vietnamese dependence on U.S. air support was extremely troubling, for this support would disappear when U.S. troop withdrawals were completed.

One of the most significant and lasting outcomes of Lam Son 719 was its detrimental effect on South Vietnamese morale and esprit. Despite President Thieu's bombastic statements, the South Vietnamese forces who retreated from Laos knew they had been defeated. U.S. Marine Corps adviser Maj. William Dabney, who flew over Laos as an airborne coordinator, contrasted the Vietnamese Marines before and after operation, saying, "These were brave men, well led, well supplied, who had a certain elan and a certain confidence in themselves when they went in. When they came out, they'd been whipped. They knew they'd been whipped and they acted like they had been whipped."[75]

In the process of retreating from Laos under heavy pressure, the South Vietnamese left many of their dead on the battlefield. One ARVN officer later described the situation: "This came as a horrendous trauma to those unlucky families who in their traditional devotion to the cult of the dead and their attachment to the living, were condemned to live in perpetual sorrow and doubt. . . . Vietnamese sentiment would never forget."[76]

Although Thieu claimed victory, the soldiers and their families had no illusions about the outcome of the operation and were demoralized by what they saw as a clear defeat at the hands of the North Vietnamese. Thieu took steps to lessen the downward spiral of morale. He banned U.S. news magazines *Time* and *Newsweek* and several opposition newspapers whose coverage of the operation trumpeted the negative aspects of the operation in Laos. Additionally, he kept the hard-hit Airborne and Marine divisions in I Corps, rather than returning them to their normal bases around Saigon. He did not want these troops telling stories about the near disaster in Laos. Still, South Vietnamese morale and confidence had been dealt a serious blow.

Clearly, Lam Son 719 was a defeat for ARVN and a setback to Vietnamization; however, it nevertheless achieved at least a modicum of the original objectives. General Sutherland forwarded the following assessment to Abrams in late March: "Lamson 719 has been expensive in terms of U.S. support costs, but its achievement so far indicates that in terms of damage inflicted upon the enemy, disruption of his expected offensive operations, evidence of the effectiveness of the

Vietnamization program, and benefits which will accrue in the future it has been unquestionably a highly valuable and productive operation."[77]

Sutherland's assessment of the operation may have been a bit overblown and his comments about the effectiveness of Vietnamization certainly debatable, but ample evidence exists that Lam Son 719 at least temporarily disrupted the NVA buildup in Laos. Although the South Vietnamese losses had been severe, the North Vietnamese forces suffered as badly, if not worse, losing by some counts up to one-half of the North Vietnamese troops committed to the operation.[78] These estimates may be high, but little doubt remains that the operation cost the Communists dearly in men and equipment that probably would have been used in a major NVA offensive against Military Region I later in 1971. Lam Son 719 was an important factor in delaying the next major Communist offensive; the North Vietnamese took nearly a year to replace the resources lost in the effort to destroy the South Vietnamese along Route 9. Thus the South Vietnamese and the Vietnamization effort gained a brief, but needed respite from NVA pressure. As Keith Nolan noted in *Into Laos,* "Vietnamization had been tested, had strained but had not cracked, and now had continued room to grow."[79]

Immediately after the conclusion of Lam Son 719, President Nixon proclaimed, "Tonight I can report that Vietnamization has succeeded." Then he announced that he was accelerating the withdrawal of U.S. troops. An additional 100,000 troops would be brought home by November 1971. He promised that "American involvement in Vietnam was coming to an end," but refused to set a date for total withdrawal, saying that doing so would give away "our principal bargaining counter to win release of the American prisoners of war . . . [and] would remove the enemy's strongest incentive to end the war sooner by negotiation."[80]

The newly announced withdrawals would leave 184,000 American troops in South Vietnam at the end of 1971. In June 1971, Secretary of Defense Laird declared that 90 percent of combat responsibility had been turned over to ARVN; two months later, he announced that Phase I of Vietnamization had been completed.[81] From that time on, ground combat responsibility would be entirely assumed by the RVNAF.

Despite administration claims about the success of Lam Son 719, the operation raised serious questions about the next phase of Vietnamization. During Phase II, the South Vietnamese were to develop air and naval support capabilities and artillery, logistical capabilities, and maintenance systems to replace those that since 1965 had been supplied by the United States. How long this would take was unknown, but Lam Son 719 had demonstrated that the RVNAF still had a way to go toward the final objective of self-sustainment on the battlefield. While the South Vietnamese worked toward this goal and the remaining American ground forces gradually pulled out, the United States would need to maintain a level of combat support, particularly air support, which had been so critical in Laos. Gen. Phillip Davidson described the situation in 1971 as follows: "Lam Son 719 demonstrated that, while Vietnamization had made progress, the South Vietnamese government and its armed forces had deep flaws which made final success of the concept years, probably decades, away. Above all, the operation showed ARVN's complete dependence on the United States forces."[82]

ATTEMPTS TO REMEDY RVNAF WEAKNESSES

Immediately following Lam Son 719, General Abrams instituted new programs to overcome the weaknesses and flaws that had been so apparent during the operation. In Laos, the North Vietnamese had clearly demonstrated that they had turned away from guerrilla tactics to conventional warfare. The only way to combat this type of warfare was with combined arms operations that focused on the synchronization of infantry, armor, artillery, and air support. Abrams urged General Vien to appoint a committee to develop a combined arms doctrine suitable for RVNAF use; the committee produced the *Combined Arms Doctrinal Manual,* which was approved late in 1971. Additionally, command post exercises for ARVN units were initiated to teach air-ground coordination and combined tank-infantry operations. General Abrams directed his corps senior advisers to put together mobile advisory and support groups to work directly with the South Vietnamese corps commanders to provide "dynamic support to the early introduction of the new mode of [combined arms] tactics" within the RVNAF.[83] Later, he assigned an additional senior Army officer as "air-mobile adviser" in each corps zone to help coordinate U.S. helicopter support to South Vietnamese field units.[84]

MACV also took steps to improve RVNAF weaponry. The T-54 tanks and heavy artillery that the NVA used in Laos outmatched the ARVN M-41 tanks and lighter artillery. In an attempt to counter the heavier Communist weapons, MACV equipped one South Vietnamese tank battalion with the heavier U.S. M-48 main battle tank. Additionally, one ARVN artillery battalion received 175-mm self-propelled guns to combat the Soviet 130-mm long range guns that the NVA possessed. New equipment was a step in the right direction, but the amounts were provided in such small numbers as to have little significant impact. As General Davidson wrote, these efforts would eventually prove to be part of the continual story of "too little, too late."[85]

Equipment was not the main means for improving the fighting ability of ARVN. General Abrams noted in July 1971 that poor leadership remained the most critical South Vietnamese weakness.[86] This had only been too apparent during Lam Son 719. Abrams and his senior generals began a campaign to convince Thieu to replace weaker leaders at the top of the ARVN chain of command. Although the South Vietnamese president made a few changes, the criterion for senior command in ARVN remained political loyalty, rather than combat ability. A 1971 assessment of the RVNAF officer corps noted that the army had never been able to divorce itself from politics and that family relationships, personal loyalties, and regional, school, and business ties determined entree into the upper levels of the officer corps.[87] Even senior South Vietnamese generals realized that something had to be done. General Vien wrote after the war that "the problem of leadership should have been reviewed especially at corps and division levels. The appointment of general officers to these key command jobs should have been devoid of political considerations and based entirely on military professionalism and competence. . . . Military discipline should have been strictly enforced even with general officers especially when the conduct of a major and decisive operation was at stake."[88] President Thieu, obviously more concerned about his political support, refused to relieve incompetent officers who were loyal to him. Inadequate leadership, long prevalent in ARVN, had dire consequences in Laos; left unremedied, it would also have serious ramifications in battles to come.

Another aspect of the leadership crisis was the need to develop sufficient leaders for the expanded forces. To address this problem, Abrams urged South Vietnam to place more emphasis on the early identification of men with leadership potential, expand the number and length of leadership training courses, and elevate the standards of the leader-producing schools, which included the Vietnamese Military Academy, the Command and General Staff College, and the National Defense College.[89] These were appropriate remedies, but only time would tell if they would have a significant impact on the situation.

The South Vietnamese army was not the only subject of concern for MACV. The South Vietnamese Air Force had not played a significant role in providing close air support during Lam Son 719. Its participation and contributions had been, according to one former ARVN general, "rather modest even by RVNAF standards."[90] Despite the significant American effort that had been expended in improving the capabilities of VNAF, it still experienced severe difficulties in training, equipment, and maintenance and was in no way ready to fill the gap left by the rapidly departing U.S. Air Force. The lack of VNAF capability did not bode well for ground forces that depended so heavily on air support.

The status of Vietnamization with regard to the Vietnamese Navy was somewhat more positive. In September 1970, the VNN had assumed complete responsibility for Operation Market Time, the coastal interdiction mission, while the U.S. Navy continued to have responsibility for interdiction at sea. In mid-1971, the VNN assumed full responsibility for both missions. Additionally, VNN riverine forces took on the responsibility for escorting and protecting supply convoys on the Mekong River up to Neak Luong and Phnom Penh. By the end of 1970, they were equipped with over eight hundred river craft and assumed operational responsibilities over the entire South Vietnamese river system previously patrolled by the U.S. "brown water navy."

As the navy made great gains during this period, the United States continued to focus on the air and ground forces, who ultimately had to bear the brunt of the fighting against the North Vietnamese. Although Lam Son had revealed many problems, a 1971 year-end report provided the following upbeat assessment: "Gradual improvement in the ARVN has occurred partially as a result of the assumption of a greater portion of combat responsibilities as U.S. forces redeploy. The experience gained in the planning and execution of complex, large-scale, cross-border operations, starting with Lam Son 719 early in 1971, has been invaluable. While the ARVN command and control system has a long way to go, it has demonstrated that it can and will function under demanding combat conditions."[91]

Despite continuing difficulties, General Abrams was relatively pleased with the progress of Vietnamization. In early 1972, he declared that "the state of readiness, the alertness and activity on the part of the armed forces here in this country [South Vietnam] is the highest that I've ever seen it, though some are still asleep at the switch."[92] The U.S. troop withdrawals continued, and Abrams and his advisers in the field no doubt realized that time was running short to prepare the South Vietnamese to take over when all the Americans had left.[93] Nevertheless, the White House would continue to trumpet the "successes" of Vietnamization as more U.S. troops departed. The ultimate test for the South Vietnamese would come less than a year later during the 1972 NVA Easter Offensive.

ON THE HOME FRONT

Meanwhile, in the United States, Lam Son 719 had, like the Cambodian incursion the year before, brought out antiwar dissidents in force. Their numbers appeared to grow daily. Media coverage of the South Vietnamese retreat from Laos had a devastating effect on many Americans, most of whom were fed up with the inconclusive nature of a seemingly unending war. Popular support for President Nixon and his policies in South Vietnam fell to an all-time low. A Gallup poll on 7 March 1971 indicated that seven out of ten Americans doubted the president had told them all they needed to know about the events in Laos and South Vietnam.[94] A Harris poll published the next day revealed that only 39 percent of the population supported Nixon's handling of the war. Forty-one percent were concerned that the fighting in Laos would delay the evacuation of U.S. troops from South Vietnam, and 51 percent indicated they would favor a congressional resolution requiring the withdrawal of all U.S. troops by the end of the year.[95] April and May witnessed six weeks of demonstrations against continued U.S. involvement in the war. On 24 April, 150,000 people demonstrated in San Francisco; on the same day, 200,000 demonstrators, including a large contingent of Vietnam Veterans Against the War, hit the streets in Washington, demanding an immediate withdrawal of all U.S. troops. In the week leading up to May Day 1971, demonstrators threatened to shut down the federal government, but the mayor of the District of Columbia asked for federal help. The National Guard was called out and 12,000 protesters were arrested, effectively ending the demonstration. Nevertheless, sentiment continued unabated against the war and the administration's handling of it.

Nixon's Democratic opponents in Congress seized the moment. Between 1 March and 1 July 1971, seventeen votes in the House and Senate sought to restrict Nixon's authority to conduct the war and/or fix a date for unilateral withdrawal. House Democrats approved a resolution in late March 1971 calling for the termination of U.S. involvement in Indochina by 1 January 1973. When Nixon approved more bombing of North Vietnam during Lam Son 719, Senator George McGovern charged that the new bombing was "the most barbaric act committed by any modern state since the death of Adolph Hitler."[96] McGovern subsequently proposed to the Senate Foreign Relations Committee a bill that would force Nixon to have U.S. troops out of Southeast Asia by 31 December 1971. In hearings on the proposal conducted by committee chairman William Fulbright, supporters of McGovern's bill called for unilateral U.S. withdrawal regardless of North Vietnamese reciprocity. McGovern's bill eventually appeared in a slightly modified form as an amendment to the military conscription bill; however, on 16 June, the Senate defeated the amendment.

The anti-Nixon forces in the Congress did not give up. On 22 June, the Senate passed the Mansfield Amendment, which declared that all American troops were to be withdrawn from Vietnam within nine months of the approval of the draft extension. The wording was later changed in conference committee from "nine months from passage" to "earliest practicable date."[97] Such legislation increased the pressure on the administration and would later seriously undermine the U.S. bargaining position at the Paris peace negotiations.

THE PEACE TALKS

To quiet his critics, the president made a series of speeches in April 1971 stressing plans for continued U.S. troop withdrawals. Meanwhile, his administration tried throughout 1971 and into the new year to get the North Vietnamese to enter into serious and meaningful negotiations in Paris. Four years of official talks with them at the Majestic Hotel in Paris had settled little except the shape of the negotiating table. Accordingly, in a Paris suburb in August 1969, Kissinger had begun secret negotiations with the North Vietnamese; however, during 1970 and well into 1971, these meetings yielded little more progress than the official talks. Lam Son 719 interrupted the secret sessions, but shortly after the operation ended Kissinger requested a resumption of the clandestine talks. On 31 May 1971, he met secretly with Xuan Tuy, who was heading the North Vietnamese delegation while his colleague Le Duc Tho was temporarily in Hanoi. Kissinger repeated the proposal made by Nixon on 8 October 1970 and declared that the United States no longer required NVA troops to be withdrawn from South Vietnam as a condition for resolving the impasse in Southeast Asia. Kissinger proposed that all prisoners of war be exchanged immediately and indicated that the United States was prepared to discuss a deadline for complete U.S. withdrawal and a subsequent cease-fire when the final withdrawals began. In turn, he asked that the North Vietnamese agree to no further infiltration of outside forces into South Vietnam, Laos, and Cambodia. The North Vietnamese refused Kissinger's proposal, saying that it did not provide sufficient guarantees that NVA troops could remain in South Vietnam. Additionally, they rejected the timing of Kissinger's offer, because the proposed U.S. withdrawal would come after both the cease-fire and the exchange of prisoners, which effectively removed two of their key bargaining chips. Despite Xuan Tuy's rejection of his proposals, Kissinger left the meeting believing that "serious negotiations seemed in the offing for the first time."[98]

On 26 June, at Le Duc Tho's request, Kissinger again met secretly with the North Vietnamese in Paris. The Hanoi regime's diplomats presented nine counterproposals to Kissinger's earlier offer. Kissinger believed that seven of the proposals could be successfully negotiated, but had major objections to the last two, in which Hanoi demanded reparations and an end to U.S. support for "Thieu-Ky-Khiem so that a new administration could be set up in Saigon."[99] Once again Kissinger was heartened by events and concluded that meaningful negotiations were at hand.

On 1 July, as Kissinger was considering Hanoi's nine points, Mme Nguyen Thi Binh, the representative of the Provisional Revolutionary Government (PRG) at the official Paris negotiations, publicly issued a seven-point plan of her own, which was similar but not the same as the one presented by Le Duc Tho during the secret meetings with Kissinger. Binh called for reunification of Vietnam, a guarantee of Vietnamese neutrality, an end to Vietnamization, dismantling of U.S. military bases, inclusion of the PRG in the South's government before any elections, and a release of all political prisoners.[100] Kissinger was stunned and asked Le Duc Tho what constituted the official North Vietnamese position; Le Duc Tho replied that his was the approved position. Kissinger concluded that this contretemps was a ploy to force the United States to negotiate on Le Duc Tho's terms; they wanted to negotiate in secret, but used Madame Binh's announcement as a way to appeal to the antiwar contingent in the United States.[101] After the war, Truong Nhu Tang revealed that this may not have necessarily been the case. The former PRG minister of justice wrote that the conflicting Communist peace proposals in Paris resulted from the conflict in Hanoi between the North Vietnamese and the South Vietnamese members of the PRG.[102] Regardless of the reason for Mme Binh's announcement, it caused Congress, the news media, and the antiwar dissidents, unaware of Kissinger's secret negotiations with Le Duc Tho in Paris, to condemn Nixon for failing to respond to Binh's overture.

Kissinger met again with Tho on 12 July to discuss the discrepancies between the two North Vietnamese proposals. Le Duc Tho reiterated his original nine proposals as the basis for further negotiations. Kissinger said that reparations might be discussed, but that dismantlement of the Thieu government was non-negotiable. At an impasse, the meeting broke up, but the participants agreed to meet again on 26 July.

At the next session, the discussions went well, only to hit a wall when the Thieu issue arose. Another meeting was called for 16 August, but no progress was made. This pattern repeated itself at the next session on 13 September.

Kissinger made one more attempt to negotiate with the North Vietnamese in 1971. Trying to reach a compromise over the fate of the Thieu government,

Kissinger sent the Communist negotiators a letter on 3 October, proposing "that a new presidential election be held within six months after the signing of a final agreement. The election would be run by an electoral commission, including Communists, under international supervision. One month before the election, Thieu would resign and his function would be assumed by the president of the South Vietnamese Senate."[103] Additionally, the proposal included a new formula for the withdrawal of U.S. troops, saying that most of the troops would be gone within seven months of an agreement, leaving only a small residual force to provide "technical advice, logistics, and observation of the ceasefire."[104] The North Vietnamese agreed to discuss this proposal on 20 November, but on 17 November they canceled the meeting without commenting on Kissinger's letter.

After the war, Truong Nhu Tang wrote that the whole scenario of North Vietnamese negotiations in 1971 was a classic example of "talking while preparing to fight," in which Le Duc Tho "was treating Henry Kissinger to a brilliant display of 'talking and fighting,' using the negotiations to cover as long as possible the next real move in the war, the upcoming dry season campaign in the South."[105] Additional evidence reveals that the North Vietnamese used this time to prepare for their next offensive.

To answer his critics and in an attempt to bring the North Vietnamese back to the table, Nixon revealed in a nationwide radio and television broadcast on 25 January 1972 that Kissinger was conducting secret negotiations with the North Vietnamese in Paris. While Nixon's announcement did not quiet his critics, it nevertheless boosted the president's political fortunes early in the election year.[106] Unfortunately, the speech had no impact on the North Vietnamese. The day after the broadcast, Washington sent Hanoi a private note indicating a willingness to resume the secret talks. The North Vietnamese refused and withdrew all previous peace proposals, saying, "You should realize the difference of the conditions in 1971 and the present conditions in 1972."[107] The major condition that had changed was that the North Vietnamese were preparing to launch a general offensive in the South.

6

The Ultimate Test of Vietnamization

When 1972 began, the situation in South Vietnam appeared to be improving. The NVA, which had been kept busy refurbishing the units damaged during the allied invasion of Laos, initiated only limited offensive action in the last half of 1971. As a result, the pacification effort had made great gains. One observer, reporter and former U.S. Marine Corps colonel Robert D. Heinl, went so far as to say in 1972, "If successful pacification is the yardstick, the war in Vietnam is already settled. We have won."[1] This was an overstatement, but by the end of 1971, MACV's Hamlet Evaluation Survey indicated that 97 percent of the villages and hamlets of South Vietnam were either totally secure or relatively secure.[2] Though subject to debate, the statistics made clear that the security situation in the countryside was much better than ever before. Sir Robert Thompson, unofficial adviser to President Nixon on affairs in Vietnam, made a trip to South Vietnam in late 1970 and reported, "One of my most pleasant experiences was to drive around villages in Quang Tin province completely unescorted on the back of the District Chief's Honda, in an area where, two years before, the district town itself had been invested and only just held."[3]

The South Vietnamese ground forces had rebounded somewhat from the devastating effects of Lam Son 719. Units that had suffered serious casualties in Laos received replacements to bring them back to full strength, and the combined arms training program had begun to show signs of progress. In terms of sheer numbers, the regular South Vietnamese forces had grown to over one million men and women under arms by early 1972. A new division, the 3rd Infantry Division, had been formed in I Corps from regiments drawn from other divisions and deployed along the DMZ. The paramilitary self-defense forces had tripled in size to over four million. The VNN and VNMC had doubled in size, and the air force had become two and a half times larger. To equip these expanded forces, the United States provided 844,000 individual and crew-served weapons, 1,880 tanks and artillery pieces, a large number of bulldozers and other heavy engineering equipment, 44,000 radio sets, and 778 helicopters and fixed-wing aircraft.[4] By the start of 1972, the RVNAF, on paper, was a formidable force. It would shortly be tested in the most drastic manner.

While the Vietnamization effort intensified, U.S. troop withdrawals continued as scheduled, with 177,000 Americans departing in 1971. By January 1972, U.S. troop strength in Vietnam was 158,000, the lowest since 1965. That month, Nixon announced that he would withdraw 70,000 additional troops from South Vietnam by 1 May. As U.S. combat forces were reduced to meet this new schedule, a corresponding reduction occurred at senior American headquarters in country, including MACV, USARV, 7th Air Force, and III Marine Amphibious Force. Many of the large, complex U.S. commands that dealt with intelligence, logistics, and other types of support, such as communications, were dismantled and the American troops sent home. Accordingly, many of the larger U.S.-built bases were turned over to the South Vietnamese. For example, by the end of 1971, the U.S. Air Force had turned over ten of fifteen air bases to VNAF.

Because of continuing troop withdrawals, the advisory structure also shrank significantly. At the end of 1971, General Abrams dissolved the MACV Office of the Assistant Chief of Staff for Military Assistance, which had previously been responsible for coordinating all advisory efforts in South Vietnam, turning over its duties to the individual MACV joint staff sections.[5] The MACV Training Directorate was given the responsibility for managing the Military Assistance Program, including U.S. support of the RVNAF training effort. Early in 1972, Abrams ordered the reorganization of MACV, transforming it from an operational headquarters into a combined advisory group.[6]

While Abrams reorganized MACV headquarters, he also took steps to reduce the American advisory force in the field. The large U.S. headquarters that had previously controlled operations in each military region (corps tactical zone) were replaced by small regional advisory groups. The U.S. Army XXIV Corps and I Corps Advisory Group became the First Regional Assistance Command. I Field Force and II Corps Advisory Group became the Second Regional Assistance Group. II Field Force and III Corps Advisory Group became the Third Regional Assistance Command. Delta Military Assistance Command and IV Corps Advisory Group combined to form the Delta Regional Assistance Command.

The commander of each regional assistance command was the senior U.S. commander in the region (an army major general), who commanded U.S. elements in the region and served as the senior adviser to the corps commander. The one exception to this arrangement was in Military Region II, where Abrams appointed a civilian, John Paul Vann, as the head of the Second Regional Assistance Group. Because he was a civilian, he had a U.S. Army general officer as his deputy, who exercised command over the military members of the advisory group and other U.S. forces left in the region.[7]

At the lower levels, Abrams ordered that the division combat assistance teams be reduced, closing out the battalion advisory teams by 30 June 1971 and beginning the phaseout of regimental teams in September. By early 1972, only 5,416 tactical advisers remained in all of South Vietnam.[8] The province, district, school, training center, and other advisory elements took commensurate cuts in strength, and the number of CORDS advisory personnel at MACV and the province and district levels fell by over one-half during 1971 (6,147 to 2,682).[9]

Despite their relatively small numbers, the advisers had assumed increasingly more important roles as U.S. combat forces withdrew, performing critical functions as the efforts to turn over the war to the RVNAF gained momentum. As U.S. combat forces left South Vietnam, the tactical advisers in the field became the focal point for liaison and coordination between the RVNAF and the U.S. combat-support assets still left in country. Although by this time few American forces were operating in ground combat roles in Vietnam, U.S. tactical air power was still much in evidence throughout the theater of operations. U.S. Air Force and Marine aircraft operated from bases in South Vietnam and Thailand, while U.S. Navy and other Marine aircraft operated from carriers in the South China Sea. B-52 heavy bombers flew missions regularly from bases in Guam and Thailand. Additionally, U.S. Army helicopters continued to fly ground support missions throughout South Vietnam. The U.S. advisers on the ground provided an invaluable link between the South Vietnamese and this support, a role that would prove critical during the action to follow in 1972.

THE NORTH VIETNAMESE DECIDE TO ATTACK

The North Vietnamese Politburo in Hanoi had begun discussing the possibility of a general offensive at the Nineteenth Plenary Session of the Lao Dong (Workers) Party in December 1970 and January 1971, but the leadership split over the issue. First Secretary Le Duan and Gen. Vo Nguyen Giap, hero of Dien Bien Phu, were among the more militant advocates of an all-out offensive. Le Duan was a southerner who maintained that the total subjugation of the South was the only ideologically proper path to follow. Possibly, as Gen. Dave Palmer suggests, Giap's motive for pushing the offensive may have been that he was still "smarting over the failure of his 1965 and 1968 offensives" and was looking for a final decisive victory that would win the war.[10] Nevertheless, Giap and Le Duan were opposed by a more conservative faction led by Truong Chinh, who wanted to concentrate on rebuilding the North while postponing any attempt to force unification with the South. Eventually, Giap and Le Duan won out.

In May 1971, the Party Central Committee met in Hanoi to discuss the outcome of the South Vietnamese operation in Laos. Giap and Le Duan were emboldened by their experience with the South Vietnamese in Laos. Lam Son 719 seemed to reinforce the NVA's belief that, with modern weapons and conventional tactics, it could easily defeat South Vietnam's armed forces once U.S. combat troops had been withdrawn.[11] The weaknesses demonstrated by the South Vietnamese in Laos—Saigon's lack of substantial strategic reserves and its inability to shift forces rapidly within South Vietnam—were all too apparent. As for possible American action against any contemplated offensive, the North Vietnamese felt that continued U.S. troop reductions would reach a point where the United States would not have enough forces left to influence the strategic situation. Furthermore, Giap and Le Duan did not think that the political situation in the United States would permit Nixon to commit any new troops or combat support to assist the South Vietnamese once the NVA launched its invasion. They also felt that Nixon, in pursuit of detente with the Soviets, would be reluctant to take any measures to blunt an offensive that might upset the strategic arms control talks. For these reasons, Giap and Le Duan believed that North Vietnam could attack South Vietnam with little or no significant interference from the United States. Additionally, they thought that a resounding NVA military victory would humiliate the U.S. president, destroy his war politics, and perhaps foil his bid for reelection in November. If they could inflict a defeat on Saigon, the damage to the Vietnamization program and the Nixon Doctrine might contribute to the defeat of the American president as well.[12] Because all of Nixon's potential election opponents appeared more or less inclined to take the United States out of Vietnam, anything they could do to contribute to his defeat was a plus. In this same vein, Truong Nhu Tang wrote after the war that an additional objective of the offensive was to spur antiwar dissidence in the United States.[13]

The international situation also influenced Hanoi's decision to launch the offensive. More than a little apprehensively, the North Vietnamese leaders watched Washington's evolving diplomacy with Moscow and Beijing. They were uncertain how these warming relations would affect the North's continued relationship with its Communist benefactors, or the aid it received in support of the war effort against the South. Thus, a general offensive was Hanoi's only possible means of forcing a settlement on its own terms.[14]

Once the Politburo decided to launch the offensive, its members debated the question of when the attack should begin. North Vietnamese leaders had noted Nixon's troop withdrawal announcements, watched U.S. forces departing South Vietnam, and calculated that American troop strength would probably fall below 65,000 by April 1972. This number would include headquarters and combat service support elements, but only a few combat battalions and some tactical aircraft and helicopters, a force that the NVA considered to be militarily insignificant. Some in the Politburo argued that the best course of action was to wait until 1973, when virtually all U.S. troops would be gone. Le Duan and his supporters rejected the argument, making a strong case that pacification and Vietnamization programs were beginning to show signs of progress. They maintained that if these programs were allowed to continue unimpeded for the rest of 1972, the United States would continue to pump weapons and equipment into South Vietnam and ARVN would grow stronger, thus making the future military conquest of South Vietnam much more difficult. Le Duan and Giap succeeded in convincing their colleagues at the Central Military Party Committee meeting in June 1971 that they should not wait, and the committee subsequently decided to "develop our strategic offensive posture in South Vietnam to defeat the American 'Vietnamization' policy, gain a decisive victory in 1972, and force the U.S. imperialists to negotiate an end to the war from a position of defeat."[15]

Having decided to launch the invasion in 1972, planners then had to determine the exact timing. As always, the monsoon seasons dictated the best times for combat operations in South Vietnam. If the North Vietnamese waited until too late in the spring dry season to start their offensive, torrential rains in late May could seriously impede later phases of the operation. Another consideration was that detection of their forces before the invasion would provide lucrative targets for U.S. tactical air support; therefore, the longer the North waited before beginning the operation, they more they put their forces at risk. The Communist leaders also wanted to initiate the invasion in time to have a maximum impact on the U.S. election in November, something that could be done only by starting the offensive earlier, rather than later. Finally, if they could inflict a defeat on South Vietnam while U.S. forces were still in country, North Vietnam could claim a military victory against the humiliated Americans. For these reasons, the Party Central Committee decided to launch the offensive in March 1972.[16]

To prepare for the attack, the North Vietnamese initiated a "logistics offensive." Le Duan went to Moscow to request assistance in the form of new weapons and equipment.[17] An appeal was also made to Beijing.[18] Subsequently, the North Vietnamese received massive quantities of modern weapons from the Soviet Union and China, including MIG-21 jet fighters, SAM antiaircraft missiles, T-54 tanks, 130-mm guns, 160-mm mortars, 57-mm antiaircraft guns, and, for the first time, shoulder-fired, heat-seeking SA-7 "Strela" antiaircraft missiles.[19] The North Vietnamese also began stockpiling spare parts, ammunition, and fuel in much greater amounts than ever before reported.[20] Divisions of the NVA general reserves were ordered to move south to position themselves for the invasion.

THE PLAN

The North Vietnamese dubbed the invasion the "Nguyen Hue" campaign in honor of Nguyen Hue, the birth name of Emperor Quang Trung, a Vietnamese national hero who dealt invading Chinese troops a resounding defeat just outside the imperial capital of Hue in 1789. In the United States, the North Vietnamese invasion would become known as the "Easter Offensive."

The architects of Nguyen Hue were General Giap and his chief of staff, Gen. Van Tien Dung. According to captured documents and information obtained from NVA prisoners of war after the invasion, Giap's campaign was designed to destroy as many ARVN forces as possible, thus permitting the North Vietnamese to occupy key South Vietnamese cities. In this posture, the Communist forces could threaten President Nguyen Van Thieu's government. At the same time, Giap hoped to discredit Nixon's Vietnamization and pacification programs, cause the remaining U.S. forces to be withdrawn, and, ultimately, seize control of South Vietnam.[21] Although the North Vietnamese hoped to achieve a knockout blow and the total defeat of the South Vietnamese forces, the offensive, at the very least, would undoubtedly seize enough terrain to strengthen the Communist position in any subsequent peace negotiations.

Giap's plan included a massive, three-pronged invasion of South Vietnam aimed at three critical areas. The first thrust would be made against the provincial capital of Quang Tri in Military Region I; the second at An Loc, in Binh Long Province, Military Region III, northwest of Saigon; and the third at Kontum in the Central Highlands, Military Region II (see map 8).

In the north, the 304th and 308th divisions, plus three separate infantry regiments, reinforced by two hundred tanks and several artillery regiments, would attack across the DMZ to seize Quang Tri. At the same time, the 324B Division would attack from the west to take Hue, while threatening the airport and harbor at Da Nang. The objective of the northern attack was to expel all South Vietnamese forces from Quang Tri and Thua Thien, the two northernmost provinces, thus effectively extending North Vietnam's border to the south.

The southernmost attack would also include three NVA divisions (5th VC, 7th NVA, and 9th VC) and would be aimed at seizing An Loc, the capital of Binh Long Province, just sixty-five miles from Saigon. From An Loc, the NVA would attack down Route 13 to threaten Saigon itself. It should be noted here that although some NVA divisions were called "VC" divisions, they were actually NVA divisions that carried the "VC" designation only as an honorific; they were organized, manned, and equipped just like all other NVA mainforce divisions.

The third prong of the invasion would be an attack in the Central Highlands against Kontum and Pleiku by the 2nd and 320th divisions, supported by a tank regiment. Additionally, the 3rd "Gold Star" Division would conduct a supporting attack in the coastal province of Binh Dinh. The ultimate objective in this region was for the forces attacking Pleiku and Kontum to link-up with the 3rd Division in Binh Dinh to cut South Vietnam in two along Route 19, a major east-west road from the coast to the Highlands. At the same time, the NVA 711th Division would threaten Da Nang from the southwest.

Additional NVA forces in Military Region IV, including the 1st Division, in the vicinity of the Cambodian border area west of the Mekong River, and other NVA units in the U Minh Forest (Chuong Thien Province) would join in the offensive with local attacks to seize territory and tie down ARVN forces so they could not be moved north to reinforce ARVN forces under attack in the other military regions. A total of fourteen NVA infantry divisions and twenty-six separate regiments (the equivalent of more than twenty ARVN divisions), including over 130,000

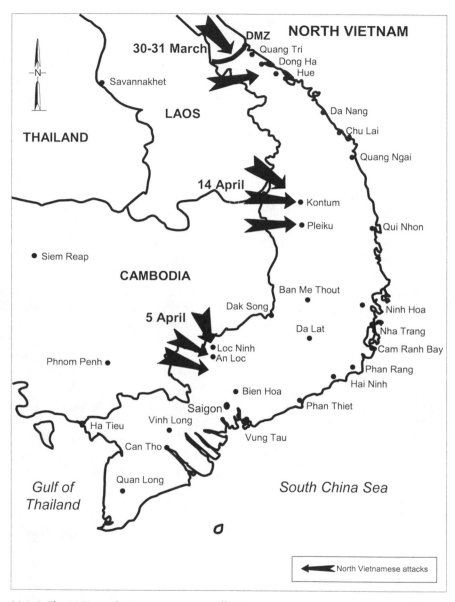

Map 8. The 1972 North Vietnamese Easter Offensive.

Communist troops and 1,200 tanks and other armored vehicles, would participate in the offensive. This represented the entire North Vietnamese combat force, less the 316th Division, which continued to operate in Laos for the duration of the offensive.

Giap's plan was audacious and somewhat risky, but he counted on the simultaneous attack of three major areas to disorganize the RVNAF and thus prevent Saigon from decisively committing its national reserves. Any of the three prongs of the attack, if successful, could have a major impact on the course of the war. The northern attack could sever the two northern provinces. The attack in the Central Highlands could cut South Vietnam in two. The southern attack might eventually propel North Vietnamese forces into the capital city itself. Realizing any of these goals would put the North Vietnamese in a superior position in later negotiations. If all three attacks were successful, the war would be over and the South Vietnamese would be defeated, thus negating the need for negotiations. One way or the other, the North Vietnamese stood to gain. As a Communist B-5 Front (northern South Vietnam) communique stated before the attack, "[R]egardless of whether the war is ended soon . . . or not, we will have the capability of gaining a decisive victory."[22]

D-DAY

The scope of the North Vietnamese preparations for offensive operations escaped allied intelligence analysts until very late in 1971. Recognition of these preparations was delayed despite numerous reports of increased heavy vehicle traffic on the Ho Chi Minh Trail during the summer of 1971. (The reports had come from the super-secret Studies and Observation Group [SOG], long-range reconnaissance teams that were inserted at key points along the trail to monitor enemy activity.[23]) Apparently ignoring these indications, the CIA's official estimate of enemy intentions for 1972, issued in early November 1971, stated: "One thing Hanoi cannot do in the remaining months of this dry season—it cannot launch a nation-wide military offensive on anything approaching the scale of Tet 1968." That same month, another intelligence estimate concurred, predicting "that the North Vietnamese were making no special effort" for a big offensive in 1972.[24]

A flurry of new reports significantly changed the intelligence picture in December: large troop formations with tanks and heavy artillery were staging in the North and beginning to move down the Ho Chi Minh Trail. Other reports told of new units being formed and moving south. Late in December, the allies received a copy of an unnumbered North Vietnamese policy resolution that outlined guidance for future operations. The resolution indicated a shift in tactics from protracted warfare to conventional war, calling for "tilting the balance of forces through the use of main-force warfare and political initiative."[25] By the end of the year, both U.S. and South Vietnamese intelligence analysts agreed that a North Vietnamese attack in early 1972 was probable.

Late in 1971, the North Vietnamese had broken off negotiations in Paris; it became apparent that they were making preparations for offensive operations against the South. When the NVA shelled Saigon a few days after refusing to meet Kissinger for the scheduled 20 November meeting, Nixon ordered that bombing raids be reinstated south of the twentieth parallel to impede the Communist buildup. The bombing would prove insufficient in achieving the president's goal.[26]

In late December, allied intelligence warned that North Vietnam had the capability for a major offensive and predicted that it would probably initiate the attack sometime before the Tet new year holiday, probably in late January.[27] On 16 January, General Abrams sent a message to Admiral McCain, saying that intelligence indicators "all point quite clearly in my view to a major military action by the North Vietnamese in the weeks ahead. In fact, it is my view that it will evolve into the maximum military effort the North is capable of making in the next few months."[28] Three days later in a follow-up message, he said that "the enemy is preparing and positioning his forces for a major offensive. Although we cannot be sure at this time of his precise plan of attack it is apparent that he is going to attempt to face us with the most difficult situation of which he is capable."[29]

However, nothing happened in January, and a subsequent intelligence estimate predicted that the attack would come during the Tet holidays in mid-February. Another intelligence estimate indicated that the attacks, when they came, would most likely occur in Quang Tri and Thua Thien provinces in Military Region I, and Kontum and Pleiku provinces in Military Region II.[30] Ambassador Bunker, failing to foresee the scope of the coming North Vietnamese offensive, predicted that the North Vietnamese would launch "a heavy and sustained set of ground attacks for a period of weeks," but speculated that "the enemy's objectives . . . are not military, but political and psychological."[31] Nevertheless, the Joint General Staff ordered ARVN commanders to cancel leaves during the holiday period and keep their troops in the barracks ready for action, but Tet passed without any significant enemy activity.

The U.S. news media, which had severely criticized the military for being surprised in 1968, now ridiculed them for predicting an attack that did not happen. The 24 March 1972 issue of *Life* magazine said in an editorial: "Remember all the predictions about this year's Tet offensive? 'The enemy advertised an offensive as they have advertised no other offensive in Vietnam,' said Defense Secretary Mel Laird in January. Army Chief of Staff Westmoreland predicted it would take place in February, and Pentagon speculation was that it would be timed to embarrass the President on the eve of his trip to Peking. Well, Tet and the President's trip are past, and the offensive never happened."[32]

Intelligence indicators still pointed to a North Vietnamese attack, but the two false alarms had raised the frustration level among the advisers in Vietnam. In early March, a U.S. civilian province adviser summed up the uncertainty about North Vietnamese intentions: "On again, off again, gonna come, didn't come—it has been a virtual merry-go-round this month of pending action that never materialized. It is very hard to actually ascertain the enemy's present intention."[33] General Abrams, while also frustrated, remained convinced that the North Vietnamese were preparing a major offensive, but he was not certain about its actual timing.[34]

As the allies debated the probability of a major Communist attack, the North Vietnamese completed preparations for the invasion of South Vietnam. On 30 March, the North Vietnamese commenced the offensive with a massive artillery preparation on 3rd ARVN Division positions all along the DMZ (see map 9). These

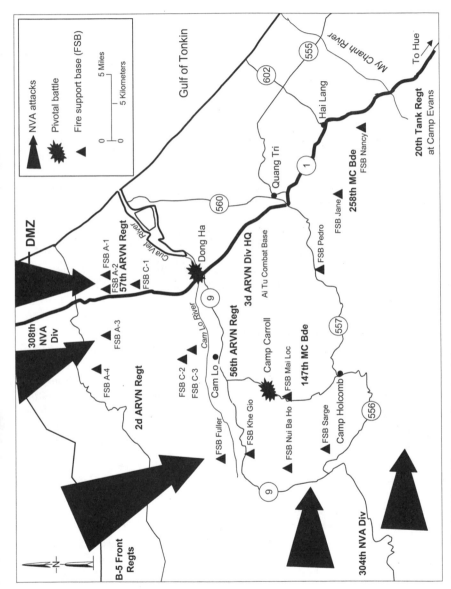

Map 9. The 1972 North Vietnamese Invasion, I Corps.

artillery barrages were closely followed by ground attacks across the DMZ and from the west along Route 9. The unexpected enemy attacks by the NVA 304th and 308th divisions, three separate infantry regiments of the B-5 Front, two tank regiments, and at least one sapper battalion, totaling an estimated 30,000 Communist troops, caught the 3rd ARVN Division repositioning forces and not ready for a fight. Additionally, the South Vietnamese were outgunned and usually outnumbered locally three to one. The 3rd Division, a new unit that was unprepared for large-scale conventional tank-infantry attacks supported by massive heavy artillery strikes, reeled from the intensity of the NVA onslaught.

General Lam, I Corps commanding general (who had previously commanded the South Vietnamese forces that went into Laos in Lam Son 719), was also not ready for a Communist attack of such scope. Lam, having seen no cause for alarm in the warnings from Saigon about an impending attack, had consequently made no special preparations to prepare his troops.[35] The corps commander expected any enemy attack in MR I to come from the west out of Laos rather than across the relatively flat and open Demilitarized Zone, so he was caught completely by surprise when the NVA poured across the DMZ in force.

Having achieved surprise, the enemy directed two attacks at the 56th Regiment of the 3rd Division in the vicinity of FSB Fuller and FSB A4. Two more attacks were aimed at the 57th Regiment positions at FSB A2 and FSB A1. Additional NVA forces struck the 147th Marine Brigade at Nui Ba Ho, FSB Sarge, and FSB Holcomb. The enemy attacks continued all day and increased in intensity as the day progressed. Because of clouds, fog, and drizzle, the availability and effectiveness of allied tactical air support were greatly reduced; lacking this support, the South Vietnamese forces pulled back, usually in disorder. Nui Ba Ho was evacuated late in the evening of 31 March and Sarge was overrun during the early hours of 1 April. Meanwhile, heavy NVA pressure forced elements of the 56th Regiment near FSB Fuller and those of the 2nd Regiment near Khe Gio to withdraw. By evening on 1 April, all South Vietnamese positions along the northern perimeter had either fallen back or been evacuated: the 56th withdrew to Camp Carroll and was under attack; the 57th fell back to north of Dong Ha; and the 2nd pulled back to Cam Lo. The Vietnamese Marine units remained at Mai Loc and FSB Pedro, giving a good account of themselves against the NVA attackers.[36]

At 1800 on 1 April, Brig. Gen. Vu Van Giai, Commanding General of the 3rd ARVN Division, ordered the withdrawal of all divisional forces north of Dong Ha, directing his forces to establish a line of defense south of the Cua Viet and Mieu Giang rivers. Giai ordered the RF and PF units in Dong Ha to hold a line along the southern bank of the Cua Viet River from the coastline to approximately five kilometers inland. The 57th Regiment would establish its line from the end of the RF/PF line to Dong Ha. The 2nd Regiment was to occupy a line from Dong Ha west to Cam Lo, where it would tie in with the 56th Regiment, which was ordered to hold Camp Carroll. This line would be extended southward to join the 147th Marine Brigade positions around Mai Loc. The 20th Tank Squadron, which was hastily thrown into combat as it was completing unit training at Camp Evans, was given responsibility for Dong Ha itself.

By 2 April, General Giai's new defensive line was established and in fairly good shape. However, later that day the enemy launched simultaneous attacks on Dong Ha and Camp Carroll. The 57th Regiment, although initially successful in throwing back the Communist assault, watched a steady stream of terrified refugees fleeing down Route 1 into Dong Ha. The panic was infectious and the troops eventually lost their nerve, broke, and ran, joining the chaotic exodus south. The NVA also hit Camp Carroll with intense artillery and human-wave attacks supported by T-54 tanks. U.S. adviser Lt. Col. William Camper later said that he felt that the South Vietnamese could have held out for at least another week, but Col. Pham Van Dinh, commander of the 56th Regiment at Camp Carroll, informed Camper that a "cabal" of his own officers had forced him to negotiate a surrender.[37] Over Camper's objections, Dinh surrendered his entire regiment: 1,500 ARVN troops and twenty-two artillery pieces, including a 175-mm battery and numerous quad-50s and twin-40s, the largest assemblage of heavy weapons in Military Region I.[38] Camper and his assistant, Maj. Joseph Brown, were rescued by U.S. helicopter. On 3 April, Radio Hanoi carried an appeal from Colonel Dinh urging all ARVN soldiers to lay down their arms and surrender to the NVA.[39]

With the loss of Carroll and its artillery, the Vietnamese Marine elements at Mai Loc were forced to withdraw toward Quang Tri City. Over the next few days, the relentless NVA attacks forced the South Vietnamese defenders into a perimeter that was only eleven kilometers in diameter, barely encompassing Dong Ha and Quang Tri City. By 5 April, there came a momentary lull in the fighting as the NVA repositioned artillery and replenished ammunition supplies.

In Washington, the White House was receiving mixed signals about the severity of the new Communist offensive. On 31 March, Secretary of Defense Laird advised the president and his national security adviser that the fighting in Military Region I constituted a major attack, but Kissinger recalls that for some reason, the Pentagon continued to issue "soothing" accounts.[40] He later speculated that the civilians in the Defense Department concealed the scope of the NVA attack in order to preclude Nixon from fulfilling his oft-stated threat to react strongly to any North Vietnamese offensive.[41] Laird, ever the politician, apparently did not want the president to react and thus incur the ire of the American public in an election year.

On 2 April, however, any ambiguity about the attack was removed when Ambassador Ellsworth Bunker cabled Kissinger and Nixon that "ARVN forces are on the verge of collapse in I Corps."[42] It was now clear to the White House that the attack in MR I was part of a full-blown Communist offensive and that the South Vietnamese, reeling from the intensity of the attacks, were in danger of folding. If the North Vietnamese succeeded in inflicting a major defeat on the South Vietnamese, Nixon's three-year-old policy of Vietnamization would be exposed as a fraud and his run for reelection in November would be seriously imperiled. Further, Nixon was scheduled to meet in Russia with Soviet premier Leonid Brezhnev, and he could not go to Moscow in the wake of a military defeat inflicted largely by Soviet-supplied weapons.[43] Nixon was in a difficult position. If he responded in a strong fashion to the North Vietnamese invasion, it might cause the Soviets to cancel the summit and destroy his hopes for detente. A strong response also might anger the Chinese, whom Nixon was also trying to court. Yet, if Nixon did not resort to bombing, virtually the only weapon left to him with most of the U.S. combat troops already having departed South Vietnam, the North Vietnamese would most likely overrun Saigon's troops, inflict a military defeat on ARVN, and compromise the U.S. strategic position throughout the world. At home, it was an election year, and opposing segments of American society would readily condemn Nixon for either failing to act to prevent the collapse of South Vietnam or for responding with anything that looked like an escalation of the war. Despite the dangers involved, Nixon had come to the conclusion that "Defeat . . . was simply not an option."[44] He and Kissinger agreed that something had to be done quickly to assist the faltering South Vietnamese, and they determined that the best way to do that was to "carry the war to North Vietnam."[45] Given this situation, bombing was the only answer to prevent the fall of South Vietnam.

Late on 4 April, Nixon, removing previous restrictions that had existed since 1968, ordered air strikes in North Vietnam all the way up to the eighteenth parallel. Civilians in the State and Defense Departments advised the president not to initiate new bombing, maintaining that if Vietnamization was to be truly tested, the South Vietnamese should be required to resist the invasion without extra aid.[46] Nixon was not prepared to take the risk that this course of action entailed. According to U.S. Air Force general John W. Vogt, who at the time was in Washington for briefings prior to flying to Saigon to assume command of the 7th Air Force, Nixon told him, "I want you to get down there and use whatever air you need to turn this thing around . . . stop this offensive."[47] On 6 April, as part of "Operation Freedom Train," American fighter-bombers attacked Communist targets sixty miles north of the DMZ. On 10 April, twelve B-52s struck supply depots near the port of Vinh, about 150 miles north of the DMZ. This was the first time that the Nixon administration had used B-52s on North Vietnam. By mid-month, B-52s were attacking targets within a few miles of Hanoi and Haiphong.

With Nixon's initiation of intensified air operations against North Vietnam, squadrons of additional aircraft and many American ships were alerted and began moving toward Southeast Asia to comply with the president's orders to stop the NVA invasion. Within sixty days, U.S. forces available for use in Vietnam would increase by one hundred B-52s, hundreds of tactical warplanes, four additional aircraft carriers, and thirty-two more combat ships.

As the Nixon administration responded to the initial North Vietnamese attack and the NVA pounded the 3rd ARVN Division in and around Quang Tri, additional NVA forces struck in Military Region III. The 24th and 271st NVA regiments attacked elements of the 25th ARVN Division in several firebases near the Cambodian border in northern Tay Ninh Province. As in Quang Tri, the NVA attacked with infantry and tanks (including American-made M-41s previously captured from ARVN forces). Although the South Vietnamese were surprised at the intensity of the battles and the use of tanks, the attacks themselves coincided with previous expectations that any significant NVA move in the region would be aimed at Tay Ninh.[48] However, these attacks proved to be only a diversion, designed to mask the movement of three NVA divisions (totaling over 35,000 NVA troops, counting artillery and other support elements) to final assault positions in preparation for the main attack down Route 13 through Loc Ninh and An Loc toward Saigon.[49] The NVA plan called for the 5th VC Division to begin the campaign by capturing Loc Ninh, the northernmost town in Binh Long Province. Once Loc Ninh was secured, the 9th VC Division, considered one of the elite NVA divisions, would take An Loc. Concurrently, the 7th NVA Division would cut Route 13 south of An Loc to interdict any attempts to resupply or reinforce the city.

At 0650 on the morning of 5 April, the 5th VC Division crossed the Cambodian border and attacked Loc Ninh with infantry and tanks supported by heavy artillery fire (see map 10). Only the effective employment of tactical air strikes prevented the defenders from the 9th ARVN Regiment, 5th ARVN Division, from being completely overrun. On the morning of 6 April, the NVA attacked again. Repeated air strikes by fighter-bombers and close support by AC-130 Spectre gunships broke the first attack and two others that followed. However, the sheer force of NVA numbers prevailed, and the defenders were eventually overwhelmed. Only one hundred ARVN soldiers escaped to An Loc, and six of seven U.S. advisers were killed or captured.[50]

After overrunning two ARVN firebases manned by Task Force 52 south of Loc Ninh, near the junction of Routes 13 and 17, the NVA moved on An Loc. As the attacks on Loc Ninh and TF 52 unfolded, Maj. Gen. James F. Hollingsworth, commander of Third Regional Assistance Command, came to the conclusion that An Loc, not Tay Ninh, was the primary objective of the NVA's main attack. He and his counterpart, Lt. Gen. Nguyen Van Minh, III Corps commander, convinced President Thieu that if An Loc fell, the NVA forces would have very little between them and Saigon. Accordingly, the decision was made to hold An Loc at all costs; Thieu radioed the senior ARVN officers in An Loc that the city would be "defended to the death."[51]

As the ARVN forces in An Loc girded for the coming attack, the defenders around Quang Tri attempted to hold the line against increasingly heavy enemy pressure. The loss of Camp Carroll and Mai Loc had initially taken a heavy toll on South Vietnamese morale, but spirits improved with every successful defense against the repeated NVA attacks. Additionally, reinforcements were received with the arrival in Quang Tri of the 369th Marine Brigade and the 1st, 4th, and 5th Ranger groups. With these new forces, General Lam began to contemplate a counterattack. General Giai, however, disagreed and strongly urged that the new troops be used to reinforce the defensive line. By this time, Giai's span of control included nine brigades (two regiments of his own, two marine brigades, four ranger groups, and one armor brigade, plus all the territorial forces), which totaled twenty-three

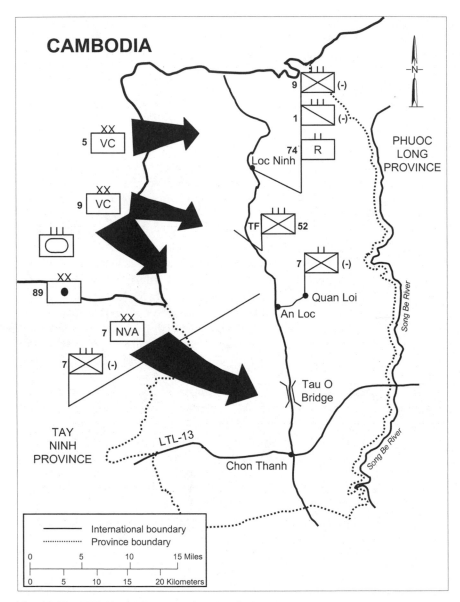

Map 10. The 1972 North Vietnamese invasion, III Corps.

battalions. Giai, who had been a colonel commanding a regiment just the previous year, was now hopelessly overburdened with the task of controlling so many units. General Lam could have remedied the situation by placing I Corps in control of the marine elements under the Marine Division, and by giving the Marine Division and the Ranger Command separate responsibility for one sector each on the defensive line. However, Lam did none of these things, and Giai retained the burden for the conduct of the entire defense of the Quang Tri area, a situation that contributed to the coming disaster.

By 10 April, limited ARVN successes had convinced Lam, despite the continued protests from General Giai, that he was right about the advisability of conducting a counterattack. He wanted to launch an attack across the Cua Viet River to retake all the lost territory between the river and the DMZ. After much discussion, the idea was discarded because it would draw too many troops away from the defensive line. Lam then decided that the counterattack should be focused on reestablishing the western portion of the original defensive line, retaking Cam Lo, Camp Carroll, and Mai Loc in the process. The counteroffensive, called Quang Trung 729, was scheduled to begin on 14 April.

As Lam's forces prepared for the counterattack in I Corps, the NVA hit An Loc with everything it had. On 7 April, elements of the 9th VC Division seized the Quan Loi airstrip, just three kilometers southeast of An Loc. The move, coupled with the closing of Route 13 south of the city by the 7th NVA Division, meant that An Loc was surrounded and cut off from the outside; a prolonged siege began. General Hollingsworth urged General Minh to order the 1st Airborne Brigade to attack north to secure Route 13, but when members of the brigade were inserted along the highway, they came under heavy attack from the entrenched NVA. Unable to make any significant progress up the road, they were subsequently airlifted by helicopter to landing zones east of An Loc, where they provided much-needed reinforcement for the defenders inside the city.

Having cut off the South Vietnamese in An Loc from further ground reinforcement and resupply, the NVA launched an all-out attack. During the early morning hours of 13 April, the Communists began a massive artillery preparation. A total of seven thousand shells and rockets would fall on the city during the next fifteen hours, a rate of one round every eight seconds.[52] Shortly after dawn, the NVA gunners shifted their fire and the Communists launched a combined tank and infantry attack from the northeast. Soviet-made T-54s and PT-76s moved down the main north-south street toward the 5th ARVN Division command post in the middle of the town. The panic-stricken South Vietnamese forces, most of whom had never before confronted tanks in battle, fell back in the face of the NVA attack. The situation was stabilized somewhat by two factors. First, the NVA was extremely inept in its coordination of armor and infantry in the attack. The tanks attacked without infantry support, persisted in advancing along roads when cross-country movement would have been safer, and, when speed and initiative were called for, proceeded slowly and indecisively. This failure to apply the most basic tenets of combined arms tactics left the NVA tanks unprotected against the ARVN defenders, who found them easy prey for their M-72 light antitank weapons (LAWs) once they overcame the initial shock of facing tanks in the attack.[53]

The more important factor in thwarting the initial and subsequent attacks on An Loc was the well-executed air support that struck the enemy well forward of the ARVN positions and prevented the NVA from reinforcing its initial successes in the northern part of the city. While U.S. Air Force, Navy, and Marine Corps fighter-bombers dropped their ordnance on NVA forces massing around the city for the attack, the ARVN forces, supported by U.S. Army AH-1G Cobra attack helicopters and Air Force AC-119K Stinger and AC-130 Spectre gunships, were able to defend against the reduced number of NVA infantry and tanks that escaped the air strikes.[54] This pattern of air support, which continued for the next three months, repeatedly proved to be the difference between victory and defeat for the South Vietnamese defenders.

For the next two days, battle raged in An Loc, marked by intense house-to-house fighting and constant enemy artillery bombardment of the South Vietnamese defensive positions. While the battle continued inside the city, General Hollingsworth directed B-52 strikes on NVA staging areas just outside the city. Each B-52 strike, code-named Arc Light, consisted of three aircraft, each carrying 108 500-pound conventional bombs (MK-82s). One such strike caught an entire battalion in the open before it reached the northwest approach to the city, killing an estimated one hundred attackers, destroying three tanks, and breaking the back of the NVA attack on that part of An Loc.[55] The defenders continued to pound the NVA with tactical airpower and B-52 strikes. Brig. Gen. John R. McGiffert, deputy commanding general, Third Regional Assistance Command, said of the importance of the air strikes after the battle, "I really believe that without these the city would have fallen, because I think the infantry would have gotten in with the tanks."[56] During the first two weeks of the battle for An Loc, over 2,500 air strikes were flown in and around the city in support of the South Vietnamese defenders.[57] The key to the success of these missions was that U.S. advisers on the ground in An Loc were able to coordinate with the forward air controllers to make maximum use of the strikes.

Despite the devastating effect of U.S. airpower, the NVA continued to attack An Loc for the next three days. The battle was fought at close quarters, with the NVA attackers almost taking the 5th ARVN Division command post twice, but still ARVN held. General Hollingsworth reported on 16 April to General Abrams that "there was a great battle at An Loc today, perhaps the greatest of this campaign. The enemy hit us hard all day long with all he could muster—and we threw it back at him. The forces in An Loc realized that they had to fight and they fought well."[58]

President Thieu, seeing that he had to hold An Loc to prevent a direct thrust on Saigon, ordered the 21st ARVN Division to move from its base in the Mekong Delta to reinforce III Corps forces. General Minh immediately ordered the 21st to attack north from Lai Khe to open Route 13 to An Loc. The division moved to Lai Khe and launched their attack, but quickly ran into heavy resistance from the entrenched 7th NVA Division. The North Vietnamese would tie the South Vietnamese forces down for the next two months, blocking any relief of An Loc by road.

Back in the city itself, there was a momentary lull in the battle. The enemy's initial plan to seize An Loc had been thwarted. The main attack, conducted by the 9th VC Division, supported by the 3rd and 5th battalions of the 203rd Tank Regiment, was supposed to result in the occupation of the city by 20 April.[59] However, the attack had been unsuccessful—largely due to the continuous pounding by B-52s, fighter-bombers, AC-130 Spectre gunships, and attack helicopters.

Although they had stymied the NVA's first attempt to take the city, the South Vietnamese defenders were in trouble. Col. William Miller, senior adviser to Brig. Gen. Le Van Hung, commander of the 5th ARVN Division inside An Loc, reported to General Hollingsworth on 17 April that the city continued to sustain extremely heavy shelling and that he thought the NVA forces were girding themselves for another all-out assault. He was very pessimistic regarding the capability of ARVN to carry on: "The division is tired and worn out; supplies minimal, casualties continue to mount, medical supplies are low; wounded a major problem, mass burials of military and civilians, morale at a low ebb. In spite of incurring heavy losses from U.S. air strikes, the enemy continues to persist."[60]

On 19 April, the NVA launched its second full-scale attack on the city with five regiments. The battle raged for three days under a continuous bombardment. The fighting was intense, but tactical air support and B-52s permitted the defenders to stave off the NVA attackers, although ARVN now held only a very small area in the southern portion of the city. The South Vietnamese defenders, completely surrounded and under constant artillery fire, lived underground and ventured outside their trenches and bunkers only at great risk. One adviser put the odds of surviving five minutes outside in the open at fifty-fifty.[61] By the end of April, the South Vietnamese defenders held An Loc, but it was a tenuous foothold at best.

While South Vietnamese forces in Quang Tri and An Loc fought for their very survival against the initial attacks by the NVA in their sectors, Lt. Gen. Ngo Dzu, II Corps commander, and his adviser, Mr. John Paul Vann, made preparations for what they were sure would be an imminent Communist attack in Military Region II. They had been watching the enemy buildup in Base Area 609 in the tri-border area of Vietnam, Cambodia, and Laos since the first of the year and were increasingly alarmed at reports of tanks, heavy artillery, and antiaircraft weapons seen moving through the area. Accordingly, they called for B-52 and tactical air strikes on the base area and began bolstering the defenses of the provincial capitals of Kontum and Pleiku. Early in February, they moved the 22nd Infantry Division headquarters and the 47th Regiment from their rear base in Binh Dinh Province to the Tan Canh-Dak To area to join the 42nd Regiment, which had been deployed there for some time. The purpose of the move was to put the better part of an ARVN division between the NVA staging areas and the town of Kontum.

While Dzu and Vann made preparations to counter the impending NVA attack, the Communist forces prepared to launch the offensive in MR II. Under control of the B-3 Front, the 2nd, 3rd, and 320th NVA divisions, totaling more than twenty thousand troops and four hundred supporting tanks, assumed attack positions.[62] Although contacts with the enemy increased in February and early March, the NVA did not launch an all-out attack. On 30 March, the NVA began placing heavy artillery fire on the FSBs lining the "Rocket Ridge" area west of Kontum and

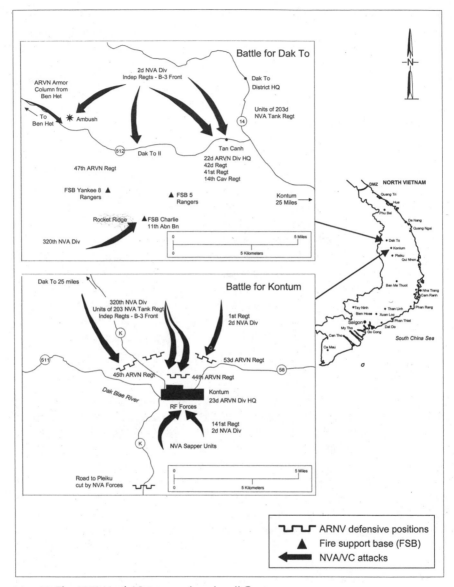

Map 11. The 1972 North Vietnamese invasion, II Corps.

southwest of Tan Canh, but still the NVA did not launch the massive ground attacks that were underway in MRs I and III. II Corps intelligence analysts felt at the time that "the NVA have had a great difficulty coordinating, and it didn't appear as if they had everything set up, ready to go."[63] (See map 11.)

On 3 April, sappers attacked the airfield at Phung Hoang, near Dak To. A soldier from the 400th Sapper Regiment (NVA) who was taken prisoner during this assault indicated that the B-3 Front campaign in MR II, called "*Truong Song Chuyen Minh*" (Western Mountains Rise Up), was to be conducted in two phases. In Phase I, NVA forces were to destroy ARVN military bases in Kontum Province and open routes for further enemy movement into the region. During Phase II, the NVA would take Ben Het, Dak To, Tan Canh, and eventually the town of Kontum.[64] The pattern of artillery attacks and light ground probes continued for a number of days as the NVA forces maneuvered to their final attack positions. Meanwhile, Dzu and Vann kept the pressure on the NVA with B-52 and tactical air strikes.

On 11 April, the NVA launched its offensive in MR II with a heavy attack on FSBs Charlie, Six, Zulu, and Yankee, as well as the Ben Het Ranger Camp west of Dak To. At the same time, the NVA attempted to interdict the vital supply line connecting the cities of Qui Nhon and Pleiku. Apparently, the Communists were trying to separate the coast from the Central Highlands in order to deny Saigon the ability to reinforce and resupply South Vietnamese forces in the Highlands. On 14 April, ARVN abandoned FSB Charlie under heavy enemy pressure, but the withdrawal was orderly and the South Vietnamese made the NVA pay dearly for its victory. A U.S. forward air controller reported, "The people on Charlie were far outnumbered, but they held on. . . . They never did break. They made the reds take bunker by bunker. They just did not give up and run. . . ."[65]

Unfortunately, such praiseworthy performance by ARVN would not always be the case during the coming heavy action. By 20 April, Tan Quan and Hoai An, district capitals in Binh Dinh Province, had fallen to the NVA attackers. On 23 April, the NVA struck Tan Canh, the headquarters of the ARVN 22nd Division, in full force with tanks, infantry, and artillery. The NVA also used Soviet-made AT-3 "Sagger" wire-guided antitank missiles for the first time in South Vietnam. Simultaneously, the NVA cut Route 14 in three places above Dak To and south of Tan Canh, effectively isolating Tan Canh and Dak To from the town of Kontum. At this point, according to Col. Phillip Kaplan, senior adviser to the 22nd Division, Col. Le Duc Dat, the commander, broke under the pressure. "Dat was really demoralized," Kaplan recalled, reporting that Dat said, "We're going to lose, we're going to be overrun, we will all be killed or captured."[66] Aware that Dat still had 1,200 soldiers inside the compound, Kaplan urged him to hold on, but Dat was paralyzed by fear and so were his soldiers. On 24 April, as the ARVN defenders waited terrified in their bunkers, the Communists surrounded Tan Canh and took the base with little difficulty, entering the 22nd Division command post virtually unopposed. Despite the ever-present fighter-bombers and Spectre gunships, ARVN had collapsed; shortly thereafter the NVA took Dak To. A senior U.S. Army adviser later described the situation: "I think the reason they broke and ran initially was the surprise of the tanks. They had never fought tanks before. They had plenty of anti-tank devices, but no one could visualize a bunch of T-54s and T-59s. . . . The best units when completely surprised might run and break."[67]

The 22nd Division, not among the best ARVN units, succumbed to the psychological impact of the intense attacks. As the South Vietnamese fled in terror from the Tan Canh-Dak To area, they abandoned twenty-three 155-mm howitzers, ten M-41 tanks, and 16,000 rounds of ammunition to the enemy. After these battles and the subsequent retreat, the 22nd ARVN Division ceased to be a combat effective unit, and the division commander was ultimately relieved. The only thing that had slowed the enemy assault was tactical airpower. U.S. casualties among the 22nd Division advisory personnel during these battles were four KIA, one WIA, and ten missing in action; Kaplan and eight of his fellow advisers were evacuated by U.S. helicopters as the NVA overran the South Vietnamese positions at Tan Canh.[68] While the NVA took Dak To, additional Communist forces cut Route 1, drove most of the South Vietnamese units guarding the road from their bases, and effectively gained control over almost all of Binh Dinh Province.

As the NVA pursued the attacks against An Loc and MR II, it continued to increase the pressure in Quang Tri. General Lam, I Corps commander, had initiated Operation Quang Trung 729 on 14 April. Rather than the counteroffensive Lam unrealistically hoped for, the operation was little more than a continuation of the same action that had been ongoing. The South Vietnamese forces were already in contact with the NVA and were reluctant to advance. By the end of the week, ARVN had moved forward less than five hundred meters from the line of departure. As one former ARVN general wrote after the war, "QUANG TRUNG did not resemble an offensive, but rather had settled into a costly battle of attrition in place in which the ARVN battalions were steadily reduced in strength and effectiveness by the enemy's deadly artillery fire."[69] South Vietnamese morale in I Corps plummeted.

New command and control problems surfaced. The Marine Division headquarters and the Ranger Command, both of which continued to be left out of the command and control structure, nevertheless questioned General Giai's orders and even issued directives and orders counter to those given by Giai, thereby complicating and confusing the chain of command in I Corps and inhibiting the conduct of an effective defense against the NVA attacks. On 18 April, the NVA began a concerted effort to take Quang Tri with a major attack against the western sector of the 3rd Division. Much as had happened in An Loc, U.S. tactical air support and B-52s broke the back of the attack and gave ARVN a good opportunity to counterattack. However, the South Vietnamese refused to seize the moment and remained in their bunkers.

The following week the defensive line at Dong Ha and along the Cua Viet River collapsed, not because of enemy action, but as a result of ARVN panic. The commander of the 1st Armored Brigade ordered his 20th Tank Squadron on the Cua Viet line to reposition to the south along Route 1 in order to clear the enemy elements there. The ARVN troops along the line, seeing the tanks moving south, panicked and broke ranks, fleeing down the highway toward Quang Tri. The Cua Viet defense, which had been very effective for nearly a month, was abandoned without a fight. The 3rd Division commander learned of the debacle too late to do anything and attempted to reestablish a defensive line west of Quang Tri and north of the Thach Han River.

During the days that followed, the defenders, already shaken, were further demoralized by their continual pounding by NVA artilleiy. On 27 April, the NVA, trying to take advantage of worsening weather, initiated a new push to take the city of Quang Tri. For the entire day, virtually all units of the 3rd ARVN Division were in close contact with the enemy. The next day, enemy tanks approached the Quang Tri Bridge, only two kilometers southwest of the city. Frightened by the tanks, the South Vietnamese defenders quickly lost their discipline and abandoned their positions, fleeing south along Route 1.

Meanwhile, elsewhere on the defensive line, enemy artillery and repeated ground attacks had rendered the 57th Regiment combat ineffective. On 30 April, General Giai decided that his defensive line was untenable and ordered his forces to prepare to withdraw south of the Thach Han River, leaving the 147th Marine Brigade the only unit north of the river. The next morning, as the units were preparing to move, General Lam called General Giai and countermanded the division commander's order, saying that the 3rd Division and its attached units were to remain where they were and hold their positions at all costs. The last-minute change in orders resulted in total chaos.[70] Some units had already moved to their new positions, others were on the way, and in still others, the unit commanders refused to give their troops the new orders. Consequently, the 3rd ARVN Division defense totally collapsed. Units to the north of the river streamed back across and "continued their way south with the uncontainable force of a flood over a broken dam."[71] The mechanized elements that reached Quang Tri Bridge were unable to cross, because the bridge had already been destroyed in the confusion. They left their vehicles and equipment and forded the river on foot. On the southern bank of the river, those soldiers in the infantry units that had established new positions along the river, seeing the ever-growing throng of ARVN soldiers, tanks, and vehicles heading south at a high speed, deserted their positions and joined the flood of humanity running from the NVA.

As tanks and vehicles ran out of gas, the drivers and crews abandoned them and continued on foot. The commander of the 147th Marine Brigade, still north of the river and the only unit left defending the city, decided for himself that the situation was hopeless and ordered his unit to withdraw, leaving the 3rd Division commander and his skeletal staff all alone in the undefended city. General Giai and his staff officers then boarded three armored personnel carriers and attempted to catch up with their fleeing troops. U.S. helicopters came in to rescue the division's advisory personnel and their Vietnamese employees. Unable to join his troops, Giai's party returned to the old command post, where they were also picked up by U.S. helicopters. When the NVA entered the city, Quang Tri became the first provincial capital to fall into Communist hands during the war. General Giai was subsequently relieved and court-martialed for dereliction of duty and abandoning his division. Many Americans thought that General Lam should have been court-martialed, as well, but Giai became the scapegoat for the entire debacle in Military Region I.

During the capture of the capital, NVA gunners targeted the mass of military and civilian humanity streaming down Route 1, which became known as "Terror Boulevard." By 2 May, the entire province of Quang Tri was in NVA hands, and the Communists could turn their attention on Thua Thien Province and the imperial capital at Hue. Abrams, doubting that Kontum and Hue could hold, cabled Washington that "the senior [South Vietnamese] leadership had begun to bend and in some cases break . . . losing its will, and cannot be depended on to take the measures necessary to stand and fight."[72]

STALEMATE IN PARIS AND OPERATION LINEBACKER

That same day, 2 May, Kissinger again met secretly with Le Duc Tho in Paris. The meeting was a disaster. Kissinger attempted to persuade the North Vietnamese to agree to a cease-fire and a mutual troop withdrawal, but he was not negotiating from a position of strength, because the North Vietnamese held all the cards. The South Vietnamese were under fire throughout the country: Quang Tri had fallen the day before, Kontum was surrounded, Loc Ninh had fallen, An Loc was besieged, and Saigon was bracing for a direct attack. Malcolm M. Brown of the *New York Times* reported on 15 April that the previous twenty-four hours had seen 107 NVA-initiated actions in South Vietnam, the highest such figure since the Communists' Tet offensive in 1968.[73]

The North Vietnamese were winning on every front, and a South Vietnamese collapse appeared imminent. After a three-hour diatribe about American treachery and North Vietnamese heroism, the North Vietnamese negotiators demanded the immediate resignation of Thieu and abandonment of Vietnamization. According to Kissinger, the Communists had ceased to negotiate and were dictating terms.[74] The meeting adjourned with nothing accomplished. Kissinger had previously counseled the president to delay an all-out response to the North Vietnamese until all diplomatic avenues had been exhausted, but on his return to Washington, he told the president that, in his opinion, the North Vietnamese in Paris believed that the complete rout of the South Vietnamese was only days or weeks away and that the situation was beyond U.S. capacity to reverse by retaliation. When Nixon had sent Kissinger to Paris, he directed him to tell the North Vietnamese to cease the invasion and "Settle or else!"[75] Now Kissinger was back, relating the arrogance and recalcitrance of the North Vietnamese negotiators; he advised the president that any U.S. retaliation "had to provide a shock that would give the North pause and rally the South."[76] However, he warned Nixon that he might have to cancel the upcoming U.S.-Soviet summit.

While Kissinger was in Paris, the Soviet leader, Leonid Brezhnev, had sent the president a message warning against any U.S. action in Vietnam that might imperil the planned meeting of the two world leaders. General Haig counseled the president to stand tough. He told Nixon that, in his opinion, "The Russians want detente more than they need Hanoi. Let them cancel the summit if they don't like our policy. The key issue is not to lose the war; every other question is subordinate."[77] Having received the same counsel from his trusted friend John Connally, former governor of Texas, Nixon sent Brezhnev a strong message explaining that in light of the Soviet supplies that had made the North Vietnamese offensive possible, a strong U.S. response was only to be expected. He was in effect gambling with the summit and detente. Nixon pondered over his options for several days, but by 8 May, in what Kissinger described as "one of the finest hours of Nixon's Presidency," he had decided what to do.[78] That night, he announced his decision to the nation. He began by declaring that air operations against North Vietnam would be extended indefinitely. He then dropped a bombshell: "There is only one way to stop the killing. That is to keep the weapons of war out of the hands of the international outlaws of North Vietnam." To that end, "all entrances to North Vietnamese ports will be mined. . . . Rail and all other communications will be cut off to the maximum extent possible. Air and naval strikes against military targets in North Vietnam will continue."[79]

As Nixon spoke, naval attack planes took off from the aircraft carrier *Coral Sea* to mine Haiphong harbor. Over the next three days, a total of eleven thousand mines were laid in North Vietnamese waters as part of Operation Pocket Money. At the same time, Nixon ordered a full-scale air campaign against North Vietnam to destroy the ability of the NVA to continue the attack into South Vietnam. The purpose of this operation, code-named Linebacker, was the destruction of war-related industry and support infrastructure in North Vietnam, including the internal transportation system.[80] What resulted was one of the most effective bombing campaigns of the entire war. Over the next four months, U.S. planes struck roads, bridges, rail lines, troop bases, and supply depots, dropping more than 155,548 tons of ordnance on North Vietnam.[81]

Nixon's actions and the subsequent bombing campaign were condemned in the U.S. news media, which almost universally predicted that the president's announcement would doom the summit meeting. Nixon sent a four-page letter to Brezhnev explaining his reasons for stepping up the air campaign against Hanoi and arguing that events in Vietnam should not affect the summit. Soviet ambassador Anatoly Dobrynin informed the White House that the summit would take place as scheduled. Less than a week after these events, Nixon and Kissinger flew to Moscow for the summit meeting.[82] Nixon had won his gamble and at the same time put Moscow on notice that he was prepared to do whatever he had to do to keep South Vietnam from going under.

As Nixon escalated the war against the North Vietnamese homeland and played power politics with the Soviets, the situation in South Vietnam worsened. While Quang Tri was in the process of going under, the NVA in Binh Long Province made preparations for its third major attack on An Loc. On 6 May, an NVA prisoner from the 9th VC Division informed his ARVN captors that his division commander had been reprimanded for not taking An Loc in April and that the 5th VC Division commander had boasted that his troops would take the city in three days.[83] Other intelligence indicated that the E6, 174th, and 275th regiments of the 5th VC Division would attack from the east, supported by the 271st and 272nd regiments of the 9th VC Division and the 141st and 165th regiments of the 7th NVA Division. Defending against these seven regiments were barely 4,000 ARVN troops, of which at least 1,000 were already wounded. The advisers in the city doubted that ARVN could hold against another determined attack.[84] General Hollingsworth believed that the NVA was readying for a major push on An Loc; he later wrote: "I spent many hours during the course of the next few days encouraging the province chief [Col. Tran Van Nhut], the division commander [General Hung], and their advisers to hold their positions. My attempts to belittle the capability of the enemy and to strengthen friendly forces' morale seemed almost hopeless. Enemy positions and movements, intensity of antiaircraft fire, and the increase in enemy artillery and rockets against An Loc pointed to an imminent all-out attack."[85]

Preparations for the attack began on 9 May when the NVA initiated a two-day artillery barrage that far exceeded any previous attacks. The artillery preparation increased at 0035 on 11 May and for the next four hours, seven thousand rounds (or one shell every five seconds) fell on the ARVN positions inside the city.[86] At 0430 there began a thirty minute lull in the firing, but the attack started again in earnest at 0500. During the next twelve hours ten thousand artillery rounds struck the city.[87] Under cover of these fires, the NVA commenced its ground assault from all sides of the city, with the main attacks in the north and northwest. The tanks preceded the infantry and forged salients in the ARVN lines; the NVA infantry then attempted to widen these incursions. The NVA plan was to join the two salients, thereby separating the defenders into enclaves that could be defeated in detail. Once again, the only thing that saved the day was U.S. airpower. MACV declared the situation in An Loc a tactical emergency, resulting in a sharp surge of close air support. U.S. Air Force, Navy, and Marine aircraft handlers loaded all available ordnance, as aircraft made rapid turnarounds to get back into the air over An Loc in support of the defenders. The situation was so critical that the 49th Tactical Fighter Wing self-deployed from its home base in New Mexico, arrived at Takhli Air Base, Thailand, on 10 May, and went into action over An Loc the next day without normal familiarization or safety-check flights.

During the course of the battle on 11 May, 297 sorties of tactical air support were flown in support of the An Loc defense. Additionally, Cobra attack helicopters and Spectre gunships joined in the battle. While these aircraft attempted to deal with the NVA troops in close contact with ARVN, General Hollingsworth directed a total of thirty B-52 strikes against NVA staging areas during a twenty-four-hour period beginning on that morning. The battle lasted for four more days, but what one adviser termed the "almost ritualistic pattern of action and reaction" was beginning to take a heavy toll on the attackers as well as the defenders.[88] The NVA's repeated attempts to take An Loc cost the Communists dearly. Nearly their entire armored force had been destroyed, and the continual aerial bombardment had destroyed or decimated entire infantry units. The beleaguered defenders had held the city against overwhelming odds. If the third attack on An Loc represented the NVA high tide, the attack's failure represented a shift in the battle. General Hollingsworth concluded, "The enemy had lost his capability for further offensive actions in Binh Long Province."[89]

While these events were occurring in An Loc, the NVA in Military Region II, having captured Tan Canh and Dak To, turned their attention to taking Kontum. The town was defended by the 23rd ARVN Division, which had been moved from its previous base at Ban Me Thuot. The enemy pressure had taken its toll on General Dzu, the II Corps commander. He doubted that his forces could defend the city and spent his time calling President Thieu for guidance. Thieu, believing that Dzu had lost his nerve, would eventually replace him on 10 May with Maj. Gen. Nguyen Van Toan.

Col. Ly Tong Ba, commander of the 23rd ARVN, was placed in charge of the Kontum defense. He actually commanded only one regiment, the 53rd, but had operational control over four ranger battalions, an airborne brigade, and territorial forces. These units tended to maintain communication channels with their parent organizations, thus Colonel Ba faced the same command and control difficulties that had bedeviled General Giai at Quang Tri. The ranger battalions were arrayed in blocking positions at Vo Dinh, twenty kilometers northwest of Kontum, and at Polei Kleng, a border ranger camp. On 1 May, the units at Vo Dinh came under attack, and the ranger group commander ordered them to withdraw to Ngo Trang, just thirteen kilometers from Kontum. On 9 May, Polei Kleng fell to a massive tank-infantry assault. By the end of the second week in May, the NVA was poised around Kontum. On 14 May, the 320th NVA Division began the attack, but the initial assault was broken up when the defenders destroyed the lead NVA tanks. However, the attack continued for the rest of the day, and by nightfall an NVA battalion had broken through a gap between two of the defending regiments. Two preplanned B-52 strikes were used to blunt this penetration, killing several hundred NVA attackers. Kontum had been saved for the time being, but it had come very close to falling. Over the next two weeks, the ARVN defenders, supported by B-52s and tactical air support, defeated several more NVA attempts to take the town. Colonel Ba launched several limited offensive operations in the areas north and northwest of the city within range of ARVN artillery.

On 21 May, General Toan, the new corps commander, initiated a major effort to clear Route 14 from Pleiku north to Kontum. Despite U.S. air support, the II Corps relief column was unsuccessful in opening the road to Kontum. On 25 May, the NVA made a last-ditch attempt to take the provincial capital. The monsoon season was starting, and the Communists needed to achieve a quick victory or withdraw for refitting and replenishment. They began their attack with an extensive artillery preparation, followed by two sapper battalion attacks. From the north and northeast, the enemy tanks and infantry attacked and forged a penetration in the ARVN lines. The next day, the Communists tried to reinforce their success, but B-52s once again blunted the NVA effort. On 27 May, two NVA regiments and a tank company attacked the 44th ARVN Regiment. The South Vietnamese defenders fought back, halting the attack, but the NVA retained its position inside the ARVN lines, and by the night of 28 May, ARVN and the NVA were engaged in hand-to-hand, house-to-house fighting. However, the NVA started to experience severe resupply problems, and the attrition caused by air strikes and gunships began to take its toll.

Flying in support of the South Vietnamese for the first time were U.S. Army UH-1B helicopters, armed with the experimental airborne TOW (tube-launched, optically tracked, wire-guided) missiles. John Paul Vann, the II Corps senior adviser, had lobbied for and received operational control of a test unit, the 1st Aerial TOW Team, from Fort Lewis, Washington, which had been rushed to South Vietnam when the offensive began. The unit destroyed twenty-four tanks during the first three days of its deployment at Kontum.[90] Having successfully defended the town, Colonel Ba ordered a counterattack, which regained most of the lost territory in and around Kontum. The provincial capital was saved again. By the end of July, other II Corps units took back most of the areas previously taken by the NVA. However, Vann, who had played such a key role in the victory in II Corps, would not get to see the fruits of his labor because he was killed in a helicopter crash on 9 June; he was succeeded by Brig. Gen. Michael Healy.

TURNING THE TIDE IN I CORPS

As the battles at An Loc and Kontum unfolded, the NVA continued its assault in MR I. During the month of April, the 1st ARVN fought back several attempts by the 324B NVA Division to take the western and southwestern approaches to Hue. These battles were inconclusive, but the ARVN defenders managed to forge a defensive line in the foothills west of Hue that extended from Camp Evans in the north, through FSB Rakkasan, then southeast through FSBs Bastogne and Checkmate to link up with FSB Birmingham. Bastogne and Checkmate were the keys to this defensive line because they were all that stood between NVA forces in the west and Hue. During the last two weeks of April, these critical positions came under repeated heavy enemy attacks that left the ARVN strength at both firebases at less than 50 percent. Only tactical air support prevented the NVA from overrunning the positions. On 28 April, the sheer weight of the NVA attack by the 29th and 803rd regiments of the 324B NVA Division overwhelmed the defenders at FSB Bastogne; the survivors fled to the east. With the fall of Bastogne, FSB Checkmate became vulnerable and its defenders were ordered to evacuate. The loss of the two bases exposed Hue to a direct enemy attack.

By the first of May, South Vietnam's strategic position was extremely precarious. After more than a month of constant heavy fighting that ranged the length of the country, the South Vietnamese were close to breaking. They had lost Quang Tri, Tan Canh, and Dak To; Kontum faced an imminent attack; and An Loc was in the midst of a battle for its very life. Saigon entered a dark hour, and national morale fell to an all-time low. The situation was particularly bleak in I Corps; the fall of Quang Tri had been a serious psychological blow to both the military and the local population. The continuing flow of terrified refugees south down Route 1 toward Da Nang had a debilitating effect on the defenders at Hue. Additionally, throngs of deserters and dispirited troops, some from units that no longer existed, "roamed about, haggard, unruly and craving for food"; their presence added to the atmosphere of terror and chaos that reigned throughout Hue.[91]

President Thieu realized that he was in danger of losing Military Region I in its entirety. Accordingly, he replaced General Lam with Lt. Gen. Ngo Quang Truong, commander of IV Corps in the Mekong Delta. Truong, a well-respected officer, had previously served in Military Region I and knew the area well. Upon arriving in the region, he immediately established a forward headquarters at Hue to take personal charge of the coming battle. With his senior U.S. adviser, Maj. Gen. Frederic J. Kroesen (later succeeded by Maj. Gen. Howard H. Cooksey), Truong took steps to stabilize the situation, establishing clear-cut lines of command and assigning missions to each I Corps subordinate unit. Using the three brigades of the Marine Division and the two regiments of the 1st ARVN Division, Truong established an in-depth defense around Hue, focusing on blocking the NVA approaches from the west and north. At the same time, he reestablished control inside the city, restoring discipline and order, picking up stragglers and deserters, and assisting the civilian population and refugees. Truong requested and received reinforcements in the form of the two airborne brigades, which were redeployed from other battle areas in Military Regions II and III.

Once General Truong had stabilized the situation in MR I, he ordered his forces to launch a series of limited counterattacks to catch the North Vietnamese off balance. These operations, conducted during the latter part of May and June by heliborne assaults and amphibious landings, and supported by very effective tactical air strikes by U.S. Air Force and Navy fighter-bombers, achieved the desired result. The South Vietnamese successfully retook FSBs Bastogne and Checkmate, and several other key areas previously captured by the NVA. These successes greatly boosted South Vietnamese morale in the region. On 21 May, the NVA attacked marine positions along the My Chanh River. The marines there held, while the Marine Division launched an amphibious landing at My Thuy, ten kilometers north of the defensive line, and a heliborne assault into Co Luy, six kilometers west of the coastline. After several days of operations behind NVA lines, the marines returned to their positions along the My Chanh. By the end of May, Truong and his forces had regained the initiative and, with the arrival of an airborne brigade as reinforcements, the I Corps defense had been restored to good shape.

Truong instituted a refitting and retraining program to bolster those South Vietnamese units that had suffered severe losses or had disintegrated during the first two months of the NVA offensive. The ARVN casualties and materiel losses had been severe. The 1st Armored Brigade alone had sustained 1,171 casualties and lost 43 M-48 tanks, 66 M-41 tanks, and 103 M-113 armored personnel carriers.[92]

In addition to the tank losses, I Corps had lost 140 artillery pieces, the equivalent of ten ARVN artillery battalions. The 3rd ARVN Division had been left with only a skeletal staff, and the remaining two regiments and the ranger battalions had all lost at least half of their original strength. Truong called on Saigon for assistance in putting his forces back together. In response, the ARVN Central Logistics Command and MACV accomplished almost superhuman efforts in replacing the lost equipment. Truong ordered an accelerated training program for the large number of arriving personnel replacements. He also directed that certain units, such as the 20th Tank Squadron, undergo unit retraining.

Having reconstituted his forces and stabilized the tactical situation, he prepared an audacious plan to retake Quang Tri. When Truong presented his plan to President Thieu, he was told that it was too ambitious and that he was to conduct a more limited spoiling attack instead. Upset with this decision, Truong returned to Hue very discouraged. The next day, he flew to Saigon and presented a stronger case for his plan, securing Thieu's reluctant approval.

On 28 June, Truong launched Lam Son 72, a two-pronged counteroffensive in which the Airborne Division made the main attack along the southwest side of Route 1 toward La Vang, accompanied by a supporting attack by the Marine Division along Route 555 toward Trieu Phong. While the paratroopers and marines attacked north, the 1st ARVN Division conducted operations to pin down NVA forces southwest of Hue and the 2nd ARVN Division conducted search-and-destroy operations in Quang Tin and Quang Ngai provinces. The 3rd ARVN Division, having completed its reconstitution and refitting, assumed responsibility for the defense of Da Nang.

The attack north initially made progress, but as the South Vietnamese forces approached the Thach Han River, NVA resistance became heavier. Nevertheless, on 7 July, the first airborne elements reached the outskirts of Quang Tri City. The NVA defenders responded violently and it became clear that the Communists were planning to defend the city to the last man. As General Truong later explained, "Quang Tri City suddenly became a 'cause celebre' . . . a symbol and a major challenge."[93] Determined to hold the city at all costs, the NVA forces reinforced their defenses, thus stalling the ARVN drive. By then, elements of six NVA divisions occupied Quang Tri and Thua Thien provinces. Truong modified his plan, but the retaking of Quang Tri against such difficult odds became a long, laborious process that lasted into September. Using tactical air support, naval gunfire, artillery, and B-52s, the South Vietnamese were able to continue the attack, but the advance remained tedious and costly. On 8 September, Truong, seeing an opportunity, ordered an all-out assault by the airborne and marine forces. Supported by a diversionary false amphibious assault by ARVN forces on a beach north of the mouth of the Cua Viet River, the attackers made slow but steady progress. It was a fierce fight, but on 16 September, the marines raised the South Vietnamese flag in the old citadel in the center of the city.

While the North Vietnamese Army had prosecuted large-scale, conventional attacks in Military Regions I, II, and III, it tried a different tack in the Mekong

Delta. As the battles in the other MRs began to develop, the situation in the Delta remained relatively quiet. After the war, it was determined that the North Vietnamese strategy in the Delta was twofold. First, the NVA wanted to pin down IV Corps forces (7th, 9th, and 21st ARVN divisions) so they could not be redeployed to reinforce RVNAF troops in one of the other corps areas. Second, the NVA wanted to disrupt the pacification effort in the Delta.[94] To do this, the North Vietnamese moved the 1st NVA Division into Cambodia adjacent to the Delta's westernmost provinces. Additionally, two other enemy regiments, 18B and 95B, moved north from the U Minh Forest to Chuong Thien Province. In early April, just after Saigon ordered the 21st ARVN Division north to Lai Khe in MR III to try to open Route 13 to An Loc, the Communist forces in the Delta began attacking ARVN and territorial forces positions. The South Vietnamese forces remaining there were further reduced a month later when Saigon also redeployed the 15th Regiment of the 9th ARVN Division to MR III to assist in the relief of An Loc. Less than two South Vietnamese divisions were left to handle the increasing NVA presence in the Delta. Throughout the rest of the summer, the NVA kept the pressure on IV Corps units and the territorial forces. The battles in the Delta never reached the same magnitude and intensity as those that raged in the other regions, but the steady action tied down a significant number of ARVN troops. Nevertheless, Major General Nguyen Vinh Nghi, who had replaced Major General Truong as IV Corps commander when Truong was given command of I Corps in early May, was able to contain the North Vietnamese. Despite some gains, the NVA was unable to achieve significant advances in population control; not one district town in the Delta fell to the Communists.

Although fighting continued in all the military regions throughout the rest of the year, the level was much reduced, and, by the end of September, the Nguyen Hue Offensive had largely ended. The South Vietnamese, despite serious setbacks at the beginning, had held; as Douglas Pike observed, "ARVN troops and even local forces stood and fought as never before."[95] Unfortunately for Saigon, the RVNAF did not have the strength to eject the remaining North Vietnamese forces from their territory, a situation that would cost South Vietnam dearly in the months to come.

The South Vietnamese had held against the NVA onslaught, but only at great cost. In only the first two months of fighting in 1972, the South Vietnamese sustained over 12,000 killed in action, 34,000 wounded, and 15,000 missing.[96] A closer examination of only one of the major battles demonstrates in more human terms just how much the defense had cost the South Vietnamese. In An Loc, for example, the continuous shelling, estimated at over 78,000 rounds during the three-month period, had reduced the city to almost total ruin.[97] Over 80,000 refugees had been forced from their homes in Binh Long Province and a like number were dead or missing.[98] The ARVN defenders in An Loc had sustained 5,400 casualties, including 2,300 killed or missing. U.S. advisers stated that every man in the 5th ARVN Division was a casualty; even those that survived had sustained one or more wounds during the course of the fighting in An Loc.[99] As one adviser described the city after the battle, "The graves, the burned out vehicles, and the rubble were mute testimony to the intensity of the battle that had been fought there."[100] This situation was repeated in Quang Tri and Kontum, which were left virtually in ruins by the intense fighting.

In spite of these costs, the South Vietnamese defenders and their advisers, with the help of tactical airpower, had decisively defeated a fourteen-division NVA attack (see table 8). Estimates placed North Vietnamese casualties at 10,000 soldiers killed and 15,000 wounded during the battle at An Loc alone.[101] Allied intelligence estimates put the total NVA killed in action at over 100,000. Over 450 tanks, almost the entire NVA armored force, were destroyed, as well as innumerable artillery pieces, trucks, and other vehicles.[102]

Interrogation of NVA prisoners indicated the extent of the Communist defeat. In An Loc, for example, a prisoner from the 95C Regiment of the 9th VC Division reported on 10 June that only thirty to forty men remained in each battalion in his regiment. He said that his battalion commander and all company commanders in his unit had been killed. The situation was much the same in other NVA units. Prisoners from the 141st and 165th regiments of the 7th NVA Division reported their units almost 100 percent destroyed.[103] These losses were repeated in most of the NVA units, particularly those that were involved in the pitched battles at places like Quang Tri and Kontum. Giap's chief of staff, Gen. Van Tien Dung, told the senior cadre of COSVN that the Communists had sustained such catastrophic casualties that they could mount no new offensive action for another three to five years.[104]

ASSESSING NGUYEN HUE

Despite the North Vietnamese casualties, the 1972 Nguyen Hue offensive was at least partially successful for the Communists. One of the objectives of the offensive had been to seize territory, and in a sense that was accomplished, for Communist troops remained in the South, putting Hanoi in a good position when the negotiated cease-fire went into effect in 1973.

The other area in which the offensive was somewhat successful was the impact that it had on the pacification program. Craig Whitney reported in the *New York Times* that "the [South Vietnamese] strategic reserve force was inadequate and the government has had to deprive many relatively pacified areas of the country of their regular defenses" to throw them into the fighting.[105] Thus, the offensive achieved two of its goals: occupying territory in South Vietnam and derailing, or at least setting back, the pacification effort.

However, the offensive failed to achieve the knockout blow that Giap had hoped for. The South Vietnamese had stood up against the North Vietnamese onslaught and remained intact both as a nation and as a military force. For a number of reasons, the offensive did not overwhelm the South Vietnamese as Giap had planned. First, the North Vietnamese had underestimated the effectiveness of U.S. airpower. Although most of the American ground combat troops had left Vietnam and those that remained had not been a factor in thwarting the NVA offensive, U.S.

Table 8. Fixed-Wing Strike Sorties in South Vietnam, 1972

	March	April	May	June
USAF tac air	247	3,032	7,516	5,310
USAF gunships	24	407	491	325
US Navy	128	4,683	3,247	2,040
USMC	—	537	1,381	1,937
VNAF tac air	3,118	4,612	5,276	3,950
VNAF gunships	31	292	310	182
USAF B-52s	689	1,608	2,223	2,207
Totals	4,237	15,171	20,444	15,951

Source: Colonel Donaldson D. Frizzell and Col. Ray L. Bowers, eds., *Airpower and the 1972 Spring Invasion*, USAF Southeast Asia Monograph Series (Maxwell Air Force Base, Ala.: Air Command and Staff College, 1973), 2:106.

airpower in its many forms was still available, and President Nixon was not reluctant to use it to assist the South Vietnamese in turning back the Communist invasion. Nixon's use of airpower directly against North Vietnam itself was also a contributing factor toward blunting the invasion. *Quan Doi Nhan Dan,* the NVA's official military newspaper, admitted the serious damage done to North Vietnam's transportation and communications systems and to its industrial production capacity in a three-part series of articles published during the first week of June.[106]

Second, the North Vietnamese plan was flawed strategically. In an attempt to overwhelm the South Vietnamese at three critical points, the NVA dispersed its mainforce units and permitted President Thieu to move his strategic reserve forces around the country to employ them where and when they were most needed to counter the NVA attacks. For example, elements of the Airborne Division were first deployed to An Loc, then to Military Region II, and ultimately to I Corps to assist in the action that retook Quang Tri. Had Giap massed the preponderance of his forces at one point of attack, Thieu would have had difficulty in mustering the combat power to overcome the sheer numbers that the NVA could have brought to bear. When Quang Tri fell, Giap could have used several more divisions that were committed elsewhere and driven south along Route 1. Thieu would have been hard-pressed to stop them. The same could be said for the attacks at An Loc and Kontum. When Giap's diluted forces came up against heavy South Vietnamese resistance in those two places, he did not have the reserves to overcome the resistance and maintain the momentum of the attack.[107] Additionally, the three prongs of the attack were difficult to sustain logistically. For example, the NVA required almost a week to resupply its forces after taking Loc Ninh, delaying its attack on An Loc and giving the defenders there much-needed time to prepare their defenses. In another example, during the battle of Kontum, one U.S. adviser with the 44th ARVN Regiment found an abandoned NVA T-54 tank with no apparent damage. Upon closer examination, he found that the gas tanks were completely empty.[108]

Another strategic failure was that the North Vietnamese high command let their forces become involved in battles of attrition long after the significance of certain terrain objectives had passed. For example, three divisions were tied down at An Loc in order to achieve what was basically only a psychological victory when they could have bypassed the city and driven down Route 13 to threaten Saigon directly. The same pattern also held true for the battles in Military Regions I and II. Speaking of the battles at An Loc and Kontum, Gen. Phillip B. Davidson said: "An experienced armor commander would have loaded his infantry on the decks of the tanks and bypassed the two towns. The terrain and weather would have permitted it, and a sizable NVA armored force showing up in ARVN's rear areas would have panicked the already jittery South Vietnamese troops. . . . If an Abrams or Hollingsworth had commanded the NVA troops at Kontum or An Loc, those battles might well have gone quite differently."[109]

The last strategic error was timing of the attack. Had the North Vietnamese waited until 1973, when virtually all U.S. forces would have already departed from South Vietnam, they no doubt would have had a much easier time of it.

In addition to strategic errors, the North Vietnamese made several tactical errors that contributed to the failure of Nguyen Hue. Although employing vast numbers of Soviet- and Chinese-made tanks, the NVA continually demonstrated its inability to coordinate the use of infantry and armor in the attack. Lt. Gen. Tran Van Quang, deputy chief of the general staff of the North Vietnamese Army, making a report on the conduct of the offensive before the Soviet Politburo in Moscow in June 1972, acknowledged this situation, saying, "[W]e still have not sufficiently established a clear system of command and control of our forces . . . among a number of our commanders, there is a lack of high quality tactical training and combat experience. . . . These represent the main reasons for the heavy losses of our forces."[110]

Lacking training and experience in handling combined arms in an attack, the NVA, rather than take advantage of the inherent shock action of tanks and their ability to conduct deep thrusts into enemy lines, repeatedly used the tanks hesitantly, primarily as infantry support vehicles against heavily prepared defensive positions. Thus, the NVA forfeited the advantages of having tanks in large quantities. After overcoming the initial shock of facing tanks and seeing how easily they could be destroyed, particularly in city fighting, the South Vietnamese defenders were successful in most cases in handling the NVA armor. Had the NVA been more skillful in coordinating infantry and armor, they probably would have overrun the South Vietnamese in many cases.

The second tactical error had to do with the nature of the NVA infantry attacks. Enjoying superior numbers in most of the key battles, the NVA commanders squandered their soldiers in repetitive human-wave attacks. Massing for such attacks made them lucrative targets for B-52s and tactical air support, which wrought devastation on them, often saving the day for the South Vietnamese defenders. The attrition resulting from the human-wave attacks was a major factor in the loss of momentum for the North Vietnamese.

The last and perhaps most significant factor that contributed to the defeat of the North Vietnamese invasion was that the leadership in Hanoi underestimated the ability of the South Vietnamese to endure the intense level of combat against

ARVN in Laos; the NVA leadership expected the southerners to fold under the weight of the fourteen-division attack. When the South Vietnamese, backed by their advisers and U.S. air support, managed to hold on, the NVA became bogged down in meaningless battles that severely diminished their combat power.

EVALUATING SOUTH VIETNAMESE COMBAT PERFORMANCE

The RVNAF performance warrants more scrutiny, but one must remember the bottom line: the South Vietnamese ultimately held against everything the NVA could throw at them. In addition to inflicting a military defeat on the enemy, the ARVN defenders won a decisive psychological victory. They had stood up against the very best of the North Vietnamese Army, defeated them, and prevented them from establishing their "liberation government" in the South. President Thieu and his regime emerged from the crisis stronger than ever, at least on the surface. He and his army had been victorious. The victory seemed a turning point for South Vietnam.

As in Lam Son 719, the actual performance of the RVNAF on the battlefield was mixed. The crucible of the NVA offensive demonstrated only too well the continuing severe shortcomings in leadership and morale within the RVNAF. At Quang Tri, the inexperienced troops of the newly organized 3rd ARVN Division broke and ran in the face of the NVA attack. This was not an isolated case. Desertion under fire by South Vietnamese troops was a continual problem for the duration of the Communist offensive.

According to General Abrams, leadership continued to be the single most critical failing in the RVNAF.[111] For example, General Lam, I Corps commander, demonstrated the same failings that had almost spelled disaster during Lam Son 719. He refused to make decisions even when it was imperative that he do so. Most of the division commanders were little better, including the commander in An Loc. According to Col. William Miller, senior adviser to the 5th ARVN at the beginning of the battle, "a spring came loose inside General [Le Van] Hung" when the NVA overran Loc Ninh, and he failed to exercise command when it was needed most.[112] According to Brigadier General McGiffert, deputy commander of Third Regional Assistance Command, Hung "choked" under the pressure and "just didn't do a damn thing for a long time."[113] During the offensive, Thieu changed commanders "in each case where inadequate performance had been brought to his attention," but Abrams felt that the real problem was the lack of experienced leaders to promote.[114]

The leadership problem went further down the chain of command. After the battle, McGiffert said that the regimental commanders at An Loc, with a few exceptions, were no better than mediocre, stating that "there was no control. There was no supervision; there was no command emphasis to get out in the crew positions."[115] One South Vietnamese official at Quin Nhon, speaking of the failure of the South Vietnamese to stop the NVA in Binh Dinh Province, told Craig Whitney of the *New York Times*, "The Americans were sincere, they tried to help the

Vietnamese armed forces, and from A to Z they brought equipment here, but one thing the Americans cannot bring here is leadership—they cannot bring that in from their arsenal."[116]

The intensity of combat brought out the worst in some South Vietnamese, best demonstrated by what one adviser in An Loc called the "olympic wounded."[117] Reminiscent of similar events during Lam Son 719, evacuation helicopters braved intense ground fire to land in or near An Loc to pick up casualties only to have "wounded" ARVN soldiers drop their more severely wounded compatriots to clamber aboard the departing helicopters. The incident was not an isolated one, happening similarly at Quang Tri and Kontum.

In many cases, the South Vietnamese refused to fight and often gave up with only token or no resistance. In relating the fall of Tan Canh, for example, a correspondent for *Time* magazine quoted one of five American officers who had survived the disaster, writing, "Tan Canh fell because ARVN never got off its ass and fought."[118] Even when effective air strikes provided ARVN troops a window of opportunity to counterattack the NVA, they refused to seize the moment, often remaining in their holes instead of closing with the enemy. Such was the case in the early days of the battle for Quang Tri, in which one U.S. officer observed that "most of the ARVN plans [for a counteroffensive] would have succeeded had the ground commanders taken action to take advantage of the massive air support provided."[119] Unfortunately, the commanders were often the root of the problem. Ill-led, many South Vietnamese soldiers lost heart and panicked. Such was the case in Quang Tri, where the South Vietnamese totally collapsed as a fighting force. Paul A. Daly, Quang Tri senior adviser, later said that the NVA did not "win" Quang Tri Province, but rather that the South Vietnamese "lost" it. He was quoted in a CORDS afteraction report: "Psychologically the NVA scored heavily with the introduction of 130mm artillery and tanks. In justifying their collapse, a number of South Vietnamese used this for an excuse—without considering that they had more artillery and better tanks, not to mention TACAIR, B-52 strikes, and naval gunfire. Rumors, refugees, and retreating troops did the rest."[120]

Although the most visible instance of ARVN's failure to fight was at Quang Tri, a similar story could be told of the South Vietnamese on many battlefields during the dark days of 1972. For example, at Bong Son, a town on the seacoast to the east of Kontum, *New York Times* reporter Craig Whitney, in describing the situation there, quoted the senior American adviser in the area, Maj. George H. Watkins Jr.: "[T]here was a lot of cowardice. . . . The troops' morale was just broken. Some broke and ran and didn't know where to go. Some deserted to the VC. They just didn't know what to do, and that was because of their lack of leadership in any depth."[121]

When the South Vietnamese stood and fought, they did so often only grudgingly. In many cases, troops who did not wish to be there had no choice but to fight in order to survive. In An Loc, some U.S. advisers felt that the city would probably have fallen if the NVA had left the road open to the south so the ARVN troops could have escaped.[122] The same held true for Kontum, where one adviser said that the NVA made a mistake in cutting the road between Kontum and Pleiku, because, in doing so, it had "left the ARVN no alternative but to fight."[123]

Leadership and discipline were so bad in some of the ARVN units that the civilians had nothing but scorn for these soldiers, many of whom had seemingly spent as much time looting as fighting.[124] In An Loc, looting incidents and firefights between friendly troops over the airdrops that made it into the city indicated the breakdown of discipline among some of the South Vietnamese. Unfortunately, their behavior was by no means the exception. Sydney Schanberg of the *New York Times* wrote of the situation in Hue on 4 May: "South Vietnamese Army runaways from the scattered Third Division, which abandoned the northern city of Quang Tri to North Vietnamese forces on Monday without a fight, were roaming through Hue today like armed gangsters—looting, intimidating and firing on those who displeased them."[125]

Another dimension of the problem with the South Vietnamese leadership involved tactical competence. A November 1972 report stated:

Operations in a conventional environment necessitated by the recent enemy offensive . . . have indicated that there are two operational areas which will require continuing US adviser support. There is a continuing need for expertise in the area of fire support coordination, and control. The problem is not a lack of technical knowledge, but one arising from the failure of the commanders to insure that fires are properly integrated into the maneuver plans of the ground gaining units. The second operational area needing advisory assistance is combined arms planning and employment. As with the integration of fires, the technical aspects of the problem are relatively easily mastered, but they must be constantly and consistently applied by the appropriate commander. . . . Time and time again, during the spring offensive, these deficiencies were glaringly apparent.[126]

In part, blame for these deficiencies lay with the U.S. advisory effort, which had been working with ARVN commanders for years. During training, much emphasis had been placed on planning and conducting tactical operations; the focus, however, was mostly on small-scale operations, such as search-and-destroy missions. The situation during the 1972 NVA offensive was far removed from the type of circumstances that even the best ARVN commanders had previously experienced. Facing tanks was a far cry from chasing guerrillas. As one adviser later described the situation that existed in An Loc, "Regimental and higher level leadership was not tactically or psychologically prepared for a battle of the duration and intensity of the Binh Long campaign; battalion level leaders lacked preparation for the close coordination necessary between fire and maneuver elements."[127]

Despite these instances of lapses in leadership and courage, many other South Vietnamese soldiers, marines, and territorial forces fought valiantly, often in the face of overwhelming odds. When ably led, the South Vietnamese soldiers fought hard and in many places well. The Vietnamese Marines in I Corps maintained discipline and order throughout the offensive, even when superior enemy strength caused them to abandon defensive positions. The besieged defenders in An Loc repeatedly threw back NVA human-wave assaults, standing toe-to-toe with the Communist attackers, holding out longer than the French did at Dien Bien Phu.

To be perfectly objective, however, it must be noted that when the South Vietnamese stayed and fought, it was often because of the support provided by U.S. airpower. Members of the U.S. Senate Committee on Foreign Relations traveled to Saigon in late 1972 to investigate the conduct of the defense against the Easter Offensive. They later cited U.S. air support as the key ingredient to the ARVN victory. During one of the briefings presented to the committee members at MACV Headquarters, the briefer was asked what would have happened if U.S. air support had not been available; the briefer replied: "We would be meeting some other place today."[128]

General Abrams, who departed Saigon in June to become Army chief of staff, had earlier observed that American airpower, and not South Vietnamese arms, had caused the enemy's losses.[129] Participants at all levels later echoed his evaluation. The after-action report of the 21st ARVN Division stated, "The accuracy, devastation, and responsiveness of U.S. tactical air meant the difference between victory and defeat."[130] Brigadier General McGiffert, who had been General Hollingsworth's deputy at Third Regional Assistance Command when the offensive began, was even more emphatic in his evaluation of the impact of U.S. airpower. During the battle for An Loc, he was quoted as saying that the B-52 force was "the most effective weapon we have been able to muster" and asserted that the threat of bomber strikes "forces the enemy to break up his ground elements into small units and makes it difficult to mass forces for an attack."[131] When asked after the battle what he thought about the ability of the ARVN to hold An Loc without American tactical air support, McGiffert replied, "No contest—never would have hacked it."[132]

Even South Vietnamese officials shared McGiffert's sentiment. Gen. Cao Van Vien wrote after the war: "The tremendous firepower unleashed by the USAF, especially B-52 strikes, effectively blunted all enemy efforts on three fronts, disrupted enemy supply lines, and helped the RVNAF conserve their ground forces. It also gave the RVNAF much-needed respite to recover from the initial enemy shock, consolidate their lines of defense, and regroup for the counterattack." He further stated, "Without this support, the RVNAF success in stalling the enemy invasion would have been impossible."[133]

While tactical airpower was critical to South Vietnamese success on the battlefield, the air campaign against North Vietnam was equally important. It significantly reduced Hanoi's ability to sustain the offensive. U.S. intelligence analysts estimated that strikes against North Vietnam decimated North Vietnam's overland supply system, cutting imports coming overland from China from 160,000 tons to 30,000 tons per month.[134] By the end of the campaign, U.S. bombs had destroyed virtually all of North Vietnam's oil storage facilities and three-quarters of the country's generating capacity. Such damage severely hampered Hanoi's ability to keep supplies flowing to their forces in the South.

Gen. Frederick C. Weyand, who assumed command of MACV from General Abrams, summed up the collective role of airpower in all its forms when he said that it was "unlikely that the South Vietnamese forces could have stopped the invasion without the tremendous effectiveness of airpower. . . . [He could not] see how anybody in any service, could question the decisive role played by the fixed-wing gunships, TACAIR, and the B-52s. . . ."[135]

Another important factor in the South Vietnamese victory was the presence of American advisers on the ground, where they served in several key roles. First, the advisers, who usually stayed with their counterparts throughout the battle and shared their fate on a daily basis, provided a tangible demonstration of American resolve, which encouraged their counterparts. Raising the spirits of the defenders was of particular importance in the darkest hours of the repeated North Vietnamese attacks. When advisers were evacuated, often against their own wishes, the South Vietnamese units they left more often than not collapsed. When the advisers stayed in and around An Loc to coordinate U.S. support, all the while remaining in constant contact with General Hollingsworth, their excellent leadership by example greatly encouraged the South Vietnamese defenders. Lt. Gen. Phillip Davidson wrote that the advisers "stiffened the morale of the ARVN commanders in time of desperate peril."[136]

Second, the American advisers played an important role in the delivery of critical U.S. air support. They were the link between the ARVN defenders and the American tactical aircraft and helicopters supporting the South Vietnamese. Without the advisers and their radios, the defenders on the ground would have been unable to talk to the aircraft. After the battle, General McGiffert said that the ARVN defenders in An Loc could not have held out if the advisers had not been there controlling the air strikes. He said of the advisers, "[T]heir primary duty and their primary reason for existence was coordination of US tacair [tactical air support] and without them it [the defense of An Loc] would have just been damn near impossible."[137]

Third, the advisers provided the only source of "ground truth" to senior American commanders who controlled the air assets. When confusion and near panic often reigned, determining exactly what was going on during critical battles was key. Thus, speaking of An Loc, General McGiffert noted, "It was the only way we could get any kind of objective analysis of what was really going on in there, it was talking to them [the advisers] everyday."[138]

Finally, but perhaps most important, was the less tangible role played by the American advisers. Many of the ARVN troops fought bravely and maintained their fighting edge under trying conditions; unfortunately, as has already been discussed, others allowed panic and fear to rule and fought less than valiantly. On several occasions in critical battles, the situation was only a razor's edge away from crumbling. In many of these cases, the Americans stepped into the void and assumed virtual command of the ARVN units they accompanied. In doing so, they provided badly needed leadership and expertise in handling battles of such magnitude, making up for the inabilities of South Vietnamese commanders to command and control conventional battles against combined arms attacks. The Senate Committee on Foreign Relations reported, "No one with whom we talked, American or Vietnamese, thought that the South Vietnamese could have held had there not been American advisers."[139] In case after case, General McGiffert said that the advisers "were the glue that kept them [ARVN] together."[140]

In the final analysis, the South Vietnamese armed forces remained too dependent on the United States. American airpower saved South Vietnam. The South Vietnamese in I Corps even relied on U.S. naval gunfire to supplant the artillery pieces that were captured by the North Vietnamese as the Saigon troops withdrew from Quang Tri.[141] American transport aircraft moved RVNAF troops and supplies around the country. American advisers bolstered their counterparts and coordinated American firepower. The South Vietnamese had survived the 1972 NVA invasion, but they owed much of their success to the United States and not to their own ability to defeat the NVA on the battlefield. In his recently revised study of the Easter Offensive, Dale Andradé concluded that "Despite Vietnamization, the South Vietnamese army exhibited many of the same problems in 1972 as it had ten years earlier, a fact made painfully clear during the Easter Offensive. . . . The Easter Offensive showed that this partnership [between the United States and ARVN] could work, but only as long as American firepower remained abundantly available."[142]

NIXON PROCLAIMS VIETNAMIZATION A SUCCESS

Despite the reality of the situation in 1972, the ultimate outcome of the battles in 1972 (discounting the impact of U.S. advisers and American airpower) could be used as evidence that Vietnamization had worked, or at least, was working. The Nixon administration trumpeted this idea to all who would listen, using the South Vietnamese victory to declare the president's Vietnamization policy a success.[143] As Henry Kissinger's assistant Les Janka told General Haig, "How this offensive plays in the American press may be the actual ultimate test of the success of Vietnamization . . . since it is our own people we must convince."[144] Accordingly, the administration began an immediate campaign to put the best face on South Vietnamese battlefield performance. As early as 26 April, when the fighting still raged on three fronts and was still very much in doubt, Nixon had gone on national television to bolster support for the South Vietnamese. He reported:

> The South Vietnamese are fighting courageously and well in their self-defense. They're inflicting very heavy casualties on the invading force, which had not gained the easy victory some predicted it would three weeks ago. . . . [T]he South Vietnamese will have demonstrated their ability to defend themselves on the ground against future enemy attacks. . . . I have decided that Vietnamization has proved itself sufficiently that we can continue our program of

withdrawing American forces without detriment to our overall goal of insuring South Vietnam's survival as an independent country. And, consequently, I am announcing tonight that over the next two months 20,000 more Americans will be brought home from Vietnam. This decision has the full approval of President Thieu and of General Abrams. It will bring our troop ceiling down to 49,000 by July 1, a reduction of half a million men since this administration came into office.[145]

Although Nixon also announced in this speech that the bombing of North Vietnam would continue until the Communists stopped their offensive, he failed to mention that, despite the troop reductions, he was sending more air and naval power to the region to ensure that the South Vietnamese were not overrun.

After the offensive was over, administration spokesmen downplayed the role of U.S. airpower and American advisers and praised the steadfastness of the South Vietnamese. Citing the "fierce determination of its Vietnamese defenders," they proclaimed the victories at An Loc and Kontum as clear proof that the policy of turning the war over to the South Vietnamese was working.[146] An air force report published shortly after the end of the offensive proclaimed, "Vietnamization, in terms of the capability of the Republic of Vietnam (RVN) ground and air military forces to confront and withstand the Communist surge, had proven itself a success."[147] Many in the U.S. military in Vietnam agreed with this statement. Published MACV reports at the time lauded the performance of the South Vietnamese defenders. Col. Theodore C. Williams Jr., senior adviser, 9th ARVN Division, wrote in his senior officer debriefing report that "The U.S. advisory effort, reinforced by U.S. air support, has successfully completed its mission of assisting RVNAF to mold itself into a strong, viable force."[148] Similarly, Col. John C. Evans, senior adviser, 18th ARVN Division, reported that "it can be unequivocally stated that the 18th Infantry Division, ARVN, is capable of sustained combat without U.S. advisers."[149] Such reports, although understandable in the natural euphoria that follows a successful and hard-fought battle, failed to reveal just how close the outcome of the battle had been.

The Nixon administration, having established the "success" of Vietnamization, did not want to hear anything to the contrary. Col. Bill Miller, upon his return to the United States from An Loc in May 1972, was called before the House Armed Services Committee to testify about ARVN performance at An Loc. During these hearings (and in additional discussions with Senator John Stennis, Alexander Haig, and other high government officials and members of the media), Miller testified that in his opinion, ARVN had not really won, but had merely avoided defeat with the help of its advisers and American air power.[150] He also said that removing the advisers and U.S. air support prematurely would result in disaster for the South Vietnamese.

Ultimately, Miller's warnings and those of others who held the same opinions received little credence. In August, Defense Secretary Laird, wanting to reduce the number of American advisers in South Vietnam, asked the Joint Chiefs of Staff to review the status of the advisory effort. The resulting report approved the scheduled elimination of 1,700 more advisory positions and the reduction of the division advisory teams from thirty-six to fifteen.[151] A separate Department of Defense study recommended a 2,500–man advisory force for 1973 and a reduced role for combat advisers in favor of more emphasis on territorial security and staff management.[152] Thus, when the advisers were needed most to help put the RVNAF back together after the near debacle of the NVA offensive, their numbers were being reduced and they were being removed from the field. At this point, having been declared a resounding success, the Vietnamization effort began to wane. The South Vietnamese "victory" in 1972 became one of the underlying rationales for complete U.S. withdrawal and Nixon's "peace with honor."

In his address to Congress on 1 June, upon his return from the summit in Moscow, President Nixon had said: "I emphasize to you once again, this Administration has no higher goal—a goal that I know all of you share—than bringing the Vietnam war to an early and honorable end. We are ending the war in Vietnam, but we shall end it in a way which will not betray our friends, risk the lives of the courageous Americans still serving in Vietnam, break faith with those held prisoners by the enemy, or stain the honor of the United States of America."[153]

Just how this "early and honorable end" would unfold for the South Vietnamese remained to be seen. The United States was obviously on its way out of South Vietnam; the real test for Thieu, his troops, and his nation would come after U.S. forces, including the ubiquitous airpower that had been so critical in 1972, had left and the RVNAF had to stand on its own. That would be the ultimate measure of Vietnamization.

Secretary of Defense Melvin Laird and U.S. Ambassador Ellsworth Bunker arrive at President Thieu's Office, March 1969. (National Archives Photo)

President Richard Nixon and President Nguyen Van Thieu announce new American policy of "Vietnamization" at Midway conference, 8 June 1969. (National Archives Photo)

President Nixon, on a surprise visit to Saigon, departs Independence Palace with President Nguyen Van Thieu enorute to a joint press conference, July 1969. Behind them, from right, are U.S. Ambassador Ellsworth Bunker, Vice President Nguyen Cao Ky, and Henry Kissinger. (National Archives Photo)

US artillery adviser from Advisory Team 40 observes ARVN soldiers performing section drill on a 155mm howitzer at Duc My, April 1970. (National Archives Photo)

Members of the 8th Vietnamese Marine Battalion and their advisers prepare to launch airmobile operation into Bai Loc Valley, September 1970. (National Archives Photo)

Major H. Lee, Vinh Long Province Phoenix Adviser, discusses the day's mission with his counterpart, 1LT Nguyen The, July 1970. (National Archives Photo)

Captain Thomas Trumble, MACV Advisory Team 76, looks on during a class on motor maintenance at the ARVN Armor School, Thu Duc, May 1970. (National Archives Photo)

Adviser Staff Sergeant Douglas Smith observes a class on search and seizure demonstration at the Vietnamese National Training Center, Quang Trung, April 1970 (National Archives Photo)

Private First Class Jerry Sanders and Sergeant John Grantham, 124th Signal Company, demonstrate the breakdown of an M-16 rifle to two members of the Popular Forces, Pleiku, March 1970. (National Archives Photo)

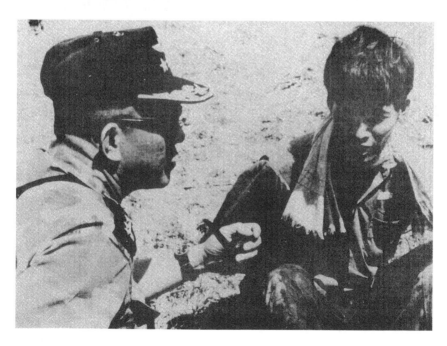

Lieutenant General Do Cao Tri, III Corps Commander, questions a captured enemy soldier in Cambodia during the Incursion of 1970. (U.S. Army Photo)

Soldiers from 25th ARVN
Division with weapons
captured during the
Cambodian Incursion, June
1970. (Douglas Pike Photo
Collection, The Vietnam
Archive, Texas Tech University)

South Vietnamese soldiers move along part of the Ho Chi Minh Trail in Laos
during Operation LAM SON 719, March 1971. (Douglas Pike Photo Collection,
The Vietnam Archive, Texas Tech University)

American helicopters are preparing to carry South Vietnamese forces across the Laotian border into battle as part of Operation LAM SON 719, April 1971. (Douglas Pike Photo Collection, The Vietnam Archive, Texas Tech University)

Unknown U.S. adviser and ARVN counterpart discuss roadclearing operation in Military Region I, May 1971. (National Archives Photo)

Le Duan (white shirt), secretary general of the Communist Party of Vietnam, at a military conference in July 1971. With him are Generals Vo Nguyen Giap and Van Tien Dung (second and third from the left). (Douglas Pike Photo Collection, The Vietnam Archive, Texas Tech University)

The ARVN flag flies over the old 101st Airborne Division Headquarters following turnover ceremonies, Camp Eagle, 1 February 1972. (National Archives Photo)

Emergency White House meeting to discuss the ongoing North Vietnamese invasion, 13 April 1972. (National Archives Photo)

NVA troops running through abandoned ARVN artillery position in the vicinity of Quang Tri, May 1972. (Douglas Pike Photo Collection, The Vietnam Archive, Texas Tech University)

Sappers and locals clear road for North Vietnamese armor in the Quang Tri–Thua Thien Front area in April 1972. (Douglas Pike Photo Collection, The Vietnam Archive, Texas Tech University)

North Vietnamese T-54 tank destroyed during the battle of An Loc, April-June 1972. (Neal Ulevich Photo)

People inspect a display of captured NVA weapons in Lam Son Square, Saigon, 14 May 1972. (National Archives Photo)

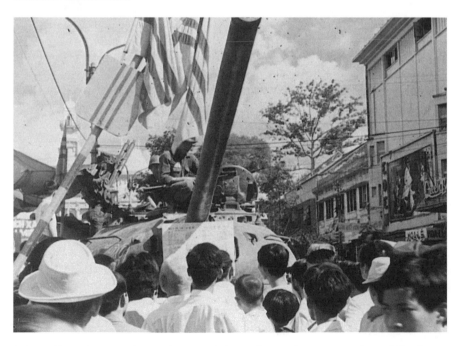

Saigon citizens inspect a T-54 tank captured during the North Vietnamese Easter Offensive, May 1972. (National Archives Photo)

NVA soldiers firing unidentified artillery piece in the Quang Tri area in November 1972. (Douglas Pike Photo Collection, The Vietnam Archive, Texas Tech University)

U.S., South Vietnamese, and Communist representatives sign the "Agreement on Ending the War and Restoring Peace in Viet Nam" in Paris, 27 January 1973. (National Archives Photo)

President and Mrs. Richard Nixon depart the White House after he had resigned his office, 9 August 1974. (National Archives Photo)

A South Vietnamese C-130 aircraft, trying to take off was hit by a North Vietnamese SA-7 Strela missile and burns on the runway at Ton Son Nhut, 29 April 1975. (National Archives Photo)

Two U.S. Marine CH-53 helicopters set down in a parking lot on the north side of Saigon during Operation FREQUENT WIND, the evacuation of the U.S. Embassy. (National Archives Photo)

7

Cease-Fire and "Peace with Honor"

As the fighting continued in Vietnam, Richard Nixon prepared for his reelection campaign, the key issue of which proved to be the continuing war. Nixon had been severely criticized in the media for "escalating" the conflict when he ordered the mining of Haiphong harbor. Furthermore, bombing North Vietnam in response to the Easter Offensive had been a political gamble, and the question was whether he would get away with it and win the election in November. The odds improved somewhat when he announced in June that troop withdrawals would continue, reducing U.S. military strength in South Vietnam to thirty-nine thousand by 1 September 1972. Additionally, Nixon said that draftees would no longer be assigned for duty within South Vietnam unless they volunteered for service there.[1]

On 12 July, South Dakota senator George McGovern, a leading political figure in the antiwar movement since 1965, won the Democratic presidential nomination. McGovern primarily based his subsequent campaign on opposition to Nixon's handling of the war. Two days after his nomination, he pledged: "Within 90 days of my inauguration, every American soldier and every American prisoner will be out of the jungle and out of their cells and back home in America where they belong. . . . If the war is not ended before the next Democratic administration takes office, we pledge, as the first order of business, an immediate and complete withdrawal of all United States forces in Indochina."[2]

Missouri senator Thomas Eagleton, McGovern's running mate, charged that Nixon and the Republicans were "keeping troops in Vietnam until the last minute" and would pull them out "just before the election."[3] Nixon responded to this charge in his acceptance speech at the GOP convention in Miami Beach by asserting that the Democratic leadership was in effect telling the leadership of North Vietnam "Don't negotiate with the present administration; wait for us, we will give you what you want—South Vietnam." He stressed that his administration would not surrender Vietnam, declaring, "We will never abandon our prisoners of war. We will not join our enemies in imposing a Communist government on our allies—the seventeen million people of South Vietnam. And we will never stain the honor of the United States of America."[4] The American people may have been tired of the war, but a large majority was not prepared to just give up in South Vietnam. As journalist Arnold R. Isaacs maintains, the electorate was willing to let Nixon do what he had to do, as long as the American war was fought from the air by professionals, not draftees.[5] Consequently, despite the political risks incurred by bombing North Vietnam, Nixon began to widen his lead over McGovern.

The election campaign did give impetus to the Nixon administration's pursuit of Paris negotiations with the North Vietnamese. Kissinger, in particular, wanted to reach a negotiated settlement before the November election. He believed that the North Vietnamese would be more prone to make concessions before the election, particularly if it seemed that Nixon was going to win. On the other hand, Nixon listened to the advice of Charles Colson, who reported that pollsters had determined that "any agreement we reached before the election would appear to be a political ploy."[6] Additionally, Nixon believed that by winning reelection he would have a mandate to carry out additional acts of war if necessary to force the North Vietnamese to accept concessions. Nevertheless, Nixon knew that the war had to be ended sooner or later. He told his advisers, "Only great events can change things in the campaign now and Vietnam is the only great event happening."[7] To win the election, Nixon wanted to play on his efforts to end the war, highlighting the contrast between his "peace with honor" and what he called McGovern's "peace by surrender."[8]

"PEACE IS [NOT] AT HAND"

The military situation in Vietnam supported Nixon's approach. Although the South Vietnamese initially staggered under the North Vietnamese invasion in 1972, they eventually stabilized the situation, winning some credibility for the president's Vietnamization strategy, thereby permitting him and Henry Kissinger to pursue the "other" strategy: negotiations.

When Nixon had gone on national television and radio on 8 May 1972 to announce the mining of Haiphong harbor, popular reaction to the bombing proclamation had overshadowed the terms of settlement offered the North Vietnamese in the same speech—a standstill cease-fire, release of prisoners, and a total American withdrawal within four months (with no mention of a corresponding withdrawal of North Vietnamese troops from the South).[9] Riding a high tide on the battlefield, the North Vietnamese did not respond to Nixon's offer. However, as the momentum of their attack slowed, the North Vietnamese proved more willing to discuss a negotiated peace. In addition, they were under pressure from Russia and China. President Podgorny of the Soviet Union traveled to Hanoi in June and bluntly told the North Vietnamese leaders that it was time to negotiate.[10] The Soviets were interested in detente with the United States and the continued war in Vietnam threatened to derail the process. The Chinese were also interested in fostering better ties with the Americans. In the summer of 1972, Zhou Enlai urged the North Vietnamese Communists to be more flexible.[11] Thus, Nixon and Kissinger, by focusing their diplomatic efforts on bettering relations with the Soviet Union and China, had isolated North Vietnam politically.

Still under aerial bombardment at home and beginning to lose ground on the battlefield and the support of their Communist benefactors, the North Vietnamese turned to negotiations. The Nixon administration was eager to settle as well. Beset by problems with Congress and the ever-present antiwar element, the White House desperately wanted a way out of Vietnam, but one that would give some semblance of "peace with honor." Into this situation stepped Nguyen Van Thieu. According to General Davidson, Thieu had heretofore not been overly concerned by U.S. negotiating points, even when he disagreed with them, because he always felt that Hanoi would reject any terms offered by the United States.[12] However, as 1972 progressed, he realized that Nixon was seeking a negotiated exit from Vietnam and that the North Vietnamese, unable to achieve a victory with the Nguyen Hue offensive and reeling from the effects of the U.S. bombing campaign, were more open to serious negotiations. For Thieu and his regime, which relied completely on the United States for its very existence, a negotiated settlement that called for the withdrawal of all American forces and support was a frightening thought. As Kissinger later wrote in his memoirs, "The South Vietnamese after eight years of American participation, simply did not feel ready to confront Hanoi without our direct involvement. Their nightmare was not this or that clause but the fear of being left alone."[13] Thieu was afraid that Nixon and Kissinger, wanting to extricate the United States from Southeast Asia any way they could, would make an unfavorable settlement behind his back.

In June, Hanoi replied by telegram to a note from Washington requesting a resumption of the secret talks, saying, "The DRV side, clothed by its goodwill, agrees to private meetings."[14] Kissinger quickly responded and a date of 19 July 1972 was set for the next meeting. When Kissinger and Le Duc Tho met in Paris, Kissinger detected an immediate change in attitude among the North Vietnamese negotiators. However, Tho and his colleagues neither offered any new proposals nor backed away from previous demands. Their continuing hardline approach was best summed up by Prime Minister Pham Van Dong in a February 1972 speech:

Nguyen Van Thieu and his machine of oppression . . . constitute the main obstacle to the settlement of the political problem in South Vietnam. Therefore, Nguyen Van Thieu must resign immediately, the Saigon administration must end its warlike policy, disband at once its machine of oppression and constraint against the people, stop its "pacification" policy, disband the concentration camps, set free those persons arrested on political grounds and guarantee . . .

democratic liberties. . . . After the above has been achieved, the Provisional
Revolutionary Government of the Republic of South Vietnam will discuss
with the Saigon administration the formation of a three-segment government
of national concord with a view to organizing general elections [for] the definitive government of South Vietnam.[15]

Little was accomplished at this meeting, but the link with the North Vietnamese had been reestablished; they agreed to meet with the American negotiator
again on 1 August. Kissinger was encouraged because he noted a softening of the
North Vietnamese attitude that hopefully portended a major change in their previous negotiating stance. Although they had not explicitly said that they had given
up on their demand that Thieu resign, their use of terms like "two administrations,"
"two armies," and "three political groupings," implied for the first time that they
were at least titularly recognizing the validity of the Thieu government. Kissinger
reported to Nixon that the North Vietnamese negotiators were about "as positive
in this first session as we would expect if they do want to settle."[16]

At a subsequent meeting on 14 August, Kissinger received further encouragement. The North Vietnamese said that the United States had to stop supporting the Thieu administration and agree to a coalition. They, however, did not specifically mention Thieu's removal or speak of dismantling Saigon's army; instead,
they alluded to three political forces—Saigon, the Communists, and a neutral "third
segment." Although nothing firm came from this session, Kissinger considered the
discussions a major shift in the right direction, with the North Vietnamese adopt-
ing a more conciliatory tone.[17]

After the meeting, Kissinger flew to Saigon to brief President Thieu regarding the discussions in Paris. Since early May, Kissinger and Ambassador Bunker
had endeavored to reassure Thieu that the United States would continue "full support" and promised to "keep him promptly and fully apprised" of any discussions
with the North Vietnamese.[18] In June, Bunker informed Kissinger that he had met
with Thieu to assure him again "of the President's continued support and that we
have no intention of conceding to the enemy at the negotiating table what he has
been unable to achieve on the battlefield."[19] Thieu told Bunker that he understood
the "game plan." However, he remained fearful of a settlement that would benefit
the United States and North Vietnam while ignoring the needs of South Vietnam.
When Kissinger informed Thieu of the seeming shift in negotiating attitude at the
August session, the South Vietnamese leader was not impressed. He was upset
about the idea of an in-place cease-fire and opposed anything that looked even re-
motely like a coalition government. Additionally, he was terrified of a negotiated
peace that included both the complete withdrawal of U.S. forces and the continued presence of North Vietnamese troops in the South. Accordingly, he bombarded
Nixon and Kissinger with objections to the agreement right up until Kissinger's
next meeting with the North Vietnamese on 15 September. Nixon sent Thieu a letter at the end of August that promised continued support for South Vietnam, say-

ing that "the United States has not persevered all this way, at the sacrifice of so many American lives, to reverse course in the last few months of 1972. . . . The American people know that the United States cannot purchase peace or honor or redeem its sacrifices at the price of deserting a brave ally. This I cannot do and will never do."[20] At the same time, Nixon cabled Kissinger, who had gone to Moscow to confer with Soviet leaders about the situation in Vietnam, that "the American people are no longer interested in a solution based on compromise. [They] favor continued bombing and want to see the United States prevail after all these years."[21] Thus, the president charged Kissinger to be "tough" with the North Vietnamese when he returned to Paris.

On 11 September, Hanoi issued a statement saying that the "solution to the internal problem of South Vietnam must proceed from the actual situation that there exist in South Vietnam two administrations, two armies, and other political forces."[22] This heartened Kissinger because for the first time the North Vietnamese indicated that they would not demand a tripartite coalition government to supercede Thieu's government in South Vietnam. However, at the meeting in Paris on 15 September, Le Duc Tho once again proposed a coalition government, which Kissinger promptly rejected. However, Kissinger believed that he was making progress with the North Vietnamese and, at Tho's urging, agreed to an "agreement in principle" by 15 October.[23]

Tho and Kissinger met again on 26 September and largely solved the remaining military issues. In a major change from previous discussions, Tho dropped the demand for a coalition government and instead proposed a "Provisional Government of National Concord," whose only function would be to arrange elections for South Vietnam within ninety days after the war had ended. Kissinger deferred discussion on this proposal, saying he needed time to study it overnight. They parted company with Tho promising that the next meeting would be "decisive."[24] Two days later, the North Vietnamese sent Kissinger a note that said their delegation would come to the next meeting "in a constructive spirit and serious attitude, in a last effort at arriving at an agreement of the essentials with the American side."[25]

Still concerned that Thieu could scuttle any agreement that Kissinger worked out, Nixon sent General Haig to Saigon to confer with the South Vietnamese president. Haig carried with him a personal message from Nixon to Thieu: "I give you my firm assurance that there will be no settlement arrived at, the provisions of which have not been discussed personally with you beforehand." He also included a not-so-subtle hint to "avoid the development of an atmosphere which could lead to events similar to those which we abhorred in 1963"—a reference to the coup that had resulted in the death of President Ngo Dinh Diem.[26]

Thieu feared that the United States might be preparing to make a separate deal with the North Vietnamese. On 2 October, with Haig still in Saigon, Thieu told the South Vietnamese National Assembly: "A political solution is a domestic affair of the South. It is a right and responsibility of the southern people to settle it among themselves. No one is allowed to interfere. . . . Only the present Republic of Vietnam government is competent to discuss and approve any domestic political solution for the South, and no one has the right to do it in its place."[27] Despite his fears, there was little that Thieu could do. As Nguyen Tien Hung, one of Thieu's closest advisers, wrote after the war, the South Vietnamese president "could not allow himself the luxury of an open rift with the United States."[28]

When Haig returned to Washington, he and Kissinger met with Nixon to discuss the Thieu situation. The president listened to Haig's report and told Kissinger that "the tail cannot wag the dog": if Kissinger persuaded Le Duc Tho to accept the offer the United States made in September, he should go to Saigon and "cram it [the agreement] down his [Thieu's] throat."[29]

As Kissinger and Haig prepared to leave for Paris, Nixon met with Soviet foreign minister Andrei Gromyko in Washington for the official signing of the Strategic Arms Limitations (SALT) agreements. During their meeting, Nixon warned that the offer Kissinger would make at the next Paris talks was final, and that if Tho turned it down, the United States would "have to turn to some other methods after the election."[30]

The president and his national security adviser were at odds over the negotiating strategy. Kissinger was pressing for an immediate agreement, but Nixon wavered. Kissinger believed that the North Vietnamese, fearing Nixon and the new mandate that would result from his defeat of McGovern, would be more likely to reach an agreement before the election. Nixon took the opposite view, arguing he would have more power to react after the election if the North Vietnamese proved difficult in the final negotiations; thus, he instructed Charles Colson, one of his chief political advisers, to "tell him [Kissinger] it will hurt—not help us—to get the settlement before the election."[31]

The next meeting between Kissinger and the North Vietnamese took place as scheduled on 8 October. Tho presented a nine-point proposal that included an immediate cease-fire, a prisoner exchange, American troop withdrawal, a cessation of movement of new NVA troops into South Vietnam, and the creation of an Administration of National Concord composed of representatives from the Thieu government, the PRG, and mutually agreed upon representatives of South Vietnam's uncommitted "third force," loosely described as the "neutrals." This body, like the previously proposed Provisional Government of National Concord, would resolve political matters, including supervision of elections, but it would be more advisory in nature than a "government." In the interim, the Saigon regime and the Communists would each control the areas that they occupied at the beginning of the cease-fire. Additionally, he proposed the "replacement of armament," dropping the previous demand that the United States cease all aid to the Saigon regime, saying that the Americans could extend continued military assistance to Saigon; this effectively left Hanoi free to resupply its troops in the South. Lastly, Tho proposed that the United States provide postwar economic assistance to Hanoi as previously offered by President Johnson. Le Duc Tho's proposals now closely mirrored those made by Nixon on 8 May, indicating that he was now prepared to accept a military settlement separated from the political one.

Although Tho's proposal represented a major breakthrough, some troubling aspects still remained. Tho proposed a cease-fire in South Vietnam, but ignored Laos and Cambodia. The proposals did not mention a North Vietnamese troop withdrawal, and Kissinger was also unhappy about the vagueness of the North Vietnamese proposal with regard to the cessation of further NVA troop movements and the functions of the Administration of National Concord. Nevertheless, Kissinger was elated by the progress being made and felt that the details could be worked out. At the conclusion of the session, he embraced his assistant Winston Lord and exclaimed, "We have done it."[32]

Kissinger and Tho met again on 9, 10, and 11 October. Most issues were settled fairly quickly. The Administration of National Concord was renamed the National Council of Reconciliation and Concord and was no longer required to reach a political settlement within ninety days, but rather was charged to "do their utmost." The replacement of military equipment was placed on a "one-for-one" basis, rather than the previously proposed "equality" basis, which would have permitted North Vietnam to build its forces in the South to a parity with the RVNAF. Linking the return of American prisoners of war to the release of political prisoners held by Saigon was one point of contention, but the details were to be worked out between Kissinger and Xuan Tuy, Tho's deputy, on 17 October. Tho, agreeing in principle to the cease-fire in Cambodia and Laos, settled on a tentative timetable with Kissinger for the implementation: 21 October—cessation of American bombing in North Vietnam; 22 October—initialing of the agreement in Hanoi; and 30 October—formal signing of the agreement in Paris.

Kissinger was elated; if everything went well, the war would be over in three weeks. He later called the forging of the October agreement his "most thrilling moment in public service."[33] However, when Kissinger returned to Washington on 12 October, some of his staff members were less than ecstatic about his breakthrough in Paris. His specialist on Vietnam, John Negroponte, argued that leaving North Vietnamese troops in South Vietnam was a big mistake. Kissinger exploded, telling Negroponte and his other staff members who shared this opinion, "You don't understand, I want to meet their terms. I want to reach an agreement. I want to end the war before the [U.S.] election. It can be done, and it will be done. . . . What do you want us to do: Stay there forever?"[34] Kissinger explained later that he thought the United States had no choice but to acquiesce to continued North Vietnamese presence in South Vietnam because a North Vietnamese withdrawal had been "unobtainable through ten years of war. We could not make it a condition for a final settlement. We had long passed that threshold."[35] Kissinger was probably right, but so was Negroponte. The situation would ultimately prove disastrous for South Vietnam.

Undaunted by the opinion of his staffers, Kissinger went to brief Nixon, jovially announcing, "Well, Mr. President, it looks like we've got three out of three."[36] Kissinger was referring to the diplomatic success with China and the Soviet Union, and now Vietnam. Nixon was also pleased, declaring that the proposed accords were "a complete capitulation by the enemy; they were accepting our terms."[37] He approved the tentative agreement, but directed Kissinger to bring Thieu along and not to leave him out of the process.

Kissinger flew back to Paris on 17 October to work out the remaining language in the agreement and to hammer out an acceptable compromise on the release of American POWs. He and his assistants made progress on all fronts, but they could reach no accommodation on the POW problem, which prevented finalization of the agreement. Kissinger warned the North Vietnamese that he would not sign the agreement until the final changes were made.

On 18 October, Kissinger departed Paris for Saigon to discuss the situation with Thieu. Nixon, softening his earlier stance, told Kissinger to convince Thieu to accept the settlement, but to do it gently, saying, "Thieu's acceptance must be wholehearted so that the charge cannot be made that we forced him into a settlement. . . . It cannot be a shotgun wedding."[38] While Kissinger was en route to Paris, Nixon wrote Thieu that he saw "no reasonable alternative" to the agreement and promised that the North Vietnamese would face "the most serious consequences" if they violated it.[39]

Anticipating a cease-fire, both sides began "land-grabbing" operations in South Vietnam to expand their respective zones of control before the cease-fire went into effect. On 11 October, Kissinger had cabled Thieu to "seize as much territory as possible," especially in the III Corps area surrounding Saigon.[40] The NVA forces received similar orders from Hanoi and made their move on 20 October. They made some minor gains, but ARVN exacted a heavy toll, killing or capturing over five thousand NVA soldiers. The result of this "land-grabbing" by both sides was, as one former ARVN general described after the war, "a pattern as crazy as the spots on a leopard."[41] (See map 12.)

Kissinger arrived in Saigon on 18 October. For the next four days, he, Bunker, and General Abrams, who had also flown in from Washington, tried to convince Thieu to support the tentative agreement that Kissinger had made with Le Duc Tho.[42] Thieu adamantly refused, raising four major objections. First, he objected to the stated purpose and function of the National Council of Reconciliation and Concord, seeing it as a Communist ploy to establish a coalition government by another name in South Vietnam. Second, the draft agreement referred to three Vietnamese states—North Vietnam, South Vietnam, and the portion of South Vietnam occupied by North Vietnamese forces. Thieu rejected any such division of South Vietnam. Third, the draft agreement required no withdrawal of North Vietnamese troops from South Vietnam. Fourth, there was no reestablishment of the DMZ, which to Thieu implied that there would be only one Vietnam, not two sovereign states.[43]

Thieu also had major objections to the translation of the agreement, maintaining that haste had resulted in substantive differences between the English and Vietnamese versions, further clouding the exact nature of the agreement in the four critical areas discussed above. The same day that Kissinger and the U.S. party arrived in Saigon, North Vietnamese prime minister Pham Van Dong added more impetus to Thieu's

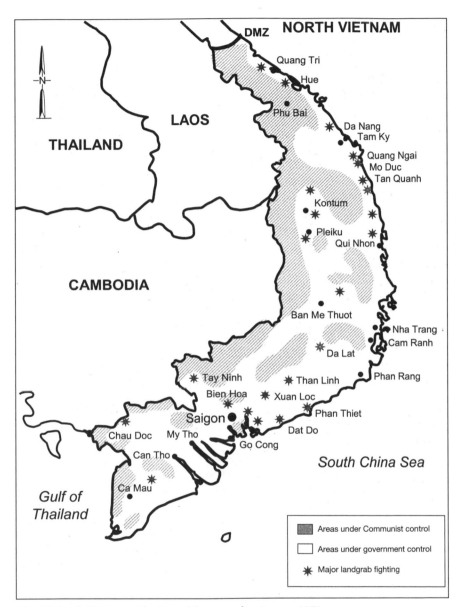

Map 12. South Vietnam at the time of the cease-fire, January 1973.

disagreement with the settlement when, during an interview with journalist Arnaud de Borchgrave in Hanoi, he referred to the National Council of Reconciliation and Concord as a "three-sided coalition of transition."[44] Thieu remained adamant in refusing to consider a coalition government for South Vietnam, and Dong's comments only inflamed his resistance to Kissinger's negotiated settlement.

On 22 October, at Kissinger's urging, Nixon scaled back the Linebacker raids in North Vietnam, establishing a restriction against further bombing north of the twentieth parallel.[45] The same day, the president cabled Thieu, threatening to cut off American support and warning him that his intransigence "would have the most serious effects upon my ability to continue support for you."[46] At the same time, Nixon ordered Kissinger to "push Thieu as far as possible," even to the point of threatening to sign a separate treaty with the North Vietnamese if he continued to fight the settlement. Thieu publicly denounced both the bombing reduction and the draft treaty, and told his forces that the Communist apparatus in the South "must be wiped out quickly and mercilessly."[47] In an official statement issued by the RVN Ministry of Foreign Affairs, Thieu said that South Vietnam had not been consulted about the peace settlement and would not "accept a peace at all costs, especially a peace that would pave the way to the subjugation of 17 million South Vietnamese people by the Communists."[48] In a meeting on 22 October, Thieu accused Kissinger and the United States of "conniving" with China and the Soviet Union to sell out South Vietnam. He completely rejected the agreement and presented a list of 129 demands that included a recognition of the DMZ and South Vietnamese sovereignty, the withdrawal of all North Vietnamese forces from the South, and the acknowledgment of the existing governmental structure in South Vietnam. Kissinger cabled Nixon: "Thieu has just rejected the entire plan or any modification of it and refuses to discuss any further negotiations on the basis of it. . . . It is hard to exaggerate the toughness of Thieu's position. His demands verge on insanity."[49]

On 23 October, Kissinger notified Tho that the tentatively agreed upon schedule could no longer be met and that he would not be traveling to Hanoi to sign the agreement as originally planned before Thieu balked. While Kissinger returned to Washington, Nixon sent a cable to the North Vietnamese in Paris. He cited Dong's comments and the NVA's "land-grabbing" as major hindrances toward reaching a peaceful settlement that was more palatable to Thieu, saying, "[T]he breach of confidence committed by the DRV side with respect to the Arnaud de Borchgrave interview bears considerable responsibility for the state of affairs in Saigon." Trying to make the North Vietnamese understand that he was in a precarious position with regard to Thieu's role in the peace deliberations, he wrote further, "The DRV side is aware of the fact that the constant U.S. position has been that it will not impose a unilateral solution on its allies and that it will move ahead only on the basis of consultation."[50]

On 26 October, the North Vietnamese broadcast a summary of the proposed peace agreement and charged the Americans with attempts to "sabotage" it, arguing that "the United States has not respected [it]" and further saying, "The Democratic Republic of Vietnam denounces the frivolous attitude of the Nixon administration."[51] Nixon and Kissinger decided that Kissinger would use a previously scheduled news conference that morning "to undercut the North Vietnamese propaganda maneuver and to make sure that our version of the agreement was the one that had great impact."[52] Kissinger began his remarks by declaring,"We believe that peace is at hand. We believe that an agreement is within sight."[53]

Kissinger's unfortunate statement made headlines around the world and raised expectations in the United States.[54] It also infuriated Thieu, who denounced the draft treaty as "humiliating . . . a surrender."[55] Kissinger admitted afterward that his comments had been a mistake that would "haunt me from then on."[56] Nixon was not happy with Kissinger's statement because he felt that it showed weakness toward the Communists. It also took much of the limelight away from the president himself, violating what Nixon biographer Stephen Ambrose described as a "cardinal rule" in the Nixon White House.[57] However, Nixon aide H. R. Haldeman did not think Kissinger's pronouncement such a bad thing. The Watergate scandal was beginning to heat up, and Haldeman felt that Kissinger's "peace is at hand" speech had taken "the corruption stuff [Watergate] off the front pages."[58] Nevertheless, Nixon was displeased with Kissinger's statement. He later wrote that he "knew immediately that our bargaining position with the North Vietnamese would be seriously eroded and our problem of bringing Thieu . . . along would be made even more difficult."[59] Accordingly, he attempted to distance himself from Kissinger's announcement. On 2 November, in a campaign speech, Nixon acknowledged the political breakthrough that Kissinger had made in the negotiations, but warned, "We aren't going to allow an election deadline or any other kind of deadline to force us into an agreement which would be only a temporary truce and not a lasting peace. We are going to sign the agreement when the agreement is right, not one day before—and when it is right, we are going to sign without one day's delay."[60] The next day in a speech in Rhode Island, he said, "[W]e are going to end this war and end it in a way that will lay the foundation for real peace in the years to come. That is what all Americans want."[61]

On 7 November, Nixon and his running mate, Spiro T. Agnew, won a landslide victory, with 47 million votes, or 60.7 percent of the total, to McGovern's 29 million, or 37.5 percent. He received 521 electoral votes against McGovern's 17, winning every state except Massachusetts and the District of Columbia. Many observers believe that Kissinger's "peace is at hand" statement helped Nixon at the polls, but it proved to be a short-lived victory.

Having won the election, Nixon was ready to be done with Vietnam so he could move on to other issues. He decided that Thieu, rather than the NVA, was rapidly becoming the major stumbling block to ending the war and extricating the United States from Southeast Asia. Thus, he intensified his efforts to win over the South Vietnamese president. The first step was to show Thieu that Nixon did not plan to abandon him. In early November, the Pentagon began implementing the plan that General Abrams had outlined for President Thieu while accompanying Kissinger to Saigon during the October talks. This plan, called Enhance Plus, involved a massive airlift of military equipment into South Vietnam. It was a continuation of the Enhance program, an earlier effort carried out to replace the weapons and equipment lost by the RVNAF during the Easter Offensive (see table 9).

Table 9. Operations Enhance and Enhance Plus

Enhance (May-Oct. 1972)	Enhance Plus (Oct.-Nov. 1972)
39 175-mm guns (3 battalions)	28 A-1 fighter-bombers
120 M48A3 tanks	90 A-37 jet fighter-bombers
37 CH-48 helicopters	116 F-5A jet fighters
32 UH-1H helicopters	32 C-130 transport planes
2 F-5E jet fighters	277 UH-1H helicopters
5 F-5A jet fighters	72 M48A3 tanks
48 A-37 jet fighter-bombers	117 M113 armored personnel carriers
23 AC-119K Stinger gunships	8 M706 armored cars
12 C-119G maritime patrol aircraft	44 105-mm howitzers
14 RC-47 photo recon aircraft	12 155-mm howitzers
23 EC-47 electronic recon aircraft	1,302 2½-ton trucks
28 C-7 transport planes	424 5-ton dump trucks
100 TOW antitank weapons	
32 twin 40-mm antiaircraft guns	
96 quad-.50 caliber machine guns	
3 high-speed endurance cutters	
4 fast patrol craft	

Source: William E. Le Gro. *Vietnam from Cease-Fire to Capitulation* (Washington, D.C.: U.S. Army Center of Military History, 1981), 17.

Enhance Plus was designed to complete the Vietnamization process, at least in terms of supplies and equipment, by giving the South Vietnamese as much equipment as possible before the peace agreement was signed. It would also serve to convince both Saigon and the North Vietnamese that the U.S. government was determined to "insure that South Vietnam had an even chance to make a go of it, once American forces were withdrawn."[62] The U.S. "borrowed" over $2 billion in materiel originally destined to American aid recipients such as Taiwan, South Korea, and the Philippines, who were promised replacements for the materiel that went to South Vietnam. The majority of this new equipment was flown into Tan Son Nhut airport in Saigon. In addition to the equipment brought in, the South Vietnamese also received materiel and equipment turned over to them by departing U.S. and allied units, including most of the equipment of two complete South Korean divisions, which were returning to Seoul.

In an attempt to circumvent a clause in the tentative agreement that called for the dismantling of U.S. bases in South Vietnam, the Americans began secretly transferring installations and associated equipment to the Saigon forces. Altogether, South Vietnam received an impressive amount and array of sophisticated military equipment that not only replaced the losses from the NVA offensive, but also provided an extensive stockpile for future use. One American general was reported to have said, "If we had been giving this aid to the North Vietnamese, they could have fought us for the rest of the century."[63]

Unfortunately, this massive influx of equipment proved to be more a political ploy than a sound military effort to assist the South Vietnamese. The decision to initiate Enhance Plus was made with no recommendation by the Joint Chiefs, who had previously indicated that no buildup over and above the replacement of

RVNAF combat losses was necessary. The White House's approval of the program was clearly designed to convince Thieu to go along with Kissinger's efforts at the Paris talks. However, much of the equipment received was not appropriate to South Vietnam's combat needs, and a large preponderance of the materiel went into storage and stayed there until Saigon fell in 1975. Bui Diem, the former South Vietnamese ambassador to Washington and later Thieu's political adviser, commented later:

> This . . . costly equipment was considered at the time as a gesture from the U.S. Administration to induce the Thieu government to sign the Agreement. It had perhaps its political value—practically everything which could be construed as a form of guarantee from the U.S. not to abandon South Vietnam was welcomed by Mr. Thieu. But it was hastily planned and ill-conceived, and the whole program had little military value; in fact, a lot of this equipment could not be effectively used by the South Vietnamese armed forces who later complained that they needed men and money just for the maintenance of this unusable equipment.[64]

This statement is particularly true with regard to the aircraft buildup. The South Vietnamese had 1,397 aircraft in June 1972, and by the completion of Enhance Plus that number had shot up to 2,075. By the end of 1972, South Vietnam, in terms of airframes, had the fourth largest air force in the world.[65] Unfortunately, they did not have enough pilots and ground crew to man such a force. As a U.S. Air Force study later concluded, this force was "completely beyond their [VNAF's] capability to maintain."[66] Thus, although the equipment provided under Enhance Plus may have served the purpose of sending a signal to Thieu, in the long run, it did little to assist the South Vietnamese in the coming confrontation with the North Vietnamese.

Despite the ultimate realities of the equipment transfer, Nixon hoped the new equipment would persuade Thieu to go along with the negotiations in Paris. On 8 November, he wrote a letter to the South Vietnamese president and sent Alexander Haig to Saigon to deliver it in person. In the letter, Nixon told Thieu that he had instructed Kissinger to work on improving the terms of the agreement with which Thieu disagreed. He wrote, "We will use our maximum efforts to effect these changes in the agreement," but he also warned, "I wish to leave you no illusion, however, that we can or will go beyond these changes in seeking to improve an agreement that we already consider to be excellent." Therefore, he urged Thieu to "take the political and psychological initiative by hailing the settlement and carrying out its provisions in a positive manner."[67]

Thieu, unimpressed with Nixon's letter, once again insisted that the NVA troops be removed from South Vietnam, stating that American estimates placing North Vietnamese military strength in the South at 140,000 were "imaginary" and "misleading" and suggesting instead that the actual figure was not less than 300,000.[68] He again demanded recognition of both his government's sovereignty over all of South Vietnam and of the DMZ's status as the permanent boundary between North and South Vietnam. Haig cabled Nixon of Thieu's continued opposition, and on 14 November, the president sent Thieu another letter in which he gave the South Vietnamese president his "absolute assurance" that he would "take swift and severe retaliatory action" if the North Vietnamese violated the agreement once it was signed. However, he warned that he had to have the support of Congress and the American people to carry out such actions and closed by saying, "I cannot overemphasize the urgency of the task at hand nor my unalterable determination to proceed along the course we have outlined. . . . In order to do this effectively it is essential that I have public support and that your government does not emerge as the obstacle to a peace which American public opinion now universally desires."[69]

Thieu responded to Nixon's letter by presenting Haig with sixty-nine modifications to the proposed settlement agreement that were designed to limit the role of the Communists in any future South Vietnamese government and force the evacuation of the NVA troops from the South. Haig said he would give the modifications to Kissinger for consideration but told Thieu that President Nixon wanted an agreement with North Vietnam. Speaking for Nixon, he promised additional military aid to Saigon and more bombing if the North violated the cease-fire, but he made clear that, one way or another, the United States would be out of Vietnam within six months.[70]

Having put Thieu on notice, Nixon gave instructions to Kissinger for his next meeting with the North Vietnamese in Paris. He commiserated with Kissinger about Thieu's impeding the settlement process but urged his adviser to work with the South Vietnamese president, stating, "What we are concerned about is to save South Vietnam and that's why we had to temporize with Thieu as much as we did, because our interest is in getting South Vietnam to survive and Thieu at present seems to be the only leader who could lead them in that direction." However, Nixon, a realist, added that if Thieu would not go along, "we shall simply have to make our own deal, have our withdrawal . . . and then say that Vietnamization has been completed and Thieu can do what he likes."[71] Having said that, Nixon directed Kissinger to present Le Duc Tho with the sixty-nine amendments to the draft agreement that Thieu had proposed; Kissinger, already frustrated with Thieu's recalcitrance, regarded these proposals as "preposterous" and going "far beyond what we had indicated publicly and privately," but agreed to submit them as directed when he resumed talks with Le Duc Tho on 20 November.[72]

Meanwhile, Le Duc Tho had declared upon his return to Paris that if Washington really wanted a settlement, it should "abide by the provisions agreed upon between the two parties" or "the Vietnamese people will have no other way than resolutely carrying on their fight."[73] When Kissinger and the North Vietnamese negotiators met at the scheduled session on 20 November, Le Duc Tho not surprisingly rejected Thieu's proposed modifications. The next day, he presented a set of new demands of his own. Tho withdrew the previously offered concession that American POWs would be released before political prisoners held by Saigon were freed. He also demanded that all American civilian technicians depart along with the U.S. military. The latter demand was key and, if granted, would have a debilitating impact on South Vietnamese military effectiveness, because a large number of civilian contract personnel were needed to service and maintain the sophisticated equipment the South Vietnamese had received under the Enhance programs.

When Kissinger informed Nixon of the new North Vietnamese demands, the president angrily sent his chief negotiator a new set of instructions. Unless Le Duc Tho showed "the same willingness to be reasonable that we are showing," he said, "I am directing you to discontinue the talks and we shall then have to resume military activity until the other side is ready to negotiate." He told Kissinger to warn the North Vietnamese that "with the election behind us, he [the president] will take whatever action he considers necessary to protect the United States' interest."[74] Nixon was clearly losing patience with the North Vietnamese; Kissinger later wrote in his memoirs that this period was marked by "the darkest and perhaps most malevolent frame of mind of [Nixon's] Presidency."[75]

The next meeting between Kissinger and the North Vietnamese negotiators produced no results; the negotiations were hopelessly deadlocked. Kissinger sent Nixon a message that presented two options: increase the bombing on North Vietnam to force them back to the negotiating table or wait until January to resume negotiations and take a hard line then to hammer out an acceptable agreement.[76] According to Nixon, Kissinger recommended pursuing the first option, but Kissinger later maintained that he had not.[77] Subsequently declassified White House documents have so far failed to settle the major discrepancy in their recollections or shed any new light on the genesis of what would become known as the Christmas bombing. Regardless of who first advocated a renewal of the bombing, the events of the following weeks resulted in new attacks on Hanoi.

After the talks reached an impasse, Nixon sent Kissinger a series of conflicting instructions. He initially sent a message telling Kissinger to work with Tho to reach a settlement, because "we must recognize the fundamental reality that we have no choice but to reach agreement along the lines of the 8 October principles."[78] Then, not wanting to take the bombing "chip" off the table, he told him to "suspend" the talks for a week and that he was prepared to use bombing if necessary to force an agreement. Nixon said, "I recognize that this is a high-risk option, but our aim will continue to be to end the war with honor. And if because of the pursuit of our strategy and the accident of timing of the elections we are now in a public relations corner, we must take our lumps and see it through . . . even though the cost in our public support will be massive."[79]

The next day, the president flip-flopped again and ordered Kissinger to keep the talks going. However, Kissinger had already arranged for a recess. He flew back to Washington to meet with the president. Nixon told him to "back off the position that we really had a viable option to break off the talks with the North and resume the bombing for a period of time. It simply isn't going to work. . . . We must have no illusions that we now have no option except to settle."[80] Instead of increasing the ongoing bombing that had begun in response to the 1972 invasion, he directed that it be reduced.

Nixon was indecisive because he was in a difficult position. The American people were ready for the war to be over. The North Vietnamese had been prepared to sign the 8 October agreement, but Thieu and his incessant demands for revision caused a backlash from them and resulted in an impasse in Paris. Nixon had to end the war, but not in such a manner that he appeared to be selling out Thieu and the South Vietnamese. Thus, the president was trying to walk a tightrope between the North Vietnamese and Thieu, which may explain the vacillation in his instructions to Kissinger.

On 23 November, Nixon sent Thieu another letter, promising "to take massive action against North Viet-Nam in the event they break the agreement," but warned him that leading American senators, including many of those from the president's own party who still strongly supported the administration's policy on Vietnam, "were not only unanimous but vehement in stating their conclusion that, if Saigon is the only roadblock for reaching agreement . . . they will personally lead the fight when the new Congress reconvenes on January 3 to cut off all military and economic assistance to Saigon." He urged Thieu not to delay the progress of the negotiations further, saying, "If you fail to join us in concluding a satisfactory agreement . . . you must understand that I will proceed at whatever costs."[81]

On 29 November, Nixon met in the White House with Nguyen Phu Duc, Thieu's personal representative to the Paris talks, who presented a fourteen-page letter from Thieu restating all his objections to the proposed settlement and asking for a Thieu-Nixon summit conference before any agreement was concluded with Hanoi. Nixon bluntly refused and reiterated to Duc the same warnings and assurances that he had been repeatedly sending Thieu. He said that the time had come for Saigon to "face the reality" that if the settlement was not worked out at the next scheduled session on 4 December, the Ninety-third Congress would perceive that Thieu had prevented a peace agreement and would end the war by cutting off appropriations.[82] However, Nixon reassured Duc that if Thieu agreed to the settlement, the United States would retaliate strongly if the North Vietnamese violated the peace agreement.

Thieu was not reassured by Nixon's promises. He was well aware that Congress could cut off the funding at any time and leave the South Vietnamese isolated to deal with the North Vietnamese on their own. Therefore, Thieu was less inclined to make concessions than Nixon and Kissinger, who just wanted the war over and the United States out of Southeast Asia. In a speech before the National Assembly, he said that if the North Vietnamese troops were permitted to stay in the South, "the annexation of South Vietnam through military and political means will only be a question of time." He added that the Republic of Vietnam "does not hesitate to continue the struggle, but it needs assistance." He concluded by saying that "the simplest way to achieve peace is to make North Vietnam end its war of aggression in the South. We do not demand that the war end with a victory . . . only in justice and with minimum righteousness, that is, that the invaded must cease to be invaded and that the aggressor must go home."[83] A point of contention was created by Nixon's and Thieu's drastically different ideas of "peace" in South Vietnam: Nixon wanted the United States out of Southeast Asia in an "honorable" manner, but Thieu was worried about the survival of his nation.

The day following his meeting with Nguyen Phu Duc, Nixon met with the Joint Chiefs of Staff. He wanted the chiefs to help him convince the American people that the agreement being hammered out by Kissinger in Paris was tantamount to an American victory. He also wanted their assistance in reassuring Thieu that the United States would respond if the North Vietnamese violated the agreement. Adm. Elmo Zumwalt, chief of naval operations, later wrote that Nixon warned them not to let the American people know about his secret promises to support the South Vietnamese after the cease-fire, because the president wanted the public to believe that the agreement "meant the end of any kind of American involvement in Vietnam no matter what happened there after the cease-fire."[84] Nixon then told the Joint Chiefs to begin preparing contingency plans for a renewed bombing of the North if the negotiations continued to be deadlocked, but under no circumstances were they to plan for the use of American ground forces.[85]

The president's approach to solving the Vietnam issue put Kissinger in an almost untenable position. Nixon himself described the situation: "[Kissinger] had not only to convince the North Vietnamese that we would stay in and continue fighting unless they agreed to a settlement, but to convince the South Vietnamese that we would stop fighting and get out unless they agreed to one."[86] Doing so became an increasingly difficult proposition.

Kissinger flew back to Paris to meet with the North Vietnamese. Le Duc Tho opened the meeting on 4 December by rejecting Kissinger's proposals and demanding that the United States accept the October draft accords as written. After a week of inconclusive negotiations, the North Vietnamese presented new demands of their own in the form of a set of "protocols" that contained sixteen alterations to the original document. According to Kissinger, these protocols "reopened a whole list of issues that had been settled, or we thought had been settled in the agreement. They contained provisions that were not in the original agreement, and they excluded provisions that were in the original document."[87]

The talks went back to square one. Little evidence exists to explain why Hanoi balked at negotiations in the last minute, but the North Vietnamese may have wanted to delay the signing for several reasons. Having failed to accomplish their goal of signing the agreement before the U.S. election, Hanoi had little incentive (at least initially) to speed up the process. Additionally, further delays in signing might benefit the North by widening the growing rift between Washington and Saigon. With Kissinger's "peace is at hand" speech, public opinion in the United States might force Nixon to reach a separate peace with Hanoi if Thieu remained recalcitrant. Finally, the longer the North Vietnamese delayed, the more opportunity they would have to resupply and replenish their units in the South. All of these reasons no doubt played some role in Hanoi's decision-making process. Regardless of the exact reasons, the negotiations were deadlocked. Neither side would give, and on 13 December, Le Duc Tho broke off the talks, saying he needed to return to Hanoi for consultation.

Kissinger returned to Washington to brief the president. According to Nixon, Kissinger was enraged at the North Vietnamese: "They're just a bunch of shits. Tawdry, filthy shits. They make the Russians look good."[88] The president, angry and frustrated, sent Hanoi an ultimatum to begin "talking" seriously within seventy-two hours or suffer "grave consequences." As Nixon biographer Stephen Ambrose points out, "Because he [Nixon] was a frustrated President, he was a dangerous President."[89] Nixon told the Joint Chiefs to prepare to execute the previously directed plans for massive air attacks against North Vietnam. He lifted all restrictions and told them to prepare to hit rail yards, power plants, radio transmitters in Hanoi, and the docks and shipyards in Haiphong.

On 16 December, Kissinger issued a statement, saying that the peace settlement was "99 percent completed" but blaming the North Vietnamese for the failure to complete the agreement. He warned that "we will not be blackmailed into an agreement. We will not be stampeded into an agreement, and . . . we will not be charmed into an agreement until its conditions are right."[90] Nguyen Thanh Lee, the North Vietnamese spokesman in Paris, responded to Kissinger's charges, saying that it was "completely untrue" that North Vietnam had demanded changes to the agreement and further stated that "if the United States really wants to settle the Vietnam War peacefully . . . it should sign the agreement agreed upon without delay and without any change."[91] At a 19 December press conference in Paris, Xuan Thuy stated, "The deliberate distortion by the U.S. side of facts related to the private meetings since November 20, 1972, is aimed at deceiving U.S. and world opinion, in an attempt to lay the blame on the D.R.V.N. side and concealing the wicked U.S. scheme of intensifying the bombing of North Viet Nam, continuing the Vietnamization policy on South Viet Nam, using military force in order to force the Vietnamese people to accept the terms imposed by the United States."[92] Peace was obviously not at hand.

THE CHRISTMAS BOMBING

Convinced that the North Vietnamese were extending the negotiations just when the agreement was so close to being finalized, Nixon gave the order to launch Operation Linebacker II, the full-scale resumption of air operations against North Vietnam.[93] Nixon wrote in his diary, "The North Vietnamese figure that they have us where the hair is short and are going to continue to squeeze us. That is why we had to take our strong action."[94] He wanted to demonstrate to both the North Vietnamese and Thieu that he could still punish North Vietnam if he had to. Kissinger later wrote that this was "Nixon's last roll of the dice . . . helpful if it worked; a demonstration to the right wing if it failed that he had done all he could."[95] In his memoirs, Nixon wrote that this was "the most difficult decision" he had to make in the war, but added that "it was also one of the most clear-cut and necessary ones."[96] Having made the decision, he told Admiral Moorer, "I don't want any more of this crap about the fact that we couldn't hit this target or that one. This is your chance to win this war, and if you don't, I'll hold you responsible."[97]

As the bomber crews prepared to carry out their new orders, Nixon wrote Thieu once again. Fearing that the South Vietnamese president would see the resumption of bombing as a signal that the peace settlement was dead, Nixon sent General Haig back to Saigon with the letter for Thieu. Nixon assured the South Vietnamese president that he intended to go ahead with the peace agreement as soon as the North Vietnamese came back to the negotiating table. At the bottom of the letter, he added in his own handwriting: "I have asked General Haig to obtain your answer to this absolutely final offer for us to work together in seeking a settlement along the lines I have approved or to go our separate ways. Let me emphasize in conclusion that General Haig is not coming to Saigon for the purpose of negotiating with you. . . . You must decide now whether you desire to continue our alliance or whether you want me to seek a settlement with the enemy which serves U.S. interests alone."[98]

Beginning on 18 December and for the next eleven days, U.S. B-52s, F-105s, F-4s, F-111s, and A-6s struck targets all over North Vietnam, flying over 3,000 sorties and dropping over 40,000 tons of bombs.[99] The Hanoi-Haiphong area was struck particularly hard, but the damage was extensive everywhere. It was reported that "Virtually all industrial capacity [of North Vietnam] was gone. Power generating plants and their transmitting grids were smashed. Gas and oil storage dumps were burned-out shells. Railroad marshalling yards looked like lunar landscapes. Roads and canals were clogged with shattered transport, SAM [surface-to-air missile] storage areas, tank, artillery and truck parks were pulverized. Military traffic dwindled to a trickle."[100]

The North Vietnamese air defenders retaliated, shooting down fifteen B-52s and eleven other aircraft, but the U.S. planes kept coming.[101] By the latter part of the campaign, Hanoi's air defense cover was destroyed and North Vietnam was nearly defenseless against air attack; former MACV intelligence officer General Davidson reported that during the last three days of the campaign, U.S. aircraft drew virtually no fire.[102] Unhampered by North Vietnamese antiaircraft fire, the U.S. bombers had finished taking out most of their priority targets. Approximately 80 percent of North Vietnam's electrical power was knocked out, and nearly 25 percent of the nation's petroleum supplies were destroyed. In testimony before the House Appropriations Committee later in the year, Admiral Moorer claimed that the December bombing had reduced Hanoi's warmaking ability to "less than one-half" what it had been before its ports were mined in May 1972.[103]

Reaction to the renewed bombing was swift, both at home and overseas. The Europeans were appalled. Sweden's prime minister, Olaf Palme, compared the bombing to Nazi atrocities in World War II. Roy Jenkins, the normally pro-American leader of the British Labor Party, called the raids a "wave of terror." The *London Daily Mirror* said that the raids "made the world recoil in revulsion." The Hamburg newspaper *Die Zeit* described the bombing as "a crime against humanity." Pope Paul VI called the bombing "the object of daily grief."[104] In the United States the reaction was just as severe. The media outcry against the bombing was almost universal: an editorial by James Reston in the *New York Times* called Nixon's bombing campaign "Stone Age barbarism" and "war by tantrum"; *Newsweek* magazine called it "diplomacy by terror"; and the *Washington Post* called the raids "savage and senseless."[105]

Congressional response was also immediate. Although Congress was adjourned for the holidays, leading Democrats condemned Nixon's actions and made plans to introduce new legislation to end U.S. involvement in Southeast Asia. Senator Edmund Muskie called the bombing "disastrous" and said he would "demand an explanation." Senator Jacob Javits threatened to cut off funds for the operation, and Senator William A. Saxbe suggested that Nixon appeared to have "taken leave of his senses."[106] In a poll taken several days after the bombing began, forty-five of seventy-three senators polled opposed the action; only nineteen supported it. Forty-five senators declared themselves ready to support legislation to end the war.[107]

The Nixon administration had expected a strong negative reaction to the bombing, but according to Kissinger, "Charges of immorality and deception were thrown around with abandon; 'barbaric' was another favorite adjective. It seemed to be taken for granted that North Vietnam was blameless and that we were embarked on a course of exterminating civilians."[108] Such was not the case, however. Stanley Karnow reports that the so-called "carpet bombing" of Hanoi and Haiphong, which many in the media compared to another Hiroshima, produced only 1,318 civilian casualties in Hanoi and 305 in Haiphong. (The atomic bomb that was dropped on Hiroshima on 6 August 1945 killed between 130,000 and 150,000 people.) Although there were some mistakes, such as the accidental bombing of the Bach Mai hospital, Karnow asserts that the American pilots went out of their way to avoid civilian casualties.[109]

Undeterred by either the reaction of the press or the loss of U.S. airmen, Nixon continued the bombing until 30 December. On 22 December, he sent Hanoi a message that he would halt the bombing above the twentieth parallel beginning on 31 December if the North Vietnamese would agree to resume the talks in Paris by 3 January. Hanoi failed to respond, so he launched the heaviest attack to date on 26 December, in which 120 bombers struck ten targets in Hanoi and Haiphong in a fifteen-minute period. Shortly thereafter, Hanoi sent a message requesting a resumption of the talks on 8 January. Nixon replied that he wanted technical negotiations to commence on 2 January and stipulated that the North Vietnamese should not bring up matters already covered by the basic agreement. If they agreed, he would stop bombing within thirty-six hours. They did so, and on 29 December, Nixon announced the cessation of Linebacker II. In his memoirs, Nixon called

Hanoi's returning to the negotiations a "stunning capitulation," which had been forced by the bombing.[110]

Because not everyone agrees with Nixon's assessment, the impact of the Christmas bombing on the negotiations has become a contentious issue. Many historians, like Nixon biographer Stephen Ambrose, believe that the bombing had little effect on the ultimate outcome of the negotiations and that "Nixon bombed Hanoi to get the North Vietnamese to agree to an agreement that they had already agreed to."[111] However, others take the view that Linebacker II and the devastation that it wrought brought the North Vietnamese back to the negotiating table. Historian Earl Tilford writes,

The "Eleven-Day War" became shrouded in myth and the subject of controversy. Within the Air Force in the post-Vietnam Era, it was an article of faith that Linebacker Two had "brought Hanoi to its knees." Simultaneously, "the Christmas bombing" gained near iconic status in anti-war theology, especially among those who would hold that it constituted "another Dresden." Both interpretations are wrong . . . Linebacker Two's contribution was much more in accordance with traditional concepts of strategic bombing—it had a psychological impact on Hanoi's leadership. That, coupled with the destruction of North Vietnam's air defense system, finally compelled a return to meaningful peace negotiations.[112]

Even those who question the role of the bombing in bringing the North Vietnamese back to the negotiating table agree that it may have had another equally important impact. Stanley Karnow, while believing that the bombing accomplished little diplomatically, has asserted that Nixon's main motivation was not diplomacy but rather a way to reassure Thieu and warn the Communists that he would not hesitate to bomb North Vietnam again should the armistice break down.[113] Karnow's assertion is correct; Nixon himself later wrote that he used the bombing to demonstrate his "own unilateral capability to prevent violation" as well as to maintain "credibility in policing the agreement."[114] There is little doubt that Nixon's willingness to use his bombers against Hanoi was an important factor in partially alleviating Thieu's fears about continued U.S. support, which contributed toward his eventual acquiescence to the peace accords. No one but the North Vietnamese know for sure (and they have not said to date) how much the Christmas bombing influenced their decision to resume negotiations. The fact remains, however, that they returned to the negotiating table.[115]

Nixon, anticipating that the bombing had paved the way for a breakthrough in the negotiations, sent Thieu another letter on 5 January. He told the South Vietnamese leader that Kissinger would present Thieu's continued concerns at the meeting in Paris but neither expected nor would require Hanoi to accept them. Nixon said that the problem of North Vietnamese troops in the South was "manageable" and added that if U.S. terms were met on the remaining issues, "we will proceed to conclude the settlement. The gravest consequences would then ensue if your government chose to reject the agreement and split off from the United States." As always, he promised to "respond with full force should the settlement be violated by North Vietnam."[116]

The same day that Nixon sent the letter, he and his advisers met with Bui Diem, Thieu's ambassador-at-large. Diem was given the same message that had been sent to Thieu. In a follow-on meeting, General Haig told Diem, "I have no doubt about the determination of our president to proceed. . . . If your president decides to reject it, it will be the end of everything—in other words, the abandonment of South Vietnam."[117]

RETURN TO PARIS AND THE SIGNING OF THE PEACE ACCORDS

Kissinger departed for Paris on 7 January. The next day he met with Le Duc Tho, and they quickly worked out the remaining details of the agreement. With the exception of minor cosmetic language changes that strengthened the dividing line at the DMZ, the agreement was essentially the same as the one Nixon had rejected in November—the U.S. negotiators failed to gain any new concessions. The final agreement completely ignored Thieu's main objection—the continued presence of NVA troops in the South—and also failed to address an Indochina-wide cease-fire. Kissinger, when asked by one of his assistants why he did not press Hanoi for more concessions, replied, "Look, you don't understand my instructions. My orders are to get this thing signed before the inauguration."[118] Having followed those orders, Kissinger cabled Nixon that there had been "a major breakthrough in the negotiations. In sum, we settled all the outstanding issues in the text of the agreement."[119]

Nixon, foreseeing Thieu's continued intransigence, sent General Haig to Saigon once again to give the South Vietnamese president an ultimatum. On 16 January, Haig, conducting the sixth high-level mission to win Thieu's support of the peace agreement, delivered a letter from Nixon informing Thieu of the agreement negotiated by Kissinger and stated, "I have . . . irrevocably decided to proceed to initial the Agreement on January 23, 1973, and to sign it on January 27, 1973, in Paris. I will do so, if necessary, alone." In that case, he warned, "I shall have to explain publicly that your government obstructs peace. The result will be an inevitable and immediate termination of U.S. economic and military assistance." Having threatened Thieu, Nixon tried to reassure him. If Thieu would sign the agreement, Nixon would make it "emphatically clear that the United States recognizes your government as the only legal government of South Vietnam; that we do not recognize the right of any foreign troops to be present on South Vietnamese territory; that we will react strongly in the event the agreement is violated."[120] He also promised to continue full economic and military aid. These were hollow promises. The promise of aid was doubtful, given the antipathy in Congress toward any continued involvement in Southeast Asia. Nevertheless, it was clear that the United

States was going to sign the agreement one way or the other. Still, Thieu would not budge. He sent a letter to Nixon listing the same objections to the "surrender agreement" that he had been making all along.[121]

Nixon was losing patience. He was to be inaugurated for his second term on 20 January 1973, and he had hoped to be able to announce the signing of the peace accords in his inaugural speech. Thieu's refusal to accept the terms precluded such an announcement. On 20 January, Nixon sent Thieu a final ultimatum, saying that if he had no "positive" answer from Thieu by noon, Washington time, on 21 January, he would tell Kissinger to initial the agreement without South Vietnam's concurrence.[122] Thieu realized that he had finally run out of options and had no choice but to accede to Nixon's wishes. Accordingly, he cabled Nixon on 22 January that he would approve the agreement.

On the evening of 23 January 1973, President Nixon addressed the nation on radio and television, issuing a formal statement announcing the end of the war:

> We today have concluded an agreement to end the war and bring peace with honor in Vietnam and Southeast Asia. At 12:30 Paris time today, January 23, 1973, the agreement on ending the war and restoring the peace in Vietnam was initialed by Dr. Henry Kissinger on behalf of the United States and Special Adviser Le Duc Tho on behalf of the Democratic Republic of Vietnam. The agreement will be formally signed by the parties participating in the Paris Conference on Vietnam on January 27, 1973, at the International Conference Center in Paris. The cease-fire will take effect at 2400 Greenwich Mean Time, January 27, 1973. The United States and the Democratic Republic of Vietnam express the hope that this agreement will insure stable peace in Vietnam and contribute to the preservation of lasting peace in Indochina and Southeast Asia.[123]

With the signing of the "Agreement on Ending the War and Restoring the Peace in Vietnam," Nixon had brought the Vietnam War to an end, at least as far as the United States was concerned. However, as Stephen Ambrose points out, the convoluted negotiations and the bombing of North Vietnam had resulted in a peace settlement that was scarcely different from the one that had been proposed in October. Nevertheless, President Nixon later declared that, by 1973, when the Paris Peace Accords were signed, "We had won the war in Vietnam. We had attained the one goal for which we had fought the war. The South Vietnamese people would have the right to determine their own political future."[124] What they actually got was the right to fight the Communists on their own, because the peace settlement did not resolve the issue over which the war had been fought in the first place — as Le Duc Tho had stated earlier, "the problem of power in South Vietnam."[125] Although the accords stopped the fighting for a very brief period of time, the agreement was doomed to failure because it mandated the departure of the remaining U.S. forces from Vietnam, but not that of the estimated 150,000 NVA troops encamped in the Central Highlands and elsewhere throughout South Vietnam who could be very easily reinforced after the Americans had left.[126]

The situation was made worse by the fact that the agreement provided no effective means to enforce the cease-fire. The Joint Military Commission and the International Commission of Control and Supervision, both of which were supposed to help enforce the cease-fire, worked on the principle of unanimity, giving North Vietnam a veto on the Joint Commission and the Communists the same blocking power on the International Commission.[127] What ensued was what the Communists called "half war and half peace."[128] As Stanley Karnow predicted in a January 1973 article in *The New Republic,* the cease-fire proved to be only "an interlude" that preceded "the beginning of what could become the third Indochina war." He added that it remained to be seen "whether the struggle that lies ahead can be waged without American involvement."[129] For the United States, the war was over. For the South Vietnamese, the war was just beginning another phase. The efficacy of Nixon's Vietnamization policy and the force that it built would be put to the final test without U.S. support of any kind—South Vietnam would have to face the Communists completely on its own. In early February, Kissinger told journalist Marvin Kalb that "it had always been our intention to enable the South Vietnamese to take over the burden of their own military defense and we believe we have left them in a position where they can handle most of the challenges that we can now foresee."[130] This was a hopeful assessment; unfortunately, the Vietnamization program that Kissinger alluded to had not solved the many long-standing problems of the RVNAF. Additionally, the massive equipment provided by the United States as it departed Southeast Asia had given the South Vietnamese "airplanes they couldn't fly, ships they couldn't man, and tanks and other equipment they couldn't maintain."[131] The bitter results of this situation would be realized over the next two years.

U.S. WITHDRAWAL

The cease-fire went into effect at eight o'clock Sunday morning Saigon time on 28 January (midnight, Greenwich Mean Time, 27 January 1973). At MACV Headquarters, Maj. Jere K. Forbus, the briefing officer, announced to assembled reporters, "All offensive military operations by U.S. forces in the Republic of Vietnam stopped at 0800 today."[132] The war was over for the United States. Lt. Col. William B. Nolde, the senior adviser to the Binh Long Province chief in An Loc, was killed by an NVA artillery shell at nine o'clock the night before the cease-fire went into effect. He was the 46,941st American killed in action and the last officially listed U.S. casualty of the war.

Under the terms of the cease-fire agreement, the United States agreed to "stop all its military activities against the territory of the Democratic Republic of Vietnam" and remove remaining American troops, including advisers, from South Vietnam within sixty days.[133] U.S. forces departed South Vietnam as agreed, with the last troops leaving Saigon on 29 March 1973.[134] That day, the last sixty-one American POWs known to be held by the North Vietnamese were released.[135]

For better or worse, Vietnamization had officially ended once and for all; the South Vietnamese were on their own. The only residual U.S. military presence in South Vietnam (aside from the 159 marines who remained to guard the U.S. Embassy in Saigon) was the newly formed Defense Attache Office (DAO) under Maj. Gen. John E. Murray, U.S. Army. The DAO included 50 officers and approximately 1,200 American civilians, many of whom were retired middle and higher ranking officers. Its mission was to monitor South Vietnamese military activities while providing technical assistance in such areas as communications and intelligence, but in accordance with the cease-fire agreement, giving no advice on military operations or tactics.[136] To support DAO and to prepare contingency plans for the possible resumption of the air war in Southeast Asia should the United States decide to do so, the U.S. Support Activities Group, commanded by Gen. John W. Vogt Jr., U.S. Air Force, was established at Nakhon Phanom in northeast Thailand.

Gen. Frederick Weyand formally deactivated U.S. Military Assistance Command, Vietnam, on 29 March 1973. In a final assessment of the military situation in Vietnam, Weyand cautiously declared RVNAF "capable of defending the South Vietnamese from any but a major power supported attack of massive proportions." He believed that if the cease-fire agreement was honored, the armed conflict would gradually fade away to a political contest. However, if the cease-fire did not take, he predicted that "we will be faced with the difficult decision of U.S. reinvolvement and the inevitable questioning of the validity of our past involvement." He noted the North Vietnamese buildup in South Vietnam and estimated that the NVA would be capable of launching a major offensive in the I and III Corps areas by 1974. Weyand believed that South Vietnam's ability to meet this threat hinged on Thieu's skill in attracting domestic and international support, reducing internal corruption, and improving military leadership, as well as on "the continuation of adequate levels of U.S. military and economic assistance."[137]

On the day that the last U.S. soldier left Saigon, Nixon went on national television and radio and reported that "for the first time in twelve years, no American military forces are in Vietnam. All our POWs are on their way home. The seventeen million people of South Vietnam have the right to choose their own government without outside interference, and because of our program of Vietnamization, they have the strength to defend that right. We have prevented the imposition of a Communist government by force on South Vietnam."[138]

Nixon had used Vietnamization and the negotiations in Paris as a means to achieve his promised "peace with honor" and extricate the United States from Vietnam. Many in the administration agreed with Ambassador Ellsworth Bunker, who declared in his last report to Nixon that "Vietnamization has succeeded."[139] Such optimism was not prevalent outside the executive branch, particularly among those who worked closely with the South Vietnamese military. Perhaps the best assessment of Saigon's chances was made by a DAO officer, who, when asked early in

1973 about the future prospects of the South Vietnamese against the Communists, answered, "Only time will tell if there is enough time."[140] Time always had been the key issue in the Vietnamization effort. Unfortunately, with the departure of all U.S. troops, time was beginning to run out for the South Vietnamese.

LANDGRAB 73

When the cease-fire began on 27 January, the NVA had an estimated 170,000 combat troops inside the borders of South Vietnam and about 100,000 regular troops in Laos and Cambodia (see table 10 for a summary of Communist forces in South Vietnam). Although the South Vietnamese controlled most of the populated parts of South Vietnam, the NVA controlled the extreme northern and northwestern part of Military Region I south of the DMZ and along the Laotian border, the northwestern portion of Kontum Province in the Central Highlands (Military Region II), and most of Phuoc Long Province and northern Binh Long Province in Military Region III along the Cambodian border.[141] They also controlled the "leopard spots" they had taken during the earlier landgrab in October 1972. These Communist-controlled areas would be, as ARVN general Nguyen Duy Hinh described them, "just so many knives thrust at the nation's back."[142]

The North Vietnamese ignored the peace agreement even before it went into effect. Much as they had done in October, they tried to grab as much territory as possible before the fighting was scheduled to stop. In the forty-eight hours preceding the cease-fire, the NVA attacked over four hundred villages and hamlets. The fighting was heavy, and U.S. Air Force and Navy planes flew nine hundred bombing sorties and fifty B-52 strikes in support of South Vietnamese forces during this period.[143]

Even as the North Vietnamese attempted to extend their control of South Vietnamese territory, they realized that they needed to rebuild and reinforce their troops in the South if they were going to hold the territory that had been taken. Under protection of the cease-fire, the North Vietnamese began to send troops south along the Ho Chi Minh Trail. Although they had agreed to withdraw from Laos and cease using it and Cambodia as an infiltration corridor, Hanoi leaders continued to move replacements and supplies down the trail to refurbish their units in South Vietnam in direct contravention of the peace accords. According to Gen. Nguyen Duy Hinh, the North Vietnamese "embarked on a program of force development that had never been or could ever be matched in the entire history of the Indochina War."[144]

Such reinforcement was necessary because the NVA forces in South Vietnam were in a state of total exhaustion. The Nguyen Hue Offensive had been very costly: entire units had been wiped out; a large proportion of the armored vehicles and heavy artillery had been destroyed in the fighting; and logistical stores were decimated and ammunition was low. Colonel General Tran Van Tra, the commander

Table 10. NVA Strength in South Vietnam at Beginning of Cease-Fire

	Combat Units	Admin and Rear Service Units	Guerrilla	Total
MR I	79,450	35,240	5,928	120,618
MR II	31,200	18,500	11,017	60,717
MR III	27,300	17,315	10,730	55,345
MR IV	29,050	14,065	13,325	56,440
Total	167,000	85,120	41,000	293,120

Source: Nguyen Duy Hinh, *Vietnamization and the Cease-Fire* (Washington, D.C.: U.S. Army Center of Military History, 1980), 153.

of the COSVN B-2 front, an area that included all of South Vietnam south of the Central Highlands, later wrote that "in 1973 our cadres and men were fatigued, we had not had time to make up for our losses, all units were in disarray, there was a lack of manpower, and there were shortages of food and ammunition . . . "[145] To overcome these problems while holding their positions in the South, the North Vietnamese had to initiate a massive resupply program, which was made possible by increased aid from China and the Soviet Union.[146] According to intelligence sources, North Vietnam received a total of 2.8 million metric tons of goods from Communist bloc countries in 1973, up 50 percent from 1972 aid figures; in 1974, the total increased to 3.5 million tons.[147]

To distribute this massive amount of equipment and supplies, the North Vietnamese instituted an improvement program to turn the Ho Chi Minh Trail into a network of wide macadam roads, concrete bridges, pipelines, and permanent drainage programs to support the buildup of their forces in the South.[148] Without the threat of U.S. air strikes, the NVA was able to make these improvements very quickly, rapidly increasing the infiltration of men and equipment into South Vietnam. During the early months of 1973, VNAF observation planes repeatedly reported seeing convoys of 200–300 vehicles, including tanks, trucks, and heavy artillery pieces, headed down the trail; whole units appeared to be moving south.[149] More ominously, intelligence sources reported that the North Vietnamese were greatly increasing their antiaircraft capabilities in the South. This did not bode well for the South Vietnamese, who had been taught by their American advisers to rely heavily on tactical air support.

Despite the Communist buildup in the South, the RVNAF, with over one million men under arms, was stronger in South Vietnam than the NVA and Viet Cong combined when the cease-fire started (see table 11). In addition, the South Vietnamese had just received a large influx of weapons, equipment, and supplies under Enhance and Enhance Plus. At first glance, the RVNAF appeared more than capable of handling the North Vietnamese and Viet Cong forces in the South. However, an accurate comparison of relative strengths requires more than a cursory consideration of numbers and force ratios. The RVNAF had taken a beating during the 1972 NVA offensive and was trying to recover from the traumas of that

Table 11. RVNAF and Communist Forces in South Vietnam, 1973

	MR I	MR II	MR III	MR IV	Total
RVNAF					
Divisions	5	2	3	3	13
Separate regiments and brigades	16	7	9	9	48[a]
Regular battalions	95	50	64	55	264
Ground combat troops (thousands)					
In regular units	75–90	27–29	50–60	40–50	192–229
Regional and Popular Forces	70–80	116–17	105–15	206–7	497–519
Trainees, administrative and service troops, and casuals	—	—	—	—	~200
Total troops	145–70	143–46	155–75	246–57	689–748
Communists					
Divisions	8[b]	3	2	3	16
Regimental HQ[c]	54	11	13	16	94
Battalion HQ[c]	195	73	77	79	424
Troops (thousands)[d]					
Combat troops	71	25	25	27	148
NVA regulars	68	19	20	16	123
Viet Cong	3	6	5	11	25
Administrative and service troops	25	17	16	13	71
NVA regulars	19	9	5	1	34
Viet Cong	6	8	11	12	37
Total troops	96	42	41	40	219

Source: William E. Le Gro, *Vietnam from Cease-Fire to Capitulation* (Washington, D.C.: U.S. Army Center of Military History, 1981), 28.
[a]Total includes seven ranger groups.
[b]Includes an air defense division.
[c]Includes independent regiments and battalions.
[d]In most cases, figures have been rounded down, rather than up.

eventful year. Many of the problems that had plagued the South Vietnamese military for years, such as poor leadership and high desertion rates, remained unsolved. An assessment by the U.S. Defense Attache Office in Saigon in July 1973 noted persistent corruption, poor morale, and a continuing lack of mid-level leaders and logistics resource managers.[150]

The numbers themselves were misleading. Only about 200,000 of the 450,000 ARVN regulars were in the infantry divisions and other combat units; the rest were found in the huge administrative and logistical "tail" required to support the combat forces. Saigon's problems were further compounded by Thieu's demand that all territory be held. His edict ensured continuation of the South Vietnamese forces' static nature, in which they were tied to the defense of virtually every inch of territory, thereby limiting their mobility and placing them entirely on the defensive; consequently, they abandoned the initiative to the Communist forces and let them set the terms of the coming battles.

CEASE-FIRE AND THE FALSE PEACE

As the cease-fire approached, the North Vietnamese, unable to pursue a general military offensive, decided to emphasize the political struggle, *dau tranh,* to win over the people of South Vietnam. General Giap, already discredited by the failure of the 1972 Nguyen Hue offensive, urged a general offensive against the South, but with the United States still promising aid to Thieu, the Central Committee rejected this idea as too dangerous. Instead, committee members chose to continue to prosecute a more low-key, but constant "path of revolutionary violence" against the South that would result in "half-war, half-peace" to keep the pressure on Saigon.[151] The Politburo issued orders to undertake programs designed to motivate the population, develop mass movements, and strengthen the political infrastructure. Military activities were to support the "political struggle as the base," and armed military action would be conducted according to the new situation after the cease-fire. Besides taking territory in the South, the North Vietnamese leadership ordered an intensified propaganda campaign to win over international public opinion, discredit the RVNAF, and gain support from the South Vietnamese people.[152]

A brief moment of calm followed implementation of the cease-fire, but then heavy fighting broke out all over South Vietnam as the landgrab intensified. Ambassador Bunker later wrote, quoting a U.S. pacification official in Lam Dong Province, that the "cease-fire appeared to have initiated a new war, more intense and more brutal than the last."[153] Over three thousand violations of the cease-fire occurred in the first three weeks after the official cessation of fighting. Most of these actions were small battles, fought by local forces, but in the first week of the cease-fire, the NVA captured 213 hamlets. However, within days, the South Vietnamese had retaken all but thirty-six of them. Rather than being just "a last spasm of violence" before the truce took hold, these battles were only a transition from one stage of the conflict to another, representing, according to one American military observer, "the end of the second Indochina war and the beginning of the third."[154] One South Vietnamese sergeant described the situation in simpler terms when he said, "This war will never end."[155]

Besides the initial small-scale battles, the North Vietnamese launched a number of larger attacks to secure strategically advantageous positions that could eventually be used to provide entry points for war supplies and equipment or to screen infiltration down the Ho Chi Minh Trail. On 26 January, the NVA NT-2 Division attacked and occupied the port of Sa Huynh, located in the southern part of Quang Ngai Province in MR I, but by the end of February, the ARVN 2nd Division had evicted the NVA units and reoccupied the town. In March, the North Vietnamese 9B Provisional Division launched a major attack out of Cambodia with three regiments against the South Vietnamese town of Hong Ngu, a port on the Mekong River in Kien Phong Province in the Delta (MR IV) just south of the Cambodian border. The United States, which was still bombing in Cambodia, supported the South Vietnamese by striking the North Vietnamese base areas there with B-52s;

by May, the ARVN 9th Division had retaken Hong Ngu. In early June 1973, the NVA F-10 Division attacked and captured Truong Nghia, six miles west of Kontum City in MR II. A major series of battles developed in Kontum and Pleiku provinces between the NVA F-10 and 320 divisions and the ARVN 23rd Division. After several bloody engagements, ARVN forced the Communist forces to withdraw. At the same time, North Vietnamese forces attacked the Cua Viet Naval Base in I Corps and the border ranger camp in Tong Le Chon in MR III. In these battles, the South Vietnamese forces fought well but were forced to abandon Cua Viet; Tong Le Chon held out, but was besieged. In the battle for the Cua Viet Naval Base, the South Vietnamese marines lost most of two rifle companies and an M-48 tank company, but inflicted approximately 1,000 casualties on the North Vietnamese.[156] The battles during the first three months of the truce resulted in heavy casualties on both sides. Over 6,600 South Vietnamese soldiers were killed during this period and over 200,000 refugees were driven from their homes by the fighting.[157]

In addition to the landgrabbing operations, the Communists interdicted lines of communication, shelled RVNAF-controlled cities and towns, and initiated a "flag-planting campaign" to erect the blue-and-red NLF flag in the areas under their control. South Vietnamese forces resisted and the "War of the Flags" ensued. One week after the cease-fire, nearly all the nearly four hundred hamlets that had been penetrated by the Communists were back under Saigon control.[158] Kissinger later wrote of this period: "Saigon, still the stronger side . . . gave as good as it received; it expanded its control over more hamlets than it lost."[159]

As both sides jockeyed for position in the wake of the cease-fire, the NVA buildup continued unabated and the Communist forces grew stronger every day. Intelligence reports indicated that during the first half of 1973, the NVA brought 65,000 new recruits into South Vietnam. In July 1973, Maj. Gen. Murray, U.S. defense attache in Saigon, reported in his quarterly assessment: "The position of the enemy as the result of his Easter '72 offensive, his blatant failure to adhere to the Ceasefire Agreement, and the imminent end of U.S. airpower in Indochina, make him stronger than he has ever been. His buildup of new roads, pipelines, airfields and land line communications, his input of tanks, long range artillery and antiaircraft weaponry, his stock piling of logistic resources are ominous."[160] Indeed, intelligence estimates in the same month as the DAO report estimated that the North Vietnamese had accumulated enough troops and materiel in South Vietnam to support a twelve- to eighteen-month conventional campaign of the 1972 type.[161] The Paris Accord's International Commission of Control, unable to control the situation or stop the cease-fire violations, ceased to function in any meaningful way within a few months of its establishment.[162]

Alarmed at intelligence reports of the North Vietnamese buildup and the continued significant cease-fire violations, Thieu went to the United States to confer with President Nixon in early April. However, Nixon had more pressing concerns. The Watergate scandal was gathering momentum, and the president was distracted by the mounting controversy. Thieu complained about the NVA violations of the cease-fire and told Nixon that reliable reports indicated that the Communists were preparing for a general offensive. Thieu found Nixon "preoccupied and absent minded" during the meeting, but Nixon reiterated previous promises to support Saigon, saying, "You can count on us." He told Thieu that the United States would fund the RVNAF modernization program, speaking of military aid at the "one billion dollar level."[163] Having said that, he urged Thieu to go back to South Vietnam and try to make the cease-fire work. As the South Vietnamese president boarded a helicopter to leave the presidential compound at San Clemente, Nixon again told him, "You can be sure that we stand with you."[164] Despite Nixon's promises and encouraging words to Thieu, Kissinger wrote later that "Nixon clearly did not want to add turmoil over Indochina to his mounting domestic perplexities."[165]

Thieu, not privy to Kissinger's assessment and wanting to believe Nixon's promises of continued support, returned to Saigon. As his plane took off from California, he had a champagne celebration to mark his pleasure and relief at his talks with Nixon.[166] He still feared that Nixon could not sustain these promises forever and thought that the United States would eventually abandon South Vietnam. For the time being, however, he believed that Nixon would intervene with U.S. airpower to save South Vietnam. His misconception was reinforced in large part by the activities of the Defense Attache Office in Saigon and the U.S. Support Activities Group in Nakhon Phanom, Thailand. The four ARVN corps commanders were flown to Nakhon Phanom and briefed on the procedures for requesting U.S. air strikes.[167] Secret communications equipment was installed linking the corps commanders and the Joint General Staff in Saigon with the U.S. headquarters in Thailand. ARVN plans subsequently assumed the availability of B-52s and close air support; no one on the American side discouraged such planning.[168] The Vietnamese commanders routinely submitted target lists to the DAO for transmittal to the Support Activities Group and U.S. 7th Air Force. According to former ARVN general Dong Van Khuyen, "Our leaders continued to believe in U.S. air intervention even after the U.S. Congress had expressly forbidden it. . . . They deluded themselves into thinking that perhaps this simply would take a longer time to come because of the complex procedures involved."[169]

Laboring under the misconception that U.S. airpower would be forthcoming if the situation became dire enough, Thieu decided to intensify efforts to gain every advantage over his Communist adversaries before Nixon's hands were tied by Congress and the promised support became unavailable. He emphasized what became known as the "Four Nos": no negotiations with the enemy, no Communist activity south of the DMZ, no coalition government, and no surrender of territory to the NVA or PRG.[170] His policy all but abrogated the Paris Accords. The last point was key: Thieu's refusal to give up territory would be one of the reasons for the ultimate demise of him and his nation. His adamant desire to hold all territory would have dire consequences in 1974 and 1975, causing him to overextend his forces, particularly in the remote border areas, and thus reducing the availability of troops that could have been better used as mobile reserves elsewhere in more critical areas.

Shortly after Thieu returned to Saigon, Kissinger met again with Le Duc Tho in Paris to discuss the cease-fire.[171] Unfortunately, the United States, with Nixon under fire over Watergate and with all U.S. forces having departed South Vietnam, was in a poor position to exact concessions from North Vietnam. When Kissinger charged that the Communists were violating the cease-fire, Tho countered that Saigon was responsible for the continued fighting. The best that Kissinger could wrest from Tho was a renewed commitment to the cease-fire. In reality, Tho was correct; Thieu's "Four Nos" policy was in direct contravention of the letter, as well as the intent, of the Paris Peace Accords. The result of the new round of discussions in Paris was that on 13 June all four signatories to the Paris Agreement issued a "joint communique" reasserting enforcement of the cease-fire. What became known in Saigon as "Cease-fire II" or "Son of Cease-fire" initially seemed to work, as no one flagrantly violated the cease-fire for a while, but then the fighting resumed at its old intensity.

On 22 September, the NVA 320th Division, using an infantry regiment supported by tanks, attacked and overran the Le Minh ranger border camp, twenty-five miles west of Pleiku. The camp sat on terrain that dominated an infiltration route from lower Laos into the Central Highlands. Having secured Le Minh, the Communists then attacked a long chain of border outposts designed to control enemy infiltration and collect intelligence. The North Vietnamese were obviously attempting to secure their north-south infiltration routes in preparation for renewed offensive action.

Thieu knew that the North Vietnamese were reinforcing their forces in the South and that their strength was growing daily. To take advantage of his military superiority at the moment, he put the RVNAF on the offensive. Accordingly, ARVN forces struck in the coastal lowlands, the Mekong Delta, the western mountain area close to Cambodia, and the provinces surrounding Saigon. Unfortunately, the NVA, steadily improving its offensive posture with the rapid infiltration of replacements, equipment, and new units, was already a lot stronger than Thieu had believed. The South Vietnamese had great difficulty dislodging the North Vietnamese, particularly those units that held areas around the capital seized during the 1972 offensive. The Vietnamese Air Force attempted to assist in these battles, but proved largely ineffective in providing close air support. Because of the new concentrations of anti-aircraft artillery and SA-7 shoulder-fired ground-to-air missiles introduced by the NVA in violation of the cease-fire agreement, the VNAF pilots remained at high altitudes and most of their bombs landed miles from their targets. A South Vietnamese air force general later confided that the poor results were due to "poor targeting, poor execution and low VNAF morale."[172]

The South Vietnamese found themselves in a fight for survival. Fox Butterfield reported the following assessment of the "cease-fire" in a September *New York Times* article:

> . . . despite the withdrawal of the last American military forces, the shooting has continued unabated, Vietnamese officers say, with an average of 100 South

Vietnamese soldiers killed or wounded every day this year in the Delta alone. That is a rate equal to the number of casualties during the big communist offensive last year, and higher than in many previous periods during the interminable war.

All you can safely say so far of the situation since the cease-fire, an experienced American official remarked, is that both sides are pushing full steam ahead with their separate programs, and they are going to continue to collide.[173]

As Thieu's forces attempted to hold the Communists at bay, the South Vietnamese president's worst fears about continued U.S. support began to materialize. With the approach of the cease-fire, many U.S. officials had demonstrated that they were ready for the United States to be done with South Vietnam. In early January 1973, Defense Secretary Laird told newsmen that the RVNAF was "fully capable" of defending its nation, which warranted "the complete termination of American involvement."[174] Not everyone in the Nixon administration agreed with Laird, but those who favored continued support for Saigon would find it increasingly difficult to counter those who shared Laird's viewpoint.

With the Watergate scandal becoming a hot issue, Nixon himself faced a hostile Congress. As he became more embroiled in the Watergate fiasco, Congress asserted itself and began to take a dominant position on getting America completely out of the war in Southeast Asia. In June 1973, Congress passed legislation that cut off all funds for combat action in the air or on the ground in Cambodia and Laos. The president vetoed the bill, but after a great deal of legislative maneuvering, on 1 July, Congress passed and the president reluctantly signed a bill that prohibited direct or indirect combat activities over, on, or near Laos, Cambodia, and both Vietnams after 15 August 1973. Nixon was not pleased with the turn of events, but by this time he was almost totally consumed by the Watergate scandal.[175] In addition, other events captured his and the American public's attention. In the fall of 1973, war broke out between Israel and Syria and Egypt. The subsequent oil embargo by the Organization of Petroleum Exporting Countries (OPEC) caused an economic crisis in the United States and the rest of the industrial world in the winter of 1973–74. Beset by these difficulties, and with all the U.S. troops out of South Vietnam and the POWs finally home, few Americans were concerned about the events in South Vietnam. Thieu's fears of American abandonment appeared to be coming true.

Nixon, involved in a virtual war with Congress, was in deep trouble. On 21 October, he dismissed Archibald Cox, the special prosecutor investigating Watergate. The firing ignited a firestorm of protest, and the House of Representatives commenced impeachment proceedings against the president. Nixon's presidential power and ability to influence the action in Southeast Asia was effectively gone.

Congress, concerned about continued fighting in South Vietnam, Cambodia, and Laos, took measures to limit the authority of the president and on 7 November overrode Nixon's veto of the War Powers Act. Under the legislation, the president was required to notify Congress, if possible, before introducing U.S. forces into an area where hostilities might take place. Once those forces were employed, they could remain no longer than sixty days unless Congress granted specific authority for them to stay.[176] The legislation did not specifically prohibit U.S. support to South Vietnam, but the law made providing assistance decidedly more difficult. Congress gave yet another indication of its intentions regarding the war in Southeast Asia when it modified the fiscal year 1974 military aid bill for Vietnam. The administration had requested $1.6 billion in aid, but Congress reduced the figure to $1.126 billion.

The aid bill and the implications of the struggle between Congress and the president over U.S. support to South Vietnam were not lost on the North Vietnamese, who were much aware that Nixon, critically wounded by the Watergate scandal, would be hard pressed to do anything if the Communists raised the stakes in South Vietnam. As time went along, U.S. aid for Thieu and his government appeared less and less likely. Accordingly, the North Vietnamese Central Committee convened the Twenty-first Communist Party Plenum in October 1973 to reassess their strategy and discuss how to proceed. The Communist forces, previously not strong enough in the South to prosecute an all-out military offensive, had focused military action to support the political struggle. However, by the time of the plenum in October 1973, the Communists had rebuilt their forces in the South and were growing stronger every day. At this meeting, Gen. Van Tien Dung, who had replaced Giap as the chief North Vietnamese military planner, advocated a new offensive, saying, "The U.S. imperialists would find it very difficult to intervene directly. . . . They cannot save the Saigon regime from collapse."[177] However, the civilian leadership of the Politburo, including Premier Pham Van Dong and party First Secretary Le Duan, urged caution. Having seen the effects of U.S. airpower during the Nguyen Hue offensive, they felt that undertaking major offensive action without Soviet and Chinese backing might result in the reintroduction of U.S. forces. Additionally, they believed that a general offensive would drain resources from the effort to reconstruct the North. After much discussion, the two factions reached a compromise. The North Vietnamese decided to increase the pressure on Saigon by shifting their efforts in South Vietnam from a primary focus on *dau tranh,* the political struggle, to one that emphasized military action, "war in peace," in preparation for a general military offensive at some time in the future after forces had been sufficiently built up to support such a move. Acknowledging that the struggle would be "protracted and complex" and that victory might take many years, they ordered "all officers and men of the main forces army, the regional army, the militia, and all guerrilla, home-guard, and security forces across South Vietnam to . . . fight back at the Saigon administration, as long as it has not discontinued its war acts, any place and with appropriate forms and force, thus compelling the other side to implement the Paris agreement seriously and scrupulously and to put a complete stop to all its acts of war and sabotage."[178] In addition to this critical change of strategy, the Twenty-first Plenum also decided upon the following measures: intensification of political and propaganda efforts against the United States so that Congress would further cut South Vietnamese aid; improvement of the "logistics corridor" down the border of South Vietnam from Khe Sanh to Loc Ninh to provide support for the proposed offensive; escalation of attacks against ARVN outposts; and continued application of military pressure on Saigon and other major cities to prevent the shift of South Vietnamese forces.[179]

Almost immediately, South Vietnam felt the effects of the Twenty-first Plenum's fateful decisions. The first blow of the new campaign came in Quang Duc Province, along the Cambodian border, where a division-sized North Vietnamese force overran ARVN outposts at Bu Prang and Bu Bong. Two days later, another NVA regiment routed the ARVN defenders at Dak Song, cutting off Gia Nghia, the capital of Quang Duc Province, and severing the only road to Phuoc Long Province. Then the NVA forces in Bu Bong attacked south toward Kien Duc district town, reaching the outskirts of the city by 21 November. There they were stopped by elements of the ARVN 23rd Division. Meanwhile, the II Corps commander, Maj. Gen. Nguyen Van Toan, ordered the ARVN 44th Infantry Regiment to retake the critical road junction at Dak Song, which they did on 28 November. The South Vietnamese forces acquitted themselves relatively well until 4 December when the 205th NVA Regiment, reinforced by tanks and sappers, drove ARVN from Kien Duc. However, a few days later, the ARVN 45th Infantry Regiment counterattacked and retook the city.

The new North Vietnamese military strategy became evident throughout South Vietnam. The fighting was intense, particularly at the remote bases and outposts in the outer areas and along the "rice road" from the Mekong Delta to Saigon, where both sides lost thousands of soldiers.[180] The NVA rocketed Bien Hoa Air Base, destroying three F-5A jet fighters, and sappers attacked the Nha Be petroleum tank farm on the Saigon river, igniting over nine million gallons of fuel. In mid-December, the Communist forces attacked a party from the U.S. Joint Casualty Resolution Center at Binh Chanh only sixteen kilometers southwest of Saigon, killing Capt. Richard M. Rees.[181]

At year's end, the combat in South Vietnam continued unabated. The U.S. Defense Attache Office's final report for 1973 stated, "Fighting continues with little adherence to the accords by either side."[182] Overall South Vietnamese combat performance during the period after the cease-fire had been adequate. Ambassador Graham Martin, who had replaced Ellsworth Bunker in Saigon, cited South Vietnamese battlefield gains as an argument for continued U.S. support. He noted the "increasingly evident self-confidence and up-beat morale of the GVN and ARVN" and stated, "The ARVN has not only held well, but has up to now kept the other side off balance. If we remain constant in our support, and determined to carry out the commitments we have made at the highest level, we have every right to confidently expect the GVN can hold without the necessity of U.S. armed intervention."[183]

The support that Martin so strongly urged was not to be forthcoming. The South Vietnamese had held their own during the fighting in 1973, but the "seeds of disaster" had been sown—a hostile U.S. Congress and the "virtual certainty of no American retaliation" when the North Vietnamese openly violated the Paris Accords in the future.[184] These seeds would begin to bear fruit for the South Vietnamese in 1974, and that fruit would turn deadly in 1975 when Vietnamization failed its final test.

8

The Fateful Year

THE "THIRD INDOCHINA WAR"

As 1974, the "Year of the Tiger," began, the fighting continued with the South Vietnamese performing reasonably well against the North Vietnamese on the battlefield. They had retaken most of the territory captured by the NVA in January 1973, with the exception of a few isolated fire-support bases and border outposts retained by the North.[1] Additionally, they had retaken 15 percent of the total land area controlled by the NVA at the time of the cease-fire, including 779 hamlets that had been either completely or predominantly under Communist control after the land-grab in 1973.[2] These gains had come at a high cost. The South Vietnamese suffered 25,473 battle deaths in 1973, exceeding that of any previous year in the war with the exception of 1968, the year of the Tet offensive, and 1972, the year of the NVA Easter invasion.[3] Despite these losses, the U.S. DAO in Saigon reported in February that the South Vietnamese were holding their own and that "uneasy equilibrium" existed on the battlefield.[4]

When the U.S. forces departed South Vietnam in 1973, President Thieu naturally assumed control of his own strategy. The few Americans left in the DAO had no role in advising Thieu and his generals on strategy after the cease-fire took effect. Col. William Le Gro, intelligence chief of the DAO, wrote:

> The cease-fire agreement in Vietnam signaled the end of the American advisory effort in that country. The senior officials of DAO scrupulously avoided any offer of operational advice to the Vietnamese with whom they worked intimately and continuously. The technical assistance provided by military and senior civilian officials of DAO and by the contractors was essential to the RVNAF's modernization and expansion, but the South Vietnamese military would get no advice on military operations, tactics, or techniques of employment. The war

199

belonged to the Vietnamese, and they were going to fight it. The RVNAF knew what to do but had to be provided the means.[5]

While the few remaining Americans concerned themselves with helping the South Vietnamese maintain the tools of war, Thieu's strategy remained, simply put, "hold all and at all costs."[6] As one of Thieu's advisers described it, "Everywhere there was a Communist attack or infiltration, the South Vietnamese forces must respond immediately. So the flag of South Vietnam should be everywhere, even over the remotest outpost of the country."[7]

Thieu's strategy had several serious drawbacks that eventually produced dire consequences for the Saigon regime. First, the RVNAF, trying to follow the president's orders, was stretched very thin and was always on the defensive. As such, it could only react to the movements of the North Vietnamese, who were able to set the terms of battle and thus achieve numerical superiority at the place and time of their choosing. According to Gen. Cao Van Vien, former chairman of the RVNAF Joint General Staff, Thieu's order "amounted to sacrificing a substantial number of troops who could be employed effectively elsewhere."[8] Second, ARVN possessed a limited strategic reserve, and even these forces were committed to a static defense role. Third, the local popular forces were tied down in small outposts with little or no mobility. Finally, ARVN had few troops to spare to mount any continuing mission to interdict the massive North Vietnamese reinforcement and resupply effort streaming down the Ho Chi Minh Trail into staging areas in Laos and Cambodia. Thus, Thieu's strategy, which demanded the utmost in mobility to respond to all NVA threats, resulted in just the opposite: most of his forces were immobile and on the defensive.

Shortly after the start of the new year, Thieu announced the beginning of the "Third Indochina War," saying that he was sending his forces on "appropriate punitive actions" that would be launched "not only right in our zones of control, but also right in the areas in which North Vietnamese Communist troops are still stationed."[9] Accordingly, during the second week of February, ARVN IV Corps commander Maj. Gen. Nguyen Vinh Nghi ordered troops of the 7th and 9th ARVN divisions to attack the 5th NVA Division (the former 5th VC Division that had played a major role in the battle for An Loc in 1972) in the Tri Phap area at the juncture of Dinh Tuong, Kien Phong, and Kien Tuong provinces in the Mekong Delta. The South Vietnamese took the Communist forces by surprise, forcing the NVA to fall back with heavy losses in men, ammunition, and supplies. For the next two months, intense fighting raged in the Tri Phap area, but ARVN performed very well, killing over one thousand North Vietnamese soldiers and capturing 5,000 tons of rice, over 600 weapons, 8 tons of ammunition, and a large quantity of other military equipment.[10] The South Vietnamese suffered seven hundred wounded, but fewer than one hundred killed. In the process, three NVA regiments (Z-15, Z-18, and Dong Thap 1) were badly mauled. By the end of May, the South Vietnamese were firmly in control of Tri Phap and the surrounding area.

The 5th NVA Division withdrew to the Parrot's Beak area in Svay Rieng Province, Cambodia, just west of Saigon. From that location, the North Vietnamese began to launch attacks against ARVN positions in Tay Ninh, Hau Nghia, and Kien Tuong provinces. ARVN III Corps commander Lt. Gen. Pham Quoc Thuan, deciding to hit the NVA in its sanctuaries in Cambodia, began positioning over twenty South Vietnamese maneuver battalions around the Parrot's Beak in preparation for an attack on the North Vietnamese base area around Svay Rieng.[11] On 27 April, Thuan gave the order to go and the ARVN infantry and armor forces attacked. The tank columns pushed sixteen kilometers into Cambodian territory, and infantry units lifted by helicopters took blocking positions behind the North Vietnamese defenders. The fighting was heavy, but ARVN, with VNAF close air support, maintained the momentum of the attack until 10 May, when the South Vietnamese forces withdrew across the border. The operation was a success: the ARVN attackers had killed 1,200 Communist troops, captured an additional 65, destroyed large quantities of supplies, and disrupted NVA communications and logistics throughout the area.[12]

These successes were short-lived, however, and the Svay Rieng campaign would be the last major offensive mounted by South Vietnamese forces; 1974 would prove to be a fateful year for South Vietnam. Eventually, Thieu's "hold at all costs" strategy would join with two other factors to seal the fate of South Vietnam. These factors were the loss of U.S. support and the subsequent demoralization of the RVNAF, which together would eventually lead to the fall of Saigon and the demise of South Vietnam as a sovereign nation. Although these events would not come to pass until 1975, the die was cast and the "unraveling of South Vietnam was already well under way."[13]

The withdrawal of U.S. combat forces left a void that the South Vietnamese, despite an increase in RVNAF force structure, were unable to fill. In 1969, the United States and South Vietnam fielded twenty-two divisions together; in 1974, the South Vietnamese mustered only thirteen divisions on their own. Conversely, the Communist forces in the South numbered 646 battalions by the beginning of 1974, a vast increase from the 1969 total of 352. Thus, the disparity in relative troop strength between the South and North widened, as the North Vietnamese forces grew daily in South Vietnam.

Even more important than the withdrawal of U.S. ground combat troops was the loss of American airpower, which was no longer available to the South Vietnamese. For a force that had learned to depend on the constant presence of U.S. aircraft for support, the drastic reduction in combat power would have dire consequences. Ironically, Nixon's Vietnamization policy had worked very well to the extent that it taught the South Vietnamese to fight "American-style," using air mobility, tactical air support, and lavish expenditure of ammunition and other materiel. Now they found themselves trying to prosecute such a war in situations where the requisite air support, ammunition, equipment, and supplies were either in short supply or unavailable. Involved in a life-or-death struggle with the North

Vietnamese, the South Vietnamese were neither willing nor able to restructure their forces and operational concepts to correspond to the new situation dictated by the drastic cuts in U.S. military aid to Saigon.

Some attempts were made at consolidating and reorganizing combat units to conform to the new situation. The general reserve was enlarged (the Airborne and Marine divisions each received an additional brigade) and two new ranger groups were organized. Additionally, the JGS transformed sector headquarters into mobile regional group commands, hoping to free regular divisions from territorial concerns and give the military regions a sizable combat force to confront enemy territorial units. These attempts at reorganization were less than effective because they did not address the central problem: the RVNAF's fighting style. The forces still tried to fight using the American way of war, but without all the requisite materiel and weapon systems that it demanded. As one observer aptly stated, "[T]he RVNAF had to fight a rich man's war on a pauper's budget."[14]

Thieu and his generals acted as if American assistance were guaranteed for the indefinite future. When the Americans left in 1973, the South Vietnamese made few adjustments and continued to prosecute the war on a "business as usual" basis. Former 3rd ARVN Division commander Maj. Gen. Nguyen Duy Hinh later wrote that "the RVN could not possibly think of tightening its belt for the simple reason that military aid was forced into its hands and no one could foresee a day when this aid would be reduced. So when aid was suddenly reduced, the RVN was really in trouble."[15] Hinh's characterization of "forced" aid is debatable, but his assessment of the results of reduced aid is certainly correct.

The well began to run dry in 1974. In 1972–73, South Vietnam received $2.2 billion in U.S. assistance. In 1973–74, that figure was slashed to $964 million, more than a 50 percent reduction.[16] In early 1974, Maj. Gen. John Murray, DAO in Saigon, advised Ambassador Martin that Thieu and his generals should be told that they needed to begin economizing at once in order to avoid a crisis later. Fearing that this would be "too unsettling politically" for the South Vietnamese, Martin forbade Murray to broach the subject.[17]

At first glance, it would appear that the South Vietnamese had enough war materiel to continue indefinitely the fight against the North Vietnamese. They had received $753 million worth of new airplanes, helicopters, tanks, artillery pieces, and other military equipment under the Enhance and Enhance Plus programs. However, as discussed above, much of this equipment was either inappropriate to the RVNAF's needs or could not be used and maintained because the South Vietnamese were not able to meet the management and maintenance requirements to keep it operational. Consequently, much of the new equipment, as one U.S. official noted, remained in storage "sitting around rusting."[18] Unfortunately, the mere presence of this vast amount of equipment gave the South Vietnamese a false sense of security as they assumed that the United States would continue to provide the spare parts, fuel, and ammunition needed to operate the new weapons and machinery.

Although the RVNAF leadership eventually instituted controls on expenditures to conserve fuel, ammunition, and supplies, the South Vietnamese still tried to fight the way they had been taught. With no change in basic tactics and operational concepts that relied on a significant amount of artillery and air support, the new controls did not work. The South Vietnamese began to use up the fuel and ammunition that they had on hand; by early 1974, the supply line dried up and "the system was never to recover."[19] They had nearly run out of everything that they had become accustomed to under the U.S. support umbrella. Such scarcity rapidly undermined South Vietnamese combat power and had a detrimental impact on their will to continue the fight. By the middle of 1974, ammunition supplies had dwindled, placing severe restrictions on combat operations. For example, artillery batteries in the Central Highlands, which had previously been firing one hundred rounds a day, were reduced to firing only four daily.[20] By the summer, each ARVN soldier was restricted to only eighty-five bullets per month. Hand grenades and other essential munitions were rationed. Even communications suffered, as radio batteries were in short supply.[21]

The shortage of fuel was a critical problem that affected both combat power and mobility. Restrictions in fuel allotments permitted only 55 percent of South Vietnamese vehicles—trucks, tanks, armored personnel carriers, river patrol craft, helicopters, airplanes—to operate, and those that could did so only at greatly reduced operational levels.[22] About half of the RVNAF's truck fleet was put in mothballs for lack of fuel and parts. An ARVN general officer in I Corps noted that "the ambulance units were so short in gasoline that in order to evacuate the wounded, they had to tow four ambulances in a row with a 2 1/2–ton truck."[23] In the Mekong Delta, the VNN was forced to deactivate half of its units because it could not maintain or refuel all its river craft. The VNAF was hit particularly hard: because of the fuel shortage and lack of spare parts, strategic mobility through the use of helicopters and cargo aircraft shrank by 50 to 70 percent.

In mid-1974, Gen. Pham Quoc Thuan, commander of ARVN III Corps, aptly described the harmful effects of the shortages:

In the last quarter of 1973 . . . fuel and ammunition supply was 30% as compared to the first quarter, or 60% if compared to the same period of the previous year. The supply was further reduced 30% in the first quarter of 1974, and another 20% in the next quarter. . . . At the beginning of 1973, III Corps was allotted 200 tactical air sorties a day; by the end of 1973, only 80 sorties were made available, and during the first half of 1974, the number of sorties allocated fluctuated between 30 and a maximum of 60. This huge reduction in air sorties stemmed not from a shortage of aircraft but from a shortage of fuel, bombs, and ammunition.[24]

For a force that had been taught to employ massive firepower and ordered to "hold everywhere," the situation was critical. According to Colonel Le Gro, the success of the South Vietnamese armed forces during 1973 had been made possible largely because of their ability to move quickly to reinforce threatened positions or attack suspected North Vietnamese troop concentrations, but that mobility "all but vanished with the decline in funding for maintenance requirements and the sky-rocketing cost of all supplies, particularly fuel."[25]

In addition to materiel shortages, the South Vietnamese began to experience a personnel shortage. Maintaining the RVNAF at its authorized strength of 1.1 million men under arms became increasingly difficult for Saigon. According to Gen. Cao Van Vien, former chief of the Joint General Staff, overcoming the attrition caused by combat losses, normal deaths, desertions, and discharges from the service required a yearly contingent of 200,000 to 240,000 replacements; however, the draft amounted to only somewhere between 100,000 and 150,000 men, resulting in a perennial deficit of 90,000 to 100,000 soldiers.[26] Consequently, many units were understrength, particularly in the combat forces that were bearing the brunt of the fighting. One DAO study of Military Region II in early 1974 found that only 65 percent of authorized ARVN manpower was present for duty.[27]

Not surprisingly, the manpower shortfall, coupled with equipment and supply shortages, had a devastating effect on troop morale. A lower number of replacements arrived in the combat units; a reduced supply of ammunition led to more ARVN casualties; and a dearth of operational helicopters delayed the timely evacuation of the wounded. Once at the hospitals, the wounded faced shortages of medicines, antibiotics, and bandages (which in many cases had to be washed and used again).[28] That the South Vietnamese soldier's will to fight began to waver under these conditions is understandable.

Saigon, faced with increasing shortages of funds and resources, cut soldiers' pay allowances, which severely affected the South Vietnamese troops and their families.[29] The DAO conducted a survey in 1974 in an attempt to determine the effects of these cuts on the economic status of South Vietnamese soldiers. The final report, prepared by Tony Lawson, director of DAO Special Studies, concluded that "South Vietnamese military personnel are forced to live at less than reasonable subsistence levels and that performance and mission accomplishment are seriously affected . . . [this situation] has caused a deterioration of performance which cannot be permitted to continue, if the South Vietnamese military is to be considered a viable force."[30] A South Vietnamese marine officer demonstrated the validity of Lawson's assessment when, responding to a survey conducted by the Rand Corporation for the Department of Defense, said with bitterness: "Yeah, you are a soldier, you are a squad leader with your squad, and you get the order to defend a hill to the death. You cannot defend to the death, when every week you hear from your family that they don't have enough food to eat. And you look to Saigon, the rich had food, liquor, they have money, they relax, have a good time. Why fight to the death? For whom?"[31]

Saigon did little or nothing to rectify the situation. The result was a sharp increase in desertions. Soon 15,000 to 20,000 South Vietnamese were fleeing their units every month. To make matters worse, many of those who stayed with their units made arrangements with their commanders to work elsewhere rather than at their duty place in order to make enough money to support their families. Those who worked away from their units were called *linh bong,* flower soldiers, and usually paid their commanders for the privilege of being gone from the unit, further reducing the organization's combat strength.

Still other soldiers made extra money by selling their weapons, ammunition, and equipment to the enemy. According to a February 1974 DAO assessment, "[C]ommanders in MR I freely admit that they cannot keep sufficient ponchos, entrenching tools, mechanic tool kits, etc., on hand, because, soldiers, whose families are in desperate need, sell these items on the black market to buy food."[32] Some South Vietnamese soldiers began to prey on their own countrymen. A peasant woman working a rice field near the American-built Chu Lai Air Base told an American reporter, "They [the ARVN troops] rob us all the time. The people can do nothing because they have guns—we can do nothing but weep."[33]

Senior leaders could have stepped in to assist their troops and ensure that they did not abuse the local villagers, but most did nothing. Many senior commanders appeared more interested in their own livelihood than the plight of their soldiers. Rather than curbing corruption, they more often than not joined in, raising it almost to an art form. A 1974 study conducted by Nguyen Van Ngan, one of President Thieu's closest aides, charged that more than two-thirds of sixty ARVN generals and full colonels were involved in some form of illegal activity.[34] Another study of corruption in the military, conducted by the RVNAF Military Security Service, found: "Since the cease-fire, military operations of our forces have become less active because of the declining morale of the soldiers, who either did not want to endure hardship or were too confident in the cease-fire agreement. A remarkable factor taking place beside the enthusiastic fighting of the majority of the soldiers is the corruption of a number of command echelons who escape responsibility, avoid hardship, and engage in activities for personal gain."[35]

The same report also said that lower "command echelons, especially battalion and company commanders," were selling weapons and equipment, embezzling public funds, extorting money from subordinates, and "devoting their attention to private business." Some commanders made money by pocketing the pay of nonexistent "phantom" soldiers on the unit rolls. One former South Vietnamese observer wrote after the war that the maintenance of "ghost soldiers" on unit rosters was a widespread practice particularly in Military Region IV in both regular and regional force battalions. He cited a 1974 report that most RF battalions in the Delta had an actual combat strength of 150 to 250 soldiers. However, the number of effectives reported on unit rolls was often over 400. Thus, the commanders in these battalions could collect and pocket the pay of roughly 200 "ghost soldiers."[36]

Other commanders made money from "ornament soldiers" who paid money to get safe assignments. Still others demanded protection money from villagers. Naval commanders in the Delta sold much-needed diesel fuel for personal profit.

There were even reports that some helicopter pilots were charging money for the evacuation of wounded soldiers from the battlefield.[37] Former ARVN general and minister of defense Tran Van Don later said that "virtually everyone who was able took advantage of his position and engaged in profiteering."[38]

The debilitating corruption and poor leadership led to a rapid decline of the RVNAF in the field. Discipline deteriorated and morale reached new lows. Alcoholism and heroin addiction increased. While the fighting dragged on and casualties mounted, soldiers watched their families go hungry, leaders often took more interest in personal gain than fighting the enemy, and replacements and supplies dwindled daily. The result, according to General Davidson, was that "a paralysis began to grip the RVNAF—a lethargic acceptance that the war was going increasingly against them and would eventually be lost."[39] This state of affairs was ominous, because the North Vietnamese were preparing to increase the pressure on the battlefield.

Despite clear signals that the United States would not reenter the war, President Thieu, who had received repeated promises from Nixon, clung to the belief that American intervention would save the day. Consequently, he took no drastic steps to stop the steepening downward spiral of his forces. General Davidson, writing after the war, placed at least part of the blame for Thieu's failure to act on the senior South Vietnamese military leaders: "The JGS, always weak and cowed by Thieu, studied no other options for the degenerating situation. Passivity and prayer were its recipe."[40]

Thieu also had to deal with the virtual collapse of the South Vietnamese economy. The South had long depended on U.S. aid and the revenue produced by the presence of large numbers of American troops to fuel its economy. With the troops gone and U.S. military aid drastically reduced, the economy all but came to a halt, leaving widespread unemployment.[41] Refugees who fled into the cities to avoid the continued fighting exacerbated the economic problem.

The U.S. Agency for International Development (USAID) estimated in 1974 that nearly one million workers, about 20 percent of the civilian work force, were unemployed.[42] The cost of living, which had surged upward to 65 percent in 1973, climbed an additional 27 percent during the first six months of 1974. The price of gasoline jumped from 31 to 105 piasters per liter.[43] The price of everything else also skyrocketed: rice was up 100 percent; sugar, 107 percent; cooking oil, 139 percent; and kerosene, 112 percent.[44] At the same time, per capita income fell by 25 percent. In the countryside, labor was in short supply, and despite record rice harvests in 1973, agricultural production could not meet the country's needs. By mid-1974, South Vietnam was solidly enmeshed in a recession that only promised to worsen with time. Thieu took steps to slow the momentum of the economic decline, but they proved inadequate.[45]

Compounding the dire economic situation was rampant corruption, which was just as prevalent in the public sector as in the South Vietnamese military. Smuggling was widespread, and untaxed whiskey, soap, and other goods flooded the black market, depriving the government of much-needed revenue. Profiteering in commodities such as rice, sugar, and fertilizer resulted in scandals that implicated high government officials, senior military officers, and even Buddhist and Catholic priests. A Saigon expression of the time said, "The house leaks from the roof on down," and many South Vietnamese held President Thieu directly responsible for the wholesale *tham nhung* (corruption) that permeated everyday life.[46] They were not far from wrong, because ample evidence exists that Thieu either tolerated or directly profited from the pervasive corruption. Some of Thieu's closest advisers and friends, such as Gen. Dang Van Quang, special assistant for military and security affairs, were among the most corrupt people in South Vietnam.[47]

The widespread corruption had a crippling effect on South Vietnam society. Writing after the war, former ARVN lieutenant general Lam Quang Thi described the situation:

> Corruption always engenders social injustice. In Viet Nam, a country at war, social injustice appeared to be more evident than in any other country. Corruption had created a small elite which held all the power and wealth, while the so-called "middle-class" composed mainly of army officers and civil servants became poorer and poorer joining the ranks of peasants, workers, and soldiers. The lower social classes were the people who shouldered the burden of the war and made all the sacrifices. It was the peasants who paid the taxes to the government, the bribes to the police, who bought fertilizers at exorbitant prices and sold their rice at a price fixed by the government. It was these people who sent their sons to fight and die for the country while government officials and wealthy people sent their sons abroad. . . . The government professed to win the hearts and minds of the people, but all it had accomplished was to create a widening gap between the leadership and the masses.[48]

Corruption and the deepening economic crisis had a devastating impact on the morale of the South Vietnamese people, which was already low due to the continual bloodletting of the "no war, no peace" situation that had prevailed since the peace accords were signed. Now, facing renewed military pressure from the North Vietnamese and in the midst of an economic disaster, the South Vietnamese people felt increasingly abandoned not only by the United States, but by their own government as well. According to General Davidson, "[I]n 1974 the fight went out of them; they sensed that the RVN was doomed; and that even without an enemy attack the Thieu regime was on the point of collapse."[49] Nguyen Ba Can, the RVN's last prime minister, agreeing with this assessment, later said that "the war had lasted too long, had been too costly, and had offered too few prospects of favorable termination."[50] The result, according to Stuart Herrington, an intelligence officer assigned to DAO, was "the erosion of the people's confidence in ultimate victory. There was a growing sense that one was sitting on a time bomb, and that the North Vietnamese were adding new sticks of dynamite to that bomb every day."[51]

THE "STRATEGIC RAIDS" AND THE NVA SUMMER OFFENSIVE

Herrington's assessment was correct. It was within the context of the South Vietnamese malaise that the North Vietnamese decided to take the "war in peace" to a new level. When Hanoi had stepped up military action in October 1973, the North Vietnamese leaders had watched closely for the reaction of the United States. Not only did the Americans fail to respond, but Congress passed the War Powers Act in November, further restricting the president's military options in Southeast Asia. The new legislation, coupled with the lack of an American military response, encouraged the hawks in the Hanoi Politburo, who renewed their demands for a drastic escalation in the fighting. At the party's Twenty-second Plenum in December 1973, the moderates in Hanoi once again successfully argued that a general offensive had to be put off until reconstruction of the North was complete. However, attendees decided to increase the military confrontation in the South to a level that, though falling short of a general offensive, would increase the pressure on Saigon. Accordingly, COSVN issued Resolution 12 late in December 1973 or early January 1974. The resolution, asserting that Communist forces in the South were in a stronger military position than at any time since 1954, charged those forces to attack "point by point, grasping partial victories and advancing toward final victory."[52] The order called for combined arms operations against not only isolated outposts, but also against more important targets such as district towns, subsector headquarters, rear bases, and division headquarters. By increasing the combat tempo, the North Vietnamese hoped to regain the military initiative in the South.

The Twenty-second Plenum's assessment of the growing strength of the North Vietnamese forces in the South was justified. By the beginning of 1974, the North Vietnamese were well prepared to increase the scope and pace of operations against the RVNAF. While U.S. support for South Vietnam dwindled, the North Vietnamese continued to receive weapons and munitions from both the Soviets and the Chinese. (One report said that the North was receiving roughly twice the amount of arms that the Americans were giving the South.[53]) RVNAF intelligence estimated that Russian and Chinese aid to North Vietnam in 1974 amounted to $1.7 billion, compared to $700 million in 1973.[54] Clark Dougan and David Fulghum assert that although the Soviets and Chinese had reduced military aid to Hanoi in mid-1973, the Soviets, upset with the failure of the United States to grant them most-favored-nation status, increased military aid to the North Vietnamese in late 1974 and early 1975.[55] However, Gareth Porter disputed these figures, citing CIA sources that said aid to the North Vietnamese from their Communist benefactors declined in both 1973 and 1974.[56] The actual amount of aid is obviously subject to debate, but the sheer volume of new equipment and weapons that the North Vietnamese employed during the final offensive in 1975 was most impressive, demonstrating few if any shortages.

Regardless of the specific amount of aid Hanoi received, the North Vietnamese made good use of the time following the cease-fire to replenish and reinforce their forces in the South, moving vast quantities of troops and supplies down the much improved Ho Chi Minh Trail. ARVN general Hinh later estimated that the North Vietnamese introduced more than 200,000 men into South Vietnam in 1973 after the cease-fire took effect.[57] The amount of new equipment moving south was staggering: The number of North Vietnamese tanks grew to over 650, compared with the cease-fire figure of 100. Additionally, the North Vietnamese had over 400 artillery pieces, including a new supply of 122-mm and 130-mm guns that far outranged RVNAF artillery. By the end of 1973, the North Vietnamese had twenty antiaircraft regiments in South Vietnam, and most were equipped with advanced air defense weapons and radar; some antiaircraft units were equipped with the SA-2 antiaircraft missiles mounted on mobile launchers. In addition to new weapons and equipment, the North Vietnamese sent vast quantities of food, spare parts, and ammunition to their units in the South. In Military Region I alone, an estimated 10,000 tons plus of supplies and ammunition were infiltrated in each month of 1974.[58]

To handle the increased volume of troops and equipment moving south, the North Vietnamese began constructing a new supply route, called the Truong Son Corridor, or Corridor 613. Unlike the Ho Chi Minh Trail, which ran through Laos and Cambodia, the new route ran inside South Vietnam, from north of the DMZ to Loc Ninh, just one hundred kilometers from Saigon. Completing the route required two years and the services of thirty thousand troops and multitudes of young men and women volunteers from the Communist Vanguard Youth organization.[59] The Truong Son Corridor was to play a key role in NVA operations in 1975.

While the North Vietnamese continued to build-up troops and materiel in the South, they also substantially reorganized their forces. According to senior NVA general Van Tien Dung, "To stage large-scale annihilating battles and firmly defend the newly liberated areas, it was no longer advisable to field only independent or combined divisions."[60] Therefore, separate regional and mainforce battalions were formed into regiments, and separate regiments were formed into divisions. Later in 1974, the North Vietnamese high command established several corps headquarters to command the increased number of mainforce divisions. I Corps was formed from divisions around Hanoi in May 1974. II Corps, organized in July 1974, assumed command of NVA divisions around the DMZ and two northern provinces of South Vietnam. IV Corps was established in the Southern Highlands and Cambodia, and III Corps was formed later in the Central Highlands. The establishment of corps headquarters portended increased combined-arms operations on a much wider scale than ever before.

The North Vietnamese Central Military Party Committee met in March 1974 and concluded that "The Vietnamese revolution may develop through various transitional stages, and it can only achieve success by way of violence with the support of political and military forces; if the war resumes on a large scale, a revolutionary war will be waged to win total victory."[61] Consequently, the military command ordered its subordinate headquarters in the South to commence what were described as "strategic raids" against the South Vietnamese forces. The operations were designed to regain the initiative on the battlefield, to gain control of additional territory and people, to wear down ARVN forces, to lower South Vietnamese morale through aggression and attrition, and "to hone the fighting abilities" of the Communist troops and staffs in preparation for the future general offensive.[62] While testing the resistance of the South Vietnamese forces and their will to continue the fight, the operations were planned to remain just below the threshold that might provoke a U.S. response.

The operations' specific objectives varied by region. Forces in the Mekong Delta would attempt to gain land and popular support. However, forces in the region surrounding Saigon would move to cut the capital city off from the Mekong Delta in the south, from the sea on the southeast, and from central South Vietnam to the north. Additionally, the North Vietnamese hoped to eliminate ARVN outposts that blocked Communist lines of communication and avenues of approach toward Saigon, both of which would be used during the general offensive, whenever it came. In Military Region I, the North Vietnamese wanted to isolate the old imperial capital of Hue, push ARVN forces out of the key cities, and eliminate the remaining outposts along the new logistical corridor. Meanwhile, the Communist forces in Military Region II also wanted to secure their part of the logistical corridor and the routes into central South Vietnam, while at the same time isolating the cities of Kontum and Pleiku.

During the month of May 1974, the North Vietnamese struck at bases and outposts throughout Quang Tin, Quang Ngai, and Thua Thien provinces in MR I. On 4 May, elements of the NVA 1st and 2nd divisions attacked Tien Phuoc district town and the village of Ky Tra. By the next day, Ky Tra had fallen, as well as all the outposts surrounding Tien Phuoc. Concurrent with the attacks on Tien Phuoc and Ky Tra, the NVA shelled and rocketed the 2nd ARVN Division headquarters at Chu Lai and the airfield at Tam Ky. The North Vietnamese next struck at the town of Gia Vuc near the Quang Ngai-Kontum Province border. These battles lasted until mid-June, when the North Vietnamese withdrew across the border to their sanctuaries in Laos. ARVN managed to successfully defend Tien Phuoc, but in the course of the fighting, three battalions from the 2nd ARVN Division were rendered combat ineffective.

The next move in MR I came in July, when the North Vietnamese mounted a new attack into Quang Nam Province under the command of the newly activated III Corps. The objective of this attack was the strategic Khe Le Valley, which provided access to the populated coastal regions. On 18 July, the NVA 304th and 2nd divisions began their attack in the area with artillery and rocket barrages on the Nong Song ranger camp and an ARVN base at Da Trach, followed by tank and infantry ground assaults. The South Vietnamese defenders at both bases were initially successful at holding back the attackers, but the next afternoon, a five-battalion infantry attack overwhelmed the defenders at Da Trach. The following day, Nong Song also fell. As these battles unfolded, NVA gunners shelled Duc Duc subsector headquarters and the air base at Da Nang while forces totaling eleven infantry battalions attacked additional government outposts and district towns. Former 3rd ARVN Division commander Maj. Gen. Nguyen Duy Hinh later wrote of these battles: "His [the NVA] combat tactic was clearly a model of mobile conventional warfare. Enemy forces attacked only during daylight and with the support of artillery and armor. The deadly enemy artillery firepower, the increase in other types of fire, and in particular the use of AA guns for direct ground support were factors that caused some concern to our troops. Enemy bodies displayed new equipment, modern first-aid kits, and modern combat rations."[63]

By the end of July, elements from three NVA divisions were besieging ARVN positions throughout eastern Quang Nam and Quang Ngai provinces. On 29 July, the 29th NVA Regiment struck Thuong Duc, the westernmost remaining ARVN position in Quang Nam. After intense shelling and numerous ground attacks, the ARVN garrison succumbed on 5 August, becoming the first district capital lost to the Communists since the cease-fire. By the end of August, the North Vietnamese 324th Division had taken key positions in the high ground south of Phu Bai in Thua Thien Province and was threatening the old imperial capital at Hue. During August and September, the North Vietnamese mounted successful assaults throughout MR I, capturing many more district towns and ARVN positions. General Truong, ARVN I Corps commander, counterattacked and used his forces skillfully. However, ARVN was stretched too thin, and Truong did not have enough reserves to stave off all the Communist attacks in the region. Additionally, the continuous combat had seriously depleted the ARVN ammunition supply in MR I.

As the North Vietnamese attacks unfolded in MR I, additional Communist forces attacked in the Central Highlands. They initially focused on eliminating ARVN outposts that threatened the logistics corridor. At the same time, the North Vietnamese commander ordered his forces to attack the ARVN positions in the Highland foothills in an attempt to force them down onto the coastal plain so that NVA units could move into assault positions near the major coastal cities. In April, two regiments of the NVA 320th Division struck at Outpost 711, just southeast of Pleiku. The small garrison there held out long enough for the 22nd ARVN Division to rush reinforcements from Pleiku into the battle, which turned the tide and forced the NVA to withdraw. Other South Vietnamese outposts in the region were not so fortunate. By mid-year, the NVA had taken the ARVN outposts at Dak Pek and Tieu Atar, while effectively laying siege to Plei Mei. In August, Mang Buk, an outpost located near a Communist supply route connecting Kontum with Quang Ngai and Binh Dinh provinces, fell to the NVA onslaught. As in I Corps, the North Vietnamese pattern of attack included massive artillery fires and overwhelming combined-arms ground assaults. Unlike ARVN, the NVA showed neither any evidence of ammunition shortages for its heavy artillery and tanks nor any reluctance to use what it had. Like his counterpart in I Corps, the ARVN II Corps commander, Lt. Gen. Nguyen Van Toan, was unable to move his troops around the region fast enough to counter all the NVA attacks; by October, Chuong Nghia, the last major

ARVN outpost in western Kontum Province had fallen. The North Vietnamese had succeeded in pushing the South Vietnamese out of the foothills, permitting NVA units to establish positions within artillery range of every major city and district town in the central region. In the process, they had exhausted two ARVN divisions by causing them to be "whiplashed" back and forth in response to widespread NVA attacks; in addition to severely depleting ARVN of experienced leaders and soldiers, the newly organized NVA III Corps gained valuable experience in planning and conducting a major offensive campaign.[64]

NVA general Tran Van Tra, commander of the B-2 Front, oversaw the operations around Saigon. He wanted to isolate Tay Ninh and Phuoc Long provinces, interdict the routes between Saigon and the Mekong Delta, and secure territory favorable to future operations. In April, elements of the 7th NVA Division struck at the small firebase at Chi Linh, forty-eight kilometers north of Saigon along Highway 14, which was the main route connecting Saigon and Phuoc Long. Shortly thereafter, other North Vietnamese troops finally overran the ARVN outpost at Ton Le Chan, west of An Loc, which had held out since the Communists had first besieged it in April 1972.

Tra ordered the 5th NVA Division to attack from Cambodia to take the Duc Hue ranger base in Hau Nghia Province just west of Saigon. Although the NVA was unsuccessful in dislodging the defenders, they quickly occupied and secured most of the area between the Vam Co Dong River and the Cambodian border. Ultimately, however, the 25th ARVN Division, reinforced by the 3rd Armored Brigade and a ranger group, counterattacked and forced the North Vietnamese back into Cambodia. In May, elements of the 7th NVA Division captured three ARVN outposts in the strategic Iron Triangle area, just northwest of Saigon. In a supporting operation designed to further isolate Saigon, Tra ordered a major attack by the 33rd and 274th regiments toward Xuan Loc, a major communications hub in Long Khanh Province, thirty-seven miles northeast of Saigon. Xuan Loc sat astride Highways 1 and 2, critical routes that connected Saigon with central South Vietnam and the coast, respectively. By the end of May, the ARVN forces had managed to halt the NVA advance on Xuan Loc.

The North Vietnamese had attempted to cut Saigon off from the west, northwest, and east, but they failed to hold any of the areas in MR III that they captured. However, they had successfully overextended the ARVN forces and inflicted serious casualties upon them. By early fall, III Corps commander Lt. Gen. Pham Quoc Thuan had successfully blunted the attacks around Saigon, but his forces remained in heavy contact with the NVA throughout the region; "the Communist thrusts in MR III had simply opened too many wounds for the RVNAF to heal."[65]

The story was no different in the Mekong Delta, although the battles were less dramatic than those in the other regions. The North Vietnamese increased the tempo of their operations, gaining control of villages and hamlets in Kien Giang, An Xuyen, and Chuong Thien provinces, including Hung Long, the first district capital ever lost in the Delta region.

The attacks from March to October 1974 accomplished exactly what the North Vietnamese leadership wanted. The NVA retook the initiative while occupying additional territory and gaining valuable experience in combined arms operations for its new units and staffs. They battered the South Vietnamese forces, causing them to expend large quantities of ammunition, and seriously depleted ARVN of experienced leaders and soldiers, lowering ARVN morale in the process. Additionally, they secured avenues of approach and, in some cases, even "jump-off points" that could be used for the major offensive when it came.[66] At the same time the North Vietnamese forces continued to grow in troops and equipment. Although the North Vietnamese suffered significant casualties during these operations, they were now receiving replacements faster than were the South Vietnamese. A DAO estimate reported that by September 1974, the North Vietnamese force in South Vietnam had grown to ten divisions, which included an overall combat strength of 200,000 men, 700 tanks, and 450 artillery pieces.[67] Still more equipment and men streamed down the Truong Son Corridor, which by this time was a twenty-six-foot-wide, all-weather road. From this main north-south route, spurs had been built running eastward to the battle fronts. This system, according to NVA senior general Van Tien Dung, resembled "strong ropes inching gradually, day by day, around the neck, arms, and legs of a demon, awaiting the order to jerk tight and bring the creature's life to an end."[68] Put less elegantly, the NVA forces were forging victories on every front and growing stronger every day, while the South Vietnamese grew progressively weaker.

U.S. ATTITUDES AND NEW MILITARY AID REDUCTIONS

As the events of 1974 unfolded, the official Nixon administration line in the United States on South Vietnam was "relentless optimism."[69] Although the ARVN forces acquitted themselves reasonably well at the beginning of the year, the situation quickly changed, belying the administration's optimism as the year progressed. By this time, Nixon was almost completely consumed by the Watergate scandal, but other administration spokesmen continued to extol the virtues of the RVNAF, even as they began to falter on the battlefield. Defense Secretary James Schlesinger reported that "The armed forces of South Vietnam are giving an excellent account of themselves when there are flare-ups of hostilities. . . . To many who observed the ARVN of six or seven years ago, the account they are now giving of themselves is splendid."[70] Henry Kissinger echoed these sentiments in testimony before Congress, saying that Saigon's military strength was sufficiently formidable to make its defeat "not an easy assignment for Hanoi."[71] Assistant Secretary of State Robert Ingersoll declared, "South Vietnam is stronger militarily and politically than ever before."[72]

The official optimism, particularly as the tide began to turn against the South Vietnamese, apparently was designed to elicit funds from a Congress that had lost interest in the war in Vietnam and just wanted it to go away. Administration officials hoped that by building up the South Vietnamese, they could justify asking for continued aid for "just a few more years" until Saigon could finally turn the corner.

Perhaps the most vocal supporter of the South Vietnamese was Ambassador Graham Martin. Testifying before the Senate Foreign Relations Committee in the summer of 1974, he painted a glowing picture of Thieu's government, reporting that "politically the South Vietnamese government is stronger than ever."[73] Most in Congress, however, were not buying his pitch. When a Defense Department official repeated Martin's assertions and predictions about Thieu's continued viability before a congressional committee, Representative Patricia Schroeder (D-CO) replied, "I have a feeling you believe in the Tooth Fairy."[74] Later, many in Congress came to the conclusion that Martin deliberately distorted the facts about the strengths and weaknesses of the Saigon government and the South Vietnamese armed forces. After comparing reports from U.S. representatives in the provinces with the reports that were forwarded to Washington, Senate investigators stated in 1974 that "the thrust of information submitted from the field to Saigon is sometimes altered and . . . on occasion significant information is withheld altogether."[75] Although Martin vociferously denied these charges, the damage had been done; both he and the Nixon administration, which was already reeling from the Watergate scandal, rapidly lost any remaining credibility with regard to the viability of the South Vietnamese, particularly in light of the difficulties that the RVNAF was now experiencing on the battlefield.[76]

President Nixon had submitted a supplemental aid request to Congress for the fiscal year 1974 budget to cover increased operational expenses and the replacement of lost and damaged war materiel, plus another $266 million to make up for the deficit incurred in the previous year. On 18 March, the House Armed Services Committee convened its hearings on Nixon's request. Adm. Thomas Moorer, chairman of the Joint Chiefs of Staff, and William P. Clements, deputy secretary of defense, appeared before the committee to state the administration's case for increased aid for South Vietnam, requesting that the House raise the ceiling on military aid to Saigon and approve the supplemental request. They warned that if additional aid was not appropriated, the South Vietnamese war effort would be seriously damaged, perhaps beyond repair.

On 19 March, the Senate Armed Services Committee began deliberations regarding the supplemental request. Senators Edward M. Kennedy (D-MA) and James B. Pearson (R-KS) tried to delete altogether the portion of the supplemental request earmarked for Saigon. Senator Alan Cranston (D-CA) urged the Committee "to phase out, as rapidly as possible, future military funds for the Thieu government."[77] On 6 May, the Senate rejected the removal of the ceiling on Saigon military aid. However, it approved the spending of the additional $266 million that had been discovered as a result of a bookkeeping adjustment. Senator Kennedy immediately submitted an amendment to block the expenditure of these funds. The Kennedy amendment was approved by a vote of 43 to 38. When the House-Senate conference committee met to iron out the differences over the bill, the appropriations ceiling was allowed to remain and the administration was prohibited from using the additional monies. The president, despite his disagreement with the outcome of the budgetary deliberations, signed the bill on 8 June. The South Vietnamese were upset by this turn of events, but the budget situation was to get much worse.

President Nixon submitted his foreign aid request for fiscal year (FY) 1975 (1 July 1974–30 June 1975) to Congress on 24 April 1974. The total aid package came to $5.18 billion, of which $1.45 billion was earmarked for military aid to Saigon. Additionally, the Pentagon asked that $150 million in already appropriated funds be allocated to South Vietnam.

The House Committee on Foreign Affairs debated the administration's request throughout June and July. As part of the effort to justify the budget, the administration presented the findings of a joint U.S.-South Vietnamese study that asserted that even with the full $1.45 billion requested in the defense budget, Saigon's ability to hold against a major Communist offensive was questionable. Further, the report maintained that anything below the 1974 program of $1.126 billion "would seriously affect both the capabilities and morale" of the South Vietnamese armed forces, which "would no longer have the capabilities to defend the entire territory under [its] control even if fighting continued at the same level" as the previous year.[78] Citing the joint report during testimony before the committee, Henry Kissinger strongly urged Congress to approve the $1.5 billion military aid bill, insisting that the United States had a moral obligation to South Vietnam and warning that failure to uphold it would have a "corrosive effect on our interests beyond Indochina."[79]

During committee deliberations, Secretary of Defense James Schlesinger was asked what would happen if the amount of ammunition provided to the South were sharply reduced because of budget cutbacks; he replied: "The ability of the [South Vietnamese] government to survive would be severely compromised. As you recall, at the time of the cutoff of tactical air support last summer, there was some question whether the government could survive. It pulled itself together, but it is dependent upon its own forces and the munitions that are supplied to these forces. Without such munitions, it is hard to see how it could survive."[80]

While the Foreign Affairs Committee debated the advisability of further aid to Saigon, the House Appropriations Committee was also dissecting the aid appropriation request. After much debate, the Appropriations Committee recommended that the requested $1.45 billion be reduced to $922.6 million, plus $77.4 million in unused funds. When the bill reached the floor of the House on 6 August, John J. Flynt (D-GA) offered an amendment to reduce the appropriation to $622.6 million, saying that the United States was not going to keep sending billions of dollars to President Thieu so he could "avoid the political realities of his own country."[81] The appropriation bill containing the Flynt Amendment was approved by the House on a vote of 350 to 43.

The administration's budget request received much the same treatment in the Senate, where many Senators apparently felt like Senator Hubert Humphrey (D-MN) who said that more "money [for the South Vietnamese] might buy time, but it won't buy peace."[82] Although some legislators spoke in favor of the administration's request, Senator Kennedy, one of the most vocal critics of the Saigon government, voiced the consensus when he said that it was time to terminate America's "endless support for an endless war."[83] The sentiment against increasing support for the South Vietnamese ran so strong in the Senate that a bill introduced by William Proxmire (D-WI) to further cut the appropriation for Saigon was only narrowly defeated by a vote of 47 to 44.

Despite dire warnings from the Pentagon and the White House, Congress eventually rejected all supplemental aid requests and slashed the final appropriation for 1975 to $700 million, a drastic reduction from the amount requested by the administration. The final amount appropriated included operating costs for USDAO, shipping costs, and certain undelivered FY 1973–74 equipment, leaving less than $500 million to be applied to the operational requirements of the South Vietnamese.[84]

According to General Vien, the army and people of South Vietnam were shocked at the reduced appropriation, which came at a time when North Vietnamese–initiated action had increased 70 percent since the previous year, a fact that only added impetus to the growing malaise.[85] A stunned Thieu lamented to Nguyen Tien Hung, his special adviser:

This is incredible. First the Americans told me at Midway to agree to the withdrawal of a few thousand troops and I would still have half a million Americans left to fight with me. Then, when they withdrew more troops, they said, "Don't worry, we are strengthening you to make up for the American divisions that are being withdrawn." When the pace of withdrawal speeded up in 1972, they told me, "Don't worry, you'll still have residual forces and we are making up for the withdrawals with an increase in air support for your ground troops." Then after there was a total withdrawal and no more air support, they told me, "We will give you a substantial increase in military aid to make up for all that. Don't forget the Seventh Fleet and the air bases in Thailand to protect you in case of an eventuality." Now you are telling me American aid is cut by sixty percent. Where does that leave us?[86]

Thieu was not the only one alarmed and frustrated over Congress's refusal to fund the war at the requested levels. Over the next eight months, the administration would send Congress a series of proposals asking for more funds, but none passed. In turn, the South Vietnamese would be encouraged by each new effort, then disheartened when each was turned down. General Vien later wrote, "For the first time in the war, our armed forces were in the decided position of underdog. It now became clear that the most [we] could hope to achieve was a delaying action pending restoration of U.S. military aid to its former level."[87] The funding was never restored, and the reduction in U.S. aid, according to North Vietnamese general Vo Nguyen Giap, represented "a fundamental turning point in the balance of forces."[88]

General Murray tried to convince anyone who would listen that the RVNAF was in desperate trouble. He testified before Congress in person, saying, "Vietnamese blood is being used as a substitute for American ammunition."[89] Returning to the United States in August to retire, he wrote in his final report as the chief of USDAO that without adequate support, "the South Vietnamese would lose, perhaps not right away but soon."[90] Despite Murray's pleas, Congress remained steadfast in its refusal to provide any more funds for the Thieu regime. Unfortunately, Thieu and his generals could not bring themselves to believe that the American people would let Saigon go under after having spent so many lives and so much treasure to support the South Vietnamese up to that point. Ironically, according to journalist Arnold Isaacs, Saigon's failure to adjust to the new funding realities stemmed in part from the budget deliberations and, in particular, the joint U.S.-South Vietnamese study that had played such a prominent role in the administration's case before Congress. Isaacs observes that

> to the Vietnamese the [joint] study became part of their doctrine, a basic premise of their strategy that made it even more unthinkable that aid could be denied. Different American advice might have persuaded them to examine what they could do with less aid: what territory might be given up, what units might be drawn from exposed or vulnerable positions. This was, after all, one of the implications of the joint study. In mid-1974 there were still space and time to try to adapt to new realities. But the Americans gave no such advice and the Vietnamese shrank from such decisions. Instead, they dithered purposelessly while telling themselves and everyone else what they couldn't do with $700 million.[91]

Wanting desperately to believe that the United States would save them at the last minute with an emergency injection of funds, Thieu and his regime refused to make the hard decisions that might have changed the ultimate outcome in 1975. Isaacs wrote, "In this state of strategic paralysis, already gripped with the premonition of disaster and with no clear-eyed or useful advice from Washington, Saigon awaited the next Communist blows."[92]

NIXON RESIGNS

The next blow to the South Vietnamese came not from the Communists, but from their staunchest ally. On 9 August 1974, two days after the House passed the military aid bill, Richard Nixon resigned from the presidency. Thieu and his countrymen had always relied on Nixon's promises to intervene if the North Vietnamese violated the cease-fire in force. Now, in the midst of the largest Communist offensive since the cease-fire, Nixon was leaving office. Thieu was stunned and, according to Nguyen Tien Hung, in a "state of high tension" and "in seclusion in his office."[93] The situation was best described by General Vien, who wrote after the war: "As the principal architect of Vietnamization and the Paris Agreement, in our view, he [President Nixon] was the only American official who bore the moral obligation of enforcing the cease-fire. He was also the only credible man who had the courage to take bold and forceful action when it was required."[94] The man who had repeatedly promised Thieu that he would stand by South Vietnam was no longer president. Thieu was heartened for a moment on 10 August when he received a letter from the new president, Gerald Ford, who promised that "the existing commitments this nation has made in the past are still valid and will be fully honored in my administration."[95] According to one of the South Vietnamese president's closest advisers, Thieu had been thinking about taking the advice of General Murray, who had urged him to think about shortening his defensive lines, concentrating his remaining troops and ammunition, and focusing on the defense of more-populated enclaves along the coastal areas. Ironically, Ford's letter convinced Thieu that American help was on the way, and he tabled any plans to change strategy.[96]

In the months to come, Ford would continue to reassure Thieu, but it soon became clear that the new president would not be able to change the mind of Congress. In the fall election of 1974, as a result of the Watergate scandals, the Democrats gained forty-three seats in the House, giving them 291 to the Republicans' 144. In the Senate, the Democrats gained three seats, leaving 61 Democrats and 39 Republicans. The formidable Democratic majority would all but tie President Ford's hands in 1975 when the North Vietnamese launched their final assault.

In the long run, Nixon's resignation and the reduction in aid appropriation were a one-two punch from which the South Vietnamese never recovered. "These two setbacks alone," wrote Stuart Herrington, "would have eroded the fighting spirit of the Vietnamese, but they were accompanied by stepped-up combat, escalating corruption, and worsening economic stagnation. The result was an unprecedented crisis in morale."[97]

The aid cutback and the abrupt departure of Nixon further undermined the Thieu government and led to the most serious political challenge of his career. Thieu had been able to contain the dissidents against his government largely on the basis of his relationship with Nixon and his ability to maintain U.S. support. When those evaporated, the political situation in Saigon came undone. On 8 September, a group of Catholic lay and religious leaders led by Father Tran Huu Thanh, a staunch anti-Communist priest, issued "Indictment No. 1," which charged Thieu with protecting the widespread corruption that permeated every aspect of South Vietnamese life. Moreover, the document charged Thieu and his family members with illegal speculation, skimming from public funds, and heroin trafficking.[98] The indictment concluded that the "present rotten, dictatorial family regime . . . [was] a national disaster and a national shame, a betrayal of all those who have been sacrificing themselves for the hard, protracted struggle of our people and army for more than a quarter of a century."[99]

The direct attack on Thieu and his claim to leadership of the nation set off a chain reaction of other protests. Three Saigon daily newspapers published the indictment, but their editions were confiscated by government troops and national police, which only fanned the flames of protest. A group of Buddhist religious leaders and political leaders formed the "National Reconciliation Force" and demanded that Thieu implement the Paris Agreement. Shortly thereafter, in quick succession, an "Anti-Famine Movement," a "Women's Movement for the Right to Life," and a campaign for the release of political prisoners appeared and added to the protests against Thieu and his regime. The frustration of the South Vietnamese people had finally boiled over, generating what one of Thieu's advisers described as "a vast anti-government crusade."[100]

Urged by Ambassador Martin to defuse the situation, Thieu at first tried to reason with the dissenters. He even went so far as to dismiss four cabinet members and fired or demoted four hundred field-grade officers in the RVNAF. However, the protesters regarded his actions as being too little too late. Father Thanh, vowing that the demonstrations would continue, explained: "Personnel changes are not important. We want a change of stance and policy."[101] Thieu, making the most substantial concessions of his seven-year presidency, removed three of his four regional commanders. Even this failed to satisfy the dissenters. One National Assembly deputy proclaimed, "Dropping a few technocrats will not change things. The man at the top must be changed."[102]

Thousands of protesters once again took to the streets of Saigon. Thieu, whose forces were being hard pressed on the battlefield, was prepared to allow the dissidents only so much leeway. Matters worsened for the beleaguered South Vietnamese president on 8 October when the Provisional Revolutionary Government announced that it would no longer negotiate with his regime. "As long as Nguyen Van Thieu and his gang remain in power in Saigon," the PRG statement said, "the sabotage of the Paris agreement will go on, and it will still be impossible to achieve peace and national concord." Therefore, Thieu must be overthrown and replaced by "an administration that desires peace and national concord and is willing to implement the Paris agreement on Vietnam in a serious way."[103]

Thieu, vowing that he would not let the protesters deliver the country to the Communists, struck back. When he commanded the national police and government troops to bring the demonstrations under control to preserve public order, bloody clashes erupted in the streets. Eleven opposition leaders were beaten and arrested. Twenty-eight newsmen were also arrested during a raid on the Vietnam Press Club. In his National Day Speech on 1 November, Thieu announced that henceforth the dissenters would not be permitted "to propagate groundless news, to create religious divisions . . . to slander the government, to calumnify government officials, to undermine the economy."[104] In the wake of his warning and the increased show of force, the demonstrations subsided. However, the damage had been done. A public opinion survey conducted by the Saigon Government in late 1974 revealed that confidence in the performance of the government and its ability to defend the country from the Communists was at its lowest since 1968. Thieu had lost all remaining credibility with his own people.

NORTH VIETNAMESE STRATEGIC REASSESSMENT

With the demise of Nixon, favorable circumstances had converged for the North Vietnamese leadership. Their principal nemesis in Washington had been forced from office, and South Vietnamese forces were now stretched to the breaking point. The "strategic raids" of early 1974 and the subsequent summer offensive had far exceeded the North's expectations. In addition, the RVNAF showed distinct signs that it was beginning to disintegrate as a cogent fighting force; North Vietnamese intelligence agents correctly estimated that ammunition shortages had reduced South Vietnamese firepower by 60 percent and that fuel and spare parts shortages had cut RVNAF mobility by 50 percent.[105] Given these estimates, the North Vietnamese, according to Gen. Van Tien Dung, "paid particular attention" to the battle at the district town of Thuong Duc in Quang Nam Province as a true measure of the state of the RVNAF. Thuong Duc was the westernmost ARVN outpost on the outer defensive perimeter protecting the vital city of Da Nang, which lay only 40 kilometers away. The North Vietnamese had attacked on 29 July 1974, and by 7 August they had taken the district capital, killing and capturing the 1,600-man South Vietnamese garrison in the process.[106] Dung later wrote of the battle: "This was a test of strength with what were said to be the enemy's best-trained troops. When we knocked out Thuong Duc, the enemy sent a whole division of paratroops for days of continuous counterattacks to take it back. But we inflicted heavy casualties on them, held Thuong Duc, and forced the enemy to give up."[107]

Having observed the action at Thuong Duc and the easily won objectives in the Central Highlands, Dung and the General Staff reported to the Central Military Party Committee that "the fighting ability of our mobile main-force troops was now altogether superior to that of the enemy's mobile regular troops . . . that the war had reached its final stage. The balance of forces had changed. We had grown stronger, while the enemy had weakened."[108] Their assessment, coupled with the resignation of Nixon, the cut in funding, and the mounting political crisis in Saigon, convinced many in the North Vietnamese military and civilian leadership that yet another shift in strategy was appropriate. In October 1974, the Central Military Party Committee and the Politburo met in conference in Hanoi to consider the General Staff's assessment and recommendation. According to Dung, the conference members agreed on the following:

1.   The puppet troops were militarily, politically and economically weakening every day and our forces were quite stronger than the enemy in the south.
2.   The United States was facing mounting difficulties both at home and in the world, and its potential for aiding the puppets was declining.
3.   We had created a chain of mutual support, had strengthened our reserve forces and materiel and were steadily improving our strategic and political systems.
4.   The movement to demand peace, improvement of the people's livelihood, democracy, national independence and Thieu's overthrow in various cities was gaining momentum.[109]

Although conference attendees agreed that the potential was declining for the United States to come to the aid of the Thieu regime, they were not convinced that the Americans would not react in some fashion. Thus, the key question, according to Dung, was, "Did the Americans have the ability to send troops back into the South when our large attacks led to the danger of the Saigon army's collapse?"[110] Opinion was divided on this issue, but Le Duan argued: "Now that the United States has pulled out of the South, it will be hard for them to jump back in. And no matter how they may intervene, they cannot rescue the Saigon administration from its disastrous collapse."[111] His argument persuaded Le Duan's colleagues, and by the end of October, the Politburo had decided on the strategy for 1975 and 1976. The Politburo's decision, which became known as the "Resolution of 1975," stated that the war had reached its "final stage." The North Vietnamese would launch a two-phased offensive: in 1975, they would consolidate gains, further secure the "logistics corridor," and continue the force buildup in the South; in 1976, they would begin the final general offensive.

Their decision to delay the general offensive may seem strange given the scope of the Communist buildup in 1973 and early 1974, but during the Politburo deliberations, Le Duc Tho, who by this time was the second most powerful man in North Vietnam behind Le Duan, said: "Our material stockpiles are still very deficient, especially with regards to weapons and ammunition. . . . Therefore, we must limit the fighting in 1975 in order to save our strength for 1976, when we will launch large-scale attacks. . . ."[112] The strategy was undoubtedly conservative, but Hanoi had reason to play it safe; they had tried twice before to launch general offensives (1968 and 1972), both of which proved to be premature and extremely costly in casualties. Additionally, the North Vietnamese General Staff overestimated the capabilities of the RVNAF, which had fought reasonably well during the summer and into the fall. Despite ample evidence that the South Vietnamese forces were in trouble, the North Vietnamese leadership (still unaware of just how badly South Vietnamese morale had deteriorated during the previous year) continued to believe that the RVNAF, technically at least, still held a superiority in overall strength.[113] Thus, they were not confident enough to launch the "final" campaign without further preparations.

The major field commanders and political chiefs were called to Hanoi in November to discuss how the new strategy would be implemented. Heated arguments arose about where and how to attack. ARVN was felt to be too strong in I Corps area, south of the DMZ, and the same was thought true for MR III (the area surrounding Saigon). The IV Corps area in the Mekong Delta was too far away from Communist supply lines. Therefore, several members of the committee argued for an attack in the Central Highlands (MR II). However, Lt. Gen. Tran Van Tra, B-2 Front commander, proposed that his forces launch what effectively would be a "test" attack in Phuoc Long Province, on the border of MR II and MR III, to see how well ARVN would fight and if the United States would respond. He argued that because the objective lay very close to the Truong Son Corridor, the attack could be easily supported. He presented detailed plans that he had brought with him. After much discussion and modifications of the plan, the committee approved the attack on Phuoc Long, which would commence in mid-December. Some in the Politburo disagreed with Tra's plan because they felt it had the potential to drain off men, ammunition, and equipment that might best be used in the general offensive in 1976. However, Le Duan was convinced by Tra's arguments and approved the attack. Nevertheless, he warned Tra that failure would not be acceptable, telling him, "Go ahead and attack. . . . [But] you must be sure of victory."[114]

From the North Vietnamese perspective, the decision to attack Phuoc Long was sound. A successful attack would secure the last remaining length of the Truong Son Corridor and provide easy access to positions that would dominate the approaches to Saigon. The attack would also tie down ARVN forces, leaving no reserves that could strike at the NVA resupply and replenishment effort. Meanwhile, the buildup for a general offensive in 1976 could continue uninterrupted. Additionally, a strong attack so close to Saigon would no doubt have psychological ramifications for the citizens of the capital city. If NVA forces took Phuoc Binh (the provincial capital), Thieu's forces could not longer maintain his policy of holding everywhere, which would further erode his already weakened popular support. The attack on Phuoc Long offered the potential for great gain at relatively low risk.

On 13 December 1974, the North Vietnamese launched their attack. The attack would last into the new year, and although it was not apparent at the time, the battle of Phuoc Long marked the beginning of the end for the Republic of South Vietnam.

9

Collapse in the North

THE BATTLE OF PHUOC LONG

After nearly 31,000 of its troops had been killed in action during 1974, the government of South Vietnam found itself in desperate straits at the beginning of 1975. President Thieu was under attack, a full-blown economic crisis had erupted, and the South Vietnamese people were rapidly coming to the realization that the United States was not going to provide the support that had been promised.

The battle that had begun in Phuoc Long Province in December continued into the new year. The provincial capital of Phuoc Binh (also known as Song Be and Phuoc Long City) lay seventy-five air miles north of Saigon, to which it was connected via Routes 1A and 14. The province consisted of four districts: Duc Phong, Phuoc Binh, Bo Duc, and Don Luan (see map 13). At the start of the battle, the South Vietnamese forces in Phuoc Long included five RF battalions, three reconnaissance companies, forty-eight PF platoons, and four territorial artillery sections.

The battle for the province actually began early on 7 December 1974 with diversionary attacks by the NVA 205th Independent Regiment on hamlets and RF outposts northeast of Tay Ninh City and on the ARVN radio relay station at the summit of Nui Ba Den (Black Virgin Mountain).[1] The attacks were designed to draw ARVN attention away from the main thrust in Phuoc Long. Additional attacks were launched in Binh Tuy and Long Khanh provinces to the east of Saigon. These diversions succeeded: III Corps headquarters was surprised when the major blow struck Phuoc Long. On 13 December, the 301st NVA Corps, consisting of the 7th and newly formed 3rd divisions, reinforced by two separate infantry regiments and supported by tank, artillery, and antiaircraft regiments, launched the main attack against Phuoc Long Province with probing attacks on Don Luan. The following night the NVA struck simultaneously at Duc Phong and Bo Duc. The RF

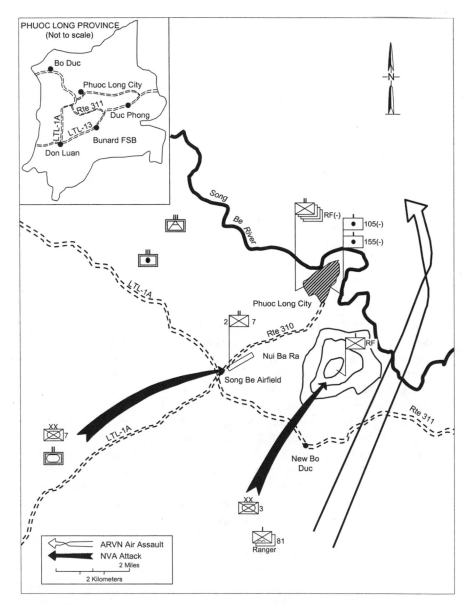

Map 13. The battle of Phuoc Long Province, December 1974.

garrison at Don Luan survived the first assault, but the South Vietnamese positions at Duc Phong and Bo Duc were immediately overrun. ARVN forces at Phuoc Binh attempted to counterattack toward Bo Duc, but the Communist troops got behind them, overrunning RF Fire Support Base Bunard and capturing four 105-mm howitzers in the process.

Lt. Gen. Du Quoc Dong, III Corps commander, reacted to the attacks by dispatching the 2nd Battalion of the 7th Regiment, 5th ARVN Division, to Phuoc Long from its base at Lai Khe. However, by this time the South Vietnamese forces in the province were in total disarray, and most had withdrawn into Phuoc Binh. Upon arriving, the regular ARVN troops tried to reorganize the RF soldiers into an effective defensive scheme, but the lightning-like NVA attacks had badly shaken the local forces. Many who had families in the area simply disappeared from the ranks to care for their relatives. The desertion by soldiers to search for and take care of family members was to become an all-too-familiar pattern in the battles to come, not just among the territorial forces, but among the regular troops as well.

Despite the burgeoning desertion problem, the regular ARVN forces launched a successful counterattack and retook Bo Duc. III Corps attempted to bring more men and supplies into the airfield at Phuoc Binh, but the NVA shelled the runway while its antiaircraft gunners fired at all aircraft in the area, severely curtailing air traffic into and out of the province. Two C-130s, one landing and the other taking off, were hit on the ground and destroyed.[2] At the same time, NVA gunners also placed the 5th ARVN Division headquarters and the airfield at Lai Khe under fire in an attempt to prevent any of its helicopters from being used to ferry reinforcements to Phuoc Long. On 22 December, the NVA recaptured Bo Duc for good. Four days later, the NVA 7th Division once again attacked Don Luan and finally overran it. With the exception of Phuoc Binh, the entire province now lay in Communist hands.

The worsening situation in Phuoc Long prompted an emergency meeting in Saigon between Thieu and his generals. The immediate question was whether or not to reinforce Phuoc Long. To reinforce III Corps, General Dong asked for at least one infantry regiment or the Airborne Division, which he would lift by helicopter into the northern part of the city. As the South Vietnamese president pondered Dong's proposal, he found himself in a position made very difficult by a number of factors. His oft-stated "defend everywhere" policy meant that he could not take troops, which were already stretched thin, from other threatened areas; at the same time, he dared not lose an entire province. The Airborne Division was deployed in MR I, where the situation did not permit its withdrawal. Forces in MRs II and IV were also decisively engaged. General Dong did not want to reinforce Phuoc Long from his own III Corps resources, because his other divisions, the 18th and 25th, were still in contact with the NVA CT-5 and CT-9 divisions on the approaches to Saigon and Tay Ninh, respectively. Even if more forces were available, it was unlikely that they could have been marshaled in time to save Phuoc Long. Nor were sufficient airlift assets available to bring in a relief force or resupply the ARVN forces defending the city. Also, any aircraft lost to the increased air defense threat in the area could not be replaced because of the reduction in U.S. military aid. Ultimately, because of these factors and Thieu's assessment that Phuoc Long was less important strategically than other areas—such as Tay Ninh, Hue, and Pleiku—the president and his generals decided not to initiate a large-scale reinforcement of the beleaguered ARVN defenders at Phuoc Long.[3] Instead, General

Dong was directed to handle the situation with his own assets, but without weakening the ARVN defenses guarding the approaches to Saigon, for which he was also responsible. Although Dong did not have many options, he decided to insert into Phuoc Long the 81st Airborne Ranger Group, which had fought so valiantly during the 1972 battle for An Loc.

As Dong pondered how to get the rangers into the battle, the NVA launched a multi-regiment infantry attack, supported by a tank regiment and corps artillery at Phuoc Binh district headquarters. By the next day, the ARVN defenders had been forced to withdraw to new defensive positions around the airfield. The NVA attempted to get between these forces and Phuoc Binh, but after a day of heavy fighting, ARVN managed to pull back in reasonably orderly fashion and establish a defensive line in the city.

At 0700, on 1 January, the NVA launched another infantry-armor attack on Phuoc Binh from the south. At the same time, the ARVN positions on Ba Ra Mountain were overrun by NVA forces, who set up forward observation posts there that allowed them to bring very accurate artillery fires on targets inside the city. Very rapidly, the NVA gunners destroyed eight ARVN 105-mm howitzers and four 155-mm guns. Additionally, the NVA placed antiaircraft weapons on the mountain, which threatened any helicopter or fixed-wing aircraft in the area surrounding the city. Still VNAF pilots did the best they could, destroying fifteen NVA tanks and assisting the ARVN defenders in holding off the NVA assault through the afternoon of 2 January.

The situation inside the city had reached a critical stage. The South Vietnamese defenders, who held only the marketplace, the provincial headquarters complex, and a small airstrip, were receiving over three thousand incoming artillery rounds per day. Although ammunition and supplies had been airdropped to the ARVN forces, their efforts to retrieve the much-needed materiel were severely hampered by the artillery fire that NVA observers on Ba Ra Mountain were directing. Also, NVA air defense weapons on the mountain prevented helicopters from evacuating hundreds of wounded soldiers.

On 4 January, two attempts to land the 81st Airborne Rangers east of the city were aborted because of rain and poor visibility; but the next day two companies successfully landed just north of the provincial administrative building. The rangers immediately launched a counterattack to retake positions lost near the sector headquarters. Their arrival stabilized the situation somewhat, but the South Vietnamese defenses were wavering, particularly among the RF units, some of which broke in the face of repeated NVA tank assaults. At midnight on 6 January, the NVA launched another major attack and drove the rangers out of their positions. The next morning, the entire defense collapsed. The defenders had fought hard, destroying sixteen NVA tanks in the process, but ultimately the NVA's overwhelming numerical superiority (estimated at four to one) won out. Of the more than 5,400 South Vietnamese troops originally committed to the battle, only 850 survived. Among those killed or captured were the province chief, the Phuoc Binh district chief, and the battalion commander from the 2nd Battalion, 7th Infantry Regiment.[4]

The entire province of Phuoc Long was now in North Vietnamese hands. One airborne trooper, a veteran of the battle at An Loc, said:

> The enemy troops were not so good and so courageous as we might have thought. There were simply too many of them. The enemy's artillery fire was fierce and many times more accurate than it had been during the battle of An Loc. Enemy tanks had something new and strange. Our M-72 rockets were unable to knock them out. We hit them; they stopped for a while then moved on. Our air support was not very effective; the planes flew too high. If only we could have had B-52s like we did in An Loc![5]

However the B-52s had left, never to return. The loss of Phuoc Long Province had a devastating effect on both the South Vietnamese civilian population and the armed forces. Making matters much worse in Saigon was the U.S. response. To the surprise of both Hanoi and Saigon, the United States did nothing.[6] In his first State of the Union message on 15 January 1975, President Ford did not even mention South Vietnam.[7] A few days later, Ford said that he could foresee no circumstances that would prompt the United States to become actively involved again in the Vietnam War.[8] The South Vietnamese were stunned. Not only had the United States cut them off materially, now it had publicly disowned them. Former ARVN general Cao Van Vien wrote after the war that this episode shook the South Vietnamese as nothing had since the Tet offensive in 1968: "The apparent total indifference with which the United States and other non-communist countries regarded this tragic loss reinforced the doubt the Vietnamese people held concerning the viability of the Paris Agreement. Almost gone was the hope that the United States would forcibly punish the North Vietnamese for their brazen violations of the cease-fire agreement. The people's belief in the power of the armed forces and the government was also deeply shaken."[9] The loss of Phuoc Long marked a major turning point in the Vietnam War. It demonstrated the impotence of both South Vietnam and the United States and signaled the beginning of a series of events that would ultimately result in the fall of South Vietnam.

MAKING NEW PLANS

Word of the ARVN defenders' capitulation at Phuoc Long reached the members of the Twenty-third Plenum while they were still in session in Hanoi. The North Vietnamese leaders reacted with jubilation. For the first time, the NVA had "liberated" an entire province, an act that would no doubt rock the already shaky confidence of the South Vietnamese. The inability of ARVN to stop the NVA assault, coupled with Ford's inaction and his public declaration, convinced the North Vietnamese leadership that the time had come to commence the final offensive.[10] First Secretary Le Duan said, "Never have we had military and political conditions so perfect or a strategic advantage so great as we have now."[11] As the Plenum came to a close, Le Duan directed the NVA military leadership to develop plans to take advantage of the situation. In his closing comments, he said that he did not think the United States would return to fight in South Vietnam; nonetheless, he warned the military leaders that, if the 1975–76 offensive did not succeed quickly, "the United States will intervene to a certain extent to save the puppets from total defeat."[12]

On 9 January, the day after the Twenty-third Plenum adjourned, the Central Military Committee and General Staff met to develop detailed plans for the follow-up to Phuoc Long. The next effort would focus on the Central Highlands (MR II). The committee, heeding Le Duan's warning that the United States might yet react (and unaware of just how badly the loss of Phuoc Long had shaken the South Vietnamese), at first took a quite conservative approach. They chose as the initial target in MR II the small border town of Duc Lap, about fifty kilometers southwest of Ban Me Thuot, the capital city of Darlac Province. The attack on Duc Lap was designed to position forces for the major thrust into the Highlands, which would not be initiated until the start of the following year. Along with this relatively limited attack in MR II, the committee also planned similar operations in MR I south of the DMZ and in the Mekong Delta. As Le Duc Tho and some of his more aggressive colleagues in the Politburo watched the development of these military plans, they became concerned that the military operations being contemplated were too limited in scope to sufficiently seize the great opportunity at hand. One of the most vocal supporters of an expanded attack was Gen. Tran Van Tra, commander of the B-2 Front, who argued for a direct attack on the provincial capital, Ban Me Thuot, which he said "would be a surprise to the enemy. We could take it from the wrong side, from the rear, where he's not watching. . . . That would be attacking the tree with a stroke of the ax at the base of the trunk. The branches and foliage will fall later."[13] Le Duc Tho agreed, arguing that a successful attack would give the North Vietnamese another province and provide staging areas and avenues of approach for a future follow-on attack to seize Pleiku, the most important city in the region. Tho and Tra eventually convinced an initially reluctant Le Duan, and they decided to focus the attack not on Duc Lap, but on Ban Me Thuot itself. Accordingly, Tho visited the Military Committee and directed them to think bigger, saying, "It would be absurd if with almost five divisions in the Central Highlands we could not attack Ban Me Thuot."[14] Although several members of the Military Committee continued to resist any changes, the original plan eventually was revised to include Ban Me Thuot as the primary objective. The Politburo approved the new plan, and Le Duan ordered General Dung to go south to take command of the new offensive — "Campaign 275."

THIEU'S RESPONSE

Even though the South Vietnamese military leaders in the JGS were not privy to what the North Vietnamese planned for the Highlands, they knew that the NVA would try to take advantage of their success Phuoc Long. The Saigon generals looked to President Thieu for guidance, but none was forthcoming, for Thieu was apparently still in a state of shock over the loss of an entire province. His decision neither to withdraw nor to reinforce the defenders in Phuoc Long had resulted in the loss of a large number of soldiers and equipment that could not easily be replaced. In addition to the mounting crisis on the battlefield, more personal concerns distracted Thieu. According to Nguyen Tien Hung, one of Thieu's closest advisers, the South Vietnamese president was "suspicious," "secretive," and "ever watchful for a *coup d' etat* against him." His wariness was only exacerbated by the NVA victories in Phuoc Long and those that followed close behind. Hung concluded: "Thieu's suspicions denied him the services of competent people, adequate staff work, consultation, and coordination. In the end his secretive nature confused his generals about his true intentions. Thieu did not share his fall-back goals with those around him until it was too late to rally his own forces and the time to develop sound operational plans had been passed."[15] His secretiveness and inability to deal with the crisis would have disastrous results when the NVA continued its offensive.

The JGS recommended to Thieu that he consider a different plan of defense that reflected the new situation on the battlefield. They advocated "truncation," or a shortening of the South Vietnamese lines to more defensible positions, and an abandonment of the "no surrender of territory" edict. No doubt realizing the political impact of giving up territory to the North Vietnamese without a fight, Thieu refused to even consider the JGS recommendations. Bui Diem, former South Vietnamese ambassador to the United States, maintains that another reason for Thieu's refusal to discuss the new strategy was that even after having lost Phuoc Long Province, Thieu continued to hold "the belief that the Americans would never tolerate a takeover of South Vietnam by the Communists, at least not in the foreseeable future."[16]

Thieu's apparent confidence was badly misplaced. In October 1974, President Ford had written the South Vietnamese president, reiterating that there had been no change in American foreign policy toward South Vietnam and giving Thieu his "firm assurance that this administration will make every effort to provide the assistance you need."[17] However, the new American president had troubles of his own. His fledgling administration was already being blamed for rising unemployment, ballooning national debt, and the continuing energy crisis that had followed the 1973 Arab oil embargo. Nevertheless, Ford wanted to honor President Nixon's repeated promises to Thieu.[18] Unfortunately, the continuing problems in the Middle East took most of his time, and even when he was able to focus on Southeast Asia, his hands were tied by Congress, which in December 1974 passed a worldwide military assistance bill that set a ceiling of only $617 million in aid for South Vietnam, Cambodia, and Laos combined.[19]

Nevertheless, Ford sought additional funds to aid the South Vietnamese. He was blocked at every juncture by an increasingly hostile Congress. On 8 January, the White House, charging that the "other side had chosen to violate most of the major provisions of this accord [Paris Peace Agreement]," asked for an additional military aid package in the amount of $522 million to fund South Vietnam and Cambodia through the end of the current fiscal year (which ended in June).[20] The administration lobbied hard for the supplemental request, trying to convince Congress that a reduction in aid would "seriously weaken South Vietnamese forces during a critical period when Communist forces in South Vietnam were getting stronger and more aggressive" and that it was imperative to "show the world that the U.S. is standing firmly by its commitments and continues to be a reliable and steadfast ally."[21] Despite the administration's efforts, neither the public nor Congress welcomed the new request for aid. Candlelight demonstrations in front of the White House protested the president's new aid request for South Vietnam, and congressional mail was overwhelmingly against increased aid. Nevertheless, the administration was betting that, in the long run, the American people did not want to see an NVA victory in South Vietnam and would not let their elected representatives cut off aid. The president's team launched a campaign to drum up sympathy for the faltering South Vietnamese.

The Ninety-fourth Congress reacted strongly. Senator Kennedy said that the administration was using "threats and scare tactics" to substantiate its aid request: "Once again we are hearing the same old arguments and the same old controversies over the same old war. The lingering and bloody conflict deserves more of our diplomacy, and not more of our ammunition."[22] Kennedy was not alone. Eighty-two members of the bipartisan Members of Congress for Peace through Law in a letter to the President said that they saw "no humanitarian or national interest" to justify aid to Southeast Asia.[23] Senate majority leader Mike Mansfield announced that he was "sick and tired of pictures of Indochinese men, women, and children being slaughtered by American guns with American ammunition in countries in which we have no vital interests."[24]

On 3 February, Ford met with the congressional leadership and suggested that a joint bipartisan delegation travel to South Vietnam to assess the military, political, and economic situation. An earlier visit to Saigon in January by Senator Sam Nunn of Georgia had convinced Nunn that military aid reductions had seriously weakened the RVNAF and "that without continued assistance from the United States, . . . failure will inevitably result."[25] Ford hoped that a second delegation would reach the same conclusion and therefore work with him to get the supplemental aid bill passed.[26] As one of his advisers put it: he wanted to put "the burden of decision on their [the congressional delegation's] shoulders."[27]

The scenario did not turn out quite the way the president and his advisers had hoped. According to Wolfgang Lehman, Ambassador Martin's deputy in Saigon, the delegation members "were unbalanced against administration policy." Although noting that "some members of the delegation . . . had a much more balanced view," including Congressman John Flynt of Georgia and Senator Dewey Bartlett of Oklahoma, Lehman felt that others, particularly Bella Abzug of New York and Donald Frazier of Minnesota, were clearly biased.[28]

Upon arrival in Saigon on 26 February, the delegation met with Ambassador Martin and his staff. According to Saigon-based CIA analyst Frank Snepp, the delegation immediately assumed an adversarial relationship and was "suspicious" of Martin, "hostile" to his staff, and "determined to rely as little as possible" on embassy personnel for briefings, input, or advice.[29] During a frantic round of meetings, discussions, and trips to the field, the delegation members quickly formed a negative opinion of Thieu, his administration, and the entire situation in South Vietnam. They were especially concerned about the jailing of journalists and political opponents and the civil unrest directed at the Thieu regime. When the delegates met with the South Vietnamese president, he confronted them directly, saying:

> During the past two decades, the people of South Vietnam have been told time and again by five U.S. presidents belonging to both parties—all of them supported by successive legislatures of the U.S.—that the U.S. is determined to provide them with adequate assistance as long as they are willing to resist Communist aggression to preserve their freedom. This solemn commitment had been renewed at the time of the signing of the Paris Agreement. The issue now boils down to one simple question: is the commitment made by the U.S. to be of any value? Is the word of the U.S. to be trusted? That is the message I want you to convey to the 94th Congress of the United States.[30]

Most members of the delegation were less than impressed with Thieu's attitude. At a dinner following his address, they assailed him with concerns and issues to the point that Ambassador Martin later apologized for what Gen. Cao Van Vien described as their "rude and contemptuous" behavior.[31] Instead of convincing the legislators to approve the additional aid for Saigon, as President Ford had hoped, the trip appeared to be having the exact opposite effect. Yet on the last day of the visit the delegation met with North Vietnamese and PRG representatives of the Joint Military Team at Camp Davis on Tan Son Nhut Air Base. Hoping to discuss American POWs and repatriation of U.S. servicemen's remains, the delegation was subjected to essentially a harangue of Communist propaganda from NVA major general Hoang Anh Tuan, the senior PRG representative, who refused to even discuss the POW issue outside of prepared statements. After a heated exchange with Representative Flynt, Tuan declared the meeting closed and walked out.[32] The behavior of the Communists reportedly changed several minds about the nature of the conflict in South Vietnam. When the delegation returned to Washington to meet with the president, all but Bella Abzug advocated some increase in military and humanitarian aid.[33] However, Representative McCloskey produced his own report concluding that the North Vietnamese "will overcome the South within three years" regardless of what the United States did with regard to additional military aid.[34] A week after the return of the congressional delegation, the Democratic caucus in both the House and Senate voted to oppose any further aid to South Vietnam and Cambodia.

If the congressional visit did not yield the results the president desired, it had an even worse impact on Thieu and his generals, who came to the conclusion that they were about to be abandoned by the United States. General Vien later wrote:

> In general, the departing visitors [from the congressional delegation] left behind a feeling of pessimism. The atmosphere was charged with rumors and speculation, all detrimental to the national cause. In the United States, we were induced to believe, our government was considered incorrigibly corrupt, despotic, and repressive. Disenchanted and troubled by its own domestic difficulties, political and economic, the United States was no longer in a position to contribute to the war effort. Aid stood no chance of being increased; on the contrary, it would be trimmed further for American attention had shifted to the Middle East.[35]

General Vien concluded that by the time the congressional delegation departed Saigon Thieu no longer held any hope for the $300 million in additional aid that had been requested.[36] However, according to Nguyen Tien Hung, former minister of planning and development and one of Thieu's closest advisers, the South Vietnamese president, despite all indications to the contrary, believed until the very end that the United States would do something to preclude the fall of South Vietnam. Hung wrote after the war: "For the Communists to accomplish a military victory over the South would be too damaging to America's credibility. The whole process of America's disengagement had been designed to uphold American honor. We could not comprehend that Ford and Kissinger would permit the eventuality of American humiliation and our own defeat to occur."[37] The reality was that Congress would not permit Ford and Kissinger to do anything to forestall a North Vietnamese victory.

When the congressional delegation departed Saigon, they took with them copies of the latest DAO intelligence report, which clearly showed that the North Vietnamese were in a position to launch a major offensive. The report said that the North had increased its strategic reserve from two divisions to seven, thereby making more than 70,000 additional soldiers available for commitment in the South to augment the 200,000 combat soldiers and 100,000 support troops already there. By this time, according to the report, the NVA had seventeen divisions in the South, supported by 500 tanks and 500 artillery pieces. Additionally, they had over 200 air defense weapons of various calibers, including surface-to-air missiles. These figures did not include 40,000 NVA soldiers operating inside Cambodia or 50,000 support personnel in Laos. Predicting an imminent major offensive in the northern half of South Vietnam, the report concluded that "the campaign is expected to assume country-wide proportions and a number of indicators point to the introduction of strategic reserve divisions from NVN."[38]

CAMPAIGN 275

The DAO intelligence estimate was surprisingly accurate. While budget deliberations continued in the United States, the North Vietnamese made preparations for
the commencement of Campaign 275. In late January, the NVA began moving additional forces into Darlac Province. During February, large truck convoys moving south down the Truong Son Corridor were sighted almost daily. Although
VNAF fighter bombers attacked as many of these convoys as they could, they were
unable to impede significantly the units and equipment flowing into the area. The
320th NVA Division based near Pleiku and the F-10 Division at Kontum began
moving toward Ban Me Thuot. Other NVA divisions, including the 312th, 316th,
and 968th, took up positions surrounding the city. In addition to the five mainforce
NVA infantry divisions, fifteen regiments of tanks, artillery, antiaircraft, and engineers operated in the area, a total of between 75,000 and 80,000 troops.[39] Defending Ban Me Thuot were one regiment from the 23rd ARVN Division, a ranger
group, and various regional forces. Thus, the Communists achieved a combat ratio
of 5.5 to 1 against ARVN in troops, 1.2 to 1 in tanks, and 2.1 to 1 in artillery in
the area around Ban Me Thuot.[40]

When General Dung arrived in the area, he set up his command post about
thirty kilometers east of Ban Me Thuot. His plan was relatively simple, employing a tactic that he had developed and first used against the French in 1952 called
"the blossoming lotus"—a plan of operation in which the attack would avoid outlying strong points and begin at the center of the enemy positions, then spread out-
wards "like a flower bud slowly opening its petals."[41] He intended to start the assault by striking elsewhere in the Central Highlands so as to misdirect South
Vietnamese attention from his main attack. He would then cut Routes 14, 19, and
21 to sever the Highland provinces from the II Corps lowlands (Pleiku and Nha
Trang), thus precluding ARVN reinforcement of the Ban Me Thuot area. Once this
was achieved, the NVA would make the main assault on the city.

Although ARVN intelligence correctly predicted that the NVA was making
preparations to take Ban Me Thuot, Lt. Gen. Pham Van Phu, II Corps commander,
disagreed with this assessment, believing that the enemy's moves toward Ban Me
Thuot were diversionary in nature and that the main objective would be either the
city of Pleiku or Kontum.[42] His perception was reinforced by the NVA's plan of
deception, which included attacks on numerous outposts and firebases north and
west of the two cities.[43] Accordingly, Phu kept the 23rd ARVN Division in place
at Pleiku. Even when the corps commander received confirmation that the 320th
NVA Division was moving on Ban Me Thuot, he sent only one regiment, the 53rd
from the 23rd ARVN Division, to the city.

The battle for Ban Me Thuot began on 1 March with diversionary attacks by
the 968th NVA Division on the firebases north and west of Pleiku. On 4 March,
NVA troops cut Route 19 in two places between Qui Nhon and Pleiku. On 5 March,
additional NVA forces blocked Route 21 in three places between Ban Me Thuot

and the coast. Still, General Phu remained convinced that the enemy target was Pleiku. On 8 March, however, the 9th Regiment of the 320th NVA Division cut Route 14 north of Buon Blech, thus completing the isolation of Ban Me Thuot. By midday on 9 March, it became apparent to even Phu that the NVA was focusing its efforts on Ban Me Thuot. He rushed the 21st Ranger Group to Buon Ho, twenty miles north of the city, and called the JGS for reinforcements, who promptly told him that none were available.

The direct assault on Ban Me Thuot began at 0200 hours on 10 March when the NVA launched a two-pronged, three-division tank and infantry attack. The honor of making the initial attack went to the 320th NVA Division, the unit that Dung had commanded earlier in his career. The division attacked from the north to take the ammunition depot and a small airstrip for light aircraft, capturing both by mid-afternoon. The 320th directed a second thrust at Phuong Duc airfield, east of the city, but the 53rd ARVN Regiment put up a stiff fight, stalling the NVA attack there.

While the 320th attacked in the north, the F-10 NVA Division and elements of the 316th NVA Division attacked from the south. Their attack, aimed at the sector headquarters, quickly became a pitched battle in which the ARVN defenders fought well, inflicting heavy losses on the enemy. However, the tide turned when ARVN, demonstrating a long-standing inability to coordinate fire support, dropped an artillery round intended for the attacking NVA tanks on the sector command post, knocking out communications and killing and wounding many key personnel. At that point, the ARVN defense virtually fell apart. The survivors withdrew under heavy pressure to the command post of the 23rd ARVN Division (a forward element commanded by the 23rd's deputy commander, Col. Vu The Quang) at the airfield, where they were quickly surrounded by NVA tanks and infantry. By nightfall, the NVA controlled most of the center of the city while the South Vietnamese retained isolated positions on the airfield and along the perimeter to the east, west, and south. The battle continued into the night with the North Vietnamese using flame throwers to rout out the ARVN defenders. During the early evening hours, the remainder of the 316th Division closed on Ban Me Thuot, completing the encirclement of the city. By this time, the remaining ARVN defenders were hopelessly outnumbered. Making matters worse, a flight of VNAF A-37s mistakenly dropped its bombs on the 23rd Division Forward Command Post, knocking out all communications between Colonel Quang and the division headquarters at Pleiku. Unable to communicate with division superiors, the South Vietnamese could not coordinate much-needed air support. The next day, the NVA, unhampered by VNAF fighter-bombers, increased the intensity of its attack. By noon on 11 March, the NVA had captured the forward command post and most of the remaining ARVN positions, seizing many senior officers in the process, including the province chief and Colonel Quang.

THE FATAL DECISION

As the North Vietnamese prepared their final attack on Ban Me Thuot, President Thieu made a momentous decision, one that would eventually prove the undoing of his nation. Reeling from the disastrous loss of Phuoc Long and knowing that Darlac Province was under heavy attack, Thieu concluded that he had to take drastic action before all was lost.[44] The RVNAF was overextended and stretched dangerously thin, and the preponderance of the strategic reserve was already committed. Previously, Thieu had stood firm regarding his "Four Nos," demanding that everything be held "at all costs." However, the loss of Phuoc Long in January and the impending fall of Ban Me Thuot convinced the South Vietnamese president that his strategy was no longer viable.

On 11 March 1975, as the NVA was in the process of overrunning the 23rd Division Command Post in Ban Me Thuot, Thieu met over breakfast with General Vien and Lt. Gen. Dang Van Quang, his assistant for security affairs. Thieu said, "Given our present strength and capabilities, we certainly cannot hold and defend all the territory we want."[45] He had decided instead that RVNAF forces should focus on protecting only the populous areas deemed most essential. Looking at a small-scale map, he outlined the areas he considered most critical (see map 14). He said that MRs III and IV were vital and had to be held at all costs; any territory already lost in these regions had to be recaptured. These military regions, which contained most of South Vietnam's population and national resources, would become the "untouchable heartland, the irreducible national stronghold." With regard to MRs I and II, Thieu, according to General Vien, appeared less sure of himself. Combat had raged almost continuously in MR I since the cease-fire, and the NVA was particularly strong there. Still Hue and Da Nang were important. Therefore, in MR I, it would be a matter of "hold what you can." In the Central Highlands, Ban Me Thuot had to be held because of its economic and demographic importance, and the key coastal cities also had to defended. To accomplish what he wanted, Thieu drew a series of phase lines on the map that indicated how the RVNAF would withdraw if unable to stand against the NVA onslaught. If the South Vietnamese were strong enough, they would hold the territory up to Hue or Da Nang. If not, they were to redeploy farther south to Quang Ngai, then Qui Nhon, and, ultimately, a final defensive line just north of Tuy Hoa. His new strategy, later described as "light at the top, heavy on the bottom," revealed that Thieu was planning to trade space for time.[46] He was effectively "truncating" South Vietnam, just as his generals had previously recommended. General Vien later wrote that he vocally supported the president's new plan during the meeting, but privately had serious doubts because he "believed it was too late for any successful redeployment of such magnitude."[47] Vien did not voice his misgivings because, as he later wrote, it appeared that the president had already made up his mind and did not desire further discussion. Thieu was, after all, the man who "made all the decisions as to how the war should be conducted."[48]

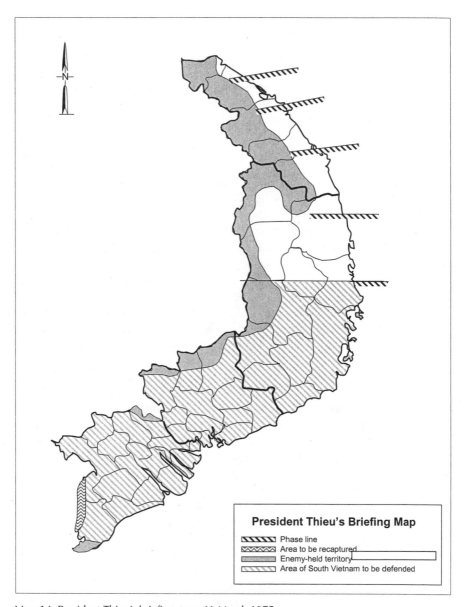

Map 14. President Thieu's briefing map, 11 March 1975.

Thieu's decision was not a bad one from a purely military standpoint. Seven of the ARVN's thirteen divisions were deployed in MRs I and II, defending only one-fifth of the population. Shortening his lines and withdrawing these forces to assist in the defense of MRs III and IV, where over twelve million people resided, made sense. However, withdrawal of forces under fire is one of the most difficult military maneuvers to attempt. If not conducted in an orderly and controlled fashion, the maneuver can turn quickly into a disaster. Thieu's strategy might have worked if it had been applied earlier, but the poorly planned and even more poorly executed massive withdrawal under heavy enemy pressure came too late. Thieu's decision, which resulted in the unraveling of the South Vietnamese armed forces, would have fatal ramifications for all of the Republic of Vietnam.

COUNTERATTACK FAILS

By 11 March, the day after Thieu had made his fateful decision, the NVA had captured most of Darlac Province. However, remnants of two ARVN battalions still fought inside Ban Me Thuot, and the South Vietnamese still held Phuoc An airfield, about thirty kilometers east of the city. Lt. Gen. Phu, II Corps commander, attempted a counterattack to recapture Ban Me Thuot and relieve the surrounded defenders. He first ordered the 21st Ranger Group to move south from Buon Ho to Ban Me Thuot.

The ranger attack initially went well as the forces advanced toward Ban Me Thuot against light resistance, driving the NVA ahead of them into the city. The rangers had almost reached the outskirts of Ban Me Thuot when Brig. Gen. Le Van Tuong, commander of the 23rd ARVN Division, halted them and ordered them to secure a landing zone outside of the town to ensure safe evacuation of his wife and children by helicopter.[49] Having lost the momentum, the rangers tried to resume the attack, only to run into stiff resistance from NVA reinforcements who had been rushed into the fight while the rangers evacuated Tuong's family. A perfect opportunity to relieve Ban Me Thuot had been lost.

Shortly after the ranger attack stalled, President Thieu ordered General Phu to mount another counterattack. Phu ordered the 44th and 45th regiments of the 23rd Division to be airlifted to Phuoc An from Pleiku. Once all the forces were marshaled in Phuoc An, the counterattack would be launched west along Route 21 to link up with the ARVN survivors holding out at the airfield in Ban Me Thuot and retake the city.

The relief forces from the 23rd ARVN Division encountered major problems with helicopter support. Over a three-day period, the number of operational CH-47 helicopters being used for the movement to Phuoc An dwindled from twelve to one due to maintenance problems and the lack of spare parts. The result was that by 14 March, only the 45th Regiment and one battalion from the 44th had arrived at Phuoc An. Many of the soldiers in the relief force had families in Ban Me Thuot (which was the rear base for the 23rd Division) and as they waited at Phuoc An until the rest of the force could be brought in, they watched a steady stream of soldiers and civilian refugees fleeing the provincial capital along Route 21 toward Nha Trang. Fearing for their own loved ones, many soldiers deserted to find and evacuate their families.[50]

The counterattack was finally launched from Phuoc An on 15 March. The lead unit advanced only a few kilometers down Route 21 when it ran into elements of the NVA F-10 Division in blocking positions astride the road. Because of poor planning and continued helicopter availability problems, ARVN had commenced the counterattack without artillery or tank support. When confronted by the NVA, the South's forces were hopelessly outgunned. The situation was made worse by the poor leadership that extended all the way to the top. On 16 March, General Tuong, the 23rd ARVN Division commander who had aborted the successful ranger advance, once again demonstrated that he was unfit for command. He received a very slight facial wound and, rather than continuing to lead the counterattack, he had himself evacuated by helicopter to the safety of a hospital at Nha Trang. Not surprisingly, the attack, beset by inadequate leadership and continued wholesale desertion, stalled. Indeed, by the next day, it turned into a retreat as the would-be attackers joined columns of refugees fleeing east. The remaining ARVN positions in Ban Me Thuot were overrun and the South Vietnamese holdouts were either killed or captured. On 18 March, the NVA overran the airfield at Phuoc An, thus eliminating the last staging area from which ARVN could launch a counterattack. All of Darlac Province had fallen to the Communist troops.

In the final analysis, much of the blame for this defeat belongs to General Phu, because the II Corps commander refused to act on sound intelligence revealing that four NVA divisions were closing on Ban Me Thuot. Consequently, he did not provide sufficient forces to defend the city. Convinced that he knew where the enemy would strike, he did not reassess the situation when new information to the contrary became available. By the time he realized that Ban Me Thuot was the main target, it was too late to get sufficient reinforcements to the scene. The North Vietnamese, having taken another province, were on the march.

DISASTER IN THE HIGHLANDS

The fall of Ban Me Thuot was only a prelude to further disaster. The rapidity of the South Vietnamese collapse in Darlac Province surprised the North Vietnamese leadership. Maj. Gen. Tran Con Man said after the war: "In the attack in Ban Me Thuot we surprised the South Vietnamese. On the other hand, the South Vietnamese troops surprised us, too, because they became so disorganized so quickly. We did not expect that to happen. We thought that after the attack on Ban Me Thuot the South Vietnamese would draw the line there and fight back. We had expected a very intense and long battle with the South around Ban Me Thuot."[51]

Just as surprising to the North Vietnamese was the fact that the United States had done nothing to come to the aid of the faltering RVNAF. General Dung recovered quickly from his surprise and saw the great opportunity before him. He realized that with the defeat of ARVN in Darlac Province, no organized South Vietnamese forces stood between the NVA and the South China Sea. Dung was very close to cutting South Vietnam in two, isolating RVNAF units at Kontum, Pleiku, Binh Dinh, and farther north in MR I. Attempting to seize the advantage, Dung advised Hanoi that he planned to turn his forces north to take Pleiku and Kontum.

While Dung made new plans, Thieu and his generals tried to decide what to do about the loss of Ban Me Thuot. They met on 14 March at Cam Ranh and Thieu asked General Phu if he could retake Ban Me Thuot. Obviously demoralized by recent events, Phu pleaded for reinforcements, only to be told that there were none. The South Vietnamese president then ordered Phu "to redeploy its [II Corps] organic forces in such a manner as to reoccupy Ban Me Thuot at all costs."[52]

Phu was stunned and at first thought the president was joking.[53] In order to gain the combat power to retake Ban Me Thuot, he would have to pull the remainder of his forces from Kontum and Pleiku, effectively abandoning these key cities to the North Vietnamese. Once he overcame his dismay at what he had been ordered to do, Phu quickly devised a plan. The main problem was finding a way to get his forces from where they were in Kontum and Pleiku to a position where they could counterattack toward Ban Me Thuot. Because all other available routes were blocked by the North Vietnamese, Phu proposed to use Route 7B, a little-used logging road that ran 200 kilometers southeast from Pleiku to Tuy Hoa on the coast, to extricate II Corps forces from Pleiku while Regional Forces screened the movement from enemy forces (see map 15).

Phu told his staff to plan on commencing the movement two days later. On each of four days, a convoy of 250 vehicles would leave Pleiku and move down Route 7B to Tuy Hoa. The 20th Combat Engineer Group would lead the first column, repairing bridges and refurbishing the road as they went. The ranger groups would bring up the rear in the last column. While the lead elements prepared to move out on the ground, the VNAF would concentrate on evacuating aircraft, personnel, and family members. Among the first to go was General Phu and his staff, who were flown to Nha Trang, where they hoped to plan for the counterattack on Ban Me Thuot once the repositioning of forces from Pleiku was complete.

When Phu departed, he left his chief of staff, Col. Le Khac Ly, to travel with the convoy. The actual command of the convoy was given to Brig. Gen. Pham Duy Tat, commander of the II Corps Rangers, who had just been promoted.[54] Tat was busy preparing his six ranger groups to move out, so the planning for the withdrawal was left to Ly. As Phu was preparing to leave, Ly asked about arrangements for evacuating the Regional Forces at Pleiku. Phu replied, "[F]orget about them. If you tell them about [the evacuation], you can't control it and you cannot get down to Tuy Hoa because there would be a panic."[55] The Popular and Regional Forces, who indeed were not informed of what was happening, consequently did not provide the screen called for in the plan. There was nothing to prevent the NVA from pursuing the South Vietnamese troops as they hastily withdrew, which is exactly what happened.

The Americans from the DAO, the CIA, and other organizations working in Pleiku also knew nothing about the evacuation until informed by Colonel Ly on

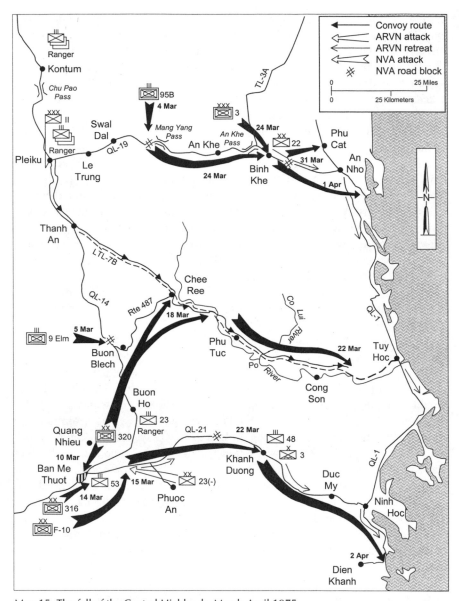

Map 15. The fall of the Central Highlands, March–April 1975.

15 March. The word was flashed to the U.S. Embassy in Saigon, which in turn ordered all American citizens out of the Central Highlands. The South Vietnamese move had taken the Americans completely by surprise, but by nightfall, the embassy, using Air America, was able to evacuate 450 American and Vietnamese employees of the various U.S. agencies in Pleiku.

The White House, already uneasy about the loss of Ban Me Thuot, was startled by the sudden South Vietnamese withdrawal from Pleiku. Ambassador Graham Martin was at his home in North Carolina convalescing from a severe infection caused by abscessed teeth. When telephoned by NSC deputy Brent Scowcroft, Martin said he was aware that Saigon planned to move the II Corps headquarters to Nha Trang, but knew nothing more than that. Martin had been anything but reluctant in the past to raise an alarm when he thought necessary. Therefore, when he failed to raise an outcry over the decision to abandon Pleiku, the Ford administration, although concerned, was initially not overly excited about the new development. Ford later wrote in his memoirs, "Everyone knew the problems in South Vietnam were serious, but no one seemed to know just how critical they were."[56] That may have been the case in Washington, but many in Vietnam recognized that the South Vietnamese were in serious trouble. As the withdrawal from II Corps unfolded, Thomas Polgar of the Central Intelligence Agency cabled Washington that "the game was over."[57] Despite such assessments, the administration continued to accentuate the positive. General Westmoreland, army chief of staff, called the redeployment "prudent action."[58] The administration's failure to recognize the serious nature of the events in Vietnam was to change very rapidly, and as the evacuation began to fall apart the White House and the Pentagon became increasingly alarmed.

While the Americans considered the ramifications of the redeployment, the circumstances on the ground in II Corps were well on the way to getting out of hand. What purportedly began as a tactical repositioning of forces rapidly began to look like a panicked withdrawal. Word of the impending move got out prematurely, and some commanders began their own evacuation without waiting for orders from II Corps. When the ranger commander at Kontum began to withdraw his forces, the province chief jumped in a jeep and joined the departing column, which quickly ran into an NVA ambush that killed the chief and a number of rangers. Nevertheless, when the NVA began shelling Kontum, more soldiers and civilians fled down the road to Pleiku.

Things were no better at Pleiku. Panic broke out when Colonel Ly informed unit commanders that they had to prepare to move. According to Ly, more than one commander asked, "Why are we withdrawing? We can fight! What is happening?" Ly later reported that he replied, "I agree with you. But now we have the President and the JGS ordering us. We are professionals. What can we do? Disobey them? Of course not. I know it's wrong. But that is the order. Do you want to start a rebellion?"[59]

As the more aggressive commanders of the regular force questioned the order to evacuate Kontum and Pleiku, the Regional and Popular Forces, perceiving rightfully that they were about to be abandoned, began to riot in the streets. Soon thereafter, as the chaos grew, the regular forces also panicked. In Colonel Ly's words, "[T]he troops, the dependents became undisciplined. Troops were raping, burning things and committing robbery. The troops became undisciplined when they heard the order. I can't blame them. There was no plan to take care of the troops' dependents."[60] In the midst of this confusion, the NVA began shelling the airfield. The demolition of ammunition dumps and fuel storage areas by departing ARVN soldiers only added credence to a growing realization that Pleiku was in imminent danger of being abandoned to the North Vietnamese.

When the first convoy departed on the night of 16 March, the panic assumed a new dimension. One reporter later wrote that physicians abandoned their hospitals, policemen shed their uniforms, and arsonists and looters committed rampant acts.[61] Civilians grabbed what meager belongings they could carry and rushed after the army. A Catholic nun remembered "babies and children were put into oxcarts and pulled. Everyone was in a panic. People were trying to hire vehicles at any price."[62]

The desperation of those seeking to flee Pleiku increased when a rumor spread that Thieu had made a deal with Hanoi. Supposedly, Hanoi would guarantee the neutrality of the remainder of South Vietnam if Thieu abandoned the northern provinces. Although the rumor was untrue, it nevertheless added to the mounting panic of both the military and the civilian population. Evidence suggests that this and similar rumors were planted by NVA propaganda units and Communist agents who had penetrated the military and civilian government of South Vietnam.[63] Regardless of their origin, the rumors had a devastating impact on members of the military, who began to question the worth of fighting against the inevitable.[64]

The retreat from Kontum and Pleiku—over secondary roads through rough country—would have been difficult under the best of conditions. However, with the North Vietnamese in close pursuit and crowds of panic-stricken civilians intermingled with the military units, the retreat rapidly degenerated into total anarchy. When the lead column reached the Ea Pa River, just a few kilometers southeast of Cheo Reo, the capital of Phu Bon Province, it had to stop for three days to construct a pontoon bridge. In the meantime, the backed-up convoys and the mass of civilian refugees following them clustered along the road outside Cheo Reo. By 18 March, over 200,000 troops and refugees were packed tight along a short stretch of road. Colonel Ly later recalled the scene that became known as the "convoy of tears": "The road from Pleiku was terrible. I saw many old people and babies fall down on the road and tanks and trucks would go over them. Accidents all the time. . . . No one could control anything. No order. The troops were mixed with the dependents and civilians and were trying to take care of all the children and wives. You can't imagine it. It was terrible. No control. . . . Refugees were strung out all the way from Cheo Reo back to the point where 7B and Route 14 fork."[65]

Chaos reigned. Unit integrity disappeared, as did all semblance of control. The units could not move because they were blocked by hordes of civilians. The civilians, many of whom had fled Pleiku carrying only what they could on their backs, had little food or water. Tormented by hunger and thirst, they were also subject to harassment by roving bands of deserters. The chaotic mass of humanity made it almost impossible for ARVN to establish a cogent defense along the road.

When ARVN began to evacuate Pleiku, General Dung recovered quickly from his initial surprise at the move. Realizing that he had a chance to destroy an entire

South Vietnamese corps, he ordered the 320th Division to move from its position along Route 14 to strike the escaping South Vietnamese in the flank.[66] At the same time, he directed the 968th Division to strike the rear of the column, while B-1 Front forces were told to cut Route 7B in front of the lead column. Attacking the head, tail, and flank simultaneously was a traditional Viet Cong ambush technique, but never before had it been applied on such a large scale.

As night fell on 18 March, the NVA opened fire on the densely packed soldiers and refugees along Route 7B. Shortly thereafter, the 320th NVA Division struck near the head of the column at Cheo Reo. At the same time, other NVA units hit the 6th Ranger Group bringing up the rear of the main column near the town of Thanh An at the crossroads of Routes 14 and 7B. Throughout the night, the NVA shelled the column and raked it with small arms, machine gun, and antitank fires. The effect on such closely packed soldiers, vehicles, and civilians was devastating. The next morning a VNAF helicopter pilot overflying the area reported, "When I flew low, I could see bodies scattered alongside the road—burning with the trucks."[67]

Mercifully, the bridge southeast of Cheo Reo was completed in the early morning of 19 March and the column began moving again. That evening General Phu ordered Colonel Ly to fly out of Cheo Reo by helicopter. Since General Tat was still directing the rear guard, no one remained in charge to control the movement of the column, and from that time on the individual units in the column were on their own. VNAF helicopters braved intense fire to pick up wounded soldiers and civilians along the route. One wounded soldier evacuated from Cheo Reo, describing the NVA attack along the road, said, "They hit us with everything. . . . People were lying all over the road as we tried to fight our way out. Soldiers died and the people died with them."[68] By nightfall on 19 March, the head of the column reached the Con River, only about forty kilometers from the coast. However, fighting all along the route remained intense. An ARVN tank battalion trying to break through earlier in the day had been mistakenly bombed by four VNAF fighter-bombers that destroyed four tanks and killed or wounded a number of soldiers and civilians. As the ARVN forces tried to fight their way down the road, the NVA hit farther back in the column, near the town of Phu Tuc. The ranger rear guard was fighting hard when another misguided VNAF air strike bombed the 7th Ranger Group, wiping out most of a battalion. In a gross understatement, Colonel Ly later said that such mistakes "made morale very, very bad."[69]

Some units fought valiantly against overwhelming odds, but most did not, and the situation rapidly deteriorated. As at Ban Me Thuot, hundreds, if not thousands, of ARVN soldiers deserted in the face of the enemy to try to find their families and take them to safety.[70] Others just tried to save themselves. General Thinh, the former commander of the Corps artillery, later praised those leaders who kept their units together, but described how things generally came apart:

We must salute the battalion commanders and lower officers for having marched with their units but they were no longer able to control their finished and tired men. The soldiers kept shouting insults at Thieu for this impossible and terrible retreat. Some reached the limit of their despair and killed the officers. An artillery battalion commander who was marching in the retreating column was shot to death by some rangers who wanted his beautiful watch. The despair was so great that at one point two or three guerrillas arriving at the scene could make prisoners of a hundred rangers. Wives and children of retreating soldiers died of hunger and sickness on the road. It was a true hell.[71]

The situation was even worse behind the main body of the last column, where the territorial forces had been left to fend for themselves. One RF soldier later reported:

Most of my friends died on the road. . . . There were many bodies on the road. Some were still alive but they had no food and no water. There was nobody to take care of them. Our commander, the lieutenant colonel, ran for his life and there was nobody in charge. . . . we only tried to fight to clear the road for ourselves, we did not protect anybody. Most of the men in my battalion are still on the road. Some are dead, some are wounded, some are trying to get through the jungle. There are more than twelve other battalions from Pleiku and Kontum and Phu Bon still left behind. They are at the back of the convoy because they never received any order to withdraw.[72]

On 21 March, the NVA forces overran the 23rd Rangers protecting the rear of the main body. Next, they quickly moved down the road and took Che Reo, completely severing Route 7B and isolating the 8th and 25th Ranger groups and about 160,000 civilians. The NVA had effectively cut the highway and the forces strung out along it into separate segments. Through General Tat, who was still at the rear of the main column, General Phu told the trapped regular elements to abandon all heavy weapons and escape any way they could. Soldiers and civilians alike took off in every direction through the jungle. The NVA gave chase. A woman from Pleiku later reported that the North Vietnamese Army "came from the jungle and told everyone to stop moving. We were on a slope. We kept moving. They just began firing on all of us."[73] To make matters worse, the soldiers and refugees who remained on the road were out of food and running low on water. VNAF helicopters tried to deliver American field rations, rice, and dried milk, but their efforts were inadequate to the monumental task at hand.

Although the ARVN forces at the front of the column reached the Ba River, their travail was not over. In order to cross the river, General Phu had requested a pontoon bridge. However, when the trucks departed Tuy Hoa for the crossing site, they ran into an NVA roadblock and could go no farther. They returned to Tuy Hoa, where the pontoon sections had to be lifted piece by piece by CH-47 helicopters borrowed from IV Corps. By 22 March, the bridge was in place. Unfortunately, the first rush of panicked soldiers and refugees across the bridge capsized an over-loaded pontoon, throwing the people and vehicles in the water. Repairing the bridge took until the end of the day, when traffic began flowing again.

The next day even the weather turned against the South Vietnamese. Move-ment on the road was hampered by cold and fog, the latter of which also impeded much-needed close air support. The journey remained tortuous. The head of the column tried to move forward against the NVA troops while the 6th Ranger Group at the back of the column attempted to fight a rear-guard action against the NVA. On 27 March, after desperate fighting to eliminate the NVA positions blocking the road to the coast, the 34th Ranger Battalion broke through and linked up with soldiers from a territorial force unit that had been fighting east of Tuy Hoa. In the process of forging the breakthrough, the 34th Ranger Battalion sustained so many casualties that it all but ceased to exist as a fighting force.

By Colonel Ly's estimate, only some 20,000 of the 60,000 troops that had started out from Pleiku and Kontum finally reached Tuy Hoa, and most of these survivors were not fit for combat.[74] Only about 700 of the original 7,000 rangers escaped. General Vien reported that in the span of just ten days "seventy-five per-cent of II Corps combat strength, to include the 23rd Infantry Division as well as ranger, armor, artillery, engineer, and signal units, had been tragically expended."[75] The withdrawal from Pleiku and Kontum had also proved a disaster for the refugees. Of the estimated 400,000 civilians attempting to flee Kontum, Pleiku, Phu Bon, and Cheo Reo, only about 60,000 to 100,000 got through.[76]

The loss of materiel and equipment was staggering. Hundreds of artillery pieces and armored vehicles had been destroyed on the road or abandoned in Pleiku. Only a handful of armored vehicles, including just thirty armored person-nel carriers, made it to Tuy Hoa. Nearly 18,000 tons of ammunition, a month's sup-ply for the corps, was left in depots in Ban Me Thuot, Pleiku, and Kontum. Scores of good aircraft were left for the enemy at Pleiku.

One former South Vietnamese general later said that the retreat from Pleiku "must rank as one of the worst planned and the worst executed withdrawal opera-tions in the annals of military history."[77] General Phu's ill-timed maneuver deci-mated almost an entire corps and led to the loss of Pleiku and Kontum virtually without a fight. Plans to retake Ban Me Thuot were now out of the question. This "self-inflicted defeat," as General Vien later described it, "amounted to a horrible nightmare for the people and armed forces of South Vietnam. Confusion, worries, anxiety, accusations, guilt and a general feeling of distress began to weigh on everybody's mind."[78] The South Vietnamese had lost six entire provinces in a very short period of time, and their confidence was fatally shaken. Arnold Isaacs, Saigon correspondent for the *Baltimore Sun,* witnessed the debacle in II Corps and wrote: "There was a feeling of a vital part come loose. After suffering so much for so long for so little reward, these [ARVN] soldiers had now experienced a betrayal that even their remarkable resilience could not bear. Deserted by their officers and left to the terrible shambles of the road from Pleiku, they had been robbed even of the chance to redeem their pride by fighting back. . . . It was impossible to believe they would ever again be an army."[79] As bad as the defeat was in the Central Highlands, an even worse calamity was unfolding two hundred miles to the north.

DEBACLE IN MR I

The disaster in II Corps had serious repercussions for I Corps in MR I. As refugees fled the Highlands, the population in the northernmost provinces, terrified that they might be cut off, panicked and began streaming south along the coastal road toward Saigon. Their flight made matters extremely difficult for Lt. Gen. Ngo Quang Truong, the I Corps commander who, as one of Thieu's best field generals, had established a sound defense in his area of operations.[80] Truong had five divisions at critical locations. The elite Marine Division defended Quang Tri. The 1st Division, considered by many to be the best ARVN division, and an armored brigade occupied the critical ridgeline that ran west and south of Hue.[81] The Airborne Division, also an elite force, protected the Hai Van Pass and the outposts to the west of Da Nang. The 3rd ARVN Division, reconstituted after being decimated at Quang Tri during the 1972 NVA Easter Offensive, defended Da Nang. The 2nd ARVN Division took responsibility for securing Quang Tin and Quang Ngai provinces, the former of which included the seaport of Chu Lai.

During the first two months of the year, Truong's forces had done very well, successfully countering NVA attacks at Quang Tri and Hue and along Route 1. Their fortunes changed with the fall of Ban Me Thuot and the disaster in II Corps. President Thieu was convinced that the target of the new North Vietnamese offensive was ultimately Saigon, and at the urging of the JGS began to pull forces back to protect the capital city. On 11 March, he ordered Truong to release the Airborne Division for immediate redeployment to the Saigon area. On 13 March, Truong flew to a meeting with the president at Independence Palace to plead his case for retaining the Airborne Division, one of the linchpins of his entire defense. In a three-and-a-half hour meeting, Truong explained to Thieu that he currently had a good defensive scheme in I Corps, but that detaching the airborne could very well mean the eventual loss of Quang Tri Province and possibly Hue as well. According to General Vien, who attended the meeting, Thieu launched into a discussion of his new strategy, emphasizing that the loss of four provinces meant there was little he could do except redeploy forces to hold the vital areas around the capital.[82] Thus, he was taking the Airborne Division to reconstitute a strategic reserve. Thieu then told Truong that he was to hold Da Nang, implying that he was to consider the rest of MR I expendable.[83] At the same time, the president ordered Gen. Nguyen Van Toan, the new commander of III Corps, to pull his forces back from An Loc to protect Saigon. Essentially, Thieu had awarded the NVA another province (Binh Long) with virtually no fight.

Truong was both disheartened by the detachment of the Airborne Division and confused by the president's orders, but he returned to Da Nang determined to carry them out to the best of his ability. Due to Thieu's ambiguous directions, Truong believed that he had been ordered to give up most of I Corps, keeping only Da Nang, its seaport, and the immediate surrounding area.[84] Under that assumption, he began the redeployment of his forces to protect Da Nang. He pulled the Marine brigades out of Quang Tri, sending the 369th Brigade to new positions along the Bo River just north of Hue, the 285th Brigade to a position north of the Hai Van Pass to relieve the airborne brigade, and the 147th Marine Brigade to the old airborne positions west of Da Nang. He also ordered the withdrawal of the 20th Tank Regiment and several batteries of 175-mm guns from Hue to an area south of Da Nang. As these forces began to redeploy from Quang Tri and Hue, the local people became frightened, suspecting that they were to be abandoned to the North Vietnamese. Consequently, civilians began fleeing Quang Tri for Da Nang. The people of Hue, watching the evacuation of Quang Tri and remembering what had happened during the 1968 Tet offensive, left their homes and joined the throng streaming south down Route 1.[85] By 18 March, the highway was inundated with terrified refugees frantic to escape to Da Nang. On 19 March, the NVA reoccupied the ruins of Quang Tri without a fight.

That day General Truong returned to Saigon to consult with President Thieu yet again. The purpose of the meeting was to discuss the cost and difficulty of trying to hold on to both Hue and Da Nang. Since the meeting on 13 March, Truong and his staff had devised a plan whereby both Hue and Chu Lai would be retained for as long as possible. When he arrived to speak with Thieu, he presented this plan, arguing that Hue and Chu Lai could be used as intermediate defensive areas to wear down the NVA attack before their assault on Da Nang. If necessary, these troops later could be withdrawn by sea for the final defense of Da Nang, which would become a stronghold to block the NVA advance south. According to Nguyen Tien Hung, one of Thieu's senior advisers, the South Vietnamese president was at first reluctant to agree to Truong's plan, but eventually the general persuaded him.[86] Before departing, Truong pointed out that the refugee problem was getting out of hand and hampering ARVN troop movements. Truong told the president about the persistent rumor that Thieu had struck a "deal" with the Communists in which he ceded the northern provinces to North Vietnam; the rumor was increasing the flow of refugees and demoralizing his soldiers. Thieu did not respond, leaving the refugee problem to Truong.[87] As the I Corps commander prepared to depart Saigon, Prime Minister Tran Thien Khiem took him aside and privately hinted that the president might also soon pull the Marine Division from I Corps.

Truong returned to Da Nang determined to "fight a historic battle."[88] However, in his absence, the situation had deteriorated. The flow of refugees into Da Nang grew daily, and long-range NVA artillery had begun shelling the I Corps forward headquarters near Hue. North Vietnamese troops had swept aside the regional forces screening the withdrawal of the South Vietnamese troops from Quang Tri and were now attacking the next ARVN defensive line along the My Chanh River, halfway to Hue. South of Hue, the 324B and 325C NVA divisions attacked the 1st ARVN Division and 15th Ranger Group in their positions along Route 1 (see map 16). Additionally, the NVA had begun to shell the highway itself, which was jammed with motorcycles, autos, buses, trucks, and masses of people on foot.

By this time, the South Vietnamese forces in MR I faced the equivalent of nearly nine enemy divisions: five NVA mainforce divisions, nine separate infantry regiments, three sapper regiments, three tank regiments, eight artillery regiments, and twelve antiaircraft regiments. The NVA plan was to attack the South Vietnamese positions in I Corps simultaneously from the north, west, and south to drive Truong's forces into Da Nang, where they could be destroyed. As the first move, General Dung ordered the B-4 Front and II Corps to cut Route 1 and isolate Hue. A series of unclear orders between Saigon and II Corps ultimately conspired to make these tasks much easier for the North Vietnamese.

On the morning of 20 March, General Truong flew to the Marine Division Command Post just south of the My Chanh line to address a gathering of his subordinate commanders. Telling them of Thieu's order to hold Hue, he then dispatched the commanders to carry out the order. At 1330 that afternoon, a recorded radio message from President Thieu went out over the airwaves ordering that Hue be held "at all costs."[89]

When Truong returned to his headquarters in late afternoon, he was stunned to receive a "flash" (high priority) secret message from Saigon stating that the JGS had decided that they did not have the resources to resupply all three enclaves in MR I (Hue, Da Nang, and Chu Lai) and that he was "free" to redeploy his forces to Da Nang if he saw fit.[90] Truong was totally baffled by the complete turnaround from what had been discussed at the palace the day before. To further confuse matters, the prerecorded presidential order to hold Hue was still being broadcast over the radio hourly. Truong was not sure about what he should do.[91] He sent a message to the JGS asking for clarification and stating his reservations about the new order. The next day he received a reply from General Vien: "The situation is very critical. Try to do your best."[92] The officer who drafted the message later said that he had meant that Truong was given the discretion of withdrawing only if the situation so dictated. Left to his own devices, however, Truong thought he was being told to pull his troops back to Da Nang. General Vien later admitted that the language in the JGS message was unnecessarily ambiguous, leading to General Truong's confusion and the subsequent withdrawal of all his forces to Da Nang.[93] That was putting it mildly. A U.S. observer best explained the situation, telling a *Time* magazine correspondent: "It was like a yo-yo. First, Thieu gave the order to pull back and defend Danang. Then he countermanded it and ordered that Hue be held. Then he changed his mind again and told the troops to withdraw. A reasonably orderly withdrawal turned into a rout."[94]

On 21 March, the NVA forces increased their attacks on Route 1 between Hue and Da Nang. The 1st ARVN Division and 15th Ranger Group, using massive ar-

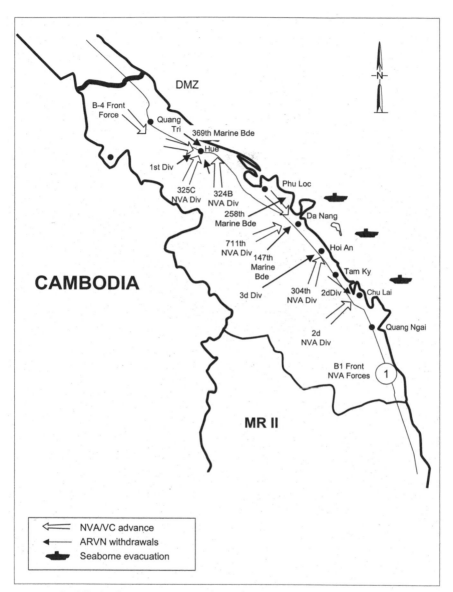

Map 16. The fall of Military Region I, March-April 1975.

tillery and VNAF air strikes fought well throughout the day, but the NVA moved in reinforcements during the night. By mid-afternoon on 22 March, both the 1st ARVN and the rangers, suffering heavy losses, had been overcome and the highway effectively cut at Phu Loc, thereby isolating Hue.

The surviving rangers and remnants of the 1st ARVN Division conducted a withdrawal north into Hue. On the north side of the city, the rangers along the My

Chanh River withdrew under heavy pressure to the defensive line established by the marine brigade along the Bo River about eight kilometers north of Hue. On 24 March, General Truong, believing he had been told in the JGS message to abandon Hue, ordered his forces to pull back through the port town of Tan My, ten kilometers northeast of Hue, for evacuation by ship. The 1st ARVN Division was to provide cover for the marines, who would lead the withdrawal to the sea. Once the marines had embarked, the 1st would then conduct its own withdrawal to the coast. When the South Vietnamese forces reached the coast, the infantry units were to be ferried by all available vessels to Vinh Loc Island, which paralleled the coastline for thirty kilometers south toward Da Nang. The ARVN and marine units would move down the island, cross the Tu Hien Estuary, which would be bridged by ARVN engineers, travel overland to catch Route 1 south of Phu Loc, and then proceed into Da Nang. Although sound, the plan rapidly fell apart during its execution.   .

The marine units reached the coastal village of Tuan An in good order, but they found the docks and beaches clogged with civilians and heavy military equipment. Furthermore, the orders to abandon Hue were not well received by the 1st ARVN Division's soldiers, many of whom had families in the area. Brig. Gen. Nguyen Van Diem, an ARVN division commander, told his men, "We've been betrayed. We have to abandon Hue. It is now *sauve qui peu* [every man for himself]. . . . See you in Da Nang."[95] Under such guidance the withdrawal of the division quickly became a fiasco. The roads to the coast were already overrun with civilian refugees, and as the chain of command broke down under General Diem's edict, many ARVN soldiers simply melted into the crowd and began to look for their families. While this disaster was in the making, the NVA entered the Citadel in Hue unopposed.

The marines and ARVN soldiers who made it to the island began moving south to the estuary. On the morning of 26 March, the sea turned rough, delaying the emplacement of the critical bridge and making difficult the passage from the beaches to the island. The NVA, who had discovered what the South Vietnamese were trying to do, turned their guns on the crowds waiting on the beaches and on the troops and civilians awaiting completion of the bridge at Tu Hien, spreading havoc and inflicting heavy casualties.

The commodore in charge of the sealift, Ho Van Ky Thoai, saw the potential disaster developing at Tu Hien and ordered a flotilla of small boats to be sunk in order to form a causeway across the inlet on which the troops and refugees could walk. However, by this time, discipline had completely broken down, and a group of renegade soldiers took the commodore captive and forced him to take them to Da Nang. Attempts to construct the causeway ceased. Some of the remaining soldiers tried to swim across the inlet, but were drowned by the incoming tide.

The VNN again attempted to mount a sealift and managed to pull about 7,700 people off Vinh Loc Island, but rough seas and increasingly accurate NVA artillery fire hampered their efforts. Although some of the army transportation troops who manned the landing craft refused to approach shore, one regiment of the 1st ARVN

Division was eventually rescued. Another boatload of about six hundred marines also managed to escape. However, two large landing craft full of soldiers were swamped by the rough seas and another was sunk by a direct hit. Bodies littered the water around the island.

The withdrawal from Hue had been an unmitigated disaster. The South Vietnamese had started the battle in northern I Corps in reasonably good condition. Many soldiers and marines fought valiantly, but confusing orders leading to the abandonment of strong defensive positions demoralized the troops.[96] Poor leadership, the disintegration of unit integrity and discipline, and concern over family members quickly led to panic and total chaos. The situation was so bad that the troops did not even bother to destroy the weapons and equipment they left behind. One officer reported that he had left thirty-seven tanks, all fueled and operational, on the beach when he and his men rushed to the boats.[97] Another senior officer, coming ashore at Da Nang, summed up the general attitude when he told a reporter, "I don't know even know where my wife and family are. Why should I care about my division command?"[98] Only about one-third of the troops finally made it to Da Nang, and untold numbers of civilians died in the panic-stricken evacuation. The 1st ARVN Division, the pride of the army, "was lost as an identifiable unit" and never reconstituted.[99]

While this disaster was unfolding, General Truong also had to deal with the NVA attacks in southern MR I, where the situation was not much better. After several hard-fought battles, the 2nd ARVN Division, augmented by the 12th Ranger Group and commanded by Brig. Gen. Tran Van Nhut (the former Binh Long Province chief and one of the heroes of the Battle of An Loc in 1972), had stopped the NVA attack on Tam Ky, the provincial capital of Quang Tin; but on 24 March, the 52nd Independent Brigade of the NVA 711th Division struck again with reinforcing armor elements. By noon, the city had fallen to the Communists. Truong ordered the 2nd Regiment of the 3rd ARVN Division to Quang Tin to assist in the withdrawal of the ARVN forces falling back from Tam Ky. As happened elsewhere the operation was made more difficult by the thousands of civilians moving north out of the area to the supposed safety of Da Nang. Additionally, NVA sappers and artillery forward observers probably gained access to the city by joining the refugees.[100]

Farther south in MR I, the NVA had stepped up its attacks on Quang Ngai Province, cutting Route 1 midway between the city of Quang Ngai and Chu Lai. As the marines and the 1st ARVN Division in the north withdrew from Hue and tried to escape down Vinh Loc Island, Truong ordered the 2nd ARVN Division, along with Quang Ngai territorial forces and their family members, to move to the coast, where they were to be picked up and taken to Re Island, twenty miles offshore from Chu Lai. Fortunately for the South Vietnamese, this evacuation by sea was more successful than the one up north.

Meanwhile, the situation in Da Nang itself had deteriorated significantly. From the north, the NVA 324B and 325C divisions, reinforced by a tank regiment and two artillery regiments, attacked along Elephant Valley against the western flank of the city. From the south, the 711th and 304th divisions, augmented by 44th Front forces, attacked the district towns of Duc Duc and Dai Loc. As the NVA pressed Da Nang from all sides, the mass of humanity, both military and civilian, inside the city became totally disarrayed. By this time, the city of 300,000 was inundated with nearly 2 million refugees from Quang Tri, Hue, and Quang Tin, all clamoring to get out. Thousands of stragglers and deserters who preyed on the refugees and looted the city only added to confusion and panic. A high-ranking officer from I Corps later recalled that Da Nang was "seized by convulsions of collective hysteria."[101] Consequently, according to General Murray's replacement in the Saigon DAO, Maj. Gen. Homer Smith, "the pandemonium which overtook reason in Da Nang literally wrested control of the city from all official presence."[102] All order and discipline had broken down. An attempt to stage a massive airlift failed when hordes of refugees overran the airfield and mobbed the airplanes as they tried to take off; over two hundred operational aircraft were then left on the airfield.[103]

From Saigon, Thieu tried to rally his forces. On 26 March, he went on the radio and issued an order of the day urging his soldiers to stop the enemy advance "at all costs" and demanding that "all combat orders must be strictly carried out. . . . All of you must be determined and strong like a fortress which the aggressors, no matter how brutal and fanatical they may be, will be unable to shake. The aggressors will be defeated in the end. I have led you through many dangerous circumstances in the past. This time, I am again by your side and, together with you, determined to fight and win!"[104] Unfortunately, the troops and civilians in I Corps were long past rallying. Thieu's exhortation had no effect.

Nevertheless, on 28 March, General Truong met once again with his commanders at I Corps headquarters in an attempt to restore order and forge a last-ditch defense of the city. Once again, unit integrity had completely disintegrated and many units had ceased to exist as cogent fighting forces. General Truong's chief of staff later reported that "even at I Corps headquarters, the men deserted. Our drivers, our communication people, men from the headquarters companies, they deserted."[105] By 1400, the territorial forces manning the outer rings of outposts abandoned their positions and joined the crowd in Da Nang. By nightfall, the North Vietnamese troops were entering the outskirts of the city. Meanwhile, the NVA cut Route 1 between Da Nang and Hoi An, thus isolating the city from the south.

As night fell, the NVA forces shelled the Da Nang airport and the naval base. At the same time, they fired on the I Corps command post and other key military installations in the city. ARVN's attempted counter-battery fire with 175-mm guns was largely ineffective, and the NVA kept firing into the city. Under this pounding, Da Nang's remaining defenses collapsed and General Truong called President Thieu to request immediate evacuation of the city. General Vien reported that Thieu, although very concerned about the situation, was very noncommittal in his response to Truong's request.[106] Apparently, the president did not want another disaster like the one in the Central Highlands, but as in previous instances, he did not provide direct guidance to the I Corps commander. As soon as General Truong hung up the telephone, the NVA shelling severed the lines between Da Nang and Saigon. Truong, believing that the situation was hopeless, decided to withdraw what was left of his forces from Da Nang and ordered the displacement of his troops to three embarkation points—the end of Hai Van Pass, the foot of Non Nuoc (Marble) Mountain, and the edge of Hoi An Estuary.

At dawn on 29 March, I Corps began the evacuation. The dense fog that had settled in along the coast and the low tide prevented the ships from getting to the beach. Even though the troops had to wade and swim out to the vessels, the embarkation went smoothly at first. However, by midmorning the NVA artillery began to fall on the beaches. Chaos soon overcame the operation, which became a repeat of the disaster at Hue. Thousands of soldiers and civilians ran for the sea, where they drowned trying to reach the safety of the ships. Thousands of others died under the continuous artillery fire. An estimated 60,000 people died trying to escape Da Nang.[107] Approximately 6,000 marines and 4,000 other soldiers escaped, but in General Truong's words, "not many [others] got out."[108]

By 30 March, the NVA occupied Da Nang and controlled all of Military Region I, taking over 100,000 South Vietnamese soldiers captive in the process.[109] With a few notable exceptions, no pitched battles had occurred in the I Corps area of operations prior to the fall of Da Nang. The South Vietnamese military in the region, in most cases, merely ceased to function as a fighting force. Not many of the 50,000 South Vietnamese soldiers stationed in and around the city even raised their rifles in its defense. One observer remarked that "Da Nang was not captured; it disintegrated in its own terror."[110] Faced with superior numbers and firepower and beset by poor leadership, lack of discipline, rumor, conflicting and confusing orders, and concern for family members, the South Vietnamese troops, for the most part, quit fighting and began to fend for themselves. Among the few exceptions were the Vietnamese Marine units, long considered among the elite forces of the RVNAF; they generally maintained unit integrity and discipline even amidst chaos and disorder. Such professionalism was not the norm; one senior officer described the situation: ". . . stragglers mixed up with the populations and boarded civilian barges and commercial ships. Frustrated, hungry, and leaderless, they went wild and some of them indulged in inadmissable acts of banditry. Billions of dollars of equipment was destroyed and left to the enemy. Thus fell the second biggest city of Vietnam. She had gone through a stage of insanity before she died of suffocation."[111]

By 1 April, the NVA forces held all of MR I and most of MR II. In taking these areas they had destroyed the preponderance of two ARVN corps representing over one-half of ARVN's effective fighting strength. However, one division, the 22nd ARVN, managed to hold out in MR II, controlling the three cities of Qui Nhon, Tuy Hoa, and Nha Trang. The four regiments of the division, DAO Intelligence Chief Le Gro judged, not only "fought well, but valiantly" under Brig. Gen. Phan Dinh Niem against the 3rd and 968th NVA divisions, which were reinforced by the 95B Independent Regiment.[112] But the ARVN defenders were overwhelmed and had to be evacuated by sea when North Vietnamese reinforcements began to flow

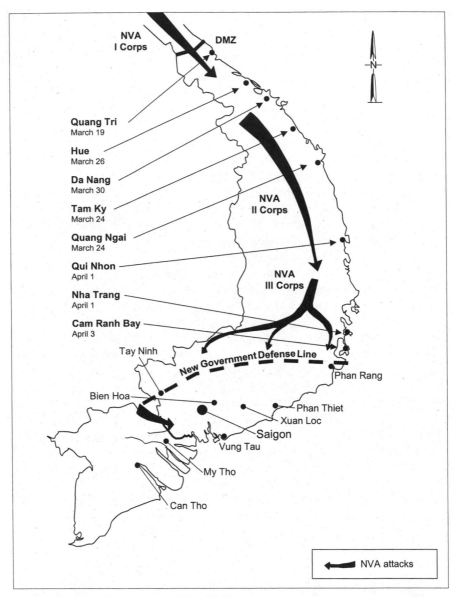

NVA I Corps

DMZ

Quang Tri
March 19

Hue
March 26

Da Nang
March 30

Tam Ky
March 24

Quang Ngai
March 24

Qui Nhon
April 1

Nha Trang
April 1

Cam Ranh Bay
April 3

NVA II Corps

NVA III Corps

Tay Ninh

New Government Defense Line

Phan Rang

Bien Hoa

Phan Thiet
Xuan Loc
Saigon
Vung Tau

My Tho

Can Tho

NVA attacks

Map 17. The loss of the coast, March–April 1975.

into the area from the north after the battle for Da Nang. Still, some wanted to stay and fight. According to General Vien, two regimental commanders of the 22nd pleaded with the division commander to stay and fight. When he denied their request, citing his orders, the two colonels refused to leave and committed suicide.[113] Only about 2,000 officers and men escaped. By mid-April, the North Vietnamese completed the destruction of the few pockets of RVNAF resistance, and the remaining provinces along the coastline "fell like a row of porcelain vases sliding off a shelf."[114] (See map 17.)

The loss of Military Regions I and II had a devastating effect on military personnel and civilians alike, rocking South Vietnam to its very foundation. Half the country had been given away with relatively little resistance. The loss of Da Nang, the nation's second largest city, was, in the words of South Vietnam's deputy premier, Dr. Phan Quang Dan, "the worst single disaster in the history of South Vietnam."[115] In addition to losing territory, the South Vietnamese, fleeing in panic, abandoned mounds of ammunition, supplies, and equipment to the advancing NVA. Over 4,410 tons of ammunition were left in the Qui Nhon depot alone.[116] The VNAF left behind thirty-three A-37 jet fighters on the runway at Da Nang and nearly sixty aircraft at Phu Cat Air Base.[117]

The evacuation of the two northern military regions, Davidson has written, turned into "a craven, every man for himself scuttle for the exits."[118] When ably led, the South Vietnamese troops fought well, in many cases demonstrating skill and valor. For the most part, however, the soldiers followed their leaders, who more often than not were the first to abandon the battlefield. One ARVN officer said that he had talked with several officers from I Corps who told him that "first the division commander disappeared, next the regimental commander disappeared."[119] Given such actions by their leaders, it is not hard to understand why the South Vietnamese army disintegrated in I and II Corps with such astonishing speed. The army collapsed, as one observer wrote, "like a house with its timbers eaten away by termites, which has continued to look sound until the moment it crumbles."[120] Since the initiation of Vietnamization, a question mark had always hung over the existence of the South Vietnamese armed forces. The question—How many years can they hold out?—became the following: How many weeks will they fight?

10

The Fall of Saigon

NEW ORDERS FROM HANOI

Observing the rapid fall of the northern half of South Vietnam and realizing that Thieu and his forces were on the ropes, the North Vietnamese Politburo decided that waiting until 1976 to launch the final offensive was no longer necessary. According to NVA general Tran Van Tra, General Giap was the first to recognize that the time was right for the final blow. Believing that U.S. interference on the battlefield was highly unlikely, Giap concluded that the South Vietnamese forces, falling at the rate of more than a battalion a day, were so weakened that they "cannot cope with the ever stronger forces of the Vietnam revolution, militarily or politically."[1] Le Duan agreed with Giap; together they convinced their colleagues in the North Vietnamese leadership that the time had come to crush the "puppet" administration with a decisive campaign designed to end the war once and for all. On 25 March, the Politburo cabled General Dung in the South to "make a big leap forward" to seize a "once in a thousand years opportunity to liberate Saigon before the rainy season," thus insuring the "reunification of the Fatherland."[2] Dung, eager to take Saigon, agreed with the Politburo's assessment, but he wanted a few more days to "attack, annihilate, and disintegrate" the remaining South Vietnamese forces on the coast between Tuy Hoa and Cam Ranh before launching a new offensive. Writing in his memoirs after the war, he explained that "The enemy was now in confusion and panic and was being closely pursued by our forces . . . [who] had sustained only marginal losses in combat; the fighting spirit of our troops had increased greatly. We were still strong logistically—only part of the ammunition earmarked for the plan had been used, and a fairly large quantity of ammunition had been seized from the enemy," but "the enemy would not disintegrate and flee if we failed to deal deadly, rapid and continuous blows."[3]

The Politburo agreed, urging Dung to wipe out the remaining resistance and move on Saigon as quickly as possible. Dung did just that, pushing his forces more than one thousand miles down the coast in rapid fashion, accomplishing one of the largest and most complex logistical feats of the war. Massive columns of troops, equipment, and vehicles, many captured from the South Vietnamese, moved down the coastal highway toward Saigon. Other elements closed on the capital city from the west and south.

On 3 April, General Dung arrived at his new command post west of Loc Ninh, only sixty miles north of Saigon. Dung now had at his disposal sixteen infantry divisions supported by tanks, sappers, artillery, and antiaircraft units and organized into five corps (1st, 2nd, 3rd, 4th, and Tactical Force 232, a newly formed corps-sized formation of four divisions).[4] As these forces maneuvered toward attack positions, Dung and his staff completed their plans. On 8 April, Dung received another order from Hanoi, reaffirming the decision to attack Saigon before the end of the month. Dung acknowledged receipt of the order and, because a code name had not been chosen, suggested that the operation be named the "Ho Chi Minh Campaign," with which the Politburo concurred by return telegram on 14 April.[5]

While Dung marshaled his forces, Thieu surveyed the South Vietnamese troops available for the defense of the capital: three divisions in ARVN III Corps (the 5th, 18th, and 25th) and three in IV Corps (the 7th, 9th, and 21st), plus remnants of the Marine and Airborne divisions, several armor battalions, some depleted ranger groups, and the survivors of the debacles in I and II Corps, a total of approximately 60,000 troops. The South Vietnamese were clearly outnumbered, but the numbers do not tell the whole tale. The loss of the two northern Corps areas, according to one Saigon official, had "dealt a serious blow to the prestige and morale of the RVN armed forces because it involved the defeat of the most capable units in ARVN."[6] While the North Vietnamese, riding a tide of victory, began to step up their offensive, the disorganized and demoralized RVNAF were already demonstrating the characteristics of a beaten army even before the climactic battle for Saigon began.

The civilian population, too, was distraught because of the unending string of North Vietnamese victories. One despairing government official said that the successive fall of provinces was "like an avalanche."[7] Unfortunately, fear and shared adversity did nothing to draw the people together behind the government and the army. Soldier and civilian alike seemed to be concerned primarily with their own fate. A journalist observing the growing sense of panic and desperation in Saigon noted "that no spirit of support or sacrifice has been summoned."[8] The thought of a Communist victory terrified the South Vietnamese at all levels, but most did little or nothing to forestall it. Terror began to spread among civil servants, members of the military, and general public. Catholics and anyone who had supported or worked with Americans in any way were particularly frightened. Ironically, statements by officials in the United States served to feed the spreading hysteria. Henry Kissinger, who had replaced William Rogers as secretary of state in 1973, testified before the Senate Appropriations Committee that those considered "seriously endangered" in

Vietnam included "all those who served in the administrative machine of the government of South Vietnam, in the various legislative bodies in the provinces, in the various police forces, [and] all those who worked for the United States in its various programs."[9] Defense Secretary James Schlesinger said that as many as 200,000 Vietnamese might be massacred in a Communist takeover.[10] Such statements were widely reported in Saigon, fueling the desperation and terror. Although the Communists' past performance in such instances as the Hue massacre provided grounds for alarm, the fear that enveloped South Vietnamese society was a gross overreaction and caused almost complete paralysis when the time came to defend the city.

The South Vietnamese became even more frightened when word spread that the United States was making plans to evacuate Americans from Saigon.[11] Ambassador Martin tried to quash such rumors. He continued to maintain the official U.S. view that the South Vietnamese, if provided additional aid, could stabilize the battlefield. His deputy, Wolfgang Lehman, told listeners at one embassy meeting a few days after the fall of Da Nang that in his view, "Militarily, the North Vietnamese do not have the capability to launch an offensive against Saigon."[12]

Lehman's statement was preposterous. By the end of the first week of April, except for a few small enclaves in Phan Rang and Phan Thiet on the coast, two-thirds of South Vietnam had fallen into North Vietnamese hands. Six of ARVN's thirteen divisions had vanished, along with many more troops in ranger, territorial, air force, and support units. Losses of weapons, supplies, and equipment were staggering. Conversely, the North Vietnamese, piling up victory after victory, were advancing on Saigon almost unscathed. General Dung wrote, "The numbers killed and wounded was very small in proportion to the victories won, and the expenditure in terms of weapons and ammunition was negligible."[13]

The speed of the NVA advance manifestly paralyzed the South Vietnamese leadership. The civil government, apparently dazed, appeared to function as if nothing had happened. The military leadership was little better. An attempt was made to devise a plan to reconstitute the divisions destroyed in the evacuation of the north, but the completed plan was based on a huge U.S. supplemental military aid appropriation to replace the equipment lost in the retreat. The planners proposed the reequipping of three infantry divisions by 15 June. Realizing that the fate of Saigon would be settled one way or the other long before then, the U.S. Defense Attache Office told the JGS that the plan was not workable and requested that they go back to the drawing board.[14] When the JGS ignored the DAO's request, Maj. Gen. Homer D. Smith, who had replaced Major General Murray as DAO in mid-1974, ordered his staff to come up with its own unit reconstitution plan. They did so, and the JGS quickly adopted the American recommendation, but refused to attach rebuilt battalions to still-functioning divisions as the DAO had suggested.[15] Instead, the South Vietnamese high command insisted on retaining the divisional commands whose units had been destroyed in the north. Extremely weak and not fully integrated into Saigon's defenses, these commands were quickly destroyed for the second time when the NVA attacked the city.[16]

NO HELP FROM WASHINGTON

The Ford administration was also stunned by the suddenness of the South Vietnamese collapse in the northern half of the country. On 22 March, President Ford had written to Thieu, pledging that he was "determined to stand firmly behind the Republic of Vietnam at this crucial hour. With a view to honoring the responsibilities of the United States in this situation, I . . . am consulting on an urgent basis with my advisers on actions which the situation may require and the law permit."[17] Thieu responded on 25 March, just as Hue was abandoned to the Communists, with a letter of his own describing the "grave" military situation and making an appeal for "the Government of the United States of America [to] live up to its pledge" to "safeguard the peace in Vietnam." He specifically requested that Ford "order a brief but intensive B-52 air strike" against the enemy's concentration of forces and logistic bases within South Vietnam and "urgently provide us with necessary means to contain and repel the offensive."[18] Ford replied with a letter to Thieu in which he said: "You and your people may be assured of my continued firm support and of my resolve to do everything I can to help the RVN. Once again, I am confident that our joint endeavors will be successful."[19] Ford added that he needed a first-hand assessment of the military situation in South Vietnam and that he was sending Army Chief of Staff Frederick Weyand to Saigon.

According to his close adviser Nguyen Tien Hung, Thieu was not impressed by Ford's assurances because he believed that Ford and his advisers were downplaying the seriousness of the situation. Thieu was slowly coming to the conclusion that the American president was backing away from previous commitments. Hung reported that Thieu complained: "Ford doesn't seem to care. He is going off on vacation to Palm Springs while we are dying. When is he going to respond?"[20]

General Weyand arrived in Saigon on 27 March. He immediately called on President Thieu and assured him of President Ford's "steadfast support." He told Thieu that he had come to Saigon to examine the "options and actions open to the United States to assist the South Vietnamese."[21] After meeting with Ambassador Martin and Major General Smith, Weyand and his party spent the next six days in making a comprehensive assessment of the military situation and conducting inspection trips to various places throughout South Vietnam. Prior to departing Saigon, Weyand told President Thieu, "We will get you the assistance you need and will explain your needs to Congress."[22]

Weyand returned to the United States on 4 April and met the next day with President Ford at Palm Springs. While deeply pessimistic about the situation, he told Ford that he thought one more infusion of dollars and arms might somehow rescue American objectives in South Vietnam. He reported that the government of the Republic of Vietnam was on the "brink of a total military defeat," but the South Vietnamese were fighting hard with all available resources.[23] Weyand said that they would not be able to recapture lost territory, but with more ammunition and equipment, they could probably establish a strong defense around Saigon. He proposed that Ford submit a supplemental aid request to Congress for $722 million to replace the materiel lost in the disastrous retreat from I and II Corps. This money would be used to provide 744 artillery pieces, 446 tanks and armored personnel carriers, more than 100,000 rifles, over 5,000 machine guns and 11,000 grenade launchers, roughly 120,000 tons of ground and air munitions, and about 12,000 trucks.[24] With this equipment, according to Weyand's assessment, the South Vietnamese could outfit eight infantry and ranger divisions and another twenty-seven independent regiments formed from existing territorial forces—a force that approximated the Communist forces advancing on Saigon. Weyand said that the supplemental request, aside from meeting the materiel needs of the RVNAF, would provide a psychological boost to the South Vietnamese people, who were "very near the brink of a slide into the kind of hopelessness and defeatism that could rapidly unravel the whole structure."[25]

Even within Ford's administration, officials disagreed about Weyand's plan and the wisdom of any attempt to obtain further aid for Saigon. First, many of the president's advisers believed that Congress was unlikely to approve such a request. One administration memo during this period stated: "Any request for supplemental military assistance, however, is likely to be turned down cold. There is strong criticism of ARVN abandonment of supplies and abuse of women and children in the chaos of retreat."[26] Ford's staffers, having polled Congress, informed the president that many legislators would not support him; others would actively oppose any new aid requests.[27] Some advisers doubted that the South Vietnamese could hold out long enough for the aid to reach them, even if by some miracle Congress authorized part or all of the funds. They cited a Defense Intelligence Agency assessment of 3 April that gave South Vietnam only thirty days.[28]

Other counsel came from White House photographer David Kennerly, who had accompanied Weyand to South Vietnam. After he returned, he went in to see the president privately. Having left Weyand in Saigon and gone "upcountry" to see for himself what was happening, Kennerly evaluated the situation much differently than Weyand. Having also flown to Cambodia, he was very upset by what he had seen in the two countries. In Nha Trang, observing the flight of the South Vietnamese army, Kennerly had flown over a ship taken over by mutinous ARVN soldiers, who fired on his helicopter. In Cambodia, he had seen hospitals full of soldiers and civilians. He told the president: "Cambodia is gone and I don't care what the generals tell you; they're bullshitting you if they say that Vietnam has got more than three or four weeks left. There's no question about it. It's just not gonna last."[29]

Despite Kennerly's assessment and those of the other presidential advisers who doubted the advisability of trying to get additional funds for Saigon, Kissinger, always mindful of the symbolism of American actions, urged Ford to request the full $722 million proposed by General Weyand in order to send a signal not only to South Vietnam, but also to America's other allies around the world, that the United States would stand by its commitments.[30]

Given the evolving disaster in South Vietnam, Ford faced an uphill battle to convince Congress to allocate more money for Thieu's forces. On 3 April, the president had suggested in a press conference that 55,000 American lives had been wasted because Congress refused to honor commitments made under the terms of the Paris Agreement. "I think it is up to the American people to pass judgment on who was at fault or where the blame may rest," he stated.[31] Not surprisingly, his remark incensed many in Congress. Senator Robert C. Byrd (D-WV) said, "Some commitments are invented where no commitments exist, and then Congress is blamed for not living up to those commitments."[32] On 8 April, Senator Henry Jackson (D-WA) charged that Nixon had made "secret agreements . . . in writing" without consulting Congress and demanded to know the nature of these promises.[33] The Ford administration responded that Nixon had promised nothing in private that he had not promised many times in public. This was true as far as Ford knew at the time, because extant evidence suggests that the new president had not himself yet seen the entire file of Nixon's correspondence with Thieu.[34] Despite Ford's explanation, many in Congress were convinced that a secret deal had been struck with Thieu.

At this juncture, President Ford, encouraged by Henry Kissinger but discouraged by domestic adviser Robert Hartmann and Press Secretary Ron Nessen, went before a joint session of Congress on 10 April to ask for the full $722 million military aid supplement and another $250 million for economic aid and refugee relief. Ford asserted that the current debacle in South Vietnam was due to "uncertainty of further American assistance," because the reduction in aid "signaled our increasing reluctance to give any support to that nation struggling for its survival." He asked Congress to help him "keep America's word good throughout the world." The president insisted that the supplemental aid to Saigon "must be swift and adequate" and that failure to act would only lead to "deeper disaster."[35] He asked Congress to approve the bill by 19 April, only nine days away. If doubt existed about the likely congressional response to the new aid request, it was quickly dispelled by the reaction on the floor to the president's speech. Not one clap of applause greeted Ford's appeal for additional aid for Saigon, and two Democrats even walked out in the middle of the speech.

Despite the administration's efforts, the supplemental aid request was doomed from the beginning. Events in Cambodia did not help the situation. The Communist Khmer Rouge had been on the verge of completely overrunning Cambodia for some time. Two hours before the president spoke to Congress, Ambassador John Gunther Dean cabled from Phnom Penh requesting initiation of Operation Eagle Pull, the final phase of the American evacuation from the Cambodian capital. The end of U.S. involvement in Cambodia, which included five years of effort and the expenditure of more than one billion dollars, occurred on the morning of 17 April when the victorious Khmer Rouge entered Phnom Penh.

The shadows of the imminent fall of Cambodia and the ongoing disaster in South Vietnam loomed as Congress considered the president's military aid request. As White House staffers had predicted, even previous supporters of U.S. policy in South Vietnam, such as Senator Byrd, again spoke against new aid for Saigon. Byrd announced that "any additional military support for either Cambodia or South

Vietnam would fall into the hands of those we are now opposing" and expressed "considerable doubt that additional expenditure of American funds, except for humanitarian purposes, would change the course of events."[36] Other legislators were even more adamant. Representative Bella Abzug (D-NY) wrote the president, charging that the "wrong policies and illegal military intervention for the past decade" of the U.S. government were "largely responsible for the current tragic plight of the South Vietnamese." She demanded that Ford "cease at once all military aid to the discredited government of President Thieu."[37]

Administration representatives were severely grilled during congressional hearings on the aid request. Secretary of State Kissinger testified before the House Committee on Appropriations, saying "South Vietnam has nowhere else to turn. Without our help, it has no hope, even of moderating the pace of events which it has bravely resisted for years." He further warned that "if the U.S. projects the impression of abandoning people who have dealt with us for so long, totally—without making any effort to achieve control over the situation, it would not help our international position."[38] Such pleas fell on deaf ears.

Other administration officials conveyed grave doubts, even when trying to make a case for the additional funds. When Defense Secretary Schlesinger testified, he was asked if the RVNAF could hold the territory it currently occupied even with the equipment and weapons to be paid for with the supplemental request. He answered, "We must recognize that the probabilities are against it . . . [but] there is a chance."[39] When General Weyand testified about the supplemental aid bill before the House Appropriations Committee, he was asked by Representative Jamie Whitten of Mississippi, "Is there any basis for your request except to maintain an appearance, perhaps in the press and in the news media, when we know the end is inevitable?" Weyand replied weakly, "Well, sir, let me say this: that sometimes the style with which we do things, or the appearance, as you say, are equally as important as substance."[40] Such testimony did little to support the administration's case for the supplemental aid package. Not surprisingly, Congress denied the president's request and then focused its attention on the expected evacuation of U.S. citizens. When the administration asked for a waiver of legal restrictions on military force so that Vietnamese citizens who had worked for the United States could be evacuated with the Americans, liberals in both houses denounced the proposal in the most extreme terms. In the House of Representatives, Bella Abzug loudly pronounced: "This legislation is just an excuse to enable the United States to remain in Vietnam and to use military force if necessary to maintain control . . . so that if we do not happen to like what happens there we can again re-engage the United States in the affairs of that country. . . . It borders on a new Gulf of Tonkin resolution."[41]

A 14 April *Time* magazine poll of three dozen congressmen who had toured their districts during the Easter recess revealed that many of their constituents were "fed up and turned off" by events in South Vietnam. An article that accompanied the poll quoted Democrat Don Bonker of Washington, who observed, "People are drained. They want to bury the memory of Indochina. They regard it as a tragic chapter in American life, but they want no further part of it." Typical of the comments the congressmen heard, according to the article, was the angry observation of Dan Merwin, a fireman in Girard, Ohio, who said of the South Vietnamese: "They're going down the drain without a fight, and we're talking of sending them hundreds of millions of dollars? I don't understand it. We've got people starving in West Virginia."[42] Such attitudes as depicted in the *Time* article and other journals, coupled with the belligerent stance of Congress, made it all too apparent that the South Vietnamese would receive no further help from the United States.

Thieu was demoralized by the inability of the Ford administration to convince Congress to pass the emergency military aid bill. In a nationally televised speech on 4 April, he blamed everyone for the military defeats, attributing the disasters to treachery by Montagnard troops (in the territorial forces), cowardice and defeatism in the armed forces, the intrigues of foreign agents, and even the broadcasts of "foreign radio stations such as the BBC and the Voice of America." Rather than personally accepting a large part of the responsibility, he then attacked the United States for failing to come to South Vietnam's aid as two presidents had promised. "One wonders," he said, "whether U.S. commitments can be trusted and whether U.S. words have any value." Having bitterly chastised the Americans, Thieu then said that only the United States could provide the miracle that would save the day. If American aid continued to arrive "drop by drop . . . we will lose our land gradually to the North Vietnamese Communists until the day when we lose it all. Therefore, I hope that the American people and Congress now will see clearly the real situation . . . and the consequences of their actions over the past two years and that they will assist us in a more practical, more rapid, more efficient and more adequate manner so that we can defend our remaining territory."[43]

Such was not to be the case. How far the fortunes of Thieu and his nation had fallen was made clear on 8 April when 1st Lt. Than Trung, a VNAF F-5E fighter pilot, made two bombing runs on Independence Palace and then flew to the NVA-occupied airfield at Phuoc Long, where he landed to a hero's welcome.[44] Thieu, long frightened about the possibility of a coup, was all but immobilized by the attack on the palace. Although later found to have been an isolated act and not part of a coup, the bombing of the palace clearly demonstrated that the situation was beginning to unravel.

THE HO CHI MINH CAMPAIGN

While Thieu worried about coup attempts and President Ford and his advisers battled with Congress, General Dung, his staff, and field units finalized preparations for launching the Ho Chi Minh Campaign. Shortly before the attack was to kick off, Le Duc Tho arrived at Dung's headquarters in Loc Ninh, after traveling from Hanoi by airplane, car, and motorcycle. He brought with him the final attack order, which began "Forward to Final Victory!"[45] The order confirmed Dung as the overall commander of the campaign and named Politburo member Pham Hung, the senior southern-born Communist, as chief political officer. Tran Van Tra and Le Duc An were named as military deputies to Dung.

Dung's campaign plan called for a three-pronged attack on Saigon. The main attack would be in the east and would be led by NVA IV Corps, consisting of the 6th, 7th, and 341st NVA divisions. They were to leave their positions in Tay Ninh and Binh Long provinces north and northwest of Saigon, march easterly along the foothills of the Southern Highlands, occupy Lam Dong Province, and then attack from there to take Xuan Loc, capital city of Long Khanh Province and the key ARVN stronghold defending Saigon along Route 1. In order to tie down the ARVN forces in and around Saigon so they could not reinforce Xuan Loc, the recently organized 232nd Tactical Force, consisting of four NVA divisions, would drive up from the Delta and cut Route 4. At the same time, NVA III Corps would increase its attacks in the Tay Ninh area to keep the 25th ARVN Division in place and divert attention away from the move east by NVA IV Corps.

THE BATTLE OF XUAN LOC

By 8 April, IV Corps had moved into positions around Xuan Loc. The next day the 341st NVA Division launched the main attack from the northwest after a 4,000-round mortar, artillery, and rocket barrage, which set a large part of the city on fire (see map 18). Supporting attacks were conducted from the north-northeast and east by the 7th and 6th NVA divisions, respectively. Attacking with T-54 tanks, the 341st Division pushed toward the heart of the city. By dawn the next day, the North Vietnamese held the police station, the CIA compound, and the local ranger base. However, the 18th ARVN Division, under Brig. Gen. Le Minh Dao, put up a stiff fight, fighting hand-to-hand in many cases while conducting an orderly withdrawal into the city where they set up a hasty, but sound defense. One of the reasons that these soldiers fought so well is that they were ably led. General Dao defiantly proclaimed, "I vow to hold Xuan Loc. I don't care how many divisions the other side sends against me, I will knock them down."[46] He and his officers stayed and fought alongside their men, a situation not often seen in the earlier debacles to the north in MRs I and II. Too, the soldiers fought hard because they were not worried about their family members, most of whom had been evacuated to Saigon before the main battle began. Another factor in the initial success of the ARVN defense in Xuan Loc was that the 341st NVA Division, manned largely by young, inexperienced soldiers, was not an elite unit.[47]

On the morning of 10 April, the 43rd ARVN Regiment conducted repeated counterattacks against the NVA, causing it to yield ground. Maj. Gen. Le Trong An, the NVA corps commander, ordered reserve regiments from the 6th and 7th NVA divisions into the fight, but ARVN doggedly held onto its positions in and around Xuan Loc. Dung, who had become accustomed to gaining ground without

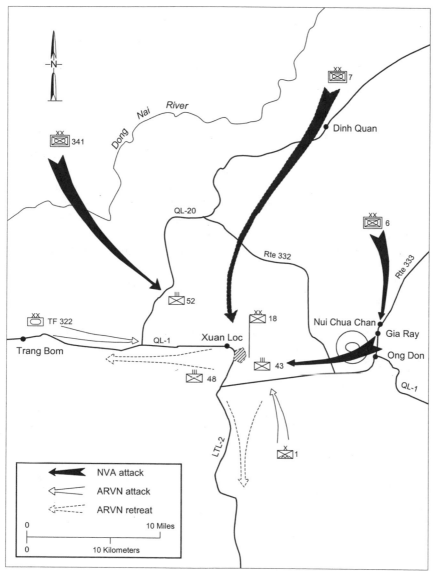

Map 18. The battle of Xuan Loc, April 1975.

a fight, was impressed with "the stubbornness of the enemy."[48] By this time, Xuan Loc itself was a burning pile of rubble. *Time* magazine photographer Dirck Halstead reported that "virtually every building was in ruins. Blackened bodies of North Vietnamese soldiers littered the streets, where heavy house-to-house fighting had obviously taken place not long before."[49] Despite the horrible conditions inside the city, the ARVN forces refused to yield. Unfortunately, they were on their own, because the NVA had blocked the highway west of the city, thus precluding reinforcement from Saigon. On 11 April, the NVA once again made a major push, striking the 52nd Regiment northwest of the city along Route 20 and the 43rd Regiment and 82nd Ranger Battalion in the center of the city. The JGS, fearing that the NVA was trying to encircle Xuan Loc, ordered additional troops from Cu Chi to attack the roadblocks along Route 1 and airlifted two battalions of the 1st Airborne Brigade by helicopter into an area just south of Xuan Loc. Now committed to the defense of Xuan Loc were more than 25,000 ARVN troops, representing almost one-third of the remainder of the Army of the Republic of Vietnam.

With VNAF flying close support, the soldiers of the 18th ARVN began to get the upper hand in the battle.[50] The 43rd Regiment had pushed the NVA out of the center of the city, the 52nd Regiment still held their positions along Route 20, and the 1st Airborne was fighting its way in from the south. Encouraged by the RVNAF's determined resistance, General Smith sent a message to the Joint Chiefs, declaring that the South Vietnamese "had won round one" of the battle for Xuan Loc. He lauded the "valor and aggressiveness of GVN troops" and concluded that their performance "appears to settle for the time being the question, 'Will ARVN fight?'"[51]

Both the South Vietnamese and the Ford White House were momentarily encouraged by the valiant stand of the 18th ARVN at Xuan Loc. For several weeks, Ford's advisers had provided the president with increasingly pessimistic estimates about the potential for a total collapse of the South Vietnamese armed forces. Admiral Gaylor, CINCPAC, had reported from Honolulu that "Saigon can hold out only a few weeks. . . . Barring massive U.S. intervention or a deliberate North Vietnamese pause it is going to go."[52] Now finally came good news. The administration hoped that the stand at Xuan Loc would convince Congress that South Vietnam could be saved, but it did not. Despite the valor of the 18th ARVN soldiers in Long Khanh Province, most congressmen felt as did Illinois Republican Robert Michael, who reported that his constituents believed that the reluctance of the South Vietnamese armed forces to fight dictated that America "only provide humanitarian assistance."[53]

As Washington and Saigon watched the battle in Long Khanh Province unfold, General Dung, not wanting to get tied down in a battle on the periphery of Saigon, urged his forces to redouble their efforts to annihilate the defenders at Xuan Loc. He moved the armor-supported 95B NVA Regiment into the battle against the 52nd Regiment. At the same time, he ordered Artillery Group 75 to train its long-range 130-mm guns on the air base at Bien Hoa to keep the VNAF on the ground. He told NVA II Corps, which was in the process of taking Phan Rang, to continue south along the coast to seize Phan Thiet, then swing westward to hit Xuan Loc if the South Vietnamese still held the city by the time they got there. The battles that ensued were hard fought on both sides. The South Vietnamese forces acquitted themselves extremely well, but during the evening of 14 April, as the NVA forces in contact pressed the ARVN defenders, elements of the 6th NVA Division stealthily slipped around the South Vietnamese positions and moved down Route 1 toward Trang Bom on the way to Bien Hoa, the last obstacle between the North Vietnamese and Saigon.

The 18th ARVN Division had fought valiantly, but by 15 April, sheer numbers and superior firepower turned the tide. One Western military analyst observed: "It's like running a twenty mile race with one contestant going the distances while the other runs a four-man relay. There's simply no way ARVN can win."[54] General Dao was forced to evacuate his forces from inside the city. On 16 April, helicopters extracted the survivors of the 43rd Regiment. That same day, the NVA finally overran the 52nd Regiment, which by this time had lost 70 percent of its original strength. The North Vietnamese had taken Xuan Loc in what would prove to be the last major battle of the war. According to one observer, the South Vietnamese had fought "splendidly," forcing the NVA high command to use the battle as a "meat grinder," sacrificing its own units to destroy irreplaceable ARVN forces.[55] The 18th ARVN had held out for three weeks against overwhelming odds, destroying thirty-seven NVA tanks and killing over 5,000 attackers.[56] Had the rest of the South Vietnamese fought as hard and courageously as the 18th ARVN Division, the outcome of the war might have been drastically different.

The fall of Xuan Loc dealt a death blow to President Ford's supplemental aid request. When testimony by members of the administration failed to convince Congress to act, Ford went on the attack. On 16 April, speaking before the American Society of Newspaper Editors, the president again accused Congress of reneging on U.S. obligations to support South Vietnam. He said, "It just makes me sick that at the last minute of the last quarter the country would not make that special effort, [that] small, additional commitment in economic and military aid" needed to avert "this tragic situation."[57] Such comments did not help Ford's case, because they stirred up additional animosity in Congress over supposed "secret" commitments by Nixon and stoked the ire of those already adamantly against further aid for Saigon.

On 16 April, as the survivors of the battle at Xuan Loc were being evacuated, Nguyen Tien Hung, acting as President Thieu's personal emissary, arrived in Washington to plead Saigon's cause. With him, he brought the file that contained letters from Nixon and Ford promising support for the South Vietnamese. His mission was to seek a postponement of the vote on the supplemental appropriation while he pursued an alternative to the bill. He would petition Ford for a loan of $3 billion per year for three years, at an interest rate to be determined by Congress. In a letter that Hung presented to Ford, Thieu said this money would be a "'freedom loan,' a loan that would permit us to defend ourselves against the aggressors and give us a reasonable chance to survive as a free country."[58] Thieu believed that he could still hold on and resist the Communists in the Mekong Delta if assured of continued American support. Hung was sent, he later admitted, "to play the part of a cabinet minister turned beggar."[59]

It was too late even for begging. On 17 April, the administration's aid request was effectively killed when the Senate Armed Services Committee voted not to approve the additional aid for Saigon. Earlier in the week, the committee members had met with Ford to discuss the situation in Southeast Asia. Ford wrote in his memoirs that the meeting was tense and that "the [Senators'] message was clear: get out, fast."[60] New York Republican Jacob Javits of New York said, "I will give you large sums for evacuation, but not one nickel for military aid."[61] Although the bill was still being debated in other committees, it was a dead issue. Hung later wrote that he was overwhelmed by the news of the Armed Services Committee vote. His mission disintegrated because "there was no one to talk to about the Freedom Loan."[62]

THIEU RESIGNS

Thieu's position and even his personal safety had become precarious. On 18 April, NVA sappers struck the Phu Lam radar station on the outskirts of Saigon. When General Toan, III Corps commander, called to inform the president of the new attack on the radar site, he also confirmed that the defense in Xuan Loc was on the verge of collapse and that Phan Rang had fallen. Then he told Thieu that ARVN soldiers had "bulldozed and leveled" Thieu's ancestral grave site outside Phan Rang.[63] The terrible insult demonstrated just how far Thieu had fallen in the eyes of his countrymen. By now, wrote former ARVN lieutenant general Lam Quang Thi, Thieu had become "the most hated man in Viet Nam."[64]

Later that day, a group of political moderates and opposition figures confronted Thieu and told him that they would publicly demand his resignation if he did not voluntarily step down within six days. Thieu responded by arresting several high-ranking military officers, including II Corps commander General Phu, who he insisted were more responsible than he for the military disaster. General Dong Van Khuyen wrote after the war that Thieu had believed until almost the last moment that the Americans would not let him and his countrymen go down in defeat; but the South Vietnamese president finally realized that time had run out.[65] His capital was surrounded by the North Vietnamese Army, his people no longer supported him, and it was now painfully clear that the United States had abandoned him.

On the day after the supplemental aid request was voted down, Ambassador Martin had cabled Kissinger that he believed members of the Joint General Staff might make a move to remove the South Vietnamese president once it became clear that the United States would provide no further aid. Martin said that he intended to go to Thieu "unless instructed to the contrary" and tell him that "his place in history would be better assured with the recording of all the truly significant things he has accomplished," and that if Thieu insisted on remaining in power, he would be " remembered for failing to permit the attempt to be made to save what is left of Vietnam as a reasonable free state." Martin would make "absolutely crystal clear" that he was speaking only for himself "as a friend" and further say that it was his "dispassionate and objective conclusion that if he does not do this [leave office voluntarily], his generals will force him to depart."[66] In the same message, Martin also strongly urged the secretary of state to convince the Soviet Union and China to use their influence to get the North Vietnamese to accept a cease-fire and new negotiations.

Kissinger replied the same day in a message marked "Secret Sensitive Exclusively Eyes Only via Martin Channels." He told Martin: "I have discussed your Saigon 710 [message] with the President. There is no objection to your proceeding as you indicate in Paragraph 9."[67] The president had given the go-ahead for Martin to try to convince Thieu to step down.

Kissinger had already met with Anatoly Dobrynin, Soviet ambassador to the United States, to ask for assistance. The Soviets later passed on word that the North Vietnamese did not plan to attack Saigon during their current campaign. This may have been Moscow's impression, but the North Vietnamese, having no doubts that the ultimate military victory was within their grasp, were determined to seize their chance. A South Vietnamese agent who had long been inside COSVN came in from the field on 17 April and reported that the NVA was planning to take Saigon; any talk of negotiations, with or without Thieu, was out of the question. He said that the Communist high command had vowed to be in Saigon to celebrate Ho Chi Minh's birthday on 19 May.[68]

On Sunday evening, 20 April, Ambassador Martin called on President Thieu. He brought with him the latest CIA intelligence estimate.[69] The picture he painted was desperately bleak. He told Thieu: "I believe that in a few days your generals will come to tell you to step down." Additionally, Martin said that the North Vietnamese gave clear indications that they would not negotiate as long as Thieu remained president. Martin stopped short of telling Thieu that he should resign, but, saying that he was speaking only as a friend and not in an official capacity, commented that the decision to leave office was Thieu's and Thieu's alone to make. The South Vietnamese president asked whether his resignation might have a positive effect on the aid vote in Congress. Martin replied that it might help, but probably not—that it was a "bargain whose day had passed." Thieu listened quietly to all this and assured the ambassador that he would "do what is best for the country."[70]

Later that day, Thieu was visited by French Ambassador Jean-Marie Merillon, who also told the president that he had heard rumors that various generals were prepared to force him out if he did not resign.[71] Whether a movement really existed to remove Thieu is unclear. General Vien, the JGS chairman, later maintained that Martin and Merillon were wrong: "I am certain that on our side there was absolutely no pressure from any general to force [Thieu] to resign."[72] However, Vien admitted meeting with a group that included Defense Minister Tran Van Don, Prime Minister Nguyen Ba Can, and Economics Minister Nguyen Van Hao, but insisted that this group met to discuss the situation and not to plot against Thieu. Some observers maintain that this group planned to call on Thieu to convince him to resign.[73]

Regardless of the nature of the meetings, the next day, in an effort to preempt any ouster, Thieu called the key members of his government to Independence Palace. He began by relating the details of his discussions with Ambassadors Martin and Merillon. He then said he would base his decision on their reaction and whether they considered him an obstacle to peace. No one said a word. According to presidential adviser Hung, Thieu decided at that moment to resign.[74]

The next day Thieu appeared before a joint session of the National Assembly.

In this nationally televised three-hour speech, a rambling and emotional tirade, he vilified the United States for failing to live up to its commitments: "The United States has not respected its promises. It is inhumane. It is not trustworthy. It is irresponsible."[75] Likening the recent congressional debate over the supplemental aid request to "bargaining at the fish market," he said that he "could not afford to let other people bargain over the bodies of our soldiers." He then announced his decision to resign and turn over the government to Vice President Tran Van Huong. Thieu concluded: "I depart today. I ask my countrymen, the armed forces, and religious groups to forgive me my past mistakes I made while in power. The country and I will be grateful to you. I am very undeserving. I am resigning, but I am not deserting." The next day, with the assistance of U.S. officials, Thieu departed Saigon for Taiwan.

By the time Huong assumed office, the battle at Xuan Loc, although not yet over, had already been decided. The North Vietnamese, moving closer to Saigon every minute, were not interested in negotiating with the new president or anyone else. The official North Vietnamese news agency called the change in leadership a "puppet show" and denounced the new government as the "Thieu regime without Thieu."[76]

Nevertheless, Huong attempted to reach out to the Communists. He called for an immediate cease-fire and the establishment of the National Council of Reconciliation called for in the Paris Peace Accords. He also proposed to send Brig. Gen. Phan Hoa Hiep as a special emissary to Hanoi. The North Vietnamese scornfully replied that Huong's proposal for a cease-fire "fools no one" and "will hardly help the Americans out of their defeat."[77]

By this point, American attention had shifted to the evacuation. On 23 April, Ford spoke at Tulane University in New Orleans. The president said, "America can regain the sense of pride that existed before Viet Nam. But it cannot be achieved by refighting a war that is finished as far as America is concerned."[78] That same day, Ambassador Martin cabled Kissinger that it would soon be time to execute Operation Frequent Wind, the American evacuation of Saigon.[79]

THE FALL OF SAIGON

While the new South Vietnamese government vainly searched for a way to save Saigon, General Dung and his staff completed preparations for the final assault. On 22 April, Dung had received a message from the Politburo instructing him to launch "the attack against the enemy from every direction without delay. To act in time now is to guarantee with the greatest certainty that we will gain total victory."[80] Dung's plan, a variation of the "blossoming lotus" tactic used so effectively at Ban Me Thuot, called for quick thrusts to seize five key points in the city: Independence Palace, Joint General Staff headquarters, the National Police headquarters, Tan Son Nhut Air Base, and the Special Capital Zone headquarters, whose commander controlled the ARVN troops defending the city. Dung reasoned that once these vital "nerve centers were smashed . . . the Saigon army and administration would be like a snake without a head. What remained of their system of defense and repression would fall apart, the masses would rise up . . . and Saigon would be quickly liberated."[81]

Saigon was now defended by the remnants of five ARVN divisions arrayed in a ring thirty to fifty kilometers from the center of the city. Dung neither wanted a prolonged battle with these forces nor their withdrawal into the city, where his troops would have to fight them house-to-house. Therefore, he proposed to divide his forces. While one part of his troops tied down the ARVN troops on the outer perimeter, the other force would drive for the center of the city. To facilitate this scheme, he planned to send forces to secure the major roads, bridges, and key positions leading into Saigon to prepare the way for an armored thrust that would strike the key installations. At the same time, he proposed to use artillery, a battery of SA-2 antiaircraft missiles, and a group of captured A-37 bombers to shut down Tan Son Nhut Air Base.

Dung set the attacks on the perimeter for 26 April and the main attack on the city center for the following day. After finalizing the plan, Dung ordered his forces, now totaling over 130,000 troops, into attack positions (see map 19). NVA IV Corps (three divisions), having captured Xuan Loc and Trang Bom, would continue down Route 1 from the east to attack Bien Hoa and then Saigon itself. NVA II Corps (four divisions) moved down Route 2 toward Ba Ria and Vung Tau.

In the southwest, the 232nd Tactical Force (four divisions) and several independent regiments prepared to attack the ARVN positions along Route 4 to cut off access to Saigon from the Mekong Delta. In the northwest, NVA III Corps (four divisions) prepared to attack the 25th ARVN Division in their positions along Route 1 in the vicinity of Trang Bang and Cu Chi. As the other corps completed their moves, the three reserve divisions of NVA I Corps arrived at assembly areas east of Ben Cat. The climactic battle for the survival of the Republic of South Vietnam was about to begin.

On 26 April, the North Vietnamese launched supporting attacks by the 6th, 7th, and 341st NVA divisions against Bien Hoa and the former U.S. base at Long Binh. At the same time, the 304th and 325th NVA divisions attacked ARVN positions at Long Thanh in an attempt to cut Route 15, the remaining overland link between Saigon and Vung Tau on the coast. The 312th Gold Star Division struck Ba Ria, at the base of the Vung Tau Peninsula. The supporting attacks would hold ARVN defenders in place, so that they could not reinforce Saigon when the city came under direct attack.

In the early morning hours of 27 April, the NVA main attack on Saigon began. Following a rocket barrage, the NVA forces "attacked like a hurricane" from five directions.[82] They made rapid progress. To the east, NVA IV Corps closed in on Bien Hoa, while two divisions overran Long Thanh after one of the most intense tank battles of the war. To the south, the 232nd Tactical Force cut Route 4 nineteen kilometers outside the city, engaging elements of the ARVN 7th, 9th, and 22nd divisions. To the southeast, the 3rd NVA Division hammered the rebuilt 3rd ARVN Division and remnants of the 1st Airborne Brigade, driving them out of Ba Ria and

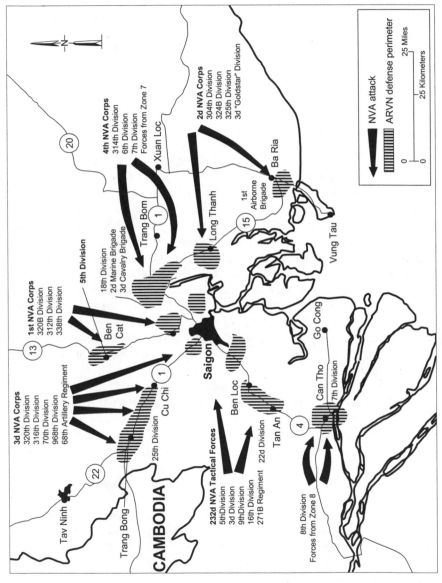

Map 19. The Ho Chi Minh Campaign, April 1975.

3d NVA Corps
320th Division
316th Division
70th Division
968th Division
68th Artillery Regiment

1st NVA Corps
320B Division
312th Division
338th Division

5th Division

18th Division
2d Marine Brigade
3d Cavalry Brigade

4th NVA Corps
314th Division
6th Division
7th Division
Forces from Zone 7

2d NVA Corps
304th Division
324B Division
325th Division
3d "Goldstar" Division

232d NVA Tactical Forces
5thDivision
3d Division
9thDivision
16th Division
271B Regiment

8th Division
Forces from Zone 8

Tay Ninh

Trang Bong

CAMBODIA

Cu Chi

25th Division

Ben
Cat

Saigon

Ben Loc

Tan An

22d Division

Can Tho
7th Division

Go Cong

Trang Bom

Xuan Loc

Long Thanh

1st
Airborne
Brigade

Ba Ria

Vung Tau

NVA attack
ARVN defense perimeter

0   25 Miles
0   25 Kilometers

272

closing in on Vung Tau. To the north and northwest, NVA III Corps blocked Route 1 between Tay Ninh and Saigon, surrounding the 25th ARVN Division at Cu Chi.

As the NVA closed in on the city, South Vietnamese politicians debated who should lead the nation. Although many felt that President Huong would step aside soon after assuming office in favor of someone stronger who could either lead the fight against the Communists or negotiate an accommodation, he had not done so. Huong was a well-meaning man, but he suffered from asthma and arteriosclerosis and was not up to the demands of the crisis at hand. He soon came under intense pressure to relinquish his office. After a period of vacillation, Huong, citing a respect for the constitution, said that if the National Assembly no longer wanted him as president, it was up to them to vote him out of office. The assembly replied that it was up to Huong to resign. At the same time, a heated debate broke out in the assembly between old-line Thieu supporters, those who supported the elevation of General Duong Van ("Big") Minh, and still others who believed that Air Vice Marshal Nguyen Cao Ky should be made president to carry on the fight.

While debate about the presidency raged, the North Vietnamese Army continued to close the ring around Saigon. Finally, on 27 April, shortly after four NVA rockets landed in the city, Huong recalled the National Assembly "to choose a political personality to replace the head of state and negotiate with the other side."[83] At 6:45 in the evening, Senate President Tran Van Lam called the assembly into session and read a letter from President Huong. Conceding that "we are lost" and "have no choice but to negotiate," Huong announced that he was prepared to turn over the reins of government to General Minh, who long had boasted of contacts in the Communist camp.[84] After the letter was read, Defense Minister Tran Van Don, along with General Vien of the Joint General Staff and Lt. Gen. Nguyen Van Minh, commander of the Saigon defenses, gave a briefing on the bleak military situation. Shortly thereafter, the assembly, with one-third of the members abstaining, voted to make Minh president, charging him to "carry out the mission of seeking ways and means to restore peace to South Vietnam."[85] Those who voted for the new president clearly hoped that he would use his contacts to open negotiations with the North Vietnamese.[86] Such hope was unrealistic. The Communists held the upper hand on the battlefield, and final victory was in sight. The Politburo had already unanimously decided against a negotiated settlement, regardless of any political changes in Saigon.[87]

At dawn on 28 April, NVA commandos from IV Corps took the far end of the Newport Bridge, only five kilometers from the center of Saigon, cutting the only remaining land route between the capital and Bien Hoa.

NVA infiltrators had been entering the city for several days, joining the columns of refugees streaming into Saigon to get away from the fighting. Once inside the city they reconstituted themselves in groups of ten to fifteen men. Each group had an assigned target. The target list included key installations such as barracks, munition dumps, and police stations. These groups would go into action as the main NVA body began its attack on Saigon. Other infiltrators were assigned to protect bridges to preclude the South Vietnamese from trying to block NVA tank and mechanized columns from entering the city. An Italian reporter later wrote that he had been told by a high ranking North Vietnamese officer that over fifteen hundred commandos infiltrated the city in the week before the South Vietnamese surrendered.[88]

At 5:15 in the afternoon of 28 April, as the North Vietnamese were making final preparations for the assault on Saigon, President Huong officially stepped down in a ceremony at Independence Palace. Huong spoke first, addressing Minh: "General, your mission is very heavy, [but] if you wholeheartedly save the country . . . and strive to restore peace and ensure that bloodshed stops, the meritorious service you render will be remembered forever by younger generations."[89] When Minh took the podium, he said, "I can make you no promises. In the days ahead we will have nothing but difficulties, terrible difficulties. The decisions to be taken are grave and important, our position is a difficult one."[90] He paused for a moment and one reporter later wrote that he and his colleagues present thought that Minh was going to announce surrender.[91] However, the new president continued, "The order to our soldiers is to stay where they are, to defend their positions, to defend with all their strength the territory remaining to us." Then he announced: "I accept the responsibility for seeking to arrive at a cease-fire, at negotiations, at peace on the basis of the Paris Accords. I am ready to accept any proposal in this direction." As a gesture of good faith, he announced that he would release all political prisoners and lift the restrictions on the press.[92] He concluded by appealing to those attempting to flee the country to "remain here to join us and all those with good will in building a new South for the future."

Just as Minh finished his speech, five captured A-37s made an attack on Tan Son Nhut, destroying three AC-119s and several C-47s.[93] Thus, the sole North Vietnamese air strike of the war served as an answer to Minh's attempt to foster negotiations. The Communists also broadcast the following response over Radio Liberation one hour after Minh's speech:

> After the departure of the traitor Nguyen Van Thieu, those who are replacing him, namely the clique Duong Van Minh, Nguyen Van Huyen and Vu Van Mau, are holding fast to their war, to keep their present territories while calling for negotiations. It is obvious that this clique continues stubbornly to prolong the war in order to maintain American neocolonialism. But they are not fooling anyone. The fighting will not stop until all of Saigon's troops have laid down their arms and all American warships have left South Vietnamese waters. Our two conditions must be met before any cease-fire.[94]

While North Vietnamese pilots attacked Tan Son Nhut and the South Vietnamese transferred power to General Minh, NVA forces moved into position for the final assault on Saigon. To the southeast of the city, the 325th NVA Division reached the town of Nhon Trach, from which its long-range 130-mm guns could fire on Tan Son Nhut. To the west of the capital, another NVA division under Maj. Gen. Di Thien Tich spent the daylight hours under cover. When it became dark, the force moved into attack positions along the Van Co River, which flowed along Saigon's southwestern edge. Dung later wrote that "there was no longer any safe place" for the government forces.[95]

To the east of Saigon, following an overnight artillery barrage, the final assault on Bien Hoa began. Lt. Gen. Nguyen Van Toan, ARVN III Corps commander, had already left Bien Hoa for Saigon. When the artillery fire began, the rest of Toan's staff also fled.[96] *Time* magazine, reporting that Toan had privately conceded the battle for Saigon was already lost, quoted a U.S. military observer as saying that most of the ARVN top leadership had virtually resigned themselves to defeat: "Their morale and their leadership was just flowing away."[97] The leaders' bleak outlook had a devastating impact on the forces supposed to be fighting the climactic battle for Saigon. As one young pilot from the South Vietnamese air force later said, "We—the young ones—we expected to continue fighting. But how could we fight when there were no generals to lead us any more?"[98]

In the early morning hours of 29 April, the NVA began a rocket attack on Tan Son Nhut. During the attack, two U.S. Marine security guards were killed. LCpl. Darwin Judge and Cpl. Charles McMahon Jr. were the last American servicemen to die in the Vietnam War.[99] The NVA followed the rocket attack by firing shells from the long-range 130-mm guns in Nhon Trach. Chaos broke out as South Vietnamese soldiers and airmen tried to board anything that flew. The crew of one already overloaded C-130 pushed soldiers off the rear cargo ramp so that the aircraft gained enough ground speed to take off. Another plane, a C-7 Caribou transport, spun off the runway, crashed, and burned. VNAF pilots manned anything that would fly and took off for Thailand; eventually 132 aircraft were flown to U Tapao Air Base in Thailand.[100] Later that day, Lt. Gen. Tran Van Minh, VNAF commander, and a group of thirty armed senior air force officers rushed into the DAO compound at Tan Son Nhut and demanded that they be evacuated immediately. General Smith directed his assistant air attache, Lt. Col. Dick Martin, to inform the officers that they would be shot on the spot unless they surrendered their weapons and calmed down. They did so and Martin placed them under lock and key. Later, they were evacuated. In its final assessment, the DAO later reported that this incident "signalled the complete loss of command and control" of the air force "and magnified the continued deterioration of an already volatile situation."[101]

While desperation and terror reigned at Tan Son Nhut, President Ford convened a meeting of his advisers in the White House. After much discussion, President Ford directed the implementation of the final phases of Frequent Wind.[102] The artillery and rocket attacks had effectively ruled out Tan Son Nhut for any further evacuation by fixed wing aircraft. Over the next several days, U.S. helicopters airlifted some 7,100 American and South Vietnamese military and civilian personnel out of Saigon, many of them from the roof of the embassy. Navy ships ferried more than 70,000 South Vietnamese to American vessels in the South China Sea. In one of the many tragedies of the war, the Americans left behind 420 South Vietnamese who had worked for them and had been promised evacuation. Col. Harry

Summers, an army officer assigned to the U.S. Embassy, later wrote that this incident was "a shameful day to be an American" and that the evacuation of the embassy was "the Vietnam War writ small."[103] As had happened in the larger sphere, the Americans had made promises that they did not fulfill.

When the American evacuation began in earnest, chaos engulfed the city. Mobs took to the streets, overturning cars, setting fire to buildings, and looting. Former residences and offices of Americans were the primary targets for the looters, who took everything they could carry, even bathroom fixtures. One reporter later wrote: "In a flash it became an orgy of people opening drawers, ripping down curtains, emptying refrigerators, taking sheets, blankets, dishes. . . . It was an impressive show of rage, frenzy, and joy by people bent on plunder."[104]

The NVA columns advanced slowly on the center of the city, encountering very little resistance. The Saigon military command virtually ceased to exist. Shortly before 7:00 P.M., the new chief of the Joint General Staff, Lt. Gen. Vinh Loc, issued his first and only order of the day, admonishing his officers and soldiers against "running away like a mouse," and promising, "From now on, I and the commanding generals will be present among you . . . day and night."[105] Shortly afterward, Loc boarded a helicopter for the evacuation ships. Most other senior commanders had already bailed out. A reporter who observed the collapse of the South Vietnamese armed forces and the civil government in Saigon later wrote: "Like a puppet no longer supported by its strings, the whole government apparatus of Saigon was collapsing. There was no order, no army, no authority other than that of the guns and weapons that many, a great many still had and were using."[106]

Just after 5:00 A.M. on 30 April, Ambassador Martin, carrying the furled American flag that he had taken from his office, departed by CH-46 helicopter for the *U.S.S. Blue Ridge* standing off the coast in the South China Sea. At 10:24 A.M., President Duong Van Minh announced the unconditional surrender of the Republic of Vietnam. Almost immediately, the South Vietnamese soldiers began to divest themselves of weapons and uniforms, attempting to melt into the crowds to avoid retribution from the victors. Some chose another way. One ARVN colonel went to Lam Son Square, site of the memorial to South Vietnamese war dead. He saluted the huge statue of a South Vietnamese soldier and shot himself with his pistol.[107]

By noon, General Dung's II Corps tanks rumbled through the outskirts of Saigon and rolled into the city unimpeded, followed by open trucks full of heavily armed NVA soldiers. One column of tanks rolled down Thong Nhut Avenue across Cong Ly Boulevard toward Independence Palace. The lead tank, Number 843 commanded by NVA major Nguyen Van Hoa, crashed through the gate of the palace.[108] Other tanks followed, parking in a semicircle on the palace grounds in front of the staircase. One NVA soldier jumped down from his tank, ran up the steps, and began jubilantly waving the blue and red flag with the yellow star of the Provisional Revolutionary Government. Neil Davis, a war correspondent for Reuters, asked the soldier his name and the young man replied, "Nguyen Van Thieu."[109] On that ironic note, the Vietnam War came to an end.

Conclusion

North Vietnamese forces controlled all of South Vietnam by 3 May 1975. Only fifty-five days after the original attack on Ban Me Thuot on 10 March, the armed forces of the Republic of Vietnam had completely collapsed, resulting in the total defeat of a million-man army, the loss of $5 billion of weapons and equipment, and the demise of South Vietnam as a sovereign and independent nation. After the war's end, various theories and explanations emerged about how and why the war had been lost. Many faulted the fatally flawed Paris Peace Accords that ensured the defeat of South Vietnam by leaving 100,000 NVA soldiers in the South after the cease-fire. Others, arguing that Saigon could have averted defeat with American assistance, charged that the United States had abandoned the South Vietnamese. Those taking this stance blamed Congress for refusing to allocate funds for additional military aid. Still others maintained that Nixon, had he remained in office and not been weakened by the Watergate scandal, would have responded strongly to North Vietnamese military moves in 1975. All of these viewpoints possess some validity, but all are also open to argument. Because the larger issue of why the war was lost cannot be resolved, the issue at hand here is to assess the somewhat more manageable question of whether Vietnamization, as a policy, contributed to the defeat of South Vietnam.

Any evaluation of Vietnamization must occur on two levels. The first level of analysis deals with the stated purpose of the program. Nixon wanted to "reverse the 'Americanization' of the war . . . withdraw the half million troops from Vietnam in a way that would not bring collapse in the south . . . negotiate a cease-fire and a peace treaty."[1] Ultimately, he desired to pull the United States out of Vietnam and achieve "peace with honor." Considered dispassionately (especially if one happens to be American and not South Vietnamese), Vietnamization did just that. U.S. troops were withdrawn, a peace treaty was signed, a cease-fire (short-lived though it may have been) was initiated, and South Vietnam had survived for two more years. A 1980 BDM Corporation report on strategic lessons learned in the Vietnam War noted: "In light of the goals set by the Nixon Administration (i.e., the withdrawal of US forces from RVN and to bring about a negotiated settlement of the war), Vietnamization has to be considered a success."[2]

However, that report acknowledged in an excessively mild fashion that the United States was ultimately thwarted in its Vietnamization goal of increasing the RVNAF's ability to hold off the enemy.[3] Other observers were much less charitable. Some said that Vietnamization gave the United States a face-saving way out of an unwinnable war and that the Paris Accords were signed to achieve a "decent interval" after U.S. departure before an inevitable South Vietnamese surrender. One of the harshest critics of the policy was retired Army brigadier general Douglas Kinnard, who wrote in 1985 that "as the American people watched the debacle on television in the spring of 1975, they were seeing an event that had many causes. Suffice it to conclude here that if it had not been previously evident enough, the final rout exposed Vietnamization for the fraud and deception that it was."[4] Another historian, Joan Hoff, also criticized Vietnamization, maintaining that it "led to the covert as well as overt expansion of the war in Indochina, a result that had not been anticipated by either the opponents or the proponents of the concept in the first months of the new administration."[5] Both of these assessments faulted Nixon and the political aspects of the Vietnamization policy. However, it must be remembered that the Nixon administration inherited the situation in Vietnam. While without question Nixon's policy, as ultimately executed, was flawed, Vietnamization was doomed to failure for a number of reasons—some attributed to the way the Nixon administration implemented the policy, but also some coming into play long before Richard Nixon took office. Why did Vietnamization fail? What were the fundamental reasons for the collapse of a force on which the United States had spent so much time, effort, and money?

The first of two primary reasons had to do with the timing of Vietnamization; the second, closely related to the first, with the attempt to shape the RVNAF in the image of the U.S. military. Vietnamization, as an official policy, was not instituted until 1969. A 1974 survey of American general officers revealed that most seemed to approve of the Vietnamization program but believed that Washington had waited too long to begin it.[6] The United States had mounted an advisory effort since the 1950s, but after the large American conventional combat force buildup in South Vietnam began in 1965 the advisory effort took a secondary role.[7] With the formal initiation of Vietnamization in 1969, the pendulum swung to improving the RVNAF; unfortunately, U.S. forces began to withdraw faster than the South Vietnamese could or would improve. The shift in emphasis from large-scale U.S. combat operations to preparing the South Vietnamese to assume the burden of the fighting came too late. Given many long-standing problems in the RVNAF, little could be accomplished in the relatively short period of time between Nixon's order to Vietnamize the war and final U.S. withdrawal. "By far the widest loophole of the Vietnamization program was its failure to provide the RVN with enough time for an overall improvement," wrote former ARVN general Nguyen Duy Hinh. "The program was initiated out of American political considerations, and it was implemented with too much haste. While the increase in troop strength could be achieved fairly rapidly, it was almost impossible to ignore the quality and technical capabilities of a one-million strong military force within the span of a few years."[8]

Hinh was correct. Indeed, his comments apply not only to the formal program of Vietnamization, but also to the entire American effort to train the South Vietnamese armed forces dating back to the earliest days of U.S. involvement in Southeast Asia. Many of the problems that contributed to the collapse in 1975 could have been alleviated by instituting a more deliberate approach to "Vietnamizing" the war during the early days of the conflict. This is true in terms of both command emphasis and the type of force to be developed.

Although subsequent evidence has demonstrated that the South Vietnamese were dealing with largely an internal insurgency at the beginning of the conflict, the emphasis of the earliest U.S. advisory efforts was on building a South Vietnamese conventional force to repel a Korean-style invasion from the North.[9] Therefore, rather than structuring forces made up of small, mobile, local units that could combat insurgents, the South Vietnamese army became a mirror image of the 1960s' U.S. Army with its heavy divisions and reliance on firepower and technology.[10]

The 1980 BDM Corporation report on strategic lessons learned cited a number of reasons for this erroneous approach to building up the South Vietnamese military. Chief among them were a failure to learn from the French experience, a failure to perceive the seriousness of the counterinsurgency threat, superficial similarities to the Korean experience leading Americans to believe tactics could be transplanted, and a habitual overconfidence that tended to tune out Vietnamese voices and discourage careful study of the situation.[11] Echoing these findings, military analyst Andrew Krepinevich Jr. charges in *The Army and Vietnam* that the U.S. Army gave "only lip service to counterinsurgency doctrine" and insisted on fighting the war in South Vietnam just like the conventional conflict it was preparing for on the plains of Europe.[12] The approach had a tremendous impact on the effort to build a viable South Vietnamese force. Less than comfortable with the "new" counterinsurgency approach and believing that the nature of the conflict in South Vietnam was primarily an invasion from the North, U.S. Army leaders set out to build a force around what Krepinevich called the "concept" or the "big unit war" based on helicopters, massive firepower, and attrition of enemy forces.[13] From the earliest days of its inception, ARVN received very little counterinsurgency training from the American advisers, who were part of the conventional U.S. Army and had been trained in that system. Therefore, building an army that looked and fought like the U.S. Army remained the thrust of the early advisory effort and continued under the Vietnamization program from its formalization in 1969 until U.S. withdrawal in 1973. The Americans' approach certainly made more sense during the latter period of the war than it had during the earlier phases of the conflict. Nevertheless, the overall result was a very expensive force, primarily devoted to static defense and dependent on technology and large quantities of ammunition and other munitions. As historian Gabriel Kolko later wrote, "[T]he ARVN soon had all of the liabilities of American technology and few of its assets"; thus, technology became a source of dependency and distraction for ARVN.[14]

Once the early direction had been determined, the RVNAF could not be turned around. By the time persuasive evidence surfaced that the immediate threat was internal and not a matter of cross-border attack, it was too late to make major changes in the South Vietnamese force structure and operational concept.[15] Ironically, when the North Vietnamese turned to conventional tactics later in the war and began to send large numbers of combat troops into the South, the RVNAF, trained to fight that kind of war, proved woefully inadequate for the task. Having become so dependent on U.S. support, the South Vietnamese proved incapable of continuing the war once American assistance was no longer available.

The problems involved in forging a sound South Vietnamese military capability were compounded by the arrival of U.S. combat troops in 1965. The U.S. forces arrived on the scene ready to fight a "big war" against the North Vietnamese invaders. As a result, the South Vietnamese were virtually shunted aside and relegated to a supporting role; the feeling among many U.S. commanders was that U.S. forces alone could defeat the Communists with minimal ARVN participation.[16] When the Americans arrived, the "locals" were essentially told to stand by and watch the professionals. As former ambassador Bui Diem said, "Vietnamization began in 1965, not in 1968, but Americans never got around to implementing it because they expected early victory without Vietnamese participation."[17] Such ethnocentrism promoted a misplaced confidence that denigrated not only the South Vietnamese, but also earlier French efforts as well. The Americans' hubris had a detrimental effect on South Vietnamese morale and motivation. One former ARVN officer wrote after the war that "the spectacular battles the Americans fought so well and with so much firepower and such large formations caught the eyes of all elements of the press. . . . The result was the unavoidable but erroneous impression that the Americans were doing all the fighting for the Vietnamese. This gave the Communists more propaganda ammunition for their political war: 'The Viet Cong were fighting the Americans to save Vietnam.' It was a very effective line; it even convinced a lot of Americans."[18] By the time that Nixon assumed office and initiated the Vietnamization program, the foundation for disaster had already been laid. Col. Vu Van Uoc, former chief operations officer of the South Vietnamese air force, commented: "Even in joint U.S./Vietnamese operations, ARVN was only given a minor role and . . . tactics were placed under the supervision of American advisers. In that situation, ARVN felt a too heavy dependence upon U.S. forces and one can hardly say these operations were under Vietnamese jurisdiction. . . . so that ARVN completely lost the notion of being an independent army."[19]

As the U.S. forces began to withdraw, General Abrams and MACV were given what proved to be the insurmountable task of trying to get the South Vietnamese ready to assume responsibility for the war. Conscious of long-standing problems in the RVNAF that would take years to fix, the Americans turned much of their attention to the easiest solution: the physical buildup of the RVNAF in terms of manpower and sophisticated equipment and weapons systems. The effort produced one of the strongest military forces in the world, at least numerically. However, as Gen. Phillip Davidson points out in *Vietnam at War,* "Such an army may improve superficially as foreign equipment and training are lavished on it, but such improvement is deceptive, for the foundation of the force remains rotten."[20]

Ironically, the expansion of the force, long touted as a measure of the "success" of the Vietnamization effort, only exacerbated the problem, leading to a decline in the proportion of soldiers actually in fighting units. Expanding the RVNAF lowered the quality, diluted the competence of the units, and overtaxed the few good officers, as illustrated by the establishment and subsequent demise of the 3rd ARVN Division, which virtually collapsed in the face of the North Vietnamese attack on Quang Tri in 1972.

Concurrent with the vast buildup of the RVNAF was an improved advisory effort to increase South Vietnamese participation in the defense of their own nation. Unfortunately, the increased emphasis on the advisory effort, well intentioned though it may have been, had some unforeseen consequences. Buu Vien, a close personal adviser to President Thieu, said after the war: "The presence of American advisers at all levels of the military hierarchy created among the Vietnamese leadership a mentality of reliance on their advice and suggestions. Even though some officers didn't like the intrusive presence of their counterparts, most of them felt more confident when they had their advisers at their side. The ideas might be theirs, but they felt more assured when those ideas were concurred in by American advisers than when they were suggested by their superiors."[21]

Bao Long, a former ARVN officer, told journalist Paul Hendrickson: "[T]he Americans came and took over and shoved us aside. We lost our character."[22] According to one former ARVN general, character was not the only thing lost when the advisers took over:

> The power and influence of US advisers in the field did tend to overshadow the role of Vietnamese unit commanders. For example, activities of a unit tended to follow along the lines recommended by the adviser. In many instances, it was the adviser who won the battle by calling effective tactical air or firepower support from US resources. This gradually produced overreliance and sometimes total dependence on US advisers. As a consequence, the initiative, responsibility, and prestige that the unit commander usually wielded were greatly affected and, over the long run, the presence of advisers resulted in reduced opportunity for ARVN cadres to develop their command capabilities and leadership.[23]

South Vietnamese officers were not the only ones holding this view; one U.S. general, responding to General Kinnard's study in 1974, said: "There were too many advisers. The result was, advisers became operators and diverted the energy of their ARVN counterparts from their primary mission and at the same time left little incentive for the ARVN commanders to take actions of their own."[24] Gen. Melvin Zais, former commander of the 101st Airborne Division in Vietnam, probably stated it best:

> We were not very good at working with the Vietnamese and I was beginning to work up sort of an internal discontent in my own mind and thinking to myself, "This war will never end until the Vietnamese get good enough to win it. We must be working ourselves out of a job, but we're not. We're not coaching the team; we're like five college football players who have come down to coach a high school team and have inserted ourselves into the lineup." . . . there had to come a time when we couldn't play anymore and the ARVN would have to take over.[25]

When that time came, the U.S. forces had done a poor job of preparing ARVN to take over. Ex-CIA official Douglas Blaufarb wrote that the "panic" of the Vietnamese leadership at the decline of U.S. support was "caused, one can only surmise, by the realization of the Vietnamese officer corps that it really was not up to its job. In the final analysis, those who had played out the charade had never been fooled by it." Only the Americans, Blaufarb added, were deceived, "largely as a result of their own blindness to the political realities of a land where they lived and worked for so many years without learning the most elementary truths of the scene about them."[26]

Despite the ambitious attempts to build-up the RVNAF and increase the advisory effort, the political realities that Blaufarb alluded to reflected long-standing systemic problems within the South Vietnamese society and military that mitigated against success in Vietnamizing the war and making the South Vietnamese a viable fighting force. Corruption, which began at the apex of society, permeated every walk of life and had a devastating impact on the military. It destroyed morale and fighting spirit, contributed to a fantastically high desertion rate, and fatally weakened the entire fabric of South Vietnamese combat capability.

Compounding the crippling corruption was the political nature of the military hierarchy. The RVNAF was actually an extension of Thieu's political apparatus; thus, the real purpose of the army was not military but political. The key commanders were political appointees chosen for their loyalty rather than their expertise as commanders, a practice, according to Blaufarb, that guaranteed corruption and incompetence: "Combat merit goes unrewarded; the soldiers go uncared for; and the demands of the martial spirit—Duty, Honor, County—go unanswered."[27] Lt. Gen. Hoang Xuan Lam, commander of the debacle in Laos, was a prime example of the corrupt political appointees who filled the key posts. Thieu's generals were rivals for both his good graces and the fruits of corruption, making the creation of an integrated command structure that focused on fighting the war impossible. One ARVN general described "dissension verging on insubordination" that prevented any cogent chain of command or overall operational concept.[28]

Another factor contributing to the ultimate failure of Vietnamization and the subsequent demise of the South Vietnamese forces was Thieu himself: he was a disaster as commander in chief. After the departure of U.S. forces, he became excessively rigid, exercising tight control of the military and involving himself in operational matters best left to commanders in the field. Deprived of flexibility in decision-making and on the wrong end of confusing and often conflicting orders, the military commanders, many of whom were political appointees and ill-suited for command of large unit formations against a skilled enemy like the North Vietnamese, were not up to the demands of the moment. This confusion and ineptitude at the top resulted in the lack of a viable strategy.[29] As one ARVN officer explained after the war, "*Vietnamization* really meant *Americanization.* . . . It was not possible to return (or revert) to a Vietnamese-style war. It was going to have to be fought the American way. . . . It shortly became clear to all participants in the struggle that the crucial elements of the South's firepower advantage—U.S. air and naval power—would not be used. But South Vietnamese leaders were too slow to perceive these permutations in the overall strategy."[30] Thus, when the North Vietnamese began to step up their operations after the fall of Phuoc Long, Thieu and his generals were unable to put together a defensive plan to stop the Communist onslaught. Thieu's disastrous order to abandon the Central Highlands resulted in panic and hastened the North Vietnamese victory.

The situation in 1975 might have been saved, despite the mistakes made at the top, if South Vietnamese forces had been well led on the battlefield. However, leadership had been one of the most critical and long-standing problems that Vietnamization, despite all the funds and effort expended, could not redress. South Vietnamese soldiers, sailors, and airmen fought very well when ably led, but these instances, such as at An Loc in 1972 and Xuan Loc in 1975, were the exception rather than the rule, due to abysmal combat leadership.

The leadership problem included poor tactical competency, as well as the lack of fighting spirit. The political nature of the senior military leadership meant that many leaders obtained offices for which they were not qualified; unqualified leaders were prevalent at the lower echelons of command as well. More often than not, family connections, financial status, and formal education dictated officer selection and subsequent promotions. A systematic means of recruiting or selecting potentially good leaders from the ranks was never developed. Instead, the system by which Thieu maintained his power ("purchased power," as General Davidson called it) guaranteed that inept political supporters and incompetent cronies would be in positions of leadership, while the all-prevalent corruption undermined morale and discipline.[31] As one former ARVN officer said, "[T]he majority of the high-ranking commanders were servants to the Thieu regime and they brought up a number of lazy, corrupted and unqualified generals for their servile obedience . . . so destroying the fighting morale of the young ARVN officers."[32] Such officers were seldom motivated to get in front of their troops and lead them into battle. One former senior South Vietnamese general said, "It was common usage that in the case of heavy fighting the commanders took off in their helicopters, leaving the fighting to the troops on the ground. This had a negative effect on troop morale [and]. . . . the performance of units greatly suffered from this. . . . in an Oriental society where the prestige, the bravery and the wisdom of the leader are of the highest importance, these negative characteristics of leadership were very detrimental."[33] As Robert Komer, deputy for CORDS wrote in 1972, "[N]o matter how well trained, equipped, and organized the GVN and RVNAF became, poor leaders all too often remained its Achilles Heel."[34] Komer was correct. Under poor leaders, the valor and endurance of the common South Vietnamese soldier were often squandered. Air Force major Thomas N. Bibby, in a study written at the Marine Corps Command and Staff College, eloquently summed up the situation, writing that "the leadership within the South Vietnamese armed forces encompassed all the worst possible features. It lacked the competence to do the job when the crisis arose; the aggressiveness to take and gain the initiative from the enemy; and ultimately, the moral credibility to maintain the loyal support of its soldiers, and the South Vietnamese people."[35] The situation reached its nadir when the entire force collapsed in 1975, but it is essential to note that the leaders, not the soldiers, collapsed. As Arnold Isaacs notes, "[T]he army did not collapse in its foxholes, or for lack of supplies. It disintegrated when its senior officers—the class of South Vietnamese society that had virtually monopolized the material and political rewards of the American alliance—deserted it."[36]

The early advisory effort and the subsequent Vietnamization program failed to produce a self-sufficient combat force. This fact, coupled with the endemic weaknesses and failures of the Thieu regime, resulted in a disaster in 1975. Confronted with a crisis of cataclysmic proportions, Thieu refused to believe that the United States would not intervene, even after Congress passed legislation forbidding the White House to do anything. His self-imposed delusion, fueled by Nixon's repeated promises, prevented the South Vietnamese from developing a cogent, workable strategy within the framework of the resource-constrained circumstances that followed the cessation of U.S. military aid. The North Vietnamese, much more flexible, were able to seize the moment when presented an opportunity to do so and routed the South Vietnamese forces, toppling the Saigon regime in the process. One former South Vietnamese colonel put it as follows: "Vietnamization was more than modernization, and expansion of the RVNAF; it was essentially a strategy that would require the Vietnamese to survive with greatly reduced American participation. Had President Thieu and the Joint General Staff fully realized this fact, perhaps they would have begun to build a strategy to cope with it. Instead, the RVNAF made no adjustments in doctrine, organization or training to compensate for the departure of American troops and firepower."[37]

Although the United States stood by and did nothing when the North Vietnamese attacked, the sudden collapse of the South Vietnamese cannot be blamed simply on American inaction or the reduction in U.S. military aid. "Saigon's forces did suffer significant logistical shortages in the last year of the war," wrote Arnold Isaacs, "but those shortages were not as crippling as was later alleged in the effort to blame Congress exclusively for the defeat, and material shortages were obviously not the only or even necessarily the chief cause of the Saigon regime's military and political deterioration. The psychological damage of the aid cuts was almost certainly greater than the real. To a military and bureaucratic elite that gravely lacked self-confidence, the cuts were a symbolic act of American abandonment, a blow from which the South Vietnamese leadership never recovered."[38]

The United States military had made the RVNAF in its own image, but the result was a hollow likeness. Consequently, the North's final offensive in 1974 revealed that Vietnamization was an abysmal failure. As the final report of the Army Division, DAO Saigon, stated: "To summarize, the U.S. forces tutored ARVN in combat, combat support tactics and management techniques in an arena not bounded by dollar limitations, but with freedom to determine and execute tactical decisions and order of battle plans based on security needs of the country—a philosophy totally reversed by constraints established with low order funding levels and incremental releases against program authorizations. The result was manifested in confusion, insecurity, reluctance to execute tactical plans, degradation of leadership and control, and finally, military defeat."[39]

Clearly, the process of Vietnamization began too late, stifled South Vietnamese initiative and induced dependence on U.S. support, and failed to address the fundamental weaknesses that led to the ultimate downfall of the RVNAF. Gabriel Kolko, quoting several ARVN generals after the war, wrote that "the United States managed to turn an already inadequate army into a yet worse one, making it wholly dependent on American equipment and doctrine."[40] In the absence of continued U.S. support, that force crumbled in 1975 in less than two months.

Did it have to be that way? Working through alternative outcomes to the fall of South Vietnam in 1975 is difficult—too many variables exist. The outcome may have been different if the Paris Peace Accords had not permitted North Vietnamese troops to remain in place in the South after the cease-fire. The outcome may have been different if President Nixon had not been forced to resign by the Watergate scandal or if President Ford had been able to convince Congress to provide monetary and/or military support to Saigon in 1975. The outcome may have been different if Thieu had instituted internal reforms and considered alternate military strategies before it was too late. The impact of such events has been debated by historians and military analysts, and various arguments have been offered regarding the ultimate impact of changing one or more of these variables. Manifestly, permitting North Vietnamese troops to remain in South Vietnam hastened the demise of the South Vietnamese, as did the lack of internal reform and the lack of U.S. military aid. However, these factors do not fully explain the complete and sudden collapse of the South Vietnamese military, which in the final analysis was woefully unprepared to fight the North Vietnamese. Despite the "victories" proclaimed during the Cambodian incursion, the Laos cross-border operation, and the successful confrontation with the NVA during the 1972 invasion, Vietnamization, in the final analysis, failed and failed miserably. The idea was not in and of itself bad. Perhaps the outcome in 1975 might have been different if the United States had taken an alternate approach to preparing the South Vietnamese to defend themselves.

First, the effort should have begun in earnest from the earliest days of the conflict. Self-sufficiency should have been the priority mission and not the sideshow that it became when compared with the "big war" waged by U.S. divisions and brigades. Had the program been undertaken in, say, 1963, perhaps the South Vietnamese would have been able to defend themselves beginning with the early internal insurgency; thus, there would have been no need to insert the massive numbers of U.S. troops that ultimately saw duty in Southeast Asia. In that case, the United States would have had no need later to "Vietnamize" the war as a cover for withdrawal of those same troops.

Second, the United States should have helped the South Vietnamese construct a force in consonance with the actual threat at the time that the American effort began. In the early days, all signs pointed to the main threat being an insurgency. Therefore, the type of force needed was a counterinsurgency force—organized, trained, and equipped to fight guerrillas. Such tactics require specialized training and are best executed by small, mobile units that can close with the guerrillas and deny them the support of the populace. More emphasis on the pacification programs would have complemented this type of force and led to increased support for the government in Saigon.

Third, a need may well have emerged at some time during the evolution of the RVNAF for a force to fight a "big war." However, this conventional force should have been trained to fight by maneuver and fire, and not to rely on heavy firepower and technology, as the RVNAF had done during Lam Son 719 and the 1972 NVA Easter Offensive. Even the most casual observer of the American political scene could have predicted in 1974–75 that U.S. logistical support could not and would not last forever. Unfortunately, by the time that Thieu and his regime came to the realization that military aid would no longer be available, it was too late to change the operational concept under which ARVN had been trained. General Vien wrote after the war, "By overrelying on the U.S. promise of continued support and assistance, the GVN had become complacent and too shortsighted to develop an acceptable strategy for defending South Vietnam in the long term. As a result, faced with the stark reality of North Vietnamese intentions in 1975, it was already too late."[41] Having tied themselves to an American style of warfare, the South Vietnamese were unable to function in a resource-constrained environment.

Last, the United States made a great mistake by not urging the South Vietnamese to address underlying fundamental problems that prevented forging a viable fighting force. The United States had an opportunity at an early stage to press Saigon to clean its own house. American officials should have threatened a drastic reduction in U.S. support unless the South Vietnamese reduced corruption in the military, depoliticized the officer ranks, and instituted far-reaching domestic political reform. Demanding such reforms, which would have been a hard call at the time of initial U.S. involvement in South Vietnam, probably would have risked the fall of Saigon to the Communists, but doing so might have prevented the loss of 58,000 American and countless Vietnamese (both North and South) lives.[42] With no impetus to reform itself, the corrupt system became an easy target for the Communist propaganda apparatus and caused the average soldier to ask why he should fight for this country that was controlled by and beneficiary to a small clique.

Nonetheless, we are left with an incomplete evaluation of Vietnamization's effectiveness. The process was, after all, not carried out to completion. The United States neither stayed the course (as we did and continue to do in South Korea) nor provided the promised support to the South Vietnamese, thus truncating the program before it had been fully implemented. When the Paris Peace Accords permitted 100,000 North Vietnamese troops to remain in the South and the Americans withdrew promised support, the South Vietnamese became doomed: Vietnamization had no chance of precluding the ultimate outcome of the war under these circumstances.

Vietnamization was not the sole cause of South Vietnam's defeat, but it proved a major factor when coupled with a debilitated Thieu regime, the resurgence of the North Vietnamese after the cease-fire, and the withdrawal of American support. The U.S. desire to exit Vietnam, the flawed Paris Peace Accords, and the belated and ultimately incomplete Vietnamization policy set the stage for the collapse of the South Vietnamese armed forces. Thinking they had all the answers upon entering the war, the Americans shouldered the South Vietnamese aside. But after the Americans found they could not win the war, President Nixon began to withdraw U.S. troops while striving to increase the combat capabilities of the South Vietnamese. However, after the Paris Peace Accords were signed, it became apparent that the United States had not done an adequate job in preparing the South Vietnamese to fight their own battles. As former General Vien said, "The strength of South Vietnam and its armed forces had been built primarily on foreign aid, not on its national resources. The fate of South Vietnam, therefore depended on its American friends."[43] When those "friends" decided to abandon the struggle, the ultimate result was the fall of Saigon and the demise of South Vietnam as a nation.

Still, the South Vietnamese deserve a large part of the blame themselves, because they lacked the will necessary to save themselves. Vietnamization could do nothing to remedy the lack of will, but it may have set the preconditions for the South Vietnamese collapse. The most prescient comment about the efficacy of Vietnamization was offered by a U.S. general officer in response to General Kinnard's survey on the war in 1974. He said, "We erroneously tried to impose the American system on a people who didn't want it, couldn't handle it and may lose because they tried it."[44] Unfortunately, that assessment proved correct in 1975.

What does this painful, tragic story tell us? To be victorious, a military force must be trained and equipped to fight the right enemy, be led by men of courage and skill, and have purposes worth fighting and dying for. U.S. policymakers should remember these simple lesson in the future if contemplating similar intervention. The best intentions in the world are meaningless if leadership and cohesion are not present in any force with which an alliance is forged. In the case of Vietnam, the United States should have pushed "Vietnamization" much earlier and brought influence to bear to achieve radical changes in South Vietnamese society and stayed the course when the going got tough. The eventual outcome might have been much different if American military and civilian leaders had remembered the quotation attributed to T. E. Lawrence about assisting armies of other countries: "Better they do it imperfectly than you do it perfectly, for it is their country, their war, and your time is limited."[45] No one, it appears, remembered those prophetic words during America's long involvement in Vietnam's nightmare.

Notes

ABBREVIATIONS IN NOTES

ABRAMS: Abrams, Creighton W. Papers. U.S. Army Center of Military History,
          Washington, D.C.

CARL: Combined Arms Research Library, Fort Leavenworth, Kansas.

FORD: Gerald R. Ford Presidential Library, Ann Arbor, Michigan.

NPM: Nixon Presidential Materials, National Archives and Records
          Administration, College Park, Maryland.

PIKE: Douglas Pike Indochina Collection, Texas Tech University Archive of
          the Vietnam Conflict, Lubbock, Texas.

Viet. Hist.:   *Vietnam: A History in Documents.* Edited by Gareth Porter. New York:
          New American Library, 1981.

RecMACV: *Records of the Military Assistance Command Vietnam.* Pt. 1, *The War in
          Vietnam, 1954–1973,* MACV Historical Office Documentary Collection.
          Bethesda, Md.: University Publications of America, 1988. Microfilm.

USACMH: U.S. Army Center of Military History, Washington, D.C.

USAMHI: U.S. Army Military History Institute, Carlisle Barracks, Penn.

USMACV: U.S. Military Assistance Command, Vietnam.

INTRODUCTION

1. Louis A. Fanning, *Betrayal in Vietnam* (New Rochelle, N.Y.: Arlington House, 1976), 11.

2. House Committee on Appropriations, *Hearings before Subcommittees of the Committee on Appropriations: Supplemental Appropriation Bill, 1971,* 91st Cong., 2nd sess., 1970, 1249.

3. The People's Army of North Vietnam, or PAVN, was more popularly known as the North Vietnamese Army (NVA); this more popular term will be used in this study.

1. VIETNAMIZATION

1. Lewis Sorley, *A Better War: The Unexamined Victories and Final Tragedy of America's Last Years in Vietnam* (New York: Harcourt Brace, 1999), 69.

2. Lyndon Baines Johnson, *Public Papers of the Presidents of the United States, 1968–69,* bk. 1 (Washington, D.C.: GPO, 1970), 469–76.

3. Robert B. Semple, "Nixon Vows to End War with a 'New Leadership,'" *New York Times,* 6 March 1968.

4. Richard M. Nixon, *RN: The Memoirs of Richard Nixon* (New York: Warner Books, 1978), 298. Nixon biographer Stephen E. Ambrose writes that Nixon "did not say, as was later reported and widely believed, that he had a 'secret plan to end the war.' In fact, he said the opposite: that he had no gimmick, 'no push-button technique' to end the war." *Nixon*, vol. 2, *The Triumph of a Politician, 1962–1972* (New York: Simon and Schuster, 1989), 142.

5. Robert B. Semple, "Nixon Sharpens Attack on Johnson," *New York Times*, 8 March 1968.

6. Robert B. Semple, "Nixon Withholds His Peace Ideas," *New York Times*, 11 March 1968.

7. Clayton Knowles, "Nixon Delays War Statement," *New York Times*, 2 April 1968.

8. Nixon, *Memoirs*, 308.

9. John Finney, "G.O.P. Rift Widens on Vietnam Plank," *New York Times*, 4 August 1968.

10. Nixon, *Memoirs*, 308.

11. Ambrose, *Triumph of a Politician*, 182.

12. Nixon, *Memoirs*, 324.

13. Ibid., 327–28.

14. According to Stephen Ambrose, Nixon contacted Thieu through an intermediary, Mrs. Anna Chan Chennault, wife of World War II hero Gen. Claire Chennault, and implied that Nixon would make Vietnam his top priority and see that Vietnam got better treatment from his administration than it had under the Democrats. *Triumph of a Politician*, 207–8. According to Nguyen Tien Hung and Jerrold L. Schecter, Nixon sent John Mitchell to see Mrs. Chennault to get her to convince Thieu to refuse to go to the negotiating table. *The Palace File* (New York: Harper & Row, 1986), 23–24. How much real influence Mitchell's attempt had is unknown, but the fact remains that Thieu refused to enter the peace talks.

15. George C. Herring, *America's Longest War: The United States and Vietnam, 1950–1975*, 3rd ed. (New York: McGraw-Hill, 1996), 244–45.

16. H. R. Haldeman, *Ends of Power* (New York: Times Books, 1978), 81.

17. Nixon, *Memoirs*, 337–38. Despite the antipathy of many of the United States' allies toward continued American involvement in the Vietnam War, this line of reasoning dominated the subsequent actions of the Nixon administration. Kissinger, who became the idea's main proponent, wrote in January 1969 that a defeat in Vietnam would "unloose forces that could complicate prospects for international order" and that U.S. credibility was at risk. "The Vietnam Negotiations," *Foreign Affairs* 47 (January 1969): 218–19, 234.

18. Memorandum by Clark Clifford, "Notes of Pres's Meeting with President-Elect Richard Nixon," 11 November 1968, Clark Clifford Papers, Lyndon Baines Johnson Presidential Library, Austin, Texas.

19. Nixon, *Memoirs*, 336.

20. John Finney, "Johnson-Nixon Talk Today Seen Focusing on Vietnam," *New York Times*, 11 November 1968.

21. Nixon, *Memoirs*, 341.

22. Ibid.

23. Ibid., 357–58.

24. Ibid., 349–50.

25. Ibid., 349.

26. Ibid.

27. Ibid., 350.

28. National Security Study Memorandum (NSSM) 1, Henry A. Kissinger, Special Assistant for National Security, for the Secretaries of State and Defense and the Director of Central Intelligence, 21 January 1969, DepCORDS Papers, USACMH.

29. Henry Kissinger, *White House Years* (Boston: Little, Brown, 1979), 238.

30. Message, Wheeler JCS 14581 to Abrams 120217Z Dec 68, sub: RVNAF capabilities, ABRAMS.

31. William M. Hammond, *Public Affairs: The Military and the Media, 1968–1973* (Washington, D.C.: U.S. Army Center of Military History, 1996), 78.

32. Unsigned Memo, Feb 69, sub: Vietnam Has the Resources But Lacks the Motivation To Win, President's Personal Files, Memos, 1969, NPM.

33. Memo, Henry A. Kissinger for Members of the National Security Council Review Group, 14 Mar 69, sub: Summary of Responses to NSSM 1 Vietnam Questions, DepCORDS Papers, USACMH. Actual agency responses are found in the Thomas C. Thayer Papers, folders 13, 20, 134, and 136, USACMH.

34. Kissinger, *White House Years,* 238.

35. Letter, Headquarters, III MAF (I CTZ), to COMUSMACV, 25 Jan 1969, sub: Situation in Vietnam, *RecMACV,* reel 1, frame 0451.

36. Message, Kerwin (III CTZ) to Corcoran, Chief of Staff, MACV, 251545Z Jan 69, *RecMACV,* reel 1, frame 0379.

37. Message, Abrams to Johnson, sub: Situation in Vietnam, *RecMACV,* reel 1, frame 0104.

38. Ibid.

39. NSSM 1 responses can also be found in *Congressional Record,* 92nd Cong., 2nd sess., 118 (10 May 1972): 16750–836.

40. Kissinger, *White House Years,* 239.

41. Ibid., 227–28.

42. Draft Memo, Kissinger for the President, Sep 71, sub: Vietnam, NSC files, Alexander M. Haig Special File, box 1013, General Haig's Trip to Vietnam, Sep 1971, NPM.

43. Herring, *America's Longest War,* 198.

44. Joan Hoff, *Nixon Reconsidered* (New York: Harper Collins, 1994), 211.

45. Message, Wheeler to Abrams, 28 Jan 69, JCS 01181Z, ABRAMS; Kissinger, *White House Years,* 239–42.

46. Gen. Andrew J. Goodpaster, interview by Col. William D. Johnson and Lt. Col. James C. Ferguson, transcription, 1976, Andrew J. Goodpaster Papers, USAMHI.

47. Jerry Friedheim (Deputy Assistant Secretary of Defense, 1969–1973), interview by William H. Hammond, 3 Oct 86, USACMH.

48. Memo, Laird to the President, 13 Mar 69, sub: Trip to Vietnam, NPM.

49. Kissinger, *White House Years,* 272. By all accounts, "Vietnamization" became the accepted term for Nixon's new policy at this meeting. However, Abrams biographer Lewis Sorley maintains that Abrams started the process of helping the South Vietnamese armed forces become more capable when he assumed command from General Westmoreland in 1968 and that Nixon and Laird merely adopted the "Vietnamization" label and, instituting U.S. troop withdrawals, formalized it as administration policy. *Thunderbolt, from the Battle of the Bulge to Vietnam and Beyond: Creighton Abrams and the Army of His Times* (New

York: Simon and Schuster, 1992), 254–56. Nixon virtually confirms this assessment in *No More Vietnams* (New York: Touchstone, 1990), 105.

50. House Committee on Armed Services, *Hearings on Military Posture,* 91st Cong., 2nd sess., 1970, pt. 1, 7023–24.

51. Alexander M. Haig Jr., with Charles McCarry, *Inner Circles: How America Changed the World, A Memoir* (New York: Warner Books, 1992), 226.

52. Kissinger, *White House Years,* 262.

53. Nixon, *Memoirs,* 392.

54. Haig, *Inner Circles,* 225–29.

55. National Security Study Memorandum 36, Kissinger to SecState, SecDef, and DCI, 10 Apr 69, sub: Vietnamizing the War, USACMH; Nixon, *Memoirs,* 392; Kissinger, *White House Years,* 272.

56. Richard M. Nixon, *Public Papers of the Presidents of the United States, 1969* (Washington, D.C.: GPO, 1971), 443. Abrams would assess onsite both the RVNAF progress and the level of enemy activity.

57. Nixon, *Memoirs,* 392.

58. Ibid.

59. Kissinger, *White House Years,* 274; Henry Kissinger, *Ending the Vietnam War* (New York: Simon and Schuster, 2003), 84.

60. Talking Paper, Office of the Assistant Secretary of Defense, 3 Oct 69, sub: U.S. Objectives in Southeast Asia, Thomas C. Thayer Papers, USACMH.

61. News Summaries, 17 July 1969, NPM; Kissinger, *White House Years,* 276.

62. Nixon, *Public Papers, 1969,* 549.

63. Kissinger, *White House Years,* 224.

64. "The Nixon Doctrine: From Potential Despair to New Opportunities," policy speech delivered by Secretary of Defense Melvin R. Laird, undated, White House Central Files, NPM.

65. Hoff, *Nixon Reconsidered,* 165.

66. Kissinger, *White House Years,* 276–77.

67. Nixon, *Public Papers, 1969,* 901–9.

68. Kissinger, *White House Years,* 306.

69. Richard M. Nixon, *Real War* (New York: Warner Books, 1980), 106.

70. Richard M. Nixon, *A New Road for America* (Garden City, N.Y.: Doubleday, 1972), 681.

71. George Gallup, "Nixon Backed on War Handling," *Washington Post,* 10 April 1969. Louis Harris wrote that Nixon's support began to slip in September 1969. The July Harris poll revealed that although Nixon's personal popularity remained high and two out of three Americans supported his decision to turn over more of the fighting to the South Vietnamese, 52 percent of those questioned expressed dissatisfaction with his overall handling of the war. *The Anguish of Change* (New York: Norton, 1973), 69. These numbers would only worsen.

72. Rowland Evans and Robert Novak, "Secret Laird Plan Will Allow Early Troop Pull Out," *Washington Post,* 24 March 1969; Hedrick Smith, "Nixon to Reduce Vietnam Force, Pulling Out 25,000 G.I.'s By the End of August," *New York Times,* 9 June 1969; William Beecher, "The Problem Is How to Disengage Without Causing a Collapse," *New York Times,* 22 June 1969.

73. The French tried their own version of Vietnamization in 1951. They called it *jaunissement,* or "yellowing." France established the Vietnamese National Army, and according to the ill-fated Navarre Plan of 1953–54, the Vietnamese, once sufficiently trained, would assume more responsibility for combat against the Viet Minh so that French troops could be brought home. It was no more successful than the U.S. plan would be.

74. Department of State Bulletin, 11 Dec 1967, 785–88.

75. Nguyen Duy Hinh, Maj. Gen., *Indochina Monographs: Vietnamization and the Cease-Fire* (Washington, D.C.: U.S. Army Center of Military History, 1980), 11.

2. IMPLEMENTING THE NEW STRATEGY

1. Kissinger, *White House Years,* 1111.

2. Ibid., 272–73.

3. House Committee on Appropriations, Subcommittee on Department of Defense, *Hearings on Department of Defense Appropriations for 1971,* 91st Cong., 2nd sess., 1970, pt. 1, 311.

4. Nguyen Duy Hinh, *Vietnamization and the Cease-Fire,* 45.

5. Ibid., 39–40.

6. Ibid., 31.

7. Message, COMUSMACV to CINCPAC, 271422Z Apr 68, sub: RVNAF Improvement and Modernization, Southeast Asia Branch Files, USACMH.

8. Memo, Nitze to Chairman, JCS, 25 June 68, sub: RVNAF Improvement and Modernization, Southeast Asia Branch Files, USACMH.

9. Jeffrey J. Clarke, *Advice and Support: The Final Years* (Washington, D.C.: U.S. Army Center of Military History, 1988), 298–99.

10. Planning Paper, Joint General Staff, 8 June 1969, sub: RVNAF Improvements Program, Southeast Asia Branch Files, USACMH.

11. Military History Branch, Headquarters, USMACV, "Command History, 1969," 2:VI-4–15.

12. Ibid., 2:VI-12.

13. Ibid., 2:VI-14–VI-15.

14. Clarke, *Advice and Support,* 354.

15. Memo, Laird to Chairman, JCS, 10 Nov 69, sub: Vietnamization—RVNAF Improvement and Modernization Aspects and Related U.S. Planning, ABRAMS.

16. Clarke, *Advice and Support,* 355; Military History Branch, Headquarters, USMACV, "Command History, 1969," 2:VI-151–57.

17. Clarke, *Advice and Support,* 356.

18. Memo, Laird to President, 14 Feb 70, sub: Trip to Vietnam and CINCPAC, 10–14 Feb 1970, Laird Files, NPM.

19. Military History Branch, Headquarters, USMACV, "Command History, 1970," 2:VII-4–16.

20. House Committee on Armed Services, *Hearings on Military Posture,* 91st Cong., 2nd sess., 1970, pt. 1, 7610.

21. Nguyen Duy Hinh, *Vietnamization and the Cease-Fire,* 39.

22. Ibid., 42.

23. Ibid., 45.

24. Cao Van Vien, et al., *Indochina Monographs: The U.S. Adviser* (Washington, D.C.: U.S. Army Center of Military History, 1980), 10.

25. The senior U.S. commanders were III Marine Amphibious Force Commander in I Corps, I Field Force Commander in II Corps, and II Field Force Commander in III Corps. IV Corps never had a corps-level headquarters, but a designated U.S. Army major general served as the senior adviser to the IV Corps commander.

26. For a detailed discussion of the province advisory teams, see Richard A. Hunt, *Pacification: The Struggle for Vietnam's Hearts and Minds* (Boulder, Colo.: Westview Press, 1995), 94–96.

27. Cao Van Vien, et al., *U.S. Adviser,* 7–8, 10.

28. Fact Sheet, MACMA-PP, 13 Aug 1969, sub: Combat Assistance Team (CAT), *RecMACV,* reel 40, frame 0983.

29. Cao Van Vien, et al., *U.S. Adviser,* 16.

30. Fact Sheet, MACMA-PP, 13 Aug 1969, sub: Combat Assistance Team (CAT), *RecMACV,* reel 40, frame 0983.

31. Clarke, *Advice and Support,* 371.

32. David Fulghum and Terrence Maitland, *The Vietnam Experience: South Vietnam on Trial, Mid-1970 to 1972* (Boston: Boston Publishing, 1984), 55.

33. James Lawton Collins Jr., *The Development and Training of the South Vietnamese Army, 1950–1972* (Washington, D.C.: Department of the Army, 1975), 105. Bolton had previously been the chief of the military assistance program on the MACV staff before being reassigned to the Pentagon.

34. Quoted in Fulghum and Maitland, *South Vietnam on Trial,* 54.

35. Clarke, *Advice and Support,* 317.

36. Fulghum and Maitland, *South Vietnam on Trial,* 56–57.

37. Ibid., 56.

38. Cao Van Vien, et al., *U.S. Adviser,* 175.

39. Memo, Laird to Service Secretaries, 16 Dec 69, sub: Quantity and Quality of U.S. Advisers in Vietnam, ABRAMS.

40. This was the author's personal experience; advisory duty was not seen as "career enhancing."

41. The author, as a newly promoted captain with two years in the army and not even having commanded a company, was assigned in late 1971 as an adviser to a South Vietnamese infantry battalion commander.

42. Memo, Resor to Secretary of Defense, 2 Feb 70, sub: Quantity and Quality of U.S. Advisers in Vietnam, ABRAMS.

43. Memorandum for Record, Brigadier General Albert H. Smith, Jr., MACV J-1, 15 Dec 69, sub: General Abrams' Guidance on Selecting Advisors, ABRAMS. See also Sorley, *Better War,* 181–84.

44. Memo, Secretary of Defense Laird to the Service Secretaries, 16 Dec 69, sub: Quantity and Quality of U.S. Advisors in Vietnam, ABRAMS.

45. Fulghum and Maitland, *South Vietnam on Trial,* 56.

46. Military History Branch, Headquarters, USMACV, "Command History, 1970," 2:VII-63–79.

47. Nguyen Duy Hinh, *Vietnamization and the Cease-Fire,* 19.

48. Ibid., 19–20.

49. Ibid., 20.

50. Ibid.

51. Cao Van Vien and Dong Van Khuyen, *Indochina Monographs: Reflections on the Vietnam War* (Washington, D.C.: U.S. Army Center of Military History, 1978), 92.

3. THE RVNAF IN ACTION

1. Central Office for South Vietnam (COSVN) Directive No. 71, 31 January 1969, PIKE.

2. Henry Kissinger, *White House Years,* 239–47.

3. Bruce Palmer, *The 25-Year War: America's Military Role in Vietnam* (Lexington: University Press of Kentucky, 1984), 97–98.

4. Kissinger, *White House Years,* 242.

5. For the most complete narrative of the Menu secret bombing, see William Shawcross, *Sideshow: Kissinger, Nixon and the Destruction of Cambodia* (New York: Simon and Schuster, 1979).

6. Shawcross, *Sideshow,* 26–35; Phillip B. Davidson, *Vietnam at War: The History 1946—1975* (Novato, Calif.: Presidio Press, 1988), 534–36.

7. Sorley, *Better War,* 138–43.

8. 101st Airborne Division, "After-Action Report, Battle of Dong Ap Bia," reprinted in *Congressional Record,* 91st Cong., 2nd sess., 116 (29 December 1970): S210403; Col. Joseph B. Conmy, "I Led a Brigade at Hamburger Hill," *Washington Post,* 27 May 1989. One of the most comprehensive narratives of the Battle of Dong Ap Bia, or Hill 939, is Samuel Zaffiri, *Hamburger Hill, May 11–20, 1969* (Novato, Calif.: Presidio Press, 1988).

9. *Congressional Record,* 91st Cong., 1st sess., 115 (20 May 1969): S13003.

10. "The Grim and Inaccurate Casualty Numbers Game," *The New York Times,* 1 June 1969.

11. "How Nixon is Trying to End the War," *U.S. News & World Report,* 26 May 1969, 27; "Hamburger Hill, the Army's Rationale," *Washington Post,* 23 May 1969.

12. Sorley, *Thunderbolt,* 261.

13. Kissinger, *Ending the Vietnam War,* 81.

14. Kissinger, *White House Years,* 272.

15. Sorley, *Thunderbolt,* 263–64.

16. Sorley, *Better War,* 113, 128.

17. Message, Wheeler JCS 04800 to Abrams, 192113Z Apr 69, and Message, Wheeler JCS 05386 to Abrams, 021455Z May 69. Both in ABRAMS.

18. Kissinger, *White House Years,* 271.

19. Ibid.

20. Ibid., 274.

21. Clark Clifford, "A Viet Nam Reappraisal," *Foreign Affairs,* 47, no. 4 (July 1969): 610.

22. Nixon, *Public Papers, 1969,* 472.

23. Kissinger, *White House Years,* 275.

24. Military History Institute of Vietnam, *Report to General Vo Nguyen Giap, A Consolidated Report on the Fight Against the United States for the Salvation of Vietnam by Our People,* Hanoi, 1987, 26. Despite their intent, the North Vietnamese soon found that

they could not sustain the August attacks because they had not fully recovered from the losses incurred during the 1968 Tet offensive, the Third Offensive in August–September 1968, and the fighting of Tet 1969.

25. Kissinger, *White House Years,* 283.

26. Memorandum, Kissinger to Nixon, sub: Our Course in Vietnam, 10 Sep 1969, reprinted in *White House Years,* 1480–82.

27. Kissinger, *White House Years,* 283.

28. Nguyen Duy Hinh, *Vietnamization and the Cease-Fire,* 26–27.

29. Talking Paper, AVHGC-P, USARV, 17 Jul 69, sub: NSSM 36—Vietnamization, Southeast Asia Branch Files, USACMH.

30. Before assuming his position with the CIA, Cushman had been the commander of all U.S. Marines in South Vietnam.

31. Kissinger, *White House Years,* 276.

32. Ibid.

33. Message, Wheeler JCS to McCain and Abrams, 6 Aug 1969, ABRAMS.

34. Kissinger, *White House Years,* 276.

35. Ibid.

36. Nixon, *Public Papers, 1969,* 901–9.

37. Message, Abrams to Wheeler, 19 Apr 1969, ABRAMS.

38. Clarke, *Advice and Support,* 362.

39. Samuel Lipsman and Edward Doyle, *The Vietnam Experience: Fighting for Time* (Boston: Boston Publishing, 1983), 53.

40. JGS-MACV Combined Campaign Plan 1969, 30 Sep 1968, Southeast Asia Branch Files, USACMH.

41. Ngo Quang Truong, *Indochina Monographs: RVNAF and U.S. Operational Cooperation and Coordination* (Washington, D.C.: U.S. Army Center of Military History, 1980), 162.

42. For detailed discussion of U.S./RVNAF combined operations, see Jeffrey J. Clarke, "The Role of USARV Units in Vietnamization," CMH Monograph 192M (Washington, D.C.: U.S. Army Center of Military History), 1974.

43. Ngo Quang Truong, *RVNAF and U.S. Operational Cooperation and Coordination,* 115.

44. Davidson, *Vietnam at War,* 553. Richard A. Hunt, *Pacification: The American Struggle for Vietnam's Hearts and Minds* (Boulder, Colo.: Westview Press, 1995), 221–22, also provides a good discussion of the change in mission in what is arguably the most comprehensive treatment of the pacification effort in South Vietnam.

45. This initiative had begun earlier under U.S. Marine Corps general Robert E. Cushman, when he was commander of III Marine Amphibious force. Cushman considered the 1st ARVN Division to be equal to any American division.

46. William R. Peers, Senior Officer Debriefing Report, 23 June 1969, USACMH.

47. Ngo Quang Truong, *RVNAF and U.S. Operational Cooperation and Coordination,* 135.

48. Message, Ewell to Abrams, 29 Nov 1969, ABRAMS.

49. Clarke, *Advice and Support,* 406.

50. Message, Abrams to Wheeler, 2 June 1969, ABRAMS.

51. Office of the Assistant Secretary of Defense, Talking Paper, sub: Redeployment of U.S. Units from Vietnam, Public Affairs Guidance, Washington, D.C., June 1969.

52. Julian Ewell, "Impressions of a Field Force Commander in Vietnam" (USACMH, 15 Apr 1970, unpublished paper), 1.

53. Clarke, *Advice and Support,* 409.

54. II FFORCEV Circular Number 525–1, 26 June 1969, sub: The Dong Tien (Progress Together) Program, Long Binh, South Vietnam, CARL.

55. Ngo Quang Truong, *RVNAF and U.S. Operational Cooperation and Coordination,* 147–48.

56. Dong Van Khuyen, *Indochina Monographs: The RVNAF* (Washington, D.C.: U.S. Army Center of Military History, 1979), 198.

57. Ibid., 151.

58. Lipsman and Doyle, *Fighting for Time,* 70.

59. Message, Wheeler to Abrams, 4 Jul 1969, sub: Publicizing ARVN Performance; Message, Abrams to Wheeler, 8 Aug 1969, sub: Publicizing ARVN Achievements, both in ABRAMS.

60. Gen. William B. Rosson, Senior Officer Debriefing Program, 1968, USAMHI.

61. In addition to Richard Hunt's previously mentioned treatment of pacification, see also William Colby, with James McCargar, *Lost Victory* (Chicago: Contemporary Books, 1989), and Tran Dinh Tho, *Indochina Monograph: Pacification* (Washington, D.C.: U.S. Army Center of Military History, 1980).

62. Colby, *Lost Victory,* 238.

63. Nguyen Duy Hinh, *Vietnamization and the Cease-Fire,* 80; Hunt, *Pacification,* 197–98.

64. Headquarters, USMACV, "One War: MACV Command Overview, 1968–1972," undated, 15, ABRAMS.

65. Tran Dinh Tho, *Pacification,* 24.

66. Hunt, *Pacification,* 217–20; Military History Institute of Vietnam, *Report to General Giap,* 26.

67. Nguyen Duy Hinh, *Vietnamization and the Cease-Fire,* 83.

68. Ibid.

69. Message, Bunker to the President, 9 Dec 1969, in *Bunker Papers,* 3:740–41.

70. Tran Dinh Tho, *Pacification,* 24.

71. Senate Committee on Foreign Relations, *Hearings on Vietnam: Policy and Prospects, 1970: Civil Operations and Rural Development Support (CORDS) Program,* 91st Cong., 2nd sess., 17–20 March, 3–4, 17, 19 May 1970, 709, 714.

72. Davidson, *Vietnam at War,* 551.

73. United States Embassy, Saigon, "A Preliminary Report on Activities during the 1969 Autumn Campaign," Vietnam Documents and Research Notes No. 82, July 1970, 3.

74. Nixon, *Memoirs,* 391–92.

75. Kissinger, *White House Years,* 270–71.

76. Nixon, *Memoirs,* 393.

77. Haig, *Inner Circles,* 229; Nixon, *Memoirs,* 392.

78. Nixon, *Public Papers, 1969,* 910.

79. Nixon, *Memoirs,* 393–94.

80. Herring, *America's Longest War,* 249.

81. Nixon, *Memoirs,* 393.

82. Kissinger, *White House Years,* 284–85; Seymour Hersh, *The Price of Power: Kissinger in the Nixon White House* (New York: Summit Books, 1983), 125–30.

83. Nixon, *Memoirs,* 396.

84. Ibid.; Kissinger, *White House Years*, 280–82.

85. Kissinger, *White House Years*, 282.

86. Nixon, *Memoirs*, 397.

87. Ibid.

88. Kissinger, *White House Years*, 262–63.

89. Memorandum, Laird to Nixon, 4 Sep 1969, White House Central Files, NPM.

90. Nixon, *Memoirs*, 397.

91. Nixon, *Public Papers, 1969*, 718.

92. Ambrose, *Triumph of a Politician*, 302.

93. Nixon, *Public Papers, 1969*, 749.

94. Nixon, *Memoirs*, 400.

95. Ibid.

96. Ibid.

97. Memorandum, Nixon to Kissinger, 1 Oct 1969, White House Central Files, NPM.

98. "Fulbright to Hold Hearings on Vietnam," *The New York Times*, 5 Oct 1969.

99. Nixon, *Public Papers*, 1969, 798–800; Nixon, *Memoirs*, 403; John Pierson, "Nixon Letter Seeks to Defuse Protest on Vietnam," *Wall Street Journal*, 14 Oct 1969.

100. Nixon, *Memoirs*, 403.

101. Kissinger, *White House Years*, 285.

102. Thompson was a counterinsurgency expert noted for his experiences in Malaya and the Philippines. An unofficial adviser to Presidents Kennedy, Johnson, and Nixon, he was a proponent of the ill-fated strategic hamlet program attempted by the United States in South Vietnam in the early 1960s. Interestingly, he proposed to President Kennedy in April 1963 that he reduce U.S. advisers in South Vietnam and prepare the South Vietnamese to take over the responsibility for their own defense.

103. Nixon, *Memoirs*, 404–5.

104. Ibid.

105. Ibid., 405.

106. Ibid., 408.

107. Nixon, *Public Papers, 1969*, 901–9.

108. Nixon, *Memoirs*, 409.

109. James Reston, "Nixon's Mystifying Clarifications," *New York Times*, 5 Nov 1969.

110. James Keough, *President Nixon and the Press* (New York: Funk & Wagnalls, 1972), 171–90.

111. "Nixon Support Soars in Poll after Speech," *Washington Star*, 14 Nov 1969.

112. Nixon, *Memoirs*, 410.

113. Ibid., 410–11.

114. Ibid., 411.

115. George Gallup, "One in Five Americans Backs Protesters' Goal of Quick Withdrawal," *Philadelphia Enquirer*, 27 Nov 1969.

4. RAISING THE STAKES

1. COSVN Directive 53, April 1969, PIKE.

2. Hoang Ngoc Lung, *Indochina Monographs: The General Offensives of 1968–1969* (Washington, D.C.: U.S. Army Center of Military History, 1978), 128. For a discussion of

the change in North Vietnamese tactics, see the Military History Institute of Vietnam, *Victory in Vietnam: The Official History of the People's Army of Vietnam, 1954–1975*, trans. Merle L. Pribbenow (Lawrence: University Press of Kansas, 2002), 246–47.

3. COSVN Resolution 14 on Guerrilla Warfare, July 1969, PIKE.

4. Hoac Ngoc Lung, *General Offensives,* 126. The exact translation from the Vietnamese is "fighting while negotiating."

5. Davidson, *Vietnam at War,* 559.

6. Message, Saigon to State, 24 Jan 1970, sub: Estimate of Enemy Strategy, NSC Convenience Files, NPM.

7. Kissinger, *White House Years,* 435.

8. Memorandum, Laird for the President, 4 Apr 1970, sub: Vietnam, White House Central Files, NPM. In *A Better War,* Lewis Sorley reports that General Abrams saw Resolution 9 as a positive sign that South Vietnam had seized the initiative from the Communists (156–57).

9. Ibid.

10. "Vietnamization: Will It Work?," *Newsweek,* 9 Feb 1970, 31.

11. Nixon, *Memoirs,* 448.

12. Nixon, *Public Papers, 1970,* 373–77.

13. Sorley, *Better War,* 179; Kissinger, *White House Years,* 478–79.

14. Nixon, *Memoirs,* 445.

15. Ibid., 467.

16. House Committee on Armed Services, Special Subcommittee on National Defense Posture, *Report of the Vietnam Conflict and Its Impact on U.S. Military Commitments Abroad* (Washington, D.C.: GPO, 1968), 17.

17. Dave Richard Palmer, *Summons of the Trumpet* (San Rafael, Calif.: Presidio Press, 1978), 229.

18. Kissinger, *White House Years,* 460.

19. Dave Palmer, *Summons of the Trumpet,* 228.

20. Message, McCain to Wheeler, 14 Feb 1970, sub: Reduction of NVA Sanctuary in Cambodia, ABRAMS.

21. Historical Division, Joint Secretariat, U.S. Joint Chiefs of Staff, *The Joint Chiefs of Staff and the War in Vietnam, 1969–1970* (Washington, D.C.: GPO, 1976), 232–33.

22. Message, Abrams to McCain, 30 Mar 1970, ABRAMS.

23. Quoted in James S. Olson and Randy Roberts, *Where the Last Domino Fell: America and Vietnam, 1945 to 1990* (New York: St. Martin's, 1991), 234.

24. Kissinger, *White House Years,* 475.

25. Ibid., 489–90; Nixon, *Memoirs,* 448–49.

26. Kissinger, *White House Years,* 490.

27. Ibid.

28. Ibid.

29. Ibid.

30. Nixon, *Memoirs,* 449.

31. Message, Moorer JCS 5623 to McCain, Abrams, 23 Apr 1970, sub: Operations in Cambodia, ABRAMS.

32. Sorley, *Better War,* 200–201.

33. Kissinger, *White House Years,* 491.

34. Nixon, *Memoirs,* 449; Kissinger, *White House Years,* 490.

35. Kissinger, *White House Years,* 492.

36. Ibid., 495.

37. Ibid.

38. Haig, *Inner Circles,* 237.

39. Ibid., 235.

40. Marvin Kalb and Bernard Kalb, *Kissinger* (Boston: Little, Brown, 1974), 160–61.

41. Nixon, *Memoirs,* 450.

42. Kissinger, *White House Years,* 490.

43. Message, Moorer to Abrams and McCain, 25 Apr 1970, ABRAMS.

44. Kissinger, *White House Years,* 497.

45. Ibid.

46. Ibid., 501.

47. Nixon, *Memoirs,* 450.

48. Message, Abrams to Wheeler and McCain, 22 Feb 1970, ABRAMS.

49. Nixon, *Public Papers, 1970,* 405–10.

50. John W. Finney, "Senators Angry, Some Seek to Cut Off Funds for Widened Military Action," *New York Times,* 30 Apr 1970.

51. "At War with War," *Time,* 18 May 1970, 6.

52. Quoted in Lipsman and Doyle, *Fighting for Time,* 164.

53. Ibid., 165.

54. Tran Dinh Tho, *Indochina Monographs: The Cambodian Incursion* (Washington, D.C.: U.S. Army Center of Military History, 1979), 76–77.

55. Ibid., 79–80. Rock Island, Illinois, is one of the largest army depots in the United States.

56. Nixon, *Memoirs,* 454.

57. Truong Nhu Tang, *A Vietcong Memoir—An Insider Account of the Vietnam War and Its Aftermath* (New York: Harcourt Brace Jovanovich, 1985), 177.

58. Quoted in Lipsman and Doyle, *Fighting for Time,* 170.

59. Tran Dinh Tho, *Cambodian Incursion,* 114.

60. Lipsman and Doyle, *Fighting for Time,* 172.

61. Hersh, *Price of Power,* 202.

62. Fact Sheet, "Impact of the Enemy of the Cambodian Operations," released in Saigon, 14 May 1970, Southeast Asia Branch Files, USACMH.

63. "Cambodia: Now It's 'Operation Buy Time,'" *Time,* 25 May 1970, 28.

64. Sir Robert Thompson, *Peace is Not at Hand* (New York: David McKay, 1974), 76–77.

65. Peter R. Kann, "Uneasy Alliance," *Wall Street Journal,* 2 Jul 1970.

66. Clarke, *Advice and Support,* 418.

67. Sidney Schanberg, "Looting by Saigon Units Stirs Cambodian Hatred," *New York Times,* 2 Jul 1970.

68. Bruce Palmer, *25-Year War,* 104.

69. A version of the Cooper-Church Amendment was incorporated into the Special Foreign Assistance Act (Public Law 91–652), which was signed by President Nixon on 5 January 1971. Section 7(a) of this bill stated: "In line with the expressed intention of the President of the United States, none of the funds authorized or appropriated pursuant to this or any other Act may be used to finance the introduction of United States ground combat troops into Cambodia, or to provide United States advisers to or for Cambodian military forces in Cambodia."

70. Editorial, *Washington Post,* 28 Aug 1970.

71. Quoted in Lipsman and Doyle, *Fighting for Time,* 184–85.

72. Ibid.

73. Nixon, *Memoirs,* 467.

74. Nixon, *Public Papers, 1970,* 476–80.

75. Headquarters, U.S. Army Advisory Group, III Corps, "After Action Report—TOAN TANG 42," 24 July 1970, CARL.

76. Headquarters, 1st Cavalry Division Airmobile, "Combat Operations After-Action Report," 11 July 1970, CARL.

77. Lipsman and Doyle, *Fighting for Time,* 174; J. D. Coleman, *Incursion* (New York: St. Martin's, 1991), 263.

78. Tran Dinh Tho, *Cambodian Incursion,* 170.

79. Dave Palmer, *Summons of the Trumpet,* 236.

80. Memo, the President for Haldeman, 11 May 1970, White House Central Files, NPM.

81. Message, Collins to Abrams, 23 Apr 1970, Arthur S. Collins Papers, USAMHI.

82. Coleman, *Incursion,* 263.

83. The advisers were not the only ones worried. Brig. Gen. Douglas Kinnard reported that at a Saigon luncheon in May 1970 a senior ARVN general had confided to Kinnard that he thought the United States was departing too rapidly and that the chances of the ARVN forces making it on their own were slight. *The War Managers* (Wayne, N.J.: Avery Publishing Group, 1985), 142.

84. Tran Dinh Tho, *Cambodian Incursion,* 180.

85. Message, Sutherland to Rosson, DEPCOMUSMACV, 10 Aug 1970, Southeast Asia Branch Files, USACMH.

86. "A Different Scene," *Newsweek,* 8 June 1970, 35.

87. ARVN suffered a serious setback when both Lieutenant General Tri and Lieutenant General Thanh, the IV Corps commander, were later killed in separate helicopter crashes.

88. *Christian Science Monitor,* 10 Feb 1970. The situation improved somewhat when the division commander was replaced with a former brigade commander from the ARVN Airborne Division.

89. Memorandum, Westmoreland to SecDef, SecArmy, Chairman JCS, 4 Aug 1970, sub: Trip Report (7–21 Jul 1970), Westmoreland Papers, USACMH.

90. Tran Dinh Tho, *Cambodian Incursion,* 170. Tho states, however, that "for some ARVN units with missions to be carried out within well-defined time limits and requiring the support and assistance of U.S. combat support assets, the presence of U.S. advisers was still necessary because they could obtain fire support, medevac helicopters and resupply more rapidly and in a more reliable manner." Tho's assessment would be proven in 1971 when the South Vietnamese crossed into Laos without their advisers for Operation Lam Son 719, which is covered in the next chapter.

91. Cable for the President from Bunker, 30 Jan 1971, in *Bunker Papers,* 3:807.

92. Quoted in Olson and Roberts, *Where the Last Domino Fell,* 231.

93. George S. McGovern, Statement before U.S. Senate Committee on Foreign Relations, 4 Feb 1970, quoted in *Vietnam Documents: American and Vietnamese Views of the War,* ed. George Katsiaficas (Armonk, N.Y.: M. E. Sharpe, 1992), 151–54.

94. Point Paper, Vietnam Briefing, Annex to Fact Book, 3 Aug 1970, White House Central Files, NPM.

95. Nixon, *Memoirs*, 468.

96. Nixon, *Public Papers, 1971*, 7–22.

97. Kissinger, *White House Years*, 971.

98. Stemple, Robert B., Jr., "Nixon Urges Supervised Truce in Vietnam, Cambodia and Laos and a Wider Peace Conference," *New York Times*, 8 Oct 1970.

99. Kissinger, *White House Years*, 974.

100. "Peace Plan Gets Wide Praise from Hill Leaders and Media," *Washington Post*, 11 Oct 1970.

101. Henry Giniger, "Nixon Peace Plan Assailed by Reds at Talks in Paris," *New York Times*, 9 Oct 1970.

102. Nixon, *Memoirs*, 469.

103. Kissinger, *White House Years*, 986.

104. Ibid.

5. LAM SON 719

1. Fulghum and Maitland, *South Vietnam on Trial*, 65.

2. Ibid.

3. Haig, *Inner Circles*, 273.

4. Memorandum, 19 Jan 1971, sub: Meeting Between the President, Secretary Rogers, Secretary Laird, the Chairman of the Joint Chiefs of Staff, Henry Kissinger, Richard Helms, Vietnam Subject Files, NPM.

5. Message, McCain to Abrams, 110253Z Oct 1970, ABRAMS.

6. Message, McCain to Abrams, 062132Z Dec 70, ABRAMS.

7. Message, McCain to Abrams, 080435Z Dec 70, ABRAMS.

8. Message, Moorer to Abrams, 080435Z Dec 70, ABRAMS.

9. After the operation, many of the principals involved in putting together this plan made significant efforts to distance themselves from the original decision to launch the operation. In his memoirs, Kissinger blamed General Abrams for having misled him about the operation's prospects for success (this appears to be a case of Kissinger wanting to be absolved from responsibility after the fact). The South Vietnamese also disavowed any responsibility for the controversial decision to launch the operation; one former ARVN officer, Col. Hoang Ngoc Lung, wrote: "The Cambodian foray in 1970 and the Laos operation to Tchepone in 1971 came into being only because MACV originated them, promoted them, and supported them." *Indochina Monographs: Strategy and Tactics* (Washington, D.C.: U.S. Army Center of Military History, 1980), 73. Such was not entirely the case, as Gen. Cao Van Vien, chairman of the South Vietnamese Joint General Staff, had been proposing a similar operation since 1965. Moreover, he and President Thieu both agreed to the raid into Laos when General Abrams presented it to them. Lewis Sorley maintains that when the option was first discussed, Abrams warned against "the ever present danger of RVNAF indigestion from too much too soon" and that the plan was pushed by Haig and McCain. *Better War*, 230–36. It is clear from the message traffic that Abrams received his marching orders from Washington via CINCPAC and that he devised the plan based on the guidance that he had been given.

10. Kissinger, *White House Years*, 991.

11. Ibid., 994.

12. Ibid., 994–95.

13. Ibid., 999.

14. Memorandum, 19 Jan 1971, sub: Meeting Between the President, Secretary Rogers, Secretary Laird, the Chairman of the Joint Chiefs of Staff, Henry Kissinger, Richard Helms, Vietnam Subject Files, NPM; H. R. Haldeman, *The Haldeman Diaries* (New York: G.P. Putnam's Sons, 1994), 239.

15. Haldeman, *Diaries*, 239.

16. Willard J. Webb, *The Joint Chiefs of Staff and the War in Vietnam, 1971–1973* (Washington, D.C.: GPO, 1979), 19.

17. Haig, *Inner Circles*, 273.

18. Ibid.

19. Kissinger's concerns were transmitted to Abrams in Message, Moorer to McCain and Abrams, 262124Z Jan 71, ABRAMS.

20. Kissinger, *White House Years*, 999. Davidson writes that Moorer, a "distinguished navy airman, but one who never served in Vietnam . . . understood little of the complexities of ground operations and virtually nothing about the peculiarities of infantry fighting in Indochina." *Vietnam at War*, 576. Perhaps that explains the chairman's faith in airpower to protect the South Vietnamese and produce decisive results. This is an age-old (and continuing) debate between those who fight on the ground and those who fight in the air. One would have thought that the army chief of staff at the time, Gen. William Westmoreland, could have pointed out the dangers in such an operation as Lam Son 719, but Davidson was told by Westmoreland that he had not been consulted about the operation until after it had been launched. Davidson reports that both Moorer and Laird rebutted Westmoreland's claim, saying that he had been consulted prior to the operation and concurred with it. Kissinger agreed that Westmoreland knew beforehand. *White House Years*, 1005.

21. Memo, Haig for Kissinger, 1 Feb 1971, sub: Meeting With the Vice President, et al., 29 Jan 1971, White House Central Files, NPM.

22. Kissinger, *White House Years*, 999–1000. Kissinger maintains that even though Nixon approved execution of the mission, he was concerned with follow-on phases of the initial assault that called for the ARVN airborne forces to be lifted by U.S. helicopters to overwatch positions along Route 9. Nixon questioned whether the touching down of American helicopters on Laotian soil constituted "ground combat in Laos," proscribed by the Cooper-Church Amendment. He directed Admiral Moorer to study whether this part of the attack could either be eliminated or made without American airlift. Kissinger asserts that Nixon had already made up his mind to go through with the whole operation, but that his question added a level of uncertainty among his senior military advisers. Kissinger writes: "The uncertainty and hesitation suggested by his [Nixon's] request for further study of the airborne operation was bound to be magnified as it moved down in the military hierarchy" (1000).

23. Message, CJCS to MACV, 042053Z Feb 1971, ABRAMS.

24. In fact, both General Sutherland's XXIV Corps staff and General Lam's I Corps staff worked on independent plans for the operation until 7 January 1971, when authorization was given for combined planning. A combined planning cell was established, and the completed plan was briefed on 16 January. The U.S. XXIV Corps/ARVN I Corps combined plan was approved for execution by the Joint General Staff and General Abrams on 21 January. Headquarters, XXIV Corps, "Combat Operations After Action Report, Operation LAMSON 719," 14 May 1971, 3, CARL.

25. Headquarters, XXIV Corps, "Operations Order, LAMSON 719," 23 Jan 1971, 2.

26. The original Dewey Canyon had been a 1969 marine operation directed in the area south of Khe Sanh; it was hoped that designating Phase I of Lam Son 719 as Dewey Canyon II would have some deception value.

27. Donn A. Starry, *Armored Combat in Vietnam* (New York: Bobbs-Merrill, 1980), 190–91.

28. Lieutenant General James Sutherland, Senior Officer Debriefing, 31 Aug 1971, USAMHI. Many sources maintain that the enemy infiltrated planning of the operation, but that is unlikely. Communist accounts make no mention of U.S. or South Vietnamese planning for Lam Son 719. More likely, they anticipated the offensive merely because it was a logical step after the Cambodian incursion.

29. Terence Smith, "U.S. B-52's Strike Foe's Laos Bases around the Clock," *New York Times,* 1 Feb 1971; "Some Daylight on the Blackout," *Washington Daily News,* 4 Feb 1971; Ralph Blumenthal, "U.S. News Blackout in Saigon Tried to Keep Even Its Existence Secret," *New York Times,* 5 Feb 1971.

30. Colonel Arthur S. Pence, Vietnam Series interview by 1LT Thomas Turlenko, 6 May 1971, USACMH.

31. Maj. Gen. Nguyen Duy Hinh reported that an NVA sergeant from the 24B Regiment, 304th Division, who defected to the South Vietnamese side during the battle said that his unit had been given orders to counteract a possible ARVN offensive along Route 9 five months before it was launched. *Indochina Monograph: Lam Son 719* (Washington, D.C.: U.S. Army Center of Military History, 1980), 168.

32. Why there was not more concern with the enemy and his potential for rapid reinforcement is unknown. Gen. Phillip Davidson, former MACV J-2 (Intelligence), wrote that numerous U.S. intelligence reports estimated that the NVA could reinforce the Tchepone area with at least eight NVA infantry regiments and associated artillery support within two weeks; thus, it was apparent that the ARVN assault troops, numbering less than three divisions, might find themselves fighting at least four NVA divisions, with possibly more on the way. *Vietnam at War,* 579. The discounting of these estimates was clearly a failure in the planning process that would have dire consequences on the ultimate outcome of the operation.

33. Nguyen Duy Hinh, *Lam Son 719,* 164.

34. Bruce Palmer, *25-Year War,* 110.

35. Ibid.

36. The engineers estimated that they would need four days to make the Khe Sanh airfield operational again, but they were off by over a week. The condition of the old airstrip was such that virtually a new one had to be built, delaying the landing of the first airplanes there until 15 February.

37. Despite the efforts of the ARVN engineers to repair the road, it remained virtually impassable to all but tracked-vehicle traffic for the remainder of the operation. Because no wheeled vehicles could negotiate the road, the ARVN forces in Cambodia relied entirely on U.S. helicopters for resupply of fuel, ammunition, rations, and critical spare parts.

38. There is some question about the order to halt the South Vietnamese advance. Nguyen Tien Hung and Jerrold L. Schecter wrote that "Thieu insists he never gave such an order." *Palace File,* 44.

39. Nguyen Duy Hinh, *Lam Son 719,* 73.

40. The B-52s usually flew in three-ship cells and bombed from high altitude. Consequently, they required large targets and a three-kilometer safety zone between friendly

positions and the enemy to preclude bombs from accidentally falling on friendly troops. The NVA, aware of these restrictions, refrained from massing until the last minute and tried to stay as close to the ARVN forces as possible.

41. Fulghum and Maitland, *South Vietnam on Trial,* 78–79.

42. Craig Whitney, "Saigon's Rangers Driven from an Outpost in Laos," *New York Times,* 22 Feb 1971.

43. Quoted in Fulghum and Maitland, *South Vietnam on Trial,* 79–80.

44. Message, Sutherland to Abrams, 021420Z Mar 1971, ABRAMS.

45. Bruce Palmer, *25-Year War,* 112.

46. Starry, *Armored Combat,* 195.

47. Message, Sutherland to Abrams, 100850Z Mar 1971, ABRAMS.

48. Sorley, *Better War,* 255.

49. Message, Abrams to Moorer, 11 Mar 1971, ABRAMS.

50. Bruce Palmer, *25-Year War,* 112.

51. Quoted in Fulghum and Maitland, *South Vietnam on Trial,* 90.

52. During Operation Lam Son 719, South Vietnamese forces from III Corps attacked the NVA base in the Chup rubber plantation in Cambodia. The attack went reasonably well at first, but when the corps commander, Lieutenant General Tri, who had led the earlier campaign into the Parrot's Beak, was reassigned and subsequently killed in a helicopter crash, the operation came to a halt.

53. Quoted in Fulghum and Maitland, *South Vietnam on Trial,* 90.

54. Nixon, *Public Papers, 1971,* 160.

55. Nixon, *Memoirs,* 499.

56. The most comprehensive study of the Nixon administration's confrontation with the U.S. news media over the conduct and meaning of Lam Son 719 can be found in William H. Hammond, *Public Affairs: The Military and the Media, 1968–1973* (Washington, D.C.: U.S. Army Center of Military History, 1996), 401–92.

57. James McCartney, "S. Vietnamese 'Succeed' by Backing Away," *Philadelphia Enquirer,* 18 Mar 1971.

58. "Hanoi Supplies Still Moving," *Cleveland Plain Dealer,* 12 Apr 1971.

59. "'Hacking' It in Laos," *Philadelphia Bulletin,* 23 Mar 1971.

60. Quoted in Fulghum and Maitland, *South Vietnam on Trial,* 90.

61. "Assessing the Laos Invasion," *Newsweek,* 5 Apr 1971, 25–26. The NVA claimed 16,400 allies killed, including 200 Americans.

62. Headquarters, XXIV Corps, "Combat Operations After Action Report, Operation LAMSON 719," 14 May 1971, 90, CARL.

63. Directorate of Operations Analysis, Headquarters Pacific Air Forces, *Contemporary Historical Examination of Current Operations (CHECO) Report—LAM SON 719, 30 January–24 March '71, The South Vietnamese Incursion into Laos.* Honolulu, 24 March 1971, 123.

64. Davidson, *Vietnam at War,* 585.

65. Headquarters, XXIV Corps, "Combat Operations After Action Report, Operation LAMSON 719," 14 May 1971, 91, CARL. The report acknowledges that it differs with ARVN reports on some numbers.

66. Quoted in Fulghum and Maitland, *South Vietnam on Trial,* 91.

67. Message, COMUSMACV to JCS, 031015Z Apr 71, sub: Vietnamization, Southeast Asia Branch Files, USACMH.

68. Lt. Gen. Le Nguyen Khang, commander of the Marine Division, actually outranked Lieutenant General Lam.

69. Bruce Palmer, *25-Year War,* 109.

70. Quoted in Fulghum and Maitland, *South Vietnam on Trial,* 91.

71. Ibid., 72.

72. Cao Van Vien and Dong Van Khuyen, *Reflections on the Vietnam War,* 102.

73. Quoted in Keith William Nolan, *Into Laos* (Novato, Calif.: Presidio Press, 1986), 360.

74. John J. Tolson, *Vietnam Studies: Air Mobility, 1961–1971* (Washington, D.C.: U.S. Department of the Army, 1973), 251–52.

75. Quoted in Fulghum and Maitland, *South Vietnam on Trial,* 90.

76. Nguyen Duy Hinh, *Lam Son 719,* 140.

77. Message, Sutherland to Abrams, 211040Z Mar 71, ABRAMS.

78. Nolan, *Into Laos,* 360.

79. Ibid., 361.

80. Nixon, *Public Papers, 1971,* 524–26.

81. Nguyen Duy Hinh, *Vietnamization and the Cease-Fire,* 68.

82. Davidson, *Vietnam at War,* 588.

83. Message, Abrams to Major Subordinates, 18 Apr 1971, ABRAMS. See also Sorley, *Better War,* 272.

84. Message, Abrams to Major Subordinates, 300448Z Nov 1971, sub: VNAF/RVNAF Helicopter Operations, ABRAMS.

85. Davidson, *Vietnam at War,* 594.

86. Message, Abrams to Major Subordinates, 050611Z Jul 1971, ABRAMS. For additional observations with regard to South Vietnamese leadership during Lam Son 719, see Sorley, *Better War,* 257–59.

87. Report, Department of Defense (Vietnam Task Force), 27 Aug 1971, sub: Daily Highlights of Vietnamization and Pacification: An Assessment of the RVNAF Officer Corps, ABRAMS.

88. Cao Van Vien and Dong Van Khuyen, *Reflections on the Vietnam War,* 103.

89. Military History Branch, Headquarters, USMACV, "Command History, 1971," 1:I-5.

90. Nguyen Duy Hinh, *Lam Son 719,* 155.

91. Military History Branch, Headquarters, USMACV, "Command History, 1971," Volume 1:I-2.

92. Sorley, *Better War,* 309.

93. Ibid., 223–24.

94. George Gallup, "The Gallup Poll," *Washington Post,* 7 Mar 1971.

95. Louis Harris, "The Harris Survey," *Washington Post,* 8 Mar 1971.

96. Terrence Smith, "Fulbright Hopes to Force Nixon's Advisers to Testify," *New York Times,* 1 Mar 1971.

97. Louis A. Fanning, *Betrayal in Vietnam* (New Rochelle, N.Y.: Arlington House, 1976), 85–86.

98. Kissinger, *White House Years,* 1020.

99. Ibid., 1023.

100. Ibid., 1024; Qiang Zhai, *China and the Vietnam Wars, 1950–1975* (Chapel Hill: University of North Carolina Press, 2000), 197.

101. Kissinger, *White House Years,* 1025.

102. Truong Nhu Tang, *Vietcong Memoir,* 186–200.

103. Kissinger, *White House Years,* 1039.

104. Ibid.

105. Truong Nhu Tang, *Vietcong Memoir,* 194.

106. "The Same Old Shell Game," *Washington Post,* 27 Jan 1972; "Reaction Is Mixed," *New York Times,* 26 Jan 1972.

107. Quoted in Fulghum and Maitland, *South Vietnam on Trial,* 111.

6. THE ULTIMATE TEST OF VIETNAMIZATION

1. Robert D. Heinl, "On Basis of Pacification, Vietnam War Has Been Won," *Armed Forces Journal,* February 1972, 50.

2. Nguyen Duy Hinh, *Vietnamization and the Cease-Fire,* 83; Tran Dinh Tho, *Pacification,* 165. The Hamlet Evaluation Survey (HES) was a system devised to rate the security status and pacification level of individual hamlets.

3. Sir Robert Thompson, *Peace Is Not at Hand,* 78.

4. Nguyen Duy Hinh, *Vietnamization and the Cease-Fire,* 47; Sorley, *Better War,* 306.

5. Military History Branch, Headquarters, USMACV, "Command History, 1971," 1:VIII-72–83.

6. Message, Abrams MAC 02304 to Major Subordinates, 140537Z Mar 1972, sub: Reorganization of Military Assistance Command Vietnam, ABRAMS.

7. Neil Sheehan presents a detailed look at Vann's life and times in *Bright Shining Lie: John Paul Vann and America in Vietnam* (New York: Random House, 1988).

8. Clarke, *Advice and Support,* 452.

9. Ibid.

10. Dave Palmer, *Summons of the Trumpet,* 245; Brian M. Jenkins, *Giap and the Seventh Son* (Santa Monica, Calif.: Rand Corp., 1972), 4.

11. Lt. Gen. Ngo Quang Truong, *Indochina Monographs: The Easter Offensive of 1972* (Washington, D.C.: U.S. Army Center of Military History, 1980), 8.

12. Central Office for South Vietnam (COSVN), Directive 42, Dec 1971, p. 1, PIKE; Military History Institute of Vietnam, *Report to General Giap,* 30; Truong Nhu Tang, *Vietcong Memoir,* 204.

13. Truong Nhu Tang, *Vietcong Memoir,* 210.

14. William J. Duiker, *Sacred War: Nationalism and Revolution in a Divided Vietnam* (New York: McGraw-Hill, 1995), 234–35; Qiang Zhai, *China and the Vietnam Wars,* 202.

15. Military History Institute, *Victory in Vietnam,* 283.

16. This summary of North Vietnamese strategic thinking is drawn from David W. P. Elliott, *NLF-DRV Strategy and the 1972 Spring Offensive* (Ithaca, N.Y.: Cornell University, International Relations of East Asia, IREA Project, January 1974), and Ilya V. Gaiduk, *The Soviet Union and the Vietnam War* (Chicago: Ivan R. Dee, 1996), 231.

17. Gaiduk, *Soviet Union and the Vietnam War,* 231–32.

18. Qiang Zhai, *China and the Vietnam Wars,* 195–96. Qiang Zhai maintains that China had already begun to increase weapons shipments to North Vietnam earlier in 1971 to convince the Politburo in Hanoi that China's opening to America would not undermine their war effort. China's aid to North Vietnam would reach record levels in 1972–73. See

Chen Jian, *Mao's China and the Cold War* (Chapel Hill: University of North Carolina Press, 2001), 228, for table showing China's military aid to Vietnam, 1964–75.

19. Ngo Quang Truong, *Easter Offensive,* 8–9. Fanning asserts that the Soviets provided more than just equipment (*Betrayal in Vietnam,* 105). Citing Hanoi International News Service in English, 29 March 1972, he writes that the Soviets also provided high-ranking advisers for the invasion. According to Fanning, the Soviet delegation included Marshal Pavel F. Batitsky, a member of the Central Committee of the Communist Party of the Soviet Union; Lt. Gen. A. N. Sevchenko, representing the General Political Department of the Soviet Air and Naval Forces; and Lt. Gen. of Artillery F. M. Bolarenko, Soviet Antiaircraft Missile Forces. According to the cited article, the members of the delegation spent their time visiting "various air force missile, navy and infantry units."

20. Dave Palmer writes that 350 Soviet ships brought weapons and equipment to North Vietnamese ports in 1971 (*Summons of the Trumpet,* 248). Fulghum and Maitland estimate that Red China and the Soviets sent $1.5 billion in military aid during 1970–72 (*South Vietnam on Trial,* 120).

21. Central Office for South Vietnam (COSVN), Directive 42, Dec 1971, 1, PIKE; Headquarters, USMACV, "Special Intelligence Report (Declassified): The Nguyen Hue Offensive—Historical Study of Lessons Learned," Saigon, January 1973, C-1.

22. Quoted in Fulghum and Maitland, *South Vietnam on Trial,* 122.

23. The best discussion of SOG and its activities in Laos and Cambodia is found in John L. Plaster, *SOG: The Secret Wars of America's Commandos in Vietnam* (New York: Simon and Schuster, 1997).

24. Both November intelligence estimates are quoted in Dale Andradé, *America's Last Vietnam Battle: Halting Hanoi's 1972 Easter Offensive* (Lawrence: University Press of Kansas, 2001), 9.

25. Ibid.; Ngo Quang Truong, *Easter Offensive,* 157.

26. Nixon stated in his *Memoirs* that he limited the attacks to the period 26–30 December to coincide with the absence of students on college campuses due to the Christmas vacation. He hoped to avoid a new round of protests, but the response was "immediate and intense" with the dissidents protesting that Nixon was once again widening the war (584).

27. Ngo Quang Truong, *Easter Offensive,* 9.

28. Message, Abrams to CINCPAC, 200425Z 17 Jan 1972, ABRAMS.

29. Message, Abrams to CINCPAC, 200945Z Jan 1972, ABRAMS.

30. Headquarters, USMACV, "Periodic Intelligence Report (PERINTREP)," February 1972, 1.

31. Memorandum, Bunker to Nixon, 26 Jan 1972, White House Central Files, NPM.

32. "The Tet That Wasn't," *Life,* 24 Mar 1972, 38.

33. Quoted in Fulghum and Maitland, *South Vietnam on Trial,* 126.

34. For a discussion of Abrams's perspective on the preinvasion intelligence buildup, see Sorley, *Better War,* 307–17. When the attack came on 30 March, both General Abrams and Ambassador Bunker were outside Vietnam visiting their families for Easter in Thailand and Nepal, respectively (Bunker's wife was U.S. ambassador to Nepal).

35. Ngo Quang Truong, *Easter Offensive,* 21.

36. Military History Branch, Headquarters, USMACV, "Command History, 1972–1973," 2:L-7–8.

37. Memorandum, Lieutenant Colonel William C. Camper, Senior Adviser, 2nd Regiment, and Major Joseph Brown Jr., Deputy Senior Adviser, 2nd Regiment, to Senior Adviser, MACV Advisory Team 155, 3d Division, 13 Apr 1972, sub: Surrender of Camp Carroll, 1, ABRAMS.

38. Ibid., 30.

39. Fulghum and Maitland, *South Vietnam on Trial,* 140.

40. Kissinger, *White House Years,* 1099–1101.

41. Ibid., 1097–98.

42. Quoted in Olson and Roberts, *Where the Last Domino Fell,* 247.

43. Kissinger, *White House Years,* 1098–99.

44. Nixon, *Memoirs,* 588.

45. Kissinger, *White House Years,* 1113.

46. Ibid., 1108–9; Haig, *Inner Circles,* 282.

47. Quoted in Fulghum and Maitland, *South Vietnam on Trial,* 142.

48. Military History Branch, Headquarters, USMACV, "Command History, 1972–73," 2:J-1.

49. Headquarters, USMACV, "Periodic Intelligence Report (PERINTREP)," Apr 1972, C-1.

50. Maj. Thomas A. Davidson, part of the Binh Long Province advisory team, escaped through the wire at Loc Ninh just as the NVA entered one end of his command bunker. He and his Vietnamese interpreter evaded the NVA for the next four days, barely avoiding capture on numerous occasions and finally reaching an ARVN Ranger battalion in the northern part of An Loc. Andradé, *America's Last Vietnam Battle,* 373–74.

51. James H. Willbanks, *Thiet Giap! The Battle of An Loc, April 1972* (Ft. Leavenworth, Kans.: U.S. Army Combat Studies Institute, September 1993), 24. Major John D. Howard, "The War We Came to Fight: A Study of the Battle of An Loc, April–June 1972" (U.S. Army Command and General Staff College, Ft. Leavenworth, Kansas, June 1974, unpublished paper), 29.

52. Ian Ward, "North Vietnam's Blitzkreig—Why Giap Did It: Report from Saigon," *Conflict Studies,* Oct 1972, 5.

53. During the confusion of the initial attack, one NVA tank unit demonstrated that even the NVA had troops who "didn't get the word." Thinking that the city had been secured by NVA infantry, the tank crews rolled into the city with all hatches open, completely oblivious to the fact that the soldiers in the fighting positions were ARVN, not NVA. The lead tank made it all the way to the center of the city before it was knocked out by a South Vietnamese soldier with an M-72 LAW.

54. Stinger and Spectre gunships provided excellent support of the South Vietnamese defenders during the Easter offensive. They were cargo planes converted to platforms for a variety of gun systems. The Stinger was an AC-119 gunship, while the Spectre was an AC-130, a much more advanced aircraft, which had sophisticated target acquisition capabilities and was armed with 20-mm and 40-mm automatic gun systems. The PAVE AEGIS version, AC-130E, also mounted a 105-mm gun, which was particularly effective against tanks and other vehicles.

55. John Morrocco, *Rain of Fire, Air War, 1969–1973* (Boston: Boston Publishing, 1985), 105.

56. Brigadier General John R. McGiffert, interview by Walter S. Dillard, 10 Oct 1972, MACV, SJS-History, ABRAMS.

57. Frizzell, Donaldson D., Colonel, and Col. Ray L. Bowers, eds., *Airpower and the 1972 Spring Offensive,* U.S. Air Force Monograph Series 2 (Maxwell Air Force Base, Ala.: Air Command and Staff College, 1976), 85.

58. Message, Major General James F. Hollingsworth to General Abrams, "Backchannels: Daily Commander's Evaluation, 151000H-161000H April 1972," in *RecMACV,* reel 44, frames 0496–0500.

59. Headquarters, USMACV, "Special Intelligence Report (Declassified): The Nguyen Hue Offensive—Historical Study of Lessons Learned," January 1973, C-2.

60. Military History Branch, Headquarters, USMACV, "Command History, 1972–1973," 2:J-14.

61. Major General James F. Hollingsworth, "Communist Invasion in Military Region III," unpublished narrative in *RecMACV,* reel 44, 16; Philip C. Clarke, "The Battle That Saved Saigon," *Reader's Digest,* Mar 1973, 154.

62. Directorate of Operations Analysis, Headquarters Pacific Air Forces, *Contemporary Historical Examination of Current Operations (CHECO) Report—Kontum: Battle for the Central Highlands, 30 March–10 June 1972,* Honolulu, n.d., 5.

63. Ibid., 8.

64. Ibid., 15–16.

65. Ibid., 14.

66. Quoted in Fulghum and Maitland, *South Vietnam on Trial,* 154.

67. Directorate of Operations Analysis, Headquarters Pacific Air Forces, *CHECO—Kontum: Battle for the Central Highlands,* 24.

68. Military History Branch, Headquarters, USMACV, "Command History, 1972–73," 2:K-9.

69. Ngo Quang Truong, *Easter Offensive,* 37.

70. Message, Kroesen to Abrams, 021325Z May 1972, sub: General Assessment MR I, ABRAMS.

71. Ngo Quang Truong, *Easter Offensive,* 44.

72. Message, Abrams to Laird, 011601Z May 1972, sub: Personal Assessment of the Situation in RVN as of 1 May 1972, ABRAMS.

73. Malcolm M. Brown, "Battle for An Loc Raging as Enemy Moves in 10 Tanks," *New York Times,* 15 April 1972.

74. Kissinger, *White House Years,* 1172.

75. Nixon, *Memoirs,* 594.

76. Kissinger, *White House Years,* 1175.

77. Haig, *Inner Circles,* 286.

78. Kissinger, *White House Years,* 1175.

79. Nixon, *Public Papers, 1972,* 583–87.

80. Earl H. Tilford Jr., *Crosswinds: The Air Force's Setup in Vietnam* (College Station, Tex.: Texas A&M University Press, 1993), 149.

81. For the most-detailed description of Operation Linebacker, see Mark Clodfelter, *The Limits of Airpower: The American Bombing of North Vietnam* (New York: Free Press, 1989), 151–76.

82. At the summit meeting, Nixon negotiated treaties regulating anti-ballistic missiles and establishing temporary limits on the numbers of intercontinental ballistic missiles and submarine-launched missiles each side could have until a permanent agreement was signed.

83. Directorate of Operations Analysis, Headquarters Pacific Air Forces, *Contemporary*

Historical Examination of Current Operations (CHECO) Report—Battle for An Loc, 5 April–26 June 1972, Honolulu, n.d., 40.

84. Military History Branch, Headquarters, USMACV, "Command History, 1972–1973," 2:J-22.

85. Hollingsworth narrative, 17.

86. Directorate of Operations Analysis, *CHECO—Battle for An Loc,* 42.

87. Nguyen Duy Hinh, *Vietnamization and the Cease-Fire,* 104.

88. Howard, "The War We Came to Fight," 24.

89. Message, Hollingsworth to Abrams, "Backchannels, 151000H-161000H May 1972," in *RecMACV,* reel 44, frames 0416–0418.

90. Fulghum and Maitland, *South Vietnam on Trial,* 158.

91. Ngo Quang Truong, *Easter Offensive,* 50.

92. Ibid., 61.

93. Ibid., 67.

94. Ibid., 139.

95. Douglas Pike, *PAVN: People's Army of Vietnam* (Novato, Calif.: Presidio Press, 1986), 224–25.

96. U.S. Information Agency, Office of Policy and Plans, "Talking Paper: Facts on the Current North Vietnamese Invasion," 20 June 1972, p. 3, PIKE; Craig A. Whitney, "U.S. Aides Believe Saigon Can Withstand Foe's Drive," *New York Times,* 29 June 1972.

97. Philip C. Clarke,"The Battle That Saved Saigon," *Reader's Digest,* March 1973, 153.

98. U.S. sources estimated that the NVA invasion resulted in over 800,000 South Vietnamese refugees.

99. Craig A. Whitney, "U.S. Aides Believe Saigon Can Withstand Foe's Drive," *New York Times,* 29 June 1972.

100. Howard, "The War We Came to Fight," 1.

101. Ngo Quang Truong, *Easter Offensive,* 134.

102. Davidson, *Vietnam at War,* 634.

103. Hollingsworth narrative, 27.

104. Quoted in Davidson, *Vietnam at War,* 634.

105. Craig A. Whitney, "Saigon Holding in the North," *New York Times,* 24 Apr 1972. The pacification effort suffered its greatest setback in the Mekong Delta when the preponderance of the ARVN forces were sent elsewhere to shore up South Vietnamese offenses against the NVA invasion.

106. *Quan Doi Nhan Dan,* 1, 2, and 5 June 1972, PIKE.

107. Thompson, *Peace Is Not at Hand,* 110–12.

108. Fulghum and Maitland, *South Vietnam on Trial,* 158. The author saw the same thing at An Loc in mid-June.

109. Davidson, *Vietnam at War,* 710.

110. Report of PAVN Lieutenant General Tran Van Quang on 1972 Easter Offensive to the Soviet Politburo (translated from Vietnamese and Russian), 26 June 1972, p. 13, PIKE.

111. Message, Abrams to Laird, 020443Z May 1972, ABRAMS; Kissinger, *White House Years,* 11–112.

112. Col. William Miller, letter to author, 17 March 1993.

113. McGiffert, interview, 22.

114. Message, Abrams to Agnew, 171034Z May 1972, sub: MEMCON of Meeting at TSN Base Operations VIP Lounge, ABRAMS.

115. McGiffert, interview, 23.

116. Craig R. Whitney, "Allied Program Fails a Key Test," *New York Times*, 2 May 1972.

117. Major John D. Howard, "An Infantryman Remembers An Loc and the Air Force" (U.S. Army Command and General Staff College, Fort Leavenworth, Kansas, Mar 1974, unpublished paper), 14. The author witnessed the phenomenon personally on numerous occasions at An Loc.

118. "Settling in for the Third Indochina War," *Time*, 8 May 1972, 28.

119. Directorate of Operations Analysis, Headquarters Pacific Air Forces, *Contemporary Historical Examination of Current Operations (CHECO) Report—The 1972 Invasion of Military Region I: Fall of Quang Tri and Defense of Hue*, Honolulu, 15 Mar 1973, 31–32.

120. USMACV, Civil Operations for Rural Development Support (CORDS), "Operational Report for Period 30 Mar 1972 to 1 May 1972," 15 May 1972, 3, ABRAMS.

121. Craig R. Whitney, "As Town Falls, American Sees Valor and Cowardice," *New York Times*, 30 Apr 1972.

122. An Loc advisers, conversations with author, April 1972.

123. Senate Committee on Foreign Relations, *Staff Report: Vietnam, 1972* (Washington, D.C.: GPO, 1972), 5.

124. Headquarters, Third Regional Assistance Command, "Debriefing Report of Advisers Returning from An Loc," June 1972, ABRAMS.

125. Sydney H. Schanberg, "'It's Everyone for Himself' as Troops Rampage in Hue," *New York Times*, 4 May 1972.

126. Headquarters, USMACV, "Sustaining US Advisory Support—ARVN Division," 16 Nov 1972, 2–3, ABRAMS.

127. Colonel Jack Conn, Senior Officer Debriefing Report, Feb 1973, USMACV, K-1–3, USAMHI.

128. Senate Committee on Foreign Relations, *Staff Report: Vietnam, 1972*, 2.

129. Message, Abrams to Laird, 011601Z May 72, sub: Personal Assessment of the Situation in RVN as of 1 May 1972, ABRAMS.

130. Colonel Jack Conn, Senior Officer Debriefing Report, K-3, USAMHI.

131. Quoted in Donald Mrozek, *Air Power and the Ground War in Vietnam: Ideas and Actions* (Maxwell Air Force Base, Ala.: Air University Press, 1988), 144.

132. McGiffert, interview, 32.

133. Cao Van Vien and Dong Van Khuyen, *Reflections on the Vietnam War*, 109.

134. Dale Andradé, *Trial by Fire* (New York: Hippocrene Books, 1995), 521.

135. Quoted in Edgar Ulsamer, "Airpower Halts an Invasion," *Air Force Magazine*, Sep 1972, 61.

136. Davidson, *Vietnam at War*, 637.

137. McGiffert, interview, 26.

138. Ibid.

139. Senate Committee on Foreign Relations, *Staff Report: Vietnam, 1972*, 11.

140. McGiffert, interview, 27.

141. Davidson, *Vietnam at War*, 633, writes that the U.S. Navy, from May to July, fired a high of 7,000 rounds a day and a low of 1,000 rounds in support of the ARVN forces at Quang Tri and Hue, and a total of 16,000 tons of munitions between April and September.

142. Dale Andradé, *America's Last Vietnam Battle*, 487–88.

143. "Vietnam: the Specter of Defeat," *Newsweek*, 15 May 1972, 25.

144. Memorandum, Les Janka for Alexander Haig, 3 Apr 1972, sub: Handling of Vietnam Offensive, White House Central Files, NPM.

145. Nixon, *Public Papers, 1972*, 551–52.

146. "A Record of Sheer Endurance," *Time*, 26 June 1972, 26.

147. Directorate of Operations Analysis, *CHECO—1972 Invasion of Military Region I*, 2.

148. Colonel Theodore C. Williams Jr., Senior Officer Debriefing Report, 24 Jan 1973, Advisory Team 60, Delta Regional Assistance Command, USAMHI.

149. Colonel John C. Evans, Senior Officer Debriefing Report, 21 Feb 1973, Advisory Team 87, Third Regional Assistance Command, USAMHI.

150. Colonel William Miller, letter to author, 17 Mar 1993.

151. Joint Chiefs of Staff, Report, sub: Appraisal of the Situation in Vietnam, Aug 1972, Southeast Asia Branch Files, USACMH.

152. Memorandum, Laird to Chairman, JCS, 26 Aug 1972, sub: U.S. Advisers in the Republic of Vietnam, ABRAMS; Memorandum, Office of the SecDef to COL Marshall, 29 Sep 1972, sub: The Future of the Advisory Effort in SVN, ABRAMS.

153. U.S. Information Agency, Office of Policy and Plans, "Talking Paper: Facts on the Current North Vietnamese Invasion," 20 June 1972, p. 8, PIKE.

7. CEASE-FIRE AND "PEACE WITH HONOR"

1. White House Press Release, 29 June 1972, NSC Convenience Files, FORD. Davidson writes that this move by Nixon took the wind out of the sails of the student antiwar movement, removing them from danger and at the same time removing their outrage at the war. He asserts, "One can only conclude that the students' professed concern for the hearts and minds of the Vietnamese people was in reality a much greater concern for a lower part of their own anatomy." *Vietnam at War*, 655.

2. Quoted in Fanning, *Betrayal in Vietnam*, 118.

3. Haldeman, *Diaries*, 485. Eagleton himself would become a campaign issue when it was revealed that he had once been hospitalized for mental illness.

4. Nixon, *Public Papers, 1972*, 744–54.

5. Arnold R. Isaacs, *Without Honor: Defeat in Vietnam and Cambodia* (Baltimore: Johns Hopkins University Press, 1983), 19.

6. Walter Isaacson, *Kissinger: A Biography* (New York: Simon and Schuster, 1992), 441.

7. Haldeman, *Diaries*, 524.

8. Ibid.

9. Nixon, *Public Papers, 1972*, 583–87. The North Vietnamese had proved intractable in Paris when winning, but they changed their attitude once their attack began to falter. This was merely a reflection of battlefield reality. Kissinger later cited a combination of measures that caused the North Vietnamese to reverse their negotiating position and agree on terms for settlement. Besides the North's defeat in the Easter Offensive, he listed the depletion of supplies caused by the mining of Haiphong Harbor, the attacks on Cambodian and Laotian sanctuaries in 1970 and 1971, the lack of political support from Moscow and

Beijing, and the fear of Nixon's reelection as major factors leading to the final negotiations that eventually ended the war. Kissinger was correct, but the fact that he and Nixon had already titularly agreed that North Vietnamese troops could remain in South Vietnam was also a factor that contributed toward the motivation of Hanoi to enter into negotiations in a more conciliatory fashion. The mutual withdrawal issue had long been a point of contention. Before 1969, the United States had refused to withdraw American troops unless there was a commensurate withdrawal of North Vietnamese troops from the South, but with the beginning of American troops withdrawals in 1969, the issue became moot—we were withdrawing troops while the North Vietnamese were sending more of their soldiers south; the United States continued to withdraw its troops even as the Vietnamese Communists launched their Easter Offensive in 1972. While President Thieu continued to insist that North Vietnamese troops would have to be withdrawn from the South as part of any political settlement, the United States had effectively decoupled the North Vietnamese withdrawal from the U.S. withdrawal. This awarded the North Vietnamese one of their prime objectives and no doubt went a long way toward convincing them to return to the negotiations in earnest.

10. Gaiduk, *Soviet Union and the Vietnam War*, 239–41.

11. Qiang Zhai, *China and the Vietnam Wars*, 205.

12. Davidson, *Vietnam at War*, 642–43.

13. Kissinger, *White House Years*, 1375.

14. Quoted in Samuel Lipsman and Stephen Weiss, *The Vietnam Experience: The False Peace, 1972–1974* (Boston: Boston Publishing, 1985), 8.

15. Speech reported by Vietnam News Agency, 4 Feb 1972, PIKE.

16. Kissinger, *White House Years*, 1313.

17. Ibid., 1318–19.

18. Message, Kissinger to Bunker, 020922Z May 1972, NSC Convenience Files, FORD.

19. Message, Bunker to Kissinger, 170430Z June 1972, State Department Letter File, FORD.

20. Nguyen Tien Hung and Schecter, *Palace File*, 68; Ambrose, *Triumph of a Politician*, 595.

21. Kissinger, *White House Years*, 1331; Tad Szulc, *The Illusion of Peace: Foreign Policy in the Nixon Years* (New York: Viking, 1978), 626.

22. Statement of the PRG, 11 Sep 1972, extract quoted in *Viet. Hist.*, 409.

23. Kissinger, *White House Years*, 1333.

24. Ibid., 1337.

25. Ibid., 1340.

26. Nguyen Tien Hung and Schecter, *Palace File*, 73–74.

27. Quoted in the *Baltimore Sun*, 29 Sep 1972.

28. Nguyen Tien Hung and Schecter, *Palace File*, 16–17.

29. Kissinger, *White House Years*, 1339–40.

30. Nixon, *Memoirs*, 689.

31. Hersh, *Price of Power*, 581–82.

32. Quoted in Lipsman and Weiss, *False Peace*, 12.

33. Kissinger, *White House Years*, 1345–46.

34. Quoted in Karnow, *Vietnam: A History* (New York: Viking, 1983), 648; Kissinger, *White House Years*, 1366, alludes to Negroponte's objections.

35. Kissinger, *White House Years*, 1347–48.

36. Nixon, *Memoirs,* 691.
37. Ibid., 692.
38. Quoted in Isaacson, *Kissinger,* 454.
39. Nixon, *Memoirs,* 695–96.
40. Kissinger, *White House Years,* 1357–58.
41. Nguyen Duy Hinh, *Vietnamization and the Cease-Fire,* 126–28. In mid-October 1972, an ARVN unit operating in Quang Nam Province captured an enemy document that turned out to be the Communist plan for the period before and following the imposition of the anticipated cease-fire. This document described three phases. During Phase I, the Communist cadres were directed to study the Cease-Fire Agreement closely and be prepared to use it to further the "struggle." They were instructed to prepare NLF flags to be used on the day of the cease-fire "in every house, every hamlet, and on every hill" to demonstrate Communist presence in the south. Major units would conduct military operations to tie down the RVNAF and seize as much territory as possible. In Phase II, which encompassed the actual day of the cease-fire, the Communist forces were told to hold the territory that they had seized, while armed propaganda teams would increase efforts to proselyte the South Vietnamese villagers, especially in contested areas. In Phase III, the post-cease-fire or consolidation phase, the Communist cadres were to consolidate the gains made during the first two phases while continuing to conduct the propaganda campaign against the Thieu government. When the cease-fire did not occur later in the month as anticipated, many of the lower echelon Communist units carried forth with their previous instructions and launched the "land grab."
42. Abrams had departed South Vietnam in June 1972 to become army chief of staff. He was succeeded at MACV by Gen. Frederick C. Weyand.
43. Nguyen Tien Hung and Schecter, *Palace File,* 438–41.
44. Kissinger, *White House Years,* 1381.
45. The United States had conducted more than 41,000 bombing sorties over North Vietnam since 1 April 1972.
46. Nixon, *Memoirs,* 700; Kissinger, *White House Years,* 1377.
47. Quoted in Olson and Roberts, *Where the Last Domino Fell,* 252.
48. Statement by RVN Ministry of Foreign Affairs, 24 Oct 1972, in *Viet. Hist.,* 410.
49. Nixon, *Memoirs,* 702.
50. Kissinger, *White House Years,* 1388–89.
51. Statement of the DRV Government, 26 Oct 1972, in *Viet. Hist.,* 411–15.
52. Nixon, *Memoirs,* 705.
53. Kissinger, *White House Years,* 1399; text of news conference is found in *Viet. Hist.,* 415–17. North Vietnamese spokesman in Paris, Nguyen Thanh Le, later said that "Peace is at the hand of a pen." Quoted in Kissinger, *White House Years,* 1401.
54. "Kissinger Asserts That 'Peace Is at Hand'; Saigon Says It Will Agree to Cease-Fire," *New York Times,* 27 Oct 1972; "U.S. Confident a Truce Accord Will Soon Come," *New York Times,* 28 Oct 1972; "Peace 'Within Reach,' U.S. Says," *Washington Post,* 27 Oct 1972.
55. *Baltimore Sun,* 29 Oct 1972.
56. Kissinger, *White House Years,* 1399.
57. Ambrose, *Triumph of a Politician,* 643.
58. Haldeman, *Diaries,* 524. The scandal had been brewing since 17 June 1972 when a team of burglars led by G. Gordon Liddy and E. Howard Hunt, working for the Committee

to Re-Elect the President (CREEP) broke into the offices of the Democratic National Committee in the Watergate office building. The discovery of the subsequent cover-up and Nixon's involvement eventually led to his resigning in disgrace.

59. Nixon, *Memoirs*, 705.

60. Bernard Gwertzman, "Nixon Bars Truce for Vietnam War till Pact Is Right," *New York Times*, 3 Nov 1972; Department of State Bulletin, "A Look to the Future," 20 Nov 1972.

61. Nixon, *Public Papers, 1972*, 1108.

62. Walter S. Dillard, *Sixty Days to Peace, Implementing the Paris Peace Accords, Vietnam 1973* (Washington, D.C.: National Defense University, 1982), 15.

63. Quoted in Allan E. Goodman, *Lost Peace: America's Search for a Negotiated Settlement of the Vietnam War* (Stanford, Calif.: Hoover Institute Press, 1978), 147.

64. Quoted in Stephen T. Hosmer, Konrad Kellen, and Brian Jenkins, *The Fall of South Vietnam: Statements by Vietnamese Military and Civilian Leaders* (Santa Monica, Calif.: Rand Corp., 1978), 7–8.

65. South Vietnam also had the fourth largest army and the fifth largest navy in the world.

66. Quoted in William W. Momyer, *The Vietnamese Air Force, 1951—1975, an Analysis of Its Role in Combat*, U.S. Air Force Southeast Asia Monograph Series 3 (Maxwell Air Force Base, Ala.: Air Command and Staff College, 1975), 55–56.

67. Kissinger, *White House Years*, 1411.

68. Quoted in Message, Bunker to Kissinger, 3 Nov 1972, NSC Convenience Files, NPM.

69. Nixon, *Memoirs*, 718; Kissinger, *White House Years*, 1411–12; text of letter is found in *Viet. Hist.*, 417–19.

70. Nguyen Tien Hung and Schecter, *Palace File*, 120–24.

71. Nixon, *Memoirs*, 719.

72. Kissinger, *White House Years*, 1417.

73. Quote reported by New China News Agency, 19 Nov 1972, PIKE.

74. Nixon, *Memoirs*, 721; Isaacson, *Kissinger*, 419.

75. Kissinger, *White House Years*, 1417.

76. Nixon, *Memoirs*, 733.

77. Ibid., 721; Kissinger, *White House Years*, 1420–21.

78. Nixon, *Memoirs*, 722.

79. Ibid., 723.

80. Ibid.

81. Message, Kissinger to Bunker, 260510 Nov 1972, NSC Convenience Files, NPM; Nguyen Tien Hung and Schecter, *Palace File*, 137.

82. Nixon, *Memoirs*, 723–24.

83. Foreign Broadcast Information Service, 12 Dec 1972, PIKE.

84. Elmo R. Zumwalt Jr., *On Watch* (New York: Quadrangle, 1976), 412–15. Zumwalt, disgusted by "Nixon's duplicity," said, "There are at least two words no one can use to characterize the outcome of that two-faced policy. One is 'peace' and the other is 'honor.'"

85. Memorandum, Haig for the President, 30 Nov 1972, sub: The President's Meeting with the Joint Chiefs of Staff, 30 Nov 1972, NSC Convenience Files, NPM.

86. Nixon, *Memoirs*, 724.

87. Department of State, Bulletin, Bureau of Public Affairs, "Vietnam Peace Talks: Status of Negotiations," 1972, quoted in Fanning, *Betrayal in Vietnam*, 127.

88. Nixon, *Memoirs*, 732–33.

89. Stephen E. Ambrose, *Nixon,* vol. 3, *Ruin and Recovery, 1973–1990* (New York: Simon and Schuster, 1991), 37.

90. Kissinger, *White House Years,* 1451; full text of statement is found in *Viet. Hist.,* 419–22.

91. "Kissinger's Charges Untrue, Hanoi Aide in Paris Says," *New York Times,* 17 Dec 1972.

92. Press conference statement by DRV delegation chief Xuan Thuy, Paris, 19 Dec 1972, in *Viet. Hist.,* 422–23.

93. Secretary of Defense Laird believed that escalating the bombing after Kissinger's "peace is at hand" statement would lead to a cataclysmic reaction from the Congress, the media, and the student protesters. Events would prove him right.

94. Nixon, *Memoirs,* 732.

95. Kissinger, *White House Years,* 1449.

96. Nixon, *Memoirs,* 733–34.

97. Ibid., 734.

98. Kissinger, *White House Years,* 1459–60; Nixon, *Memoirs,* 737.

99. Not all of the sorties involved dropping bombs; over one-third of the flights provided support to the bombers—inflight refueling, fighter cover, antiaircraft missile suppression, and electronic countermeasures. Detailed accounts of the Christmas bombing can be found in James R. McCarthy and George B. Allen, *Linebacker II: A View from the Rock,* U.S. Air Force Southeast Asia Monograph Series 6 (Maxwell Air Force Base, Ala.: Air War College, 1979), and John T. Smith, *The Linebacker Raids: The Bombing of North Vietnam, 1972* (London: Cassell & Co., 1998).

100. "B-52 Toll Laid to Lack of Earlier Strikes," *Aviation Week and Space Technology Magazine,* 1 Jan 1973, 16–17.

101. The downing of the fifteen B-52s resulted in ninety-three missing American airmen, of which thirty-one became POWs.

102. Davidson, *Vietnam at War,* 654.

103. House Committee on Appropriations, *Hearings on Department of Defense Appropriations—Bombing of North Vietnam,* 93rd Cong., 1st sess., 9, 17, and 18 Jan 1973, 16.

104. International reactions were reported in "Key British Laborite Bids Heath Speak Up against U.S. Bombing," *New York Times,* 29 Dec 1972; "Diplomacy of Terror," *Newsweek,* 8 Jan 1973, 10–11; "Nixon's Blitz Leads Back to the Table," *Time,* 8 Jan 1973, 9–11.

105. James Reston, "Back to the Stone Age," *New York Times,* 20 Dec 1972; "Diplomacy of Terror," *Newsweek,* 8 Jan 1973, 10–11; "Bombing: The Damage at Home," *The Washington Post,* 24 Dec 1972.

106. Richard L. Strout, "Congress Glares at Bombing," *Christian Science Monitor,* 21 Dec 1972; Richard L. Lyons, "New Bombing Causes Distress in Senate," *Washington Post,* 21 Dec 1972.

107. Gabriel Kolko, *Anatomy of a War: Vietnam, the United States, and the Modern Historical Experience* (New York: Pantheon, 1985), 441–42.

108. Kissinger, *White House Years,* 1453.

109. Karnow, *Vietnam: A History,* 653–54. See also Thompson, *Peace Is Not at Hand,* 134–36.

110. Nixon, *Memoirs,* 741.

111. Ambrose, *Ruin and Recovery,* 46. Nguyen Tien Hung and Schecter quote Kissinger aide John Negroponte as saying, "We bombed the North Vietnamese into accepting our concession." *Palace File,* 146.

112. Tilford, *Crosswinds,* 170.

113. Karnow, *Vietnam: A History,* 654.

114. Nixon, *Memoirs,* 724–25, 734–35.

115. One cannot underestimate the role that China and the Soviet Union played in convincing North Vietnam to return to the talks. Qiang Zhai suggests that the Chinese advised them to return to the negotiating table. *China and the Vietnam Wars,* 204–6. When Zhou Enlai met with Le Duc Tho in Beijing on 3 January 1973, he stated his belief that the Americans obviously wanted a settlement and exhorted Hanoi to let them leave as quickly as possible. With the Americans gone, the North Vietnamese could then pursue the final solution to reunifying their country. Gaiduk reports that Soviet ambassador Shcherbakov met with Pham Van Dong in Hanoi on 23 December urging North Vietnam negotiators to return to the negotiating table "for the purpose of concluding the agreement as soon as possible." *Soviet Union and the Vietnam War,* 245.

116. Nixon, *Memoirs,* 724–25, 734–35.

117. Quoted in Isaacs, *Without Honor,* 59.

118. Quoted in Lipsman and Weiss, *False Peace,* 30.

119. Kissinger, *White House Years,* 1464; Nixon, *Memoirs,* 746. The final agreement included the following major provisions: a cease-fire in place; the withdrawal of U.S. troops and an exchange of POWs within sixty days; a prohibition against the United States and North Vietnam from sending more troops into South Vietnam; replacement of equipment only on an item-for-item basis; the creation of two commissions—the Joint Military Commission (South Vietnam, North Vietnamese Army, and the Viet Cong) and the International Commission of Control and Supervision (Hungary, Poland, Indonesia, and Canada) to enforce the cease-fire and compliance with the agreement; the establishment of a National Council of Reconciliation and Concord to organize free elections in South Vietnam; and the recognition of the DMZ as defined by the terms of the 1954 Geneva Accords.

120. Nixon, *Memoirs,* 749–50; Nguyen Tien Hung and Schuster, *Palace File,* 148. Nixon also had Senators John Stennis (D-MS) and Barry Goldwater (R-AZ) make public statements suggesting that if Thieu blocked the agreement, Congress would cut off further aid to South Vietnam.

121. Nixon, *No More Vietnams,* 167.

122. Kissinger, *White House Years,* 1469–70.

123. Department of State, Bulletin, Bureau of Public Affairs, "Address of the President as Delivered on Live Radio and Television, Jan 23, 1973," 1973.

124. Nixon, *No More Vietnams,* 97.

125. New China News Agency, 13 May 1972, PIKE.

126. William B. Le Gro, *Vietnam from Cease-Fire to Capitulation* (Washington, D.C.: U.S. Army Center of Military History, 1985), 2.

127. Davidson, *Vietnam at War,* 657. The best discussion of the experiences of the International Commission of Control and Supervision and the Four-Party Joint Military Commission is found in Dillard, *Sixty Days to Peace.*

128. COSVN Directive 2/73, 19 Jan 1973, PIKE.

129. Stanley Karnow, "The Vietnam Accord: Truce or Peace?" *New Republic,* 27 Jan 1973, 19–20.

130. Transcript of Kissinger interview, 1 Feb 1973, Philip Buchen Files, FORD. Some have charged that the United States had cut South Vietnam loose and was only looking for a "decent interval" between U.S. departure and a North Vietnamese victory. Kissinger maintains in his memoirs that this was not the case: "We had no illusions about Hanoi's long-term goals. Nor did we go through the agony of four years of war and searing negotiations simply to achieve a 'decent interval' for our withdrawal. We were determined to do our utmost to enable Saigon to grow in security and prosperity so that it could prevail in any political struggle. We sought not an interval before collapse, but lasting peace with honor. But for the collapse of executive authority as a result of Watergate, I believe we would have succeeded." *White House Years,* 1470.

131. Davidson, *Vietnam at War,* 657.

132. Quoted in Isaacs, *Without Honor,* 12.

133. The Agreement on Ending the War and Restoring the Peace in Vietnam consisted of twenty-three articles, divided into nine chapters. Excerpts of the agreement can be found in *Vietnam Documents,* ed. George Katsiaficas, 171–76. The entire agreement, including the protocols on the cease-fire and the Joint Military Commission, prisoners and detainees, the International Commission of Control and Supervision, and mine clearing in North Vietnam is found in Dillard, *Sixty Days to Peace,* 187–225.

134. By July 1972, fewer than 49,000 Americans remained in South Vietnam. By September, the total dipped to 39,000, and by the end of the year it reached 24,000, about the same strength in country when the United States began its buildup in 1965. Joining the last Americans in departing were 25,000 Koreans and a few hundred assorted Thais, Filipinos, and Nationalist Chinese military personnel, the remnants of the Free World Military Forces who had come to fight with the South Vietnamese.

135. The North Vietnamese held 591 POWs when the Paris Accords were signed. By the terms of the agreement, they would return all within sixty days of the signing of the accords. In return, the United States would have all troops out of South Vietnam by the same deadline. Whether the North Vietnamese turned over all American POWs has long been a point of contention, but no concrete evidence has ever been found to prove that POWs remained in North Vietnam after the release of the prisoners in 1973.

136. Clarke, *Advice and Support,* 495.

137. Message, COMUSMACV to JCS, 070930Z Mar 1973, sub: Assessment of RVNAF, Southeast Asia Branch Files, USACMH.

138. Nixon, *Public Papers, 1973,* 234–38.

139. Message, Bunker to President, 5 May 1973, *Bunker Papers,* 3:852–62.

140. Defense Attache Office, U.S. Embassy Saigon, RVNAF Quarterly Assessment, 4th Qtr FY 73, 24 Jul 1973, 12-2.

141. Le Gro, *From Cease-Fire to Capitulation,* 5–15, 27–31; Henry Kissinger, *Years of Upheaval* (Boston: Little, Brown, 1982), 16, 36–43, 332.

142. Nguyen Duy Hinh, *Vietnamization and the Cease-Fire,* 166.

143. Robert D. Schulzinger, *A Time for War: The United States and Vietnam, 1941–1975* (New York: Oxford University Press, 1997), 305.

144. Nguyen Duy Hinh, *Vietnamization and the Cease-Fire,* 154.

145. Tran Van Tra, *Vietnam: History of the Bulwark B-2 Theater,* vol. 5, *Concluding the 30–Years War* (Ho Chi Minh City: Van Nghe Publishing, 1982), 33.

146. Odd Arne Westad, et al., eds., *77 Conversations between Chinese and Foreign Leaders on the Wars in Indochina, 1964–1977* (Washington, D.C.: Woodrow Wilson Center,

1998), 187–91. In meetings with Le Duan in Beijing on 5–6 June 1973, Zhou Enlai promised to provide aid to the DRV at the 1973 level for the next five years.

147. Nguyen Duy Hinh, *Vietnamization and the Cease-Fire,* 154.

148. The NVA built several oil pipelines to support its forces in the South. One terminated adjacent to Thua Thien Province. Another ran from Mu Gia Pass in North Vietnam nearly to the DMZ. This line was later lengthened to reach Quang Duc Province in MR III. The NVA would no longer have the fuel resupply problems that plagued it in 1972.

149. In addition to sending new units south, several of the units that had been decimated during the 1972 offensive (the 308th, 312th, 316th, and 320th) were withdrawn to Laos or North Vietnam for a major refitting process before being sent back to South Vietnam.

150. Defense Attache Office, U.S. Embassy Saigon, RVNAF Quarterly Assessment, 4th Qtr FY 73, 24 Jul 1973, 12-1.

151. COSVN Directive No. 2/CT/73, 19 Jan 1973, PIKE.

152. U.S. Embassy Saigon, *Vietnam Documents,* No. 113, June 1973, 14–15, PIKE.

153. Message, Bunker to Kissinger, 2 Mar 1973, NSC Convenience Files, NPM.

154. Le Gro, *From Cease-Fire to Capitulation,* 32; Isaacs, *Without Honor,* 84.

155. Quoted in Lipsman and Weiss, *False Peace,* 37.

156. Ibid., 32.

157. Defense Attache Office, U.S. Embassy Saigon, RVNAF Quarterly Assessment, 2nd Qtr FY 75, 1 Feb 1975, 32–33, USACMH.

158. Nguyen Duy Hinh, *Vietnamization and the Cease-Fire,* 137–38.

159. Kissinger, *Years of Upheaval,* 32.

160. Defense Attache Office, U.S. Embassy Saigon, RVNAF Quarterly Assessment, 4th Qtr FY 73, 24 Jul 1973, 1, USACMH.

161. Nguyen Duy Hinh, *Vietnamization and the Cease-Fire,* 158; Cao Van Vien, *Final Collapse,* 36.

162. Alan Dawson, *55 Days: The Fall of South Vietnam* (Englewood Cliffs, N.J.: Prentice-Hall, 1977), 99. The International Commission of Control and Supervision never fulfilled its mission to control the cease-fire. Stuart A. Herrington, who served in the DAO in 1975 as a captain, wrote after the war that the initials ICCS stood for "I Can't Control Shit." "The Third Indochina War, 1973–1975: A Personal Perspective" (thesis, Air Command and Staff College, Maxwell Air Force Base, Alabama, May 1980), 89. However, as Arnold Isaacs asserts, since the warring sides made no effort to make the cease-fire work, the ICCS "never had a chance," *Without Honor,* 97.

163. Nguyen Tien Hung and Schecter, *Palace File,* 163; Kissinger, *Years of Upheaval,* 315; Ambrose, *Ruin and Recovery,* 98–99.

164. R. W. Apple Jr., "Nixon Pledges Aid to Thieu But Not U.S. Intervention," *New York Times,* 4 Apr 1973, 1, 13.

165. Kissinger, *Years of Upheaval,* 318.

166. Hosmer, Kellen, and Jenkins, *Fall of South Vietnam,* 10–15.

167. Le Gro, *From Cease-Fire to Capitulation,* 62.

168. Dong Van Khuyen, *RVNAF,* 386–87.

169. Ibid., 387.

170. Dillard, *Sixty Days to Peace,* 62–63; Schulzinger, *A Time for War,* 312–13. The "Four Nos" were not new; Thieu had been espousing this position since 1969.

171. Kissinger had visited Hanoi in February 1973 to discuss the cease-fire, as well as other topics, including North Vietnamese information on American MIAs, U.S. financial

assistance to DRV, and the continuing hostilities in Cambodia and Laos. Kissinger and the North Vietnamese were unable to reach any meaningful agreements, thus establishing an unfortunate pattern that would repeat itself.

172. Quoted in Isaacs, *Without Honor,* 141.

173. Fox Butterfield, "In the Mekong Delta, a War with Two Faces," *New York Times,* 8 Sep 1973.

174. Eric Pace, "Laird Says Saigon is Ready on Arms," *New York Times,* 9 Jan 1973.

175. Two reporters from the *Washington Post,* Robert Woodward and Carl Bernstein, had exposed the whole story. It had become clear that a number of top administration officials were involved in the planning and financing of the break-in. On 30 April 1973, two of Nixon's closest advisers, John Ehrlichman and H. R. Haldeman, resigned when they were implicated in the cover-up. Senator Sam Ervin of North Carolina chaired the Select Committee on Presidential Campaign Activities, which eventually learned that Nixon had been personally involved in the cover-up as well. The House Judiciary Committee began impeachment hearings against the president late in 1973. On 9 Aug 1974, Nixon would resign from office.

176. John Hart Ely, *War and Responsibility: Constitutional Lessons of Vietnam and Its Aftermath* (Princeton, N.J.: Princeton University Press, 1993), 48–53.

177. Quoted in Olson and Roberts, *Where the Last Domino Fell,* 258.

178. People's Liberation Armed Forces Command Order, 15 Oct 1973, in *Viet. Hist.,* 438–39.

179. Van Tien Dung, *Our Great Spring Victory: An Account of the Liberation of South Vietnam* (New York: Monthly Review Press, 1977), 10–11; Cao Van Vien, *Final Collapse,* 38–39; Tran Van Tra, *Bulwark B-2 Theater,* 53, 65; Truong Nhu Tang, *Viet Cong Memoir,* 229.

180. Isaacs, *Without Honor,* 139.

181. Ibid., 132; *New York Times,* 16 and 17 Dec 1973.

182. Defense Attache Office, U.S. Embassy Saigon, RVNAF Quarterly Assessment, 2nd Qtr FY 74, 1 Feb 1974, 4, USACMH.

183. Quoted in Le Gro, *From Cease-Fire to Capitulation,* 81–82.

184. Davidson, *Vietnam at War,* 668–69.

8. THE FATEFUL YEAR

1. The North Vietnamese retained the bases they had overrun at Le Minh (Plei D'jereng), Ngoc Bay Mountain Base in Kontum Province, and Bach Ma Mountain Base near Da Nang, among others.

2. Senate Committee on Foreign Relations, *Staff Report: Vietnam, May 1974* (Washington, D.C.: GPO, 1974), 4; House, *Vietnam: A Changing Crucible—Report of a Study Mission to South Vietnam* (Washington, D.C.: GPO, 1974), 4.

3. Dong Van Khuyen, *RVNAF,* 118.

4. Defense Attache Office, U.S. Embassy Saigon, RVNAF Quarterly Assessment, 2nd Qtr FY 1974, 1 Feb 1974, 1, USACMH.

5. Le Gro, *From Cease-Fire to Capitulation,* 19.

6. Cao Van Vien and Dong Van Khuyen, *Reflections on the Vietnam War,* 124.

7. Quoted in Lipsman and Weiss, *False Peace,* 146.

8. Cao Van Vien, *Final Collapse*, 39.

9. President Nguyen Van Thieu's 4 Jan 1974 speech at Can Tho, transcript in Message, Martin to Kissinger, 5 Jan 1974, NSC Convenience Files, FORD.

10. Le Gro, *From Cease-Fire to Capitulation*, 91.

11. The attack included eighteen battalions from III Corps and a supporting attack by two IV Corps battalions from the Moc Hoa sector, which Lt. Gen. Thuan had coordinated with General Nghi.

12. Le Gro, *From Cease-Fire to Capitulation*, 92–95.

13. Lipsman and Weiss, *False Peace*, 124.

14. Davidson, *Vietnam at War*, 672.

15. Nguyen Duy Hinh, *Vietnamization and the Cease-Fire*, 185.

16. Anthony James Joes, *The War for South Viet Nam, 1954–1975* (New York: Praeger, 1989), 125.

17. Le Gro, *From Cease-Fire to Capitulation*, 80.

18. Lipsman and Weiss, *False Peace*, 144.

19. Le Gro, *From Cease-Fire to Capitulation*, 81–82.

20. The most comprehensive discussion of the impact of the 1974 U.S. military aid reduction is found in ibid., 80–87.

21. Ibid., 86–87.

22. Ibid., 87.

23. Hosmer, Kellen, and Jenkins, *Fall of South Vietnam*, 8.

24. Nguyen Duy Hinh, *Vietnamization and the Cease-Fire*, 173–74.

25. Le Gro, *From Cease-Fire to Capitulation*, 86.

26. Cao Van Vien, *Final Collapse*, 44.

27. Lipsman and Weiss, *False Peace*, 149. Le Gro wrote that such reports were gathered by DAO personnel who had regular contact with knowledgeable Vietnamese officers and were given access to South Vietnamese units. *Vietnam from Cease-Fire to Capitulation*, 79.

28. Nguyen Tien Hung and Schecter, *Palace File*, 229; Le Gro, *From Cease-Fire to Capitulation*, 84–87; Hosmer, Kellen, and Jenkins, *Fall of South Vietnam*, 7–9.

29. A full ARVN colonel with twenty years' service earned about 40,000 piasters a month, or about $80, with which he supported an extended family group. A sergeant with fourteen years' service earned only the equivalent of $25 a month. The Defense Attache Office found that 90 percent of enlisted men and junior officers were not receiving enough pay to sustain their families. RVNAF Quarterly Assessment, 3rd Qtr FY 1974, 1 May 1974, USACMH.

30. Anthony B. Lawson, "Survey of the Economic Situation of RVNAF Personnel," Special Studies Section, USDAO, U.S. Embassy Saigon, 1974, 7, PIKE.

31. Hosmer, Kellen, and Jenkins, *Fall of South Vietnam*, 57.

32. Defense Attache Office, U.S. Embassy Saigon, RVNAF Quarterly Assessment, 2nd Qtr FY 1974, 1 Feb 1974, 15-1–2, USACMH.

33. Isaacs, *Without Honor*, 297.

34. Lipsman and Weiss, *False Peace*, 138.

35. Quoted in Stuart A. Herrington, *Peace with Honor? An American Reports on Vietnam, 1973–1975* (Novato, Calif.: Presidio Press, 1983), 45–47.

36. Lam Quang Thi, *Autopsy: The Death of South Vietnam* (Phoenix: Sphinx Publishing, 1986), 170.

37. Le Gro, *From Cease-Fire to Capitulation*, 72; Herrington, *Peace with Honor*, 22.

38. Lam Quang Thi, *Autopsy*, 169–70.

39. Davidson, *Vietnam at War,* 673.

40. Ibid., 674.

41. In 1969, about 160,000 South Vietnamese worked directly for the United States in one capacity or another. After the U.S. withdrawal, most of these people became unemployed. Additionally, the vast industry that had grown up to service the American war machine in South Vietnam now had no one to service; its workers entered the ranks of the jobless as well.

42. Report cited in *American Aid and Vietnam Economy,* Office of the [South Vietnamese] Deputy Prime Minister in Charge of Economic Development, Saigon, RVN, Mar 1975, 300, PIKE.

43. Herrington wrote that the increase in prices greatly affected the South Vietnamese military. Herrington was told by a South Vietnamese officer that he was allocated only twenty liters of gasoline a month for his jeep and that he had to pay for any additional fuel needed out of his own pocket. *Peace with Honor,* 22.

44. Lipsman and Weiss, *False Peace,* 140.

45. With 60 percent of the GVN budget spent to maintain its million-man army and another 20 percent going to support refugees and veterans, very little was left for the measures necessary to reconstruct the South Vietnamese economy.

46. Herrington, *Peace with Honor,* 45.

47. Lam Quang Thi, *Autopsy,* 165–66. General Thi asserts that in the final days before Saigon fell in 1975, General Quang, who controlled passports and exit visas, "had the effrontery to ask for up to 17 million piasters ($28,000 U.S.) for each person who wanted to obtain a passport." Thi also maintains that Quang, who controlled senior officer appointments, "sold" division commands for 2 million piasters.

48. Lam Quang Thi, *Autopsy,* 173.

49. Davidson, *Vietnam at War,* 676.

50. Hosmer, Kellen, and Jenkins, *Fall of South Vietnam,* 60.

51. Herrington, *Peace with Honor,* 41.

52. Nguyen Duy Hinh, *Vietnamization and the Cease-Fire,* 132.

53. Goodman, *Lost Peace,* 175.

54. Lam Quang Thi, *Autopsy,* 141.

55. Clark Dougan and David Fulghum, *The Vietnam Experience: The Fall of the South* (Boston: Boston Publishing, 1985), 17–18.

56. Gareth Porter, *A Peace Denied: The United States, Vietnam, and the Paris Agreement* (Bloomington: Indiana University Press, 1975), 187–88.

57. Nguyen Duy Hinh, *Vietnamization and the Cease-Fire,* 171.

58. Lam Quang Thi, *Autopsy,* 141. Timothy J. Lomperis states that fifty thousand Chinese engineering troops maintained the transportation system inside North Vietnam, which allowed Hanoi to focus on maintaining the routes into South Vietnam. *The War Everyone Lost—And Won* (Baton Rouge: Louisiana State University Press, 1984), 75.

59. Military History Institute, *Victory in Vietnam,* 348–51.

60. Van Tien Dung, *Our Great Spring Victory,* 2.

61. Ibid., 1.

62. Military History Institute, *Victory in Vietnam,* 354.

63. Nguyen Duy Hinh, *Vietnamization and the Cease-Fire,* 177.

64. Le Gro, *From Cease-Fire to Capitulation,* 124. Le Gro and several of his colleagues traveled to the field to personally observe many of the actions in 1974 and early 1975. He

also wrote that field reports from the various U.S. consul generals were "especially copious and usually reliable." Charles J. Timmes provides a thorough summary of combat operations in the 1973–75 time frame in "Military Operations after the Cease-Fire Agreement, Part I," *Military Review,* Aug 1976, 63–75, and "Military Operations after the Cease-Fire Agreement, Part II," *Military Review,* Sep 1976, 21–29.

65. Lipsman and Weiss, *False Peace,* 164.

66. The most detailed discussion of the 1974 "strategic raids" can be found in Le Gro, *From Cease-Fire to Capitulation,* 96–132.

67. Defense Attache Office, U.S. Embassy Saigon, RVNAF Quarterly Assessment, 1st Qtr FY 1975, 1 Nov 1974, I-1. The total number of divisions did not include seven reserve divisions located north of the DMZ.

68. Van Tien Dung, *Our Great Spring Victory,* 15.

69. Isaacs, *Without Honor,* 303.

70. House Committee on Foreign Affairs, *Hearings on Fiscal Year 1975 Foreign Assistance Request,* 93rd Cong., 2nd sess., 4–5, 11–13, 18–20, 26 June, 1–2, 10–11 July 1974, 58.

71. Senate Committee on Appropriations, *Hearings on Foreign Assistance and Related Programs Appropriation FY1975,* 93rd Cong., 2nd sess., 25 February, 6, 11, 25 March, 7, 24, 28 May, 13–14, 17–19, 25 June 1974, 1318.

72. Quoted in Isaacs, *Without Honor,* 303.

73. Senate Committee on Foreign Relations, *Hearings on Foreign Assistance Authorization,* 93rd Cong., 2nd sess., 7, 21, 26 June, 24–25 July 1974, 386–89.

74. Quoted in Isaacs, *Without Honor,* 303.

75. Senate Committee on Foreign Relations, *Staff Report: Vietnam—May 1974* (Washington, D.C.: GPO, 1974), 13–14.

76. According to Arnold Isaacs, Col. William E. Le Gro, the DAO intelligence chief, later recalled that the reports from the field had not been censored before being forwarded to Washington, but in 1975, a State Department team determined that in fact the messages from Saigon "showed really just one side." *Without Honor,* 308.

77. *Congressional Record,* 93rd Cong., 1st sess., 120 (19 March 1974): 7106–7.

78. Passages from joint report quoted in Dong Van Khuyen, *RVNAF,* 282–85.

79. House Committee on Foreign Affairs, *Hearings on Fiscal Year 1975 Foreign Assistance Request,* 54–56.

80. Quoted in Fanning, *Betrayal in Vietnam,* 173.

81. Ibid., 175.

82. Quoted in Lipsman and Weiss, *False Peace,* 173.

83. *Congressional Record,* 93rd Cong., 2nd sess., 120 (20 Aug 1974): 29176–80.

84. Le Gro, *From Cease-Fire to Capitulation,* 87.

85. Cao Van Vien, *Final Collapse,* 47–48.

86. Nguyen Tien Hung and Schecter, *Palace File,* 234–35.

87. Cao Van Vien, *Final Collapse,* 53–54.

88. Vo Nguyen Giap, *How We Won the War* (Philadelphia: Recon Press, 1976), 24.

89. *Congressional Record,* 94th Cong., 1st sess., 121 (6 Mar 1975): H1454–55.

90. Defense Attache Office, U.S. Embassy Saigon, RVNAF Quarterly Assessment, 4th Qtr FY1974, 1 Jul 1974, foreword, USACMH.

91. Isaacs, *Without Honor,* 320.

92. Ibid.

93. Nguyen Tien Hung and Schecter, *Palace File*, 238–40.

94. Cao Van Vien, *Final Collapse*, 80.

95. Ford to Thieu, 10 Aug 1974, White House Central Files, FORD.

96. Nguyen Tien Hung and Schecter, *Palace File*, 240–41.

97. Herrington, *Peace with Honor*, 103–4.

98. Lam Quang Thi charges that Thieu's special assistant for military and security affairs, Gen. Dang Van Quang, was "the man in charge of the narcotics traffic under Thieu." *Autopsy*, 173–75.

99. Quoted in Isaacs, *Without Honor*, 323, and in Lipsman and Weiss, *False Peace*, 175.

100. Quoted in Isaacs, *Without Honor*, 323, and in Lipsman and Weiss, *False Peace*, 180.

101. Quoted in Isaacs, *Without Honor*, 325.

102. Quoted in Lipsman and Weiss, *False Peace*, 180. The relieved corps commanders, all lieutenant generals, were Nguyen Van Toan of II Corps, Pham Quoc Thuan of III Corps, and Nguyen Vinh Nghi of IV Corps.

103. New China News Agency, 10 Oct 1974, PIKE.

104. Ibid.

105. Van Tien Dung, *Our Great Spring Victory*, 17–18.

106. Military History Institute, *Victory in Vietnam*, 354–55.

107. Van Tien Dung, *Our Great Spring Victory*, 12.

108. Ibid.

109. Van Tien Dung, "Great Spring Victory," Radio broadcast, 7 June 1976, Foreign Broadcast Information Service, transcript, PIKE, 5.

110. Van Tien Dung, *Our Great Spring Victory*, 19.

111. Ibid., 20.

112. Tran Van Tra, *Bulwark B-2 Theater*, 93, 96–98.

113. Davidson, *Vietnam at War*, 681.

114. Quoted in Dougan and Fulghum, *Fall of the South*, 17.

9. COLLAPSE IN THE NORTH

1. Le Gro, *From Cease-Fire to Capitulation*, 133–34. As chief intelligence officer of the Saigon Defense Attache Office, Colonel Le Gro had access to both U.S. and South Vietnamese intelligence; thus, his perspective provides the most comprehensive view of events on the battlefield between the signing of the cease-fire in 1973 and the surrender of the South Vietnamese in April 1975.

2. Because the VNAF only had thirty-two C-130 aircraft, the destruction of two at Song Be was a significant loss.

3. Cao Van Vien, *Final Collapse*, 64.

4. Le Gro, *From Cease-Fire to Capitulation*, 137; Olivier Todd, *Cruel April: The Fall of Saigon* (New York: Norton, 1987), 36.

5. Quoted in Vien, *Final Collapse*, 67. Todd reported that the North Vietnamese tanks were reinforced with exterior armor plate that diffused the effects of the exploding M-72 antitank rockets fired by the South Vietnamese soldiers, making the tanks much more difficult to kill (*Cruel April*, 34–35).

6. The United States did move the aircraft carrier *USS Enterprise* and its accompanying task force out of the Philippines closer to Vietnam. Additionally, it alerted the

Marine Division on Okinawa. However, these actions, nothing more than political gestures by the Ford administration, had no impact whatsoever on the situation in South Vietnam.

7. Ford, *Public Papers, 1975*, bk. 1, 36–46.

8. Ibid., 56.

9. Cao Van Vien, *Final Collapse*, 67–68.

10. Tran Van Tra, "Concluding the 30–Years War," Foreign Broadcast Information Service, PIKE, 134; Military History Institute, *Victory in Vietnam*, 359.

11. Quoted in Dougan and Fulghum, *Fall of the South*, 22, and in Military History Institute, *Victory in Vietnam*, 360.

12. Ibid.

13. Quoted in Todd, *Cruel April*, 81.

14. Van Tien Dung, *Our Great Spring Victory*, 27.

15. Nguyen Tien Hung and Schecter, *Palace File*, 259–60.

16. Quoted in Dougan and Fulghum, *Fall of the South*, 28. According to PRG minister of justice Truong Nhu Tang, Thieu's faith in the Americans was due to the "ingrained Confucianism" of Vietnamese culture: "Among the very deepest feelings one raised in a Confucian society has, is the inhibition against betraying those with whom one enjoys a relationship of trust . . . [Thieu was] betting on the American geopolitical investment in South Vietnam . . . a relationship of personal commitment had been created. Trapped in his Vietnamese habits of thought, Thieu imagined that this relationship must prevail, regardless of apparent political realities and logic." *Fall of the South*, 30.

17. Ford to Thieu, 24 Oct 1974, White House Central Files, FORD.

18. David L. Anderson, "Gerald R. Ford and the Presidents' War in Vietnam," in *Shadow on the White House: Presidents and the Vietnam War, 1945–1975*, ed. David L. Anderson (Lawrence: University Press of Kansas, 1993), 187–88.

19. Ford, *Public Papers, 1974*, 244; Edward P. Haley, *Congress and the Fall of South Vietnam and Cambodia* (East Brunswick, N.J.: Associated University Presses, 1982), 45–46.

20. Quoted in Dougan and Fulghum, *Fall of the South*, 31. This request included $300 million for South Vietnam and $222 million for Cambodia.

21. Memorandum, Timmons to Ford, sub: Foreign Aid Legislation, 12 Aug 1974, William E. Timmons Files, FORD.

22. "Democrats See 'Scare Tactics,'" *Washington Post*, 30 Jan 1975.

23. Members of Congress for Peace through Law to Ford, 6 Feb 1975, White House Central Files, FORD.

24. John W. Finney, "Drive to Step Up War Aid to Saigon Opens in Congress," *New York Times*, 31 Jan 1975.

25. Senate Committee on Armed Services, *Report of Senator Sam Nunn: Vietnam Aid— The Painful Options*, 94th Cong., 1st sess., 12 February 1975, 9. Rep. Leo J. Ryan had visited Saigon in December 1974 and come to the same conclusion as Nunn.

26. Memorandum, Wolthuis to Marsh, 14 Jan 1975, John O. Marsh Files, FORD.

27. Memorandum, Linwood Holton to Kissinger, sub: Vietnam: Visit by Members of Congress, 21 Jan 1975, Robert K. Wolthuis Files, FORD.

28. Wolfgang J. Lehman, Senior Officer Debriefing Program, interview by LTC Tommy Stiner and LTC Andrew Tinker, 1982, USAMHI. The other members of the delegation were Representatives Millicent Fenwick (NJ), William Chappell (FL), and John Murtha (PA).

29. Frank Snepp, *Decent Interval* (New York: Random House, 1977), 162.

30. Transcript of Thieu address to Congressional Delegation, 1 Mar 1975, Robert K. Wolthuis Files, FORD.

31. Vien, *Final Collapse*, 76; Nguyen Tien Hung and Schecter, *Palace File*, 259–62.

32. In *Peace with Honor*, Stuart Herrington, who attended the meeting, provides a detailed discussion of the confrontation (128–38).

33. Memorandum of Conversation, President Ford and Members of the Congressional Delegation, 5 Mar 1975, NSC Convenience Files, FORD.

34. U.S. Congress, House of Representatives, Extension of Remarks, Report of Representative Paul N. McCloskey Jr., "The North Vietnam-South Vietnam Confrontation," reprinted in *Congressional Record*, 94th Cong., 1st Sess., 121 (14 Mar 1975): 6775–79; Paul N. McCloskey Jr., "Report, Vietnam Fact-Finding Trip, February 24–March 3, 1975," 14 Mar 1975, Robert K. Wolthuis Files, FORD.

35. Cao Van Vien, *Final Collapse*, 76.

36. Ibid.

37. Nguyen Tien Hung and Schecter, *Palace File*, 322.

38. USDAO Saigon, Monthly Intelligence Summary and Threat Analysis, Jan 1975, Robert K. Wolthuis Files, Vietnam Fact Sheets, FORD.

39. Military History Institute, *Victory in Vietnam*, 364.

40. Lam Quang Thi, *Autopsy*, 143; Todd, *Cruel April*, 32.

41. Van Tien Dung, *Our Great Spring Victory*, 31–32.

42. Cao Van Vien, *Final Collapse*, 69; Le Gro, *From Cease-Fire to Capitulation*, 149.

43. Vo Nguyen Giap, *How We Won the War*, 49.

44. Cao Van Vien, *Final Collapse*, 77.

45. The description of this fateful meeting comes from Cao Van Vien, *Final Collapse*, 77–82.

46. Rowland Evans and Robert Novak, "Why the Vietnamese Collapsed," *Washington Post*, 5 Apr 1975.

47. Cao Van Vien also wrote: "I said something to the effect that this redeployment was indeed necessary, and I had embraced such an idea for a long time. But so far I had kept it to myself and considered it an improper proposal. First of all, it conflicted with the prevailing national policy, and second, if I had made such a suggestion, it could well have been interpreted as an indication of defeatism." *Final Collapse*, 78.

48. Ibid. Phillip Davidson draws an interesting comparison between Thieu and his generals and Hitler and his generals: both national leaders refused to surrender any ground, even when it made sense militarily; both were actively involved in the nuts and bolts of directing their armies; and both lived in constant fear of coup d'etat and assassination. Davidson notes that "the two men differed vastly in other ways, but their similarities in the military field were striking." *Vietnam at War*, 696–98.

49. Hosmer, Kellen, and Jenkins, *Fall of South Vietnam*, 84.

50. Ibid., 85; Cao Van Vien, *Final Collapse*, 75.

51. Quoted in Larry Engelmann, *Tears before the Rain: An Oral History of the Fall of South Vietnam* (New York: Da Capo, 1997), 302. In this comprehensive oral history, soldiers and civilians, both American and Vietnamese, describe their experiences in the spring of 1975 as the NVA carried out its final offensive against the Republic of Vietnam. The book provides the perspectives of a wide range of participants and observers, including soldiers, generals, ambassadors, journalists, children, doctors, and even those from the other side.

52. Cao Van Vien, *Final Collapse*, 86.

53. Dawson, *55 Days*, 58. According to Dawson, a UPI reporter who was in Vietnam in 1975 and reported on the fall of South Vietnam, Thieu told Phu to carry out the order or be replaced and jailed.

54. Colonel Ly assumed a subordinate role as head of the corps staff and logistical units. However, General Phu muddied the command and control arrangement by appointing Brig. Gen. Tran Van Cam, his assistant for operations, to oversee the withdrawal.

55. Quoted in Hosmer, Kellen, and Jenkins, *Fall of South Vietnam*, 188.

56. Gerald R. Ford, *A Time to Heal: The Autobiography of Gerald Ford* (New York: Harper & Row, 1979), 250–51.

57. Quoted in Engelmann, *Tears before the Rain*, 63.

58. Drew Middleton, "Saigon Defenses Now Are Stretched," *New York Times*, 20 Mar 1975.

59. Quoted in Engelmann, *Tears before the Rain*, 229.

60. Quoted in Hosmer, Kellen, and Jenkins, *Fall of South Vietnam*, 94.

61. Denis A. Warner, *Certain Victory: How Hanoi Won the War* (Kansas City, Mo.: Sneed, Andrews and McKeel, 1978), 60–61.

62. Quoted in Dougan and Fulghum, *Fall of the South*, 58.

63. Lam Quang Thi, *The Twenty-Five Year Century* (Denton: University of North Texas Press, 2001), 357. Thi was the deputy commander of I Corps. Rumors were also cited in Dawson, *55 Days*, 13, and Cao Van Vien, *Final Collapse*, 146.

64. Warner, *Certain Victory*, 71.

65. Quoted in Hosmer, Kellen, and Jenkins, *Fall of South Vietnam*, 95.

66. Military History Institute, *Victory in Vietnam*, 375–76.

67. Quoted in Dawson, *55 Days*, 77.

68. Quoted in Dougan and Fulghum, *Fall of the South*, 60.

69. Quoted in Hosmer, Kellen, and Jenkins, *Fall of South Vietnam*, 95.

70. Defense Attache Office, U.S. Embassy Saigon, RVNAF Final Assessment, 15 June 1975, 16–B–5.

71. Quoted in Hosmer, Kellen, and Jenkins, *Fall of South Vietnam*, 95–96.

72. Quoted in Isaacs, *Without Honor*, 342.

73. Quoted in Dougan and Fulghum, *Fall of the South*, 60.

74. Quoted in Hosmer, Kellen, and Jenkins, *Fall of South Vietnam*, 96.

75. Cao Van Vien, *Final Collapse*, 95.

76. Olson and Roberts, *Where the Last Domino Fell*, 259.

77. Hosmer, Kellen, and Jenkins, *Fall of South Vietnam*, 96.

78. Cao Van Vien, *Final Collapse*, 95.

79. Isaacs, *Without Honor*, 345.

80. Kinnard, *War Managers*, 86. Truong had previously commanded the 1st ARVN Division and had repeatedly demonstrated his leadership and tactical skills, particularly during the 1972 campaign to retake Quang Tri after he assumed command of I Corps.

81. Lam Quang Thi, *Autopsy*, 38–39. Some said that the 1st ARVN Division was the equal to any American division, which may have been an overstatement; however, the force was undoubtedly one of the better-led South Vietnamese divisions.

82. Cao Van Vien, *Final Collapse*, 98–99.

83. Defense Attache Office, Final Assessment, 1–8, FORD.

84. Lam Quang Thi, *Twenty-Five Year Century*, 347–48.

85. After the Communist occupation of Hue during the Tet offensive, 2,800 civilians were found buried in mass graves, many with their hands tied behind their backs, indicating that they had been executed. The best account of this massacre is found in Don Oberdorfer, *Tet!* (Garden City, N.Y.: Doubleday, 1971), 210–34.

86. Nguyen Tien Hung and Schecter, *Palace File*, 272. According to Hung and Schecter, Thieu had been advised by Vice President Tran Van Huong that "to hold Hue would be too costly. If you hold Hue, you will lose thirty thousand troops." Nevertheless, General Truong convinced Thieu that he could do it.

87. Thieu later made several ineffectual broadcasts on television and radio denying that any deal had been struck, but the damage had already been done. It was later revealed that the Communists had planted the rumors to spread fear and dissension among the South Vietnamese populace.

88. Nguyen Tien Hung and Schecter, *Palace File*, 272; Lam Quang Thi, *Twenty-Five Year Century*, 349.

89. Nguyen Tien Hung and Schecter, *Palace File*, 273.

90. Lam Quang Thi, *Twenty-Five Year Century*, 349.

91. Ibid., 350.

92. Nguyen Tien Hung and Schecter, *Palace File*, 273–74.

93. Lam Quang Thi, *Twenty-Five Year Century*, 349–50; Vien, *Final Collapse*, 104.

94. "The Anatomy of a Battle," *Time*, 14 Apr 1975, 16–17.

95. Quoted in Hosmer, Kellen, and Jenkins, *Fall of South Vietnam*, 109.

96. On the last day of the evacuation, five battalion commanders from the marine brigade, obviously distraught over the way things had gone, gathered on the beach, walked away from the crowd, said their final farewells to each other, and then committed suicide by shooting themselves.

97. Don Oberdorfer, "Danang Diary: From Threat to Panic to Collapse," *Washington Post*, 7 Apr 1975.

98. Bernard Weintraub, "Saigon's Forces Are in State of Shock after Decision to Quit Northern Area," *New York Times*, 27 Mar 1975.

99. Defense Attache Office, Final Assessment, 5–15, FORD.

100. Cao Van Vien, *Final Collapse*, 105.

101. Quoted in Hosmer, Kellen, and Jenkins, *Fall of South Vietnam*, 111.

102. Homer D. Smith, Major General, U.S. Army (Ret.), "The Final Forty-Five Days in Vietnam" (USACMH, 22 May 1975, unpublished paper), 6.

103. Momyer, *Vietnamese Air Force*, 76.

104. Broadcast quoted in Isaacs, *Without Honor*, 365.

105. Quoted in Hosmer, Kellen, and Jenkins, *Fall of South Vietnam*, 111. Gen. Tran Van Don reporting to Hosmer, Kellen, and Jenkins what General Truong later told him, said, "When he [Truong] came to find his people, his staff, he said nobody was there. He was alone" (111).

106. Cao Van Vien, *Final Collapse*, 108.

107. Warner, *Certain Victory*, 75.

108. Quoted in Hosmer, Kellen, and Jenkins, *Fall of South Vietnam*, 111, and Lam Quang Thi, *Autopsy*, 158–59.

109. An estimated two million civilian refugees were left stranded in MR I after the evacuation of Da Nang.

110. Isaacs, *Without Honor*, 363.

111. Quoted in Hosmer, Kellen, and Jenkins, *Fall of South Vietnam,* 112.

112. Le Gro, *From Cease-Fire to Capitulation,* 161–62.

113. Cao Van Vien, *Final Collapse,* 118.

114. Isaacs, *Without Honor,* 380.

115. Quoted in "Growing Gloom in a Shrunken Land," *Time,* 7 Apr 1975, 28–33.

116. Defense Attache Office, Final Assessment, 6–31.

117. Momyer, *Vietnamese Air Force,* 76.

118. Davidson, *Vietnam at War,* 706.

119. Quoted in Hosmer, Kellen, and Jenkins, *Fall of South Vietnam,* 114.

120. Isaacs, *Without Honor,* 361.

10. THE FALL OF SAIGON

1. Tran Van Tra, *Bulwark B-2 Theater,* 125.

2. Van Tien Dung, *Our Great Spring Victory,* 120–21.

3. Ibid.

4. Le Gro wrote that Dung had sixteen divisions in Military Region III (which included Saigon) (*From Cease-Fire to Capitulation,* 177). Cao Van Vien said that the NVA force surrounding Saigon included fifteen divisions, plus supporting units (*Final Collapse,* 129). Le Gro's number, including units not necessarily surrounding Saigon but nonetheless capable of being committed to the battle if needed, is probably more accurate. This number would increase when the NVA reserve divisions arrived in the Saigon area later in the month.

5. Van Tien Dung, *Our Great Spring Victory,* 155–56, 160.

6. Quoted in Hosmer, Kellen, and Jenkins, *Fall of South Vietnam,* 116.

7. Isaacs, *Without Honor,* 392.

8. "The Communists Tighten the Noose," *Time,* 21 Apr 1975, 14.

9. Senate Committee on Appropriations, *Hearings on Emergency Military Assistance and Economic and Humanitarian Aid to South Vietnam,* 94th Cong., 1st sess., 15 Apr 1975, 35–36.

10. John W. Finney, "Pullout of 5,000 to Leave 1,000 Americans in Saigon," *New York Times,* 16 Apr 1975.

11. The detailed and complex story of the U.S. evacuation, not covered in this book, was controversial. Tension existed between evacuating American citizens in a timely manner and sending a signal to the South Vietnamese that the United States had given up and was abandoning them entirely. Superimposed over this difficult situation was the obligation to do something about the South Vietnamese who had worked for the United States and would face severe consequences should the North Vietnamese prevail. Many observers and participants faulted Ambassador Martin for waiting too late to activate the evacuation. The story of this aspect of the fall of Saigon is fully discussed by Stuart A. Herrington, *Peace with Honor,* and Frank Snepp, *Decent Interval.*

12. Quoted in Herrington, *Peace with Honor,* 172.

13. Van Tien Dung, *Our Great Spring Victory,* 62.

14. Le Gro, *From Cease-Fire to Capitulation,* 172–73.

15. Army Division, Defense Attache Office, U.S. Embassy Saigon, "Army Division Final Report," vol. 9, 18 June 1975, USACMH.

16. Defense Attache Office, Final Assessment, 5–33 to 5–35, 5–50 to 5–51, USACMH; Le Gro, *From Cease-Fire to Capitulation,* 172–73.

17. Ford to Thieu, 22 Mar 1975, NSC Convenience Files, FORD.

18. Thieu to Ford, 22 Mar 1975, White House Central Files, FORD; Nguyen Tien Hung and Schecter, *Palace File*, 286–87.

19. Ford to Thieu, 25 Mar 1975, NSC Convenience Files, FORD.

20. Nguyen Tien Hung and Schecter, *Palace File*, 291.

21. Memorandum for the President from Weyand, 4 Apr 1975, NSC Convenience Files, FORD.

22. Nguyen Tien Hung and Schecter, *Palace File*, 300.

23. Memorandum for the President from Weyand, 4 Apr 1975, NSC Convenience Files, FORD.

24. House Committee on Appropriations, *Hearings on Emergency Supplemental Appropriations for Assistance to the Republic of South Vietnam for Fiscal Year 1975*, 94th Cong., 1st sess., 21 Apr 1975, 3.

25. Memorandum for the President from Weyand, 4 Apr 1975, NSC Convenience Files, FORD.

26. Memorandum, Kempton B. Jenkins to Jack Marsh, 2 Apr 1975, J. O. Marsh Files, FORD.

27. Memorandum, Wolthuis to Marsh, 2 Apr 1975, J. O. Marsh Files, FORD.

28. Le Gro, *From Cease-Fire to Capitulation*, 171.

29. Ford, *A Time to Heal*, 253.

30. Transcript, Kissinger Press Conference, 5 Apr 1975, Vernon Loen and Charles Leppert Files, FORD.

31. Ford, *Public Papers, 1975*, bk. 1, 420–21; Transcript of Press Conference, 3 Apr 1975, David Gergen Files, FORD.

32. "Seeking the Last Exit from Vietnam," *Time*, 21 Apr 1975, 8.

33. "Criticism of the Congress is Muted by Schlesinger," *New York Times*, 7 Apr 1975.

34. Anderson, "Gerald R. Ford and the Presidents' War in Vietnam," 196. The best account of the Nixon-Thieu letters is found in Nguyen Tien Hung and Schecter, *Palace File*. Altogether, there were twenty-seven letters from Nixon to Thieu and four from President Ford. On 21 April, Ford was interviewed on live television and radio by Eric Sevareid and Bob Schiefer about the situation in South Vietnam. When the president faulted Congress for not appropriating the requested military aid, he was asked about "secret agreements" between Nixon and President Thieu; he replied that "The personal correspondence between President Nixon and President Thieu corresponds with the public record." The transcript of this program can be found in the David Gergen Papers, 1974–77, General Subject File, FORD.

35. Address by President Gerald R. Ford to Joint Session, 10 Apr 1975, Loen and Leppert Files, Congressional Liaison Office, FORD, and Ford, *Public Papers, 1975*, bk. 1, 459–73.

36. Byrd's comments quoted in Memorandum from Kempton B. Jenkins to J. O. Marsh, John O. Marsh Files, FORD.

37. Abzug to Ford, 3 Apr 1975, Robert K. Wolthuis Files, FORD.

38. Transcript of Kissinger testimony before Committee on Appropriations, 21 April 1975, Nessen Papers, FORD.

39. *Baltimore Sun*, 16 Apr 1975.

40. House Committee on Appropriations, *Hearings on Emergency Supplemental Appropriations for Assistance to the Republic of South Vietnam for Fiscal Year 1975*, 94th Cong., 1st sess., 21 Apr 1975, 10. The idea that the administration was not serious in

attempting to obtain supplemental funding was a recurring theme in the media during this period. The *Baltimore Sun* reported on 12 April 1975 that in off-the-record conversations held with White House personnel on the day after Ford's speech to the joint session, the administration officials said that President Ford did not really believe that the supplemental bill would pass and also did not think that additional aid would make a difference in South Vietnam anyway. According to these sources, the president did not want to give Thieu the perception that the United States was turning its back on him, because he feared that the South Vietnamese might use the seven thousand American citizens still in Vietnam as hostages, either explicitly or implicitly, for continued aid. *Time* carried a similar story (21 April 1975). Although an examination of the available evidence in the Ford presidential papers reveals that the president and his advisers harbored no illusions about the chances for the passage of the supplemental aid bill, there is no documentation to support the *Sun*'s allegations.

41. *Congressional Record*, 94th Cong., 1st sess., 121 (22 Apr 1975): 11268.

42. "Fed Up and Turned Off," *Time*, 14 Apr 1975, 20.

43. Speech quoted in Isaacs, *Without Honor*, 414–15.

44. Van Tien Dung, *Our Great Spring Victory*, 82. Italian journalist Tiziano Terzani quotes Col. Con Man, editor of *Quan Doi Nhan Dan*, the North Vietnamese armed forces newspaper, on the incident:

> Nguyen Than Trung has been a Party member ever since he was a student. It was the Party that ordered him to join the Saigon air force and go to the United States where he obtained his pilot's license. Such a man was important for a crucial occasion, and for this reason Trung did not reveal himself and had never been used before. The bombing of Doc Lap Palace was a blow well worth the trouble. The air force was Thieu's trusted weapon, one of the foundations of his power. With the bombs of 8 April we wanted to destroy that trust, to spread suspicion within the air force itself. The attack succeeded magnificently. (*Giai Phong! The Fall and Liberation of Saigon* [New York: St. Martin's, 1976], 39)

45. Todd, *Cruel April*, 247.

46. Nguyen Tien Hung and Schecter, *Palace File*, 336; "Next, the Struggle for Saigon," *Time*, 28 Apr 1975, 13–14.

47. Todd, *Cruel April*, 255.

48. Van Tien Dung, *Our Great Spring Victory*, 167.

49. "Next, the Struggle for Saigon," *Time*, 28 Apr 1975, 13–14.

50. The importance of close air support was demonstrated in this battle. VNAF fighters, using cluster bombs, were instrumental in permitting the South Vietnamese defenders in Xuan Loc to hold out against superior numbers. In the absence of U.S. B-52s, VNAF used 15,000-pound "daisy cutter" bombs that were rolled out of the back of C-130 cargo planes. VNAF proved very effective until the NVA began to shell the air base at Bien Hoa, which severely curtailed air operations in support of the Xuan Loc defenders.

51. Message, Smith to CJCS, 13 Apr 1975, NSC Convenience Files, FORD.

52. Message, CINCPAC to JCS, 2 Apr 1975, President's Handwriting File, FORD.

53. Memorandum, Charles Leppert to John Marsh, 21 Apr 1975, J. O. Marsh Files, FORD.

54. Quoted in Dougan and Fulghum, *Fall of the South*, 131.

55. Le Gro, *From Cease-Fire to Capitulation*, 173. Although the VNAF had done an admirable job in the early phases of the battle for Xuan Loc, a large part of the NVA victory was due to its extremely accurate artillery fire on Bien Hoa Air Base; the fire degraded VNAF close air support by damaging six F-5A fighters and fourteen A-37 Dragonfly fighter-bombers and seriously curtailing air operations from the base. The South Vietnamese, already greatly outnumbered, were unable to hold their positions in the absence of effective close air support.

56. Hosmer, Kellen, and Jenkins, *Fall of South Vietnam*, 133; Todd, *Cruel April*, 298. Even in withdrawal, the 18th ARVN evacuated its forces in an orderly manner.

57. *Time*, "Vietnam: No More Arms," 28 Apr 1975, 10–11.

58. Letter in Nguyen Tien Hung and Schecter, *Palace File*, 320–21.

59. Ibid., 323.

60. Ford, *A Time to Heal*, 255.

61. Ibid.

62. Nguyen Tien Hung and Schecter, *Palace File*, 327.

63. Ibid., 326.

64. Lam Quang Thi, *Autopsy*, 187.

65. Dong Van Khuyen, *RVNAF*, 387.

66. Message, Martin to Kissinger, 18 Apr 1975, NSC Convenience Files, FORD.

67. Message, Kissinger to Martin, 18 Apr 1975, NSC Convenience Files, FORD.

68. Snepp, *Decent Interval*, 366–68.

69. Snepp wrote the report for CIA Station Chief Thomas Polgar. According to Snepp, Polgar told him to "Make it as bleak as you can" because the ambassador wanted to use it to convince Thieu to step down. Snepp wrote that he did not have to manufacture any intelligence because the truth was bad enough. *Decent Interval*, 382.

70. Account of the meeting from Nguyen Tien Hung and Schecter, *Palace File*, 330.

71. Ibid., 335–36; Todd, *Cruel April*, 293–94.

72. Cao Van Vien, *Final Collapse*, 143.

73. Snepp, *Decent Interval*, 324.

74. Nguyen Tien Hung and Schecter, *Palace File*, 331.

75. Ibid., 331–32.

76. Quoted in Isaacs, *Without Honor*, 422.

77. Ibid., 431–32.

78. *Washington Post*, 25 Apr 1975; Ron Nessen, *It Sure Looks Different from the Inside* (Chicago: Playboy Press, 1978), 108.

79. Message, Martin to Kissinger, 23 Apr 1975, NSC Convenience Files, FORD.

80. Van Tien Dung, *Our Great Spring Victory*, 209.

81. Ibid.

82. Ibid., 216–18.

83. Radio broadcast quoted in Terzani, *Giai Phong!*, 22.

84. Quoted in Isaacs, *Without Honor*, 439.

85. Ibid.

86. According to Isaacs and Terzani, the French ambassador, Jean-Marie Merillon, was a strong proponent of what became known as the "Minh solution" and tried to convince everyone he knew in the Saigon government that the elevation of Minh might save Saigon. *Without Honor*, 432–33, and *Giai Phong!*, 23–24, respectively.

87. Tran Van Don, *Our Endless War* (San Rafael, Calif.: Presidio Press, 1978), 253.

88. Terzani, *Giai Phong!*, 26. The Military History Institute reported that "six sapper regiments and four battalions and 11 teams of commandos" secretly deployed their forces into the city while 1,700 "cadre" were dispatched to the precincts of the inner city and the suburbs to prepare to launch a "mass uprising" in coordination with the main attack. *Victory in Vietnam*, 409.

89. Quoted in Isaacs, *Without Honor*, 440; Todd, *Cruel April*, 341.

90. Speech quoted in Isaacs, *Without Honor*, 442–43, Todd, *Cruel April*, 342–43, and Terzani, *Giai Phong!*, 41.

91. Terzani, *Giai Phong!*, 41.

92. In order to demonstrate to the North Vietnamese his sincerity, Minh later wrote to Ambassador Martin requesting the evacuation of all American personnel in the Defense Attache Office "within twenty-four hours beginning April 29, 1975, in order that the question of peace for Viet Nam can be settled early." Quoted in Nguyen Tien Hung and Schecter, *Palace File*, 478.

93. Defense Attache Office, Final Assessment, 16–E-14, USACMH.

94. Quoted in Todd, *Cruel April*, 343.

95. Van Tien Dung, *Our Great Spring Victory*, 109.

96. Brigadier General Tran Quang Khoi, "Fighting to the Finish," *Armor*, March-April 1996, 23.

97. "Preparing to Deal for Peace," *Time*, 5 May 1975, 12–14.

98. Quoted in Engelmann, *Tears Before the Rain*, 248.

99. Defense Attache Office, Final Assessment, 16–B-4; Colonel Harry G. Summers Jr., "Final Days of South Vietnam," *American History*, Apr 1995, 67. Two other marines died taking part in the evacuation when their helicopter crashed into the sea. They were Capt. William C. Nystul and 1st Lt. Michael J. Shea.

100. Momyer, *Vietnamese Air Force*, 79. Among the aircraft that reached U Tapao Air Base in Thailand were 26 F-5 fighters, 27 A-37 fighter-bombers, several gunships, and numerous transport planes.

101. Defense Attache Office, U.S. Embassy Saigon, Final Assessment.

102. Ford, *A Time to Heal*, 256; Snepp, *Decent Interval*, 292–99.

103. Summers, "Final Days of South Vietnam," 68. Another tragedy that also had similar symbolic implications to many was the 4 April crash of an Air Force C-5A transport loaded with 243 "Baby Lift" children and thirty-seven American women, mostly secretaries and staff from the U.S. Embassy. Schulzinger wrote: "Americans saw it all on television. For many of them the plane crash symbolized much of the horror and futility of the American involvement in Vietnam. Whatever their good intentions, the Americans had never comprehended Vietnamese culture or politics. Modern technology seemed mocked and defeated by Vietnamese tenacity." *A Time for War*, 322.

104. Terzani, *Giai Phong!*, 76.

105. Quoted in Isaacs, *Without Honor*, 467, and Terzani, *Giai Phong!*, 66–67. General Cao Van Vien, former chief of the Joint General Staff had departed with his family by airplane for the United States, without even bothering to turn in his resignation.

106. Terzani, *Giai Phong!*, 77.

107. Dawson, *55 Days*, 7–8; Terzani, *Giai Phong!*, 87.

108. Major Hoa's experiences were related in "The Final 10 Days," *Time*, 24 Apr 1995, 25–35.

109. Olson and Roberts, *Where the Last Domino Fell*, 263; Dougan and Fulghum, *Fall of the South*, 175.

CONCLUSION

1. Nixon, *Real War*, 106.

2. BDM Corporation, *A Study of Strategic Lessons Learned in Vietnam: Omnibus Executive Summary* (McLean, Va.: BDM Corp., April 1980), V-15. The BDM report was a massive, eight-volume study that focused on a myriad of areas, including U.S. foreign policy and Vietnam, U.S. domestic considerations that influenced war-making decisions, planning and conduct of the war, and operational and functional analyses.

3. Ibid.

4. Kinnard, *War Managers*, 156. In September of 1974, Kinnard, who had served in Vietnam, sent out an extensive questionnaire to the 173 army generals who had managed the war during the period from 1965 to 1972. A total of 67 percent of those surveyed responded. Kinnard then personally interviewed 20 of the respondents. *The War Managers* is a compilation and analysis of the surveys and subsequent interviews.

5. Hoff, *Nixon Reconsidered*, 167.

6. Kinnard, *War Managers*, 144–45. On the topic of Vietnamization, 58 percent of those surveyed agreed that the program was "soundly conceived," but 73 percent said that the program should have been "emphasized years before."

7. Clarke, *Advice and Support*, 498; Ngo Quang Truong, *RVNAF and U.S. Operational Cooperation and Coordination*, 163.

8. Nguyen Duy Hinh, *Vietnamization and the Cease-Fire*, 190.

9. After the war, former ARVN generals Cao Van Vien and Dong Van Khuyen stated: "From the beginning to the end, the Vietnam War had always been an insurgency war sustained by infiltration and supported by offensive attacks from North Vietnam. Because of its ultimate goal—overthrowing the RVN government—insurgency was the most important element of the war with mainforce units playing the supporting role. It was insurgent or subversive activities that affected the people's security and their attitude toward the government more than fierce battles fought in the DMZ or border areas." *Reflections on the Vietnam War*, 142. The best discussion of the early U.S. advisory effort is Ronald Spector's *Advice and Support: The Early Years, 1941–1960* (Washington, D.C.: U.S. Army Center of Military History, 1983).

10. Cao Van Vien, et al., *U.S. Adviser*, 186.

11. BDM Corporation, *Study of Strategic Lessons Learned*, 6:12-7.

12. Andrew F. Krepinevich Jr., *The Army and Vietnam* (Baltimore: Johns Hopkins University Press, 1986), 56–57. Harry C. Summers, a former U.S. Army colonel argues the opposite in *On Strategy: A Critical Analysis of the Vietnam War* (Novato, Calif.: Presidio Press, 1982). The heated debate between Krepinevich and Summers and their respective supporters continues, both in academic circles, as well as within the U.S. military establishment.

13. Krepinevich, *The Army and Vietnam*, 164–68. Krepinevich, writing that many in the U.S. military hierarchy did not see anything particularly special about the requirements of counterinsurgency, quoted Gen. George H. Decker, army chief of staff from 1960 to 1962: "Any good soldier can handle guerrillas" (37). Not all Americans agreed with trying to build

the South Vietnamese armed forces as a mirror image of their American counterparts. Edward G. Lansdale, noted counterinsurgency expert, advocated small, highly mobile South Vietnamese units who could fight on the same level with the guerrillas. He was joined by a number of South Vietnamese officers such as former colonel Nguyen Huy Loi, a veteran staff officer with the Joint General Staff, who prepared a study calling for the establishment of the type of forces advocated by Lansdale. The recommendations of those like Lansdale and Loi fell largely on deaf ears. Lansdale wrote of his experiences in Vietnam in *In the Midst of Wars: An American Mission to South East Asia* (New York: Harper & Row, 1972).

14. Kolko, *Anatomy of a War,* 378, 380.

15. Kinnard, *War Managers,* 88.

16. Ngo Quang Truong, *RVNAF and U.S. Operational Cooperation and Coordination,* 166.

17. Bui Diem, "Commentary," in Peter Braestrup, ed., *Vietnam as History: Ten Years After the Paris Peace Accords* (Washington, D.C.: University Press of America, 1984), 62.

18. Hoang Ngoc Lung, *Strategy and Tactics,* 135.

19. Hosmer, Kellen, and Jenkins, *Fall of South Vietnam,* 30.

20. Davidson, *Vietnam at War,* 477.

21. Hosmer, Kellen, and Jenkins, *Fall of South Vietnam,* 29.

22. Quoted in Paul Hendrickson, *The Living and the Dead: Robert McNamara and Five Lives of a Lost War* (New York: Knopf, 1996), 330.

23. Ngo Quang Truong, *RVNAF and U.S. Operational Cooperation and Coordination,* 163.

24. Kinnard, *War Managers,* 91.

25. General Melvin Zais, Senior Officer Debriefing Program, interview by Cols. William L. Golden and Richard C. Rice, 1977, USAMHI.

26. Douglas S. Blaufarb, *The Counter-Insurgency Era: U.S. Doctrine and Performance, 1950 to the Present* (New York: Free Press, 1977), 304–5.

27. Ibid., 302–5.

28. Nguyen Duy Hinh, *Lam Son 719,* 151.

29. Lam Quang Thi, *Autopsy,* 187.

30. Hoang Ngoc Lung, *Strategy and Tactics,* 136.

31. Davidson, *Vietnam at War,* 711.

32. Hosmer, Kellen, and Jenkins, *Fall of South Vietnam,* 30–31.

33. Ibid., 57–58.

34. Robert W. Komer, *Bureaucracy Does Its Thing: Institutional Constraints on U.S.-GVN Performance in Vietnam* (Santa Monica, Calif.: Rand Corp., 1972), 124.

35. Thomas N. Bibby, "Vietnam: The End, 1975" (U.S. Marine Corps Command and Staff College, Quantico, Virginia, April 1985, unpublished paper), 80.

36. Isaacs, *Without Honor,* 502.

37. Quoted in Col. Harry Summers, *On Strategy: A Critical Analysis of the Vietnam War* (Novato, Calif.: Presidio Press, 1982), 176.

38. Isaacs, *Without Honor,* 502.

39. Army Division, Defense Attache Office, U.S. Embassy Saigon, "Army Division Final Report," executive summary, 18 June 1975, 17, USACMH.

40. Kolko, *Anatomy of a War,* 379.

41. Cao Van Vien and Dong Van Khuyen, *Reflections on the Vietnam War,* 134.

42. For details of America's early days in Vietnam, see Lansdale, *In the Midst of Wars.*

43. Cao Van Vien and Dong Van Khuyen, *Reflections on the Vietnam War,* 135.

44. Kinnard, *War Managers,* 92.

45. Quotation of T. E. Lawrence, by Col. E. F. Pelosky, USA Chief Army Division, in Defense Attache Office, U.S. Embassy Saigon, "Army Division Final Report," executive summary, 18 June 1975, USACMH. The attribution to Lawrence is questionable because the quote does not describe his relationship and experience with the Arabs during World War I; nevertheless, the words certainly apply to the situation in South Vietnam and U.S. efforts to prepare the South Vietnamese to defend themselves.

Bibliography

Because this book was drawn from a myriad of primary and secondary sources, I have chosen to divide the bibliography into several sections. The first section includes papers and document collections; the second contains public documents; the third includes official publications; the fourth includes North Vietnamese and Viet Cong sources; the fifth contains unpublished primary source material (including after-action reports, senior officer debriefing reports, and other associated material); and the sixth includes memoirs, autobiographies, and biographies. The last two sections include books and periodicals.

PAPERS AND DOCUMENT COLLECTIONS

Abrams, Creighton W., General, U.S. Army. Papers. U.S. Army Center of Military History, Washington, D.C.

Bunker, Ellsworth. *The Bunker Papers: Reports to the President from Vietnam, 1967–1973*. 3 vols. Edited by Douglas Pike. Berkeley: Institute of East Asian Studies, University of California, 1990.

Clifford, Clark. Papers. Lyndon Baines Johnson Presidential Library, Austin, Texas.

Collins, Arthur S., Jr., Lieutenant General, U.S. Army (Ret.). Papers. U.S. Army Military History Institute, Carlisle Barracks, Penn.

Cooksey, Howard H., Lieutenant General, U.S. Army (Ret.). Papers. U.S. Army Military History Institute, Carlisle Barracks, Penn.

Corcoran, Charles A., Lieutenant General, U.S. Army (Ret.). Papers. U.S. Army Military History Institute, Carlisle Barracks, Penn.

DepCORDS (MACV Deputy for Civil Operations and Revolutionary Development Support) and Pacification Files. U.S. Army Center of Military History, Washington, D.C.

Ford, Gerald R. Presidential Papers. Gerald R. Ford Presidential Library, Ann Arbor, Mich.

———. *Public Papers of the Presidents of the United States: Gerald R. Ford*. 6 Books. Washington, D.C.: GPO, 1973–75.

Gettys, Charles M., Lieutenant General, U.S. Army (Ret.). Papers. U.S. Army Military History Institute, Carlisle Barracks, Penn.

Goodpaster, Andrew J., General, U.S. Army (Ret.). Papers. U.S. Army Military History Institute, Carlisle Barracks, Penn.

The History of the Vietnam War. Ann Arbor, Michigan: University Microfilms International, 1991. Microfiche.

Johnson, Lyndon B. *Public Papers of the Presidents of the United States: Lyndon B. Johnson, 1968–69.* Book 1. Washington, D.C.: GPO, 1970.

Kroesen, Frederick J., General, U.S. Army (Ret.). Papers. U.S. Army Military History Institute, Carlisle Barracks, Penn.

Laird, Melvin R. Papers. National Archives and Records Administration. College Park, Md.

McCaffrey, William J., General, U.S. Army (Ret.). Papers. U.S. Army Center of Military History, Washington, D.C.

Montague, Robert M. Papers. U.S. Army Military History Institute, Carlisle Barracks, Penn.

Nixon, Richard M. Presidential Papers. Nixon Presidential Materials Project, National Archives and Records Administration, College Park, Md..

——. Pre-Presidential and Post-Presidential Papers. The Richard Nixon Library and Birthplace, Yorba Linda, Calif.

——. *Public Papers of the Presidents of the United States: Richard M. Nixon.* 6 vols. Washington, D.C.: GPO, 1971–75.

Pike, Douglas. Indochina Collection. Texas Tech University Archive of the Vietnam Conflict, Lubbock, Tex.

Public Statements by the Secretaries of Defense. Edited by Paul Kesaris. Frederick, Md.: University Publications of America, 1983. Microfilm.

Records of the Military Assistance Command Vietnam. Pt. 1, *The War in Vietnam, 1954–1973.* Edited by Robert Lester. MACV Historical Office Documentary Collection. Bethesda, Md.: University Publications of America, 1988. Microfilm.

Rosson, William B., General, U.S. Army (Ret.). Papers. U.S. Army Military History Institute, Carlisle Barracks, Penn.

Southeast Asia Branch Files, U.S. Army Center of Military History, Washington, D.C.

Sutherland, James W., Jr., Lieutenant General, U.S. Army (Ret.). Papers. U.S. Army Military History Institute, Carlisle Barracks, Penn.

Thayer, Thomas C. Papers. U.S. Army Center of Military History, Washington, D.C.

U.S. Armed Forces in Vietnam. Edited by Paul Kesaris. Frederick, Md.: University Publications of America, 1983. Microfilm.

U.S. Army Build-up and Activities in South Vietnam, 1965–1972. Edited by Robert Lester. Bethesda, Md.: University Publications of America, 1989. Microfilm.

Vann, John Paul. Papers. U.S. Army Military History Institute, Carlisle Barracks, Penn.

Westmoreland, William C., General, U.S. Army (Ret.). Papers. U.S. Army Center of Military History, Washington, D.C.

Woodward, Gilbert H. Papers. U.S. Army Military History Institute, Carlisle Barracks, Penn.

PUBLIC DOCUMENTS

Nixon, Richard M. *U.S. Foreign Policy for the 1970s: A Report to Congress.* Washington, D.C.: GPO, 25 February 1971.

State of Vietnam, Ministry of National Defense. "Memorandum: Principles Authorizing TRIM Advisers with Units and Formations of the Vietnamese National Armed Forces." Saigon, 10 April 1955.

State of Vietnam, Office of the Deputy Prime Minister in Charge of Economic Development, "American Aid and Vietnam Economy." Saigon, March 1975.

U.S. Congress. *Congressional Record.* 1970–75. Washington, D.C.

U.S. Congress. *Vietnam: A Changing Crucible—Report of a Study Mission to South Vietnam.* 93rd Cong., 2nd sess., 1974.

———. Committee on Appropriations. *Hearings on Defense Appropriation for 1975.* 93rd Cong., 2nd sess., Part 1, 9 January, 13 and 26–28 February, 5–6 March 1974.

———. Committee on Appropriations. *Hearings on Aid to Vietnam and Cambodia.* 94th Cong., 1st sess., 3 February 1975.

———. Committee on Appropriations. *Hearings on Department of Defense Appropriations— Bombing of North Vietnam.* 93rd Cong., 1st sess., 9, 17, and 18 January 1973.

———. Committee on Appropriations. *Hearings on Department of Defense Appropriations—Oversight of Fiscal Year 1975 Military Assistance to Vietnam.* 94th Cong., 1st sess., 30 January and 3 February 1975.

———. Committee on Appropriations. *Hearings on Emergency Supplemental Appropriations for Assistance to the Republic of South Vietnam for Fiscal Year 1975.* 94th Cong., 1st sess., 21 April 1975.

———. Committee on Appropriations. *Hearings before Subcommittees of the Committee on Appropriations: Supplemental Appropriation Bill, 1971.* 91st Cong., 2nd sess., 1970.

———. Committee on Appropriations. Subcommittee on Department of Defense. *Hearings on Department of Defense Appropriations for 1971.* Part 1. 91st Cong., 2nd sess., 1970.

———. Committee on Armed Services. *Hearings on Military Posture.* Part 1. 91st Cong., 2nd sess., 1970.

———. Committee on Foreign Affairs. *Hearings on Fiscal Year 1975 Foreign Assistance Request.* 93rd Cong., 2nd sess., 4–5, 11–13, 18–20, 26 June and 1–2, 10–11 July 1974.

———. Committee on Foreign Affairs. *Staff Report on U.S. Aid to Indochina.* 93rd Cong., 2nd sess., 25 July 1974.

———. Committee on Government Operations. *Hearings before Subcommittee on Foreign Operations and Government Information—U.S. Assistance Programs in Vietnam.* 92nd Cong., 1st sess., 15–21 July and 21 August 1971.

———. Extension of Remarks. Report of Representative Paul N. McCloskey Jr. "The North Vietnam-South Vietnam Confrontation." Reprinted in *Congressional Record,* 94th Cong., 1st sess., 14 March 1975, 6775–79.

———. Special Subcommittee on National Defense Posture. *Review of the Vietnam Conflict and Its Impact on U.S. Military Commitments Abroad.* 90th Cong., 2nd Sess., 1968.

———. Subcommittee on Asian and Pacific Affairs. *Hearings on the Situation in Southeast Asia.* 93rd Cong., 2nd sess., 3 February 1974.

U.S. Congress. Senate. Committee on Appropriations. *Hearings on Emergency Military Assistance and Economic and Humanitarian Aid to South Vietnam.* 94th Cong., 1st sess., 15 April 1975.

———. Committee on Appropriations. *Hearings on Foreign Assistance and Related Programs Appropriation FY1975.* 93rd Cong., 2nd sess., 25 February, 6, 11, 25 March, 7, 24, 28 May, 13–14, 17–19, 25 June 1974.

———. Committee on Armed Services. *Hearings on Bombings in Cambodia.* 93rd Cong., 1st sess., 1972.

———. Committee on Armed Services. *Hearings on the Causes, Origins and Lessons of the Vietnam War.* 92nd Cong., 2nd sess., 9–12 May 1972.

——. Committee on Armed Services. *Hearings on Vietnam: Policy and Prospects.* 91st Cong., 2nd sess., 1972.

——. Committee on Armed Services. *Report of Senator Sam Nunn: Vietnam Aid—The Painful Options.* 94th Cong., 1st sess., 12 February 1975.

——. Committee on Armed Services. *Staff Report, Vietnam 1972.* 92nd Cong., 2nd sess., 1972.

——. Committee on Foreign Relations. *Background Information Relating to Southeast Asia and Vietnam.* 7th rev. ed. 1974.

——. Committee on Foreign Relations. *Hearings on Foreign Assistance Authorization.* 93rd Cong., 2nd sess., 7, 21, 26 June, 24–25 July 1974.

——. Committee on Foreign Relations. *Hearings on Vietnam: Policy and Prospects, 1970: Civil Operations and Rural Development Support (CORDS) Program.* 91st Cong., 2nd sess., 17–20 March, 3–4, 17, 19 May 1970.

——. Committee on Foreign Relations. *Report: Cambodia: May 1970.* Prepared by Richard Moose and James Lowenstein. 91st Cong., 2nd sess., 1970.

——. Committee on Foreign Relations. *Report: Laos, April 1971.* Prepared by Pat Holt and Richard Moose. 92nd Cong., 1st sess., 1971.

——. Committee on Foreign Relations. *Staff Report: Vietnam, May 1974.* 93rd Cong., 2nd sess., 5 August 1974.

U.S. Department of State. Bulletins. 1967–73. Washington, D.C.: GPO.

——. *United States Treaties and Other International Agreements.* Washington, D.C.: GPO, 1974.

U.S. Embassy, Saigon. "COSVN Resolution No. 14 (October 30, 1969)." Vietnam Documents and Research Notes No. 81. July 1970.

——. "Central Office for South Vietnam." Vietnam Documents and Research Notes No. 96. July 1971.

——. "A Preliminary Report on Activities during the 1969 Autumn Campaign." Vietnam Documents and Research Notes No. 82. July 1970.

U.S. National Security Council. *National Security Council Study Memorandum No. 1*, 14 March 1969.

——. *National Security Council Study Memorandum No. 36*, 10 April 1969.

——. *Vietnam Documents*, No. 113, June 1973.

OFFICIAL PUBLICATIONS

Berger, C., J. S. Ballard, and R. L. Bowers. *The United States Air Force in Southeast Asia: 1961–1973.* Washington, D.C.: Office of Air Force History, 1977.

Clarke, Jeffrey J. *Advice and Support: The Final Years.* Washington, D.C.: U.S. Army Center of Military History, 1988.

Collins, James Lawton, Jr. *The Development and Training of the South Vietnamese Army, 1950–1972.* Washington, D.C.: GPO, 1975.

Dillard, Walter S. *Sixty Days to Peace: Implementing the Paris Peace Accords, Vietnam 1973.* Washington, D.C.: National Defense University, 1982.

Directorate of Operations Analysis, Headquarters Pacific Air Forces. *Contemporary Historical Examination of Current Operations (CHECO) Report—Kontum: Battle for the Central Highlands: 30 March–10 June 1972.* Honolulu, n.d.

——. *Contemporary Historical Examination of Current Operations (CHECO) Report—LAM SON 719, 30 January–24 March '71, The South Vietnamese Incursion into Laos.* Honolulu, 24 March 1971, 123.

——. *Contemporary Historical Examination of Current Operations (CHECO) Report—The Battle for An Loc, 5 April—26 June 1972.* Honolulu, n.d.

——. *Contemporary Historical Examination of Current Operations (CHECO) Report—The 1972 Invasion of Military Region I: Fall of Quang Tri and Defense of Hue.* Honolulu, 15 March 1973.

——. *Contemporary Historical Examination of Current Operations (CHECO) Report—U.S. Air Deployments in Response to the NVA 1972 Offensive.* Honolulu, March 1973.

Frizzell, Donaldson D., Colonel, and Col. Ray L. Bowers, eds. *Airpower and the 1972 Spring Invasion.* U.S. Air Force Southeast Asia Monograph Series. Vol. 2. Maxwell Air Force Base, Ala.: Air Command and Staff College, 1976.

Hammond, William J. *Public Affairs: The Military and the Media, 1968–1973.* Washington, D.C.: U.S. Army Center of Military History, 1996.

Head, William. *War from Above the Clouds: B-52 Operations during the Second Indochina War and the Effects of the Air War on Theory and Doctrine.* Maxwell Air Force Base, Ala.: Air University Press, July 2002.

Historical Division, Joint Secretariat, U.S. Joint Chiefs of Staff. *The Joint Chiefs of Staff and the War in Vietnam, 1969–1970.* Washington, D.C.: GPO, 1976.

Le Gro, William E. *Vietnam from Cease-Fire to Capitulation.* Washington, D.C.: U.S. Army Center of Military History, 1981.

McCarthy, James R., and George B. Allison. *Linebacker II: A View from the Rock.* U.S. Air Force Southeast Asia Monograph Series 6. Maxwell Air Force Base, Ala.: Air War College, 1979.

Momyer, William W. *The Vietnamese Air Force, 1951—1975, an Analysis of Its Role in Combat.* U.S. Air Force Southeast Asia Monograph Series 3. Washington, D.C.: GPO, 1975.

Mrozek, Donald J. *Air Power and the Ground War in Vietnam: Ideas and Actions.* Maxwell Air Force Base, Ala.: Air University Press, 1988.

Ott, David Ewing. *Vietnam Studies: Field Artillery, 1954–1973.* Washington, D.C.: Department of the Army, 1975.

Scoville, Thomas W. *Reorganizing for Pacification Support.* Washington, D.C.: U.S. Army Center of Military History, 1982.

Spector, Ronald. *Advice and Support: The Early Years, 1941–1960.* Washington, D.C.: U.S. Army Center of Military History, 1983.

Tobin, Thomas G., Arthur E. Laehr, and John F. Hilgenberg. *Last Flight from Saigon.* U.S. Air Force Southeast Asia Monograph Series 4. Maxwell Air Force Base, Ala.: Air Command and Staff College, 1979.

Tolson, John J. *Vietnam Studies: Air Mobility, 1961–1971.* Washington, D.C.: U.S. Department of the Army, 1973.

Trask, Roger R. *The Secretaries of Defense: A Brief History, 1947–1985.* Washington, D.C.: Historical Office, Office of the Secretary of Defense, 1985.

Webb, Willard J. *The Joint Chiefs of Staff and the War in Vietnam, 1971–1973.* Washington, D.C.: GPO, 1979.

NORTH VIETNAMESE/VIET CONG SOURCES

Bui Tin. *Following Ho Chi Minh: The Memoirs of a North Vietnamese Colonel*. Honolulu: University of Hawaii Press, 1995.

——. *From Enemy to Friend*. Annapolis, Md.: Naval Institute Press, 2002.

Chien Dich Tien Cong Nguyen Hue (1972) [The Nguyen Hue Offensive Campaign (1972)]. Hanoi: Vietnam Institute for Military History, Ministry of Defense, 1988.

Hoang Van Thai. *History of the People's Army*. Vol. 2. Hanoi: People's Army Publishing House, 1994.

——. *The Decisive Years: Memoirs of Senior General Hoang Van Thai*. Washington, D.C., Joint Publications Research Service Report JSPS-SEA-87–084, 23 June 1987.

Hoang Van Thai, General. *How South Vietnam Was Liberated*. Hanoi: Gioi Publishers, 1992.

Le Duan. *Letters to the South*. Hanoi: Su That Publishing House, 1985.

Lich Su Quan Doi Nhan Dan Viet Nam [History of the People's Army of Vietnam]. Hanoi: People's Army Publishing House, 1990.

Military History Institute of Vietnam. *Report to General Vo Nguyen Giap, A Consoli-dated Report on the Fight Against the United States for the Salvation of Vietnam by Our People*. Translated by Duong Bui. Hanoi: Military History Institute of Vietnam, 1987.

——. *Victory in Vietnam: The Official History of the People's Army of Vietnam, 1954–1975*. Translated by Merle L. Pribbenow. Lawrence: University Press of Kansas, 2002.

Mot So Tran Danh Cua Bo Doi Thiet Gap, Tap IV [A Number of Battles Fought by Our Armor Troops, Volume 4]. Hanoi: Armor Command, General Staff Printing Plant, 1983.

Nguyen Huu An, Colonel General, and Nguyen Tu Duong. *Chien Truong Moi: Hoi Uc* [New Battlefield: A Memoir]. Hanoi: People's Army Publishing House, 2002.

Su Doan 9 [9th Division]. Hanoi: People's Army Publishing House, 1990. Translated by Foreign Broadcast Information Service. FBIS, October 1995.

Tran Van Don. *Our Endless War*. San Rafael, Calif.: Presidio Press, 1978.

Tran Van Tra. *Vietnam: History of the Bulwark B2 Theater*. Vol. 5, *Concluding the 30–Year War*. Southeast Asia Report 1247. Ho Chi Minh City: Van Nghe Publishing, 1982.

Truong Nhu Tang. *A Vietcong Memoir—An Insider Account of the Vietnam War and Its Aftermath*. New York: Harcourt Brace Jovanovich, 1985.

Van Tien Dung. *Our Great Spring Victory: An Account of the Liberation of South Vietnam*. New York: Monthly Review Press, 1977.

Vo Nguyen Giap. *How We Won the War*. Philadelphia: Recon Press, 1976.

——. *People's War, People's Army*. New York: Praeger, 1968.

Xuan Thieu. *North of the Hai Van Pass, 1975*. Hanoi: People's Army Publishing House, 1977.

UNPUBLISHED PRIMARY SOURCE MATERIAL

Army Division, Defense Attache Office, U.S. Embassy Saigon. "Army Division Final Report." 18 June 1975.

Battreall, Raymond R., Colonel. Interview by Major Walter Scott Dillard. 14 January 1973. Military History Branch, United States Military Assistance Command, Vietnam.

Collins, Arthur S. Lieutenant General, U.S. Army (Ret.). Senior Officer Debriefing Program. 1981. U.S. Army Military History Institute, Carlisle Barracks, Penn.

Conn, Jack, Colonel. Senior Officer Debriefing Program. February 1973. U.S. Army Military History Institute, Saigon.

Cooksey, Howard, Lieutenant General, U.S. Army (Ret.). Senior Officer Debriefing Program. 1981. U.S. Army Military History Institute, Carlisle Barracks, Penn.

Corcoran, Charles A., Lieutenant General, U.S. Army (Ret.). Senior Officer Debriefing Program. 11 April 1975. U.S. Army Military History Institute, Carlisle Barracks, Penn.

Davidson, Michael R., General, U.S. Army (Ret.). Senior Officer Debriefing Program. 20 February 1976. U.S. Army Military History Institute, Carlisle Barracks, Penn.

Defense Attache Office. U.S. Embassy Saigon. RVNAF Final Assessment. 15 June 1975.

——. RVNAF Quarterly Assessments. July 1973 through February 1975.

——. Special Studies Section. "Survey of the Economic Situation of RVNAF Personnel," by Anthony B. Lawson. 1974.

Dolvin, W. G., Lieutenant General. Senior Officer Debriefing Report. 15 December 1972.

Evans, John C., Colonel. Senior Officer Debriefing Report. 21 February 1973. Third Regional Assistance Command.

Ewell, Julian. "Impressions of a Field Force Commander in Vietnam." Unpublished paper, U.S. Army Center of Military History, Washington, D.C., 15 April 1970.

Fifth Division Combat Assistance Team, Headquarters, Advisory Team 70. "After-Action Report, Binh Long Campaign, 1972." October 1972.

Ginger, Walter D., Lieutenant Colonel. Headquarters, Advisory Team 87. "After-Action Report, Task Force 52." May 1972.

Haney, Raymond, Major, Adviser, Task Force 52. Interview by Major John Cash, Military Assistance Command, Vietnam, SJS-History. 19 April 1972. 3rd Field Hospital.

Headquarters, Airborne Division Advisory Detachment, "Combat Operation After Action Report, Toan Thang 43." 11 July 1970.

Headquarters, Delta Regional Assistance Command. "Senior Officer Debriefing Report— Colonel William E. Davis, Senior Advisor, 7th Division (ARVN)," 28 January 1973.

Headquarters, 11th Armored Cavalry Regiment. "After-Action Report, Operation Dong Tien II and Toan Thang 43, December 9, 1970." 1971.

——. "Operational Report, Lessons Learned, for Period Ending 31 July 1970."

Headquarters, 1st Airborne Brigade, Combat Assistance Team. "Combat After-Action Report, 1st Airborne Brigade." July 1972.

Headquarters, 1st Cavalry Division Airmobile. "Combat Operation After-Action Report." 11 July 1970.

——. "Operational Report, Lessons Learned, for Period Ending July 31, 1970." N.d.

Headquarters, First Regional Assistance Command. "After Action Report—Battle of Quang Tri." N.d.

Headquarters, MACV Advisory Team 155, 3rd Infantry Division (ARVN), "Senior Advisor's Debriefing Report." 27 January 1973.

——. Letter to First Regional Assistance Command, sub: Implications of the Reduction in Strength of Advisory Team 155. 13 November 1972.

Headquarters, 101st Airborne Division (Airmobile). "After Action Report Lam Son 719." 1 May 1971.

Headquarters, Second Regional Assistance Command. "After Action Report, 10 November 1972–28 March 1973." 24 March 1973.

Headquarters, Third Regional Assistance Command. "Debriefing Reports of Advisers Returning from An Loc." June 1972.

Headquarters, Third Regional Assistance Command. "Senior Officer Debriefing Report of COL W. F. Ulmer, Jr., Senior Advisor to 5th ARVN Infantry Divsion (RCS CSFOR-74)." 10 January 1973.

Headquarters, Third Regional Assistance Command. "Tactical Operations Center Duty Logs," April-June, 1972.

Headquarters, 21st Infantry Division (ARVN). "After-Action Report, Binh Long Campaign, 1972." 1972.

Headquarters, XXIV Corps. "Combat Operations After Action Report, Operation LAMSON 719." 14 May 1971.

——. "Assessment of Result of Lam Son 719." 31 March 1971.

——. "Operations Order, LAMSON 719." 23 January 1971.

Headquarters, U.S. Army Advisory Group, III Corps. "After Action Report: TOAN TANG 42," 24 July 1970.

Headquarters, United States Military Assistance Command, Vietnam. "Capability Study of U.S. and ARVN Infantry Battalions." MACEVAL Study No. 2–68. 1968.

——. "Command History, 1969." 3 vols. 1969.

——. "Command History, 1970." 4 vols. 1970.

——. "Command History, 1971." 2 vols. 1971.

——. "Command History Supplement, 1971." April 1972.

——. "Command History, 1972–1973." 2 vols. June 1973.

——. "Daily Operational Summary Reports to Joint Chiefs of Staff, March, April, May 1972." 1972.

——. MACV Command Briefing, "The Changing Nature of the War." 1972.

——. "One War: MACV Command Overview, 1968–1972." N.d.

——. "Periodic Intelligence Report (PERINTREP)—April 1972." 1972.

——. "Periodic Intelligence Report (PERINTREP)—Feb 1972." 1972.

——. "Special Intelligence Report (Declassified): The Nguyen Hue Offensive—Historical Study of Lessons Learned." January 1973.

——. "Vietnamization, Lessons Learned No. 76," 22 November 1969.

——. Army Advisory Group. "Sustaining US Advisory Support—ARVN Division." 16 November 1972.

——. Civil Operations for Rural Development Support (CORDS). "Operational Report for Period 30 Mar 1972 to 1 May 1972," 15 May 1972.

Hemingway, John, Brigadier General, U.S. Army. Senior Officer Debriefing Program. 30 July 1971. U.S. Army Military History Institute, Carlisle Barracks, Penn.

Hill, John, Major General, U.S. Army. Interview by Major Michael Dunn and Robert Nixon. Tape recording. 31 January and 1 February 1986. Combat Studies Institute, Fort Leavenworth, Kans.

Hollingsworth, James F., Major General. "Communist Invasion in Military Region III." Unpublished narrative, 1972. In Records of the Military Assistance Command Vietnam, pt. 1, The War in Vietnam, 1954–1973, edited by Robert Lester, MACV Historical Office Documentary Collection, reel 44, frames 1004–1037. Bethesda, Md.: University Publications of America, 1988. Microfilm.

——. Message to General Creighton Abrams. "CG's Back Channels Communication: Daily Commander's Evaluation." 7 February 1972–31 May 1972; 1 June 1972–20

August 1972. In *Records of the Military Assistance Command Vietnam*, pt. 1, *The War in Vietnam, 1954–1973*, edited by Robert Lester, MACV Historical Office Documentary Collection, reel 44, frames 0392–0655; 0656–0871, respectively. Bethesda, Md.: University Publications of America, 1988. Microfilm.

Kessler, Melvin M. Letter to Dr. Jeffrey C. Clark, 25 February 1975. Army Center of Military History, Washington, D.C.

Kroesen, Frederick J., General, U.S. Army (Ret.). Senior Officer Debriefing Program. 1987. U.S. Army Military History Institute, Carlisle Barracks, Penn.

Lawson, Anthony B. *See* Defense Attache Office. U.S. Embassy Saigon. Special Studies Section.

Lehman, Wolfgang J. Senior Officer Debriefing Program. 1982. U.S. Army Military History Institute, Carlisle Barracks, Penn.

Logan, Laddie B., Lieutenant Colonel. Senior Officer Debriefing Report. 7 February 1972.

MacKinnon, Robert N., Major General. Senior Officer Debriefing Report. 1 July 1972. Saigon.

McClellan, Stan L., Major General. "Vietnamization—A Point of View." Unpublished paper, n.d.

McCoid, C. B., Colonel. Senior Adviser's Debriefing Report. 16 February 1973.

McGiffert, John R., Brigadier General, Deputy Commanding General, Third Regional Assistance Command. Interview by Major Walter S. Dillard, Military Assistance Command, Vietnam, SJS-History. 10 October 1972. USACMH.

Miller, William H., Colonel, U.S. Army (Ret.). Letters to author, 17 March 1993–18 May 1994.

Peers, William R. Senior Officer Debriefing Report. 23 June 1969. U.S. Army Center of Military History, Washington, D.C.

Pence, Arthur, Colonel, U.S. Army. Vietnam Series interview by 1st Lt. Thomas Tulenko. 6 May 1971. U.S. Army Center of Military History, Washington, D.C.

Rosson, William B., Lieutenant General. Senior Officer Debriefing Report. 1968. USAMHI.

"RVNAF Improvement and Modernization and Management System Report." 4th Qtr., 1969. 1970.

"RVNAF Improvement and Modernization Progress Report." 24 April 1970.

Smith, Homer D., Major General, U.S. Army (Ret.). Memorandum for General Kerwin, sub: "What Happened to the RVNAF." 11 August 1975.

——. Senior Officer Debriefing Program. 1982. U.S. Army Military History Institute, Carlisle Barracks, Penn.

——. "The Final Forty-Five Days in Vietnam." Unpublished paper, U.S. Army Center of Military History, Washington, D.C., 22 May 1975.

——. "They Did Not Lose Their Will to Fight." Unpublished paper, U.S. Army Center of Military History, Washington, D.C., 15 July 1975.

Smith, Mark A., Captain. "Battle of Loc Ninh, RVN, 5–7 April 1972." Unpublished narrative, Fort Bragg, N.C., 21 October 1976.

Summers, Harry G., Colonel, U.S. Army. Senior Officer Debriefing Program. 1982. U.S. Army Military History Institute, Carlisle Barracks, Penn.

Sutherland, James, Lieutenant General, U.S. Army. Senior Officer Debriefing Report. 31 August 1971. U.S. Army Military History Institute, Carlisle Barracks, Penn.

Tarpley, Thomas M., Major General, U.S. Army. Senior Officer Debriefing Report. Undated. U.S. Army Military History Institute, Carlisle Barracks, Penn.

Ulmer, W. F., Colonel. Senior Officer Debriefing Report. 10 January 1973. Third Regional Assistance Command.

Vaught, James B., Lieutenant General, U.S. Army (Ret.). Senior Officer Debriefing Program. 1987. U.S. Army Military History Institute, Carlisle Barracks, Penn.

Westmoreland, William. Interview by North Vietnamese Army colonel Bui Tin. 5 February 1995. Paris, France.

Williams, Theodore C., Colonel. Senior Officer Debriefing Report. 24 January 1973. Delta Regional Assistance Command.

Woodward, Gilbert H. Senior Officer Debriefing Program. 1981. U.S. Army Military History Institute, Carlisle Barracks, Penn.

Yoder, Harry A., Colonel. Senior Officer Debriefing Report. 16 February 1973. Third Regional Assistance Command.

Zais, Melvin, General, U.S. Army (Ret.). Senior Officer Debriefing Program. 1977. U.S. Army Military History Institute, Carlisle Barracks, Penn.

Zumwalt, Marvin C., Captain, Adviser, 52nd Infantry. Interview by Major John Cash, Military Assistance Command, Vietnam, SJS-History. 18–19 April 1972.

MEMOIRS, AUTOBIOGRAPHIES, AND BIOGRAPHIES

Ambrose, Stephen E. *Nixon*. Vol. 2, *The Triumph of a Politician, 1962–1972*. New York: Simon and Schuster, 1989.

——. *Nixon*. Vol. 3, *Ruin and Recovery, 1973–1990*. New York: Simon and Schuster, 1991.

Bui Diem, with David Chanoff. *In the Jaws of History*. Boston: Houghton Mifflin, 1977.

Cannon, James. *Time and Chance: Gerald Ford's Appointment with History*. New York: Harper Collins, 1994.

Chanoff, David, and Doan Van Toai. *Portrait of the Enemy*. New York: Random House, 1986.

Clifford, Clark. *Counsel to the President*. New York: Random House, 1991.

Colby, William, with James McCargar. *Lost Victory*. Chicago: Contemporary Books, 1989.

Currey, Cecil B. *Victory at Any Cost: The Genius of Viet Nam's General Vo Nguyen Giap*. Washington, D.C.: Brassey's, 1997.

Ehrlichman, John. *Witness to Power: The Nixon Years*. New York: Simon and Schuster, 1982.

Ford, Gerald R. *A Time to Heal: The Autobiography of Gerald R. Ford*. New York: Harper & Row, 1979.

Gardner, Lloyd C. *Pay Any Price: Lyndon Johnson and the Wars for Vietnam*. Chicago: Ivan R. Dee, 1995.

Greene, John Robert. *The Presidency of Gerald R. Ford*. Lawrence: University of Kansas Press, 1995.

Haig, Alexander M., Jr., with Charles McCarry, *Inner Circles: How America Changed the World, A Memoir*. New York: Warner Books, 1992.

Haldeman, H. R. *The Haldeman Diaries*. New York: Putnam, 1994.

——, with Joseph di Mona. *The Ends of Power*. New York: Times Books, 1978.

Hargrove, Thomas R. *A Dragon Lives Forever*. New York: Ivy Books, 1994.

Hearden, Patrick J. *The Tragedy of Vietnam*. New York: Harper Collins, 1991.

Herring, George C. *LBJ and Vietnam: A Different Kind of War*. Austin: University of Texas Press, 1994.

Herrington, Stuart A. *Peace with Honor? An American Reports on Vietnam, 1973–1975*. Novato, Calif.: Presidio Press, 1983.

———. *Silence Was a Weapon: The Vietnam War in the Villages*. Novato, Calif.: Presidio Press, 1982.

Hersh, Seymour. *The Price of Power: Kissinger in the Nixon White House*. New York: Summit Books, 1983.

Hoff, Joan. *Nixon Reconsidered*. New York: Harper Collins, 1994.

Hoopes, Townsend. *The Limits of Intervention*. New York: David McKay, 1969.

Isaacson, Walter. *Kissinger: A Biography*. New York: Simon and Schuster, 1992.

Johnson, U. Alexis. *The Right Hand of Power*. Englewood, N.J.: Prentice-Hall, 1981.

Kalb, Marvin, and Bernard Kalb. *Kissinger*. New York: Little, Brown, 1974.

Kiem Do, and Julie Kane. *Counterpart: A South Vietnamese Naval Officer's War*. Annapolis, Md.: Naval Institute Press, 1998.

Kissinger, Henry. *Diplomacy*. New York: Simon and Schuster, 1994.

———. *Ending the Vietnam War*. New York: Simon and Schuster, 2003.

———. *White House Years*. Boston: Little, Brown, 1979.

———. *Years of Renewal*. New York: Simon and Schuster, 1999.

———. *Years of Upheaval*. Boston: Little, Brown, 1989.

Lam Quang Thi. *The Twenty-Five Year Century*. Denton: University of North Texas Press, 2001.

Lansdale, Edward Geary. *In the Midst of Wars: An American Mission to South East Asia*. New York: Harper & Row, 1972.

MacDonald, Peter. *Giap: The Victor in Vietnam*. New York: Norton, 1993.

McNamara, Francis Terry, with Adrian Hill. *Escape with Honor: My Last Hours in Vietnam*. London: Brassey's, 1997.

Morris, Roger. *Uncertain Greatness: Henry Kissinger and American Foreign Policy*. New York: Harper & Row, 1977.

Nessen, Ron. *It Sure Looks Different from the Inside*. Chicago: Playboy Press, 1978.

Nguyen Cao Ky. *Buddha's Child: My Fight to Save Vietnam*. New York: St. Martin's, 2002.

———. *Twenty Years and Twenty Days*. New York: Stein and Day, 1976.

Nguyen Khac Ngu. *Final Days of the Republic of Vietnam*. Montreal: n.p., 1979.

Nguyen Ngoc Nhan, with E. E. Richey. *The Will of Heaven: A Story of One Vietnamese and the End of His World*. New York: E. Dutton, 1982.

Nixon, Richard M. *A New Road for America*. Garden City, N.Y.: Doubleday, 1972.

———. *In the Arena: A Memoir of Victory, Defeat and Renewal*. New York: Simon and Schuster, 1990.

———. *No More Vietnams*. New York: Touchstone, 1990.

———. *The Real War*. New York: Warner Books, 1980.

———. *RN: The Memoirs of Richard Nixon*. New York: Warner Books, 1978.

———. *Setting the Course: Major Policy Statements by President Richard Nixon*. New York: Funk & Wagnalls, 1970.

Safire, William. *Before the Fall: An Insider's View of the Pre-Watergate White House*. New York: Doubleday, 1975.

Schulzinger, Robert D. *Henry Kissinger: Doctor of Diplomacy*. New York: Columbia University Press, 1989.

Sheehan, Neil. *A Bright Shining Lie: John Paul Vann and America in Vietnam*. New York: Random House, 1988.

Snepp, Frank. *Decent Interval*. New York: Random House, 1977.

Sorley, Lewis. *A Better War: The Unexamined Victories and Final Tragedy of America's Last Years in Vietnam*. New York: Harcourt Brace, 1999.

————. *Thunderbolt, from the Battle of the Bulge to Vietnam and Beyond: General Creighton Abrams and the Army of His Times*. New York: Simon and Schuster, 1992.

Taylor, John M. *General Maxwell Taylor: The Sword and the Pen*. New York: Doubleday, 1989.

Taylor, Thomas. *Where the Orange Blooms: One Man's War and Escape in Vietnam*. New York: McGraw-Hill, 1989.

Tin Nguyen. *Major General Nguyen Van Hieu, ARVN*. San Jose, Calif.: Writers Club Press, 2000.

Westmoreland, William C. *A Soldier Reports*. New York: Doubleday, 1976.

Wicker, Tom. *One of Us: Richard Nixon and the American Dream*. New York: Random House, 1991.

Zumwalt, Elmo R., Jr. *On Watch*. New York: Quadrangle, 1976.

STUDIES, REPORTS, PAPERS, PROCEEDINGS, AND MONOGRAPHS

American Aid and Vietnam Economy. Saigon: Office of the [South Vietnamese] Deputy Prime Minister in charge of Economic Development, March 1975.

The American Military and the Far East: Proceedings of the Ninth Military History Symposium, U.S.A.F. Academy, 1–3 October 1980. Washington, D.C.: U.S. Air Force Academy, 1980.

BDM Corporation. *A Study of Strategic Lessons Learned in Vietnam: Omnibus Executive Summary*. McLean, Va.: BDM, April 1980.

————. *A Study of Strategic Lessons Learned in Vietnam*. Vol. 1, *The Enemy*. McLean, Va.: BDM, 1979.

————. *A Study of Strategic Lessons Learned in Vietnam*. Vol. 3, *Results of the War*. McLean, Va.: BDM, 1980.

————. *A Study of Strategic Lessons Learned in Vietnam*. Vol. 6, *Conduct of the War*. McLean, Va.: BDM, May 1980.

Bendix Aerospace Systems Division. Department of Applied Science and Technology. *Analysis of Vietnamization: Summary and Evaluation*. Ann Arbor, Mich.: Bendix Aerospace Systems Division, November 1973.

Bibby, Thomas N. "Vietnam: The End, 1975." Unpublished student paper, U.S. Marine Corps Command and Staff College, Quantico, Va., April 1985.

Cao Van Vien, General. *Indochina Monographs: Leadership*. Washington, D.C.: U.S. Army Center of Military History, 1977.

————. *Indochina Monographs: The Final Collapse*. Washington, D.C.: U.S. Army Center of Military History, 1985.

Cao Van Vien et al. *Indochina Monographs: The U.S. Adviser*. Washington, D.C.: U.S. Army Center of Military History, 1980.

Cao Van Vien, General, and Lieutenant General Dong Van Khuyen. *Indochina Monographs: Reflections on the Vietnam War*. Washington, D.C.: U.S. Army Center of Military History, 1980.

Clarke, Jeffrey J. CMH Monograph 192M. *The Role of USARV Units in Vietnamization*. Washington, D.C.: U.S. Army, Center of Military History, 1974.

Dawkins, Peter M. "The United States Army and the 'Other' War in Vietnam." PhD dissertation, Princeton University, 1979.

Dong Van Khuyen. *Indochina Monographs: The RVNAF.* Washington, D.C.: U.S. Army Center of Military History, 1979.

Elliott, David W. *International Relations of East Asia Project: NLF-DRV Strategy and the 1972 Spring Offensive.* Ithaca, N.Y.: Cornell University, International Relations of East Asia, IREA Project, January 1974.

Goodman, Allan E. "The Dual-Track Strategy of Vietnamization and Negotiation." In *The Second Indochina War — Proceedings of a Symposium Held at Airlie, Virgina, 7–9 November 1984,* edited by John Schlight, 143–52. Washington, D.C.: U.S. Army Center of Military History, 1986.

——. *An Institutional Profile of the South Vietnamese Officer Corps.* Santa Monica, Calif.: Rand Corp., 1970.

Graham, Warren, and William L. King. *Military Advising in Vietnam, 1969–1970.* HUMRRO Technical Report 73–24. Alexandria, Va.: HUMRRO, November 1973.

Hammond, William. "The American Withdrawal from Vietnam: Some Military and Political Considerations." Southeast Asia Branch, U.S. Army Center of Military History. Paper presented at the Hofstra Conference on President Richard M. Nixon, November 1987.

Herrington, Stuart A. "The Third Indochina War, 1973–1975: A Personal Perspective." Thesis, Air Command and Staff College, Maxwell Air Force Base, Ala., May 1980.

Hickey, Gerald C. *The American Military Advisor and His Foreign Counterpart: The Case of Vietnam.* Santa Monica, Calif.: Rand Corp., 1965.

Hoang Ngoc Lung. *Indochina Monographs: The General Offensives of 1968–1969.* Washington, D.C.: U.S. Army Center of Military History, 1978.

——. *Indochina Monographs: Strategy and Tactics.* Washington, D.C.: U.S. Army Center of Military History, 1980.

Hosmer, Stephen T., Konrad Kellen, and Brian M. Jenkins. *The Fall of South Vietnam: Statements by Vietnamese and Civilian Leaders.* Santa Monica, Calif.: Rand Corp., 1978.

Howard, John D., Major. "The Easter Offensive, 1972: A Strategic Appraisal." Student paper, U.S. Army War College, Carlisle Barracks, Penn.

——. "An Infantryman Remembers An Loc and the Air Force." Student paper, U.S. Army Command and General Staff College, Fort Leavenworth, Kans., March 1974.

——. "The War We Came to Fight: A Study of the Battle of An Loc, April-June 1972." Student paper, U.S. Army Command and General Staff College, Fort Leavenworth, Kans., June 1974.

Jenkins, Brian M. *A People's Army for South Vietnam: A Vietnamese Solution.* Santa Monica, Calif.: Rand Corp., November 1971.

——. *Giap and the Seventh Son.* Santa Monica, Calif.: Rand Corp., September 1972.

——. *Why the North Vietnamese Will Keep Fighting.* Santa Monica, Calif.: Rand Corp., 1972.

Kaplan, Morton. *Vietnam Settlement: Why 1973, Not 1969?* Washington, D.C.: American Enterprise Institute, 1973.

Kellen, Konrad. *1971 and Beyond: The View From Hanoi.* Santa Monica, Calif.: Rand Corp., 1971.

——. *Rand Report: Conversations with Enemy Soldiers in Late 1968/Early 1969: A Study of Motivation and Morale.* Santa Monica, Calif.: Rand Corp., 1970.

Komer, Robert W. *Bureaucracy Does Its Thing: Institutional Constraints on U.S.-GVN Performance in Vietnam.* Santa Monica, Calif.: Rand, 1972.

————. *Impact of Pacification on Insurgency in South Vietnam*. Santa Monica, Calif.: Rand Corp., 1970.

Laird, Melvin R. *Town Hall Meeting: The Nixon Doctrine*. Washington, D.C.: American Enterprise Institute, 1972.

Metcalf, D.J. "Why Did the Defense of Quang Tri Province Fail?" Student paper, U.S. Army War College, Carlisle Barracks, Penn., October 1972.

Mortensen, K. G. "The Battle of An Loc." Unpublished monograph, East St. Kilda, Australia, 25 April 1973.

Ngo Quang Truong, Lieutenant General. *Indochina Monographs: RVNAF and U.S. Operational Cooperation and Coordination*. Washington, D.C.: U.S. Army Center of Military History, 1980.

————. *Indochina Monographs: The Easter Offensive of 1972*. Washington, D.C.: U.S. Army Center of Military History, 1980.

Nguyen Duy Hinh, Major General. *Indochina Monographs: Lam Son 719*. Washington, D.C.: U.S. Army Center of Military History, 1980.

————. *Indochina Monographs: Vietnamization and the Cease-Fire*. Washington, D.C.: U.S. Army Center of Military History, 1980.

Niksch, Larry A. *Vietnamization: The Program and Its Problems*. Washington, D.C.: Congressional Research Service, 5 January 1972.

"1972 Vietnam Easter Offensive." In *Selected Readings in Tactics,* vol. 1 of *RB 100–2,* Fort Leavenworth, Kans.: U.S. Army Command and General Staff College, 1975.

Pauker, G. J. *An Essay on Vietnamization*. Santa Monica, Calif.: Rand Corp., March 1971.

Pike, Douglas. "Conduct of the Vietnam War: Strategic Factors, 1965–1968." In *The Second Indochina War—Proceedings of a Symposium Held at Airlie, Virgina, 7–9 November 1984,* edited by John Schlight, 99–119. Washington, D.C.: U.S. Army Center of Military History, 1986.

Rockett, Frederick C., and A. A. Berle. *RVNAF Effectiveness Evaluation*. Washington, D.C.: Simulmatics Corporation, 1967.

Serio, Frank E., Lieutenant Colonel. "The U.S. Military Advisory Effort in the Republic of Vietnam: Assessment and Future Trends." Thesis, U.S. Army War College, Carlisle Barracks, Penn., 9 March 1970.

Serong, F. *The Future of South Vietnam*. Strategy Papers, no. 8. New York: National Strategy Information Center, 1971.

Stephenson, Roy R. "Road to Downfall: Lam Son 719 and U.S. Airmobility Doctrine." PhD dissertation, University of Kansas, 1991.

Thayer, Thomas C., ed. *A Systems Analysis View of the Vietnam War, 1965–1972*. 12 vols. Springfield, Va.: National Technical Information Service, 1975.

Tran Dinh Tho. *Indochina Monographs: Pacification*. Washington, D.C.: U.S. Army Center of Military History, 1980.

————. *Indochina Monographs: The Cambodian Incursion*. Washington, D.C.: U.S. Army Center of Military History, 1979.

U.S. Department of Defense, Office of the Assistant Secretary of Defense (Systems Analysis). *The South East Asia Analysis Report*. Washington, D.C., November 1965 through January 1972.

Willbanks, James H. *Thiet Giap! The Battle of An Loc, April 1972*. Ft. Leavenworth, Kans.: U.S. Army Command and General Staff College, Combat Studies Institute, 1993.

BOOKS

Amter, Joseph A. *Vietnam Verdict*. New York: Continuum, 1982.

Anderson, David L. "Gerald R. Ford and the Presidents' War in Vietnam." In *Shadow on the White House: Presidents and the Vietnam War, 1945–1975*, edited by David L. Anderson, 184–207. Lawrence: University Press of Kansas, 1993.

Andradé, Dale. *America's Last Vietnam Battle: Halting Hanoi's 1972 Easter Offensive*. Lawrence: University Press of Kansas, 2001.

———. *Trial by Fire*. New York: Hippocrene Books, 1995.

Barron, John, and Anthony Paul. *Peace With Honor*. London: Hodder & Staughton, 1977.

Bender, David L. *The Vietnam War: Opposing Viewpoints*. St. Paul, Minn.: Greenhaven Press, 1984.

Bergerud, Eric M. *The Dynamics of Defeat: The Vietnam War in Hau Nghia Province*. Boulder, Colo.: Westview Press, 1991.

Berman, Larry. *No Peace, No Honor: Nixon, Kissinger, and Betrayal*. New York: Free Press, 2001.

Blaufarb, Douglas S. *The Counter-Insurgency Era: U.S. Doctrine and Performance, 1950 to the Present*. New York: Free Press, 1977.

Braestrup, Peter, ed. *Vietnam as History: Ten Years after the Paris Peace Accords*. Washington, D.C.: University Press of America, 1984.

Brigham, Robert K. *Guerrilla Diplomacy: The NLF's Foreign Relations and the Vietnam War*. Ithaca, N.Y.: Cornell University Press, 1999.

Bundy, William. *A Tangled Web: The Making of Foreign Policy in the Nixon Presidency*. New York: Hill and Wang, 1998.

Burchett, Wilfred G. *Grasshoppers and Elephants: Why Vietnam Fell*. New York: Urizen Books, 1977.

Butler, David. *The Fall of Saigon*. New York: Simon and Schuster, 1985.

Carhart, Tom. *Battles and Campaigns in Vietnam*. New York: Crown, 1984.

Chanoff, David, and Doan Van Toai. *'Vietnam,' A Portrait of Its People at War*. London: I. B. Tauriis, 1996.

Cincinnatus (Cecil B. Currey). *Self-Destruction: The Disintegration and Decay of the United States Army during the Vietnam Era*. New York: Norton, 1981.

Clodfelter, Mark. *The Limits of Air Power: The American Bombing of North Vietnam*. New York: Free Press, 1989.

Coleman, J. D. *Incursion*. New York: St. Martin's, 1991.

Davidson, Phillip B. *Secrets of the Vietnam War*. Novato, Calif.: Presidio Press, 1990.

———. *Vietnam at War: The History 1946–1975*. Novato, Calif.: Presidio Press, 1988.

Dawson, Alan. *55 Days: The Fall of South Vietnam*. Englewood Cliffs, N.J.: Prentice-Hall, 1977.

Dawson, Joseph G., ed. *Commanders in Chief: Presidential Leadership in Modern Wars*. Lawrence: University Press of Kansas, 1993.

Doleman, Edgar C. *The Vietnam Experience: Tools of War*. Boston: Boston Publishing, 1984.

Dougan, Clark, and David Fulghum. *The Vietnam Experience: The Fall of the South*. Boston: Boston Publishing, 1985.

Duiker, William J. *Sacred War: Nationalism and Revolution in a Divided Vietnam*. New York: McGraw-Hill, 1995.

Dunstan, Simon. *Armor of the Vietnam Wars*. London: Osprey Press, 1985.

———. *Vietnam Tracks: Armor in Battle, 1945–75*. Novato, Calif.: Presidio Press, 1982.

Ely, John Hart. *War and Responsibility: Constitutional Lessons of Vietnam and Its Aftermath*. Princeton, N.J.: Princeton University Press, 1993.

Engelmann, Larry. *Tears before the Rain: An Oral History of the Fall of South Vietnam*. New York: Da Capo, 1997.

Errington, Elizabeth Jane, and B. J. C. McKercher, eds. *The Vietnam War as History*. New York: Praeger, 1990.

Eschmann, Karl J. *Linebacker: The Untold Story of the Air Raids over North Vietnam*. New York: Ivy Books, 1989.

Esper, George. *The Eyewitness History of the Vietnam War, 1961–1975*. New York: Ballantine Books, 1983.

Fanning, Louis A. *Betrayal in Vietnam*. New Rochelle, N.Y.: Arlington House, 1976.

Fulghum, David, and Terrence Maitland. *The Vietnam Experience: South Vietnam on Trial, Mid-1970 to 1972*. Boston: Boston Publishing, 1984.

Gaiduk, Ilya V. *The Soviet Union and the Vietnam War*. Chicago: Ivan R. Dee, 1996.

Gelb, Leslie H., and Richard K. Betts. *The Irony of Vietnam: The System Worked*. Washington, D.C.: Brookings Institution, 1979.

Gettleman, Marvin E., Jane Franklin, Marilyn B. Young, and H. Bruce Franklin, eds. *Vietnam and America*. New York: Grove Press, 1995.

Gilbert, Marc Jason, ed. *Why the North Won the Vietnam War*. New York: Palgrave, 2002.

Goodman, Allan E. *The Lost Peace: America's Search for a Negotiated Settlement of the Vietnam War*. Stanford, Calif.: Hoover Institute Press, 1978.

Griffiths, John. *The Last Day in Saigon*. North Pomfret, Vt.: Dryad Press, 1986.

Haley, Edward P. *Congress and the Fall of South Vietnam and Cambodia*. East Brunswick, N.J.: Associated University Presses, 1982.

Hammond, William M. *Reporting Vietnam: Media and Military at War*. Lawrence: University Press of Kansas, 1998.

Harris, Louis. *The Anguish of Change*. New York: Norton, 1973.

Harrison, James. *The Endless War: Vietnam's Struggle for Independence*. New York: Columbia University Press, 1989.

Head, William, and Lawrence E. Grinter, eds. *Looking Back on the Vietnam War*. Westport, Conn.: Praeger, 1993.

Hendrickson, Paul. *The Living and the Dead: Robert McNamara and Five Lives of a Lost War*. New York: Knopf, 1996.

Herring, George C. *America's Longest War: The United States and Vietnam, 1950–1975*. 3rd ed. New York: McGraw Hill, 1996.

Hess, Gary R. *Vietnam and the United States: Origins and Legacy of the War*. Boston: Twayne, 1990.

Hunt, Richard A. *Pacification: The American Struggle for Vietnam's Hearts and Minds*. Boulder, Colo.: Westview Press, 1995.

Isaacs, Arnold R. *Vietnam Shadows: The War, Its Ghosts, and Its Legacy*. Baltimore: Johns Hopkins University Press, 1997.

———. *Without Honor: Defeat in Vietnam and Cambodia*. Baltimore: Johns Hopkins University Press, 1983.

Jennett, Richard. *A Sadness That Was Vietnam*. Framingham, Mass.: Boggastow Book Co., 1987.

Jian, Chen. *Mao's China and the Cold War*. Chapel Hill: University of North Carolina Press, 2001.

Joes, Anthony James. *The War for South Viet Nam, 1954–1975*. New York: Praeger, 1989.

Kaplan, Morton. *Vietnam Settlement: Why 1973, Not 1969?* Washington: American Enterprise Institute, 1973.

Karnow, Stanley. *Vietnam: A History*. New York: Viking, 1983.

Kattenburg, Paul M. *The Vietnam Trauma, 1945–1975*. London: Transition Books, 1980.

Keough, James. *President Nixon and the Press*. New York: Funk & Wagnalls, 1972.

Kimble, Jeffrey. *Nixon's Vietnam War*. Lawrence: University Press of Kansas, 1998.

Kinnard, Douglas. *The War Managers*. Wayne, N.J.: Avery Publishing Group, 1985.

Knappman, Edward W., ed. *South Vietnam: U.S.-Communist Confrontation in Southeast Asia, 1972–1973*. Vol. 7. New York: Facts on File, 1973.

Kolko, Gabriel. *Anatomy of a War: Vietnam, the United States, and the Modern Historical Experience*. New York: Pantheon, 1985.

Krepinevich, Andrew F., Jr. *The Army and Vietnam*. Baltimore: Johns Hopkins University Press, 1986.

Kutler, Stanley I., ed. *Abuse of Power: The New Nixon Tapes*. New York: Free Press, 1997.

Lac Hoang, and Ha Mai Viet. *Why America Lost the War*. Manchester, Ind.: Heckman Bindery, 1996.

Lam Quang Thi. *Autopsy: The Death of South Vietnam*. Phoenix: Sphinx Publishing, 1986.

Langguth, A. J. *Our Vietnam: The War 1954–1975*. New York: Simon and Schuster, 2000.

Lanning, Michael Lee, and Dan Cragg. *Inside the VC and the NVA: The Real Story of North Vietnam's Armed Forces*. New York: Fawcett Columbine, 1992.

Lee, J. Edward, and H. C. "Toby" Haynsworth. *Nixon, Ford, and the Abandonment of South Vietnam*. Jefferson, N.C.: McFarland and Co., 2002.

Lee, J. Edward, and Toby Haynsworth. *White Christmas in April: The Collapse of South Vietnam, 1975*. New York: Peter Lang, 1999.

Lewy, Guenther. *America in Vietnam*. New York: Oxford University Press, 1978.

Lind, Michael. *Vietnam: The Necessary War*. New York: Free Press, 1999.

Lipsman, Samuel, and Edward Doyle. *The Vietnam Experience: Fighting for Time*. Boston: Boston Publishing, 1983.

Lipsman, Samuel, and Stephen Weiss. *The Vietnam Experience: The False Peace, 1972–1974*. Boston: Boston Publishing, 1985.

Lomperis, Timothy J. *The War Everyone Lost—And Won*. Baton Rouge: Louisiana State University Press, 1984.

MacLear, Michael. *The Ten Thousand Day War, Vietnam: 1945–1975*. New York: St. Martin's, 1981.

Martin, Michael. *Angels in Red Hats: Paratroopers of the Second Indochina War*. Louisville, Ky.: Harmony House, 1995.

Matthews, Lloyd J., and Dale E. Brown, eds. *Assessing the Vietnam War*. Washington, D.C.: Pergamon-Brassey's, 1987.

Maurer, Henry. *Strange Ground: Americans in Vietnam, 1945–1975*. New York: Henry Holt, 1989.

McGarvey, Patrick J., ed. *Visions of Victory: Selected Vietnamese Communist Military Writings, 1964–1968*. Stanford, Calif.: Hoover Institution of War, Revolution and Peace, Stanford University, 1969.

Melson, Charles D. *The War That Would Not End: U.S. Marines in Vietnam, 1971–1973.* Central Point, Oreg.: Hellgate Press, 1998.

Miller, John G. *The Bridge at Dong Ha.* Annapolis, Md.: Naval Institute Press, 1989.

Millett, Allen Reed. *A Short History of the Vietnam War.* Bloomington: Indiana University Press, 1979.

Moore, John Norton, and Robert F. Turner. *The Real Lessons of the Vietnam War.* Durham: Carolina Academic Press, 2002.

Morrison, Wilbur H. *The Elephant and the Tiger.* New York: Hippocrene Books, 1990.

Morrocco, John. *Rain of Fire, Air War, 1969–1973.* Boston: Boston Publishing, 1985.

Mortensen, K. G. *The Battle of An Loc, 1972.* Victoria, Australia: Gerald Griffin, 1996.

———. *Vietnam: Target for 1972 Blitzkrieg.* East St. Kilda, Australia: Gerald Griffin, 1972.

Natkiel, Richard. *Atlas of Battles: Strategy and Tactics Civil War to Present.* New York: Military Press, 1984.

Nguyen Nham Nhan. *The Will of Heaven.* With E. E. Richey. New York: E. Dutton, 1982.

Nguyen Tien Hung and Jerrold L. Schecter. *The Palace File.* New York: Harper & Row, 1986.

Nolan, Keith William. *Into Cambodia.* Novato, Calif.: Presidio, 1990.

———. *Into Laos.* Novato, Calif.: Presidio, 1986.

Oberdorfer, Don. *Tet!* Garden City, N.Y.: Doubleday, 1971.

Olson, James S., and Randy Roberts. *Where the Last Domino Fell: America and Vietnam, 1945 to 1990.* New York: St. Martin's, 1991.

Osborn, George K., et al., eds. *Democracy, Strategy, and Vietnam: Implications for American Policymaking.* Lexington, Mass.: Heath, 1987.

Palmer, Bruce. *The 25-Year War.* Lexington: University Press of Kentucky, 1984.

Palmer, Dave Richard. *Summons of the Trumpet.* San Rafael, Calif.: Presidio Press, 1978.

Papp, Daniel S. *Vietnam: The View From Moscow, Peking, and Washington.* Jefferson, N.C.: McFarland, 1981.

Parker, R. Charles, IV. *Strategy for a Stalemate.* New York: Paragon House, 1989.

Perry, Mark. *Four Stars.* Boston: Houghton Mifflin, 1989.

Pike, Douglas. *PAVN: People's Army of Vietnam.* Novato, Calif.: Presidio Press, 1986.

Pimlott, John, ed. *Vietnam: The History and the Tactics.* New York: Crescent Books, 1982.

Plaster, John L. *SOG: The Secret Wars of America's Commandos in Vietnam.* New York: Simon and Schuster, 1997.

Podhoretz, Norman. *Why We Were in Vietnam.* New York: Simon and Schuster, 1982.

Porter, Gareth. *A Peace Denied: The United States, Vietnam, and the Paris Agreement.* Bloomington: Indiana University Press, 1975.

Prados, John. *Keepers of the Keys: A History of the National Security Council from Truman to Bush.* New York: Morrow, 1991.

———. *The Blood Road: The Ho Chi Minh Trail and the Vietnam War.* New York: John Wiley and Son, 1999.

Pratt, John Clark, ed. *Vietnam Voices: Perspectives on the War Years, 1941–1982.* New York: Viking, 1984.

Record, Jeffrey. *The Wrong War: Why We Lost in Vietnam.* Annapolis, Md.: Naval Institute Press, 1998.

Schulzinger, Robert D. *A Time for War: The United States and Vietnam, 1941–1975.* New York: Oxford University Press, 1997.

Schurmann, Franz. *The Foreign Policy of Nixon: The Grand Design*. Berkeley, Calif.: Institute of International Studies, 1987.

Shaplen, Robert. *Bitter Victory*. New York: Harper & Row, 1986.

———. *The Road From War: Vietnam, 1965–1970*. New York: Harper & Row, 1970.

Shawcross, William. *Sideshow: Kissinger, Nixon and the Destruction of Cambodia*. New York: Simon and Schuster, 1979.

Smith, John T. *The Linebacker Raids: The Bombing of North Vietnam, 1972*. London: Cassell & Co., 1998.

Sorley, Lewis. *A Better War: The Unexamined Victories and Final Tragedy of America's Last Years in Vietnam*. New York: Harcourt Brace, 1999.

Spector, Ronald H. *After Tet: The Bloodiest Year in Vietnam*. New York: Free Press, 1993.

Stanton, Shelby L. *Anatomy of a Division: The 1st Cav in Vietnam*. Novato, Calif.: Presidio Press, 1987.

———. *The Rise and Fall of an American Army*. Novato, Calif.: Presidio Press, 1985.

———. *Vietnam Order of Battle*. New York: Galahad Books, 1986.

Starry, Donn A., General. *Armored Combat in Vietnam*. New York: Bobbs-Merrill, 1980.

Steinberg, Blema. *Shame and Humiliation: Presidential Decision Making on Vietnam*. Pittsburgh: University of Pittsburgh Press, 1996.

Steinman, Ron. *The Soldier's Story: Vietnam in Their Own Words*. New York: TV Books, 1999.

Summers, Harry C., Jr. *Historical Atlas of the Vietnam War*. New York: Houghton Mifflin, 1995.

———. *On Strategy: A Critical Analysis of the Vietnam War*. Novato, Calif.: Presidio Press, 1982.

Szulc, Tad. *The Illusion of Peace: Foreign Policy in the Nixon Years*. New York: Viking, 1978.

Taylor, Thomas. *Where the Orange Blooms: One Man's War and Escape in Vietnam*. New York: McGraw-Hill, 1989.

Terzani, Tiziano. *Giai Phong! The Fall and Liberation of Saigon*. New York: St. Martin's, 1976.

Thayer, Thomas C. *War without Fronts: The American Experience in Vietnam*. Boulder, Colo.: Westview Press, 1985.

Thompson, Sir Robert. *No Exit From Vietnam*. New York: David McKay, 1969.

———. *Peace Is Not at Hand*. New York: David McKay, 1974.

Thompson, W. Scott, and Donaldson D. Frizzell, eds. *The Lessons of Vietnam*. New York: Crane, Russak, 1977.

Tilford, Earl H., Jr., *Crosswinds: The Air Force's Setup in Vietnam*. College Station, Tex.: Texas A&M University Press, 1993.

Todd, Olivier. *Cruel April: The Fall of Saigon*. New York: Norton, 1987.

Tucker, Spencer C. *Vietnam*. Lexington: University Press of Kentucky, 1999.

Turley, G. H. *The Easter Offensive*. Novato, Calif.: Presidio Press, 1985.

Turley, William S. *The Second Indochina War*. Boulder, Colo.: Westview Press, 1986.

Van Dyke, Jon M. *North Vietnam's Strategy for Survival*. Palo Alto, Calif.: Pacific Books, 1972.

Vietnam: A History in Documents. Edited by Gareth Porter. New York: New American Library, 1981.

Vietnam Documents: American and Vietnamese Views of the War. Edited by George Katsiaficas. New York: M. E. Sharpe, 1992.

Walton, C. Dale. *The Myth of Inevitable U.S. Defeat in Vietnam.* London: Frank Cass, 2002.

Warner, Denis A. *Certain Victory: How Hanoi Won the War.* Kansas City: Sneed, Andrews and McKeel, 1978.

Werner, Jayne S., and David Hunt, eds. *The American War in Vietnam.* Ithaca, N.Y.: Southeast Asia Program, Cornell University, 1993.

Werner, Jayne S., and Luu Doan Huynh, eds. *The Vietnam War: Vietnamese and American Perspectives.* Armonk, N.Y.: M. E. Sharpe, 1993.

West, Francis J. *The Village.* New York: Harper & Row, 1972.

Westad, Odd Arne, and Chen Jian, Stein Tonnesson, Nguyen Vu Tung, and James G. Herschberg, eds. *77 Conversations between Chinese and Foreign Leaders on the Wars in Indochina, 1964–1977.* Washington, D.C.: Woodrow Wilson Center, May 1998.

Willenson, Kim. *The Bad War: An Oral History of the Vietnam War.* New York: New American Library, 1987.

Woodruff, Mark W. *Unheralded Victory: The Defeat of the Viet Cong and the North Vietnamese Army, 1961–1973.* Arlington, Va.: Vandemere Press, 1999.

Young, Marilyn B., and Robert Buzzanco, eds. *A Companion to the Vietnam War.* Malden, Mass.: Blackwell, 2002.

Zaffiri, Samuel. *Hamburger Hill, May 11–20, 1969.* Novato, Calif.: Presidio Press, 1988.

Zasloff, Joseph J., and Allan E. Goodman, eds. *Indochina in Conflict.* Lexington, Mass.: Lexington Books, 1972.

Zhai, Qiang. *China and the Vietnam Wars, 1950–1975.* Chapel Hill: University of North Carolina Press, 2000.

PERIODICALS

"A Record of Sheer Endurance." *Time,* 26 June 1972, 25–26.

Ambrose, Stephen. "The Christmas Bombing." *Military History Quarterly* (winter 1992): 8–17.

Andradé, Dale. "Quang Tri Disaster." *Vietnam,* April 1994, 31–36, 59–60.

———. "Three Days on the Run." *Vietnam,* August 1990, 38–45.

Baker, Bob. "Battle of the Bilge vs. Eastertide Offensive: Lessons Unlearned." *Vietnam,* April 1999, 34–40.

Beecher, William. "Vietnamization—A Few Loose Ends." *Army,* November 1970, 13–17.

Buckley, Thomas. "The ARVN Is Bigger and Better, But—." *New York Times Magazine,* 12 October 1969, 132.

———. "Is This Written in the Stars? See It Through with Nguyen Van Thieu." *New York Times Magazine,* 26 September 1971.

Bundy, McGeorge. "Vietnam, Watergate, and Presidential Powers." *Foreign Affairs* 58, no. 2 (winter 1979–80): 397–407.

Burke, Robert L. "Back to Vietnam—Reflections on a Lost War." Interview by Major General John E. Murray. *Vietnam,* August 1997, 42–48.

Butterfield, Fox. "How Vietnam Died—By the Stab in the Front." *New York Times Magazine,* 25 May 1975.

Cerami, Joseph R. "Presidential Decisionmaking and Vietnam: Lessons for Strategists." *Parameters* 26, no. 4 (winter 1996–97): 66–80.

Church, George J. "The Final 10 Days." *Time,* 24 April 1995, 25–35.

Clarke, Philip C. "The Battle That Saved Saigon." *Reader's Digest,* March 1973, 151–56.

Clifford, Clark. "A Viet Nam Reappraisal." *Foreign Affairs* 47, no. 4 (July 1969): 609–22.

Collins, John M. "Vietnam Postmortem: A Senseless Strategy." *Parameters* 8, no. 1 (March 1978): 8–14.

Crawford, Henry B. "Operation Menu's Secret Bombing of Cambodia." *Vietnam,* December 1996, 22–28.

Daley, Jerome R. "The AH1G Versus Enemy Tanks at An Loc." *Armor,* July-August 1972, 42–43.

Davidson, Michael W. "Senior Officers and Vietnam Policymaking." *Parameters* 16 (spring 1986): 55–62.

Dillard, Walter Scott, and John Francis Shortal. "Easter Invasion Repulsed." *Vietnam* (winter 1988): 51–56.

Divine, Robert A. "Vietnam Reconsidered." *Diplomatic History* 12 (winter 1988): 79–94.

Dupuy, William E. "Vietnam: What We Might Have Done and Why We Didn't Do It." *Army,* February 1986, 22–25, 28–32, 35–36, 39–40.

Editorial. "The Tet That Wasn't." *Life,* 24 March 1972, 38.

Ellithorpe, Harold. "'Can You Hold Out for Just Eight More Minutes?'" *Life,* 24 March 1972, 51.

"Escalation in the Air, Ordeal on the Ground." *Time,* 24 April 1972, 26–28.

Gelb, Leslie H. "Vietnam: The System Worked." *Foreign Policy* 3 (1971): 140–67.

Grant, Zalin B. "Vietnam without GIs: After the U.S. Withdrawal." *The New Republic,* 19 May 1978, 19–21.

Gray, Colin S., and Jeffrey G. Barlow. "Inexcusable Restraint." *International Security* 10, no. 2 (fall 1985), 27–69.

Grayson, Eugene H., Jr. "Great Spring Victory." *Vietnam,* June 1992, 18–24.

Grinter, Lawrence E. "Bargaining Between Saigon and Washington: Dilemmas of Linkage Politics During War," *Orbis* 18 (1974): 837–67.

———. "Counter Insurgency," *Spectrum* 3 (1975): 49–78.

Hackworth, David H. "Our Advisers Must Pass the Ball," *Army,* May 1971, 61–62.

Halloran, Bernard F. "Soviet Armor Comes to Vietnam." *Army,* August 1972, 18–23.

"Hanoi's High-Risk Drive for Victory." *Time,* 15 May 1972, 8–15.

Heinl, Robert D. "On Basis of Pacification, Vietnam War Has Been Won." *Armed Forces Journal* 109, no. 6. (February 1972): 50–51.

———. "The Collapse of the Armed Forces." *Armed Forces Journal,* 7 June 1971, 30–37.

Herring, George C. "American Strategy in Vietnam: The Postwar Debate." *Military Affairs* 46 (April 1982): 57–63.

Howard, John D., Major. "An Loc: A Study in U.S. Power." *Army,* September 1975, 18–24.

———. "They Were Good Ol' Boys!" *Air University Review,* January-February 1975, 26–39.

"In Furious Battle." *Newsweek,* 24 April 1972, 31–33.

Jespersen, T. Christopher. "The Bitter End and the Lost Chance in Vietnam." *Diplomatic History* 24, no. 2 (spring 2000): 265–93.

Karnow, Stanley. "The Tenuous Peace: Reconciliation?" *The New Republic,* 10 February 1973, 13–14.

———. "Vietnam: Legacy of Desolation." *The New Republic,* 16 March 1973, 18–19.

———. "The Vietnam Accord: Truce or Peace?" *The New Republic,* 27 January 1973, 19–20.

Kiernan, Ben. "The Vietnam War: Alternative Endings." *American Historical Review* 97, no. 4 (October 1992): 1118–37.

Kissinger, Henry. "Vietnam: The End of the War." *Survival* 17, 1975, 183–86.

——. "The Vietnam Negotiations." *Foreign Affairs* 47 (January 1969): 211–34.

Komer, Robert W. "Pacification, A Look Back . . . and Ahead." *Army,* January 1969, 20–29.

Kroesen, Frank J., General. "Hiep Duc: Triumph and Tragedy." *Army,* July 1994, 45–46.

Laird, Melvin R. "A Strong Start in a Difficult Decade: Defense Policy in the Nixon-Ford Years." *International Security* 10, no. 2 (fall 1985): 5–26.

——. "Unforgettable Creighton Abrams." *Reader's Digest,* July 1976, 72–76.

Langguth, A. J. "General Abrams Listens to a Different Drummer." *New York Times Magazine,* 5 May 1968, 28.

——. "The Vietnamization of General Di." *New York Times Magazine,* 6 September 1970.

Le Gro, William E. "Tragic Postlude to 'Peace.'" *Vietnam,* June 1991, 43–49.

Lunch, William L., and Peter W. Sperlich. "American Public Opinion and the War in Vietnam." *Western Political Science Quarterly* 32 (March 1979): 21–44.

McArthur, George. "It Became Sinful." *Vietnam,* April 1995, 23–28, 66.

McCaffrey, W. J. "Vietnam in 1970: Year of Transition." *Army,* October 1970, 94–109.

McGowan, Sam. "Easter Airlift." *Vietnam,* April 1994, 47–52.

McMahon, Richard. "Saigon '75: The Inevitable Collapse." *The Retired Officer,* April 1985, 18–22.

"The Miscalculation Is Mutual." *Newsweek,* 1 May 1972, 49–52.

Moore, James K. "Giap's Giant Mistake." *Vietnam,* February 1992, 27–32.

Mueller, John. "The Search for the Breaking Point in Vietnam." *Strategic Studies* 24 (December 1980): 497–519.

Nelan, Bruce W. "Lessons from the Lost War." *Time,* 24 April 1995, 44–45.

Nihart, Brooke. "Army Reports Helicopter Success in Laos, Air Force Skeptical." *Armed Forces Journal* 5 (April 1971): 40, 44.

"Nixon's Vietnam Gamble." *Newsweek,* 22 May 1972, 18–20.

Parker, Maynard. "Vietnam: The War That Won't End." *Foreign Affairs* 53, no. 2 (January 1975): 252–75.

Pribbenow, Merle L. "North Vietnam's Final Offensive: Strategic Endgame Nonpareil." *Parameters* 29, no. 4 (winter 1999–2000): 58–71.

Record, Jeffrey. "Vietnam in Retrospect: Could We Have Won?" *Parameters* 26, no. 4 (winter 1996–97): 51–65.

Reed, David. "Vietnamization, Can It Succeed?" *Reader's Digest,* April 1970, 55–61.

Rosen, Stephen. "After Vietnam: What the Pentagon Has Learned." *The American Spectator,* October 1979, 7–11.

Rostow, W. W. "The Case for the Vietnam War." *Parameters* 26, no. 4 (winter 1996–97): 39–50.

Saar, John. "A Nervous Air Mission to An Loc and Back." *Life,* 12 May 1972, 36–37.

——. "Report from the Inferno." *Life,* 28 April 1972, 30–36.

Schemmer, Benjamin F. "Bien Hoa Air Base: Short on Toilet Paper But Long on Teamwork." *Armed Forces Journal* 109 (June 1972): 15–17.

Serong, F. "The 1972 Easter Offensive," *Southeast Asia Perspectives* (summer 1974).

"Settling in for the Third Indochina War." *Time,* 8 May 1972, 28–30.

Shaplen, Robert. "Letter from Indochina." *New Yorker,* 2 June 1973, 40–60.

——. "Letter from Saigon." *New Yorker,* 21 April 1975, 124–38.

——. "Letter from Vietnam." *New Yorker,* 24 February 1973, 100–111.

Siracusa, Joseph M. "The United States, Vietnam, and the Cold War: A Reappraisal." *Journal of Southeast Asian Studies* 5 (1974): 82–101.

Smith, Homer D. "The Final Forty-Five Days in Vietnam." *Vietnam,* April 1995, 47–52, 72–74.

Sorley, Lewis. "Courage and Blood: South Vietnam's Repulse of the 1972 Easter Invasion." *Parameters* 29, no. 2 (summer 1999): 38–56.

———. "Reassessing the ARVN." *Vietnam,* April 2003, 43–48, 65.

———. "To Change a War: General Harold K. Johnson and the PROVN Study." *Parameters* 28, no. 1 (spring 1998): 93–109.

"South Viet Nam: Pulling Itself Together." *Time,* 22 May 1972, 5–17.

Stacey, K. N. "North Vietnamese Armor Operations: The Lessons of 1972 and 1975." *Armor,* July-August 1981, 48–53.

Summers, Harry G. "The Bitter End." *Vietnam,* April 1995, 39–45, 69–70.

———. "Final Days of South Vietnam." *American History,* April 1995, 29–36, 66–68.

———. "A Strategic Perception of the Vietnam War." *Parameters* 13, no. 2 (June 1983): 41–46.

Szulc, Tad. "Behind the Vietnam Ceasefire Agreement." *Foreign Policy* 15 (summer 1974): 21–69.

Thompson, Sir Robert. "A Successful End to the War in Vietnam." *Pacific Community* (April 1971): 455–64.

Timmes, Charles J. "Military Operations after the Cease-Fire Agreement, Part I." *Military Review,* August 1976, 63–75.

———. "Military Operations after the Cease-Fire Agreement, Part II." *Military Review,* September 1976, 21–29.

Tokar, Major John A. "An Loc Airlift." *Vietnam,* December 2000, 34–40, 65.

Tran Quang Khoi. "Fighting to the Finish." *Armor,* March-April 1996, 19–25.

Turley, G. H., and M. R. Wells. "Easter Invasion 1972." *Marine Corps Gazette,* March 1973, 18–28.

Ulmer, Walter F., Jr., Colonel. "Notes on Enemy Armor at An Loc." *Armor,* January-February 1973, 14–20.

Ulsamer, Edgar. "Airpower Halts an Invasion." *Air Force Magazine,* September 1972, 61.

Verba, Sidney. "Public Opinion and the War in Vietnam." *American Political Science Review* 61 (June 1967): 317–33.

"Vietnam: The Specter of Defeat." *Newsweek,* 15 May 1972, 20–22.

"Vietnamization: Will It Work?" *Newsweek,* 9 February 1970, 32.

"Vietnamization Makes Steady Gains." *Army,* November 1970, 44–45.

"The War That Won't Go Away." *Newsweek,* 17 April 1972, 16–21.

Ward, Ian. "North Vietnam's Blitzkrieg—Why Giap Did It: Report from Saigon." *Conflict Studies* 27 (October 1972): 1–11.

Weller, Jac. "RVNAF Training: The Vital Element in Vietnamization." *Military Review,* October 1972, 36–49.

West, Richard. "Saigon Keeps Its Vigil." *The New Statesman,* 4 April 1975.

Wolff, Tobias. "After the Crusade." *Time,* 24 April 1995, 46–48.

NEWSPAPERS

Baltimore Sun
Christian Science Monitor
Cleveland Plain Dealer
Los Angeles Times
New York Times
Philadelphia Bulletin
Philadelphia Enquirer
Stars and Stripes
Wall Street Journal
Washington Post
Washington Star
Die Zeit (Hamburg)

NEWS SERVICES

Foreign Broadcast Information Service
New China News Agency (Beijing)
Reuter's
Vietnam News Agency (Hanoi)

Index